MOODY GOSPEL

MATTHEW

COMMENTARY

MOODY GOSPEL
MATTHEW
COMMENTARY

ED GLASSCOCK

MOODY PRESS

CHICAGO

This commentary focuses on the text at hand and is based upon both *The Greek New Testament,* 4th rev. ed., edited by Barbara Aland, Kurt Aland, Johannes Karavidopoulos, Carlo M. Martini, and Bruce Metzger (Stuttgart, Germany: United Bible Societies, 1994) and *Novum Testamentun Graece* 26 Auflage (Stuttgart, Germany: Deutsche Bibelgesellschaft, 1985).

All Scripture quotations, unless indicated, are taken from the *New American Standard Bible* © 1960, 1962, 1963, 1968, 1971, 1972, 1973, 1975, and 1977 by The Lockman Foundation, La Habra, Calif. Used by permission.

ISBN: 0-8024-5623-5

1 3 5 7 9 10 8 6 4 2

Printed in the United States of America

To my wife, Gail,
who has been my faithful friend and supporter for thirty years.
She embodies every aspect of the Proverbs 31 woman,
who honors God and husband and
who faithfully brings up and cares for her children.
Gail is a great gift from God.

CONTENTS

ACKNOWLEDGMENTS

I am grateful to many friends and associates for their encouragement and help in completing this project. The editors at Moody Press were patient and helpful, and their assistance is appreciated. My wife, Gail, proofread and edited every page and offered numerous helpful suggestions as well as patiently encouraged me throughout the work. The support and encouragement of my colleagues at Moody Graduate School are appreciated. Gratitude to Michael Wechsler, a former student, is also expressed for his assistance in researching some of the material used in the book.

PREFACE

A commentary should not be viewed as something to tell the student what to preach or what to believe. The primary function of a commentary is to provide counsel and insights into the book being studied that will allow the reader to more honestly, objectively, and thoroughly determine what he believes the original author is saying. This book is a tool to help the student of God's Word fulfill the requirement of 2 Timothy 2:15, "Handling accurately the Word of Truth."

The reader is encouraged to allow this commentary to help in processing the gospel of Matthew but not to be dependent upon it for ultimate answers. Those must come from the conviction of the preacher, teacher, or student himself, based upon diligent study and humble dependence on the Holy Spirit. Proverbs 11:14 states, "Where there is no guidance the people fall, but in abundance of counselors there is victory." This commentary is intended to be one of those counselors. I have sought to provide grammatical, syntactical, historical, and theological observations that contribute to a more accurate understanding of the text of Matthew. The overriding hermeneutical principle governing the commentary is the exhortation of John Calvin in the preface to his work on Romans, "The first business of any interpreter is to let his author say what he did say, instead of attributing to him what he thinks he ought to say." Theories or conjecture about a supposed text behind the text are minimized, and speculative determination as to an evolution of a community-religious view is rejected. The focus of this study will be on the text at hand and will be based upon both the United Bible Societies 4th edition and Nestles 26th edition, using the NASB as the English version.

It is hoped that this commentary will be found to be a dependable and valuable counselor. Every effort has been made to provide objective and accurate information for the reader's consideration.

INTRODUCTION

The gospel of Matthew was placed first in the New Testament canon because early sources indicated it to be the first written. However, modern scholarship has called into question this order, and Matthew is no longer considered the oldest of the synoptics. This and numerous other issues have been raised in regard to the source and original nature of this record of the Lord's life and ministry. The purpose and constitution of this commentary will not allow for detailed analysis of all these issues, but the reader will be provided with quality references for consideration if desired.

If one is to be a true scholar in the contemporary arena of biblical learning, to question the synoptics' chronological order of writing and to assume their dependence upon each other as well as dependence upon noncanonical sources is considered necessary. Certainly one does not wish to be ignorant of any material that will assist him in gaining the fullest and most accurate understanding of the biblical text. In light of this assumption, consideration of some of the issues related to the present text of Matthew's gospel may be necessary.

ORIGINAL LANGUAGE

A major dispute among many biblical scholars is whether the gospel was originally written in Hebrew, Aramaic, or Greek. A remark made by Papias (Bishop of Hierapolis, a city in Phrygia, at the beginning of the second century) is normally cited as proof that the Greek version of Matthew is not the original. Eusebius states, "This is related by Papias about Mark, and about Matthew this was said, 'Matthew collected the oracles in the Hebrew language, and each interpreted them as best he could.'"[1]

The greatest problem with this issue is that the original of Papias's work is not extant, and there are many questions as to Eusebius's accuracy in quoting him, as well as many questions as to how to interpret Eusebius's words themselves. What he meant by *sunetaxsato* ("collected, composed, compiled"), *ta logia* (implying words or sayings or including events), and *Hebraidi dialektō* ("the Hebrew dialect," or Aramaic) is unclear. Scholars debate, and each can argue some legitimate reasons for his particular view. The question must surely be raised as to how justifiable focusing so much attention on something so ambiguous can be. Perhaps if the Papias document itself were available, the energies being expended would be worthy; but to place so much weight on such an obscure reference is neither good scholarship nor good stewardship.

The fact that no extant evidence of such a manuscript exists adds to the complexity of analyzing the possibility of an original Aramaic or Hebrew gospel, though other references in Eusebius offer more support to the theory. Origen, according to Eusebius, claimed Matthew's gospel was "composed as it was in the Hebrew language (*grammasin hebraikois suntetagmenon*, "arranged in Hebrew writing," or possibly "letters").[2] In another section he records, "Matthew had first preached to the Hebrews, and when he was on the point of going to others he transmitted in writing in his native language the Gospel according to himself."[3] Also Eusebius preserves a remarkable tradition concerning a missionary named Pantaenus, who was sent to India to preach the gospel. Upon arrival, he found that the Indians had already received the gospel from Bartholomew the apostle, who had left behind a written copy of Matthew's gospel "in Hebrew letters."[4] And finally, Eusebius quotes Irenaeus as saying, "Now Matthew published among the Hebrews a written gospel in their own tongue, while Peter and Paul were preaching in Rome and founding the church."[5]

These recorded comments appear to prove that an original Hebrew (more likely, Aramaic) version of Matthew's gospel existed.

But even here, so much disagreement concerning the comments continues that the serious student looking for answers becomes frustrated. One might question why Bartholomew would leave people in India a Hebrew book. Are we to assume they could read it? Did he teach them Hebrew (or Aramaic) before leaving them? Would not a translation in their own language have been more likely? The fact remains that even though different church Fathers are quoted, they are all recorded only in Eusebius. Hendriksen comments, "The interesting fact is that in many specific cases the advocates of the Aramaic theory in its extreme form reject each other's conclusions as to mistranslations."[6]

Tasker offers what he believes to be the most prominent opinion among Protestant scholars: Eusebius's comment references Papias's view that Matthew did not write a gospel but only collected the sayings (*ta logia*) of Jesus, and these sayings were subsequently written in historical narrative form as a gospel. Matthew's name was therefore attached to this later writing as the source of most of the material.[7] However, Stein in his work on the synoptic problem concludes, "Both the interpretation and the accuracy of Papias's words have been greatly debated."[8] Of course, the matter of the other quotations is still significant. Were they all basing their comments on Papias's remark? It is quite possible.

Some scholars go even further in their theories concerning the "lost" version of Matthew and promote the groundless speculation that all of the Gospels, except for some parts in John and Luke, were originally written in Aramaic.[9] Many scholars see a strong Semitic flavor to the language of the New Testament and therefore assume that demonstrates an Aramaic original. Such reasoning is more a leap of logic than a scientific theory. One should expect to see Semitic traces in documents written by Semitic writers, regardless of what language they wrote in. The foundational idea of Koine Greek is that it is the end product of numerous dialectal elements shaping its unique nature. Matthew, Mark, and John were Hebrews. They thought and expressed themselves like Hebrews. It is a rare exception for someone to learn a second or third language and not maintain the distinctive expressions of his native tongue, no matter how proficient in the second language he becomes. Hendriksen's explanation is both logical and sufficient:

There are, after all, other ways to account for the Semitic flavor of these books. Matthew, Mark, and John were Jews, and not only these three but also Luke was in close contact with Jews and used Jewish oral and written sources. When Jews speak or write Greek they do not immediately shed their Hebraistic background. The Semitisms of the New Testament may therefore be partially explained as being regional variations of Hellenistic Greek.[10]

Hendriksen confesses that there is no way to prove or disprove the early existence of an Aramaic gospel of Matthew but also strongly asserts, "That it is no translation of a Hebrew or Aramaic written Gospel is clear."[11]

Thus one can either invest time in developing and seeking to justify interesting conjecture of a "text behind the text" or invest the time and energy in working with the text at hand. Sufficient evidence offers support that the Greek text preserved through thousands of manuscripts dating back to the fourth and fifth centuries is an accurate representation of the original testimonies to Jesus Christ. The supposed text of Papias is of dubious credibility as it stands. Even Eusebius, who quotes him, questions his reliability in other areas because of his tendency to adopt apocryphal stories.[12] Henry Alford is one well-known scholar who has wrestled through this issue, and in the first edition of his commentaries on the New Testament he accepted the view of an original Aramaic text. However, after further and more careful examination of the data, he reversed his opinion:

> I can only state my own judgment on the point in debate. In the first edition of this work, I acceded to what appeared to me the irresistible weight of testimony of antiquity. But I have since then studied very closely the text itself, especially with reference to its revision in those passages which find parallels in the other Gospels, and I am bound to say that my view of the Hebrew origin is much shaken. . . . On the whole, then, I find myself constrained to abandon the view maintained in my first edition, and to adopt that of a Greek original.[13]

Other well-known scholars also accept the Greek original of Matthew.[14] This commentary will likewise approach the text before us as an actual copy of the original manuscript and will not expend energy trying to guess or assume what some unknown document may have said. This is not to belittle genuine research but to indicate the focus and intent of this work. If one is interested in a detailed explanation of the issue, D. A. Carson offers a good discussion. He concludes, "Although Matthew has Semitisms, much evidence suggests that it was first composed in Greek."[15]

Q DOCUMENT

This brings up another popular theory that must be addressed, the supposed "document Q" as the source of Matthew. Q stands for the German *Quelle,* which means "source." For more than a century and a half, theories and speculations have circulated concerning the existence of a written source of the life of Jesus Christ from which the gospel writers borrowed and constructed their own accounts. Carson traces the origin of the idea to A. E. Lessing, who (in two essays published posthumously in 1776 and 1778) "insisted that the only way to account for the parallels and seeming discrepancies among the synoptic Gospels was to assume that they all derived independently from an Aramaic *Gospel of the Nazarenes.*"[16] Linnemann suggests that the reasoning behind this were postenlightenment "allegations that the Gospels were historically unreliable."[17] When one considers the antisupernaturalism that dominated the postenlightenment era, understanding the desire to distance oneself from the idea of divinely produced documents (such as biblical inspiration would claim the Gospels to be) is easy. Certainly there are questions and issues that appear prima facie to be inconsistent or contradictory, but these can be answered by disciplined, objective hermeneutics rather than by searching desperately for a nonextant document.

Interestingly enough, the driving force in contemporary Q research is not the inconsistencies of the synoptics but their similarities. Once the theory was birthed that a common source existed from which the synoptics drew their information, the determination grew that there must have been a written source. Stein comments, "The exactness of wording between the synoptic Gospels is better explained by the use of written sources than oral ones."[18] Thus, the proof of Q has not been established by manuscript discoveries, nor by any record that such a document existed, but only by conjecture based upon human reasoning that consistency of witness required it. So, on the one hand, inconsistency brought the integrity of the synoptics into question, but consistency allowed for the creation of a document that has never been proven to exist. Some will certainly explain that the issue is much too complex to be understood without the immense scholarship of the higher critical school; however, the complexities are created by lack of evidence and historical documentation. Devising and supporting theories that have no factual basis always include complexity.

Stein argues that "the extensive agreement in the order of material cannot be explained by any other means than a common written tradition."[19] This is a dogmatic assertion based upon what is supposed, not upon what can be verified by material evidence. Is it not possible that divine inspiration could account for the harmony? Is the Spirit of God not capable of directing the recording of such events and sayings by each individual writer because there is purpose and design in them? In all the extensive arguments to justify a nonextant document Q, no consideration is given to any supernatural element of scriptural revelation. Support for the possibility of a document Q has been reduced to what is plausible to human reasoning and the assumed traditions of the religious community. Seeking a literary origin for the Gospels is effectively stating that they are no more than religious tradition. Eta Linnemann, who was once dedicated to source criticism, has concluded:

> Now we discover the truth: Q, the hypothetical sayings gospel, is the lever needed to pry the Christian faith out of its biblical moorings. Not the Gospels, but Q must be faith's new anchor, inasmuch as Q is earlier than the Gospels and does not agree with them. Q settles the matter.[20]

Though not directly linked to Q research, one extreme to which such attitudes have been taken is demonstrated by the Jesus Seminar, in which the validity of a text is voted on by dropping colored beads into a basket, based upon whether or not an academician felt the text was certainly, likely, or possibly an original account or whether it was certainly, likely, or possibly *not* a part of the original document.

The primary premise behind this reconstruction of the New Testament is that the gospel records are not trustworthy and other sources must be sought to validate genuineness. This group of approximately two hundred scholars has determined that at least "eighty-two percent of the parables, aphorisms and other *mots* put in Jesus' mouth by New Testament scribes were never uttered by him."[21] Though these scholars claim their judgments are based upon empirical data, they decided the Lord's Supper never took place because "Jesus, not being a wealthy man, would not be accustomed to hosting dinners."[22]

If such methods seem absurd to conservative evangelicals, so must the search for document Q. Such efforts presuppose that the New Testament text based on the extant manuscripts is no more than a collection of greater and lesser testimonies of the early Christian community's religious views. Whether one labels it a search for the original story of Christ or a search for the historical Jesus, the energy is wasted. The assumption that Matthew was produced not by the apostle but by a redactor who reconstructed the life of Jesus based on community tradition and a missing document has no basis other than imaginative speculation. As Linnemann points out:

> It takes a robust imagination to suppose that, despite such differences, the pericopes claimed for Q based on similarities in literary sequence owe their origin to a common source. But imagination is no substitute for evidence, and guesses as to whether Matthew here or Luke there diverged from Q's sequence do not prove that Q existed.[23]

It is critical to understand that one who rejects this theory is no less scholarly than those who accept it. The issue centers on dealing with the preserved text and accepting what the earliest witnesses claimed it to be—the work of an eyewitness, an apostle named Matthew. Carson makes a significant observation:

> The major redaction-critical studies all attempt to define the historical context in which the evangelist writes, the community circumstances that call this Gospel into being (it is thought) between A.D. 80 and A.D. 100, and pay little useful attention to the historical context of Jesus.[24]

The goal of this commentary is to focus where the focus belongs—on the context of Jesus' life and ministry and on the words recorded in the gospel of Matthew. The writer desires the reader to benefit from the textual exegesis while being exposed to, though not swayed by, contemporary theories centered on the content.

MARK AS THE SOURCE

Another theory often discussed is whether Matthew actually depended upon Mark for information found in the gospel. If one accepts the authorship of Matthew, then such a theory might at first seem senseless, since he was an eyewitness and not dependent upon any source. However, the basis of the theory is the tendency of agreement and disagreement within the three synoptics. These disagreements are not to be considered errors in revelation but a reflection of the normal difficulty of clarity entailed when reading back over nineteen hundred years. Events are listed in different order and with different emphases within the synoptics. At times the same event is presented from different perspectives, dependent upon the individual gospel's purpose. In these areas of comparative studies some scholars have found that "Matthew and Mark frequently agree against Luke, and Mark and Luke frequently agree against Matthew, but Matthew and Luke seldom agree against Mark."[25] Most scholars arrive at the natural conclusion that Mark was a common source for both Matthew and Luke.

Though as a rule this view is accepted, one must remember that Mark as a common source is still theory based upon observations and involving certain presuppositions. The idea of Mark's priority did not develop until post-Reformation studies. Up until then, the consensus of the church placed Matthew as the priority gospel. Once again, Eusebius offers information concerning the early Gospels. He quotes Origen: "Having learnt by tradition concerning the four Gospels, which alone are unquestionable in the Church of God under heaven, that first was written that according to Matthew, who was once a tax-collector but afterwards an apostle of Jesus Christ."[26] However, Eusebius later makes a statement that seems to contradict: "Matthew . . . transmitted in writing in his native language the Gospel according to himself . . . and Mark and Luke had already published the Gospels according to them, but John, it is said, used all the time a message not written down."[27] That the statement was to imply Mark and Luke had already published their gospels before John is likely. The discussion begins by stating that only Matthew and John among the eleven disciples published gospels. Thus, Matthew wrote first, then Mark and Luke published before John.

The reasoning of the early church was logical: Matthew was an apostle; he was an eyewitness; he preserves more of Jesus' sayings than any of the rest; Mark's account was only an abbreviation of the gospel; and Luke was a late-appearing Gentile. Determining who said what first does not alter what was said. This commentary takes the view that the Spirit of God gave oversight to the writings, and thus all are equally valuable and authoritative. The premise of this book will be that Matthew probably wrote first, but no conclusive evidence supports either view.

AUTHORSHIP

The generally accepted author for the gospel of Matthew is the apostle Matthew, but the text does not reveal the author. As Mounce points out, the witness of the early church Fathers supports the apostolic authorship—Origen, Irenaeus, Eusebius, and Jerome included[28]—prompting some scholars to argue that the Matthean authorship was universally accepted.[29] Carson notes that "the universal testimony of the early church is that the apostle Matthew wrote it, and our earliest textual witness attributes it to him (*kata matthaion*)."[30] Nothing is overtly stated in the gospel to cause doubt, but some scholars see certain implied inconsistencies, which they feel create difficulty for Matthean authorship.

Meyer argues that "the many indefinite statements of time, place, and other things which are irreconcilable with the living recollection of an apostolic eye-witness and a participator in the events, even upon the assumption of a plan of arrangement carried out mainly in accordance with the subject matter" is evidence that the original text did not proceed from the hand of the apostle Matthew.[31] Meyer's arguments, however, are not conclusive. If the author is Matthew, no other writings by him exist that would allow for style comparison. To assume that he must be definite concerning time and events is an assumption without warrant. To see his account of events as less accurate than John's or others' is to assume that his purpose and design were the same as John's and that he must use the same manner of expression as the other writers. Such assumptions are unnecessary.

Even Meyer comments that the superscription *Euanggelion kata Matthaion* "has the oldest and best witnesses in its favor."[32] Although such superscriptions are not a part of the original document, it does testify to a very early date of ascription of the work to Matthew. To assume that such early witness to the authorship and such strong witness of the Fathers should not be taken at face value would be strange. Hendriksen concludes:

> Use of this Gospel in the earliest patristic writings that have been preserved (those ascribed to Barnabas, Clement of Rome, Ignatius, and Polycarp) is abundantly attested. The Didache also adds its testimony. In fact, one can say without exaggeration that external evidence of the early use of this Gospel, and of its ascription to Matthew as soon as ascriptions were made, is unanimous. It would be hard to explain how within a period of perhaps sixty years since this Gospel was composed the name of its true author could have been lost and a fictitious name substituted.[33]

Mounce asks, "If the apostle did not write the Gospel, how did his name become attached to it?"[34] The question is legitimate. There seems to have been no question as to Matthean authorship until modern scholars began to read between lines, assume certain stylistic rules, and accept obscure evidence. Another interesting element is that no other name was ever associated with the book, and no internal or external proof exists against Matthew's authorship.

Some interesting characteristics in the book certainly lend internal witness to the authorship of Matthew. One observation is that both Luke and Mark use the name *Levi* in referencing the apostle prior to his apostolic appointment (Mark 2:14; Luke 5:27, 29), but Matthew never uses *Levi*. In referring to his call to follow Jesus, he uses the name *Matthew* (Matt. 9:9). A similar attitude is seen in Paul's writings, where he uses only his postconversion name. Meyer explains that customarily the Jews adopted new names upon life-changing occasions and thus Matthew's intent was to emphasize his new identity.[35] It is also interesting to note that in all the lists of apostles, Matthew is always recorded as Matthew, not Levi, but in Matthew's list alone is the negative qualifier "the tax collector" used. That Matthew would use that title of himself—and no one else did, because of its offensiveness to the Jews—is logical. It is as though Matthew remembered that Christ sought him, though considered unworthy in the religious leaders' eyes. Somewhat reminiscent of John's omitting his personal name and referring to himself as "the disciple whom He [Jesus] loved," (John 19:26) Matthew seemed overwhelmed that Jesus loved him and would call him, a despised tax collector, to service.

Numerous novel theories exist concerning authorship, but pursuing the endless, intricate arguments is not a prudent use of time for either commentator or reader. The arguments and theories are available through a broad range of commentaries for those interested in their development. Carson offers an objective conclusion:

> None of the arguments for Matthew's authorship is conclusive. Thus we cannot be entirely certain who the author of the first Gospel is. But there are solid reasons in support of the early church's unanimous ascriptions of this book to the apostle Matthew, and on close inspection the objections do not appear substantial.[36]

This commentary will take a more positive view of authorship and conclusively accept the unanimous voice of the church that Matthew, the tax-collector-turned-apostle, authored the text.

MATTHEW

Matthew, the apostle, was originally called Levi and identified as a tax collector, the son of Alphaeus (Matt. 9:9; Mark 2:14; Luke 5:27). His new Christian appellation was probably contracted from the Semitic *Mattathias,* which means "gift of Yaweh." A slight possibility exists that he was the brother of James the less, also one of the Twelve (Matt. 10:3; Mark 3:18; Luke 6:15; Acts 1:13). But because of the common use of the name "Alphaeus" (*Alphaiŏs*) and no attempt on the part of any of the Gospels to connect Matthew and James the less, such as the connections made between James and John or Peter and Andrew, the best hermeneutic is to assume no connection.

Tax collectors were seen as traitors, agents of the cruel Roman authorities, and because of their typical corruption were bitterly hated by the Jews. Speaking of tax collectors, Edersheim comments:

The fact that he was the symbol of Israel's subjection to foreign dom-
ination, galling though it was, had probably not so much to do with
the bitter hatred of the Rabbinists towards the class of tax-farmers
(*Moches*) and tax-collectors (*Gabbai*), both of whom were placed
wholly outside the pale of Jewish society, as that they were so utterly
shameless and regardless in their unconscientious dealings.[37]

The tax collector was a contractor who did the work of keeping up
with the citizens and making sure each paid what was due, plus
extra to get his own wages. Sperber suggests:

> As the burdens of taxation became ever more intolerable, so did the
> tax farmer or collector become a more hateful and dreaded personal-
> ity. . . . At times they even contrived to extract payments by torture
> (see Num. R. 17:5; cf Philo, spec. 3, 153-63). Being so unpopular, the
> collector's job was no easy one; indeed at times he ran great person-
> al risk, as an enraged populace was quite likely to lynch him.[38]

Jones credits Augustus for reforming the Roman tax laws but also
points out that they were very unfair to peasants:

> Augustus' system of taxation, though a great improvement on what
> had gone before, was not perfect. . . . For the great majority of tax-
> payers, who were landowners, and especially the humblest among
> them, the peasant proprietors, it could be oppressive. It was a fixed
> sum, which had to be paid every year, whether the harvest was
> good, average, or bad, and in the Mediterranean lands harvests are
> very variable.[39]

Two main taxes were enforced by Rome, the *tributum capitis* (poll
tax, a personal tax for adults) and the *tributum soli* (land/property
tax). Jones again explains:

> These taxes were based on regularly recurrent censuses, in which
> the population was counted and the land—and other property—reg-
> istered in detail . . . . The principal reason for believing that Augustus
> did introduce this system is that he is recorded, for the first time in
> history, to have conducted provincial census, in Gaul in 27 B.C. and
> 13 B.C., in Syria, through his legate Quirinius, in A.D. 6.[40]

The term "tax collector" (*telōnēs*) appears eight times in Matthew, three times in Mark, ten times in Luke, never in John, and always implies Jewish disdain. Eight times in the New Testament tax collectors are included in the same category as "sinners," "harlots," and "Gentiles." According to rabbinic literature, tax gatherers were classified as "robbers" and disqualified from acting as witnesses.[41] John the Baptist reflected the common assumption that tax gatherers took more than what was legal when he responded to their question (Luke 3:12). Tax collectors had come to hear John and wanted to be baptized, asking him what they should do, and he responded, "Collect no more than what you have been ordered to [Luke 3:13]." Notice that he did not instruct them to stop being tax collectors but to be honest in their work.

Jesus also used tax collectors to illustrate corruptness and selfishness. He warned His followers not to love only those who loved them back, because "even the tax-gatherers do the same" (Matt. 5:46). Jesus explained that an unrepentant sinner, after ample encouragement to do right, was to be treated as a "Gentile [rejected as not in a covenant with God] and a tax-gatherer" (Matt. 18:17). This association implies that tax gatherers were no more accepted in Jewish culture (even though they were often Jews by birth) than were Gentiles.

However, Jesus also marked them as objects of salvation and worthy of His company. He shocked the chief priests and the elders by saying to them, "Truly I say to you that the tax collectors and harlots will get into the kingdom of God before you" (Matt. 21:31). His reasoning is explained in v. 32: "But the tax-gatherers and harlots did believe him [John the Baptist]; and you, seeing this, did not even feel remorse afterward so as to believe him." Jesus seems to deliberately have associated with this rejected group, even to such a degree as to be labeled a "friend of tax-gatherers and sinners" (Luke 7:34). The tax collectors (and "sinners" with whom they are often associated) were frequently portrayed as "coming near Him to listen to Him" (Luke 15:1) or as being sincere regarding their spiritual condition contrasted to the Pharisees (Luke 18:13).

In this historical context where such strong feelings were openly expressed against this particular group, common sense would lead one to attempt to appease and win over the religious people by avoiding association with those of such low moral and ethical reputation. But our Lord demonstrated that He did not come to appease or win over the religious but to save sinners. He reached out to those rejected by the religious leaders and even personally chose one, Levi, a tax gatherer, to be a part of His intimate group of disciples. In Matthew's list of the twelve apostles, he qualifies himself as "Matthew, the tax-gatherer," (Matt. 10:3) but his career as a tax collector is not mentioned in the listing of apostles in the other gospels, even though qualifying remarks may be made of others. This is probably reflective of Matthew's humility at being chosen to be an apostle in spite of being rejected by the religious community.

The selection of Matthew as an apostle was not one of random choice any more than the selection of the others. It is quite likely that Matthew was among the tax gatherers who came to be baptized by John (Luke 3:12), and this would reflect a quality of character. Jesus noticed him sitting in the tax office and called him to be an apostle (Luke 5:27). He knew Matthew's character and had very likely been observing him much in the way he had observed Nathaniel (John 1:45-50). One might even speculate that the parabolic tax-gatherer of Luke 18:10-13 could have been Matthew; of course, such speculation must not be taken too seriously.

Alford refers to a comment by Clement of Alexandria indicating that Matthew was involved with an ascetic Judaistic branch of Christianity in the early development of the church.[42] Meyer refers to the same source and notes that the major focus of the sect was on following vegetarian dietary laws.[43] This is consistent with the Jewish nature of the early church, especially when compared to exhortations sent to the new churches from the Jerusalem council (Acts 15:29). Perhaps his attitude was similar to that of James in his commitment to the Lord and in rejecting halfhearted faith. However, to assume from Clement's comment that Matthew had become a legalist would be wrong. His gospel account is far too condemnatory of self-righteousness and legalism to promote such a Christian lifestyle.

Some sources report that Matthew served the Lord faithfully until an old age, covering a broad range of lands and finishing his ministry in Parthia (an area in the northern part of modern Iran near the Caspian Sea).[44] Other sources indicate that Thomas went into Parthia and evangelized India and Matthew went into Ethiopia.[45] Meyer refers to the church Father Socrates to support the view that

Matthew died in Ethiopia from natural causes.[46] Ethiopia is the most commonly accepted place for his death.

DATE AND PLACE OF WRITING

Early sources placed Matthew as the first gospel written; today some scholars contend that Mark and Luke had been composed prior to Matthew. Origen states that tradition supported Matthew's being written first. If this is true, then it must be assumed that Matthew was an early document of the church. Eusebius indicates that Matthew wrote his gospel on behalf of the Jewish believers whom he had been teaching before he left for his missionary journeys.[47] Irenaeus claims that Matthew was writing his gospel at the same time Peter and Paul were preaching in Rome.[48] This also suggests an early date, since Paul and Peter were martyred around A.D. 67-68. However, we are left with only theoretical conclusions. The internal data is difficult to interpret as it relates to time, but it is foolish to begin looking at issues such as "The existence of a Trinitarian formula for baptism (28:19) and the general impression that the church had settled into a rather fixed ethical code and pattern of organization and worship, suggest a rather late date for composition."[49] The apparent presupposition in such statements is that Matthew was not recording a message from the lips of the resurrected Lord (Matt. 28:19) but that the Christian community had evolved a formula for baptism and organization based upon tradition, which the writer was only reflecting. Such speculation is groundless and useless. We do know that Ignatius makes reference to the Matthew gospel around A.D. 110; thus it was in circulation by that time.

Hendriksen argues from a rather standard perspective that Matthew's gospel was written prior to A.D. 70, based on the omission of any reference to the destruction of the temple or the city of Jerusalem (both destroyed in A.D. 70 by Titus).[50] But the problem is that *no* New Testament writing records this catastrophe, including the book of Revelation, which was certainly written later than this event. The significant difference is that since Matthew contains so many eschatological references, especially related to Jerusalem and the temple (Matt. 24), along with his consistent reference to the fulfillment of Scripture, it would be very unlikely that he would not have called upon this event to demonstrate even further the messiahship of Jesus. There simply is not a lot of evidence to consider for a specific date, but general perimeters can be set, as has been suggested. Carson is probably correct by setting the date in the sixties,[51] and a date of approximately A.D. 65 will be assumed in this commentary.

The place from which the gospel was written, though not critical information, does offer some insight into peripheral issues. A consensus among many scholars is that Matthew composed this book at Antioch in Syria, which was closely associated with the apostolic church.[52] It is of interest that the first person to quote the gospel of Matthew seems to have been Ignatius, bishop of Antioch. This is interesting in that Antioch was primarily a Greek-speaking city.[53] So the question may be raised that if this location is correct, and if Greek was the primary language, then is it likely that Matthew would have written a Hebrew (or Aramaic) version of his gospel? This offers another perspective to be considered in the original language debate. To be fair to both sides of the issue, however, it should be noted that Antioch contained a strong Jewish population,[54] and therefore to write in Aramaic would not have been unusual since it was the common language of the Hebrews. Antioch was certainly a center of Christian activity (cf. Acts 6:5; 11:19-27; Gal. 2:11), and thus one is compelled to agree with Carson, "This is as good a guess as any."[55]

PURPOSE AND AUDIENCE

The distinctive Jewish nature of the gospel of Matthew reflects the overall purpose of the book. To believe that any particular book of the Bible has only one purpose or one "theme" is erroneous. However, it is apparent that each author of inspired Scripture was given a primary focus, which influenced what was recorded and the degree of emphasis placed upon any event or topic. Matthew's writing offers an apologetic for the messiahship of Jesus Christ. His constant references to the fulfillment of Old Testament prophecies related to Messiah, his emphasis on the genealogical rights to the throne of David, his recording of numerous kingdom parables and teachings, and his assumption that his readers understood Jewish festivals and traditions clearly indicate an intent to persuade Jews that their Messiah had come and that they had rejected Him. Carson makes a significant observation when he says, "The author goes to work according to a definite plan, setting forth that Jesus is indeed the Christ."[56]

There is some indication that Matthew did understand that his work would transcend the Jewish community. He offers some explanations that imply his assumption that there would be non-Jewish readers as well (1:23, "which translated means"; 27:33, "which means"; 27:46, "that is . . ."). However, these are relatively rare, and thus the gospel of Matthew still points to a *mainly* Jewish audience. Origen states that the tradition he was taught indicated that Matthew "published it for those who from Judaism came to believe."[57] Thus his audience would not be unsaved Jews but converts from Judaism. Alford concludes:

> We have fewer interpretations of Jewish customs, laws, and localities, than in the other Gospels. The whole narrative proceeds more upon a Jewish view of matters, and is concerned more to establish that point, which to a Jewish convert would be most important—that Jesus was the Messiah prophesied in the Old Testament.[58]

However, the purpose would still be to give these new converts an apologetic for those questioning their faith in Jesus.

CHARACTER AND STYLE OF THE GOSPEL

That Matthew intended to write a historical record of the life and works of Jesus the Messiah is unquestionable. He entrenches his writing in time and place events as well as in the context of true historical people (Matt. 1:1-19; 2:1, 16, etc.; 2:22; 3:1; 4:12; 9:9; 14:1; 26:57; 27:2, 11-26; etc.). Scott argues, "The manner in which he comments upon the Gospel events . . . show that he understood his accounts to be, and thus intended them to be, strictly historical in character.[59] Though some argue that Matthew embellishes his history for the sake of theological commentary, such accusations are not well defended exegetically, and they are based upon assumptions and usually supported by circular arguments.

It may be noted that, more often than not, the primary basis for presuming embellished stories in Matthew is comparison with secular writings, which do not fall into the category of divinely inspired literature. Their "freedom" to fabricate stories is not a legitimate parallel to statements in Scripture, which, unless placed in metaphoric, parabolic, or other figurative contexts, should be accepted as a true representation of what is claimed. The efforts of some to defend their view of midrashic style in certain parts of Matthew fall far short of acceptable hermeneutics, being far too biased toward trying to find creative literary license to be objective.

Alford states that Matthew's gospel is "written in the same form and diction which pervades the other Gospels, the Hebraistic or Hellenistic Greek.[60] This style is what should be expected from a first-century Jew. But Matthew's style is still considered "a literary masterpiece,"[61] partly due to Matthew's organization. He presents his material in blocks of teaching, divided by narrative and editorial comment. Carson also notes the "high literary craftsmanship,"[62] and this artistic merit can be attributed to the text's not being the product of mere human ingenuity. The entire Bible has been classified as a great work of artistic literature, and its reputation as such has endured for centuries, even in circles that reject inspiration.

Perhaps one of the most noticeable and most highly criticized characteristics of Matthew's style is his profuse use of the Old Testament to demonstrate the messianic credentials of Jesus Christ. Mounce counts "more than fifty clear quotations" and "innumerable single words, phrases and echoes of the Old Testament."[63] Barclay complains, "He is prepared to use as a prophecy about Jesus any text at all which can be made verbally to fit, even although originally it had nothing to do with the question in hand, and was never meant to have anything to do with it."[64] However, such a judgmental attitude toward Matthew may be reflecting a lack of understanding rather than true biblical scholarship. Carson is certainly closer to the proper approach when he says, "It is more likely, not to say more humble, to suppose that in some instances we may not understand enough of the first-century setting to be able to grasp exactly what the text says."[65] Willis offers a helpful discussion on this issue and concludes:

> Thus, all the quotations, when taken in their contexts (of which Matthew's Jewish readers would be well aware), are presenting much the same theme, that of hope of salvation brought about by

God's intervention in the human situation of captivity—which for Matthew, by analogy, has sin as the captor.[66]

Indeed, rather than challenging the intelligence or integrity of the biblical writer, perhaps we should challenge our understanding of the prophetic nature of Scripture.

In light of Matthew's heavy use of the Old Testament and his emphasis on the fulfillment of messianic prophecies in Jesus, it is natural to allow him to be the transition prophet between the Old and New Testaments. He introduces Jesus as the fulfillment of God's promises to David and the nation and, at the same time, as the provision for the sins of the world. Matthew's gospel belongs in its position in the canon, the introductory gospel that picks up where the Old Testament left off. God who sent His Son is the God of Israel. He has not forgotten His covenants with His people—Jesus the Messiah is proof of that.

ABBREVIATIONS

BAGD	Bauer, Arndt, Gingrich, and Danker, *A Greek-English Lexicon of the New Testament*
BDB	Brown, Driver, and Briggs, *A Hebrew and English Lexicon of the Old Testament*
BibSac	*BiblioTheca Sacra*
BR	*Biblical Review*
CC	Calvin's Commentaries
DAC	*Dictionary of the Apostolic Church*
DNTT	*Dictionary of New Testament Theology*
EBC	*The Expositors Bible Commentary*
EH	*The Ecclesiastical History*
EJ	*Evangelical Journal*
ET	*Expository Times*
GNTG	*Grammar of New Testament Greek*
GT	Greek Testament
JBL	*Journal of Biblical Literature*
JSNT	*Journal for the Study of the New Testament*
KJV	King James Version
LS	Liddell and Scott, *Greek-English Lexicon*
LXX	Septuagint
MCNT	*Meyer's Commentary on the New Testament*
MGC	Moody Gospel Commentary
MNTC	*The MacArthur New Testament Commentary*

NASB	*New American Standard Bible*
NIBC	New International Biblical Commentary
NIDNTT	*New International Dictionary of New Testament Theology*
NIV	*New International Version*
NTC	*New Testament Commentary: Matthew*
TDNT	*Theological Dictionary of the New Testament*
TNTC	Tyndale New Testament Commentaries
UBS4	United Bible Society, 4th edition Greek New Testament
WTJ	*Westminster Theological Journal*
ZPBD	*Zondervan Pictorial Bible Dictionary*

MATTHEW

CHAPTER

ONE

THE PROPHETIC NATURE
OF JESUS' BIRTH

The opening paragraphs of Matthew are often ignored or, at best, skimmed with little interest by today's readers. Genealogical study is hardly a modern passion. Yet, the content and value of the genealogy of Jesus Christ are unquestioned by those who are serious students of the life of the Savior. Matthew's concern is to provide his readers with proper documentation for the claims he will make concerning Jesus' right to the throne of Israel. The "book of beginnings" (*biblos geneseōs*) is simply a record of the most significant ancestors[1] of Jesus, which indicate His royal heritage and His identification with the great patriarchs of the Jewish race. The Bible has several genealogies: Genesis 35:22-26; 46:8-27; Exodus 1:1-5; and so on, the most complete being found in 1 Chronicles 1:1–9:44.

PROLOGUE TO THE GENEALOGY, 1:1

1:1 Matthew begins his introduction of Jesus Christ by establishing His credentials in relation to two great patriarchs of Israel, David and Abraham. The significance of this should not be overlooked, for it is critical in understanding the paradox involved in Israel's reaction to Jesus. Matthew identifies Him as a descendant of both these heroes, because each represents a major covenant with God.

Interesting to note, David is mentioned before Abraham. Logically, Abraham should have been first because of the chronological order of their places in history. Perhaps this is due to Matthew's intended emphasis in his gospel on Jesus as the King of Israel. David was certainly the most revered king of Israel. He symbolized the greatness of the nation and the sureness of God's further blessings. It was to David that God had promised, "I will raise up your descendant after you, who will come forth from you, and I will establish his kingdom . . . and I will establish the throne of his kingdom forever" (2 Sam. 7:12-13).[2] Matthew records evidence of the anticipation of the birth of a king in chap. 2:2, where the Magi ask, "Where is He who has been born King of the Jews?" The chief priests and the scribes knew of the promised Messiah, the "ruler in Israel" who was predicted in Micah 5:2. In John's gospel, 7:40-43, the Jews argue as to who Jesus might be, and it is noted, "Has not the Scripture said that the Christ comes from the offspring of David?" (v. 42). Also of interest is Nathanael's response to his first encounter with Jesus. His comment "You are the Son of God; You are the King of Israel" (John 1:49) certainly reflects anticipation of a coming king of divine origin.

Thus it is safe to assume that the Jewish anticipation of Messiah was that a son of David was coming to be king. Matthew therefore asserts that Jesus is demonstrated by genealogy to be that rightful king. Whereas to the modern Christian reader this would seem almost unnecessary data, for the Jews of Matthew's generation, such documentation was crucial.

In addition to connecting Jesus to David, Matthew also declares Him to be a son of Abraham. At first glance this too would appear to be rather superfluous. If Jesus was a descendant of David, it would be obvious that He also would be a son of David's ancestor Abraham. But Abraham held a special place in the theology of Israel. He was called a friend of God (Isa. 41:8; James 2:23) and was viewed as their most significant patriarch. Edersheim notes, "In fact, by their descent from Abraham, all the children of Israel were nobles, infinitely higher than any proselyte."[3] Consequently, it is no mere casual statement that Jesus, like the Jews to whom He was to minister, was a descendant of the father of the nation.

GENEALOGY OF THE MESSIAH, 1:2-17 (LUKE 3:23-38)

The two genealogies of Jesus are radically different and have led to some rather futile arguments that do not provide satisfactory conclusions. The first point of difference is name sequence. Matthew begins with deceased patriarchs (David and Abraham) and works *forward* to Jesus. Luke, on the other hand, begins with Jesus and works *backward* to Adam.

The second observation is that Matthew begins (or ends) the lineage of Jesus with Abraham, whereas Luke traces His lineage to Adam. These two starting/ending points are consistent with the purpose of the individual authors. Matthew's emphasis on Jesus as the promised Messiah required tracing His roots back only as far as David and Abraham, whereas Luke's emphasis of Jesus as the Son of Man and His connection to the whole human race necessitated lineage back to Adam.

The third distinction is more difficult to understand, and the purpose and scope of this commentary will not allow for an extensive examination of all the proposed solutions resolving this difference. The names in Luke's list do not correspond with the list in Matthew, beginning with the listing of David's sons. Matthew records the lineage of Solomon, and Luke records the lineage of Nathan. Since both were sons of David, there is no reason to question the legitimacy of the names. From David's two sons, one line leads to Joseph, the husband of Mary (Matt. 1:16), and the other leads to Eli (Luke 3:23). The question is, who is Eli? Pate sees credibility in the theory that Eli was the first husband of Jacob's wife (Joseph's father according to Matthew 1:16).[4] Another possibility, one more likely in the opinion of this writer, is that the expression "being supposedly *the* son of Joseph" (Luke 1:23) is to be understood as parenthetical. Excluding this parenthesis, the wording would be, "Jesus Himself was about thirty years of age . . . the *son* of Eli." The wording is typical of genealogical records, *tou 'Hli;* "son" is not included in the phrase. Eli was *tou Maththat,* that is, "out of Matthat." Thus, the idea is that Jesus was the one out of Eli who was out of Matthat, and so on, not meaning "a child of" but "in the line of." Jesus was in the line of Eli, just as He was in the line of Joseph. A possible reason for this different genealogy is that Matthew records Joseph's lineage to demonstrate Jesus' connection to David through Solomon, whereas Luke records Mary's genealogy to demonstrate Jesus' lineage not only to David (through his other son Nathan) but to the first man, Adam. Therefore, Jesus would be connected to David *legally* through His stepfather, Joseph, and biologically through His mother, Mary. Mary's genealogy provides the biological connection to David and Adam, because Joseph was not *biologically* linked to Jesus (the Virgin Birth excludes his genetic input).

1:2   Matthew's genealogy begins with a familiar triad: Abraham, Isaac, and Jacob. The Jews understood these three names to be the foundation of their nation and of the covenants with Yahweh, their God. The covenant given Abraham was specifically to apply to Isaac (Gen. 15:1-6; 17:1-19) and was repeated to and expanded for Jacob (Gen. 35:9-12). Judah was the son of Jacob to whom the blessing was given: "The scepter shall not depart from Judah, nor the ruler's staff from between his feet" (Gen. 49:10). Here again, the connection between Jesus and kingship is demonstrated through genealogical record.

1:3   Verse 3 continues to list the descendants but inserts an unusual property to the genealogy. Tamar, a woman of questionable moral character, is interjected. It is somewhat unusual to have women named in Jewish genealogies. However, as Unger points out, "Females are named in genealogies when there is anything remarkable about them."[4] What was remarkable about Tamar was her immoral relationship with her father-in-law, Judah (Gen. 38:6-30). Thus, Perez and Zerah were illegitimate sons, yet Perez is presented as an ancestor of the Messiah.

A significant question is, why would God include a person of Tamar's character, or why would He call attention to the immorality of Judah? The answer must also include an explanation as to why a Gentile prostitute (Rahab, v. 5) and a Moabite woman (Ruth, v. 5) and the unnamed adulteress called only "her who had been the wife of Uriah" (i.e., Bathsheba, v. 6) are included in the family line of the Messiah. Such names would certainly call to mind the grace of God in dealing with His people. Meyer comments:

> The women named entered in an extraordinary manner into the mission of continuing the genealogy onwards to the future Messiah . . . and in so doing the historical stains which cleaved to them (to Ruth also, insofar as she was a Moabitess) were not merely fully compensated by the glorious approval which they found precisely in the light in which their history was regarded by the nation, but far outweighed and even exalted to extraordinary honors.[5]

What better testimony could God have offered as to the fullness of grace that was to appear in Christ than by demonstrating His forgiving and cleansing power through those instruments He chose to bring Messiah into the world.

1:4-6 The significant names in this section of the genealogy are Rahab, Ruth, and David. Rahab and Ruth were indeed unusual persons to appear in the genealogy of the Jewish Messiah. Their presence is indicative of God's delight in accomplishing His holy tasks with those whom the world would just as soon forget. Matthew stops to make a comment when he reaches David, *"David the King."* Of course, any Jew would have known that David the son of Jesse was the great king of Israel. Matthew is simply keeping before his readers the connection between Jesus and the Davidic throne. "And to David . . . Solomon by her who had been the wife of Uriah." It may be significant that Bathsheba is the one name Matthew does not list; by giving Uriah's name, he emphasizes the horror of David's sin.

1:7-11 The next five verses give an incomplete yet significant list of kings up until the deportation of the nation into captivity. It was under Rehoboam (v.7) that the kingdom was divided (2 Chron. 10), and it was under King Hezekiah (v. 9) that there was a revival in Judah (2 Chron. 29).

1:12-15 This next section of the genealogy is not as consequential as some of the previous parts. The names are important for the flow of heritage, but—other than Jeconiah—the names will not require comment. Jeconiah, however, is quite critical. He was also called "Coniah" or "Jehoiachin" and was cursed by God, sent into deportation, and his line was cut off so as not to have an offspring on the throne of David (Jer. 22:24-30).

1:16 This verse is perhaps one of the most significant in Matthew's gospel. In the lineage of Jesus, Matthew has been listing each generation by the word *egennēsen* ("he gave birth to . . ."). For example, a literal interpretation of v. 2 would be "Abraham gave birth to Isaac, and Isaac gave birth to Jacob . . ." But in v. 16 Matthew continues by departing from that normal pattern. Here he does not say that Joseph gave birth to (*egennēsen*) Jesus. Instead he says that *Jacob gave birth to Joseph the husband of Mary, from whom Jesus, the One called Christ, was born.* The importance of this is quite obvious in light of the doctrine of the virgin birth of Christ. The Spirit's record of the Lord's supernatural birth is clearly stated in Matthew's selection of words. The original text makes it even more clear by emphasizing that Jesus was born from Mary. The text says *ex hēs egennēthē Iēsous,* "out of whom was born Jesus." The relative pronoun "whom" is feminine, which clearly eliminates Joseph as the one to whom Jesus was born.

Jesus is called the "Christ" (*Christos*), meaning "the anointed one"[6] The title is the New Testament equivalent for "Messiah," the promised divine Savior. The implication is that Jesus was the One for whom the Jews were looking (Matt. 2:4).

1:17 Matthew sums up his genealogical record by dividing it into three divisions. Each division is of fourteen names according to Matthew's own claim. The fact that there are only thirteen names in the last portion requires some searching for explanation. It could be assumed that Matthew simply made a mistake and inadvertently left out one name. Some think that Mary should be counted between Joseph and Jesus, which would make fourteen. However, since the count is generations, not names, this seems unlikely.

Meyer seems to offer the best explanation, though it is dependent upon precise use of two prepositions. In v. 11 the second series of fourteen names closes with Jeconiah and concludes with "at the time of the deportation to Babylon" (*epi tēs metoikesias Babulonos*). In v. 12, Matthew begins the third group of names with "after the deportation to Babylon" (*meta de tēn metoikesian Babulonos*). Meyer explains:

> The key to the calculation, according to which the thrice-recurring fourteen links are to be enumerated, lies in vv. 11, 12. According to vs. 11, Josiah begat Jechoniah at the time of the migration to Babylon; consequently Jechoniah must be *included* in the *terminus ad quem,* which is designated by *heōs tēs metoikesias Babulonos* in verse 17. The same Jechoniah, however, must just as necessarily again begin the third division, as the same begins with *apo tēs metoikesias Babulonos.* Jechoniah, however, who was himself *begotten* at the time of the migration, did not become a *father* until after the migration (v.12), so that he therefore belonged as *begotten* to the period *heōs tēs metoi. Babul.,* but as a *father* to the period *apo tēs metoik. Babul,* standing in his relation to the epoch of the *metoikesia* as a *twofold person.*[7]

This explanation makes sense in that Matthew is concerned with the symmetry of his genealogy and divides the list into generations rather than persons. Thus, there is Jeconiah, *epi tēs metoike-sias* ("at the time of the deportation") and the same Jeconiah, *meta tēn metoikesian* ("after the deportation"). The three critical historical epochs used by Matthew to divide the genealogy are: David's kingdom, the Babylonian captivity, and the time of the Messiah (*heōs tou Christou*).

JOSEPH'S DILEMMA, 1:18-20

Having established the legal rights of Jesus to the throne of David and His connection to Abraham, who had received the promise of an heir through whom the whole earth would be blessed, Matthew now proceeds to give details of the unique birth of Jesus. Comparison with Luke's account (Luke 1:26-38; 2:1-7) provides a broader view of the event.

1:18 The details that Matthew provides indicate his concern for preserving the uniqueness of this event. First, Matthew does not use the normal word for birth (*gennaō*) but the word *gennēsis* as in 1:1. Consequently, he states, "Now the origin of Jesus[8] Christ was thus." Three key facts are presented in this beginning: Mary, Jesus' mother, was betrothed to Joseph; Mary was pregnant before she united with Joseph; and Mary was pregnant by the supernatural work of the Holy Spirit.

The betrothal was a legally binding agreement, which carried the same accountability as marriage. According to Edersheim, "From the moment of betrothal both parties were regarded, and treated in law (as to inheritance, adultery, need of formal divorce), as if they had been actually married, except as regarded their living together."[9] Thus, Deuteronomy 22:22-24 treats infidelity of the betrothed the same as infidelity of the married. It is for this reason that Matthew clearly states, "Before they came together" (*prin ē suneltbein*) Mary was found to be pregnant. Matthew's concern is to protect not only the virtue and fidelity of Mary but also the uniqueness of Messiah's origin.

The third fact of Matthew's account is the claim that the pregnancy of Mary was from the Holy Spirit (*heurethē en gastri echousa ek pneumatos hagiou*). Luke offers more information on this event in response to Mary's question, "How can this be [her pregnancy] since I am a virgin?" (Luke 1:34). The angel's response, "The Holy

Spirit will come upon you, and the power of the Most High will overshadow you" (Luke 1:35) is not detailed and is unsatisfying to the excessively curious but clearly marks the procedure as divine. Pate remarks that "it is reminiscent of the creation of the world (Gen. 1:1); God's presence overshadowing the tabernacle via the cloud (Ex. 40:35); the Transfiguration scene (Luke 9:34); etc."[10] Indeed, the event could be compared with these other great supernatural events. It is improper to think of this event as God's having sexual intercourse with Mary (as in Greek mythology, where gods cohabited with mortal women, producing superhero offspring), or as though God were a magician working a spell. God has demonstrated in all His created work that He is a God of true science. In our contemporary age of artificial insemination, in which semen is introduced into the uterus apart from physical contact, it should not be so strange to think of God's placing in Mary's uterus the biological elements for producing the body of the Lord. Nevertheless, Pate sums up the issue well: "The exact nature of the virginal conception, historical as it was, is ultimately a miraculous mystery incomprehensible to mere mortals and to be believed by faith."[11]

1:19 Matthew's readers are now given critical information concerning Joseph. He is called a "righteous [*dikaios*] man." This should not be construed as meaning sinless or one declared "righteous" by the Law, for Scripture clearly denies such a possibility (Gal. 2:16; 3:10-11; Rom 3:9-10, 19). The idea is that he is a man who is devoted to God and God's standard. The same expression is used of Zacharias and Elizabeth (Luke 1:6) and Simeon (Luke 2:25). Matthew sets forth then the dilemma faced by Joseph. It was "found" (*eurethē*) that Mary was pregnant, and he was not the father. Gundry believes that Mary probably told Joseph herself,[12] but the text does not give this information. Carson is probably more correct in saying, "The natural way to read vv. 18-19 is that Joseph learned of his betrothed's condition when it became unmistakable, not when she told him."[13] Luke tells us that Mary spent three months with Elizabeth (Luke 1:56) after receiving the message from the angel. Elizabeth indicated that she accepted the message given Mary as truth (Luke 1:42-43). Of course, since her husband had also experienced angelic visitation and her own pregnancy was miraculous, it would be easy to understand her openness. How much of this Joseph had heard and understood is questionable. But it appears that either he had no explanation from

Mary or he did not accept what he had been told, because he was still contemplating getting out of the arrangement.

Being a man devoted to God's standards, he knew that he had the viable option of demanding her death (Deut. 22:23), though it appears this was not commonly practiced in the first century. He also realized that to take Mary as his wife would implicate him as the father, thus appearing to have himself violated the laws of the betrothal, which would certainly damage his reputation. On the other hand, he appears to have been a sensitive man, full of compassion, because he was "not wanting to disgrace her" (literally, "not desiring to publicly expose her"). Josephus illustrates how a public divorce could affect a young woman: "Divorce was social status."[14] Joseph's solution[15] was to "put her away secretly." To "put her away" is to divorce her. *Apoluō* ("send away") is used elsewhere for the act of divorce (cf. Matt. 5:31). According to Mishnah, sotah 1.5, a man could privately divorce (or cancel the engagement with) his betrothed before a minimum of two witnesses if just cause could be shown. There would be no need to bring charges, and the matter could be settled quietly. Joseph's attitude reflected a person who, though committed to the Law of God, felt compassion and concern for one who had seemingly betrayed him.

THE DIVINE MESSAGE, 1:20-23

1:20   It appears that God allowed Joseph to struggle with the issue and make a decision before He intervened. Joseph had pondered and reached what he thought was a noble and godly resolution to the dilemma. However, even the best human reasoning is often short of God's plan. An angel appeared to Joseph in a dream to explain the truth behind the seeming betrayal. The form of address, "Son of David," is consistent with Matthew's intent to emphasize the right of Jesus to the Davidic throne. It perhaps also served to signal in Joseph the significance of his role in this miraculous drama.

Joseph was told to "not be afraid to take Mary" as his wife. The text more accurately reads *Marian tēn gunaika sou,* "Mary your wife." This emphasizes the permanence of the betrothal and the sureness of God's plan. To "take" implies to "take along with" (*paralabein*), obviously referring to completing the marriage. This he did (v. 24). His fear was based upon the public disgrace that would result from a union that ignored the infidelity of the woman, or that Mary would not be a trustworthy wife. But he was not to fear (*phobeō*), because "that which has been conceived in her is of the Holy Spirit." The announcement of the divine nature of her pregnancy was to calm the fears that had plagued Joseph since he had first come to understand that his betrothed was pregnant.

Two significant terms were used by the angel. First, the angel did not say, "He who was conceived," but, *"That which"* (*to gar en autē gennēthen*) was conceived. The articular participle (*to . . . gennēthen*) is aorist passive neuter. And as Meyer points out, the neuter "places the embryo still under the impersonal material point of view."[16] The words for the object ("that which") conceived in Mary's womb were not highlighting the eternal logos, which took on flesh (John 1:1-14), but the physical body prepared for His use.[17] One might consider Hebrews 10:5, "Therefore, when He comes into the world, He says, 'Sacrifice and offering Thou hast not desired, but a body Thou hast prepared for Me.'" The Holy Spirit placed in Mary's womb the properties that generated a natural body for the supranatural being who would indwell it.

Second, the angel pointed out that the conception was not of human experience but was "of the Holy Spirit" (*ek pneumatos . . . hagiou*). The preposition *ek* with the genitive (or ablative) case (*pneumatos*) is showing the source or origin (e.g., "out of, from") or it can possibly be designating the means by which something is done ("by means of"). The angel was therefore emphasizing to Joseph that the source, or origin, of that which was in Mary's womb was the Spirit of God Himself. Consequently Joseph should have no fear of taking Mary into his home.

1:21   The angel continued by revealing that Mary would give birth to a son and that Joseph was to name Him "Jesus." The specific detail of the gender of the child Mary was carrying may have indicated to Joseph that this was indeed not just a dream but a prophetic proclamation consistent with the divine nature of the conception. Responsibility for assigning the name to the child was given to both Mary (Luke 1:31) and Joseph with the angel's instruction "You shall call His name Jesus" (*kaleseis to onoma autou Iēsoun*, the same wording in both accounts). The use of the future tense (*kaleseis*, "you shall call") is best understood with an imperatival force. The future is used to express a command in both secular and biblical Greek and "in the Mosaic Law this is particularly so."[18]

The name *Jesus* has traditionally been held to be derived from the Hebrew Jehoshua (*y hos u a*)[19], and this appears to be defensible. The Hebrew name is a compound of Je (*Y a* shortened form of *Y^ehovah*, the name of God, and *yasa*, which means to save). The name Jesus is apparently the New Testament equivalent of "Joshua," the name of the great leader who led Israel in the conquest of Palestine.[20] The significance of the name was designated by the angel: "For it is He who will save His people from their sins." The word "for" is the explanatory conjunction *gar*, which introduces the cause or reason for some action or instruction. The name was assigned because of His work of saving His people from their sins. This appellation also associates Jesus with the messianic salvific work that was anticipated by those Jews faithfully seeking their God (i.e., Simeon, Luke 2:25-30). The name *Jesus*, however, was actually a common name and is found frequently in both the LXX and Josephus, probably because of its association with Joshua, Israel's hero.

1:22   Matthew now asserts that the events spoken of by the angel had taken place (since he was writing decades after the proclamation) in accordance with Isaiah's prediction of a sign for the house of David (Isa. 7:13-14). Carson believes it is possible that vv. 22-23 are to be included in the angel's message. He explains that the words "took place" refer to the conception in Mary's womb, but it is not clear why he would not also include v. 21 ("bear a Son" and Joseph's naming the child) in what has taken place. The perfect tense (*gegonen*) and the adjective *holos* indicate that the best understanding is that all the angel predicted had taken place before Matthew wrote these words. He states that the events happened "that" (*hina*, "in order that") what was written might be "fulfilled." According to Gundry, these "fulfillment quotations" are distinctive of Matthew, and he uses the fulfillment formula eleven times in his gospel (1:22-23; 2:15, 17-18, 23; 4:14-16; 8:17; 12:17-21; 13:14-15, 35; 21:4-5; 27:9-10).[21] Hendriksen offers a more complete list of forty references in Matthew to Old Testament predictions. (For a helpful catalogue of the references, see his commentary on this gospel).[22] Matthew surely intended to convey that the virgin birth of Jesus was the fulfillment of Isaiah's prophecy. Hendriksen expresses it well: "As Matthew by inspiration sees it, whatever anticipatory fulfillments these predictions may have had during the old dispensation, they attain their consummation in Jesus Christ, in him alone."[23]

1:23 Matthew now quotes Isaiah 7:14, "Behold the virgin shall be with child." Matthew is quoting the LXX[24] except that he changes *kaleseis* (second person singular future, "you shall call") to *kalesousin* (3rd person plural future, "they shall call").[25] The Hebrew text says, "She [the virgin] shall call." Matthew's purpose in doing this is to emphasize that people ("His people," v. 21, believing Israel and, later, believing Gentiles) will recognize that He indeed was God among us (Immanuel).

Such adjustments to Old Testament references are common among all New Testament writers. Even the Lord Himself adjusted the greatest commandment, "You shall love the Lord your God with all your heart and with all your soul and with all your *might*" (Deut. 6:5, Hebrew *m'd,* LXX *dunamis*). In Matthew 22:37, He says, "You shall love the Lord your God with all your heart, and with all your soul, and with all your *mind*" (Greek *dianoia*). The New Testament use of the Old Testament often interprets the OT passage to clarify or amplify its postmessianic significance or to emphasize a particular aspect of the context. In Christ's restatement of Deuteronomy 6:5, He was emphasizing that the Jews' zeal was not the problem but rather their failure to understand the significance of God's Word brought into question whether their love was for the Lord their God or their rabbinic traditions. Matthew's change is simply emphasizing the proper recognition and worship of Christ, not by His mother or by Joseph but by all those who believe in Him.

Volumes have been written concerning the use of the word "virgin" (*parthenos*), but for the purpose of this commentary only a brief synopsis will be offered. The Hebrew text of Isaiah 7:14 states that an *alma* (*'lmh*) will bear a son. The most basic use of this word means a sexually inexperienced young woman of marriageable age (e.g., Gen. 24:43). However, it could be used of any young woman, including perhaps sexually experienced women, though this writer could find no clear reference to such in the Old Testament. The LXX, which Matthew references, uses *parthenos,* which most naturally means "virgin." Carson understands *parthenos* to "almost always" mean "virgin"[26] but sees Genesis 34:4 as an exception. He states that the "previous verse makes it clear she is no longer a virgin."[27] However, this may be overstating the argument. Genesis 34:1-2 records that Shechem the Hivite raped Dinah, the daughter of Jacob and Leah. Shechem apparently fell in love with her and desired to marry her. The LXX says that Shechem loved "the girl," or "the virgin" (*tēn parthenon*) and spoke with understanding to "the virgin" (*tēs parthenou*). It seems that after his shaming her, he fell in love with her, wanted to marry her, and consoled her about forcing her to have sex with him. He says to his father, "Get for me this maid (*paidiskē*, literally, "slave girl, maid") for a wife." The reference to her being a virgin most logically refers to her state before being raped. This reference is certainly not a "clear" indication that *parthenos* referred to women who were sexually experienced.

Regardless of what one wishes to conclude from word studies in the LXX or the Hebrew text, Matthew certainly makes clear what *he* means by *parthenos*. In vv. 18 and 20, the text emphasizes that the child in Mary's womb was not the product of sexual experience. Luke, in his gospel, also clarifies that Mary was a sexually inexperienced young girl, recording that she asked, "How can this be [her having a child], since I am a virgin?" (literally, "Do not know a man," *andra ou ginōskō*[28]; Luke 1:34).

CONCLUSION TO GENEALOGY ACCOUNT, 1:24-25

1:24   Matthew now concludes his account by explaining that Joseph arose from his sleep and followed through with the wedding contract. There is no reason to suppose that Joseph and Mary were married the next day, unless one assumes that he discovered that Mary was pregnant only after he had gone to get her at the beginning of the wedding feast. It is more likely that the explanation of the angel prepared Joseph to fulfill the marriage contract and that the wedding took place at a later time.

1:25   Matthew once again emphasizes the virgin birth by pointing out that Mary remained a virgin "until" Jesus was born. The text actually says, "He did not know her" (see fn. 28) until she had given birth to a son. The temporal preposition *heōs* implies that, following the birth, Joseph and Mary had normal conjugal relations. This is certainly consistent with Matthew 12:46 and so on. Matthew's purpose is to protect the nature of Christ by emphasizing the virgin birth, not to protect the reputation of Mary. Certainly there is no concern for making Mary a perpetual virgin.

HOMILETICAL SUGGESTIONS

As one approaches this chapter, it may be tempting to skip most of the genealogy. However, the teacher of God's Word must realize that God recorded this section just as surely as He did John 3:16 or any other portion of Scripture. Thus the one who is committed to the authority and inspiration of Scripture must communicate the first seventeen verses of chap. 1 as faithfully as the rest of the chapter. There are several key features to keep in mind: first, the names listed communicate God's grace and sovereign use of individuals, which offers hope to those who think their pre-Christian life may negate their service to God; second, the genealogy traces God's work through the covenants and demonstrates His faithfulness; third, it offers the historical context for Gentile Christians to better comprehend the work of God throughout the ages and will help properly interpret many New Testament references to Israel and messianic prophecy. The genealogy is the platform for more fully understanding the identity of Jesus Christ.

Another feature of chap. 1 is the detailed defense of the virgin birth of Jesus Christ. The Spirit of God is concerned that those who claim to believe in Jesus Christ fully understand the divine nature of this Person. He is separate from the Adamic race and is the eternal *logos,* who indwelt the flesh especially prepared by God Himself. This child is the one prophesied as God's own sign to Israel, the One who would save His people and fulfill the Davidic covenant. In teaching this section, emphasis should be placed upon the Second Adam, the One who is uniquely prepared by the Father in contrast to the rest of the human race, which is cursed by the Adamic Fall.

The characters used in God's redemptive program also deserve special attention. In vv. 18-25, Joseph is highlighted to demonstrate the character and nature of God's servant. Joseph's godly character and his concern for Mary should not be overlooked. It is also important to note that his obedience (vv. 24-25) is consistent with his reputation of v. 19, "a righteous man." Thus chap. 1 falls neatly into three major sections: the genealogy of Messiah (1:1-17); the explanation of the Virgin Birth (1:18-23); and the character and obedience of Joseph (1:19, 24-25). The first chapter introduces the birth of Messiah. Chap. 2 will offer the details of the birth itself.

MATTHEW

CHAPTER

TWO

EVENTS FOLLOWING
THE BIRTH OF JESUS

The historical veracity of this next section of Matthew's gospel has been questioned by some, who refer to the accounts in chap. 2 as "embellishments of tradition."[1] However, there is no grammatical, historical, contextual, or theological reason to dismiss the historical reality of these events. There are also accusations of trying to force harmonization between the events of Matthew and those of Luke. "Irreconcilability with Luke" is cited: "Even the most determined harmonizer should be foiled by the impossibility of reconciling a journey of the family from Bethlehem to Egypt with Luke's account of their taking the child to Jerusalem."[2]

It seems beyond comprehension to some scholars to allow each gospel writer to record those facts that are in keeping with his commission in recording a biblical narrative. Luke is concerned with Jesus' being taken by His parents to the temple in Jerusalem, only a six-mile journey, when the infant was eight days old (Luke 2:21). There must have been at least a year between the dedication in the temple and the visit by the Magi. Because he does not record the events between the temple dedication and the return to Nazareth, it is assumed that Matthew must have invented the trip to Egypt. This argument from silence indicates a predisposition toward a weak view of the integrity of Scripture. Matthew's accounts are to be taken as literally as the rest of historical narrative.

THE MAGI, 2:1-12

2:1   Regardless of holiday songs and traditions, the Magi did not have any participation in the birth of Jesus. Their arrival is carefully noted by Matthew as taking place "after" Jesus was born. He more literally states, "But Jesus having been born (*gennēthentos*, aorist passive participle from *gennaō*) in Bethlehem." The use of the aorist participle indicates that the birth of Jesus preceded the arrival of the Magi. How much later they arrived must be determined by comments made in vv. 11 and 16. These verses imply that the event must have been at least one year after the birth and not contemporaneous with the angelic message to the shepherds or their visit to the Nativity.

The Magi arrived during the reign of Herod the king. Herod founded the Idumaean dynasty and enjoyed Roman protection and support. He was both clever and violent. From 40 B.C. (when the Roman senate voted to make him king of Judea) to his death in 4 B.C., he demonstrated great ability as a military leader, a diplomat (as evidenced by winning and maintaining favor with both Octavian and Antony, who were bitter enemies), a builder of cities and great buildings (including the magnificent temple that Jesus frequented), and he left behind a legacy of both great achievement and fearful violence.[3]

Identifying the Magi is not a critical matter but adds another significant dimension to the birth of the Jewish King. The term *Magi* (*magos*) most likely refers to Persian or Babylonian wise men. The term is found in Daniel 2:2 and 10 (LXX), where they are associated with the other offices that advised the powerful monarchs of the ancient Near East. It is worth remembering that Daniel was an associate of these men and even interceded for their lives (Dan. 2:24), and Daniel 2:13 implies that Daniel was considered to be one of their community. A *magos* was probably a mixture of scientist and astronomer. Daniel's association with them may well have been the connection between the birth of the Jewish Messiah and their interpreting of the astronomical sign. Perhaps Daniel had spoken of such phenomena to his associates in Babylon, and, due to his high status, his words were orally preserved among the fraternity of wise men. God's Word does not offer any other connection. The explanation that Matthew "now turns the visit of the local Jewish shepherds (Luke 2:8-20) into the adoration by Gentile magi from foreign parts"[4] is to be rejected on both academic and biblical grounds.

The number of Magi is not given, and the assumption of three is generally drawn from the number of gifts, offering a weak explanation rather irrelevant to the visit. Equally weak is the association with kingship—prophecies of "kings" worshiping the Messiah[5] is inadequate justification for this fanciful identification.[6]

What is significant in this account is that these Gentiles have come searching for the king of Israel. It is only logical from their perspective that the king should be in Jerusalem, the seat of Jewish authority and past glory. Whereas Luke reflects the humility of Christ's birth by having it announced to humble shepherds of the fields (Luke 2:8-20), Matthew reflects the universality of Messiah's work by introducing these Gentiles, who apparently had been given some notice of the event. The importance of this is that God does not announce the birth of the Messiah, the Son of David and rightful King of Israel, to the religious leaders or to the political dynasty. God is indicating that He has no intention of using the established systems to accomplish His redemptive program or to fulfill His Davidic promises.

2:2   The Magi asked where the "King of the Jews" had been born, apparently having gone to the palace, where they expected the new king to be found. Herod "heard it and was troubled" because he was extremely jealous of his throne and suspected everyone of trying to steal his domain. The list of those whom he murdered to protect his throne, including wife and sons, is depressingly lengthy.[7] Emperor Augustus, who knew him well, spoke a parable saying, "It is preferable to be Herod's pig than Herod's son."[8] The word "pig" is the Greek *hys,* whereas the Greek word for "son" is *hyios.* This play on words seems to have been characteristic of Augustus's humor and intellect.

The Magi reported that they had seen "His star" (*autou ton astera*). Attempts to associate this star with certain conjunctions of the planets or other natural astronomical phenomena[9] are unnecessary and unprofitable. There is no need to try to justify Matthew's account with human reasoning because none of the explanations could offer more credibility to the account. Such conjunctions of planets were not normally named "stars," nor do the assumed dates match the most probable date of Jesus' birth. In reality, any attempt to explain the event by natural phenomena becomes derogatory rather than honoring to God. The star apparently moved (v. 9) and "stood over where the Child was." Had these been planets or a comet, such terminology would have been nonsensical. At best, this natural phenomenon would have indicated no less than a nation, certainly not a house. It is not the responsibility of the Christian community to make God's Word more acceptable to the world but to state the Word of God accurately.

Carson sees Matthew as alluding to Numbers 24:17.[10] Although this may be possible, it seems to be an unnecessary effort to place a prophecy of the star in the Old Testament. Such effort is not obligatory. Matthew does not claim the star was the fulfillment of any prophecy but simply records the event as historical fact. It should be noted that the star was "His" star. Matthew places the pronoun first, *autou ton astera,* indicating that the star was unique to Him. Hendriksen makes the most appropriate conclusion about the Magi and the star: "It is obvious, however, that all of these opinions as to how and why the wise men connected the appearance of this star with the birth of the Messiah are mere conjectures. We do not have the answer. We are left in the dark."[11]

What is far more important than the nature or origin of the star, or even the identity of the Magi, is the purpose for which they made the journey: they came to worship the King of the Jews. In keeping with Matthew's emphasis on Jesus as the Son of David, the King of Israel, he notes that the Magi came to worship. The significance of these noble Gentiles traveling across difficult territory and bringing expensive gifts, all to worship the Jewish king, points to the universal nature of Christ's kingdom. It also bears testimony to the deadness of Israel's faith.

2:3   Having heard of the star announcing the birth of a Jewish king, Herod became frightened. Herod was not Jewish but Idumaean[12] and had taken Jerusalem by force after the Roman senate gave him authority to do so. He knew the history of the Jews and their determination to have their own king on the throne. Thus this was not good news for him. Calvin believed that Herod was acquainted with the messianic prophecies,[13] but more likely his fear was simply based on the rumor of a challenger to his throne.

One can easily understand why Herod would have been alarmed, but Matthew continues to say that "all Jerusalem" was also troubled. The natural question is, why would the people of Jerusalem be afraid or troubled by news of a Jewish king? The answer probably most naturally lies in the terror the Romans had instilled in the people whom they ruled. They did not tolerate rebellious subjects usurping authority, and Israel had a history of rebellion and fanatical heroes. This was demonstrated somewhat by Gamaliel's warning to the Jews persecuting Peter and the apostles (Acts 5:36-37) and by the fear expressed by the town clerk of Ephesus when the city was in a riotous state (Acts 19:35-40). This is also the fear reflected in John 19:12-15: the Jews cried out, "We have no king but Caesar."

The expression "all Jerusalem" is of course hyperbolic. The point was that the arrival and question of the Magi aroused the attention of the city. Too often Christians fail to understand the significance of the impact these visitors would have had on a city such as Jerusalem. This was not just three men riding into town but a large and impressive caravan. Carrying valuable treasures and used to being prominent among the courts, these exotically dressed wise men were accompanied by ample guards, attendants, and supplies as they traversed desert areas for weeks to reach their destination. Such esteemed men would not travel in humble conditions, and a large and highly visible entourage should be envisioned. Therefore, when rumors about the seeking of a newborn king began to spread, the city could expect only trouble from either Herod (e.g., v. 16) or Rome. Contemporary Christians should understand the tensions of this real world into which God incarnated Himself.

2:4 Though Herod outwardly pretended to follow the Jewish religion, he did not know the answer to the Magi's question. Thus, he assembled the leaders of Israel's religious body and laid the question before them. Note that he exchanged the word "Christ" (*Christos*), Messiah, for the word "king" (*basileōs*). This would imply a close parallel in the thinking of the time period between the Christ (Messiah) and the rightful king of Israel. "Christ" as an appellation means "anointed one" and designated the anticipated deliverer from God, Messiah.[14] That the Jews anticipated the Messiah with great hope is clear from the numerous references to Him as the interpretive focus of Old Testament passages. Edersheim surveyed the Targumim, both Talmuds, and only the most ancient Midrashim and found 456 Old Testament passages that applied to Messiah or the messianic age. In addition, he found 558 separate quotations related to Messiah in rabbinical writings.[15] Though great confusion existed in the rabbinical literature as to exactly who or what Messiah would be or do, it was generally acknowledged that he was to be a king, the son of David.

This anticipation is reflected in several New Testament passages. For example, when John the Baptist appeared on the scene, the people became excited and sought to identify him. As Luke records, "the people were in a state of expectation and all were wondering in their hearts about John, as to whether he might be the Christ" (Luke 3:15), but his response was "I am not the Christ" (John 1:20). Herod apparently knew of this messianism and was alarmed upon hearing that the "King of the Jews" had been born. Again, the reaction of "all Jerusalem" reflected the mixed emotions of the time. The rabbis were talking about Messiah and His deliverance, but the Jews had also felt the vicious hand of Rome and the vindictive spirit of Herod. It is no wonder that the city was troubled. In a world of violence and what seemed to be unlimited military power, every family feared what the news of the arrival of Messiah would bring.

2:5-6   The religious leaders demonstrated their knowledge of the prediction concerning Messiah's birthplace. They specifically stated that He would be born in Bethlehem *of Judea* to distinguish it from Bethlehem of Zebulun (Josh. 19:15-16). Bethlehem ("house of bread"[16]), a small village about six miles south of Jerusalem, was the birthplace of David and was named by the prophet Micah as the birthplace of the Messiah.

The religious leaders' interpretation of Micah 5:2 (5:1 in the Hebrew text) is interesting. Micah refers to Bethlehem as "too little to be among the clans of Judah." The Hebrew is *ts`yr,* which means "young, insignificant," or "little."[17] The LXX likewise has *oligostos,* (verbal adjective, *oligos, ē, on*) which in the singular means "little, small, short."[18] The chief priests and scribes, however, altered it to read, "You Bethlehem, land of Judah, *are by no means least* among the leaders of Judah." Gundry assumes Matthew simply altered the Hebrew text. He asserts, "For Matthew the birth of Jesus has transformed Bethlehem from the unimportant village it was at the time of Micah's prediction into the supremely important birthplace of the

messianic king from David's line."[19] But such midrashic assumptions are unnecessary and certainly miss the point of the narrative.
Matthew is repeating what the scribes and chief priests said. In their
zeal to honor David, the great king, and his birthplace, they altered
the text to elevate the character and importance of this historically
significant site. It may also be assumed that they were working
from a text that we do not have. The main point is that there is no
reason to assume that Matthew made a mistake or changed the text
of Micah. He is only recording what these religious leaders told
Herod. The fact that Herod had selected Bethlehem as the site for
one of his Herodian palaces should be noted. It is far more likely
that these politically correct religionists should flatter Herod and
their own royal history than that the Spirit of God would have motivated Matthew to arbitrarily change the text.

They also altered the last part of the prophecy and added the
shepherd motif. Perhaps they were borrowing from 2 Samuel 5:2.
This also served two agendas of these men who had been summoned before an irrational tyrant. First, they would perhaps convey
to him that this Messiah was a shepherd-ruler, a spiritual leader, not
a political or military leader who would threaten his kingdom. Second, it recalled to their minds the Davidic rule (the shepherd who
became a great king) in association with the city of Bethlehem.

2:7-8   Apparently Herod met privately with the Magi after he
gained the desired information. His primary concern was when the
star was first seen, in order to determine how old the new king was
and if enough time had elapsed for recognition by others. The question again reflected the paranoia of this insecure and violent man.
The secret meeting probably also demonstrated his lack of trust in
the religious leaders. Herod apparently intended to kill all the
youth of Bethlehem if necessary, now that he had discovered the
birthplace. Now he only needed the time frame. Calvin points to
the confused state of Herod's mind—as a courtesy, an escort could
easily have been sent to act as a spy in locating the new king.[20]

But Herod sent the Magi on their way with instructions to
report back to him upon finding the child, under the pretense of
wishing to worship the new king. Apparently the Magi did not sus-
pect the treachery of Herod's heart, for God spoke to them in a
dream (v. 12) to alert them ("warned them") of the danger.

2:9   After leaving Herod, the Magi once again saw the star. The expression "behold" (*idou*) is a common imperatival exclamation expressing surprise at some significant event or person. Its use here implies that the star had not been visible for some time. Apparently the Magi had first seen the star while in their eastern land (or possibly, "saw the star in its rising"). It signified, either by some oral prophecy left behind by Daniel or by special revelation from God (God gave them special revelation, v. 12) that the Jewish king was born. They assumed therefore that he would be found in Jerusalem and went to that city asking for him. From there they received instructions sending them to Bethlehem. To their surprise, somewhere during that short trip the star reappeared.

Again it should be noted that the star was not a stationary light. Whatever the star was, its purpose was to lead these Gentiles to the King of the Jews. The star "went on before them" (imperfect form of the verb *proagō,* which literally should read "was going ahead of them"). How high the star was or how they perceived its moving is unknown and should not become the subject of unwarranted speculation. God is quite capable of providing any phenomena He desires to accomplish His purpose. What is clear is that the star was not like any other star. All the stars over Jerusalem would also be over Bethlehem. This star actually came to rest (aorist passive of *histēmi,* "made to stand, was placed") over the place ("house," v. 11) where the child was.

2:10 Verse 10 is apparently parenthetical only to express the emotion felt by these men. Their journey had ended in success. The audience with the long-anticipated King of the Jews was at hand. It is interesting that these men, who would certainly be used to royal persons and powerful politicians, expressed such joy, indicating the significance they placed upon this child. Again, why would Gentiles be excited about a king born to a nonroyal family in such a small and politically weak nation as Israel? They had just had an audience with Herod, a monarch who was a regular associate of Augustus (Octavian) Caesar and a friend of Cleopatra and Antony. Yet, there had been no indication of such exultation in his presence. Certainly they had information about this child that excited their hearts. And even in the humble surroundings of a carpenter's home in lowly Bethlehem, their joy was not diminished.

2:11 This verse contradicts many of the familiar Christmas traditions. The Magi did not enter a stable but a home (*oikia*[21]), whereas the shepherds found Jesus lying in a feeding trough (*phatēn,* Luke 2:7, 12, 16). Mary and Joseph had reached Bethlehem to find that all the rooms were taken, and thus they took shelter in a stable. That was where the shepherds came. The Magi, however, found the child in a house, which Joseph probably rented or perhaps where they were staying with relatives while waiting to return to Nazareth.

Upon seeing Jesus, the Magi "fell down and worshiped," a typical expression of humbling oneself before superior persons. Note that the Magi saw both the child and the mother but they worshiped Him (*prosekunēsan autō*) alone. Mary is not designated as an object of adoration. The absence of any mention of Joseph is probably not of major significance. Opening their treasures (or, more properly, "treasure box"), they presented gifts to Him, a common practice for one coming to show honor in the ancient Near East. The three gifts, gold, frankincense, and myrrh[22] were typical tokens of the time period, representing importance and great value, and probably do not offer any prophetic or metaphoric meaning. William Barclay is one who sees the three gifts foretelling His kingship, His priesthood, and His sacrifice.[23] No monetary value is placed on the gifts, but there certainly would have been enough to finance the trip to Egypt and the return to Nazareth.

2:12   As they prepared to leave, God warned the Magi in a dream to avoid any further contact with Herod. The purpose of this warning was not to protect Jesus—God would take Him to Egypt for that purpose. Rather, protection of the Magi was the issue. Certainly an unstable, violent man such as Herod would not allow them to depart, giving opportunity to tell about the newborn king they had worshiped. This verse is only one of many in the Old and New Testaments where God gives direct special revelation to people not in a covenant relationship with Him. And that indicates that God also might have given them special revelation so that they would recognize the star and its significance. Their return trip was probably along the coastal road, allowing passage without their traveling through Jerusalem or by way of Jericho, thus avoiding the king.

THE FLIGHT INTO EGYPT, 2:13-18

2:13   The language of v. 13 implies that the message from the angel followed soon after the departure of the Magi. As the wise men's caravan pulled out of Bethlehem, the warning to Joseph sounded. The passage seems to convey a clear message of urgency.

Some try to demonstrate that Matthew corrupted Luke's record: "To carry on the motif of flight from persecution Matthew changes the going up to Jerusalem by the Holy Family (Luke 2:22) into a flight to Egypt."[24] But again there is no reason to create such conjectural explanations. Herod was certainly capable of the horror Matthew records, and Egypt would be the most likely place to take refuge. According to ancient sources, almost one million Jews would have been living in Egypt at the time. Though a Roman territory, it was out of the jurisdiction of Herod. Certainly Egypt was a logical place to wait until God removed Herod and instructed Joseph to return. God was explicit that He was the One who would make the decision as to what was best for the child.

2:14   As before, Joseph obeyed the instructions of the angel. That he rose immediately to carry out the instructions is assumed from the expression "by night." However, since the journey just to the border of Egypt was approximately seventy-five miles, it may be best to assume that he arose and began to make preparations immediately and then left the following night to gain the cover of darkness. Either way, his actions again reflected Joseph's characteristic of being an obedient servant. Also interesting is his being told to take the child and His mother, and the word order may emphasize the importance of the child. Also, note the patristic responsibility of Joseph. Mary was not the focus of attention as either the receiver of the message or the primary person to be protected.

2:15   The angel told Joseph to remain in Egypt until he would instruct him to leave (v. 13), and, according to v. 15, that was until the time of Herod's death. God apparently had reason for leaving Herod in power for a period of time. Meanwhile, the child was to stay in Egypt to keep Him out of Herod's reach. We may question why God would have Joseph go to such elaborate lengths to protect the child. Certainly He could have protected the child in Bethlehem through any manner of miracle and also could have prevented the Magi from stopping by Herod's palace. But speculation is futile. The fact that God wanted Herod and the religious leaders to know is clear. The mysterious Magi had stirred all Jerusalem, and this certainly aroused the messianic anticipation of the people.

Perhaps one of the most controversial statements in Matthew

is the expression "that what was spoken by the Lord through the prophet might be fulfilled" (v. 15). Some believe that Matthew is rewriting the events of Israel's time in Egypt and deliverance through Moses, in order to compare Jesus to Moses.[25] Thus the flight into Egypt would be a fanciful embellishment on the Nativity account, made up by Matthew to draw peoples' attention to the similarity between Moses and Jesus. Though this is a simplistic way of discarding any problems of understanding Matthew's use of Hosea, it certainly brings into question the integrity of Matthew's gospel and the whole topic of inerrancy and inspiration.

Hendriksen offers a reasonable explanation, noting that Messiah is a product of Israel and that Hosea was reminding unfaithful Israel of God's deliverance based on His paternal relationship with them. When He delivered the nation from Egypt, God was indeed bringing His Son, the Messiah, out of the land with them. Had Israel perished in Egypt, so would the messianic line. Hendriksen points out a parallel idea with Christ and the church: Jesus asked the persecutor of the *church* (Saul), "Why do you persecute *Me*?" (Acts 9:4).[26]

Identification of the promised seed to the nation is clearly assumed elsewhere in Matthew's gospel. The idea of "fulfilled" also does not necessarily need to be taken as implying that every *detail* must match but rather that the intent of the original message is brought to fruition in the later event. What God said about the nation of Israel in Hosea was brought to a more complete realization through Messiah, who typically represented all that the nation was to God. Along this same line of reasoning, Jesus referred to Himself as the "'true vine" (John 15:1), whereas that analogy was used of Israel in Isaiah 5:1-7, and Psalm 80:8 describes Israel as a vine taken out of Egypt and planted in the land of promise. It does seem logical to accept Matthew's point as being that Hosea's reminder of the Exodus was to be more fully realized by the Messiah, who would likewise be brought out of Egypt.[27]

2:16   One might easily misunderstand Matthew's comment in this verse if Herod's past record and his character are overlooked. Herod's slaughter of the male children in Bethlehem and its environs flowed out of his irrational jealousy and intense thirst for power. For a man who murdered his own sons and his wife (for whom he apparently had great affection) to protect his throne from imagined threats, the slaughter of a few Jewish males in an obscure village would not be out of character. His anger at having been outsmarted by the Magi (actually by God, who instructed them) is only one of many examples of his violent and perverse nature. The fact that the Magi had not obeyed his command to report back to him (v. 8) was taken as impudence, but there can be little doubt that Herod would have taken the same drastic measures to protect his throne whether they had returned to Jerusalem or not.

Some have ridiculed Matthew's story of the slaughter of male infants because of its omission from historical records. But such skepticism is without warrant. Herod was known for violence and outrageous cruelty. Therefore, the account certainly fits his profile. For example, in one village captured during a rebellion, he slew the two thousand who remained in the surrendered hamlet and then burned it to the ground.[28] One has only to casually read the historical records of this brutal king to understand why the murder of a few Jewish babies did not get recorded. A pastor in Africa once challenged the American church for not coming to the aid of his village where hundreds were being murdered weekly by government forces. He found it difficult to believe that Americans had not heard of the atrocities, because the media simply had not reported them. Something important to him was basically ignored by the rest of the world because so many major world events were taking place.

One should understand that the village of Bethlehem was small and the percentage of children two years and younger would have been fewer than is at first assumed. In addition, when the number is further limited to only males, it is most likely that the number of children killed was less than twenty. Even though this is still a horrifying crime, compared to Herod's other brutalities, it was not notable. Had Bethlehem been a significant city, or had the children been the offspring of nobles or royalty, the slaughter certainly would have been recorded. But as these were small-town peasants, the event would not qualify for the historical records. It should also be kept in mind that many other events, not only in Matthew but in the rest of Scripture, are recorded nowhere else. Those who question Matthew's historicity based upon this argument must be consistent and reject as embellishments the events recorded in Josephus, Heroditus, and other historians who, alone, mention certain events. Josephus provides many details in the history of the Jews not found other places, yet his writings are quoted as historical fact. It could be assumed that if Josephus had recorded this event, the account would not have been questioned. This surely reflects an unjustified bias against the trustworthiness of Scripture.

Herod commanded that all the male children two years and under be put to death. His orders were calculated "according to the time which he had ascertained from the magi." This would place the age of the child as no more than two years. Hendriksen believes that since Herod "always allowed himself a very wide margin," and from what he sees as evidence from Luke 3:23 and John 2:20, that the infant was probably only two months old.[29] Such calculations are much too speculative, and it must simply be admitted that God did not give enough specific detail to accurately discover the year of our Lord's birth. This is in interesting contrast to the fact that the very hour of the day is recorded for His death. There should be little doubt that Herod would not have hesitated to kill more children than necessary to protect his kingdom, and probably from several months up to one and one-half years is a good estimate of how old Jesus was at the time of this slaughter. Or one may follow Carson's calculations in which he assumes from six to twenty months.[30]

2:17-18   Once again Matthew attributes the historical event that he is relating to the fulfillment of an Old Testament prophecy. His reference is to Jeremiah 31:15, where the context is the promise of Yahweh to gather and shepherd His people whom He had previously scattered. The Jeremiah context is intended to comfort Israel: though her children had been cut off, yet they would be restored. "Thus says the Lord, 'Restrain your voice from weeping, and your eyes from tears; for your work shall be rewarded,' declares the Lord, 'and they shall return from the land of the enemy'" (Jer. 31:16).

Ramah was a city located in the tribal area of Benjamin about ten miles north of Bethlehem and between Bethel and Gibeah.[31] It was a major Old Testament site in that it was the home of Hannah, the birthplace and burial place of Samuel (1 Sam. 1:19; 25:1), and the scene of much activity in the time of King Saul. Traditionally, Rachel, having died giving birth to Benjamin, was buried near Ramah "on the way to Ephrath (that is, Bethlehem)"[32] (Gen. 35:19). First Samuel 10:2 records that her tomb was in the territory of Benjamin at Zelzah, a town on the southern border of the Benjamite territory.

Matthew's connection is that Rachel represented the mothers of the nation, who were weeping for the fate of the children of Israel typified in the death of the male children. Binns understands Matthew's referencing Jeremiah as a type of the weeping of the mothers of the massacred children,[33] but certainly this is too limited in Matthew's scheme. It was the whole nation being wept for, not a few children in one village. Jeremiah 31:15 is to be understood as a comfort passage in that, though the tragedy of Israel's captivity has brought Rachel from her tomb to weep (figuratively), v. 16 offers comfort. God will regather those whom He has scattered. Matthew may have been saying that the slaughter of the children, bringing reminders of grief over the children of Jeremiah 31, was a forecast of the healing to come through the child spared by the intervention of God. Carson's discussion on this is helpful:

> Help comes from observing the broader context of both Jeremiah and Matthew. Jeremiah 31:9, 20 refers to Israel = Ephraim as God's dear son and also introduces the new covenant (31:31-34) the Lord will make with his people. Therefore, the tears associated with the Exile (31:15) will end. Matthew has already made the Exile a turning point in his thought (1:11-12), for at that time the Davidic line was dethroned. The tears of the Exile are now being "fulfilled"—i.e., the tears begun in Jeremiah's day are climaxed and ended by the tears of the mothers of Bethlehem. The heir to David's throne has come, the Exile is over, the true Son of God has arrived, and he will introduce the new covenant (26:28) promised by Jeremiah.[34]

RETURN TO ISRAEL, 2:19-23

2:19-21 Matthew resumes his narrative by announcing the death of Herod the Great. Josephus offers comprehensive details of the horrible death suffered by Herod after serving as king for thirty-seven years (from his appointment by Rome).[35] Bruce marks his death as taking place in March, 4 B.C.[36] The death of this tyrant opened the way for Jesus to return to Israel.

The method of communicating the instruction to return to Israel was that of an angel speaking to Joseph in a dream. This was the same method as in the account of chap. 1 when Joseph was comforted and instructed to marry Mary (1:20-24). Angelic communication through dreams was common in the Old Testament and in the early stages of the Christian era. As the author of Hebrews informs his readers, "God spoke . . . in many portions and in many ways." In the present age, we have the "more sure word of prophecy," the written Word of God.

The message was simple (v. 20): the threat was over; it was time to return to Israel. "Those" (plural) who sought the life of the child was simply a reference to Herod and his assassins. The angel does not appear to have designated any particular city in Israel, and it might be assumed that Joseph would naturally return to Bethlehem. Joseph again obeyed the angelic message and reentered the covenant land (v. 21). Matthew has already related this event to the fulfillment of prophecy (Hosea 11:1; v. 15).

2:22-23   Upon returning to Israel, Joseph learned that Archelaus, a vicious and dangerous son of Herod, was ruling Judea. Archelaus was named as the successor to his father and was publicly proclaimed king immediately after his father's death.[37] But the Jews feared him more than they had his father and did not trust his intentions for the nation. They sent a delegation to Rome to petition Caesar to remove him as king. His rule was challenged not only by the Jews but also by his brothers and by certain Roman officials who feared him as well.[38] Archelaus in turn went to Rome, where he petitioned Caesar to confirm his inheritance of the kingdom. Caesar's ruling was to make Archelaus ethnarch of Judea (ruler of half of Herod's territory) and to divide the remaining half between Philip and Antipas (tetrarchs, rulers of one-fourth), two other sons of Herod.[39]

Upon becoming ethnarch of Judea, he returned to the land and deposed the high priest Joazar, accusing him of leading seditions against him, and placed Eleazar in his place. He continued to abuse and offend the Jews through barbarous and tyrannical acts to such a degree that after ten years he was recalled to Rome, had his kingdom taken away, and was exiled without government money to Vienna, a city of Gaul.[40] It is quite likely that this historical event in Archelaus's early years was the basis for the parable Christ taught concerning His own kingdom, recorded in Luke 19:12-27. Certainly the story of Archelaus was well-known among the Jews of Jesus' time, and it would be a powerful foundation for illustrating the opposition to His own kingdom. Like all parables, the core truth was communicated without the necessity of matching every detail.

Verse 23 is among the many that are challenged by those who doubt the historical integrity of the record of Matthew. The problem here is prophetic fulfillment of "He shall be called a Nazarene." Indeed, this is a complicated issue since there is no prophetic declaration of the Messiah's being called a Nazarene. To be fair with Matthew, it should be noted that his formula for introducing this fulfillment statement is different from the others. First, he uses the plural "prophets" (*tōn prophētōn*) instead of referring to one particular prophet as in 2:17 ("Jeremiah the prophet"), 2:15 ("through the prophet"), and 2:5 ("by the prophet"). This would imply that Matthew is drawing upon a composite of several comments in prophetic literature and not a particular statement. Second, in 2:5 Matthew records that the prophecy was "written" and begins a direct quotation. In 2:15 and 17 he introduces his references with "saying . . ." (*legontos*), but in v. 23 he simply says "that [*hoti*] He will be called Nazarene." The significance of these two observations is that Matthew is not claiming to be quoting a single Old Testament passage but is compiling an image of the Messiah from several remarks of the prophets.

Calvin understands Matthew's comment to refer not to the city of Nazareth but to the Hebrew *nzyr,* "Nazirite."[41] He then associates Matthew's comment with Judges 13:5,[42] which is the prophetic reference to the birth of Samson. The connection seems to be that as Samson was to save Israel from the oppression of the Philistines, so Jesus was to save Israel from her sins. This seems too creative but yet may play some part in the combining of many Old Testament references to portray Jesus. It is not likely that "Nazarene" of Matthew 2:23 is based on the Hebrew *nzyr.*

Carson's explanation is far more acceptable. His argument focuses upon the connection between the despised reputation of the city of Nazareth with the despising of the Messiah. Carson believes that the comment of Matthew is that the Old Testament prophets portrayed Messiah as One who was to be despised, and, in fulfillment of this, Jesus would be labeled "Nazarene" because He was a citizen of the city of ill repute.[43] Nathanael's comment in John 1:46, "Can any good thing come out of Nazareth?" reveals the reputation of that city. "He shall be called a Nazarene" is somewhat like saying He would be classified as someone to be scorned. Paul was accused before Felix as being a "real pest" who "stirs up dissension among all the Jews" (Acts 24:5). As a final attack upon his character the Jews labeled him as "a ringleader of the sect of the Nazarenes," which they assumed would seal his doom by associating him with Jesus, the Nazarene.

HOMILETICAL SUGGESTIONS

It is significant that God chose to reveal the birth of His Son, Israel's King, to Gentiles (the Magi). This fact emphasizes that His program of redemption would be universal. It also points to the judgment of God against the religious community of His chosen people. Those who answered Herod's question about the location of the birth of Messiah demonstrated that they were aware of the promises of His coming. Yet they did not show interest in joining the Magi in their trip to Bethlehem. In contrast, they were troubled right along with Herod that this birth might be something that would cause difficulty for them.

It would be well to point out that one of the major thrusts of this record is that Israel had lost sight of the promises of God. The people were busy living in the "real world," and prophetic hope was not a driving force. Is it possible for Christians to do the same thing? Can Christians become so involved with the politics and economics of this life that they lose sight of the future blessings? It seems likely that a large percentage of professing Christianity has exchanged the value of things not seen for the things that are seen. The eternal has been laid aside for the temporal.

Another valuable lesson in this text is found in the horror of the slaughter of the children. Often God's plan allows the unthinkable cruelty of humanity to be a part of His redemptive work. The world is a place of brutality and greed. Herod is only one example of this. Those who deny the necessity of a savior, because they think that humanity is basically good, should learn the lesson of history. God spared His Son but not the other babies of Bethlehem. His sovereign plan provided for the protection of His servant and thus the future redemption of lost people, but humanity is still suffering from the Fall because man chose to disobey.

God used angelic messengers, a long journey into Egypt, and

the resettling of Joseph and Mary to bring the promised King into His position. It should be noted that God could have simply put angels around the child and not allowed any harm to come to Him. But God was demonstrating that He often uses everyday events and plans to accomplish His will. Joseph and Mary had to make a difficult and uncomfortable trip into Egypt. The money for such a journey and sojourn could have been provided by the gift of the Magi. When God told Joseph to return to Israel, He used the tyrant Archelaus to direct Joseph away from Judea and back to Nazareth, because that was where He wanted Him. God frequently works through the circumstances around us to direct our lives.

One final observation in this chapter is worth teaching. Though the story of their finding the "babe in the manger" may be a sentimental tradition, the Magi did not find Him in the manger but in a home. It is not honoring to God to promote error concerning His Word. Pastors and teachers need to be more careful in interpreting Scripture. To honor God, one must accurately interpret and teach His truth (2 Tim. 2:15). The life of Christ is carefully chronicled for us, and the sequence of events needs to be correctly observed. The account of these pagan Gentile astronomers is recorded so that we can better understand God's program and heart. It was to these men that God revealed the birth of the Messiah. The religious community of Israel was not privileged with such revelation because they had become careless and had confused their traditions and personal preferences with God's Word. They had become numb and apathetic toward the eternal things of God because they were too busy trying to live in the present world.

MATTHEW
CHAPTER
THREE

JOHN THE BAPTIST

Matthew now leaps from the events immediately following the birth of Jesus to the introduction of John, the messianic forerunner. John is a fascinating character in Scripture and, due to the mystery surrounding his youth and upbringing, is also the subject of great speculation and controversy. His dress, demeanor, and message made clear, as did the Magi and shepherds associated with Jesus' birth, that God was not going to be working through the established religious system.

THE PROPHET JOHN, 3:1-6

3:1 Matthew does not explain what he means by "in those days" but probably intends to designate the inauguration of the ministry of Jesus Christ. Matthew is not concerned with giving details of the Lord's childhood but is interested in getting to the issue of His messianic work. Thus, one must read Luke's account to discover what little information there is about His early years.

Luke 3:1-2 offers significant chronological data that can help give us the approximate time of John's appearance. It was the fifteenth year of the reign of Tiberius Caesar, when Pontius Pilate was governor of Judea, Herod (Antipas) was tetrarch of Galilee, Philip (his brother; both were sons of Herod the Great) was tetrarch of Ituraea and Trachonitis, and Lysanias (not a son of Herod) was tetrarch of Abilene. It was also the time when the priesthood had two high priests, Annas (the rightful high priest, who had been removed by Rome for his lack of cooperation) and his son-in-law, Caiaphas (whom Rome appointed to fill the office). From this information a date of A.D. 27-29 is derived as being the most likely for John's beginning his public ministry.[1]

All four gospels introduce the ministry of Jesus with the preparatory work of John the Baptist. This is no mere coincidence, because the Scripture clearly marks the coming of God's Anointed with the preparatory messenger. John was the son of the priest Zacharias and his wife, Elizabeth. The details of his unique birth are given in chaps. 1-2 of Luke's gospel. Josephus attributes the defeat of Herod Antipas's army to his murder of John. He records, "For Herod slew him, who was a good man, and commanded the Jews to exercise virtue, both as to righteousness towards one another, and piety towards God."[2]

Many questions remain unanswered regarding this man who came from the Judean wilderness preaching his message. Scripture makes no mention of who raised him (his parents were advanced in years at his birth). One credible theory is that he was reared in the Qumran community among the Essene sect,[3] one of the three Jewish sects listed by Josephus: Pharisees, Sadducees, and Essens (or Essenes).[4] The Pharisees and Sadducees are common characters in the New Testament, but the Essenes are never mentioned. Josephus, Pliny the elder, Philo, and Hippolytus (all first- or second-century writers) offer a sufficient amount of data to gain some knowledge of this group's beliefs and practices. The Essenes had a positive testimony for good works and work with scrolls, especially the Scriptures. John's austere appearance and lifestyle would certainly make him a likely candidate for monastic communal living.

3:2   John's message to Israel was repentance, based on the kingdom of heaven's being at hand. The command to repent is greatly misunderstood in the contemporary Christian milieu, and for proper understanding both the context and basic meaning must be considered. Such connotations as grief for sins, sorrow, turning from sin, and the like are cultural additions to the term and should not be forced into its denotation. If one could turn from his sin, then he would be capable of earning righteousness. If sorrow is the idea, then certainly Judas, whom Christ called the "son of perdition" and a "demon," repented. The word should be appreciated for its true, rich significance. The English word "repent" here is from the Greek *metanoeō,* which basically implies to change one's mind,[5] to reconsider, to think differently. The preposition *meta* is compounded here with the verb *noēō. Meta* is "frequently used to express the idea of change or difference."[6] In compound forms, the second element is defined or modified by the first.[7] Thus, the thinking process (*noēō*) is changed (*meta*) in repentance. Will a change of mind affect one's life? It should. Paul exhorts the Roman Christians to "be *continually* transformed" by "*continually* renewing the mind" (Rom. 12:2). How one perceives reality certainly will affect the way one behaves. True repentance *may* bring grief for sins, but then again it may bring extreme joy in realizing what forgiveness involves. True repentance will certainly result in a changed life, but to place a result in the position of a cause (i.e., a person is saved because he/she changed his/her life) is to present a false gospel. It is similar to the argument of faith and works. Do works contribute to salvation? Not according to Ephesians 2:8-9, Titus 3:5, and other Scriptures. But are works the *result* of true faith? Of course. Ephesians 2:10 and James 2:14-26 teach this clearly. Some seem to try to prove too much by depending on Old Testament concepts. Carson states that repentance is a "radical transformation of the entire person, a fundamental turnaround involving mind and action and including overtones of grief which results in 'fruit in keeping with repentance.'"[8] In this vein, Peter's message to the Jews would have been to "radically transform yourselves in your entire person and have grief so that your sins may be wiped away " (Acts 3:19). This certainly appears to contradict the doctrine of grace and the inability of man to earn favor with God. It also would seem to deny the doctrine of man's depravity and enslavement to sin. If the unregenerate is capable of radically transforming self, then why does one need grace? Carson is right in arguing that to change one's mind is more than mere intellectual change. But the issue is still that change of life comes from rethinking God's truth, not from an emotively driven determination to turn one's life around.

John's message of repentance was spoken to a nation that had not had a new prophetic word from God in four hundred years. The religious deadness of the nation was founded on the legalistic and self-righteous teachings of the Pharisees and on the nonsupernatural religion of the Sadducees. Christ and John the Baptist each openly opposed both parties and denounced their dead religion. Contextually, it seems far more consistent to understand John's command as a warning to the Jews to reconsider their view of God, since what they had been hearing in the religious environment of the day would not prepare them for the kingdom of heaven. Indeed they were to get sin out of their lives, but that would flow from a correct understanding of God and His standards. Such understanding would require a totally different perspective of God. The time had arrived to reevaluate their concept of pleasing Him by ritual and religious jargon. Walvoord explains the focus of John's message: "He was attacking the established religion of his day and demanding sincerity and repentance instead of hypocrisy and religious rites."[9]

Another key issue in this verse is the phrase "kingdom of heaven." Walvoord notes that only Matthew uses the term "kingdom of heaven," whereas the other writers use "kingdom of God." He sees in these two terms a deliberate distinction intended by Matthew. The kingdom of heaven refers to the outer character of the kingdom and would include all who profess to be subjects of the King. The kingdom of God, in distinction and more specific, includes only those who are born again.[10] One can sympathize with Walvoord's view and see some merit in it, but the difficulty is that in the parallel passages the other writers use "kingdom of God" in the very context where Matthew uses "kingdom of heaven" (e.g., Matt. 4:17; Mark 1:14-15). The major point in the proclamation was that the kingdom promised by God through Messiah was at hand because the Messiah was in the world. This does not challenge the dispensational view of the literal kingdom to come; though Messiah was rejected by Israel, He will return to establish the kingdom when the "times of the Gentiles" are completed. It is much too weak simply to say that the kingdom is in our hearts. This does not do justice to the Old Testament predictions of the kingdom or the Messiah's universal dominion (Dan. 7:13-14), nor does it adequately explain the humbling of the nations before the Lord's Anointed (Ps. 2).

3:3 It is significant that all four gospel writers reference Isaiah 40:3 in introducing John the Baptist. The Scripture is thereby making lucid comment about the identity of Jesus. If John is the eschatological messenger of Isaiah 40:3, then Jesus must be the one for whom the way was to be prepared, since John was preceding His ministry. Isaiah calls for the nation of Israel to meet their God; the messenger's cry is "Clear the way for the Lord." "Lord" here is *yᵉhōwah,* the covenant name of God. Isaiah continues by saying, "Make smooth . . . for our God." In view of Israel's monotheism, there can be only one Person to whom this refers. John was therefore calling Israel to prepare for the coming of their God, Yahweh. Carson states that such identification of Jesus with Yahweh is common in the New Testament and believes it "confirms the kingdom as being equally the kingdom of God and the kingdom of Jesus."[11]

The imagery of making "ready the way" and "paths straight" was a manner of expressing anticipation of a person of great rank and prestige visiting a village. It was a warning for the people to be ready to welcome and serve the dignitary with the honor to which he was accustomed. John's message to Israel was clear: the Messiah was on the way.

3:4   Matthew gives his description of John for a reason greater than just to provide interesting data. His notation of the camel's-hair garment is probably to identify him with the office of a prophet. Elijah was described as wearing a "garment of hair" and a leather belt (2 Kings 1:8 NIV is the best reading). Also, a comment in Zechariah 13:4 suggests that the garment may have identified the prophetic office: "The prophets will each be ashamed of his vision when he prophesies, and they will not put on a hairy robe in order to deceive." This seems to imply that the hairy robe marked a prophet of God. Bewer proposes that the prophets wore hairy robes as a proclamation of identity with poor peasants.[12]

John's dietary items were not as unusual as is sometimes assumed. Leviticus 11:22 identifies the locust as one of the winged insects that Jews were permitted to eat. Locusts could be cooked in oil and salted, their wings and legs removed. Even today in some parts of the world this is still not unusual food. Wild honey likewise was common and sometimes found under rocks (Deut. 32:13), in carcasses of dead animals (Judg. 14:8-9), or in underground hives (1 Sam. 14:25-26, 29). Therefore no dramatic conclusions should be drawn from John's diet; it would be normal for someone dwelling in the wilderness. The point seems to be that John had not been involved with the comforts of the world but was accustomed to the austere and separate lifestyle of the wilderness.

3:5-6   John drew crowds not only from Jerusalem but also from Judea and the Jordan Valley. His presence and message bespoke so clearly a voice from God that people were drawn to him. Jesus made reference to John's being a prophet and, more than just a prophet, the one who would announce the coming of the God of Israel (Luke 7:24-27). He also remarked that John did not eat bread or drink wine, the very basic components of Hebrew diet, and that eventually the Jews accused him of having a demon (Luke 7:33). Calvin's assessment of this event and the person of John is excellent: "John was satisfied with the food and dress of the peasants, and partook of no delicacies; but under a mean and contemptible garb, he was held in high estimation by men of rank and splendor."[13]

The baptism of John was accompanied by the confession of sin. The present middle participle (*eksomologoumenoi,* "while confessing") represents action contemporaneous with the act of being baptized (*ebaptizonto,* imperfect passive verb). To confess (*eksomologeō*) in the middle voice (as here) means to "admit, acknowledge."[14] The Jews, having heard John's announcement of the coming of Messiah, were acknowledging their sins as a part of preparing the way for receiving their God (Isa. 40:3). This act of confession certainly acknowledged their sense of need for salvation and was the proper response to John's message of repentance. They had to rethink their dependence upon the religious ritual of Israel's ceremonial laws and confess that indeed they were a sinful people. The good news that the kingdom of God was at hand and that God's deliverance was being revealed was a joyful message to people who knew their own helpless and sinful condition.

WARNING TO THE RELIGIONISTS, 3:7-12

3:7   In this context of sincere acknowledgment of sin, those who had been promoting the self-righteous religion of ceremonial piety came to be a part of this religious phenomenon. The Pharisees were the dominant religious influence in Israel. Abba Eban states, "The mass of the nation was inclined to Pharisaism, whose cardinal principle was the strict application of the law to every sphere of life in the interest of national preservation."[15] Less concerned with the strict application of the Law, the Sadducees concentrated on political and social concerns. They believed that God took little interest in human affairs.[16] Sadducees were from the priestly class and aristocracy. They were the caretakers of the temple, yet they tended toward Hellenism and in contrast to the Pharisees took little interest in oral law. They were small in number but exercised significant political power.[17]

These two religious groups came to be baptized by John. Their coming indicates that he was recognized by both as a true prophet of God (cf. Matt. 21:24-26). Certainly they would have openly condemned him had they any suspicions of his genuineness. His response must have been a shock to these leaders and also to the Jews standing by. Luke seems to imply that John's comments were to the whole crowd of Jews (Luke 3:7, "to the multitudes who were going out to be baptized by him"). Pate refers to Luke's "penchant for generalizing the audiences of John."[18] It would appear that Luke is not concerned with specifying which crowd John was attacking. Matthew's "many" (of the Pharisees) are Luke's "multitude." Matthew is more specific. His name-calling, "brood of vipers," was a great personal insult to their character and position. But John's action was not the raving of a desert madman; he knew full well their deceit and tragic misguidance of the people. Their religious jargon and pious sermons had been as deadly to God's people as the poison of the deadliest viper. Jesus, like John, identified the Pharisees with a brood of vipers (Matt. 12:34). A "brood" is actually a "product, harvest" (*genēma*) and emphasizes that they were the offspring or product of Israel's rejection of God's standards in favor of their own.

John's rhetorical question, "Who warned you to flee from the wrath to come?" should have sounded an alarm in the hearts of these men. In the typical style of the Old Testament prophet, John warned of God's impending judgment. However, he was not warning pagans but God's covenant people. Meyer's comment on this wrath is worth noting. "[It] is not the *punishment* itself, but the *holy emotion* of absolute displeasure with him who opposes His gracious will, and from this the punishment proceeds as a necessary manifestation of righteousness."[19] Paul refers to the coming wrath as the "righteous judgment of God," which comes because of man's "stubbornness and unrepentant heart" and which will "render to every man according to his deeds" (Rom. 2:5-6). Malachi 3:1-3 connects John's warning to the prediction that Messiah is coming to bring judgment upon God's people. The words of John sound somewhat ironic as he makes his point that these who were teaching others the oracles of God needed someone to warn them of the wrath of God.

3:8-9 (Cf. Luke 3:8-9)   If indeed the Pharisees and Sadducees wanted to participate in the identification of baptism of repentance, then John required them to produce evidence of repentance. According to Josephus, John "commanded the Jews to exercise virtue, both as to righteousness towards one another and piety towards God and so come to baptism . . . supposing still that the soul was thoroughly purified beforehand by righteousness."[20] Since Josephus himself was a Pharisee, he certainly chose his words carefully. John required not the self-righteous judgmental attitude that characterized the religionists but evidence that they understood their own need of forgiveness and thus evidence that they acknowledged their sins.

Their self-delusion was based upon the false security of having been born of Abraham's seed (v. 9). This Abrahamic dependence can be seen in John 8:33-53. On that occasion their answer to Jesus' offer of spiritual deliverance was "We are Abraham's offspring." Edersheim offers numerous examples from rabbinic literature of their confidence that in Abraham every Jew and every sin was forgiven:

> Abraham was represented as sitting at the gate of Gehenna, to deliver any Israelite who otherwise might have been consigned to its terrors. In fact, by their descent from Abraham, all the children of Israel were nobles, infinitely higher than any proselytes.[21]

The danger of such false security was emphasized by John's declaration that God is capable of using even inanimate objects such as stones to produce descendants for Abraham. The idea of a play on words in the Aramaic between stones and children is imaginative but not necessary to make John's point clear. The Jews should not place their hopes on biological kinship.

3:10   John warned that God's judgment had already begun, the ax was "already" (*ēdē* plus the present tense) "laid" (*keîtai*, present middle indicative from *keîmai*). The warning of the ax was analogous to God's judgment in the Old Testament (see Isa. 10:33-34). The warning is that "every tree" not producing good fruit would be cut down. The expression "every tree" is better understood as any tree fitting into the non-good-fruit-producing class of tree. Carson and Turner may stress this significance too far by claiming that the translation should be "any tree," not "every tree."[22] The fire likewise is analogous to judgment. The central idea is that God is preparing to rid His program of Israel's nonproductive dead religion. As a dead tree is cut down and burned, likewise any who do not produce genuine fruit for the kingdom will be cut down. Israel's legalistic religion could not produce the good fruit; thus, any not wishing to be cut down in judgment must demonstrate repentance from their dead ancestral religion (vv. 8-9).

3:11-12   John then drew a contrast between himself and the coming Judge. He identified himself simply as one who baptized with water as a testimony of repentance. This baptism was symbolic of the preparation of the nation or individuals of the nation to receive their God (v. 3) but offered nothing as dramatic as the two baptisms offered by the coming One. His baptism was to be of the Holy Spirit or of fire. John was emphasizing that it was not he, but the coming Judge, whom the Jews should be concerned about. The judgment to come was not to be administered by John, the messenger, but by One much mightier than the messenger. Luke 3:16 implies that John was aware of the curiosity about him and wanted to clearly distinguish between the mere messenger and the coming Lord. The coming One so surpassed John in personal greatness and authority that John felt unworthy even to serve Him as a menial servant (i.e., unlacing His sandals).

The "you" of v. 11 references Israel and the prediction that the coming One would baptize the nation either with the Holy Spirit or with fire. Carson believes that only one baptism is represented by both Holy Spirit and fire.[23] He is correct in pointing out that fire is often seen in a positive sense of purification (Isa. 1:25; Zech. 13:9; Mal. 3:2-3) and has good reason for assuming that the one preposition, *en,* governs both nouns ("Spirit" and "fire"). However, it is possible to understand that the preposition is simply qualifying baptism as the instrument or element of baptism and should not be used to connect the two. Another possibility is to associate this with the tongues of fire in Acts 2. The best approach may be to let the context and the flow of thought determine whether John intended one baptism or two. Fire certainly is used to represent judgment in both the Old and New Testaments, and v. 12 certainly establishes two antithetical acts of the Messiah. In 7:19, Matthew records the words of Jesus depicting the same type of judgmental act: "Every tree that does not bear good fruit is cut down and thrown into the fire." This commentary takes the position that John's declaration about the coming One means that He will baptize with both Spirit and fire.

Verse 12 warns that the coming One will be harvesting and separating His grain from the dead chaff. The wheat is to be gathered as a treasured product and the chaff burned in unquenchable fire. It seems best to understand the baptism just mentioned as referring to this event. Thus He comes to baptize with two baptisms: one being the immersion of the believer by the Spirit into the redeemed community (1 Cor. 12:13); the other being the immersion of the unbeliever into judgment (Matt. 13:41-42). Compare Matthew 13:24-30 as a parallel.

BAPTISM OF JESUS, 3:13-17

3:13-15 (Mark 1:9; Luke 3:21)   Matthew now records one of the most interesting dialogues in the New Testament. Jesus came to John for baptism, and it is certainly easy to identify with John's reaction. Jesus came down from the region of Galilee, where He had been living in Nazareth (2:23). According to v. 13, His stated purpose for coming was to be baptized. Matthew uses the definite article with the infinitive to show purpose (*pros ton Iwannē tou baptisthēnai,* "to John to be baptized").

Verse 14 reflects John's shock and natural hesitation at the idea of baptizing the very One whose sandals he had just proclaimed himself unworthy to unloose (v.11). John's baptism was a public identification with sin acknowledgment, demonstrating repentance toward Israel's dead religion. John's declaration that he needed to be baptized by Jesus acknowledges John's own humility and awareness of Jesus' sinless nature. Most likely John was referring to the baptism of the Spirit, which he had just proclaimed to be the function of the Messiah. However, it would not be too unlikely that he may have been referring to water baptism. John had been sent to announce the coming Messiah, but he had not yet personally met Jesus (cf. John 1:31-34). He at least suspected who Jesus was and thus hesitated to be presumptuous enough to perform this rite upon Him. After the baptism, John was fully aware of the nature of this Person.

Jesus' response in v. 15 has led to volumes of theological discourse. The explanation that Jesus was being baptized as recognizing our sin, which He took upon Himself, and was thus baptized as a sinner,[24] is stretching the limits of proper hermeneutics and good theology. The act was that which was fitting (*prepei,* "proper") to fulfill all righteousness. Notice that Jesus said it was the proper act for "us," Jesus and John. Tasker well notes, "The reply of Jesus in verse fifteen shows His awareness that both John and Himself had unique parts to play in the divine plan for man's redemption."[25] John's baptism was to demonstrate a separation from Israel's dead religion. Jesus' being baptized by John was not admission of sin but rather was the identification of Himself with the truth of John's message (that God was seeking true worshipers, not self-righteous religionists). Jesus was thus vindicating John's message and identifying Himself with the true people of God. Having received this instruction from Jesus, John baptized Him then and there.

3:16-17   Jesus went up out of the water (*anebē apo tou hudatos*), and immediately God bore witness to His approval of His Son. It seems best to understand that it was John who saw the Spirit of God descending as a dove upon Jesus (cf. John 1:32), though Luke's account implies that other people were present. The heavens opening for viewing the descent of the Spirit of God are reminiscent of Ezekiel 1:1, Acts 7:56, and Revelation 19:11, where other accounts of some manifestation of God are offered. It is as though the eyes of the beholder are empowered to see beyond the barriers of heaven to reveal God at work.

The issue of the Spirit's taking on the outward appearance of a dove has been debated, even though Luke's account would seem prima facie to imply this (Luke 3:22). The idea may be that some physical manifestation was given and the descent was like a dove landing. The imagery of a dove is fitting, as Scripture refers to the innocence of doves (Matt. 10:16; "innocent," *akeraios,* meaning "innocent, guileless, pure"). Scripture also establishes doves[26] as appropriate sacrifices for guilt offerings if one could not afford a lamb (Lev. 5:7), and for this reason doves were sold in the temple for sacrifices (Matt. 21:12; John 2:14). An offering of a pair of doves was presented on behalf of Mary and Jesus (Luke 2:24), according to the Law (Lev. 12:8).

Whatever the significance of the physical appearance, the coming of the Holy Spirit certainly marked the fulfillment of the Old Testament expectations of the divine power of the Messiah (Isa. 61:1, cf. Luke 4:18). Notation will be made later regarding Jesus' being totally dependent upon the Spirit for His power and leading. Indeed, Matthew 4 reveals Him being led by the Spirit to face the testing of the great enemy of God's redemptive plan.

The voice from heaven completed the triune manifestation (v. 17).[27] The proclamation "This is My beloved Son" would take the hearer (and reader) of Matthew to Psalm 2:7, where the Son of God is given the nations to rule as God's kingdom. The pronouncement of Jesus as God's Son and the descent of the Spirit upon Him certainly would clearly identify Him as the promised Messiah. John took this extraordinary event as the unquestioned divine attestation that his ministry was now completed with the coming of the One whom he had been announcing (John 1:29-34).

The announcement not only identified Jesus as God's beloved Son but also declared God's approval. Thus, all that Jesus had done, including His eighteen years of silence in Nazareth,[28] was well pleasing to God the Father.

HOMILETICAL SUGGESTIONS

It is significant that John was the first prophetic voice to be heard in Israel in four hundred years. God's silence had been a testimony to His displeasure with the nation, and, tragically, Israel simply carried on religiously as though they had not noticed that silence. The religious community continued to operate by rules and ritual, which had replaced their relationship with God.

Into this milieu of dead religion came the prophet John. His message was simple: Israel must realize that God sought an intimate relationship with His people, and their meaningless ritual and self-righteousness displeased Him. Acting in accordance with this message, John refused to allow the self-righteous leaders to be baptized until they demonstrated change in their thinking. He demanded humility, acknowledgment of personal sin, and a rejection of self-righteous attitudes.

There is a danger for all who claim to be religious. Pharisaism can be cloaked in Christian symbols and activities as easily as it was in Judaism. This passage is a warning to all who read the Scriptures, pray, tithe, attend church, and so on. Religious activity is not a mark of spirituality, and religion must never replace relationship with God. We should not be quick in condemning the Sadducees and Pharisees, but we all should be quick to heed the warning that God is not impressed with religious activity. Whatever our spiritual activity, let us make certain that it flows from a heart of love and sincere devotion to Him.

In contrast to the Pharisees and Sadducees, Jesus came for baptism with a humble spirit. John hesitated because he understood the significance of this event and did not see the correlation between this Person and the act of baptism of repentance. Jesus' explanation was sufficient to persuade John to baptize Him, and this act of obedience was rewarded with the dramatic testimony of the triune God. Christ's willingness to be the servant of all and His identity with true Israel were critical to God's redemptive plan. Often we may not immediately see God's design, as John did not understand, but obedience always will bring the joy of recognizing our part in God's work.

MATTHEW
CHAPTER
FOUR

THE BEGINNING OF
JESUS' PUBLIC MINISTRY

At about thirty years of age Jesus began His public ministry (Luke 3:23). Up to this time there had been no recorded sermon or miracle and, since the age of twelve, no record of any interaction with the religious leaders of His day. Jesus may have waited until He reached an age at which His peers would have recognized His authority.

The baptism by John was the first part of His entrance into the public arena, identifying Him as the servant Messiah and preparing Him by the anointing of the Holy Spirit. Then Jesus prepared for the next step into public ministry by isolating Himself for some period of time and by facing Satan directly.

THE TEMPTATION, 4:1-11 (CF. MARK 1:12-13; LUKE 4:1-13)

4:1　　It should be first noted that Jesus did not wander carelessly into temptation but was led by the Holy Spirit. Following the Spirit's descent upon Him (3:16), Jesus was led by the Spirit into the wilderness to be tempted by the Devil. Though some earlier writers imagined that Jesus was transported by the Spirit to Mount Sinai, nothing in the text offers any credence to such a theory. Christ was "led" (*anēchthē,* aorist passive of *anagō*) up to the wilderness area near the Jordan Valley. Mark's gospel uses more dramatic language, "impelled Him" (*auton ekballō*), which would imply more forceful action of the Spirit rather than just directing Him. The idea would be that Jesus did not seek this environment on His own but was sent by the Spirit to fast in the wilderness and then to face the tempter. Significantly, the stage was being set for the testing of the Second Adam even as Eden had been prepared for the temptation of the first Adam. The crucial distinction lies within the two environments: the first Adam was tested in the perfect world of God's garden, the second in the harsh fallen world of the wilderness.

The word "tempted" is *peirazō,* "put to the test," and has two basic connotations. It can mean to test the genuineness or sincerity of someone or something. In this use, man is forbidden to test God (v. 7, compound form, *ekpeirazō,* and is the exact word used in Acts 5:9, *peirazō;* see also 1 Cor. 10:9). The word is used for the trickery of the Pharisees in testing Jesus (Matt.16:1; 19:3; 22:18). The second connotation is to entice someone to evil (1 Cor. 7:5; Gal. 6:1). The simple hermeneutical principles of context and theological consistency help determine which connotation is intended. With this distinction of connotations in mind, one should understand James 1:13 as saying that God will not entice anyone to sin and that He Himself cannot be enticed to sin. However, God will test His servants *to demonstrate His power and calling in them,* and in this sense Jesus was to be tested. For this reason, James says we are to rejoice in "trials" (*peirasmos,* noun form of *peirazō;* James 1:2, 12).

God would demonstrate through this series of enticements by Satan that His servant Jesus is righteous and trustworthy. As Adam, representative of all mankind, was tested under the best of conditions and failed, plunging the human race into judgment and death (Rom. 5:12-14; 17-18), so Jesus, the Second Adam (as Paul refers to Him, 1 Cor. 15:45-47), representative of regenerate mankind, was tested under the worst conditions, passed the test, and brings life to those in Him (Rom. 5:15-21; 6:23).

As to the ability or inability of Christ to sin,[1] the issues become very complex. However, it must be remembered that though Christ did relinquish the independent exercise of His divine attributes (Phil. 2:7), He did not change in His essence or relinquish any part of His divine nature. Jesus was and is God and, thus, could not sin. To assume that the purpose of the temptation was to see whether or not He would sin is certainly incorrect. The temptation designed by God was not to entice Him to sin, though that was permitted, but was designed to demonstrate that the Messiah, the Second Adam, *would* not sin. He was the pure and spotless Lamb of God, who was qualified to pay the penalty of sin. Hendriksen offers an excellent comment on this issue:

> With Christ the case was different. The outward stimulus—*outward* in the sense that it did not originate in the Lord's own soul but was the voice of another—was there, but the *inner* evil incentive or desire to cooperate with this voice from without was not. Nevertheless the temptation—that is, the sense of need, the consciousness of being urged by Satan to satisfy this need, the knowledge of having to resist the tempter, and the struggle to which this gave rise—was real even for Christ.
>
> The soul of our Lord was not hard as a flint or cold as an icicle. It was a thoroughly human, deeply sensitive soul, affected and afflicted by suffering of every description.[2]

Thus, indeed, Christ knows our struggles because He also felt the pressure and knew the experience of conflict between the desire for human comfort and God's will.

One complexity of this event was that Jesus was tempted as a man, a true human being. Under the direction and empowerment of the Holy Spirit, He demonstrated that man under the Spirit's control will always resist sin. But this one aspect cannot be taken in isolation. The other dynamic of the temptation is that Jesus was no less God and therefore could not sin. The issue then becomes a question as to how legitimate was the temptation if He could not have sinned. Here it is important to remember the two connotations of *peirazō*. In this context it means "test." Jesus was tested to prove His sinlessness and worthiness as a sacrifice for mankind. One can test gold to see if it is pure and genuine, but the test will not alter its makeup. Testing will only demonstrate its authenticity.

It might be best to understand a twofold purpose in the testing of Jesus. First, the testing demonstrated His genuine character (sinless). Second, it also accomplished another goal. As true man, He felt the intensity of physical and emotional need, experientially learning the limitations and basic drives of the human experience. Through this, He became an intercessor who feels and understands our struggles (cf. Heb. 4:15-16).

4:2   Before facing the tempter, Jesus fasted for forty days and forty nights. Fasting, as a form of self-discipline for the purpose of focusing upon a specific task,[3] is associated in the Old Testament with humbling one's soul (Ps. 35:13) and has two modes: partial and total. The Jews practiced what was called a partial fast, which permitted eating morsels or drinking water. Daniel fasted for three weeks in that he did not eat any "desirable bread, nor meat, nor wine" (Dan. 10:3). These extended fasts may have allowed old bread and water but not the normal foods of everyday life, which would require preparation. The idea was to avoid distractions so that full attention could be given to prayer and meditation.

Total fasting involved abstaining from all food and drink and normally was restricted to a single day. Some Jews fasted two days per week (thus Christ's parable, Luke 18:11-12). Mondays and Thursdays were typically designated as fast days for the very religious.[4] From Luke's account (Luke 4:2, "He ate nothing during those days") it must be assumed that Jesus' wilderness experience was a total fast. This experience may be compared to that of Moses (Ex. 34:28; Deut. 9:9) or Elijah (1 Kings 19:8). Such extended periods of time without food or drink would certainly require divine intervention to protect the person. There is no textual reason to reduce the forty days to anything less than literal days. Admittedly, forty seems to be a number representing some significant value because of its frequent use, but simply assuming this to be a symbolic number *without literal meaning* cannot be justified. An interesting parallel is Israel's wilderness testing—for forty years, not days.

"He then became hungry." Matthew states what should have been an obvious conclusion to forty days of fasting. However, Meyer believes that Jesus did not experience hunger as a growing condition during the fast but only became hungry afterward. He writes, "The hunger did not attack Him *until* He had fasted."[5] This appears to assume too much from the expression in Matthew, but the end result of the fasting was that Jesus was hungry, a human experience. Satan used this legitimate human need as the first point of temptation.

4:3   The first temptation came in the form of a challenge to prove the truth of His title "Son of God." Apparently, when Satan approached Jesus, he knew of His position as Son. It is hard to imagine what was in the mind of this being. How arrogant, or helpless, was this creature to challenge God incarnate to prove His Person by the simple task of turning stone to bread? Meyer points out that "Son" stands in an emphatic position in the sentence, that is, "If you stand in relation to God as Son," which seems to imply that Satan knew who Christ was and was challenging His divine mission.[6] In agreement with Meyer, it should be noted that "if" (*ei*) does not necessarily imply a question. It can even assume the reality of what is questioned but seek confirmation. It is not correct, however, to go so far as to translate this "since you are the Son of God."[7] The challenge is to prove what Jesus and His followers would use as the basis of the authority for His mission: He is the Son of God.

The proof Satan demanded indeed would have been a simple task for the true Son of God. The Son of God, who is equal with God, could easily change the molecular structure of stones into that of bread. God spoke all things into existence and commanded every atom of the universe. However, the test was really to determine whether or not Jesus, God's Son and servant, would use His position and authority for selfish ends. Carson explains, "It was a temptation to use his sonship in a way inconsistent with his God-ordained mission."[8] Jesus did not need to "prove" who He was. His confidence and authority were not dependent upon the acknowledgment of Satan or of anyone else. As at the beginning of His public ministry, so at the end, the challenge was to prove His sonship by acting independently of God's plan and will (Matt.27:40).

4:4   Christ's response, both biblical and profound, reached back to the early writings of Moses (Deut. 8:3)[9] for a lesson God had tried to teach Israel: mankind is not to view human existence as dependent upon the physical sustenance of life but upon God's provisions. At His command, our every need is met. Just as God provided manna, which no Israelite had ever seen, He promises to take care of our needs. God would take care of His Son's needs; He did not need to do it Himself apart from God's permission. It was God who led Him into the wilderness to fast for forty days, and when the fast was over God would provide what He needed. To act independently and care for His own needs would be to deny God's faithfulness and God's authority over His life. What a lesson to learn. Jesus, who through miraculous power would feed more than four thousand people because He had compassion on their physical needs (Matt. 15:32-39), refused to take care of His own physical need because the Father had not yet ended the fast. Jesus was living out what He would preach to His disciples (Matt. 6:31-33) and was also demonstrating the truth of John 4:31-34.

4:5-6   The second testing was also a challenge to prove that He was the Son of God. Luke reverses the order of the second and third temptations. It is apparent that Luke is not concerned with order, since he lists the events with a simple string of conjunctions. Matthew, on the other hand, begins each part of the temptation with *tote,* a correlative adverb of time indicating that which follows in time and sequence. Matthew uses this adverb more than any other New Testament writer, marking his desire to follow historical sequence.[10] Whether the sequence is *always* historical or simply logical in the purpose of the writer is an interesting study but not significant here.

The setting for this event was more dramatic than the first. Matthew records that the devil "took Him" to the "holy city," but the method of transporting is not specified. Some writers hesitate to understand this in a sense of physical placement,[11] but there is no need to shy from this. It certainly is consistent with other scriptural comments about miraculous happenings. The expression "took Him" is *paralambanei auton* (present active indicative, third person singular from *paralambanō*) and implies "to take along with." This may be some indication as to Satan's own power to transport. Meyer points out that the expression "implies the involuntary nature of the act on the part of Jesus, and the power on the part of the devil."[12]

The expression "holy city" can refer only to Jerusalem (Pss. 122; 137:4-6; Matt. 27:51-53), for here Jesus was placed on the uppermost part of the temple (*to pterugion tou hierou*). According to the measurements of Rabbi Israel Lipschutz, the highest part would have been the roof of the sanctuary, about 150 feet high.[13] Many scholars reject this location because the entire roof was covered with eighteen-inch spikes to prevent birds from landing.[14] An important consideration is that Matthew records that Jesus was taken to the highest point of the temple (*hieron*), referring to the entire temple complex, including its outer walls, and not to the sanctuary proper. Josephus offers a dramatic description of the view from the south outer wall of the temple complex:

For while the valley was very deep, and its bottom could not be seen, if you looked from above into the depth, this farther vastly high elevation of the cloister stood upon that height, insomuch that if anyone looked down from the top of the battlements, or down both those altitudes, he would be giddy, while his sight could not reach to such an immense depth.[15]

Thus, the highest point may not refer to the tallest building but to the greatest height from which one might fall. The challenge to Jesus was, did He or did He not believe that God could supernaturally protect Him from such an apparently fatal fall?

Since Jesus used Scripture to respond to Satan's first challenge, the Devil now used Scripture to make his second challenge sound more spiritual. Satan is not afraid to quote Scripture. Also, his enticements to sin are often cloaked in spiritual-sounding arguments. As Jesus had done earlier, Satan used the LXX rather than the Hebrew text. It should not be argued that Satan perverted Scripture because the whole verse was not quoted (he omitted "to guard you in all your ways"). It was common practice of the rabbis, of Jesus, and later of the apostles to refer only to main portions for teaching purposes. Indeed, Jesus quoted only part of Deuteronomy 6:16 in response. Satan's deception continues today through misuse of the Word of God. He leads people to take God's promises out of their original context, resulting in incorrect interpretation and application. The terrible scourge of contemporary Christianity is that believers become disillusioned, thinking that God did not live up to His promises, when in reality God never made the promise they tried to claim. Satan took a beautiful psalm and tried to convince Jesus that it meant something different from what God intended. What God says in His Word to a specific person or group may or may not have any bearing upon the life of a contemporary Christian.

4:7   Jesus corrected this error by referencing another verse (Deut. 6:16). To deliberately put oneself in a hazardous position in order to make God prove that He will protect is to call into question God's faithfulness. Jesus did not need to test God's protective care —He took His word for it.

An interesting example of testing the Lord is recorded in Exodus 17:1-7. Israel was being led through the wilderness "according to the command of the Lord" (v.1) and camped in a place where there was no apparent source of water. The grumbling and complaining of the people brought God's displeasure "because they tested the Lord, saying, 'Is the Lord among us or not?'" (v. 7). Because God did not immediately meet their expectations, they questioned His faithfulness. In Acts 5:9, the error of Sapphira was in lying to cover her and her husband's deception; this was labeled by Peter as putting "the Spirit of the Lord to the test." Thus, assuming that one can deceive God is also a form of testing Him. Those who claim to believe in God must not expect Him to prove Himself either by demanding a sign or miraculous intervention to override our foolishness or by trying to get by with false claims of spirituality.

4:8-9   The third and final test relates primarily to not worshiping the Devil but, once again, obeying God. It is not important to which mountain Satan took Jesus; what is important is that from this vantage point he gave Jesus a vision of all the great kingdoms of the world. Many do not understand that this world is Satan's. He is called the ruler of this world by Jesus Himself (John 14:30), and John the apostle reminds his readers that the whole world lies under the evil one (1 John 5:19). Some scholars dismiss these and other references to Satan's control of this *kosmos,* however, and appeal to rather ambiguous verses (e.g., Rom. 16:20 or verses dealing with Christ's ultimate victory and glorification), that do not address the issue at all. This world is polluted and is already in the process of destruction (1 John 2:17). Believers are told not to love the world or the things in it (1 John 2:15-16), which would be strange if it were presently God's domain. The issue is a large subject, but it must be remembered that this earth is going to be destroyed because it has been polluted (2 Peter 3:10). For this reason, believers look for the new heavens and new earth in which dwells righteousness (2 Peter 3:13). God will subdue Satan and establish a kingdom in which His righteousness and glory will shine, demonstrating what mankind could have had if they had not fallen. It will last for a thousand years, and then rebellion will rise again and ultimate destruction of this world result (Rev. 20:1-3, 7-10; 21:1-2). This view does not in any way threaten God's ultimate sovereignty. It rather illustrates Romans 8:28—God will bring ultimate victory even from the ruin and destruction of Satan's rule over the earth.

Satan displayed the glories of the earthly kingdoms and offered them to Christ. Jesus did not argue with his right to give them away but rebuked him for the third time with Scripture. This testing was perhaps the most severe because it promised to Jesus the kingdoms of the earth, which the Father had also promised, but Satan's offer allowed for Jesus to avoid the shame and pain of death. Perhaps this is a good reminder from our Lord that some things are more shameful and destructive than physical death, namely submitting to the Devil.

4:10 Christ's response at this point was somewhat different. He commanded Satan to depart. Jesus used the present imperative from *hupagō* (the same command He would later give Peter, Matt. 16:23). At His command Satan left, which indicates the authority of Christ even in this vulnerable position. Apparently Jesus knew that the enticement to worshiping the Devil was the ultimate in testing, and thus He ended the confrontation with the stern command that His inferior foe could not disobey. Referencing Deuteronomy 6:13 added the ultimate authority of God's Word, which in every case is the final argument against any temptation. Jesus directly addressed His adversary for the first time. Meyer suggests that this was "in keeping with the growing intensity of the emotion in general, as well as with the *personal* address of the tempter in ver. 9."[16]

Luke does not record the command of the Lord and implies that Satan was not finished. He states that the devil left "until an opportune time." Some take this as a reference to his indwelling Judas in Luke 22:3,[17] which may be the case directly, but Pate is certainly correct to point out that "his behind-the-scene activity very much influenced Jesus' opponents, and even His disciples in their attempt to keep Him from going to the cross."[18] Guthrie, likewise, notes, "It must be recognized that Jesus was exposed to many more temptations than those recorded, which must be regarded as typical."[19]

4:11 After Satan's departure, angels came to minister to Jesus. Even after enduring the testing, He still demonstrated dependence upon God's provision. He did not conjure up His own food but, like Elijah in the wilderness, received God's supernatural care (1 Kings 19:5-8). Calvin notes that the mention of angels here is not to indicate that they had not been previously ministering to Jesus but that they had been removed for this period of testing. He states, "In order to allow for an opportunity for temptation, the grace of God, though it was present, was sometimes hidden from him, so far as respects the feeling of the flesh."[20] This is a good point. It reminds us that at times we may not be aware of God's care for us but that He can and will provide, even if for a little while we must endure our testing in apparent lone vigil.

JESUS MOVES HIS BASE TO CAPERNAUM, 4:12-17

4:12-13 (Mark 1:14; Luke 3:14-15)   When Jesus heard that John was arrested, He moved His base of operations from Nazareth to Capernaum. There does not seem to be any connection between the two events, though it is possible that Jesus saw John's arrest as indicating He should become more public in His ministry. Luke's account may confuse some because he places the arrest of John (3:20) before the temptation (4:1-13). However, since 3:21-22 has John baptizing Jesus, the comment in v. 20 must simply be a non-temporal remark to emphasize Herod's corruptness. Mark's record makes it clear: "Now after John had been taken into custody, Jesus came into Galilee, preaching the gospel of God."

The reference to Capernaum by the sea with specific designation of the regional (i.e., tribal heritage) names is to acknowledge the connection with Isaiah 9:1-2 (cf. vv. 14-16). The ruins of Capernaum have been unearthed at Tell Hum, including the major discovery of a second-century synagogue. The city was located on the northwest shoreline of the Sea of Galilee. Peter's home was there (Matt. 8:5-14; Mark 1:21-29), and it may be safely assumed that James and John lived there with their parents. Capernaum must have lain on the border of the tribal allotment of Zebulun and Naphtali. It was in this city that Jesus began to build His circle of disciples (4:18).

4:14-16   The prophecy of Isaiah 9:1-2 is only loosely paraphrased by Matthew, most likely depending on the LXX. The religious leaders would certainly look down on the less spiritually enlightened cities outside of Jerusalem, and Capernaum had even a more despicable reputation because of its commercial success and dominance by Gentiles. Isaiah's prophecy related to God's grace toward a people whom He had judged but who now would receive the "great light" of His revelation through the Messiah. Matthew records the move of Jesus as the fulfillment of this promise of the great light. The region is referred to as "Galilee of the Gentiles" because, since it was one of the most beautiful sites of the region, it attracted the Romans and other foreigners who of necessity had to live and do business in Israel.

Carson offers an excellent summary of the expression "upon them a light dawned": "'Dawned' (*aneteilen*) suggests that the light first shone brilliantly here, not that it was shining brightly elsewhere and then moved here."[21] The reference is certainly emphasizing the public ministry of Jesus, which focused on Galilee. The great light was seen in Jerusalem as well, but this region received special attention from the Lord. It could be symbolic of the broader work of Messiah following His death. In keeping with God's pattern thus far, that is, the humble birth of Jesus, the revelation to the Magi, and the non-conformity of John the Baptist, here God unveiled His light in a location rejected by the religious leaders instead of in Jerusalem where they would naturally assume He would focus His work.

4:17 "From that time" (*apo tote*) is not a common expression in the New Testament. Luke is the only other writer to use it, and then only once (Luke 16:16), where it certainly implies "from that point onward." In Luke's account, Jesus is rebuking the Pharisees who are scoffing at Him. He divides God's work with Israel into two separate programs—the Law and Prophets, and the message of the kingdom of God. He uses *apo tote* to separate these two foci.

Matthew uses the phrase here and again in 16:21, where it marks the beginning of Jesus' emphasis on His coming suffering, death, and resurrection. His last usage is in 26:16, where it refers to Judas as he begins to deliberately plot his betrayal of Jesus. There-fore it seems safe to assume that this phrase was intended by Mat-thew to mark a significant change in the course of God's program at this time. Tasker suggests that this expression is to indicate a summary of segments of Jesus' ministry.[22] But it is more likely to introduce a new design in His earthly task. His move to Capernaum after John's arrest marked a new emphasis in His work.

Jesus began to preach the same message that John had already began to proclaim. The word "preach" (*kērussō*) is to "proclaim" or to "announce, make known." It should not be thought of in the modern sense of a homiletical sermon but was more in the form of a public announcement with an exhortation to align oneself with the kingdom. For the content of the message, "repent, for the king-dom of heaven is at hand," see comments on 3:2.

First Disciples, 4:18-22 (Mark 1:16-20)

Selecting His disciples was a major event in the earthly work of Jesus. It should not be assumed that the account recorded in Matthew is the whole explanation. Probably John's record details the initial contact with the men who would become His closest companions. According to John's gospel, Andrew (Peter's brother) and an unnamed disciple (who could likely have been John himself, the brother of James) had followed Jesus after John the Baptist identified Him as the Lamb of God (John 1:35-40). Andrew and the other disciple met with Jesus for several hours. Andrew subsequently found Peter and introduced him to Jesus as well (1:41-42). The next day Jesus met Philip and Nathanael. Thus, according to John's account, Jesus by this time had met Andrew, Peter, the unnamed disciple (probably John), Philip, and Nathanael. These five became the first of His disciples. It is to be noted that these men were already disciples of John the Baptist and had been prepared to meet the coming Messiah. Jesus spent some time with these men before we see them in either Matthew's, Mark's, or Luke's account.

4:18   Matthew's record of the call of these disciples follows the events just discussed in John 1:35-51. Jesus came to the Sea of Galilee perhaps looking for the men with whom He had already met and discussed an itinerant ministry. He first found Simon Peter and Andrew, his brother. Matthew says they were casting their nets into the sea with the explanation "for they were fishermen." This is in exact harmony with Mark's record (1:16). It is significant that the disciples did not just jump up and leave their families and careers as is sometimes intimated in emotive preaching. The "immediately" of v. 20 must be understood in its context of having followed the former meetings and does not require any implication that they did not return to their occupation between preaching trips. Luke 5:1-11 is apparently another event following this account in Matthew. They were again at their occupation, and yet, according to 4:38, Jesus was a visitor in Peter's home.[23] It is clear from the harmony of the different accounts of the calling of the disciples that they were progressively drawn into service and had been prepared by process to make the career change.

4:19   Christ's instruction to these men was "Follow Me" (*deute opiso mou,* "come after Me"). As Carson states, the invitation "presuppose[s] a physical 'following' during Jesus' ministry."[24] The expression must be understood as a summons to discipleship. Jesus was inviting these men to join Him in a mentoring relationship, common among the great teachers of this time (e.g., John the Baptist's disciples, Matt. 9:14; and disciples of the Pharisees, Matt. 22:16). They would become His disciples (*mathētēs,* "learner, pupil"). They are so designated first in Matthew's gospel in 5:1. A disciple was to follow his teacher, learning by oral instruction as well as by observing his methods and attitudes.

The promise attached to the instruction was "And I will make you fishers of men." Carson thinks there may be some allusion to Jeremiah 16:16, but as he admits, "The allusion is uncertain."[25] Meyer sees the allusion to hunting and fishing as denoting "the winning over of souls for themselves and others."[26] However, the Jeremiah context seems too negative to correspond to the Lord's promise. Besides, there is no parallel for the hunters of Jeremiah, who are sent out with the fishermen. It is unnecessary to seek allusions from other references. The metaphor is natural enough in its own setting. Matthew has made special note to the fact that these men were fishermen (v. 18), and the concept of fishing for more followers for Jesus would certainly have communicated to them.

4:20   Some may be tempted to take the expression "immediately" too concretely and make it appear that, upon first contact with Jesus, these humble fishermen deserted family and business responsibility to dedicate their lives to the Lord. In chap. 8 Matthew records the occasion when Jesus healed Peter's mother-in-law, which is the parallel account to Luke 4:38–5:11. Since Matthew's sequence has the summoning of Andrew, Peter, James, and John prior to the healing of Peter's mother-in-law, and Luke has Peter in his fishing environment cleaning his nets—according to v. 5, he had been fishing all night after her healing—it is apparent that when they "immediately left the nets and followed Him," they were not at that time making a permanent change.

They evidently were prepared to follow and did so as He traveled to preach His message in the surrounding villages. At His summoning, they did leave their work and spent time with Him but then returned to their fishing. It is safe to assume that at some point they broke away from their careers and dedicated themselves to full-time service. This could be the significance of "they left everything and followed Him" in Luke 5:11. However, it should be noted that after the Crucifixion and Resurrection Peter went back to fishing (John 21:3). By the time of the events of Acts 6, the apostles (including Peter) seem to have clearly indicated that they were not to be distracted by other matters so that they could devote themselves totally to His service.

4:21-22   As Jesus continued along the lakeshore with Peter and Andrew, He summoned two other disciples, James and John, sons of Zebedee. They too were fishermen, working with their father. In the same manner, Jesus called them to active service. The discussion of Peter's and Andrew's vocation not changing immediately would apply here as well.

Jesus now had His basic core of disciples. (One might assume that Nathanael and Philip (John 1:43-51) had also been summoned to participate in this preaching occasion.) Three of these would become identified as His inner circle, having special privileges and receiving special attention. Peter, James, and John would witness the Transfiguration and some miracles to which the others would not have privilege. James was to become the first martyr among the Twelve (Acts 12:2). John would be preserved to write the Revelation of Jesus Christ and to be the last of the Twelve. Peter was to be the apostle who introduced the good news to the Gentiles (Acts 10) and who was certainly the most prominent of all the disciples.

THE GALILEAN MINISTRY, 4:23-25

4:23   At this time Jesus was focusing His ministry on the area of Galilee. It was at some point in this period that He and His disciples accompanied Mary to the wedding at Cana (John 2:1-11). Since this was the event where Jesus first performed a sign demonstrating His power (v.11), then it must have been one of the earliest events of the tour. Jesus may have introduced His disciples to His mother and then used that occasion as a transition between His former life in Nazareth with His family and the new life of public ministry with His disciples. Jesus' ministry in Galilee consisted of teaching in the synagogues, proclaiming the kingdom, and healing disease.

The synagogue teaching was consistent with the cultural practice of the day. Any male Jew of age was allowed to read Scripture and exhort the people of the synagogue. Deissman offers evidence for the teaching emphasis in the synagogue. He quotes an inscription from a Jerusalem synagogue dating prior to A.D. 70: "Theodotus . . . built the synagogue for the reading of the Law and for the teaching of the commandments."[27] Trepp agrees and states, "The synagogue was the House of Prayer (*Bet ha-Tefilah*), it was a House of Study (*Bet ha-Midrash*)."[28] We see Jesus doing this in Nazareth as well. Luke records that the Lord entered the synagogue and stood to read as was His custom (4:16). He read Isaiah 61:1-2 and announced that the prophet was speaking of Him (v. 21). The ultimate response of the Jews in the synagogue was outrage that a local boy whom they had known from youth, especially a common laborer's son, should claim this messianic prophecy for Himself (4:23-29). Following this rejection, He returned to Capernaum.

Jesus was also traveling through Galilee "proclaiming the gospel of the kingdom." Proclaiming (*krussō,* "herald, announce") is not the same as teaching. It is not offering exegesis or detailed explanation but simply declaring some event or significant truth. His teachings would certainly vindicate His proclamation.

It should be noted that He was proclaiming the gospel (i.e., "good news") of the kingdom. This must be understood as the announcement that John had already been spreading—that the messianic kingdom was at hand. It is not to be confused with the gospel of redemption, which would follow. The context was the fulfillment of the promise of God that He would come to His people to bring the Son of David and build the kingdom.

Many commentators confuse the promise to Israel with the resultant effect of Messiah's rejection and subsequent post-Ascension mission. Carson gives a good explanation of this phrase but then states that "God's people" were constituted as a "church,"[29] which ignores the kingdom promises to the nation of Israel and uses nomenclature not appropriate to the promise. Mounce is less clear when he summarizes this statement about the kingdom as "the long-awaited arrival of the God who would act with sovereign power in human affairs."[30] The issue is not primarily human affairs generally but fulfillment of God's promise in particular to this people. The announcement of the kingdom was a particular promise to a particular people, and the Jews knew immediately all the implications of such an announcement.

The third aspect of His Galilean ministry was healing. Jesus was certainly vindicating the promise of kingdom power to overcome every force oppressing God's people. The Old Testament offered the Jews hope that God would heal and bless His people (Isa. 35:5-7), and Christ's miracles demonstrated His right to offer the kingdom.

An interesting observation is that the references to healing diseases and every kind of sickness indicates that physiological disorders are not attributed to demons or to any particular sin. At times demons play a part in physical disorders, but certainly not every case should be treated as such.

4:24-25 These verses function as a summary to this segment of Jesus' early ministry. His reputation began to grow, and His powers were obviously the primary item of interest among the people. Syria is the broad area of the northern province of Israel. From this region, families and friends brought those who were afflicted by a great variety of distresses, including demon oppression. Hendriksen offers a good comment:

> Christ's healing miracles had a threefold significance: a. they confirmed his message (John 14:11); b. they showed that he was indeed the Messiah of prophecy (Isa. 35:5; 53:4, 5; 61:1; Matt. 11:2-6); and c. they proved that in a sense the kingdom had even now arrived, for, as has already been indicated, the concept of "kingdom" includes blessings for the body as well as for the soul.[31]

Great multitudes followed Him (v. 25). The crowds were not just from Galilee but from Decapolis (the ten-city confederacy),[32] from Jerusalem, and from "beyond the Jordan" (the region on the eastern side of the Sea of Galilee).

HOMILETICAL SUGGESTIONS

This chapter introduces the inauguration of our Lord's earthly ministry. Following His baptism and divine acknowledgment in chap. 3, He now entered the extreme environment of severe testing. He demonstrated both His holiness and His obedience as He repeatedly repelled the Devil with the authority of God's Word. One is reminded of James's exhortation and promise in James 4:7, "Submit therefore to God. Resist the devil and he will flee from you." It should also bring comfort to know that our Intercessor is One who experienced the trauma of suffering and the pressure to compromise. Though He did not fail as we do, yet He still can understand the strain of trials and can come to our aid with compassion and mercy.

As Jesus began His public ministry, He initiated the process of training followers who would eventually carry the responsibility of perpetuating His work in the world. He prepared them for ministry by taking them with Him on His journeys. They heard Him teach and watched Him perform miracles and minister to the needs of others. Their faith grew as they saw His power and observed His dealings with people. Such mentoring principles were later followed by these men, as is testified by church history and demonstrated by Paul so clearly in the New Testament (cf. 2 Tim. 2:2).

It is beneficial to observe the way in which Christ did ministry. He was obeying His Father and fulfilling the Old Testament expectations for the kingdom. However, as will be observed later in Matthew's gospel, the large following did not impress Him. He knew their response was selfish and temporary. Large crowds will certainly follow those who are doing what the crowd wants to see and hear, but Jesus' method and message would eventually drive the crowds to demand His death. Ministry is not to be designed to appeal to the masses but to obey God and honor His truth. Jesus knew well the fickleness of humans and therefore focused His primary work on His disciples. This is the major purpose behind the message of chap. 5. Matthew does not simply go from chap. 4 to 5 without design. The messages of the Sermon on the Mount are to be understood in light of this initial response to Jesus.

MATTHEW
CHAPTER
FIVE

THE DISCOURSE
ON THE MOUNT

Numerous books have been written on the subject of the Sermon on the Mount because of the material's being unique and so difficult to understand. Some have argued that the subject and instructions are kingdom ideals, which were never intended to be applied literally by Christians. C. H. Dodd states, "We are not to suppose that we are capable of loving our enemies, or even our neighbors, to the full measure in which God has loved us."[1] Certainly Dodd is correct if one is talking about the unregenerate person, but are these standards not for regenerate kingdom people, even in this fallen world? Stott is correct when he says, "It depicts the behavior which Jesus expected of each of his disciples, who is also thereby a citizen of God's kingdom."[2] Disciples were indeed chosen members of the kingdom and needed to understand at the beginning of their walk with Christ that His standards were higher than the oral traditions being propagated by the scribes and Pharisees. Though the millennial kingdom is not as yet being experienced in this world, the standards of the King are to be realized in the lives of His servants.

Some assume that this must be the same event as Luke 6:17–7:1, often referred to as the Sermon on the Plain.[3] Hendriksen is surely overly confident when he says, "It is clear that the sermon recorded by Matthew and the one reported by Luke are one and the same."[4] Carson offers argument to defend the view that both

Luke 6 and Matthew 5 are reporting the same event. His conclusion is: "It seems best, then, to take Matthew 5-7 and Luke 6:20-49 as separate reports of the same occasion, each dependent upon some shared tradition (Q?), but not exclusively so."[5]

Certainly there are some parallel teachings in the two accounts, but even Carson admits that it is not uncommon for itinerant preachers to often repeat the same sayings to different audiences.[6] Though some of the material will be repeated in Luke, the better view is that the different contexts should not be ignored. In Matthew's account, the disciples were not yet in full number; Matthew was not made a disciple until after this event (see Matt. 9:9). But in Luke's account, Matthew was already a disciple (Luke 5:27), and all twelve disciples were chosen before the event took place (Luke 6:12-16).

Other details do not match, as well. In Luke's narrative, Jesus was not sitting on a mountain but standing on a level place while coming down from a mountain with His newly appointed disciples. In Matthew's record, Jesus went up into the mountain with His disciples and sat down to teach them. Also, Luke's account has people being healed (6:18-19), which Matthew never mentions. In Matthew's gospel, following the discourse Jesus came down out of the mountain and healed a leper (8:2). In Luke, following the discourse Jesus went into Capernaum and healed the centurion's slave (7:1-10).

Commentators will always debate the harmony of the gospel events, and determining the proper sequence is always difficult. It should be remembered that to sequentially list events was not characteristic of the time or necessary in historical narrative. Whatever the recording variance, the differences are minor and do not affect the author's message. The only question is whether similar teachings were presented on two or more separate occasions or whether different details of the same event are presented by the respective authors for their designated purposes. The first option is more defensible; nothing in either text requires the reader to assume that the two accounts are of the same event. On the contrary, there is much information that suggests different times, places, and occasions. Meyer agrees: "The evangelist does not determine either the time or place precisely, yet he by no means agrees with Luke vi. 17."[7]

JESUS' AUDIENCE, 5:1-2

5:1 One misconception of the Discourse on the Mount is that Jesus was preaching to a large crowd. However, according to v. 1, the better understanding is that He went into the mountains to avoid the crowds, and His disciples followed Him. There Jesus began to address *them* concerning the difference between His kingdom and the errors of current Jewish thinking. Thus the term *sermon*[8] is incorrect. He also sat to give this address, whereas standing would have been more likely had He intended to preach to a large gathering. However, as in every other phase of His ministry, the crowd found Him and apparently began to listen to His teaching (7:28). It is best to assume that this event was intended to let His disciples and the gathering crowd know that the standards for the kingdom He had announced were quite different from those of the scribes and Pharisees. Therefore, He spoke directly to the disciples, while recognizing that the curious multitude had also gathered to hear His lesson. The term *discourse* is more appropriate than *sermon*.

The "disciples" mentioned in v. 1 do not refer to the Twelve as all were not chosen by that time (cf. Matt. 9:9). However, the term should not be taken broadly to mean the multitudes. Carson defends such a view:

> The word "disciple" must not be restricted to the Twelve . . . . Nor is it a special word for full-fledged believers, since it can also describe John the Baptist's followers (11:2). In the Lukan parallel we are told of a "large crowd of his disciples" as well as a "great number of people." (6:17)[9]

Whereas one may agree that the term is not to be restricted to the Twelve, it seems strained to assume that it should then refer to the crowd ("great multitudes") of 4:25. The comment about John's disciples is a pointless argument, because the word itself simply means "pupil, one who learns from another," and has no bearing on who they were pupils of or whom they followed, nor is salvation the issue in such usage. But these were *His* disciples, *hoi mathētai autou* (possessive), those who were His pupils, not idle curiosity seekers. Nothing more or less needs be read into the term.

Not everyone who followed Jesus out of curiosity or in search of
healing could be said to have been His disciple. Carson references
Matthew 11:2 to demonstrate the broader use of the word *disciple*,
but it is not likely that many scholars would believe that verse was
referring to a crowd of people not committed to Him. Carson bases
his argument heavily upon the theory that Luke 6 is describing the
same event as Matthew 5, and there appears to be too much left to
speculation to ignore the common significance to the word *disciple*.
Thus, Stott's view is to be preferred: "Jesus spoke the Sermon to
those who were already his disciples and thereby also the citizens
of God's kingdom and the children of God's family.[10]

5:2 Jesus began to teach His disciples. Carson believes the expression "opening His mouth" indicates a solemn or revelatory context.[11] It would certainly be a solemn and revelatory context as
Jesus began to unveil the character of His kingdom. Jesus was now
teaching (*didaskō*) His disciples. The primary idea of teaching in
Christ's ministry was not just setting forth data but always was motivational in nature, calling for a response.

THE BEATITUDES, 5:3-10

The next pericope involves a series of spiritual maxims normally referred to as beatitudes. The term *beatitude* refers to a state
of blessedness or blissfulness, which the characteristics named in
these verses would produce. It comes from the Greek *makarios,*
which is the first word of each verse from v. 3 through v. 11. It basically implies being "fortunate, blessed, happy." In some contexts it
signifies one who is worthy of praise (1 Tim. 1:11; 6:15). The word
is rich with connotations of joy and full happiness.[12] Thus one
should understand these aphorisms as divine guidelines for finding
full and genuine happiness. Jesus is not setting *conditions* for kingdom living in these first verses but is explaining the elements that
will bring true blessedness from God. What a contrast to the dead
and empty religion of self-righteousness and selfish humanity that
characterized the religious environment of Israel at this time.

The Lord used a clear formula in presenting this material. The
structure is obvious and planned. He was not randomly speaking
but making a list of people who, in contrast to what they had been
told, would find blessedness in His kingdom. The pattern is seen in

beginning each phrase with "blessed are" (*makarioi*) followed by a nominative masculine plural subject (e.g., "those who are poor in spirit," *hoi ptōchoi tō pneumati*, v. 3) and then the causal conjunction *hoti*. The pattern of the original text appears clearly:

v. 3	*Makarioi hoi ptōchoi . . . hoti . . .*
v. 4	*makarioi hoi penthountes . . . hoti . . .*
v. 5	*makarioi hoi praeis, . . . hoti . . .*
v. 6	*makarioi hoi peinōntes . . . hoti . . .*
v. 7	*makarioi hoi eleēmones, . . . hoti . . .*
v. 8	*makarioi hoi katharoi . . . hoti . . .*
v. 9	*makarioi hoi eiēenopoioi, . . . hoti . . .*
v. 10	*makarioi hoi dediōgmenoi . . . hoti . . .*

In these eight verses, Jesus names eight categories of people who are blessed and then gives the reason ("cause," *hoti*) for the blessing.[13] The eight categories are: the poor in spirit; the mourners; the gentle; the ones who hunger and thirst after righteousness; the merciful; the pure in heart; the peacemakers; and the ones who are persecuted for righteousness. Each category is offered a reason for considering its own unique condition as a blessed state.

5:3   The first condition listed that produces this bliss is an attitude of humility and spiritual honesty. The poor in spirit (*hoi ptōchoi tō pneumati*) are those who recognize their spiritual need, in contrast to the proud and self-righteous. They sense their spiritual emptiness and express humility, not arrogance. One should not assume that the poor (*hoi ptōchoi*) are those who are economically disadvantaged. *Ptōchos* may surely refer to economic circumstances but, like many words, can also be metaphoric in use. This same word is used in Revelation 3:17 of the Laodicean church, who had abundant material wealth and failed to understand their spiritual poverty.

Luke 6:20 has Christ speaking to His disciples and saying, "Blessed are you who are poor." His disciples were businessmen who may have sacrificed material wealth by leaving their professions to follow Him. He was not referring to homeless people in our modern context. This does not imply a lack of concern for the needy, but to tell economically deprived persons that they are blessed is to miss the point of the Lord's teaching and falls closer to deserving the rebuke of James 2:15-16. Luke offers no qualifier except that

Christ was speaking directly to His disciples and indicating that their commitment to the kingdom required sacrifice of material gain. Their blessedness came from participation in the coming kingdom, not in the material gain of secular employment. Of course, this would certainly be encouragement to any who were materially poor, assuming they were citizens of the kingdom; if not, then there would be little comfort. Since it is not to be assumed that Matthew's discourse on the mountain is the same as the discourse on the plain, it should not be assumed that the encouragement of Luke 6:20 is the same as of Matthew 5:3.

In Matthew's account, the prepositional phrase "in spirit" (*tō pneumati*) qualifies the kind of poverty to which Christ refers, reflecting a dependency for spiritual life that the self-righteous did not possess. Such spiritual poverty is seen in Christ's parable contrasting the two men who went into the temple to pray. The tax gatherer cries out to God, "Be merciful to me, the sinner," to which Christ responded that he was justified rather than the self-righteous Pharisee whose prayer reflects self-righteous pride instead of humility of spirit (Luke 18:9-14). Again the context of Israel's religious milieu at this time is significant. Jesus was contrasting two views of God's program, not offering economic assistance to needy people or spiritualizing away their material needs.

This category of people is blessed "because" (*hoti*) the kingdom of heaven is already theirs. The Lord used the present tense verb of being (*eimi*) to indicate that in their spiritual humility they were in harmony with the character of the kingdom. Certainly they were not living in the glory of the kingdom as yet, but they were among those who would share in its blessings when Christ came to establish it.

5:4　　If it seemed strange that the poor in spirit should be blessed, how much more those who mourn? Mourning and blessedness are apparent antitheses, but Christ indicated that they are compatible in His domain. Mounce summarizes the emphasis of this expression by identifying the mourners as those "who are filled with regret for their own waywardness and for the evil so prevalent in the world."[14] This is certainly consistent with the general nature of the Beatitudes and other teachings of our Lord.

The basic idea is that, in contrast to those who look for reward because of their self-righteous acts, those grieved by their failure in the spiritual domain will find mercy from God and thus will receive comfort from Him. Alford points out that the meaning goes beyond recognition of sin and also implies the consequences of trying to be spiritual in a nonspiritual environment. He states, "All such mourners are blessed: for the Father of mercies and God of all consolation being their covenant God, His comfort shall overbear all their mourning."[15] Perhaps the best understanding is offered by Carson, who says, "The godly remnant of Jesus' day weeps because of the humiliation of Israel, but they understand that it comes from personal and corporate sin."[16] He also appropriately references Psalm 119:136, "My eyes shed streams of water, because they do not keep Thy law" (cf. also Ezek. 9:4).

They were blessed "because" (*hoti*) they would receive comfort. The future tense is used, indicating that their comfort was forthcoming, not necessarily in their present condition. Comfort is *parakaleō,* which basically implies receiving words of comfort or encouragement and support. The cognate noun *paraklētos* is used of both the Lord ("intercessor," 1 John 2:1) and of the Holy Spirit ("Helper," John 14:26). Those who are characterized by the attitude of Psalm 119:136 and Ezekiel 9:4 will be encouraged and comforted because they are pleasing God. Again, the contrast with the religious self-content is significant.

5:5   The gentle ("meek" NIV) are to inherit the earth. This verse has been used out of context so often that it has become a proverb in much of American culture. But it is too frequently used in ways that the Lord did not intend. Jesus was most likely referencing Psalm 37:11, where the "humble" (*'ny,* adjective signifying "poor, afflicted, humble")[17] are those who patiently endure the afflictions of evildoers. The evildoers and the wicked will wither, fade, and be cut off (vv. 2, 9), but the humble will be blessed and prosper, including inheriting the earth, which the wicked have tried to claim through conquest and violence.

In this context the Lord describes a blessed person ("the meek") as one who patiently waits for God to judge with justice. He waits for God to bring about judgment of wrongdoers and does not seek to compete with them or extract personal vengeance. The idea of piety (true, not self-assumed) is also often associated with the word as well.[18]

It should be noted that meekness is not weakness. Jesus' powerful cleansing of the temple and His courageous confrontations with the Pharisees and Sadducees demonstrated that He was not a weak person. He was far from being weak, but He constantly demonstrated meekness. Out of love for those being spiritually abused by the religious leaders, and out of zeal for God's truth, He would openly confront with great boldness and aggression the enemies of God's truth and God's people. But Jesus was nevertheless meek because He was not doing it selfishly to compete with them or to usurp God's right of judgment or to extract personal vengeance.

Jesus quotes the LXX, *hoi praeis klēronomēsousin gēn* (Ps. 37:11) with the exception of adding the definite article *tēn gēn,* "the" earth, which belongs to the coming kingdom. The blessedness of the meek is that they will inherit by divine decree what the human race has struggled and killed to attain from the earliest records of civilization (cf. Eph.1:11).

5:6 The next group identified were those who crave righteousness. Hunger (*peinaō*) and thirst (*dipsaō*) are metaphors for having strong desires. Those who crave true righteousness are blessed "because" (*hoti*) true righteousness will be theirs through the work of Christ and will be the standard of conduct in the coming kingdom (2 Peter 3:13). The passive verb *chortasthēsontai* emphasizes that their hunger and thirst would be satisfied by some source other than themselves. The hunger and thirst for righteousness is satisfied in Christ. He is our righteousness (2 Cor. 5:21).

Once again a sharp dichotomy between the kingdom offered by Christ and the religious rituals of Israel was insinuated. The self-righteous environment of Israel did not satisfy the spiritual need of those who desired intimacy with God. Their desire for true righteousness was unsatisfied by ritual and legalism. Christ was offering hope to those who sensed their deep need for personal participation in God's righteousness. Meyer describes these as "such whose 'great earnestness, desire, and fervor' (Luther) are directed towards a moral constitution free from guilt."[19]

5:7 Those who show mercy are also blessed. The "merciful" (*eleēmones*) are to be contrasted with the judgmental and legalistic. They show kindness and willingness to seek reconciliation. Carson offers an excellent elucidation: "Mercy embraces both forgiveness for the guilty and compassion for the suffering and needy. No particular object of the demanded mercy is specified, because mercy is to be a function of Jesus' disciples, not of the particular situation that calls it forth."[20]

They are blessed "because" (*hoti*) they shall (future tense) be the recipients of mercy. The warning of 6:14-15 and 18:21-35 should also be considered with this statement. It is apparent that the servants of the merciful God should reflect the same nature. Those who are blessed are those who understand mercy and demonstrate it in their own lives. Stott's observation is critical to a proper application of this: "This is not because we can merit mercy by mercy or forgiveness by forgiveness."[21] We receive and thus demonstrate the attitude reflecting a spirit of humility consistent with that which brings God's mercy and forgiveness to us.

Lenski makes an interesting distinction between mercy (*eleos*) and grace (*charis*). He argues, "The noun *eleos* and its derivatives always deal with what we see of pain, misery, and distress, these results of sin; and *charis,* 'grace,' always deals with the sin and guilt itself. The one extends relief, the other pardon."[22] The blessed ones are those who understand mercy and willingly extend it to those in pain and distress, even to their enemies.

5:8   The pure in heart are those blessed by their privilege of seeing God, and the question as to their identity is not too difficult to answer. The setting for the Beatitudes is important in that these sayings draw lucid distinctions between the coming kingdom of Messiah and the present state of Israel's religion. Those who would see God were those who were inwardly pure, not those who were externally religious. The practice of Levitical purification was not sufficient to make one inwardly pure.

The heart (*kardia*) is the most inward part of our being, the innermost self. The term *heart* is used more than nine hundred times in the Old and New Testaments and almost always is used figuratively. Jeremiah 17:9 proclaims the human heart to be desperately wicked, and Christ Himself says that evil proceeds from the heart (Matt. 15:19). However, the heart can be cleansed, as David requested God to do in his case (Ps. 51:10). It is the responsibility of mankind to turn to God for cleansing. Apart from His purification, the heart's own wickedness will destroy life.

The adjective used here ("clean") is *katharos,* which implies "pureness, cleanness, innocence." The most common use of this word in the LXX translates the Hebrew *tahor,* indicating ceremonial purity, or God's declaration of something's being pure by its con-forming to His standards (Gen 7:2; Lev. 20:25; Pss. 19:9; 51:10). In the New Testament it takes on particular significance in relation to the work of Jesus and faith in Him.[23] Peter proclaimed that God has cleansed the hearts of those who have faith in Christ (Acts 15:9), which is consistent with the overall New Testament teaching of purification by faith, not by legalism.

Thus, to have a clean heart is to be clean inwardly by faith in Christ, which was in contrast to the ceremonial, external cleansing being promoted by Israel's religionists. Hendriksen points to the further significance of sincerity and truth involved with a pure heart. He summarizes this category of blessed ones as "those who, in the worship of the true God in accordance with the truth re-vealed in His word, strive without hypocrisy to please and glorify Him."[24] Those who have been cleansed inwardly are blessed "be-cause" (*hoti*) they will see (future of *horaō*) God. The sense of this word "see" is not mere visible perception but also comprehension of truth and reality (cf. Matt 13:14). However, in this context and with the future idea, it is best to assume this is the same hope John later speaks of as an eschatological hope, the ultimate revelation of Christ to His faithful saints (1 John 3:2-3).

5:9   Another beatitude popularized in the worldly arena is that of being a peacemaker, one who works out peace instead of aggres-sion. The question is, making peace with whom and by what method? Christ was certainly not considered a peacemaker by His oppo-nents but was seen as a disrupter and troublemaker. He Himself would claim *not* to have come to bring peace (Luke 12:51). As we look at Christ as an example, it becomes evident that He did not mean peace at any cost and certainly not by compromising God's truth.

This beatitude provides the only use of the noun "peacemak-er" (*eirēnopoios*), but the verbal cognate appears in Colossians 1:20 (*eirēnopoieō*), where Christ is said to have reconciled all things to Himself, "having made peace through the blood of His cross." It seems most unlikely that Jesus in His beatitude about peace was concerned primarily with interpersonal human relations, else He was a failure at this Himself. Rather, He was focused on peace between sinful humanity and God. He was the peacemaker by His death on the cross; the peacemaker of whom He speaks in Matthew

5:9 is the one who carries this message of peace to others (cf. Acts 10:34-43; Rom. 5:1). Of course, interpersonal relationships are to characterize the peace that one has from God. Paul exhorts God's people to "pursue the things which make for peace and the building up of one another" (Rom. 14:19). Ephesians 4:1-3 is also significant to this discussion. The same would be seen in the Christian's life in the secular environment as well. There is no need to argue and strive as the unregenerate who have no hope beyond this temporal and materialistic life. Carson points out:

> Our peacemaking will include the promulgation of that gospel. It must also extend to seeking all kinds of reconciliation. Instead of delighting in division, bitterness, strife, or some petty "divide-and-conquer" mentality, disciples of Jesus delight to make peace wherever possible.[25]

However, the highest good is not peace but peacemaking within the limits of God's truth. To accommodate heresy, blasphemy, immorality, or other behavior, attitudes, and characteristics that are contrary to God's revelation in the name of peace is to totally ignore this teaching in its context. Christ demonstrates how to be a peacemaker.

The peacemakers are blessed "because" (*hoti*) they shall be called the sons of God. Alford correctly indicates that the idea of "called" (future passive of *kaleō*) is to be recognized[26] as the sons of God. The idea is that at the inauguration of the kingdom the true sons (legal heirs)[27] of God, who sent His Son to establish peace, would be acknowledged as such before the whole congregation of heaven and earth. The event is the "adoption as sons" spoken of in Romans 8:23.

5:10   The final group named in the Beatitudes are those who are persecuted for the sake of righteousness. Being blessed in persecution is, again, quite contrary to the thinking of the natural mind. Whether Christ intended to follow peacemaking with persecution as a deliberate sequence is not clear, but it seems best to just take it separately and not see the persecution as a consequence of trying to be a peacemaker.[28] However, admittedly, to proclaim peace through Christ may certainly bring persecution. The issue named here is "for the sake of righteousness." Paul also counsels Timothy that "all who desire to live godly in Christ Jesus will be persecuted" (2 Tim. 3:12). Christ would later again warn His disciples that identifying with Him would bring persecution (John 15:18–16:3).

Peter, who, of course, suffered persecution for Christ's sake, brings this same comfort to his readers in 1 Peter 3:14: "If you should suffer for the sake of righteousness, you are blessed" (cf. also 1 Peter 4:14). Thus, the voice of experience is verifying Christ's teaching in this beatitude. Those who thus suffer are blessed "because" (*hoti*) they receive the kingdom of heaven. The proof of their part in the kingdom is their commitment to righteousness even in the face of persecution. Though perhaps suffering persecution now, in reality they are citizens of the kingdom whose King will ultimately and eternally reign. To be identified with the very kingdom their enemies reject is to be blessed, for that kingdom will come, and the enemies will be destroyed.

Personal Exhortations to the Disciples, 5:11-16

5:11-12   Jesus now changed the format of His lecture. He appears to have become concerned with a more personal exhortation. Even though speaking to these same men and beginning with the rather universal proclamation of third-person "those who" to identify the blessed ones, now He moved to the direct address of second-person "you." Perhaps He wanted to make sure they understood the necessity of personal application because of the persecutions awaiting them. Meyer aptly expresses the Lord's concern: "The whole of the hostility which is to assail His disciples stands even now before the soul of the Lord."[29] The disciples would be the recipients of insults, persecution, and slander on account of their association with Jesus Christ. This prediction is repeated more clearly in John 15:18-21; 16:1-4.

Their perspective was to be that this unfair treatment was a blessing. The twofold reason is stated in v. 12: first, the "great reward" awaiting them in heaven; second, identification with the honored prophets of God of whom they had heard all their lives. Promise of heavenly reward is common in the New Testament. Paul emphasized that the believer's hope is not in this world (1 Cor. 15:19) and set an example of striving for the unseen reward (2 Cor. 4:17-18). The Christian is repeatedly admonished to develop this perspective for life (Matt. 6:24-34; Rom. 8:18-25; Phil. 3:20-21; Col. 3:1-4).

The second reason Christ offered for which to rejoice, be glad, and consider themselves blessed was identification with the prophets of old. In one sense, this vindicated their genuineness as God's servants through serving Messiah (Jesus) and, in another, indicated that their suffering would win them acclaim among the people of God. This was fulfilled in the fact that their names have become household words and their "fame" is equal to or exceeds that of the great prophets of God.

SALT AND LIGHT METAPHORS, 5:13-16

Continuing His exhortation to the disciples, Jesus used two metaphors to illustrate their role in the world. The unique attributes of both salt and light are important to the concept He was communicating. Their relationship to the world would be analogous to salt in their culture and light in a dark world. Stott sees this as a lesson to "indicate their influence for good in the world."[30] Hendriksen's comment is perhaps the best summary of this pericope:

> The words of 5:13-16 show both how totally different from the world and yet how closely related to the world believers are. Worldly-mindedness or secularization is here condemned, but so is also aloofness or isolationism. Salt is a blessing when it remains truly salt; light as long as it is really light. But salt must be sprinkled over, better still rubbed into, the meat. Light must be allowed to shine into the darkness. It must not be put under cover.[31]

In the flow of Christ's teaching on the unique character of those who are blessed in His kingdom, the association of His followers with salt and light is appropriate. Like salt—an outside element added to meat or other foods for flavor and as a preservative —and like light, that which dispels darkness, His unique people are to be elements of influence in a world that is decaying and dark.

5:13   "You are the salt of the earth," Christ declared of His disciples. Such a metaphor has multiple implications. In modern America, salt is usually thought of as only a flavoring. Though this is surely a legitimate attribute and common use for salt, it was not the primary function in the ancient world. Perhaps the most common use in centuries past, including even in early America before refrigeration, was as a preservative.

Understanding both common uses for salt, one can understand the Lord's telling His disciples that they were to be seasoning in an otherwise tasteless world and a preservative in a decaying world. When used as a seasoning, the flavor of salt is distinct and is added because otherwise the food would be flavorless. The disciples were to be an outside agent to bring substance and life to the world in which they lived. Their lives were to be distinct and attractive to the unsaved.

But salt also preserves, and the word communicated to the disciples that they were left in the world to slow the process of decay. Salt is also seen in Scripture as symbolic of purification; Elisha purified water through salt (2 Kings 2:21). This is a serious matter for the disciples of Christ to consider. In what ways are Christ's followers to preserve the world, to halt or at least slow the process of its decay? Certainly not through politics or other humanistic methods. That was attempted in the last decade of American Christianity and not only failed but brought disgrace to the message of Jesus Christ. Such efforts are no more than the "weapons" of warfare "of the flesh" (2 Cor. 10:3-4).

Christ's followers are themselves the element that preserves the world from utter ruin. By the moral and ethical standards of God's people, by their higher value system, higher regard for all human life, Christ's servants offer the flavor and preserving factor of their presence. It is not political activity, nor social prestige, nor any other fleshly element that will make this world a better place in which to live. Trying to impose moral codes and to legislate spiritual standards upon the unregenerate world is casting our pearls before swine. Pharisaism attempts to legislate morality; Christianity is to demonstrate morality. If Christians were living as they should, the world would be a better place, and the seasoning would draw others to Christ. Many references to salt are in the Scriptures. It would be a worthwhile study to look into each context to develop a perspective of its numerous uses.

Jesus next made a statement that has caused some to question the inerrancy of the text: "But if the salt has become tasteless" (or, "if the salt loses its saltiness" NIV). The problem is that salt (sodium chloride), being a stable substance, normally will not or cannot "lose its saltiness." So did Christ err in His statement, or should more consideration be given to alternative explanations? First, Christ says, *"ean de to halas mōranthē,"* or literally, "if the salt be made foolish." The word *mōrainō* is "to be silly, foolish . . . make foolish, convict of folly."[32] Both here and in Luke 14:34 the context references the effectiveness of salt. In the only other New Testament uses of the word, Romans 1:22 and 1 Corinthians 1:20, the context is the foolishness of human reasoning in comparison with God's plan. Some have argued that Jesus did not intend to say that salt lost its saltiness, but in Mark 9:50 the wording is more specific, *ean de to halas analon genētai,* "if the salt becomes without salt." Therefore it is best to understand that Jesus was intending to imply salt that had lost its saltiness.

Another possibility centers on His stating a hypothetical situation that He knew could not happen. But such an explanation is weak in and of itself, seeming to leave the statement without any significance. Perhaps the best explanation is that a variety of salts were used in Palestine and some kinds were impure salt compounds. Merrill Unger offers a helpful comment: "This belief might arise from the use of impure rock salt or mixed saline and earthy deposits from the Dead Sea flats, etc., from which the salt would dissolve out, leaving only a tasteless and useless residue."[33] Carson offers a similar explanation: "Most salt in the ancient world derived from salt marshes or the like, rather than by evaporation of salt water, and therefore contained impurities. The actual salt, being more soluble than the impurities, could be leached out, leaving a residue so dilute it was of little worth."[34]

Christ's statement therefore was not contrary to science, and it made an important point to His disciples. If not fulfilling the purpose for which He sent them into the world, the disciples were useless in the kingdom work. This was not a threat of losing one's salvation but of being useless and cast aside in the ministry of Jesus Christ. The consequences of such failure does not involve loss of salvation but loss of reward at the Bema of Christ (1 Cor. 3:11-15; 2 Cor. 5:10).

5:14   The next metaphor was less complicated and more obvious in its application. Light in darkness clearly demonstrates a dichotomy of truth systems. Because of spiritual blindness, the world is in darkness; however, because of spiritual enlightenment, Christ's disciples bring the illumination of God's truth to the darkness. Jesus emphatically stated, "You ["alone" or "in particular," *humeis este*] are the light of the world." Christ Himself is called the Light that came to the world (John 1:1-5, 9), and now His followers were to perpetuate that light in their own lives. The church is to demonstrate the character of her Lord by being a light (manifestation of His glory) as expressed in New Testament terms (Eph. 5:8-9; Phil. 2:15; etc.).

The reference to a city set on a hill, serving to illustrate how a light draws attention, is not as out of place as it may at first seem. Constructed largely of white limestone, cities of the ancient Near East when placed on a hilltop would reflect the bright sun rays, allowing visibility from miles away. At night the white marble mirrored both the moonlight and burning lamps, acting as a beacon for directing travelers toward the city. Thus Christ's disciples, who are lights in the world, should be easily visible. As ancient travelers found comfort and delight in spotting these cities for refreshment and safety, likewise Christians should give hope and direction for weary pilgrims in this dangerous and futile world.[35]

5:15   The next statement illustrated the foolishness of not properly displaying a light. One lights a lamp for the purpose of illuminating an area; thus to cover the lamp with an object so as to restrict its purpose is senseless. Lenski says:

> But who lights a lamp in order to cover that lighted lamp? That would be ridiculous. If the light is not wanted, the lamp is not lit, or the light is blown out. If the light is wanted, the lamp is lit and placed upon its stand. For what do you suppose Christ lighted us? To have us hidden from sight? No, but to act as a lamp (*lamp*) to all in the house.[36]

Indeed, Christ has left His followers behind to be light in darkness, reflecting His light with their actions, attitudes, and character. For amplification of the application, notation should be made of the characteristics of a lamp. Unlike a spotlight, a typical house lamp created a small circle of light that could dimly illuminate a small room. Its intent was not to shine a beam of light on any one object but to give of itself in all directions so that the immediate environment was lit. Likewise, the purpose of Christianity is not to high-light the success or failure of an individual but to offer insight to all as to what life really is in Christ.

5:16   Next, Christ applied the metaphor in clear instructions. He equated the believer's light with good works, stating that the purpose is for mankind to glorify God. The Christian's light is to shine before men (*emprosthen tōn anthrōpōn*), in other words, to be visible witness to the world. Our lives should be analogous to a lamp lighting up a room as we work and live among the unsaved. This light is described as our "good works" (*ta kala erga*).

Meyer identifies the good works as "not their virtue in general, but, in accordance with the whole context from v. 11, their *ministry* as faithful to its obligations."[37] He acknowledges that this involves moral nature but assumes it primarily relates to their work as disciples. Carson is more nearly correct when he defines the good works as "all righteousness, everything they are and do that reflects the mind and will of God."[38] The connection between light and good works seems clear enough. Behavior, character, and attitudes that reflect the holiness, grace, and eternal values of God would certainly stand out in a world characterized by greed, self-indulgence, and violence. Such contrast may bring persecution now (see comments on vv. 10-12) but will eventuate in God's glory (1 Peter 2:12).

FULFILLMENT OF THE LAW, 5:17-20

Christ then made an unprecedented claim related to the Law—He came to fulfill the Law. These few verses are critical in properly relating to the Old Testament Law, to the purpose of Christ's coming, and to the eschatological function of the Law. Carson does not overstate the situation when he says, "The theological and canonical ramifications of one's exegetical conclusions on this pericope are so numerous that discussion becomes freighted with the intricacies of biblical theology."[39] In other words, to properly relate this pericope to the rest of Scripture is not simple and requires dedicated theological discipline not to err. Simply quoting systematic theological conclusions is inadequate to understand the text before us.

5:17   Christ's next statement was intended to prevent a misunderstanding of what He was about to say, not of what He had said up to that point. Carson correctly rejects the view that Jesus' remark implied a strong Jewish anticipation that Messiah would remove the Law.[40] Jesus was about to attack the oral interpretation of the Law, which most Jews of the time had been conditioned to accept as the Law itself. Six times in the next few verses He will challenge their oral traditions. Note the formula repeated in vv. 21-43: "You have heard that it was [v. 31 simply has "it was said"] said . . . but I say." This contrast between what the rabbis had been teaching for centuries and what Jesus Himself was about to teach could be misconstrued, so He stated plainly His intention of not doing away with the Law.

The idea of "abolish" is literally to "throw down, demolish, destroy," as in demolishing a building.[41] Jesus was not in any manner seeking to dismantle the Old Testament Scriptures. This is an important message to those who believe that He came to do away with the Law and thus now we enter the age of grace. God has always and only dealt in grace with fallen humanity; otherwise, the world would not have existed beyond the original sin of Adam. Jesus establishes the Old Testament and holds Himself accountable to fulfill all of it.

The expression "Law or the Prophets" is a typical way of saying the whole Old Testament (cf. 7:12; 11:13; 22:40; etc.); at times, a third division was added, "the Psalms [or writings]" (Luke 24:44-45). If a distinction is intended by the "or," it would be similar to saying "neither the moral code of God nor the promises of God." Jesus wanted His followers to understand that the purpose of His coming was not to discredit or nullify the intent and value of the Old Testament in either its prophetic announcements or in areas of the Law. Paul explains that the Law is good if used as it was intended (1 Tim. 1:8); in the same way, Jesus would use the Law as intended and not as the self-righteous religious leaders, who used it for their own glorification and judgment of others.

The real issue is what Jesus meant by "fulfill" (*plēroō*). Carson explains:

> The lack of background for *plēroō* ('fulfill') as far as it applies to Scripture requires cautious induction from the NT evidence. . . . Most NT uses of *plēroō* in connection with Scripture, however, require some teleological[42] force . . . and even the ambiguous uses presup-

pose a typology that in its broadest dimensions is teleological, even if not in every detail.[43]

Indeed, much confusion has been created by rash assumptions about what "fulfill" involves, but that it has some sense of bringing to completion is clear.

Hendriksen takes the phrase as explaining why His beatitudes were not contrary to the Law: "According to the beatitudes these people, convicted to their spiritual poverty, had mournfully confessed their sins and had received from God the righteousness of imputation. . . . Thus, the law was in principle being fulfilled."[44] However, this explanation artificially makes the focus of the Beatitudes as embodying the principles of the Law and brings the theological proposition of imputation into a context that does not suggest it. Hendriksen sees Christ's statement as referring to fulfillment in His own experience and also in that of His followers.[45] The implication is that Jesus' teaching and experience completed the purpose and principles of the Law.

Hendriksen's view is not totally objectionable but tries too hard to connect v. 17 to the Beatitudes. His view also assumes that vv. 11-16 must be connected to the Beatitudes. This is not a necessary correlation. It is probably best not to force the connection but allow Christ's teaching to flow to His next concern, the misuse of the Law. Before attacking their oral traditions (vv. 21-48), He was establishing in the minds of His disciples that He was not attacking the Law itself but the Jewish misapplication of it. By His teachings and His works, Christ was going to fulfill the Law. It should be noted that He was not claiming at that point to be fulfilling prophecy.

The Law is often considered to be composed of three divisions: moral, ceremonial, and civic. Some believe that Jesus intended to fulfill the moral law but was not concerned about the ceremonial and civic aspects. Nothing in the context implies such a distinction. Indeed, nothing in Jesus' life would indicate that He laid aside the ceremonial or civic dispositions of the Law. His concern was to accomplish the purpose and goal (*plēroō*)[46] of the whole Law, thereby fulfilling its demands upon the Jews and mankind in general. The One who became the Second Adam fulfilled all the Law's demands in contrast to the first Adam, who disobeyed the one prohibition and sent the human race into death. By His obedience, Christ accomplished all that the Law demanded.

5:18   Verse 18 offers explanation and further affirmation of His commitment to the authority and value of the Law. The expression "pass away" (NASB; "disappear" NIV) is aorist tense and passive voice of *parerchomai,* "passed away, come to an end, disappear."[47] The passive voice implies that the ending would not be brought upon the earth "until the heavens and earth be brought to an end." Thus, until God brings an end to the universe as we know it, the Law, even the smallest letter (*iōta,* equivalent of the Aramaic *yod,* smallest letter of the alphabet)[48] and stroke (*keraia,* the projection of part of a letter, a serif decoration on letters; also accents or breathing marks used in the Aramaic and Greek alphabets) will not pass away.[49] Christ used the same word, tense, and voice to describe bringing the Law to an end that He used for bringing the universe to an end. Thus, the universe and the Law are in effect until (*heōs,* temporal particle) all things "come to be" (*an panta genētai*). The Law has not yet been abolished, but it has been fulfilled by Jesus Christ. Those who are in Christ then have through Him met all the requirements of the Law.

5:19   Christ then made a conclusion to His statement. Since the Law is not going to be abolished by Him but rather fulfilled, anyone who is a part of His kingdom will not teach the annulling of the Law. The word annul is *lusē,* aorist subjunctive of *luō,* "set free, loose, untie, release, destroy, bring to an end, abolish, annul, tear down, destroy."[50] In the context the best idea is to "abolish" or "annul" its value and truth. Jesus' concern was that His listeners not assume that the Law was imperfect or of no value to His followers. Paul agrees with this and reminds Timothy that "the Law is good, if one uses it lawfully" (1 Tim. 1:8). To attempt to earn righteousness by mechanical obedience to part of it is not a lawful use of the Law. The Law is to reveal the meaning of loving God with all of one's heart, soul, and mind and to love one's neighbor as oneself (cf. Matt. 22:36-40). Thus understanding the Law and teaching its precepts is to properly represent Messiah's kingdom.

5:20   This verse is best understood as a transition between Christ's declaration of His purpose in fulfilling the Law and the failure of the Jews to do so because their oral traditions had become more authoritative to them than God's revelation. Brown offers an excellent synopsis.

The object of our Lord seems to us very distinctly and clearly stated by himself, in the twentieth verse. That object was to show that the system of religious and moral duty, which was to be taught and exemplified in "the kingdom of God," the new economy, was to be greatly superior to that system of religious and moral duty taught by the Scribes, and exemplified by the Pharisees.[51]

It was for this reason that Jesus stated that the righteousness of His kingdom people must exceed that of the prominent religious leaders of Israel. Their interpretation of the Law and their own life-styles were insufficient to make one righteous.

The two religious groups mentioned are often paired in the Gospels (eleven times in Matthew). Scribes (*grammateus*) were the religious scholars of the time. Their primary function was to copy and preserve the Scriptures. The scribes were also expositors of the Law, often called lawyers, and normally members of the party of Pharisees. The Pharisees were a religious party somewhat like the Democrat or Republican party in the American political system. "Scribe" was an office held by some Pharisees. The scribes are referenced more than twenty times in Matthew's gospel, usually with a negative connotation, including the seven pronouncements of "woe" and "hypocrites" in Matthew 23:13-29.

The declaration that those who enter the kingdom of heaven must have righteousness exceeding that of these two dominant religious factions was truly a shock to the hearers, especially to the scribes and Pharisees themselves. Jesus would condemn them (Matt. 23:13-29) for being hypocrites and accuse them of several failures: preventing others from entering the kingdom and not entering themselves (v. 13); taking advantage of widows and faking lengthy prayers (v. 14); winning converts only to make them two times as blind as themselves (v. 15); tithing fanatically but forgetting justice, mercy, and faithfulness (v. 23); being concerned with outward image while inwardly being robbers and self-indulgent (v. 25); appearing beautiful outwardly, but inwardly filled with death, lawlessness, and hypocrisy (v. 27); and appearing to honor the prophets of God but inwardly justifying their fathers' murder of them (v. 29). These and several other accusations clearly indicate God's displeasure with these men who were in a position to teach the people about Him.

The message is clear—external religious activity and self-righteousness are not sufficient to get one into the kingdom of heaven.

THE FIRST EXPANSION OF ORAL TRADITION, 5:21-26

5:21   "You have heard" refers to the oral traditions that had been passed from generation to generation through rabbinic teachers. Jesus expanded on these, dwelling not so much on what they taught as on how they had reduced the Word of God to their legalistic code, ignoring the Law's true purpose and value. The Pharisees were committed to the authority of these traditions and prone to equate them with the written Law of Moses. However, the Sadducees did not accept them, thus debate between these two parties could be intense. Josephus writes:

> What I would now explain is this, that the Pharisees have delivered to the people a great many observations by succession from their fathers, which are not written in the law of Moses; and for that reason it is that the Sadducees reject them . . . . While the Sadducees are able to persuade none but the rich . . . the Pharisees have the multitude on their side.[52]

In this environment, Jesus raised the issue, not to side with the Sadducees but to speak to the multitudes who had been persuaded by the Pharisees to place their traditions on an equal par with Scripture. Note, however, that Jesus contrasted the oral traditions not with the Old Testament but with *His own word.*

The first tradition had to do with murder.[53] The word Jesus used for murder was *phoneuō,* which is also used in the LXX in Exodus 20:15 (v. 13 in English). Christ was apparently quoting the LXX since He used the exact phrase, *ou phoneuseis.* He then referenced what was added, "Whoever commits murder shall be liable to the court." The point here is not that what they had been told was wrong in and of itself, for it was the Law, but that it was incomplete regarding the intended purpose of the Law. Jesus had already declared that the righteousness of the kingdom surpassed that of the scribes and Pharisees (v. 20); thus, a mere external application of the Law was not sufficient.

5:22   Jesus then explained His objection to the traditions being taught. Murder is the ultimate outward expression of a deeper problem, which the external religionist failed to grasp. Beyond merely not murdering, one is to guard against the inward attitude that could lead to the violence of murder. Whereas the scribes and Pharisees thought that as long as they did not murder anyone they were being righteous, Jesus pointed out that the crime was already being perpetrated in seed form within their hearts. Hendriksen explains it well: "He does this by pointing out and condemning the evil disposition of the heart that lies at the root of the transgression."[54]

"Everyone who is angry [*pas ho orgizomenos*] with his brother" is guilty. Looking for some hidden meaning to the word "anger" is of little value; both the Greek and English have the same meaning. A comparison with *thymos* (also "anger") offers little because of similarity in use. Note that at times *thymos* implies an outburst of anger whereas *orgizō* is more of a deliberated wrath; however, it would be incorrect to force the distinctions too far as both are forbidden for the Christian (Eph. 4:31; Col. 3:8).

Of greater significance is the object of the anger here. Christ's prohibition was clarified by the expression "with his brother" and reminiscent of Genesis 4:5-8 and 1 John 3:10-12. God warned Cain not to let his emotional response lead to destructive sin, but Cain failed to respond to the warning, and the result was murder. In similar fashion, John warns Christians to love the brothers and not be like Cain. Anger is an emotion that will be enlivened by certain stimuli, and to deny this natural emotion is foolish and perhaps prideful. The issue is, what do you do with it? Ephesians 4:26 warns, "Be angry yet do not sin" [*orgizesthe kai mē hamartanete*], "do not allow the sun to go down on your anger." In other words, when anger arises in you, it is not to be ignored, excused, or allowed to build but dealt with immediately before progressing into a destructive act.

Christ offered some common illustrations of how anger can turn to vicious attacks against brothers. "Raca" (*Raka*) is an "uncomplimentary, perh. foul epithet . . . a term of abuse."[55] Christ pointed out that even such malicious slander would be condemned by the Sanhedrin (supreme court of Israel). Another hateful slander is to call a brother "fool." The word *mōre* implies to "be foolish" or "stupid." It is used by Christ in Matthew 7:26 of those who do not heed His words and again in 23:17 of the scribes and Pharisees who have perverted the true worship of God. His warning may seem strange, since He Himself uses the word. But the difference is in stating that those who oppose God's truth are fools and in not attacking a brother out of an evil heart. The rebuke is for one whose object of anger is a brother with whom he shares a common birth (with God as Father) and not with one who opposes God's truth and thus injures those who are led away from God. Carson believes the word to the Hebrew listeners would have carried the connotation of "moral apostasy, rebellion, and wickedness."[56]

5:23-24 Christ's application to His teaching focused on the correlation of the relationship between one's brother and with God. He seems to have been making the point that worship of God is not accepted until reconciliation has been achieved with brothers with whom some offense has broken a relationship. What value is an offering to God if anger and division exists with a brother who also is God's child? God is more concerned with brotherly love than with ritualistic offerings. Here the vast chasm between Pharisaical adherence to points of the Law ("do not murder") and Christ's teaching of the heart of the Law ("do not injure a brother") is clearly seen. Both this illustration and the one following (v. 25, the opponent at law) are intended to make a distinction of internal motive, not external ritual.

5:25-26 Christ's next illustration deals with one's enemies, and certainly reconciling with a brother (v. 23) rather than with an opponent is easier to understand. The standard of Christ's righteousness emphasizes going that extra step of reconciliation—making peace with your enemy. It is interesting that Jesus stated a practical reason for this exhortation, namely, to avoid being thrown into prison. Verse 26 implies that Jesus assumed guilt for the individual and therefore settlement with an opponent (before the interference of the courts) would be better. Instead of speaking bitter words flowing from a sinful heart (which is equivalent to murder), settling the dispute and seeking reconciliation is better.

Both illustrations serve to make one point: an individual's relationship with God is connected with his/her relationship with fellow human beings, whether brothers or enemies. Psalm 34:11-14 teaches that the fear of the Lord involves seeking and pursuing peace. The New Testament commands Christians to "live in peace with one another" (1 Thess. 5:13), "pursue peace with all men" (Heb. 12:14), and "pursue the things which make for peace" (Rom. 14:19). Therefore, those of Christ's kingdom are to go beyond the mere observance of legal code—having the goal of being a peacemaker (Matt. 5:9), not just avoiding the killing of people. Those who are truly of the God of peace (Rom. 15:33) will reflect His character and follow their Lord, the Prince of Peace (Isa. 9:6). However, there is need for one qualifying point. It is not peace at any expense. Christ did not compromise God's truth and plan in order to make peace, and neither should we. For this reason, Paul exhorts, "If possible, so far as it depends on you, be at peace with all men" (Rom. 12:18). The crucial distinction is that any opposition must be over the clear and accurate understanding of God's Word, not over personal preferences. To be at peace with *our* enemies is not the same as being at peace with *God's* enemies.

THE SECOND EXPANSION OF ORAL TRADITION: LUST IS THE BASIS FOR ADULTERY, 5:27-32

5:27   The next issue also proceeded from one of the Ten Commandments (Ex. 20:14), "You have heard that it was said, 'You shall not commit adultery'" (*ou moicheuseis,* LXX, v. 13). Adultery, *moicheuō,* is prohibited not only by Mosaic Law but by legal codes in most ancient cultures. The focus of adultery in the Old Testament is on the fidelity of a married woman; men having sexual relations with prostitutes or single women is not defined as adultery in either biblical or secular documents. Genesis 16:1-4; 30:1-4; and 38:14-18 are examples of pre-Law, extramarital relationships that are not condemned as adultery because the woman involved was not married to any other living man. The law does not warn married men from sexual activity with prostitutes on the basis of adultery, and there is no penalty set up for such cases except in rape or abuse of power over a slave or as it relates to the virgin girl's father. Proverbs 6:32-35 warns of the consequences of adultery but refers only to the natural and relentless desire for vengeance on the part of the woman's husband. The law stated in Deuteronomy 22:22 is "If a man is found lying with a married woman, then both of them shall die," and when a man has violated a betrothed girl, he is to die "because he has violated his neighbor's wife" (v. 24). In the case of a man's having sexual relations with an unbetrothed or unmarried female, the punishment was a monetary payment or forced marriage, not death (Deut. 22:29). Leviticus 20:10 also states the terms of adultery as "another man's wife" or his "friend's wife."[57] As strange as this one-sided perception of adultery may seem to the modern mind, it was consistent with the culture of the Old Testament world. Reisser observes:

> Every form of sexual relationship outside marriage was forbidden to the wife, for she was the real guarantor of the integrity of the family and clan, and by adultery she broke her own marriage and she destroyed the integrity of the whole clan. A man on the contrary committed adultery only by sexual relationships with a married woman, *i.e.,* when breaking into another's arrangement.[58]

The idea is that, by committing adultery, a woman has brought another man's seed into a family or clan and thus corrupts the lineage of her husband. A man, however, cannot corrupt his own line by producing offspring with another woman. At least part of the guilt of adultery in the ancient world, then, was a matter of not maintaining the unquestioned purity of the family line.

Jesus, on the other hand, seemed to clearly imply that a man can commit adultery against his wife. He said, "Whoever divorces his wife and marries another woman commits adultery against her" (Mark 10:11). Note that there is no mention of the second woman's being married and that the adultery is committed against the man's wife. This appears to be a much clearer condemnation against male adultery than expressed in the Old Testament or similar cultures of the time period.

5:28   Jesus, however, went even further than the Mosaic code and dealt with the heart of the Law, which the oral traditions did not consider. The idea of lustful looks as being the same as the act of adultery would certainly be foreign to these externally conditioned Jews. Even in contemporary Christianity, the concept of the thought life equated with the physical act is not treated seriously. This seems similar to Paul's qualification for an elder in 1 Timothy 3:2, which is translated "husband of one wife." A more accurate translation would be "a one-woman type of man," which denotes a man not prone to flirtatious or improper behavior toward women and places the emphasis on character, not marital status.

Carson follows Haacker in arguing that the issue centers on the man's not just lusting after another woman but actually trying to get her to lust.[59] This view seems to lessen the offense of lusting and places the emphasis upon enticing someone else. However, the Lord pointed out that adultery is a matter of a wicked heart (cf. Matt. 15:19 and Mark. 7:22), not just the enticement of others or actually having sexual intercourse with the woman. Jesus warned about the intention of the wicked heart and the sinfulness of looking with wrong intent. He was not saying that every look of appreciation or pleasure equates adultery, but when the look is treasured and fantasy enacted toward that person, adultery is already in action. Jesus did not directly mention the commandment in Exodus 20:17, "Do not covet your neighbor's wife." This was because He was dealing with the broader issue of lusting for any woman, married or single, a friend's wife or a stranger. Stott reminds his readers that this is not to be turned into a "Victorian prudery,"[60] for God certainly delights in pleasure within sexual relations between husband and wife. The prohibition is in any perversion of God's beautiful provision of husband and wife intimacy.

5:29   The Lord then used rhetorical hyperbole to emphasize the horror of this internal sin. "If your right eye makes you stumble" alerted His listeners to the origin of the danger. Carson observes, "The 'eye' (v. 29) is the member of the body most commonly blamed for leading us astray, especially in sexual sins (cf. Num 15:39; Prov 21:4; Ezek 6:9; 18:12; 20:8; cf. Eccl 11:9); the 'right eye' refers to one's best eye."[61] The eye is the organ that feeds data into the brain, but the heart interprets and applies what is perceived. Thus Jesus stated that adultery comes from the heart (Matt. 15:19) but begins with what the eye views. Here the emphasis seems to be that the problem begins with how one uses this organ of perception. While being a blessing from God, sight becomes perverted by the wicked heart if one does not discipline the use of this gift. It was probably in this vein that Job declared his righteousness by saying, "I have made a covenant with my eyes; how then could I gaze at a virgin?" (Job 31:1).

Jesus offered a rather drastic answer to this dilemma: tear out the offending member. Some well-intentioned but seriously misguided zealots have castrated and mutilated themselves, trying to live up to the letter of the law, which they believe Jesus has established. However, this mechanical and external application of truth is exactly what He condemned in the religious leaders. This is certainly hyperbole, a "form of rhetorical exaggeration [that] highlights and emphasizes a point by exaggeration."[62] Jesus was not intending for anyone to literally tear out an eye, but, by comparison, that momentary action would not be as terrible as the whole body's being eternally tormented in hell.

5:30   The next verse offers another hyperbolic illustration to contrast the seriousness of the judgment on sinfulness with the relatively light affliction of losing a member of the body. The use of the term "right hand" creates a degree of curiosity, and some scholars see a euphemism for the male sexual organ.[63] It is probably best just to let the metaphor stand as the right hand symbolizing that important member for doing tasks and providing material needs. Even something as important as one's right hand is to be removed if its use will bring eternal judgment. Jesus uses the same symbolism in Matthew 18:8-9, again to emphasize the seriousness of sin. Offending God's standard is to be considered more horrifying than amputation or the loss of one's eye. If it is repulsive to think of such mutilation, then one can understand how serious immorality is to God. Therefore Christ was not advocating mutilating the body but was emphasizing the horror of sin.

THE THIRD EXPANSION OF ORAL TRADITION: FORNICATION IS THE ONLY REASON FOR DIVORCE, 5:31-32

5:31   Jesus referred to another teaching by simply stating, "It was said, 'Whoever divorces his wife, let him give her a certificate of dismissal.'" This is the shortest and least expanded of the traditions. Jesus was apparently referring to Deuteronomy 24:1, which was the center of rabbinical controversy concerning divorce. Moses required the husband who put away his wife because he found a matter of indecency in her to "write for her a certificate of divorce" (literally, "a book of cutting off," *sēpher c^{e}rithuth*). The instruction in Deuteronomy 24 was intended to restrict the casual discarding of one's wife and apparently gave the woman freedom to marry another man (Deut. 24:2) without being stoned to death, which would have been the case if her remarriage was considered adultery. Moses also forbade the first husband to take back the wife if her second husband also cast her out or even died. Once the man put her away, he relinquished any claim to her.

The great Renaissance rabbi Sforno explained, "'For it is an abomination . . .' because this is a [subtle] way of introducing adultery, the husband divorces his wife at the request of the adulterer so that he may take her for a period of time [after which] her first husband will take her back."[64] The rabbi points out how abuses to the marriage covenant could be accomplished in a form of wife-swapping and yet circumvent the law. If a *Get* (certificate of divorce) could allow a woman to remarry a second man and not be stoned, someone might conceive a plan to divorce a wife, let another man take her, and then the second put her away and the first take her back. Before one laughs at such subterfuge, consideration should be given to the undeniable evidence in human history of the depravity of man. The issue in Deuteronomy 24 will be considered in more detail at Matthew 19:7-9, where the context is more appropriate for such discussion.

5:32   Then Jesus did what He did with regard to the previous two challenges. He offered a more complete and internal perspective to the discussion. In the oral tradition of the Jews there was great diversity of opinion as to what Moses intended. The popular rabbi Hillel[65] taught that almost any weakness in the wife would allow for divorce. In strong contrast, Rabbi Shammai (Palestine born, also in the first century B.C.) taught that divorce was permitted only on the grounds of sexual immorality.[66] Josephus, a Pharisee who was contemporary with the apostles, explains the Deuteronomy 24 law in specific terms.

> He that desires to be divorced from his wife for any cause whatsoever (and many such causes happen among men), let him in writing give assurance that he will never use her as wife any more; for by this means she may be at liberty to marry another husband, although before this bill of divorce be given, she is not permitted to do so; but if she be misused by him also, or if, when he is dead, her first husband would marry her again, it shall not be lawful for her to return to him.[67]

The comment "for any cause whatsoever" is similar to the words of the Pharisees in Matthew 19:3. Again, discussion will be reserved for that context, but Jesus' answer (v. 4) was significant in that He drew their attention back to Scripture (Gen.1) rather than to the various opinions of the theological scholars of His day.

The debate of v. 32 primarily revolves around the phrase "except for the cause of unchastity" (*parektos logou porneias*). The preposition *parektos* expresses an exception to a general rule. Normally, divorce and remarriage are acts of adultery; the exception is if fornication is the main factor leading to divorce. Two questions immediately come to mind: what is fornication, and how does a man who divorces his wife not for fornication "make her commit adultery?"

Fornication (*porneia*) is a broad term involving a great variety of sexual improprieties. It is not the same as adultery (*moicheia*), which is the sexual act of a man with a married woman, or a woman with a married man, and was punishable by death (Lev. 20:10). The concept of fornication involves prostitution or improper (as defined by God's Word) sexual behavior. Reisser explains the different forms of fornication as "various extra-marital sexual modes of behavior insofar as they deviate from accepted social and religious norms (e.g. homosexuality, promiscuity, paedophilia, and especially prostitution)."[68] *Porneia* (and its cognate forms) appears fifty-five times in the New Testament; the references often warn of judgment resulting from such behavior.

Jesus therefore stated that a man creates a situation for adultery if he divorces his wife for any reason other than fornication. He was assuming that apart from some kind of improper sexual conduct this woman was innocent. What kind of sexual conduct is not mentioned? It is not adultery (*moicheia*) but rather some other deviance from God's standard of proper sexual activity (*porneia*). This might involve a woman who consistently exposes herself in intimate contact with men other than her husband, thereby disgracing him and belittling the holiness of their marriage bed.

In a genuine zeal to protect marriages, many scholars have so emphasized the evils of divorce that they have inadvertently laid aside the holiness of marriage. Divorce has been treated by some as an unpardonable sin, whereas disgracing the sanctity of sexual relations in marriage has been treated as a better option than divorce.

There is apparently little consideration of the offense against God's design and divine imagery. Many of the arguments stressing the ultimate evil of divorce ignore and omit much crucial teaching on the whole purpose and significance of marriage. Likewise, many arguments are presented to decrease the significance of Christ's exception statement, but Jesus, nevertheless, did include it in His teaching.

Another question is, how can a man by divorcing his wife make *her* commit adultery? One must understand that in that culture women were not career persons and had very few rights and options, either politically, economically, or even socially. Thus the assumption was that the divorced woman would seek remarriage. To marry a second man without proper justification for dissolution of the previous marriage was to commit adultery, because—apart from fornication—the first marriage was still binding. If fornication was not involved, then she had been put away unjustly, and she had not broken the marriage covenant. The circumstances of that cultural environment would force her to seek remarriage. Thus, though initially innocent, she would now commit adultery by joining herself to another man. This points out that a *Get* (legal term for certificate of divorce) does not necessarily end the marriage, but improper sexual conduct does justify the dissolution of the union. The complaint that divorce proceedings end the marriage is invalid; instead, the violation of the intimate privileges of marriage destroys the "two becoming one" (Gen. 2:24). God's design did not include multiple partners or casual sexual meddling. To prostitute the privilege of intimacy with someone other than one's own partner is to break the bond of oneness. The last statement, "and whoever marries a divorced woman commits adultery," indicates that if a woman has committed fornication and is sent away from her husband, she is not free to remarry. Jesus is not saying that the man who puts his wife away for fornication is committing adultery if he remarries, but that the woman who was unfaithful to her husband is already the cause of sin in the marriage dissolution. However, how does this fit into Deuteronomy 24:1-4? Moses seems to clearly indicate that a woman with a certificate of divorce could remarry. It appears that Deuteronomy 24 was written to protect women from being casually discarded by their husbands, but this had been twisted by some rabbis to give men the freedom to do just that (cf. Hillel's view).

Thus Jesus reinterpreted the passage to clarify fornication as the only justification for divorce. The divorced woman would not be executed as per the provision of the Law, since adultery was not committed, but any man marrying her *was* committing adultery before God. It must be remembered that Jesus was describing righteousness that exceeds the Pharisaical standard of external Law observance (v. 20). Here, the woman is a fornicator and has already effectively destroyed the holy matrimonial relation with her husband. One who marries her participates in her sin as well, even if she has a written certificate proclaiming her divorce.

This text does not address the issue of remarriage for the man who divorces a wife found guilty of fornication. In a similar teaching, Matthew 19:9 does mention the man's divorcing his wife—"whoever divorces his wife, except for immorality, and marries another woman commits adultery." Here the exception clause would imply that the man who divorces his wife because of fornication would not be guilty of adultery for remarriage. If a man's wife betrays him and disgraces the intimacy that should have been his, he has the option of writing a divorce certificate and sending her away. God does not then punish the man for his wife's unfaithfulness but condemns only the one who unjustly divorces his wife and marries another.

In this whole discussion, it should be remembered that permitting divorce is related to the hardness of the human heart (Matt. 19:8). This issue will be dealt with more fully in chap. 19, but note here that this is a concession to the natural cruelty of mankind and not reflective of God's ideal. Even in the case of fornication, forgiveness coupled with restoration is the more spiritual and godly choice. This writer believes that the fornication discussed here is best defined as characteristic behavior and not a one-time failure. It is also believed that adultery in this text transcends the Old Testament context and should be treated as a form of fornication, thus bypassing the legal requirement of execution. Even adultery is to be forgiven, and all attempts should be made to preserve the union as long as a dishonoring attitude toward the holiness of the marriage bond is not tolerated. Above all, in considering these lessons, the context that is built on v. 20 must be remembered: "Unless your righteousness surpasses that of the scribes and Pharisees, you shall not enter the kingdom of heaven." These standards exceed the Pharisaical rules of conduct.

THE FOURTH EXPANSION OF ORAL TRADITION:
THE MAKING OF VOWS, 5:33-37

5:33 Leviticus 19:12 states, "You shall not swear falsely by My name, so as to profane the name of your God; I am the Lord"; Numbers 30:2 adds, "If a man makes a vow to the Lord, or takes an oath to bind himself with a binding obligation, he shall not violate his word; he shall do according to all that proceeds out of his mouth"; and Deuteronomy 23:21, 23 says, "When you make a vow to the Lord your God, you shall not delay to pay it, for it would be sin in you, and the Lord your God will surely require it of you. . . . You shall be careful to perform what goes out from your lips, just as you have voluntarily vowed to the Lord your God, what you have promised." All of these verses warned the Jews to be careful of saying things that they did not live up to. The traditional paraphrase of these verses was interpreted by Christ as not to "make a *false* vow." Once again, the basis of their oral tradition was the Scripture, and this appears from one's reviewing the Old Testament texts to have been a good teaching. But Jesus made clear by His correction that they should not follow tradition but avoid oaths and vows altogether.

5:34-36 Jesus used four common objects as examples for oath taking: heaven, earth, Jerusalem, and one's own head. He forbade the swearing of oaths because of man's lack of authority over the area used as the basis for the oath: heaven is the throne of God (v. 34) and thus beyond the reach and control of man; earth (v. 35) is God's footstool and no longer man's kingdom; Jerusalem is the city of the great King and thus not man's; and man's own head is not his personal domain, as he cannot control the laws of God's design. An oath was a binding agreement, and to swear by something or someone called that thing or person into account. Since man is not the ultimate master of the things around him, he has no authority to call any of them to account.

Oath taking was common among the Jews and was assumed to demonstrate the sincerity of the one taking the oath. Jephthah is an example of the irresponsible use of vows (Judg. 11:29-39; note that the text nowhere states that God accepted or endorsed this act). Saul also made a foolish oath, which the Israelites refused to allow him to fulfill (1 Sam. 14:24-45). Josephus says of this event, "Saul sware that he would slay him [his son], and prefer the observation of his oath before all the ties of birth and of nature."[69] The solemn nature of taking an oath is undeniable, but the act had become a false show of sincerity and arrogance.

5:37   Jesus implied that oath taking was a meaningless gesture. The truly righteous man has no need of such external displays for verification of his integrity. He taught that one's word should be accepted as stated; a man's reputation is sufficient to verify the dependableness of his statement. Anything beyond a simple declaration of one's word is evil (or possibly, "from the evil one," *ek tou ponērou estin*). The Essene community likewise condemned the use of oaths as being evil, and Josephus records how their reputation reflected their view of oath taking:

> They are eminent for fidelity, and are the ministers of peace; whatsoever they say also is firmer than an oath; but swearing is avoided by them, and they esteem it worse than perjury; for they say, that he who cannot be believed without [swearing by] God, is already condemned.[70]

Certainly Jesus did not borrow His view of oaths from the Essenes, but the similarity of views reflects that other pious Jews had recognized the abuse of oath taking and realized that God was not to be so blasphemed.

One final comment is needed to guard against misunderstanding. Oaths as discussed by Jesus were specific formulaic promises involving authoritative accountability between the one making the oath and some other force, person, or holy object. This is not to be confused with the practice of calling upon God to witness the commitment of one who wishes to covenant with or proclaim loyalty to another. Thus, wedding vows are not an oath obligating God or others to perform according to the design of an oath, nor do they call upon powers beyond self for verification. Such vows are simply a public proclamation before witnesses to one's commitment to another. Paul called upon God to witness his faithfulness in prayer for the Romans (Rom. 1:9) and of his motives in not coming to Corinth (2 Cor. 1:23). The point of those comments was to proclaim his awareness that God was witness to his statements, and that such knowledge was more important than mere human accountability. Paul was not taking lightly the name of God but was demonstrating his sense of accountability before Him. One should not assume that Paul was violating Christ's instructions but rather that there is a difference between oath taking and acknowledging that God is witnessing one's acts and attitudes.

THE FIFTH EXPANSION OF ORAL TRADITION: RETRIBUTION, 5:38-42

5:38 "You have heard that it was said, 'An eye for an eye, and a tooth for a tooth.'" Jesus once again referred to the Old Testament Law (Ex. 21:24; Lev. 24:20; Deut. 19:21) as the basis of their oral tradition ("you have heard that it was said") and offered clarification in light of the standards of true righteousness. The statement "eye for an eye, and a tooth for a tooth" is only a partial quote. Old Testament references list other features as well: life for life, hand for hand, burn for burn, wound for wound, and bruise for bruise. The context of these statements deals not with personal retribution but with judgment exercised by courts of law within Israel's community. In other words, though the oral tradition implied personal vengeance, that was not the context of the original statements.

5:39-42 Christ then made individual applications, which appear to contradict the principle of retribution. He listed response to physical abuse (v. 39), lawsuits (v. 40), forced service (v. 41), and lending personal assets (v. 42) as examples of behavior contrary to the principle of personal vengeance. Again, remembering that the issue of these didactic pericopes was that true righteousness exceeded that of the scribes and Pharisees, it is best to understand that Jesus was not preaching pacifism but stating hyperbolically that one should rather suffer personal injury than to seek revenge.

He instructed His followers not to resist the evil man (v. 39). This was not an endorsement for evil to go unchecked in society but rather instructions for them not to oppose (*anthistēmi*) one attacking them personally. Neither was Jesus saying that His followers are required to stand by and watch someone else be abused without coming to his aid. The prohibition centered on defending one's pride through the medium of personal revenge. Certainly being willing as a follower to humbly lay down one's life for Christ is expected; however, to defend oneself from a crazed attacker or a thief in the night does not violate His teaching. It should be noted that a slap in the face, though humiliating and uncomfortable, is not life-threatening. If the follower of Christ is provoked or discredited through slapping of the face, he should be willing to turn the other cheek. Christ is our example (Matt. 26:67; John 18:20-23). Therefore, this is neither a generalized order to be a passivist or an injunction against the restraint of evil but a prohibition against the use of physical violence to protect one's pride.

The next injunction (v. 40) is extremely difficult to grasp in our contemporary society, where everyone is convinced of his constitutional right to defend property through legal battles. Jesus instructed His followers not to cling to worldly possessions through the court systems. Not only should one be willing to give up his inner shirt (*chitōna*) but his outer cloak as well (*himation*). The Mosaic Law forbade an Israelite to keep his neighbor's cloak (*himation*) overnight, even if it was collateral for money owed, because the garment was necessary to survive the cold (Ex. 22:25-26, LXX), yet Christ's followers were to be willing to give it up. This is to be considered hyperbole (as v. 29), emphasizing the priority of peace with one's fellow man (5:9) over material items.

Likewise, v. 41 teaches that His disciples should not resist the authority of one who makes an unfair demand but rather "go the extra mile." The history of this instruction (*aggareuō*) is probably related to the custom in the ancient Near East of compelling someone to do service for the government.[71] It is found again in Matthew 27:32, where Simon of Cyrene is "pressed into service" to carry the cross of Christ. Thus, Christ's concern here was a civil authority's enforcing the law of service. Rather than protest and resist this duty, kingdom people should demonstrate a humble servant's heart.

The last example of not seeking retribution is seen in one's willingness to share with those who have need rather than condemning them as unworthy of assistance. The Law demanded Jews to lend money to their needy brothers without charging interest (Ex. 22:25). There was no apparent contradiction of or addition to the known laws and practices of the Jews. Christ's concern seemed to be that one should not be protective of self but concerned for the needs of others. Whereas the Pharisees practiced almsgiving outwardly, Jesus reminded them of the attitude of compassion, not just religious duty.

THE SIXTH EXPANSION OF ORAL TRADITION:
LOVE YOUR ENEMIES, 5:43-48

5:43   Leviticus 19:18 commands, "You shall not take vengeance, nor bear any grudge against the sons of your people, but you shall love your neighbor as yourself; I am the Lord." One can easily relate the first part of this oral tradition to the Old Testament instructions. The word "neighbor" in this context is clearly a reference to a fellow Israelite and is not to be understood in its contemporary use, one residing next door. This is helpful in understanding the New Testament usage, which implies a fellow Christian, one bound in a relationship based upon common position in Christ. This is not to imply that one should not care for his neighborhood or other human beings in general, but the special relationship of those sharing God's name is to be a significant testimony to the world (John 13:34-35).

The second half of the oral teaching, "and hate your enemy," is what seems incongruous to modern cultural thought patterns. Though one would search in vain for an Old Testament text that commands hate for one's enemies, it is not to be supposed that Jesus or any later Christian community just fabricated this saying. Alford points out that this is a "gloss of the Rabbis" and is a "true representation of the spirit of the law, which was enacted for the Jews as a theocratic people."[72] Gundry also correctly recognizes this statement as summarizing "the OT attitude toward persecutors of God's people as voiced in Ps 139 (138):21-22; 'Do I not hate those who hate you, O Lord?'"[73] Carson adds some very helpful information from the Qumran community: "The Qumran covenanters explicitly commanded love for those within the community ('those whom God has elected') and hatred for the outsiders (cf. 1QS 1:1:4, 10; 2:4-9; 1QM 4:1-2; 15:6; 1QH 5:4)."[74] Certainly it is easily accepted that Jesus was reflecting an attitude that was orally communicated by the teachers of His day. Rabbis could refer to passages such as Deuteronomy 23:3-6; Psalms 26:5; 31:6; 139:21-22; and others, and easily teach hate for one's enemies, assuming they were also the enemies of God.

5:44   Christ then offered His antithesis, "But I say to you . . ." Whereas theocratic Israel understood that God's enemies were to be judged by Him and not pitied by them, Jesus pointed to the attitude of those of His new kingdom. Rather than hate (*miseō*) one's enemies, the servant of Messiah was to love (*agapaō*) them. *Agapaō* is not an emotive response but a sacrificial giving of one's self. The command is not to feel warm or affectionate towards one's enemies but to be generous and giving whether one feels like it or not.

The perfect demonstration of loving your enemy is to "pray for those who persecute you." Jesus, of course, is the perfect example of this (Luke 23:33-34) and is held before His followers as a role model to be imitated (1 Peter 2:21-23). As Martyn Lloyd-Jones points out, "it is not simply that we are not to strike back at them, but that we must be positive in our attitude towards them."[75] Paul, quoting Proverbs 25:21, reminds Christians that loving one's enemies is far more than just praying for them but involves meeting their physical needs as well: "If your enemy is hungry, feed him, and if he is thirsty, give him a drink" (Rom. 12:20). An Old Testament example of this very act is found in 2 Kings 6:21-23.

5:45   The NASB "in order that" may be a little misleading, since some may see this as implying a condition for becoming a son of God. Even though *hopōs* with the aorist subjunctive (as is the case here) normally implies purpose, other grammatical options and the testimony of other Scriptures argue against such an interpretation. One does not become a child of God by loving one's enemies or by any other act of religious duty (Titus 3:5; Eph. 2:8-9; etc.). Rather, loving one's enemies demonstrates that one is already God's child. Our capacity to love an enemy comes from having the character of God, which can only be the product of the new birth, not a cause for it.

Jesus literally says, "You should be . . ." (subjunctive mood, expressing what is normally expected), rather than, "You shall be. . ," which would use the future tense verb expressing a future result. It is quite likely that this should be understood as a proper grammatical substitute for the imperative[76] "Be sons of your Father," who loves His enemies. This fits well with v. 48, which summarizes vv. 20-47.

The next phrase, "for He causes . . ," explains why the child of God should love even enemies. The introductory word "for" (*hoti*) is a causal expression and could be translated "because." God's love for His enemies is demonstrated by daily provision such as sunshine and rain, which are necessary for the growing of food and other survival needs. Because God is good to both the righteous and unrighteous, His children should display that same character of goodness, not just to "neighbors" but even to enemies as God Himself does. Of course the greatest demonstration of God's love for His enemies is seen in Christ's substitutionary death (Rom. 5:8).

5:46-47   Jesus used two negative examples to illustrate why God's children are to be different. Both tax gatherers (despised by the Jews) and Gentiles (also hated by the Jews) showed love toward those who were in harmony with them. His point was that this does not require Godlike character and to be different from them by loving one's enemies requires more. Again, these comments make perfect sense when kept in the context of v. 20, "unless your righteousness surpasses that of the scribes and Pharisees, you shall not enter the kingdom of heaven." What human religion cannot accomplish, God's redemptive work in the hearts of His people will achieve. Loving one's enemies is testimony to God's redemptive work and demonstrates one's relationship with Christ.

5:48   Conclusion: be perfect! The immediate reaction to such a statement is shock because Scripture clearly teaches that all are sinners and thus perfection, as normally perceived, is impossible. The word perfect (*teleios*) actually does not mean without flaw or sinless but implies to be "complete, whole, mature."[77] The comparative phrase "as your heavenly Father is perfect" indicates that the character of God's people should reflect His character. God is perfect in that He is blameless; and in this context Jesus was teaching His disciples to be blameless in relation to the Law, which He had been expanding by His broader applications (vv. 21-47).

Carson offers an illuminating observation: "Nowhere is God directly and absolutely called 'perfect' in the OT: he is perfect in knowledge (Job 37:16) or in his way (Ps 18:30) . . . . But here, for the first time perfection is predicated to God."[78] It is best to understand Jesus' comment in light of the purpose behind the legal code. The Pharisees promoted the idea that keeping the Law made one holy, but Jesus taught that one must go beyond mere codified conformity to external behavior in order to be of the same character as God. By keeping Christ's words, one was to be complete, as God Himself is complete in the spirit of the law.

HOMILETICAL SUGGESTIONS

One should not avoid preaching the rich and powerful material of the Mountain Discourse. The Beatitudes outline the characteristics of those who will find blessedness in the kingdom of Christ. The message of Christ's disciples' being salt and light is as applicable now as ever, and the distinctions between Jesus and the religionists of His day send a powerful message to those who could possibly drift into legalism and self-righteousness.

The Beatitudes communicate the hope and promises of our glorious King. The list of eight categories of the blessed is illuminating for those wishing to understand the heart of God. The primary lessons to be learned from them are that God opposes the proud, gives grace to the humble (1 Peter 5:5), and blesses those who seriously desire righteousness—God's, not one's own. Christ's focus is stated in v. 20, "For I say to you, that unless your righteousness surpasses that of the scribes and Pharisees, you shall not enter the kingdom of heaven." The finest efforts of the most dedicated religionist, working from the divinely given Law of God, cannot earn one the right to the kingdom. It takes humility, a desire for true righteousness, which can only be found in the One who fulfilled the Law (v. 17).

The salt and light metaphors (vv. 13-16) are important in that they demonstrate how Christ's followers are to be living demonstrations of His righteousness. The distinction between His followers and the world is to be as dramatic as the distinction between light and darkness. Further, as light illuminates to reveal that which cannot otherwise be seen, Christians should offer illumination into spiritual things, which the unregenerate cannot see because of their spiritual blindness. Indeed, even as salt is a preservative and adds flavor, so Christians are to offer the world a higher standard of moral and ethical values (not through self-righteous preaching but through example and testimony), which demonstrates the superiority of God's domain. The lives of Christ's people should offer hope and dignity to the human race, which still has been created in the image and likeness of God. Our lives should point to the higher truth and ultimate goodness of God. In this way—not through protest, name-calling, and condemnation—God will preserve His truth in a lost and dark world.

One of the most critical messages in the New Testament is found in v. 20. What is God looking for in His kingdom? Not self-righteousness, not pride in piety, not religious legalism—all of these characterized the scribes and Pharisees. No, to be accepted in God's kingdom one must be even more righteous than they. Christ then explained (vv. 21-48) what this means. If a pastor is looking to mature his congregation or if a believer feels his spirituality is lacking, then these verses must be noted and accurately understood and applied. The greatest error here would be to become even more legalistic, which would miss the whole point of what Jesus was saying. An example of this would be to come to vv. 31-32 and condemn those who have been divorced and remarried. This is exactly what some factions of the Pharisees would have done. But neither is one to degrade the value of marriage by flippantly moving from relationship to relationship. This is neither another law nor an excuse to ignore God's holy standard. The higher issue of lust and coveting, of faithlessness and indifference, is what Christ wishes His followers to be concerned with, not what legal or judgmental attitudes demand. It is amazing how many wish to split hairs and quarrel over vv. 31-32 but never preach or so valiantly defend vv. 39-42.

Christ's final remark in this chapter is critical to understanding the section. Those who claim the name of God must reflect His character and nature, again not by religious zeal or spiritual disciplines,[79] which many contemporary Christians herald as signs of spirituality (as did the scribes and Pharisees), but by compassion, grace, generosity, and holiness. In today's religious environment, where the unsaved are confused about God's heart and mind, those who know the God of compassion, who loves and forgives even the vilest sinners without compromising His holiness, must reflect both personal holiness and forgiveness and humility toward the spiritually blind.

MATTHEW

CHAPTER
SIX

THE SERMON ON
THE MOUNT CONTINUES

The Lord continued to instruct His disciples and those who had drawn close to hear His astounding lessons. He finished His expansion of the oral traditions and then began giving instructions concerning worship and the attitudes that were to characterize His followers. This chapter can be divided into three concerns: warning against superficial, external righteous behavior; encouragement to build treasure for the kingdom of heaven; and prohibition against anxiety.

WARNING AGAINST PRACTICING
RIGHTEOUSNESS BEFORE MEN, 1-18

6:1   "Beware of practicing your righteousness before men." Christ continued His message that true righteousness must exceed that of the scribes and Pharisees (5:20). The word "beware" ("be careful" NIV) means literally to turn one's attention to something (*prosechō*). In other words, "be aware of this attitude of desiring other people to notice your righteousness." Some unnecessarily confuse the issue by trying to create two "dimensions" to the word *dikaiosunē*, one moral, the other religious.[1] There is a danger even in doing righteous things (*dikaiosunē*) if one's motive is to "be noticed" by others. The issue here is clearly the motive behind what one does. True followers of Christ are to live their faith openly and let good works be evident to all (5:16), but if the motive for doing righteous-ness is to gain recognition for themselves, it is going to cost them God's reward. Jesus certainly had in mind the scribes and Pharisees (5:20) and would later specifically name them as offenders in this area (Matt. 23:5).

The warning is significant in that the consequence is the for-feiture of rewards from the Father in heaven. The choice seems to be between whose reward a person desires—the recognition of men or the recognition of God. This aspect of the warning ties in with the exhortation of vv. 2-18. Jesus named three areas often used by the religious leaders of His day to display their "righteousness": giv-ing of charitable gifts; prayer; and fasting.

ALMSGIVING, 6:2-4

This pericope begins the list of righteous deeds used by the scribes and Pharisees to draw attention to themselves. Almsgiving (an act of charity toward the needy) was an important part of reli-gious duty. The Law prescribed, "I command you, saying, 'You shall freely open your hand to your brother, to your needy and poor in your land" (Deut. 15:11). Acts 3:1-10 records the healing of a crip-pled man who sat at the temple gate begging alms from the reli-gious who were about to offer worship to God. The location was chosen because the connection between almsgiving and offering worship was particularly strong.

6:2 "When therefore you give alms, do not sound a trumpet." Josephus records that trumpets were used from the time of Moses (whom he claims invented the Hebrew trumpet) to assemble the congregation of Israel and to accompany their "sacred ministra-tions" and their bringing of sacrifices to the altar.[2] No reference is made in Jewish sources concerning blowing trumpets for almsgiv-ing, but the connection between the religious ceremony of bringing sacrifices to the temple and the stretching of the practice to accom-pany the giving of alms is reasonable. It is also possible that Jesus was being sarcastic and used the ceremony of trumpet blowing as illustrating how ridiculous the Pharisees had become even in minor charities.

Jesus stated that the purpose for their action was to "be hon-ored by men." They enjoyed the "pat on the back" and sought the attention their charity offered them. This should be a warning to every follower of Jesus. If one becomes conscious of desiring recognition from fellow Christians or unbelievers, he is following the example of Christ's enemies and not of Christ Himself. John 12:43 records this condemnation of the Jews who would not confess Jesus: "They loved the approval of men rather than the approval of God." This then was their "reward in full"[3]—the short-lived and superficial praise of men. Note that three times Jesus declared this was all the reward they would receive (vv. 2, 5, 16).

6:3-4 In contrast to the hypocrites who gave to be seen of men, Christ's followers were to be subtle and unassuming in their charity. "When you give alms" assumes that His disciples *will* give charity to the needy. Jesus had already pointed out that willingness to give was to characterize His followers (5:42).

"Do not let your left hand know what your right hand is doing" expresses the unpretentious nature of genuine charity. This figure of speech is intended to communicate that giving should be so intuitive that it is done without planning or preparation, a matter so private that even in one's own action there is no premeditated stratagem. Stott offers the best explanation of this statement.

> The right hand is normally the active hand. So Jesus assumes we shall use it when handing over our gift. Then he adds that our left hand must not be watching. There is no difficulty in grasping his meaning. Not only are we to not tell other people about our Christian giving; there is a sense in which we are not even to tell ourselves. We are not to be self-conscious in our giving, for our self-consciousness will readily deteriorate into self-righteousness.[4]

This explanation is consistent with v. 4.

"And your Father who sees in secret will repay you" (v. 4) indicates that the reward that Jesus' followers were to anticipate would come from God, not man. The KJV reads "shall reward thee openly." Whereas everyone might wish to think he would be rewarded "openly," there is only weak and late manuscript evidence for this addition. It would also seem to be antithetical to what Jesus had just warned about, that is, wanting public recognition for charity. To "repay" (future of *apodidōmi*) implies equal payment for what was done. Thus, everything given to the needy will be paid back by God, who is watching the private act of giving.

The time of retribution is not stated and should not be assumed. However, vv. 19-20 and later revelation such as Romans 8:18; 2 Corinthians 4:17-18; 5:10; Colossians 3:1-4; etc., should alert us to the fact that we should anticipate reward when brought into the presence of Christ and not before. Following each warning, three times in this pericope (vv. 4, 6, 18) Jesus repeats the phrase "your Father who sees in secret will repay you."

PRAYER, 6:5-14

Jesus' followers are not to be like the hypocrites.

6:5 The negative example of prayer is giving like the hypocrites who, when giving alms, love to be seen by other people. A hypocrite (*hypokritēs*) is basically one who plays a role on the stage, an actor.[5] In classical Greek, *hypokritēs* never implied a negative connotation. It originally referred to an orator, a poet, and then an actor on a stage. However, in the New Testament (as in the LXX) it has a very disapproving connotation. Jesus alone uses the word in the Gospels and always in a condemnatory allegation.[6] These hypocrites pray in public and in the synagogues for the purpose of being seen by men ("in order to be"). They love (*phileō*, "have a fondness for") to be seen praying and therefore speak to be heard by men and not by God.

The warning is certainly clear enough: do not pray for human recognition; do not practice your prayers or pray to impress others. Jesus was not forbidding public prayer, nor was He teaching that one should be ashamed to pray. As before, the emphasis of the text is on the prideful and hypocritical display of false piety. Motive is to be questioned but not the act of praying. Once again Christ stated, "Truly [used for emphasis] I say to you, they have their reward in full" (cf. v. 2).

6:6 Prayer is required and desired by those who love the Lord. It is our most intimate communication with Him. Prayer (*prosseuchē*) is a form of worship. It demonstrates dependence upon God and acknowledges His preeminence above all other authorities, circumstances, and relationships. Therefore, to perform this privilege for the sake of winning men's approval is offensive to God. Going to the inner room (a *tameion* can be a storeroom or even a bedroom, not just a small closet) accentuates this worshipful experience. Certainly Jesus was not discouraging shared worshiping experiences of communal prayer (e.g., Acts 1:14; 12:5) but contrasting the motives in prayer. Pray to be heard by God, not man. Even if no one else hears you, pray, as "your Father who sees in secret will repay you" (cf. v. 4).

6:7 "Do not use meaningless repetition" warns against mindless muttering. Keep in mind that God is not impressed by words without genuine sentiment. What may sound pious to those standing by may be totally meaningless to the One who knows the heart. This is the second abuse of prayer that Jesus discussed. Here He mentioned the Gentiles and their prayers. Gentiles did not have a covenant with the true God, and their idols could not hear their words. Rather than conversing with a being who hears and understands, they only babbled repetitious religious sayings. One who speaks to the true God needs to speak as to a person who hears and understands. It is the content of the prayer that counts, not the quantity of words.

6:8 Simply put, "do not be like them." God's people must not fall into the trap of believing that He is impressed with the volume of verbal piety. Rather, one should relate to Him as He is, a Person. Do not offend Him with the meaningless religious jargon of the pagans who do not know the true God. God knows what His servants need, and the purpose of prayer is not to inform Him. We appeal to God as a loving Father, who already knows what is best for His own, and not to a stone idol that has no knowledge or understanding. This last comment will be brought to a more conclusive application in vv. 31-32.

THE LORD'S PRAYER, 6:9-13 (cf. Luke 11:2-4)

This pericope is often referred to as "the Lord's prayer" but is better designated as a sample prayer or formula for prayer.[7] A good translation of Christ's instruction (*houtōs oun proseuchesthe humeis*) is "Therefore, be praying in this manner." Luke's account is not to be compared to Matthew's, because, even though it contains much of the same material, the context and the introduction are very different. It is useless speculation to imagine that Matthew "removes the prayer from its original context, and inserts it here to teach that Jesus' disciples ought to pray with an economy of words."[8] The fact that Jesus used a similar formula in Luke's account is not justification for leaping to conclusions regarding borrowing and rearranging Christ's words. The message is not Matthew's but the Lord's, and it is hardly consistent with God's self-revelation that a man would be given liberty to reorganize Christ's teachings. Every itinerant preacher often uses the same text for sermons. Thus the material will be basically the same but not a word-for-word recitation. To believe that Jesus offered the same formula more than once is not difficult.[9] The formula was an exact illustration of what He had just taught (vv. 6-8) and not an appendage borrowed from another source.

6:9   "Our Father who art in heaven" introduces the formula with an intimate and familiar address. Luke's version just states "Father" without the possessive pronoun "our." In the context of Matthew, the contrast is made between the pagans, who prayed to blind and unknowing idols, and those who prayed to the true, living God. Jesus referred to God as "your Father" (vv. 4, 6, 8), which emphasized the personal relationship God desires to have with His people. Prayer to God is to be personal and intimate, not formulaic and empty.

The term "father" is to evoke the imagery of one who protects and provides, one who gives the family a name and identity. The father was the disciplinary figure (cf. Heb. 12:7-9) as well as the one who provided for his family (cf. Matt. 7:9-11). But this Father to whom we pray is not limited in understanding or in power to accomplish what is best for His children. This is probably the significance of the expression "who art in heaven" (literally, "in the heavenlies"). His domain and sphere of understanding are not limited to mere earthly influence; He is the Father who reigns from heaven. In the Lucan formula, the heavenlies are not mentioned. After addressing the prayer to "our Father in heaven," Jesus prescribed three petitions applying to God Himself.

"Hallowed be Thy name" expresses the worshipful attitude that should characterize prayer. This archaic expression is literally "Let your name be treated as holy" (*hagiastbētō to onoma sou*). Meyer agrees with Luther that the name of God is holy in itself, but "this holiness must be *asserted and displayed* in the whole being and character of believers."[10] The term "name" represents a person's being, character, and authority. Thus to do something in the name of someone (such as the baptismal prescription "baptizing them in the name of . . ." and to pray in the name of Jesus) is to perform the act as representing the person, character, or authority of the one named. The appeal to God to exalt His Person, character, and authority in holiness is the intent of the petition "Let your name be treated as holy."

6:10   The next petition of the model prayer is an appeal for God to establish His kingdom and to exercise His dominion over the sin-infected earth even as He does over heaven. The words spoken by Jesus may more literally be translated "Let your kingdom come." It should be remembered that Jesus was teaching His disciples how to pray, and the petitioning for God to bring about His kingdom certainly indicates that the world in which we live is not yet under His rule. Jesus introduced the kingdom at His appearing (cf. Matt. 4:17) but was rejected by His own people, who chose to have Caesar as their king (John 19:15). He was not declaring that the kingdom would come in the hearts of His servants but that it would exercise dominion over the whole earth (*gē*). Thus, even though He was the Messiah and brought the promise of the kingdom to the nation, the kingdom is still expressed in eschatological terms, "let it come," because it is not yet realized in human history since the Messiah was rejected and killed.

The third petition, "Let your will be done on earth even as it is in heaven," is not to be considered dependent upon the preceding plea for the kingdom to be established. Obedience to God's will is not necessarily synonymous with the kingdom, especially in light of Christ's own prayer later offered, "Not My will, but Yours" (Matt. 26:39, 42). The king was rejected, but it was God's will so that the Gentiles would be grafted into His redemptive program (Rom. 11:7-12, 17, 25). God's will is to be accomplished whether the kingdom has come or not. Once again, this petition is not found in the Luke 11 account. The focus of Matthew's context is the rebuke of the superficial religious acts of the Pharisees and the need for sincerity in His followers. This sincerity would be reflected in a desire to follow God's will, not in pursuing their own interests.

The first three petitions of the model prayer reveal that the one praying should be concerned with God's name, kingdom, and will. Therefore one important lesson to be learned about prayer is that petitioning God is not to be self-focused but God-honoring and God-centered. The second half of the exemplar prayer does focus on requests for oneself. The three areas held up for example are: daily needs; forgiveness; and protection from temptation.

6:11   The expression "daily bread" (*ton arton hēmōn ton epiou-sion*) indicates dependence upon our heavenly Father for the immediate provisions of life. "Bread" was most likely used figuratively for food in general (Gen. 3:19) and should not be taken as a reference to Jesus, who later would refer to Himself as the "bread of life" (John 6:32-41). Though one may desire to use this text for dynamic evangelistic preaching, to insert such sermonizing here ignores the context. Jesus was indicating that His disciples were to look to their heavenly Father for daily sustenance, not to worldly methods or human resources (cf. vv. 25, 31-34). This is an interesting exhortation in relation to the tangible provision of daily bread that God gave Israel in the wilderness (Ex. 16:14-15). In Luke's record, Jesus uses the present tense verb "be giving us," but Matthew continues to use the aorist tense, "give us." The aorist, apart from the indicative mood, should not be taken as indicating any particular time element (here, it is used with the imperative, not indicative), and thus there is no significant difference in the two statements. In Luke's record, Jesus may be emphasizing the continual process more than in Matthew's context.

6:12   The next request deals with forgiveness of our debts (*ta opheilēmata hēmōn*). Again we note a difference in Luke's record. There the Lord says, "Forgive us our sins [*hamartias*]," whereas in Matthew He says, "Forgive us our debts" (*opheilēmata*). It is perhaps best to understand *hamartias* and *opheilēma* as synonyms, because in both accounts the basis of appeal is how we forgive those indebted (*opheilēma*) to us. Tiedtke and Link point out that *opheilō, opheilēma* refers to moral and religious obligations as well as financial.[11] Thus, in relation to God, we are debtors to moral and ethical standards by which we fail to live; in relation to fellow humans, the debt may be in several categories. *Hamartias* is appropriate with respect to the debt to God.

The basis for the request rests upon the requester's forgiveness of those offending him. It is not likely here that the issue of forgiveness is referring to initial redemptive forgiveness (for salvation) but the forgiveness for offense against the Father in the perpetual daily life situation (for fellowship).[12] There is no salvific passage that requires the one being saved to perform any act, such as forgiving others, in order to gain forgiveness. The overwhelming testimony of Scripture is that salvation from eternal torment is a free gift not granted on the basis of any act (Eph. 2:8-9; Titus 3:5; Rom. 4:5; etc.). Matthew records the Lord's statement as "as we also have forgiven our debtors." "As" (*hōs*) implies either a comparison (i.e., "in the same way as") or is a temporal, consequential particle (i.e., "when" or "after"). Here *hōs* is used with the aorist tense (*aphēkamen*, "we forgave"), implying a temporal condition, "when" or "after."[13]

Certainly at first it seems strange that the Lord would condition forgiveness upon one's willingness to forgive others. However, Christ's point here was that if one claims to have God as Father, he should be demonstrating the same character as his Father. If the Father is expected to release someone from the debt of moral and ethical failure, it is only reasonable that that person should be willing to release those indebted to him in lesser issues. It would be blasphemous to assume that someone could offend a fellow human being in a greater way than sinful humans offend the holy God. Unwillingness to forgive others implies that the unforgiver assumes he deserves restitution more than God does. This is clearly the message of Matthew 18:21-35. Jesus offers His explanation in vv. 14-15 (which will be discussed in the following analysis). Stott's comments are a fitting summary.

> It is rather that God forgives only the penitent and that one of the chief evidences of true penitence is a forgiving spirit. Once our eyes have been opened to see the enormity of our offense against God, the injuries which others have done to us appear by comparison extremely trifling. If, on the other hand we have an exaggerated view of the offenses of others, it proves that we have minimized our own.[14]

6:13 The final petition of the model prayer deals with preservation from evil. The request for God to "not lead us into temptation" surely will sound strange to those who are cognizant of His holy character and the statement of James (1:13). The appeal "do not lead" (*mē eisenegkēs*) is best understood in connection with what had just been stated about forgiveness. Meyer is correct: "After the petition for *forgiveness* of sin, comes now the request to be *preserved* from *new* sin, negatively and positively, so that both elements constitute but one petition."[15] This connection also explains why vv. 14-15 revert to the discussion of forgiveness in v. 12. In other words, forgiveness of sin and the appeal to keep us from temptation are concerned with the same issue, forgiving others. A proper understanding of "temptation" helps one to see the association of the two ideas.

The appeal to the heavenly Father is that He not lead (*eispherō*, "to bring along into") us into temptation. The word "temptation" (*peirasmos*) seems best understood here as "testing" or "trials," as it is so translated in 1 Peter 4:12. It would be superfluous to pray for our Father not to lead us into enticement to sin, for He has stated that He would never do that (James 1:13). But if one understands *peirasmos* as trials or testings, the request is to not allow us to be tested or suffer trials. This is not to deny that the proper response to trials is joy (James 1:2), but one is to understand that suffering through trial is not a thing to be taken lightly. One should not flippantly approach the testing of one's faith; this would assume an arrogance not reflective of Jesus. The Lord Himself asked the Father to use some other means in accomplishing His purpose if it were possible (Matt. 26:39, 42, 44). The testing here, then, is the trials and struggles that Christ's followers would face. In connection with the petition for forgiveness, the idea seems to be that the trials may have a tendency to create bitterness rather than love for enemies (5:44) and therefore an unwillingness to forgive. This seems to explain, then, why v. 13 is placed in the middle of the forgiveness petition (v. 12 and vv. 14-15).

Coupled with the petition for not leading into temptation (*peirasmos,* "testing") is the appeal to "deliver us from evil." "Deliver" (*hrumai*) means simply that, to "rescue, save," or "deliver from," and the object from which we are to seek deliverance is evil. More literally it should be understood as "the Evil One" (*tou ponērou*). The clause is introduced by the strong adversative conjunction *alla* ("but") to draw the contrast between being tempted and deliverance from the Evil One. The petition of the model prayer, then, is for God not to allow us to undergo the testing but to be rescued from the snare of the Evil One, the Devil. This part of the prayer reflects confidence in the sovereignty of God even in the area of trials, testings, and temptations. One should compare 1 Corinthians 10:13 to understand God's faithfulness in this matter.

The last portion of v. 13, bracketed in the NASB and completely omitted from the NIV, is a doxology apparently added by a zealous scribe at a later date. "For Thine is the kingdom, and the power, and the glory, forever, Amen" is certainly true and an appropriate doxology with regard to deliverance from the Evil One. However, the manuscript support for it is very weak, and this portion should be omitted from the text.

6:14-15   These verses apparently are intended to offer explanation of vv. 12 and 13 relating to forgiveness of those who injure us. The topic is clearly conditional; our forgiving others is connected with our Father's forgiving us. Again, it is necessary to remember that the forgiveness here is not salvific. It is not the angry God of the universe forgiving Adamic sinfulness but our Father releasing us from offenses that block our fellowship with Him. This is the point of the parable in Matthew 18:23-35 and is similar to the teaching in Mark 11:25. An unforgiving spirit is sin, and any continued sin affects the relationship between God and His children.

FASTING, 6:16-18

The third set of examples related to the warning not to practice righteousness before men (6:1) dealt with fasting. Like almsgiving and prayer, fasting was considered a definite sign of piety. The point was the same as with the previous two: do not practice your piety to be seen by others. Again, the motive was being questioned, not the practice.

The Pharisee of Luke 18:12 brags of fasting "twice a week." This was normal for Pharisees, who set aside Monday and Thursday as fasting days and rigidly followed the law of fasting. The Didache (an early second-century manual of church instruction) refers to the practice of hypocrites fasting on Mondays and Thursdays but seems to endorse the church's fasting on Wednesdays and Fridays.[16] Whether the Didache assumed the different days made a difference or if it was rebuking Christians for assuming such is difficult to determine. It is significant, however, that the church has always struggled with the problem of hypocrisy even as Israel did.

6:16   It is safe to assume that the act of fasting is not the problem since Jesus said, "Whenever you fast," indicating that He assumed they would fast. Scripture endorses fasting at certain times (Zech. 8:19), speaking of it as an act of humility (Ps. 35:13), and reveals that at times corporate fasting was done in the church as in Israel

(Acts 13:3). However, Jesus' disciples did not fast until after His departure (Matt. 9:14-15). The point is that the hypocrites made sure everyone was aware of their fasting, believing they would be respected for their piety. Note the warning, which Christ had already stated (vv. 2, 5), "They have their reward in full."

6:17-18   In contrast, the follower of Christ, when fasting, is to give the appearance that life is being lived normally. The idea of anointing the head was normal in that culture as part of hygiene and good health.[17] Here it is stated as a contrast to a "gloomy face" and "neglecting their appearance." Verse 18 explains the motive behind the washing and anointing—"so that you may not be seen fasting by men, but by your Father." The goal of the servant of Christ is not to put on a pious show to gain the approval of others. Whether by extreme "joy" or by extreme "sobriety," if one seeks to draw attention to himself, he has failed to honor God. It is comforting to the believer to know that even if men fail to recognize his spirituality, God, who sees in secret, will repay him for genuine piety.

Thus Jesus warned His disciples not to be caught up in the hypocrisy of external religion (vv. 2-18). Giving monetary gifts, praying, and fasting can certainly be noble and godly activities; but in and of themselves these actions do not earn favor with God. If service is motivated by self-acclaim or for recognition by peers, then one forfeits the reward of God and must settle for the temporal and superficial praise of men. How ironic that those who are often held in such high esteem in Christian circles are most in danger of falling into the trap of living to maintain an image of spirituality. One must constantly examine his motive in any act of worship. Would the same effort of spiritual discipline be shown if no one would see?

THE WARNING AGAINST WORLDLY TREASURE, 6:19-24 (Luke 12:15-21)[18]

6:19-20   The second major topic of chap. 6 is introduced with a prohibition, "Do not lay up for yourselves treasures upon earth." As in the previous section, Jesus was concerned with attitudes that would hinder His followers from receiving the true wealth of heavenly reward. Human instinct will drive one to seek immediate gratification and material security; therefore Jesus was not speaking vainly to His followers who had given up careers to follow and be identified with Him. His warning reflected the real possibility of their returning to earthly things once He was gone.

Earthly treasures are those things that can be destroyed or stolen —in other words, any material possession. Jesus used the negative particle *mē* with the present imperative *thēsaurizete,* which implies that He was prohibiting something already in progress, "stop laying up treasures."[19] The implication is that He assumed cultural influences would appeal to the temporal nature of fallen mankind to accumulate material securities and comforts, but His followers were to be different. The hope and security of His disciples are not to rest in the temporal rewards and shelter afforded by this world.

Jesus used a play on words, "stop treasuring up treasures" (*thēsaurizete . . . thēsaurous*). The verb and the object are of the same root meaning to "store up, accumulate" and, in the nominal form, a "building used for storage" or an "item stored up." This construction, a cognate accusative, creates an emphasis.[20] The warning was against hoarding and depending on material things for power, happiness, or security. Stott's point is well taken that Jesus was not forbidding normal and wise management of resources: "In a word, 'lay up treasure on earth' does not mean being provident (making sensible provision for the future) but being covetous (like misers who hoard and materialists who always want more)."[21] The ant is praised in Proverbs 6:6-8 for planning ahead.

In contrast to hoarding and clinging to material things, believers should "lay up for [them]selves treasures in heaven." The follower of Christ is not losing out on rewards by avoiding covetous practices. His life of service will indeed bear ultimate reward in heaven. One should compare the promises of Romans 8:18, 1 Corinthians 3:12-15, and 2 Corinthians 5:10 to gain a better understanding of storing up treasure in heaven.

6:21   Christ's reasoning is stated in this verse. The reality is that one will set his affections and design on those things that are most valuable to him. If one perceives earthly goods as a treasure, then his heart will focus on those things. The kingdom work of Christ's followers will be hindered, and the disciple's loyalty will fail (v. 24). Paul, likewise, encourages believers to "set [their] mind on the things above, not on the things that are on earth" (Col. 3:2). His reasoning is that Christ's followers have died to all things except Christ, and they will be glorified when He is revealed and not before (Col. 3:3-4).

6:22-24   Jesus now illustrated His statement recorded in v. 21. The analogy of the lamp of the body was to point out that the eye takes in the information that will be processed by the believer. If the "eye is clear" (*haplous,* "sound, healthy" or "generous") then the body will have proper illumination to function as it should. But if the eye "is bad" (*ponēros,* "evil"), then the body will be blinded and will do evil things. In this context, Jesus was apparently saying that if one looks upon the things of the earth with a healthy, spiritual perspective, then his life will be useful. If however, one looks upon the things of the world with evil or greed in mind, then his life will be wasted.

Verse 24 goes further, explaining that divided loyalty (material things versus spiritual things) will not be accepted and cannot satisfy the one trying to cling to both. The dichotomy of two masters is a reminder that even material things are not neutral if treasured, becoming a master just as Jesus is our master. To serve one is to hate the other. Carson offers an excellent summary: "Either God is served with a single-eyed devotion, or he is not served at all. Attempts at divided loyalty betray, not partial commitment to discipleship, but deep-seated commitment to idolatry."[22]

WARNING AGAINST ANXIETY, 6:25-34 (Luke 12:22-34)

6:25   "For this reason" is to continue the thought from the previous pericope, though it is not simply a summary or continuance of the same lesson. Beyond just not hoarding things for the future, the servant of Christ must not become too focused even upon daily provisions. The reason refers to the last part of v. 24, "You cannot serve God and mammon" (*mamōnas,* "money, wealth, property"). The pursuit of mammon will not only lead to idolatry but will create anxiety as one struggles to gain and protect his wealth. Thus Christ commanded, "Stop being anxious" (again the present imperative with the negative *mē* implies to stop what is already in progress), because He knew the struggles of finding adequate material goods for those whose heart finds treasure in earthly things. To be "anxious," *merimnaō,* implies to have extraordinary concern or worry. Paul also commands believers not to be anxious. Anxiety is beyond the normal concern that prompts responsible action. It is to become so fixed upon a concern that one's thinking and energy are dominated, and a lack of trust in God's provision is demonstrated.

This is not warning against frivolous extravagances but against anxiety concerning one's life, food, drink, and clothing. The first item mentioned is "your life," or "soul," as the word *psuchē* is normally understood. Generally, the soul is misconceived as the spiritual nature of man in contrast to his body. More accurately, *psuchē* refers at times to the immaterial part of man and sometimes to the total person. In 1 Peter 3:20 *psuchē* is translated "persons" in NASB and "people" in NIV. In that context, it is the only possible translation, for certainly Peter would not imply that only the immaterial parts of Noah and his family were brought safely through the Flood. In the Septuagint the word is used of animals as well as humans (Gen. 1:20, 24, 30, etc.). Thus, the old distinction that humans have souls and animals do not is not entirely correct. It is the breath of life from God that mankind holds in distinction over the animals as well as the fact that only humans were made in His image and likeness (Gen. 1:26; 2:7).

Therefore, one should understand Christ's exhortation not to be anxious about life to be a reference to physical existence. Life itself should not be a matter of anxiety. Even food and drink, which are necessary to preserve basic life function, is not to be of extraordinary concern. Clothing one's body (*soma*) is a matter that is not to create anxiety. Carson summarizes, "If God has given us life and a body, both admittedly more important than food and clothing, will he not give us the latter?"[23] The issue is having faith in God's provision rather than becoming focused on one's own efforts to secure material and physical needs. Jesus' summary of this exhortation (v. 33) emphasized that God's program is to take priority in the lives of His followers, even over material and physical matters. Jesus prohibited becoming distracted from God's work by concern about what one will eat or drink or wear.

6:26 As testimony to God's faithful provision, Christ instructed His followers to consider the birds and the lilies. The birds of the air (literally, "of the heavens," *tou ouranou*) do not plant or harvest crops, they do not store up surplus in barns, and yet they have food to eat. The reason is that God is their provider. The explanation made is that *"your* heavenly Father feeds them" (not *their* heavenly Father), emphasizing the personal and privileged position Christ's followers have with the One who provides. Our relationship with God is not just as creature to Creator but as child to Father. A father gives what is good; God the Father does even more so (Matt. 7:9-11). "Are you not worth much more than they?" Human beings are made in the image of God. They are His creatures, appointed to represent Him in this world. Even more, the redeemed are His children. Therefore, if even simple creatures such as birds are cared for by God, how much more care shall be directed to His special ones —His own children?

6:27   What good does it do to be anxious? Christ next pointed out that worry and distress over things beyond one's control are useless. The expression "add a *single* cubit to his life's span" may appear incongruous because a cubit (*pēchus*) is a linear measure of approximately eighteen inches and a life's span is normally thought of chronologically in days or years. However, "life's span" is not the only understanding of the word *hēlikia,* translated in Luke 19:3 as "stature" (i.e., "height") and is clearly contextually correct. Christ's argument is that no matter how anxious one may be over his height, such apprehension cannot change the reality of his status. Another possibility is that "cubit" (*pēchus*) might metaphorically refer to a span of time such as a day. Tasker prefers this second possibility based on logic, concluding that "men worry more perhaps over their length of life than over their physical height."[24]

6:28-30   The next example addressed concern over one's clothing. Once again, Jesus drew attention to God's world, which He Himself designed, created, and sustains. The "lilies of the field" (*krina tou agrou*) may be the brightly colored wild flowers that bloom after the early spring rains and cover the plains of Israel— flowers so beautiful that even Solomon in all his extravagant robes could not equal them. If God is so concerned with the beauty of these simple flowers, will He not carefully cover us as well (v. 30)? God provides not just the basics but splendid abundance. Still, one is not to forget that Christ was warning His disciples against being concerned with such things. *Pursuit* of the glorious covering is not legitimate, and trusting God to provide is the point. Jesus Himself did not seek to dress in beautiful array, and neither should we. Our glory is yet to be realized (Rom. 8:18; Col. 3:4).

The rebuke "O men of little faith" (*oligopistoi*) appears three more times in Matthew: 8:26 (during the storm at sea); 14:31 (of Peter, who tried to walk on water); and 16:8 (in the parable of leaven of the Pharisees). Compare also Luke 12:28 for the same lesson content. All mentions relate to His disciples and not to the unbelieving. Hendriksen understands this as referring to "the fact that those so characterized were not sufficiently taking to heart the comfort they should have derived from the presence, promise, power, and love of Christ."[25]

6:31-32 Concerns such as food, drink, and clothing are not to be our focus. These are matters that concern the "Gentiles," who do not have a covenant with God. The "Gentiles" (*ta ethnē*) were considered by the Jews to be accursed, cut off from God, and therefore pagan unbelievers (cf. Eph. 4:17-19). Those who know God and understand His loving-kindness and faithfulness should not live with the same anxiety as pagans. We are to be trusting the heavenly Father, who "knows that you need all these things." The prohibition is not against asking God for daily needs, as that was encouraged (v. 11), but against becoming anxious about these matters, and the reason is that God knows what we need. It would be insulting to God to assume that we need to inform Him of our status. We ask Him, showing dependence, then trust rather than plotting and planning ways to meet our own needs.

6:33 The thrust of His lesson is stated in this verse, "But seek first," which reveals His concern for the priority of God's kingdom and righteousness. The comparison accentuates the priority of kingdom matters and God's standards over material commodities, including even one's own life. Jesus had already affirmed this in His own experience (Matt. 4:2-4). One's concern for food, drink, or clothing is not to become so important that it stands in the way of the kingdom of God or hinders one from exemplifying His moral and ethical standards. Carson points out that this righteousness is not to be equated with justification, which is righteousness based upon faith (Rom. 4:5).[26]

The promise of Christ is that if we make God's kingdom and righteousness our priority, then God will supply the other needs for our lives. The matters of the work and character of God are far more important than food, drink, clothing, or even life itself, and to have any other view makes one "of little faith" (v. 30).

6:34   Jesus summed up ("therefore," *oun*) and repeated the prohibition against anxiety. The conclusion then is "Do not be anxious for tomorrow." Knowing that the heavenly Father supplies what we need for today, we should assume the same for tomorrow. The connection between anxiety, seeking the kingdom, and tomorrow is important. If we are anxious about tomorrow's supplies, that will affect our service to God today. Thus we are instructed to trust God, be seeking the matters related to His kingdom and righteousness as our first priority, and not try to figure out tomorrow's problems. He takes responsibility for those things.

It is correct to ask how this relates to the exhortation about the ant referenced earlier (Prov. 6:6-8), or to Paul's command that if one does not work, neither should he eat (2 Thess. 3:10-12), or to Paul's references to planning his missionary trips. The most obvious answer is that Christ was not forbidding working or planning but rather the anxious prioritizing material needs over the things of God. The emphasis of the passage is clearly one of priority, not the exclusion of one or the other. God's supply may be through the means of a job or other sources, but it is always God who supplies. Therefore the counsel is, be busy doing God's work and living by His moral and ethical standards and do not worry over how you might eat, drink, or clothe yourself if someone should oppose your godly life. Every day brings new challenges, but God's grace is sufficient day by day. Rather than projecting tomorrow's problems into today's situation, one should keep focused on God's kingdom and righteousness.

HOMILETICAL SUGGESTIONS

The Lord continued by building on the idea that true righteousness exceeds the external deeds of religion such as the scribes and Pharisees did (fasting two times per week, praying three times per day, and memorizing great portions of Scripture). He then shifted the emphasis to problems of material concerns.

This chapter breaks down into three major sections: warning against superficial religious acts in order to appear pious before others; instruction to build up treasures in heaven; and warning against allowing material needs to create anxiety.

The first section deals with one's motive for spiritual activity. Whether in our charity, prayers, or fasting, if having others recognize our act of devotion is the primary concern, then we are no different from the hypocrites whom Jesus totally rejected. The warning is to search our hearts to determine the motivation for our actions. Would our response be the same if no one knew? Do we act because we see an unfulfilled need and because our action will reflect our God? These are serious matters, and the one who preaches the Word of God dare not fail to emphasize the need for inner purity in religious acts. When motivating Christians to be involved in spiritual service, a reminder should be given that God who sees the heart will determine the value of such service. A pastor may gain esteem if his congregation is active doing many tasks, but he must also seek to keep people serving out of love, both for Christ and others. Anything else is as offensive as Pharisaism to the One who served us because He loves us.

Jesus then shifted His emphasis to the value system of His followers—what is really important? After He warned his disciples about the praise of men being only temporary compensation, He focused on a broader scope. Are this world's temporary rewards to be the center of our desires and goals? His answer was no! He warned not to lay up earthly treasures, because such will turn the heart from Him. Worldliness is a value system that treasures temporary pleasure and immediate gratification over more important things such as character, morals, ethics, spiritual needs, and eternal fruit. To keep God's people focused on eternal things is a constant struggle (Col. 3:1-4), but this is the Lord's command. We must model for others a value system with eternal and spiritual goals and help His people to invest their lives in the more precious things.

The third section of chap. 6 flows from the second. Anxiety over material things comes from a lack of spiritual perception. If one's security and self-worth are dependent upon material things, even something as basic as food, drink, and clothing, then these things begin to dominate one's mind and energy and thus void service to Christ. If one can trust God for eternal treasures, why not for daily needs? The point of v. 32 is that one must trust the loving and powerful Father to provide essential needs, followed by v. 33, which accentuates the point that God's kingdom should have priority. If we are serving God first, He takes the responsibility to provide for earthly needs. This does not guarantee that God will give the believer anything requested; God determines "needs," and humans often become obsessed with *perceived* needs. It is a matter of trust and service. The follower of Christ is to follow Him, not become concerned with first taking care of material necessities.

Remember, there is a difference between concern and anxiety, between being obsessed with material needs and looking for God's instrument for providing. Paul reminds the Thessalonians that if one does not work, he is not to eat and that each one is to work for his own bread (2 Thess. 3:7-12); but this is not to be taken as an excuse to ignore God's work for the sake of taking care of oneself.

MATTHEW
CHAPTER
SEVEN

LAST SECTION
OF THE DISCOURSE

The topic changed as Jesus continued to sit on the hillside, lecturing His disciples and the gathered crowd. Matthew arranges this section much like a series of proverbs that provide explanations of kingdom attitudes and standards along with exhortations. Stott points out, "Matthew seven consists of a number of apparently self-contained paragraphs. Their link with each other is not obvious. Nor does the chapter as a whole follow on from the previous chapter with any clear sequence of thought."[1] He speculates that "the connecting thread which runs through the chapter, however loosely, is that of relationship."[2] This "thread," however, does not bear up under close scrutiny. The theme connecting all of Jesus' teaching since He sat down on the mountain had been the righteous standards of the kingdom, which greatly surpass those of the Pharisees. These final proverbs fit well into that theme. Carson tries to connect this pericope with Luke 6:37-38 but admits, "The relationship . . . is difficult to assess."[3] This is probably due to the fact that there actually is no relationship between them.

Some commentators argue that Matthew has pieced together, in a rather haphazard manner, material taken from other speeches of the Lord. This view reflects a failure to credit the Spirit of Truth for overseeing the recording of God's Word and will not suit the traditional concept of inspiration. Either a text is divinely inspired and considered Scripture, or the text is not divinely inspired and cannot be considered Scripture. Either Matthew's gospel is Scripture, or it is merely human religious opinion. If Matthew's gospel is Scripture, then it is God-breathed and not a clumsily pasted together collection of unrelated sermons.

This section begins with a warning about judgmental attitudes and ends with a declaration that many will not enter His kingdom despite the works they claim to have done. Christ brought the discourse to closure (vv. 24-27) by warning that only those who act upon His teachings will be able to endure the trials and tests of life.

WARNING AGAINST JUDGMENTALNESS, 7:1-6

7:1   Jesus commanded His followers not to judge others. He used the Greek negative particle *mē* with the present imperative *krinete,* to prohibit what is already in process. The command might be translated "Stop judging!" Tasker sees it as emphasizing "the habit of censorious and carping criticism" and "not the exercise of the critical faculty, by which men are able and expected on specific occasions to make value-judgments."[4] Certainly Jesus was not telling His followers that they should not make sound judgments or evaluate moral and ethical situations, as this would be contrary to everything He taught elsewhere. The prohibition was against "sitting in judgment"[5] of others. Stott adequately sums up the point:

> The censorious critic is a fault-finder who is negative and destructive towards other people and enjoys actively seeking out their failings. He puts the worst possible construction on their motives, pours cold water on their schemes and is ungenerous toward their mistakes.[6]

This view is most consistent with Jesus' theme that one's righteousness is not to be patterned after that of the scribes and Pharisees.

This key contextual focus (contrasting His kingdom standards with Pharisaism) is crucial to understanding the content of the Sermon on the Mount. Thus, He selected one of the most typical of Pharisaic faults and used it to introduce the closing lessons of His discourse. The ensuing warning about receiving the same kind of judgment one exercises toward others (7:2) is consistent with warnings of a similar type for Christians (Gal. 6:1-8) and, at the same time, adequately cautions against receiving the judgment awaiting the Pharisees.

7:2   Literally, Jesus warned, "For by what judgment you judge, you shall be judged and by what measurement you measure, it shall be measured to you." This is a sobering thought. If one shows mercy to others, he will be shown mercy, but if one is harsh and unforgiving, his judgment will likewise be harsh and unforgiving. Though popular Christian belief projects God as all-forgiving and assumes the receipt of undeserved favor, Jesus warned of consequences for being judgmental and inflexible toward the faults of others. One should review His teaching in 6:14 and the similar teaching in chap.18:21-35. Carson points out, "The judgmental person by not being forgiving and loving testifies to his own arrogance and impenitence, by which he shuts himself out from God's forgiveness."[7] If people feel so strongly about faults and guilt as to judge others, then acknowledgment must be made regarding their own faults and guilt. Stott's summary is an excellent understanding of the prohibition of vv. 1-2:

> To sum up, the command to judge not is not a requirement to be blind, but rather a plea to be generous. Jesus does not tell us to cease to be men (by suspending our critical powers which help to distinguish us from animals) but to renounce the presumptuous ambition to be God (by setting ourselves up as judges).[8]

A review of the following parallel warnings would be profitable: Romans 2:1; 14:4-13; 1 Corinthians 4:4-5; 11:31; Galatians 6:1-5.

7:3-4   Jesus illustrated His lesson with hyperbolic irony. The contrast between a speck (*karphos,* "a small splinter") and a log (a large beam of wood) is intended to magnify the offense of judgmental attitudes. Another comparison the Lord used was between the word "see" (*blepō*) for locating the speck in the brother's eye and the word "notice" (*katanoeō*) in reference to one's own failure. *Blepō* simply refers to the sense of sight, what comes into one's view, but *katanoeō* is "to observe carefully, to consider, contemplate, reflect upon something."[9] Jesus was rebuking the natural tendency to look at others and instinctively observe their faults but refuse to consider one's own problems. To try to avoid seeing guilt in oneself by noting the faults in others is instinctive to the fallen human nature. The point of v. 4 is simple: how can someone offer to remove another person's offense if his own vision is impaired by sin? If a beam protrudes from a person's eye, his vision is obstructed and therefore distorted.

This illustration emphasizes the natural inclination to exaggerate the shortcomings of others while ignoring one's own. Jesus' parable of Luke 18:9-14 indicates that this attitude was the downfall of the self-righteous religionist, whom He opposed so strongly. The Pharisee of the parable represents the very attitude that is not characteristic of those of the kingdom, and it is important to keep in mind that Christ stated at the beginning of this discourse (5:20) that one's righteousness must surpass that of the Pharisees and scribes. The contrasting of kingdom righteousness with religionist righteousness is still at the forefront of His teaching. The speck/beam comparison serves as a warning for His followers not to be as the Pharisees, who extolled their own virtues while judging others.

7:5   Jesus was not saying that there is not a responsibility to hold fellow Christians accountable, and this verse sets forth the proper procedure for dealing with the failure of others. Before one confronts a brother or sister in whom a fault is observed, the person observing the fault must examine himself with careful scrutiny and deal with his own failure first. Paul gives the same admonition in Galatians 6:1.

"Hypocrite!" is Christ's address to those who do not first judge themselves. The NASB and NIV add the personal pronoun "you," but Jesus only said "Hypocrite!" using the vocative case for direct address. The attempt of the English versions to provide a smooth translation has weakened the exclamatory power of His reproach. A hypocrite is one who plays a role and disguises his true self. Meyer points out its meaning as "the conceit of self-delusion."[10]

"First" indicates the preliminary step to correcting others. Before one can truly help others, he must first have his vision unimpaired by personal sin. A critical point is that, just as in the parable of the judgmental Pharisee (Luke 18:9-14), the "beam" often not acknowledged by the judgmental person is self-righteousness. One may not be an adulterer, a drunkard, or a thief, but the sin of self-righteousness is just as offensive to God. Failure to deal with one's pride, jealousy, hatefulness, or lack of forgiveness is as much sin as any other moral miscarriage. Hendriksen states:

However grievous the other man's error may have seemed to the eye of the would-be corrector, was it not a mere "speck" compared with his own self-righteousness, a defect so glaring that in the sight of God it amounts to a beam in the critic's eye?[11]

The one who wishes to correct others must be conscious of and willing to deal with personal failure and attitudes before speaking to others. Jesus makes this point clear in the account of John 8:3-11.

The result of dealing with one's own sin is gaining a clear perspective in addressing others' faults. Jesus used the future tense, indicating the results of self-judgment—"then you will see clearly" (*kai tote diablepheis*). This assures the one dealing with the fault of others that the action taken is not judgmental but corrective and loving. Barnes states it very well:

The beam, the thing that obscured our sight, will be removed, and we shall more clearly discern the small object that obscures the sight of our brother. The sentiment is, that our readiest way to judge of the imperfections of others is to be free from greater ones ourselves. This qualifies us for judging, makes us candid and consistent, and enables us to see things as they are, and to make proper allowances for frailty and imperfection.[12]

PEARLS BEFORE SWINE, 7:6

7:6   At first glance this verse seems to be out of place; however, upon more serious consideration it becomes clear that the other aspect of judgmental attitudes renders it appropriate. In vv. 1-5, Jesus is concerned with how believers react to other believers in relation to living up to moral and ethical standards. In v. 6, the "holy" and the "pearls" refer to God's truth and kingdom standards. Those who are disciples of Jesus are not to take the precious truth of God and cast it before "dogs" and "swine."

Both "dogs" and "pigs" were derogatory terms used by the Jews to denigrate Gentiles, and some may be shocked to hear Jesus use them. But anyone who objectively observes the life and ministry of Jesus would know that political correctness was not His major concern. It should also be noted that Jesus was not calling anyone a pig or a dog but used the metaphor in a context relating to the habits of these animals. The explanation that Jesus was concerned about a "mixed church"[13] is totally erroneous. Jesus was not concerned with having false teachers in the church but with misuse of God's precious truth. Likewise, the theory that Jesus was denying the Eucharist to the unsaved as expressed in the Didache ("But let none eat or drink of your Eucharist except those who have been baptized in the Lord's Name. For concerning this also did the Lord say, 'give not that which is holy to the dogs'"[14]) is not defensible from the context.

To understand the Lord's instruction as forbidding His followers from trying to make the unsaved live up to God's standards is best. The unsaved cannot know or obey God's truth (1 Cor. 2:11-14), and to demand that they live kingdom standards is like casting pearls before the feet of swine, resulting in something of value being trampled in the mud. To preach God's holy standards rather than the gospel to blind and spiritually dead people is like casting holy things before dogs that do not obey but become violent. The structure of v. 6 is best understood as a chiastic parallelism[15] depicting dogs turning and tearing in pieces and swine trampling the holy things under their feet. One has only to review the negative response to the social moralizing of groups that have lobbied, protested, and sued to force God's truth onto the pagan world. Rather than being light in darkness, many have tried to reform society to meet kingdom standards. The results have been exactly as the Lord predicted. Jesus' teachings are consistent with the warning of Proverbs 9:8 and 15:12. This certainly does not mean that believers should not speak out against evil, but it is a warning against attempting to make a fallen world conform to standards that cannot be understood or appreciated. The intent of evangelism is not to make the world a better place, though that would be a blessed consequence, but to save people out of this present evil world. God's truth demonstrated by the lives of those who know Christ will be seen in humble self-judgment rather than by self-righteous judgment of others (vv. 1-5).

A LESSON ON PRAYER, 7:7-11 (cf. Luke 11:9-13)[16]

Jesus next entered into one of His many lessons on prayer. This pericope is a popular text for encouraging sermons on prayer and is certainly a critical part of Christian theology. However, the passage should not be isolated from other teachings on prayer, since other conditions must be met. Scripture mentions some hindrances (such as asking with selfish motives, James 4:3; not showing proper consideration for one's wife, 1 Peter 3:7; etc.); thus, this text addresses but one area in the broad topic of prayer.

7:7 Jesus stated three imperatives: "ask" (*aiteō*), "seek" (*zēteō*), and "knock" (*krouō*). He also stated three results of obeying the imperatives, all in the future tense: "it shall be given to you" (*dothēsetai > didōmi*), "you shall find" (*heurēsete > heuriskō*), and "it shall be opened to you" (*anoigēsetai > anoigō*). All three imperatives are in the present tense, implying a continual process. Carson points out that this stresses "the persistence and sincerity required."[17] Other conditions are required for answered prayer, but here the condition is persistence, which reflects one's commitment to the power and effectiveness of prayer. Persistence also demonstrates dependence upon God. It indicates belief that only God can accomplish what really needs to be done, rather than prayer's being a ritualistic act followed by works of the flesh to accomplish what one needs.

Carson understands the three imperatives as follows: "ask" is the act of prayer, "seek" is earnest sincerity in prayer, and "knock" is the active, diligent pursuit of God's way.[18] It is interesting that Hendriksen sees the three as "the rising scale of intensity."[19] "Ask" (*aiteō*) in the New Testament usually implies that a petition from an inferior person is being presented to a greater person, demonstrating humility. Though unusual in New Testament use, at times it can have the meaning of "demanding."[20] The most common New Testament term for prayer is *proseuchomai,* but here Jesus used *aiteō* to indicate a request being made and not prayer in general, which involves praise, worship, and intercession as well.

Seeking "is asking plus acting."[21] The implication is that one not only makes his requests known to God but anticipates the response and actively pursues its result. For example, one may pray for God to give an understanding of Scripture, but 2 Timothy 2:15 insists that one must also diligently work at handling Scripture accurately. First Corinthians 2:14 states that the natural mind does not comprehend spiritual truth, and thus one must depend upon the Spirit of God to illumine, but Peter also tells us that one must be taught the Scripture so as not to develop destructive beliefs (2 Peter

3:16). Christ has provided teachers in His universal body for the purpose of teaching Scripture to others (Acts 13:1; 1 Cor. 12:28; Eph. 4:11), but that is balanced by the fact that one must still be dependent upon God for understanding what is taught. The pivotal balance in prayer is to keep on asking but also to keep on seeking.

Knocking implies a desire to be invited in for personal contact. To knock at a door is to seek entrance so as to participate and interact with the activities within. The follower of Christ should seek to be involved with the activities of the kingdom. Knocking may also imply a desire to be in fellowship with God. The often misapplied text of Revelation 3:20 illustrates how Christ's knocking is seeking entrance not into anyone's heart but into the apostate church to fellowship with any believer who will respond to Him. Therefore, believers are to pray faithfully and seek to receive all that God will provide in response to prayer but also desire to be active in the inner workings of His program and in fellowship with Him.

7:8 Verse 8 explains why one should persist in these exercises, "for" (explanatory *gar*) persistence will be rewarded. The one asking is also receiving, the one seeking is finding, and to the one knocking, it will be opened. The first two results, receiving and finding, are present tense verbs indicating that they are coincidental with the asking and seeking. The third result, however, is expressed in the future tense, "shall be opened" (*anoigēsetai*). Perhaps the reason is that even though one may presently have fellowship with the Lord, that fellowship is often interrupted by the natural propensity to sin. The future may refer to that ultimate state of uninterrupted fellowship when the saints are removed from these sinful bodies. Another viable option is the future tense's here being what is sometimes referred to as progressive future (or iterative or stative future), which implies a continuation of a condition or state. An example of this is found in 2 Corinthians 11:12, "What I am doing, I will continue to do" (*ho de poiō, kai poiēsō*).[22]

7:9-11 Jesus then offered an illustration from daily life as to why the process of asking, seeking, and knocking works, based on God's being a caring Father who will give good things to those who ask. The comparison is between human fathers and the heavenly Father. The human father, though instinctively evil because of man's fallen nature, will give good things to his children; and the heavenly Father, who is instinctively holy and good, will certainly give what is good. If a child should not question the goodness of the earthly father's gift, how much more should God's child not question the goodness of the heavenly Father's gift.

One should not make too much of the use of the bread/stone and fish/snake illustration. As common food items of the period, the giving of bread and fish implied the normal response of father to child—provision of the basic needs. For a father to give a stone in place of bread or a snake instead of a fish would have been perversion. The point is made in v. 11 by the contrast between the instinctive "evil" (*ponēros*) of human nature, "If you then, being evil,"[23] and the goodness of the heavenly Father, offering assurance of His response to the prayers of His children.

Jesus' conclusion, "How much more shall your Father who is in heaven give what is good to those who ask Him!" is to reassure His followers that asking is not in vain even if it requires persistence. James informs his readers that they may war and struggle with all their energies but they will not receive unless they ask, and ask with pure motives (James 4:2-3). When the child of God asks in faith, with consistent sincerity, God will give what is good. The good (*agathos, ē, on,* "what is good, useful, satisfactory for one's needs") that He gives may not always be what was asked, because the request was not for a good thing. For this reason, the promise is not that the heavenly Father will give what is asked, but what is good.

THE GOLDEN RULE, 7:12

7:12 (cf. Luke 6:31)   The next proverb is often labeled the Golden Rule and appears in a great variety of contexts (both sacred and secular) in various forms. A similar principle stated in the negative is found in the apocryphal book of Tobit, "And that which you hate, you should do to no one" (4:15, author's translation).[24] Rabbi Hillel is quoted in the Talmud as responding to a young critic who challenged him to teach the whole Law while standing on one foot by saying, "What is hateful to you, do not do to anyone else."[25]

A notable difference between the similar maxims with what Jesus taught is that His alone was stated in a positive form. His concern was for His followers to realize that other people feel the same needs they feel. Everyone wishes to be treated with respect and consideration. Christ's followers are to lead the way, to be role models for the world to see. What Jesus does not say is also important. He does not say, "Treat people well so that they will treat you well." The issue is not how to manipulate others so as to be treated better, but to demonstrate God's truth as taught in the Law and the Prophets. Created in the image and likeness of God, every human therefore has worth. Our treatment of others is to reflect the common respect that God's creature deserves and which we understand from our own desire as a creature made in His image.

This verse begins with "therefore" (*oun*), indicating its connection with preceding text. It is best to make the connection not just with vv. 7-11 but with v. 1 and following. One possibility here is Matthew's intent to summarize the entire discourse beginning with chap. 5. This is certainly consistent with the subsequent "this is the Law and Prophets."[26] Chapter 7 does seem to be a collection of short summary statements, and v. 12 begins to bring closure to the Lord's discourse up to this point.

THE WIDE AND NARROW GATES, 7:13-14

7:13-14   Scripture indicates a dualistic nature to life and uses pairs of items to compare alternative courses or different aspects of the same category, such as light and darkness, good and evil, human and divine, male and female, heaven and earth. Here the dichotomy is "narrow and wide," presenting the picture of two gates, probably symbolizing entrances into a course of life. One gate is narrow, implying less accessibility and popularity; the other is wide, implying approval and acceptance by the majority of people. Carson is probably correct in assuming that the allusion is to the appeal of the wide gate because it "is spacious and accommodates the crowd and their baggage."[27] The two gates lead to two destinations: the narrow to life and the wide to destruction. In response to a question as to whether or not many will be saved (Luke 13:23-24), Jesus referred to a narrow door, which many will not be able to enter. The parallel is lucid. The path most will follow is the path to destruction. The narrow way does not mean a way so legalistic or difficult that only the most righteous will be able to stay on the path—a concept that Pharisaism promoted. It simply means that only one way leads to life, and most people will not enter that way. Religion and self-righteousness will lead the majority to pursue what is assumed to be the road to salvation, only to find destruction.

FALSE PROPHETS, 7:15-20

7:15   The next pericope indicates the seriousness of Jesus' contrast between His kingdom and the religious leaders of Israel. Warnings of false prophets would assuredly sound familiar to the Jews, since Old Testament prophets constantly cautioned against both them and their message. In this context, however, an ominous variation is seen in that the false prophets were the very ones to whom they gave honor as their teachers.

"Beware" (*prosechete*) is a present imperative form of *prosechō,* which basically means "pay close attention to" or "watch carefully for." In the New Testament, it carries a connotation of intellectual alertness and at times even a connotation of the fear of danger. In this context, used with the analogy of "ravenous wolves," there can be little doubt that Christ was implying that His disciples should be alert with a sense of fear because of the vicious destructiveness of false teachers. In the contemporary Christian environment, where fear of sounding hyperconservative is greater than fear of false teachers' destroying the flock of God, such a warning is awkward.

Christ desired both His disciples and the others hearing His message to understand that both true prophets and pseudo-prophets claimed to speak for God. The true prophets spoke by divine revelation. The pseudoprophets imitated the true and spoke by their own intent, creating destruction like that of wolves in the midst of a flock of sheep. God condemns false prophets, who are "prophets of the deception of their own heart" (Jer. 23:26) and is against prophets who "steal My words from each other . . . who use their tongues and declare, 'the Lord declares' . . . and led My people astray by their falsehoods and reckless boasting; yet I did not send them or command them" (Jer. 23:30-32). In Jeremiah 23:1, God clearly warns, "Woe to the shepherds who are destroying and scattering the sheep of My pasture!" It would be well for every person who dares to speak God's Word as a prophet to read especially the warnings of Jeremiah 22-23 and understand the solemn charge of 2 Timothy 2:15. God takes His truth seriously, and in a confused generation that is totally convinced of any person's right to promote any opinion, the warning here is critical. James 3:1 also warns of impending consequences for those who presume the privileged position of teaching God's truth to God's people. The contemporary church has lost the sense of God's sending teachers, and—as any Christian bookstore demonstrates—many have taken to themselves the right to teach their own opinion of God's truth. The result of the "freedom of speech" mentality in present-day Christianity is more than three hundred denominations, several thousand "Christian" cults, more than two dozen English versions of the Bible (with serious differences), and no consistent witness to the unregenerate world.

In the immediate context, Christ's intent for false prophets being connected to the scribes and Pharisees cannot be doubted. In chap. 16 He warns two times of the "leaven of the Pharisees." In 23:13-33 He pronounces "woe" upon the Pharisees and scribes (eight times) and calls them hypocrites (seven times), blind guides (twice), fools, blind men (three times), whitewashed tombs, serpents, and a brood of vipers. He also declares to them, "How shall you escape the sentence of hell [*geennēs*, v. 33]?" In Matthew 23 He condemns their hindering people from entering the kingdom of heaven (v. 13), using religion to cover personal greed (v. 14), and neglecting the "weightier provisions of the law: justice and mercy and faithfulness" (v. 23).

The false prophets (also called false teachers, false apostles, and even false Christs in the New Testament) are described as coming to His followers in "sheep's clothing." Gundry correctly states, "Here, the donning of sheep's clothing represents the claim to follow Jesus,"[28] but he interprets the action: "The ravenousness of the wolves in sheep's clothing refers to the luxurious living of the false prophets at the expense of their followers."[29] However, the imagery of ravenous wolves is not luxury but destructiveness. Rather than emphasizing material results (gain), the analogy conveys the idea of false teaching's destructive results in the lives of God's people. Again, the straightforward language of Matthew 23 is clear as to the devastating results of incorrect theology. Most certainly the people hearing the analogy envisioned a gory slaughter of sheep by vicious wolves, not luxurious and materialistic benefits. Again, our present culture has deadened us to the horror of spiritual perversion, but this was Jesus' point. Carson connects this warning with the previous statement about the narrow gate, "They neither acknowledge nor teach the narrow way of life . . . and since the only alternative to life is destruction (vv. 13-14), they imperil their followers."[30]

7:16-18 Continuing His thoughts about the false teachers (*pseudoprophētai*), Christ stated that they will be recognized by their "fruits" (*tōn karpōn autōn*), that is, by the end product of their teaching and their lives. Fruit is a metaphor indicating the end result of one's efforts or character. The fruit is what comes from the tree; the intrinsic nature of the tree determines the product of its life (cf. James 3:12). Likewise, a false prophet is not just false by what he says but by innate nature—the false prophet speaks and lives lies.

Thus, He was saying, watch the lives of teachers to know the genuineness of their teaching. The Pharisees, for example, spoke with great skill about God, but their judgmentalness and sanctimonious attitude betrayed that they did not know or understand the God of mercy and restoration. Carson offers an excellent summary of this idea: "Living according to kingdom norms can be feigned for a time; but what one is will eventually reveal itself in what one does. However guarded one's words, they will finally betray him."[31] The same lesson is repeated often in the New Testament. Matthew 12:33-37 offers the same analogy, using the Pharisees (v. 24) as the target of the lesson.

7:19 Verse 19 proposes a serious prediction: the trees producing bad fruit are to be cut down and thrown into the fire. John the Baptist spoke these same words to the Pharisees and Sadducees (Matt. 3:10). Their "bad fruit" seems to have been (or been based upon) the false concept that being biologically linked to Abraham was sufficient to grant a place in the kingdom. Many commentators apply the "bad fruit" to some kind of moral perversion: "However attractive at first sight they may appear to be, they will *in the long run* produce a perverted morality, even if their original exponents may themselves be moral."[32] Whereas this feature has merit and appeals to one's natural desire for moral purity, it misses the point. False prophets are not moral. Their perversion of truth is evil and destructive, because every human being is by nature fallen and sinful. Their fruit is perversion of God's truth because of their corruption within. It is not that they are simply in error and their error will lead some to sin, but their product—the lies and perversions they teach

—flows from a wicked heart (Luke 6:45). This wicked heart will become evident and be held as testimony against them when they are cut down and "thrown into the fire." Fire is a common analogy for judgment in Scripture and should never be assumed as a reference to "hell," though condemnation is implied in this context.

7:20 Verse 20 is the summation of the Lord's warning. Though warned not to be judgmental (vv. 1-5), His followers are certainly to be critiquing the product of others' teachings and to make determinations as to who is true and who is false. Compare Ephesians 4:14, where Christ's gifts (named in v. 11) are given to His body for the purpose of training believers not to be deceived by false teaching. Likewise, 1 John 4:1 warns of false teachers, using the modifier "many" to indicate that their presence is not an uncommon situation. One of the duties of church elders is to refute false teachers who attempt to influence the flock (Titus 1:9). The author of Hebrews echoes a similar warning, pointing to the fruit of true teachers as verification of the legitimacy of their ministry: "Considering the result of their conduct, imitate their faith" (Heb. 13:7).

Teaching About Entering the Kingdom, 7:21-23

7:21 Jesus then made a momentous declaration: "Not everyone who says to Me 'Lord, Lord,' will enter the kingdom of heaven." Early in this discourse Jesus declared that one's righteousness must surpass that of the scribes and Pharisees in order to enter the kingdom (5:20); now He made it equally clear that rightly identifying His title is not sufficient to gain entrance into the kingdom. The question here is what He meant by "he who does the will of My Father who is in heaven."

In v. 21, the Lord challenges those who make use of His title "Lord" (*kurios*) but do not obey the heavenly Father. Jesus may have had Joel 2:32 in mind, "And it will come about that whoever calls on the name of the Lord will be delivered," to which Paul refers in Romans 10:13. The Romans context declares that no distinction exists between Jew and Gentile in God's redemptive process, but that whoever (Jew or Gentile) "calls upon the Lord" will be saved. But calling upon the Lord and saying the title are not the same. The first implies dependence and humble surrender, the latter only religious talk. Ryle believes that Jesus was teaching "the uselessness of a mere outward profession of Christianity,"[33] which is probably the best understanding of the warning.

Clarification of the significance of the term "Lord" is important, so that post-Ascension Christians do not attribute a weight to the term not intended. Often the word *kurios* was used of rabbis as synonymous with the word "teacher." However, to avoid misapplication, the concept of "teacher" in the New Testament must not be confused with its contemporary connotation. Rabbis were not just lecturers of cognitive data but were also authoritative counselors and persons who were greatly reverenced and respected. The term "Lord" (*kurios*) was used as a respectful greeting to those of authority and rank.[34] It also was used in situations expressing respect and courtesy, such as a son addressing his father.[35] The term became a distinctive title for the resurrected Lord, carrying all the authority and respect as if used of Caesar himself. In Luke 6:46, Jesus asks, "Why do you call me 'Lord, Lord,' and do not do what I say?" implying that one called Lord should be obeyed. Thus, the term should not be thought of as limited to being a synonym for "teacher."[36]

Carson believes that the repetition of the title "Lord, Lord" reflects fervency.[37] However, fervency is not sufficient to gain entrance to His kingdom. Entrance requires obedience to the "will of My Father who is in heaven." Several observations are worthy of note. First, Jesus did not mention Law, moral standards, or righteous acts as being the will of His Father. Second, entrance into the kingdom is determined by the Father's will, not the Son's. Third, the Father is designated by two crucial qualifiers: "My Father," indicating Jesus' claim to the intimacy and authority of sonship with God; and "in heaven," indicating that His origin was heaven, not the earthly stepfather Joseph.

Carson states, "It quite misses the point to say that the Father's will is simply the OT law,"[38] because, first, the keeping of the Law is beyond mere human effort and, second, no one is justified by the Law. The apostolic teaching of the church would certainly be consistent with what Jesus had taught them; and James, Peter, and the others welcomed Paul's message, rejecting any salvific merit to keeping the Law (Gal. 3:10-13 is only one example). Unquestionably, if Jesus meant that doing the will of the Father was keeping legal codes, then the scribes and Pharisees would have been leading the way into the kingdom.

The will (*thelēma*) of God is mentioned in other contexts in the New Testament. In 6:10 (also Luke 11:2), Jesus offers the model prayer and appeals to the heavenly Father to enact His will upon the earth even as He does in heaven. In 12:50 He declares that His brother, sister, and mother are those who do the will of His heavenly Father (see also Mark 3:35). In 18:14 He states what is not the heavenly Father's will: "that one of these little ones perish" (referring to the children whom He had called to Himself). The arrest, humiliation, beating, and murder of Jesus were apparently God's will (Matt. 26:42; Luke 22:42). In this last example, Jesus demonstrated doing the will of the Father. He surrendered His life into the plan of His Father, being willing to give His life to accomplish the Father's redemptive work. He declared that His whole focus in life was to be obedient to whatever the Father directed Him to do (John 4:34; 5:30; 6:38).

The question of how does one "do the will of" the heavenly Father might best be answered by the Lord in John 6:40: "Everyone who beholds the Son and believes in Him, may have eternal life." Though only an aside to Christ's explanation of how He does the will of the Father by not losing any who come to Him for salvation (John 6:38-40), this comment is still the most direct statement concerning the matter. If one considers "believing in His Son" as doing the Father's will, that helps clarify why all the religious efforts of the scribes and Pharisees were insufficient for entrance into the kingdom. Of course, God's will for particular situations and individual lives will be different, but for salvation and entrance into the kingdom, belief in His Son is essential for all.

7:22   Many will appeal to their spectacular works as a basis of salvation, only to find that works are not the basis for entering the kingdom. Three impressive works are named: prophesying, casting out demons, and miracles, all done "in the name of the Lord." Verse 22, then, deals with people who did perform those sensational deeds (Christ did not deny they did something powerful) and who claimed to be doing them in the name of Jesus Christ. Some today also put on sensational displays and claim Christ's power, but such displays are apparently not proof that one is Christ's servant. Ample proof that Satan has power to perform imitation miracles and deceive the people is found in 2 Thessalonians 2:9-10. Exodus 7:10-12 illustrates how magic arts can superficially mimic God's power (note that ultimately God's power prevailed). In Matthew 12:27, Jesus challenges the Pharisees by asking, "If I by Beelzebul cast out demons, by whom do your sons cast them out?" This would imply that the Pharisees also practiced exorcism.

7:23   Verse 23 brings the issue into focus. Not works of the Law or displays of miraculous power earmark kingdom people but rather a personal relationship with Jesus, the King. "I never knew you" is the determining factor in their condemnation. The idea of knowing (*ginōskō,* "know"), implies far more than merely knowledge about them. Of course, Jesus knew their names, character, and lives, but He did not have intimate, experiential knowledge of them. Mary used this same word in defending her virginity (Luke 1:34, *andra ou ginōskō*), which doesn't deny male acquaintances but does deny any intimate experience with a male that could lead to pregnancy. This word is also used in the Lord's prayer in John 17:3: "But this is eternal life, that they should *know* you, the only true God" (*estin hē aiōnios zōē hina ginōskōsin se*). Thus, salvation is not based upon religion but upon relationship, and these religious miracle workers did not possess that relationship. Hendriksen refers to this as "knowledge of the heart, that is, of electing love, acknowledgment, friendship, and fellowship."[39] Stott's discussion is very helpful in seeing the connection between their empty profession, "Lord, Lord," and their failure to do the Law (they "practice lawlessness").[40] However, one should not miss the point that Christianity is not a religion but a relationship—an intimate, experiential union between sinner and Savior. One final note: one must do the will of the *Father,* but it is the Son who has authority to banish unbelievers from the kingdom for not entering into a relationship with Him.

CONCLUSION TO THE MOUNTAIN DISCOURSE, 7:24-27

This final pericope in the discourse is a summary and a warning concerning all that has been presented from 5:1 to 7:23. The epilogue is introduced with the conjunctive "therefore" (*oun*), which links His conclusion to previous statements and basically says that these truths taught are the only foundation that allow one to withstand both the storms of life and final judgment. The parable is not intended to teach that Jesus Himself is the solid foundation but rather "these words of Mine," that is, what He had just been teaching is the foundation. He offered an analogy with two possible responses to His message.

7:24-25　　The first response was the correct one. "The one who hears these words of Mine and acts upon them" is the wise man—the person who realizes that the "house," no matter how carefully, skillfully, or beautifully built, will crash when the storms beat against it if placed on an unstable foundation. Hearing implies giving attention to and not just letting words fall upon the ears without evaluation and consideration. Paul strongly affirmed the Jewish zeal in service to God, but their problem was action before first understanding God's will (Rom. 10:2). The Jews, zealous as to moral behavior, faithfully performed all the rituals and religious traditions of their rich heritage but did not evaluate their actions in light of God's character and program of redemption.

Acting upon is subsequent to understanding. After evaluating and considering what is said in order to gain an accurate understanding of the will of the heavenly Father, the wise person will apply what is learned to his life. The words of Jesus may be reviewed by the following concise outline:

1. The Beatitudes of 5:3-11
2. The expansion on the oral traditions, 5:21-48
3. The warning against Pharisaical attitudes, 6:1-18
4. The warning against materialism, 6:19-33
5. The warning against judgmentalness, 7:1-5
6. The warning against false prophets, 7:15-20
7. A variety of short proverbial sayings, 7:6, 7-12, 13-14
8. The warning to the false professors, 7:21-23

The rain, floods, and winds represent the trials or pressures that will come against what one builds into his life. When the testing of life's foundation comes, only those who have responded properly to Christ's teachings will stand.

7:26-27　　The end is predictable when one's life is built upon untruth and religious effort driven by self-righteousness and pride. In contrast to those who consciously and humbly respond to the lessons of the Mountain Discourse, those who do not act upon these truths are like a foolish man who built his house upon the unstable and weak foundation of sand. When judgment comes and testing is applied to what has been built, no matter how diligently or sincerely, the building will crumble under the forces at work. To build one's life and eternal expectations upon a foundation without substance is foolishness indeed. These concluding verses should be a somber warning to all who feel secure in their own righteousness and religious rituals.

MATTHEW'S CONCLUSION 7:28-29

7:28-29   Matthew now adds his own commentary to the event of the Mountain Discourse.[41] Literally he says, "And it came about when Jesus ended these words, the people were being amazed [*exeplēssonto*, imperfect passive third person plural > *ekplēssomai*] at His teaching." The people (*hoi ochloi*) are those who gathered when they saw Jesus sit down to teach His disciples. In the account of Matthew 5:1-2, Jesus was speaking directly to the disciples but certainly intended the broader audience to hear. He was teaching kingdom standards and character, realizing that the Jews would be hearing His message.

The disciples had heard Jesus teach before and were somewhat accustomed to His authoritative and powerful style, but Matthew notes the shock of others upon hearing one teach with authority and not by repetition of rabbinical opinion as the scribes did (v. 29). The authority (*exousia*) of Christ's teaching was divinely appointed (John 5:19-30), and His mission was not to maintain the status quo in the religious environment but to bring the truth of God to the lost sheep of Israel.

HOMILETICAL SUGGESTIONS

The Mountain Discourse is perhaps one of the most powerful messages for contemporary Christianity. To believe that Christians cannot fall into the same trap as Israel's religious zealots is naive, and chap. 7 offers some critical lessons in preventing this tragic recurrence of Pharisaism.

The warning against a judgmental spirit in the first five verses is the logical beginning point for understanding what God desires from His kingdom people. First in priority is to judge oneself (Rom.

14:1-13; 1 Cor. 11:31) and deal with personal sins. Rather than look for reasons to condemn others, believers must *seek* to restore those struggling with sin (Gal. 6:1-4). Through this, the true followers of Christ will stand apart from the self-righteous religionists who misrepresent the God of mercy.

The first of the proverbs given in chap. 7 (v. 6) warns against trying to make the unregenerate live up to kingdom principles, which cannot be understood or appreciated (cf. 1 Cor. 2:14). This does not negate the responsibility of human government to restrain violence and punish social crimes. Neither does it mean that Christians should not speak out against evil or try to explain the value of spiritual morals. The distinction comes in flippantly throwing God's standards before people who are blinded and under the control of the wicked one (1 John 5:19). It is not the commission of Christ's church to reform the world or make it a better place in which to live. We should hope that such changes will result from observing the light in their darkness, but that is not the task before us. The other proverbs likewise illustrate the character and purpose of those who are kingdom citizens, dealing with trust in God, proper interpersonal relationships, the scarcity of true kingdom people, and the standards for doing God's will.

Two serious warnings conclude the teaching portion of the discourse. The first is a warning against false prophets (7:15-20). Those who would mislead the people of God, either through deliberate perversion of truth or through ignorance and pride, are to be identified and avoided. Christ has appointed teachers in the body to educate and mature believers so that the saints will not be "tossed here and there by waves, and carried about by every wind of doctrine, by the trickery of men, by craftiness in deceitful scheming" (Eph. 4:11-14), and the Holy Spirit raises up elders in local assemblies to protect the flock from such false teachers (Acts 20:28-30; Titus 1:5, 9-11). One serious weakness in contemporary Christianity is the failure of these two offices to perform the tasks of education and protection. The world has convinced the church that sermons must be man-centered and "encouraging" rather than educational and exhortative. Few believers know enough theology to discern heretical teaching, because attention is not given to God's full revelation or program. The contemporary Christian culture desires a focus on such topics as self-improvement, marriage building, child training, or how to maintain religious rituals (often called "spiritual disciplines"). Though these topics certainly are not evil, meditating upon Paul's warning in 2 Timothy 4:1-4 would be profitable. How do such subjects relate to Jesus' admonition to beware of false prophets who tell people what they want to hear? The teacher's responsibility lies in "reproving, rebuking, and exhorting, with patience and instruction," and we need to note that Paul's exhortation was to "preach the Word," not sermons (2 Tim. 4:2). Preaching the text with an explanation of words, contexts, cultural influences, and theological consistency would mature and protect the flock of God far more efficiently than all the well-intentioned moralizing done through three points and a poem.

The warning to false professors (7:21-23) is also significant in this age, when so many are seeking experiential religion. Assuming that power is truth, they do not stop to examine the source of that apparent power. The ability to work miracles, cast out demons, or prophesy smooth words is not validation of salvation. This warning is a grim reminder that self-delusion is the strongest delusion of all. Crying "Lord" and pointing to one's sensational activities are a tragic end to failure to know God and obey His will.

One should present Christ's parable of the two builders with the awareness of its context. The primary message of the Mountain Discourse is best exhibited in the caution of 5:20, "Unless your righteousness surpasses that of the scribes and Pharisees, you shall not enter the kingdom of heaven." The closing parable of 7:24-27 declares the results of either understanding or not understanding the meaning of 5:20; and the Discourse gives the keys to understanding, thus the choice of hearing and obeying or being destroyed.

MATTHEW
CHAPTER
EIGHT

MINISTRY IN CAPERNAUM

Subsequent to His lengthy discourse, Jesus left the mountain followed by a "great multitude." Though it is not recorded, the crowd was probably observing His works, particularly the sequence of miracles listed. Each synoptic writer wrote his account in such a way that the chronological flow is oftentimes difficult to ascertain, and some commentators work diligently to synchronize the four gospel accounts. However, one could dedicate more energy trying to solve the questions raised by the numerous speculations than would be worthwhile. Carson offers sufficient explanation.[1] A cursory review of Mark's account (1:21-45), reveals that apparently either Matthew or Mark did not record Jesus' ministry chronologically but by events.[2] The reader should allow Matthew's flow of argument to create the account that the Spirit of God desires rather than becoming involved with numerous speculations.

THE HEALING OF THE LEPER, 8:1-4 (Mark 1:40-45[3])

8:1-2 With the crowd following Him down the hillside (v. 1), Jesus began a series of healings: the leper, the centurion's servant, and Peter's mother-in-law. A tragic component of the ancient Near East was the treatment of lepers. Israel applied specific laws of ostracization, including required dwelling outside the city (Lev. 13:45-46).[4]

Lepers were also to be treated as unclean and thereby quarantined (Num. 5:1-4). Thus, for a rabbi to touch a leper would be unusual.

The leper approached Jesus in an attitude of worship and faith in His ability to heal him. The leper "bowed down" (*prosekunei,* imperfect of *proskuneō*), indicating either an act of worship or a demonstration of respect.[5] Unlike some other commentators, this writer will assume the first,[6] not because of his use of the word "lord" (which could simply be a title of respect, not acknowledgment of His deity) but because of the appeal for healing. It is not likely the leper would have approached a merely respectable person and asked for healing. Neither Matthew nor Mark offers any indication as to why this leper had such confidence in Jesus' ability to heal. However, Matthew 4:23-24 attests to the fame He had earned in Galilee from His healing miracles. Since Jesus was probably near Capernaum, which is at the northwest corner of the Sea of Galilee, this leper had possibly seen Him or heard of His power.

The leper phrased his request in a manner that demonstrated confidence in Christ's power but not necessarily in His willingness ("if you are willing"). Faith in His power did not imply presumption on the part of the leper, who indicated that his fate rested in Jesus' will, not in His ability.

8:3 To such faith and humility, Jesus responded, "I am willing; be cleansed." Mark's account tells us that Jesus was "moved with compassion," which agrees in motive with His instructions for the healed leper not to tell anyone (v. 4). This miracle was an act of mercy, not a public demonstration of His messianic credentials. The comment about compassion may give credence to Tasker's assumption that "Jesus allowed the constraint of divine love to take precedence over the injunction against touching a leper."[7]

Leprosy was not considered a sin but an uncleanness in the Mosaic Law, and Jesus did not forgive the man but rather commanded, "Be cleansed." It certainly was not necessary for Him to physically touch the leper, but Matthew notes the physical contact as a demonstration of Jesus' willingness to be personally and holistically involved with the needs of His people. Note that the cleansing was immediate and not a process or a partial healing.

8:4 Jesus instructed the healed leper not to speak of the healing and to present himself before the priest in Jerusalem with the required offering (Lev.14:1-32). The reason for constraining his testimony is not stated. Tasker agrees with Stonehouse that "except for restraint on his own part and on the part of others, the situation might easily have got out of hand and his public ministry brought to an untimely end."[8] Other possible reasons are that perhaps the man was to speak only to the priest until declared clean as fulfillment of the Law, or that perhaps Jesus was trying to downplay His role as a miracle worker (though not likely). According to Mark 1:45, the leper failed to obey the Lord in this matter, but Scripture reveals no indication of punishment. The phrase "for a testimony to them" (v. 4) must refer to the priest in Jerusalem.

THE HEALING OF THE CENTURION'S SERVANT,[9] 8:5-13

8:5   As Jesus completed His trip to Capernaum, a second person appealed for healing. In stark contrast to the petition of the socially rejected leper, this entreaty came from one of society's elite. In Luke's account, the centurion sent elders from the village to intercede for him, perhaps because he believed the appeal would be more acceptable coming from Jewish elders rather than from a Gentile. Matthew presents the centurion himself appealing to Christ with no reference to the elders. Rather than a contradiction between the two accounts, to understand that Matthew's concern was to contrast Israel's unbelief with the great faith of the Gentile centurion is best. The fact that the elders acted as representatives for the centurion was not significant to Matthew. Carson believes Matthew omitted the elders because his intended audience was Jewish, and he wanted to keep the racial distinctions for the purpose of his narrative.[10] This explanation is consistent with the uniqueness of divine inspiration, which allows each author to express his message in a manner consistent with his own style.

So named as military leaders in charge of 100 soldiers, centurions are mentioned often in the New Testament and always from a positive perspective. The centurion Cornelius (Acts 10), the instrument of bringing the gospel to the Gentiles, was called a "righteous and God-fearing man well spoken of by the entire nation of the Jews" (Acts 10:22). Known as the backbone of the Roman legions, centurions were highly respected for their loyalty and integrity. Secular history records numerous accounts of their faithfulness to duty.

8:6   Like the leper, the centurion called Jesus "Lord" (*kurios*). Again not assuming that he could understand all involved with the post-Ascension gravity of the word, one must understand his address as more than just a respectful greeting. He apparently believed something divine and unique was resident in the Person to whom he appealed for a miracle. The NASB and NIV both translate *pais* as "servant," which is correct in certain contexts. The word normally would imply a young boy, a son, but there is sufficient evidence in Koine Greek that it also could refer to a favorite servant.[11] Matthew again uses *pais* in 12:18, "Behold My Servant [*pais*] whom I have chosen," quoting Isaiah 42:1 and translating the Hebrew *'bd* ("slave, servant"). Luke's account has *doulos,* a "slave" or "servant," though he also uses *pais* on occasions. He probably chose to use *doulos* here because the centurion was demonstrating great concern for him, denoting affection ("highly regarded by him," Luke 7:2).

8:7 The servant was paralyzed and in great pain (v. 6); Luke adds that he was near death. Jesus immediately agreed to go, implying that He would heal him. Compassion again marked His character, and the willingness to aid even a slave testified of His humble servant's attitude.

8:8-9 The centurion's unwillingness to have Jesus come to his home illustrates three important concepts: recognition of his own unworthiness to have a person of Jesus' significance in his home ("I am not worthy," v. 8; of course, Jesus would have disagreed on this point); conviction that Jesus had power to heal even without being present ("just say the word," v. 8); and an understanding of Jesus' authority to give commands to get the work done ("I, too, am a man under authority," v. 9).

8:10 "When Jesus heard this, He marveled" reveals Jesus' response of amazement at the centurion's faith. The word "marveled" (*ethaumasen,* aorist verb from *thaumazō*) is used frequently of the people's response to His teachings or miracles (e.g., Luke 9:42-43), but its use creates conflict for some when used in relation to Jesus. With a desire to protect Jesus' deity, some scholars assume Jesus could not marvel at anything because of being omniscient. However, ignoring the reality of Jesus' full humanity, including the emotive response of amazement, is just as grievous an error as weakening His deity. The *kenosis* ("emptying," *kenōsen,* Phil. 2:7) of Christ is a reality, not a meaningless theological term. Non-use of divine attributes does not imply nonpossession. Jesus chose not to exercise those attributes so as to be dependent upon the Father and to more realistically relate to the human experience. Calvin aptly states, "*Wonder* cannot apply to God, for it arises out of what is new and unexpected: but it might exist in Christ, for he had clothed himself with our flesh, with human affections."[12] He was amazed, not only at the faith of the centurion here but also at the unbelief of Israel (Mark 6:6, *ethaumazen dia tēn apistian autōn*).

He spoke "to those who were following," which most likely refers to the great crowd that accompanied Him from the mountain (8:1). They had marveled at His authoritative teaching (7:28-29), and He used this opportunity to give another lesson, drawing their attention to the magnitude of faith demonstrated by this Gentile. The centurion rested on Christ's word and did not require presence or proof, contrary to the Jews, who demanded a sign.

8:11-12   Jesus' disclosure may have been an allusion to Isaiah 25:6-7; 49:1-13, messianic texts related to the universal impact of His kingdom. This was clearly a warning to Israel of improper response to the Messiah and the subsequent enactment of God's contingent plan, including Gentile participation in the blessings of Abraham, Isaac, and Jacob. To assume that this means Gentiles would replace Israel is erroneous, but equally erroneous is to assume that Gentiles who have faith in Christ will not be invited to share the covenant blessings promised the chosen nation. Paul reveals the mystery of the Gentiles sharing in the blessings of the kingdom (Eph. 3:1-6) but never asserts that the church is a replacement for Israel.

The sons of the kingdom being cast out into the "outer darkness" in torment refers to that generation of Jews who rejected Messiah and therefore did not have eternal life, even though they possessed a biological connection to Abraham and the covenant. Again, this is a major theme for Paul, especially in the book of Romans (e.g., Rom. 2:12-23; 3:9; 9:30-32). Carson observes:

> "But these verses affirm, in a way that could only shock Jesus' hearers, that the locus of the people of God would not always be the Jewish race. If these verses do not quite authorize the Gentile mission, they open the door to it and prepare for the great commission (28:18-20)."[13]

A strong parallel warning in Luke 13:26-35 closely links this to judgment of the Jews for rejecting their Messiah. Note in v. 35 that the temporal particle "until" (*heōs*) marks a point at which this judgment will cease. The blindness of true Israel will be removed, and the remnant will be restored.

8:13   Jesus sent the centurion on his way (in Luke, the elders and friends represent the centurion). In accordance with the believing of the centurion, the miracle took place within the hour, not "immediately" as with the leper. The Lord's working may differ, but His compassion and response in mercy are sure.

JESUS HEALS THE SICK AND DEMONIZED, 8:14-17

8:14-15   Jesus arrived at Peter's home in Capernaum[14] and found Peter's mother-in-law sick (v. 14). According to Mark (1:29-31), He had not parted from the centurion and immediately gone to Peter's house but had just come from the synagogue. Luke's account also states that it was the Sabbath and that Jesus had just cast out a demon from a man in the synagogue (Luke 4:31-38). Mark seems to indicate that Andrew lived in the same house with Peter, his wife, and his mother-in-law (1:29). First Corinthians 9:5 would also lead one to believe that Peter's wife would at times accompany him on his missions trips.

The mother-in-law was bedridden with a fever, which in that culture was treated as a disease and not just a symptom. Jesus touched the person to be healed (v. 15). Though He could heal by only speaking words, the physical contact was probably used to show personal concern and also to vividly associate the Person of Jesus with the healing. A harmony of the synoptic accounts reveals that Jesus walked into Peter's house and was approached by family members (probably including Peter's wife) concerning the illness. Jesus went to her bedside, reached down to touch her, and commanded the fever to leave. Immediately she was healed and rose up with full strength to serve the group, which had just returned from the synagogue.

8:16-17   Later that same evening, probably after sundown so as to avoid conflict with Sabbath laws, the villagers brought others who were sick or demonized. "The whole city" in Mark's account is to be understood in typical hyperbolic language to emphasize the magnitude of the crowd. Jesus is pictured as being constantly at work that evening, meeting physical needs and demonstrating both power and compassion. It is important to note that Scripture makes a distinction between illness and demonization. Two types of illness are easily identified in the New Testament: (1) illness in which no sin or demon involvement is addressed and (2) illness that is healed with simultaneous forgiveness of sin. Demonization, however, is treated differently from illness. Mark and Luke both record that Jesus instructed the demons not to reveal His identity as Messiah, and again His reasoning is not explained. This may be because He did not desire the testimony of demons or because the timing was not right for His identity to be revealed to these people.

In v. 17 Matthew again associates a major event in Christ's life with the fulfillment (*pleroō*) of an Old Testament text, Isaiah 53:4. Hendriksen points out that the message of Isaiah 53 connects the sickness and disease that Messiah removes with the sacrifice for sins.[15] The difference, however, is that illness is the natural consequence of the fallen world in which we live, and not every illness needs to be linked to personal sin. Paul's thorn in the flesh, Timothy's "often infirmity," and numerous other examples indicate that illness may be a part of God's plan for us and not judgment for sin. Matthew's connection with Isaiah points to the nature of Messiah's ministry and demonstrates its correlation with the work of Jesus Christ.

CRITERIA FOR DISCIPLESHIP, 8:18-20

Mark and Luke record that sometime after the extensive healing ministry at Peter's home, Jesus went to a private place for solitude, but His disciples sought Him out (cf. Mark 1:35-38; Luke 4:42-44). Matthew begins to describe the Lord's trip with His disciples to the other side of the lake but suddenly stops (v. 19) to discuss criteria for being a follower of Jesus (vv. 19-22). Carson believes part of Matthew's reasoning may have been that "Jesus' imminent departure to the east side of the lake (v. 18) prompted certain people to beg him to include them in the circle of disciples going with him."[16]

8:18-20   The narratives of Mark and Luke[17] proceed into different events, but Matthew interrupts his account of crossing the stormy sea to introduce the requirements for discipleship. In vv. 19-20, becoming a follower of Jesus implies relinquishing material securities. A "certain scribe . . ." (NASB) is a little misleading and would more naturally translate "and one scribe, having come up, said to him . . . " Had the adjective *tis* been in the text in conjunction with the substantive *grammateus,* one might assume a "certain" or particular scribe. But as the text reads, it was one scribe among a group. To have a crowd gather whenever Jesus appeared in public had become typical. This scribe stepped out of the crowd as he saw Jesus preparing to leave and volunteered to join Jesus' group of disciples. Reference to "another disciple" (*heteros tōn mathētōn*) in v. 21 may indicate that the scribe was already a follower of Jesus, though not one of the Twelve. His volunteering to leave home and work was to become a full-time follower like Peter and the other eleven. It probably is overly dramatic to make a big distinction between the scribe's referring to Jesus as "teacher" (*didaskalos*) rather than "Lord" (*kurios*). Jesus was rightfully called both, and for a scribe to relate to Him at this point primarily as a great teacher would be natural. Jesus did not rebuke him for using the term.

The response of Jesus was not what one would expect (but then, most of the time His responses were not what one would expect). Rather than praising the scribe for his willingness to make such a commitment or challenging his sincerity, Jesus simply referred to the unglamorous and uncomfortable conditions involved in following One who did not even own a place to sleep. Unlike the creatures of nature (foxes and birds), the Son of Man did not have a place of His own. There is no reason to assume that Jesus was rejecting the man because he was a scribe, nor can it be said that he was not one of the seventy disciples sent out by the Lord at a later time (Luke 10:1).

Volumes have been written on the title "Son of Man" and rightly so for many significant reasons. In the Old Testament, the term was repeatedly used for the prophet Ezekiel (Ezek. 2:1; 3:1; 4:1; etc.) and used eschatalogically for the Messiah in Daniel 7:13-14. In the Psalms, the title can refer to humans in general (8:4) or to the nation of Israel (80:14-19, cf. v. 8 and entire psalm).

Used eighty-one times in the New Testament, with the majority of uses in the synoptic gospels, the term certainly identified Jesus as one truly from out of mankind. But it also identified Him with eschatological expectations. Luz comments that the conviction of some Jewish apocalyptic circles was that "the messianic judge called 'the son of man' would appear and that they believed that Jesus was that son of the man."[18] He also summarizes, "The 'son of the man' therefore is a christological expression with a *horizontal dimension,* by means of which Jesus describes his way through history."[19] In other words, it is best to understand the expression "Son of Man" as emphasizing the identification of Messiah with the human experience. Carson offers excellent discussion and concludes:

> In Matthew 8:20, "the Son of Man" could easily be replaced by "I." Moreover it occurs in a setting that stresses Jesus' humanity and may foreshadow his sufferings. For postpassion Christian readers, it could only speak of the Messiah's wonderful self-humiliation.[20]

8:21-22   Whereas the earlier scribe (v. 19) appeared to be volunteering for ministry, this disciple seems to have been hesitant. Luke's account (9:59) reveals that Jesus initiated the conversation by an invitation to follow Him, and the disciple responded, "Lord, permit me first to go and bury my father." From references such as Genesis 25:9, 35:29, and 50:13, the Jews had developed the concept that to honor one's father (Ex. 20:12; Deut. 27:16), the son must take care of his burial. Jesus' response dramatically attested to the priority of kingdom responsibilities even over family devotion (cf. 10:37). Many have tried to rationalize the apparent harshness of the Lord's words "allow the dead [spiritual] to bury their own dead [physical]," but in all honesty there is no easy explanation. The best understanding is that the statement was hyperbolic, as were many of His statements, intended to draw attention to a point. The point was the priority of Jesus and His work. It is also possible that Jesus knew the insincerity of this "disciple" and called him to follow at a crucial time to dramatically point out that insincere spirit. Some argue that the father was not dead as yet but was near death, and the disciple was asking to delay following Jesus until that event. There is no grammatical or contextual support for that argument, though logically it could be appealing.

THE STORM AT SEA, 8:23-27
(Mark 4:36-41; Luke 8:22-25)

All three synoptic gospels record this event, which lends testimony to its importance. Perhaps one of the most important lessons to be learned from the account is that the disciples appear to have been, for the first time, suddenly made aware of the awesome power and authority of their Lord. One must question what they expected Him to do when they woke Him from sleep with the appeal to save them, but it is evident they did not expect to see His unparalleled display of power over nature.

8:23-24   Matthew continues the narrative he began in v. 18. Jesus had instructed His disciples to go to the other side of the lake (Lake Chinnereth, or the Sea of Galilee). While crossing the sea, Jesus apparently fell asleep and continued to sleep even though a fierce storm had begun (a "fierce gale of wind," *lailaph megalē anemou,* Mark 4:37). The intense wind stirred the sea until the whole boat shook as if experiencing an earthquake (*seismos megas,* Matt. 8:24; *seismos* is the source for the English "seismograph," a machine for measuring earthquakes). The severity of the storm was implied in the fear seen even in veteran seamen such as Peter, Andrew, James, and John, who assumed they were about to die (v. 25). One can only imagine the terror these men felt as the boat thrashed in the waves, taking on volumes of water and beginning to sink (Mark 4:37; Luke 8:23). As the experienced seamen panicked, the Lord lay undisturbed in sleep at the rear of the boat (Mark 4:38). The contrast is between One who was completely trusting God and those who were overwhelmed by the "reality" of life.

8:25-26   Matthew records that they awakened Him with the words "Save us, Lord; we are perishing" (present tense), which implies that their evaluation was a rather desperate one. Mark adds the information that they even questioned His care for them (4:38). Two observations concerning their response to the storm are noteworthy. First, panic arose because they assumed impending death. This may suggest a lack of understanding of their mission in life and of the security in God's ability to protect them for accomplishing that mission. Second, they did have enough awareness of Jesus' power to know He could help them, even though their response demonstrated failure to fully comprehend the extent of His power and authority.

Jesus took two actions when awakened (v. 26). He rebuked the disciples, then rebuked the sea. In Mark's and Luke's accounts, He stilled the sea and then spoke to the disciples. Or He could have made an immediate statement to the disciples who woke Him, stilled the storm, and then lectured them on their lack of faith. Matthew uses the temporal adverb *tote* (which he uses ninety times in his writing, far more than anyone else), which can introduce an event that follows in time in relation to another event (this and *then* this).[21] Thus, Matthew seems to be emphasizing the sequence of events—first He rebuked the disciples and then the sea.

His rebuke of the disciples raises the issue of the depth of their faith. They had seen His miracles, had heard His authoritative teaching, and had committed themselves to follow Him. Yet, when an unexpected trial came, the disciples assumed He would let them die. Prat states, "If they fancied that Jesus while sleeping did not know their danger and could not come to their help even in His sleep, their faith was still imperfect. The excitement of the moment was doubtless some excuse, for fear does not reason; but their faith had to be strengthened by this test and lesson."[22] He questioned them. "Why are you timid?" (NASB). The word "timid" is a little too polite; *deilos* is to be cowardly or afraid (thus, the NIV "afraid" is better). He then added a comment that seems to have answered His own question, "You men of little faith." It is interesting that the term "little faith" (*oligopistos*) is used five times in the New Testament, always in reference to the disciples (6:30; 8:26; 14:31; 16:8; Luke 12:28). The cognate *oligopistia* is found in Matthew 17:20, having the same meaning and also in reference to the disciples.

Faith is best understood as belief without proof (Heb. 11:1), and to have only little faith implies that the disciples believed in Him until things occurred that, according to their experience and knowledge of the sea, would surely bring death. They judged Him on the basis of their immediate circumstances and needs rather than upon the power and authority already seen in Him. They failed to understand that Jesus' power was superior to the threats and dangers of the natural world. Their faith was also "little" with regard to His love and care for them. They judged His concern based upon the condition of their comfort and apparent safety.

"Then He arose, and rebuked the winds and the sea; and it became perfectly calm." Jesus stood up in the boat, which was being tossed around and flooded by the waves, and "rebuked," literally, "commanded" (aorist tense of *epitimaō*) the winds and the sea. Mark records the words of the command: "Hush, be still." (*Siōpa, pephimōso*). *Siōpaō* means to "be silent, make no sound,"[23] much as we would say, "Be quiet!" This expression is described by John Sproule[24] as a command one would snap at a dog, "Sit!" The second command is in the perfect tense and passive voice of the verb *phimoō* and means to be "muzzled" or "tied shut."[25] Thus Christ stood and shouted into the raging storm, "Quiet, be muzzled!" The traditional reading of the King James, "Peace, be still" certainly misses the power and authority with which He spoke.

The result of His command, "it became perfectly calm," bears testimony to His authority over nature. Matthew's statement simply reads "great calmness [*galēnē megalē*] came," which is in contrast to the "great storm" (*seismos megas*).

8:27   Their shock at going from being in an intense storm to suddenly being in the midst of total calm is hard to imagine. The effect is understandable: "the men marveled." Mark's account more dramatically states, "They became very much afraid" (4:41). As the disciples suddenly realized in whose presence they were, the fear of the One whose power and authority was greater than the raging storm overcame them.

Their question, "What kind of a man is this?" is significant; the nature and power of Jesus had abruptly grasped their hearts. This was no mere man. Certainly, they had seen His miracles, which God worked through Him; but now, as though a fog had lifted from their minds, they clearly saw that the Person, not His miracles only, was extraordinary.

GADARENE DEMONIACS HEALED, 8:28-34
(Mark 5:1-20; Luke 8:26-39)

Once again, the three Synoptic Gospels differ in their accounts of this event. Matthew's version is the shortest and has two features that modify the details from both Mark and Luke. Once more the reader must resolve the differences based upon his presuppositions related to the origin of the biblical texts. If one assumes a Matthean community that reconstructed the accounts according to their traditions, then it will be determined that the redactors erred in their record or altered details to suit their particular concepts. If, on the other hand, one assumes divine inducement for Matthew to record the details as found, then the solution will be ascertained by allowing one writer to have details others did not have and to emphasize features differently so that, when the three accounts are combined, the full three-dimensional narrative is seen. There is a difference between contradiction and variety. Mark and Luke record that a "man" (singular) was demonized, whereas Matthew mentions two men. The inclusion of an additional man does not constitute a contradiction but an added feature that Mark and Luke do not mention. Mark's and Luke's accounts are not hindered by focusing their attention on one particular man.

Matthew refers to the area of this ministry as the "country of the Gadarenes," whereas Mark and Luke call it the "country of the Gerasenes." The problem is found in the variant readings of the Greek manuscripts. The manuscripts for each of the Gospels contain readings vacillating between the two. Variants are not problems with inspiration but with copyists and should not be considered a major issue here. Since there is both a Gergesa (eastern shore) and Gadara (a city on the southeast and the territory around it), either Gaderene and Gerasene could be an appropriate term.[26]

8:28   The two demon-possessed (*daimonizomenoi*)[27] men met Jesus along the road, which they apparently controlled by their violence and unnatural strength. According to both Mark and Luke, their strength was such that they could even break free of chains and shackles (Mark 5:3-4; Luke 8:29). The personal anguish of the men is also portrayed in Mark (5:5). This is not a horror story of modern Hollywood but the personal tragedy of men dominated and tormented by forces so powerful that even the strength of Roman chains could not subdue them. The power of these demons was displayed in the physical capacities the men possessed, and the whole region was terrorized by the legion of demons controlling them.

8:29   When one combines Matthew's record with Mark's and Luke's, it appears that the demonized men saw Jesus coming and somehow recognized His power. They ran and fell down before Him, begging for mercy. No attempt was made to harm Him or the disciples. They knew immediately who He was. They addressed Him as Son of God ("Son of the Most High God" in Mark and Luke), implying recognition of His divine authority (cf. Matt. 8:20, where Jesus calls Himself the Son of Man).

They feared that Jesus had come to prematurely punish them: "Have You come here to torment us before the time?" Even demons know that an appointed day awaits for their permanent removal from the presence of humanity to suffer eternal punishment. How typical of evil that even though the demons tormented the men they brutally dominated (as well as the whole region), they now begged "do not torment me" (Luke 8:28). Their power and cruelty was matched by their cowardice.

8:30-34   Jesus granted the demons' request to indwell the herd of swine. The presence of swine should not be thought inconsistent with the Mosaic prohibition of pigs, because this region was mostly Gentile. Sermons about the indwelling of swine being just punishment upon Jews for owning swine are not legitimate. Why did the demons make this request? Perhaps because, when absent from some sort of physical machine in which to function, demons sense intense frailty and insufficiency (cf. Luke 11:24). Having lost their position of being in God's presence, they may seek meaning and purpose in other forms. One can only speculate.

Another, equally puzzling, question is, why did the Lord permit it? Perhaps the reaction of the people (v. 34) was to illustrate the hardness of the human heart. In contrast to the men freed from the demons, clothed, and in their natural minds (Mark 5:15; Luke 8:35), the pigs "became insane" and were drowned. The people did not rejoice on behalf of the men but became afraid, possibly because they associated Him with a more powerful demon or feared retaliation from the demons. This was a powerful demonstration not only of His power over demons and their fear of Him but also of the ignorance and stubbornness of the human heart.

Mark 5:18-20 and Luke 8:38-39 tell us that one of the freed men sought to become a disciple (this may explain why Mark and Luke focus on only one man, whereas Matthew includes another individual, who did not seek to travel with Jesus). But Jesus sent him home to be a witness of His power and mercy.

HOMILETICAL SUGGESTIONS

The leper offered an example of faith, which pleased the Lord. The leper never seemed to doubt Jesus' power to heal but did leave in question the Lord's willingness to heal him—"if You are willing." Jesus' response indicated that He was pleased with the leper's faith and humility. There was no expressed assumption of healing or expectation that the Lord was under compulsion to grant his request. Jesus did not just command the leper to be healed but reached out and made physical contact with one who was rejected, despised, and feared because of his disease. He touched the man, indicating His compassion as well as His power. The instructions not to tell anyone but go to the priest in Jerusalem implied that Jesus was more concerned that the leper fulfill the Law than call attention to Him.

The healing of the centurion's servant was in stark contrast because of the two main characters in these accounts. The leper, a social outcast, and the centurion, a man of wealth and power, represented both extremes of the social structure. Yet the common element was the humility and faith with which they each approached Christ. Jesus praised the faith of the centurion because, though he was not Jewish, he trusted in the Jewish Messiah for this need. The third person healed represented yet another group in society. Peter's mother-in-law represented the servants of the Lord, and His care for her and her subsequent service are also instructive.

Perhaps one of the most important lessons of this chapter is seen in the calming of the storm. This account offers an ideal illustration of true worship. Contemporary Christianity tends to define worship by activities or style of music. But when the disciples "became very much afraid" (Mark 4:41), they demonstrated what true worship is—the reverent fear of One whose power and authority exceeds even the violent forces of nature. To realize one is in the presence of the Person of absolute power instinctively draws worship from the soul.

A fourth major portion of the chapter simply ties together the theme of the whole: Jesus' power and authority. The casting out of the demons was like His healing the disease of leprosy, healing the paralysis of the servant, healing the fever of Peter's mother-in-law, and muzzling the storm. Each account displayed His unquestioned authority and power.

MATTHEW
CHAPTER
NINE

PUBLIC DISPLAYS
OF JESUS' POWER

Jesus now returned to Capernaum, where He continued to draw attention with a series of demonstrations of His power. The Lord progressively unveiled His uniqueness, not only by displaying authority over illness, natural forces, demons, and even death, but also by proving His authority to forgive sins.

HEALING OF THE PARALYTIC AS DEMONSTRATION
OF THE AUTHORITY TO FORGIVE SINS, 9:1-8

9:1 (Mark 2:1-12; Luke 5:17-26)   Matthew's narrative continues from Jesus' trip across the sea to the area of Gadara back to "His own city," Capernaum (4:13). Mark and Luke agree that this event took place in Capernaum, but both place it earlier in Jesus' ministry. The sequence of events is not critical, but it is worth noting that all three place this event immediately prior to the calling of Matthew.

9:2   Mark informs us that such a large crowd gathered that no one could get into the house where He was teaching and healing (2:2). Luke adds the detail that several Pharisees and Law teachers had come from surrounding villages to hear Him (5:17).

Because the house was packed with curiosity seekers and needy people, the men who brought their paralyzed friend resorted to extreme measures. Mark and Luke explain that they actually climbed to the roof, removed the tiles, and dug through the structure to create a hole large enough to lower their friend on his pallet right in front of Jesus. This revealed two aspects of this event. First, the crowd seemed to be indifferent toward the needs of the paralyzed man; and second, the friends of the paralytic were absolutely determined to get him to Jesus. One should keep in mind that house construction of that period was rather simple and that, even though requiring great effort, what they did would not be the same as breaking through the roof of a modern house.

Jesus "[saw] their faith," the faith of the friends, and spoke to the paralytic. Note that this effort was recognized by Jesus as the product of their belief that He would help their friend. Hendriksen assumes that the faith went beyond the physical healing and that they knew Jesus would "relieve the paralytic from the burden of his guilt."[1] This would presume spiritual insight on their part, however, that is completely unjustified. There had been no reference to His forgiving sins prior to this, and the shock of the Pharisees was indication that to do so was unprecedented.

The Lord offered three expressions of great comfort and joy for the paralytic: "take courage," "My son," and "your sins are forgiven." The statement "take courage" (*tharsei*) implied that something good was about to happen for the man who had suffered as a paralytic. The second, "My son," was an address of affection, indicating that Jesus felt some tenderness toward the man's condition or attitude. The possessive pronoun "My" is not in the text but was inserted by the translation committee. Jesus did not use *huios* ("son") but *teknon* ("child"), "which is no more than an affectionate term from one's senior."[2] In some contexts it refers to spiritual children, and believers are referred to as *tekna tou Theou* ("children of God").[3] There may be some relationship between this last concept and Jesus' praise for the display of faith from the paralytic's friends and apparently from the paralytic himself.

The third statement shocked the audience. When Jesus pronounced forgiveness for sins, the scribes (v. 3) and Pharisees (Luke 5:21) began to mumble and question His authority. Forgiveness of sin is the dismissal of guilt as well as any restitution for the offense. Here, the particular sins forgiven were not mentioned. It may be assumed that it was a salvific statement covering the condition of sin every human is in until redeemed by Christ, or perhaps He meant a particular sin, which had brought paralysis as judgment. Jesus implied the former (v. 6). It should not be automatically assumed that all illness is the result of sin. Though sin can bring sickness (1 Cor. 11:28-31), several had already experienced healing up to this point with no connection being made to sin. Calvin, however, argues for sin's being the cause of the disease.[4] His arguments are sound only to a limited degree, and the forgiveness statement seems broader than that. All human ailment and suffering are related to our fallen and sinful condition, and Christ used this opportunity to demonstrate His authority over the fallen condition of mankind.

9:3   The scribes began to talk among themselves (Luke includes Pharisees as well) and challenge Jesus' right to proclaim the forgiveness of sin. Scribes were scholars in the Mosaic Law. They were exegetes of the Law and were viewed with great honor. Edersheim offers an excellent description of their class and position: "His order constitutes the ultimate authority on all questions of faith and practice."[5] Scribes and Pharisees were often seen together (seventeen times in the Synoptic Gospels) and many scribes were Pharisees, though not necessarily all. These influential teachers concluded that He was blaspheming by pronouncing forgiveness of sin. Mark (2:7) and Luke (5:21) give us their words: "He is blaspheming; who can forgive sins but God alone?" They certainly were considering verses such as Isaiah 43:25, "I, even I, am the one who wipes out your transgressions for My own sake; and I will not remember your sins." Other related passages were probably in their minds as well (Ps. 103:10-14; Isa. 1:18; 55:6-7; Jer. 31:34; Micah 7:19). Hendriksen is probably correct in his assumption of what their reasoning would have been: "Only he [God] knows what is going on in the heart of man, whether or not he has truly repented. Basically, therefore, no one else has the right and the power to grant absolution. The scribes were right in considering the remission of sins to be a divine prerogative."[6]

9:4   All three synoptics point to Jesus' perception of the hearts of the scribes. Matthew uses the term "knowing their thoughts," whereas Mark says He was "aware in His spirit" (2:8), and Luke simply says He was aware of their reasoning (5:22). These comments provide a glimpse into the spiritual discernment of the Lord. They all point to the sensitivity of the true, Spirit-filled servant of God. He knew what only the divine Spirit could reveal, the inner thoughts and intents of the human heart.

His question, "Why are you thinking evil in your hearts?" indicates His evaluation of their motives. "Evil" (*ponēra*) is an adjective referring to any worthless, bad, malignant, or wicked entity or device. When used with the definite article (*ho ponēros*), it often refers to the Devil himself. Lenski observes, "With stunning directness Jesus confronts these scribes with their own thoughts."[7] Our human tendency would be to praise the scribes for defending God's prerogative, but Jesus judged their hearts as reasoning evil, not as being confused or misunderstanding. This supernatural insight is reminiscent of John 2:24-25 and contradicts the humanistic philosophy that sees the intrinsic goodness of man. This event also reveals the early resistance toward Jesus on the part of the religious leaders.

9:5 Jesus' question was rhetorical. He made the point that He was displaying supernatural power consistent with the anticipated Messiah, who would not only heal physical infirmities but spiritual disease as well. The question, "Which is easier to say?" was to draw a comparison between the difficulty of saying without proving and saying what is immediately proved or disproved. Certainly anyone can say the words "Your sins are forgiven," and there would be no way to prove whether any action took place. If one says, "Rise, take up your bed and go home," the power and authority behind that statement can be verified or denied by watching whether or not the person is able to get up and walk.

Jesus' authority to forgive was being inwardly challenged by His critics. His words, even after the multiple healings and miracles that He displayed, were not sufficient to convince these skeptics. Therefore, now that He had their attention, He gave the second command, which is certainly more difficult, "Rise, and walk." Carson points to the heart of the matter: "If Jesus had blasphemed in pronouncing forgiveness, how could He now perform a miracle (cf. John 9:31)?"[8]

9:6-7 Jesus now transparently revealed His purpose in the dramatic proclamation of the forgiveness of sins. He would verify the reality of His forgiveness by the demonstration of His healing. The purpose clause is introduced by *hina* and declares that His intention was to let them know that He had power to forgive sins. This was not to deny their assumption that only God can forgive, but to claim for Himself the divine prerogative, thus implying His deity.

Once again Jesus used the title "Son of Man," His most common appellation for Himself and one rarely used by others to reference Him. Though many would take the title as merely an allusion to His humanity, this context certainly indicates that it would bear more weight than that by the association with His power over disease and authority to forgive sins. There can be no doubt that the appellation is associated with the Adamic race (Gen. 1:26-28; Ps. 8:4-8;), and it suggests what Adam and his race would be apart from the fall into sin. However, there can be little question that the messianic implications of Daniel 7:13-14 are intrinsic to its significance as well. The Son of Man is given dominion, glory, and a kingdom over all peoples and nations, and Jesus' demonstration of His authority over disease and sin would testify to that dominion.

After explaining His purpose, He turned to the paralytic and said, "Rise, take up your bed, and go home." All eyes must have been fixed upon the man to see if Jesus had the authority of God to forgive sins. To the crowd's amazement, "he rose, and went home" (v. 7). This should have answered the question and silenced the critics. None of the three records mentions any response directly from the scribes, but all state that the crowd was amazed and glorified God. Pate calls this "'in your face' testimony to the Pharisees and scribes."[9]

9:8 The multitudes "were filled with awe, and glorified God" because they understood that God had given such authority to a man. It is interesting that the people correctly glorified God for the work done by Christ. Mark 2:12 tells us that the crowd had never seen anything like this, forgiveness of sins verified by miraculous healing. Luke records that the multitudes were filled with fear (*eplēsthēsan phobou*) because they were seeing remarkable things (5:26), literally, "paradoxical" (*paradoxsa*) or "puzzling, incomprehensible" things. This fear was not terror but awe in respect to the phenomenal power and authority displayed before their eyes.

THE CALLING OF MATTHEW AND THE LESSON OF THE TAX-GATHERERS, 9:9-13

9:9 Jesus left the house where He had been healing and teaching and passed by a tax booth, where He saw Matthew. Mark and

Luke both refer to him as Levi (Matthew alone identifies himself by the name "Matthew"), and Mark further identifies him as the son of Alphaeus (Mark 2:14).[10] Jesus summoned Matthew to "follow" (*akoloutheō*), a word that is almost used as a technical term, denoting "the action of a man answering the call of Jesus whose whole life is redirected in obedience."[11] It should not be assumed that this was the first contact between Jesus and Matthew and that Matthew recklessly jumped up to follow Him as if in a trance. As with the other disciples, preliminary contact may have been made in which Matthew would have already been prepared for this event (cf. 4:18-20 and John 1:35-42).

9:10   Matthew does not mention that the banquet where Jesus reclined at the table with other tax gatherers and "sinners" (Luke 5:29) was held in his home. This reception apparently was an attempt by Matthew to give occasion for friends and relatives to meet Jesus and to explain why he was leaving his career.

Leonardo DeVinci's *Last Supper* has probably contributed to misconceptions of this scene. The people of that culture and time period dined while lying on mats, propped up on one elbow. Low tables were usually placed in a squared-horseshoe pattern, and servers moved in the interior area between the tables, while the diners reclined around the exterior of the horseshoe.

9:11   Observing Jesus and the disciples eating with tax gatherers and sinners, the Pharisees approached the disciples with a question. They did not come to Jesus. Perhaps after His demonstration to the scribes, the Pharisees were somewhat fearful of direct confrontation. Their question was prompted by Jesus' eating with two classes of Israelites with whom no self-respecting Pharisee would even be seen.

In that culture, the idea of sharing a meal was far more significant than in contemporary cultures. By sitting at table with these people, Jesus was showing acceptance and camaraderie (cf. 8:11). The Pharisees could not imagine that anyone who would want to be taken seriously as being from God would lower himself to associate with such immoral people. It should be noted that Jesus was not frequenting a place of ill repute, such as a modern bar, crack house, or house of prostitution. The people labeled "sinners" (*harmartōlōn*) by the Pharisees were simply those not meeting their man-made standards of holiness. This should not detract from the impact of His association with people whom the religious community rejected but simply serve to keep Jesus from being used as an excuse to live in immorality while pretending to reach the lost. Jesus recognized the reputation He was developing and used this to challenge the hypocrisy of the Pharisees (11:19).

9:12-13   Jesus overheard the slanderous question of the Pharisees and did not hesitate to step into the conversation with an answer. It would have been interesting to hear how the disciples would have answered, but Jesus did not give them opportunity. The response of Jesus was twofold. First, He used the analogy of a physician working among the sick. This was particularly appropriate in light of the healing ministry He was displaying. Second, He rebuked their lack of compassion and deliberately insulted their lack of knowledge of God's Word.

Jesus stated His point from the negative, referring to those not needing His attention (v. 12). One should not assume that He was implying that the Pharisees were not sin-sick and in need of healing. He had already publicly declared that a qualification for getting into the kingdom was to have righteousness superior to that of the scribes and Pharisees (5:20). His statement was, rather, a rebuke to those who by virtue of their position and knowledge of Scripture should have been reaching out to sinners rather than condemning them (7:1-5). His association with sinful people was not to enjoy their sinful practices but to bring them out from them. Hendriksen states:

> When he associates on intimate terms with people of low reputation he does not do this as a hobnobber, a comrade in evil, "birds of a feather flocking together," but as a physician, one who, without in any way becoming contaminated with the diseases of his patients, must get very close to them *in order that he may heal them!*[12]

Thus Jesus was saying that He was only doing what they should have been doing since they considered themselves to be healthy.

He gave these arrogant judges a stinging rebuke (v. 13). The Pharisees and scribes were experts in the Law and the traditions, capable of quoting large portions of the Torah from memory and arguing the fine points of the Old Testament. Yet, their ignorance of Scripture was exposed by His exhortation for them to "go and learn." Jesus referred them to Hosea (6:6) to learn about God's desire for mercy and compassion. Hosea was warning Israel of God's judgment and presented a terrible picture of His chastening; yet, even with rebellious and sinful Israel, God preferred to deal in mercy, not punishment. Feinberg offers a helpful summary of the context of Hosea's statement:

> Chapters 5 and 6 of the prophecy of Hosea bring vividly to us the destruction and ruin to which the sin and rebellion of Ephraim and Judah have led them. So full is the cup of iniquity of God's people that the servant of God must reprove, rebuke, and exhort by varied means. God would win back His own by loving entreaty before the hour of doom.[13]

Mercy (*eleos,* "compassion" NASB) is God's desire, not to be appeased by sacrifice (*thusia*). The religious acts of sinful men do not satisfy His longing for intimacy with His creatures. Only His mercy can restore fallen humanity. The Pharisees had failed to grasp this critical truth about God and therefore failed to pursue the sinners of their day. Messiah had come to do what religious Israel had failed to do, "call the sinners" to God.

A QUESTION ABOUT FASTING, 9:14-15

9:14-15 Jesus did not conduct His ministry as the Pharisees thought He should, and even the disciples of John the Baptist failed to understand His unusual style of spiritual leadership. Notice that John's disciples, unlike His enemies, did not fear approaching Jesus personally. Their question was a sincere one, as they did not understand how a holy man and His disciples could not fast. Perhaps the question was raised because John's disciples saw Jesus and His disciples *feasting* in Matthew's house (9:10) while they themselves were fasting (Mark 2:18). Though some commentators hesitate to see a chronological sequence in the events, that supposition seems to have some validity. Note that Matthew uses *tote* ("then") to transition between the two incidents, which could easily imply sequence. All three synoptics sequentially record the events, and a logical flow of thought (feasting raising the question of fasting) is evident.

Luke's account (5:33-35) does not record who raised the question, but Mark and Matthew identify the questioners as disciples of John. The Pharisees were known for their dedication to fasting, and Jesus often referred to this fact in His warnings against hypocrisy (6:16-18; Luke 18:11-12). Fasting is not commanded in the New Testament; neither is it a measure of spirituality, but the practice is assumed and recognized as beneficial. It is a private matter and has a purpose beyond mere physical discipline—to focus one's attention upon a task, need, or personal relationship with God even to the exclusion of concern for what one will eat. Isaiah offers God's view of a true fast (Isa. 58:6-7 in contrast to Israel's hypocritical fast, vv. 3-5). The question was reasonable, though not fully justified since Jesus and His disciples had not broken any scriptural requirements. Because the question came from disciples of John, Jesus responded with an answer, not a rebuke.

Here Jesus associated fasting with mourning, portraying it as a symbol of sorrow (*pentheō*), not as a symbol of spirituality. He used the analogy of a wedding feast, which is consistent with a common metaphor in both Old and New Testaments for Yahweh's and Christ's relationships with Their chosen people (Isa. 62:5; Jer. 2:32; 31:32; Hosea; John 3:28-29; Eph. 5:25-32). Hendriksen very aptly explains the significance of the metaphor: "Bridegrooms' attendants fasting while the feast is in progress! How absurd . . . Disciples of the Lord mourning while their Master is performing works of mercy and while words of life and beauty are dropping from his lips, how utterly incongruous!"[14] The analogy is also particularly effective because of the audience to whom He is speaking, disciples of John. John had used the bridegroom and friend of the bridegroom analogy to introduce Jesus (John 3:28-30).

Jesus proceeded to speak of a time when fasting would be appropriate for His disciples, namely, when "the bridegroom is taken away from them." To be taken away (*aparthē*, aorist passive from *apairō*, "be taken away") indicates a nonvoluntary separation. He would not desert them but would be *taken away*. The reference was definitely to His crucifixion and most likely alluded to Isaiah 53:8 (LXX, *airetai apo tēs gēs*). This will be the time of fasting (sorrow; grieving). Jesus specifically would address this issue with His disciples later (John 16:16-22), warning them of His death and of their (temporary) grief. Their grief would not last for they would witness His victory over death and receive the Holy Spirit as the

Helper who would complete Christ's work through the church. Today the church is not to be fasting in grief but living in the power of the Holy Spirit, victoriously awaiting reunion with the Lord. Fasting can still serve the purpose of focusing and spiritual refreshing, but for the church it is not a sign of sorrow.

TWO PARABLES, THE CLOTH AND THE WINESKINS, 9:16-17

9:16-17   At first, these two parables seem to be out of context and difficult to relate to any recently discussed topic. However, once again all three witnesses sequentially record the events, and therefore consideration should be given the parables in relation to His response to the disciples of John. Luke adds a third parable, which fits the pattern of the other two. Jesus probably spoke at least the three (perhaps others), but Matthew and Mark record only two. Not to consider Luke 5:39 as a separate parable but only as a comment associated with the second might be best.

The common element in both parables (or all three) is the incompatibility of old and new. The illustration of unshrunken cloth and wineskins is difficult to fully grasp in our modern culture, but both reflect common phenomena of the chemical and substance reaction when new material or new wine is introduced to old. The energy and dynamics of the new create pressure and tension with the old, and the results are disastrous. Carson sees this as teaching "that the new situation introduced by Jesus could not simply be patched onto old Judaism or poured into the old wineskins of Judaism."[15] Pate likewise makes an appropriate application: "The Judaism of Jesus' day was complacently satisfied with its old traditions, which prevented it from desiring the new message of the gospel."[16] Jesus, by not fasting or teaching His disciples to fast according to the traditions, was introducing new concepts in relationship to God. There could be no mixture of the old traditions and Christ's ministry. Verse 17 ends with the significant statement "Both are preserved," referring to the new wine and the new wineskin—the "new" truth would be kept in new forms of worship. The gospel is not contradictory to the truth of the Old Testament, but it is not to be kept in the same structure. God has provided a new configuration for worship and ministry for the mystery of Messiah's universal work. This is not to imply that the old is forever discarded; the eschatological fulfillment of the earthly Davidic kingdom will see the restitution of certain old forms of service to God.

HEALING THE OFFICIAL'S DAUGHTER AND THE WOMAN WITH THE HEMORRHAGE, 9:18-26 (Mark 5:21-43; Luke 8:40-56)

9:18-19   Matthew's account of this event is far less detailed than either Mark's or Luke's. Here the narrative says only that an unnamed synagogue official came to Jesus, requesting Him to heal his daughter. In Mark (5:22) and Luke (8:41) the name of the official is given, Jairus. The other major recorded difference concerns the girl's state: Matthew has the girl already dead; Mark has her "at the point of death"; and Luke says, "She was dying." In the much longer descriptions of Mark and Luke, the girl died before Jesus arrived at the house (Mark 5:35; Luke 8:49). The explanation that Matthew, in his more concise version, just initially states that the girl was dead is not totally satisfactory but reasonable. Lenski suggests, "So Matthew omits mention of the coming of the messengers who tell Jairus that death had just set in. Instead of adding these details, Matthew at once lets us learn the essential facts from Jairus, namely that his daughter was actually dead."[17]

Jairus is another in Matthew's long list of those who came to Jesus in time of desperate need and pled for His help. A "ruler" (*archōn*) of the synagogue and a man of great influence in his community, he knelt (*prosekuneō,* "fall down before," sometimes indicating worship) before Jesus and begged for help. Jairus had apparently either witnessed the power of Jesus' touch or believed the many witnesses to His great power. With the life of his only daughter (Luke 8:42) at stake, Jairus did not question Jesus' unorthodox methods or His power over even death. He came believing He was capable of helping his daughter. Jesus perceived this act as faith and immediately left to see the girl.

9:20-22   As Jesus traveled to the girl, His journey of mercy was interrupted by another critical need. All three synoptics record the healing of the woman with the hemorrhaging as taking place on the way to the synagogue official's home. Once again, Matthew's account is much more concise than Mark's or Luke's. The great crowds pushing to get close to Jesus (Mark 5:24) made it possible for the woman who had been suffering for twelve years to get close to Him. Medicine had not been able to relieve her, and she had depleted her funds in pursuit of help. Now she had heard of this miracle worker who had come to her land (Mark 5:26-27). Part of her desperation may have rested upon her being considered unclean according to Levitical law (Lev. 15:25-26).

Her actions revealed a new avenue of His healing ability, beyond the personal touch or spoken word. She believed even the impersonal touching of the "fringe" (*kraspedon,* v. 20, possibly the tassels of Num. 15:38-39) of His garments could heal her. Scripture does not record the basis for her assumption; however, what appears to many commentators as exaggerated superstition evidently worked. Jesus stated the reason, "Your faith has made you well" (v. 22). In view of everyone else pressing Him (Mark 5:24), it seems remarkable that this woman's touch got His attention (Mark 5:30; Luke 8:45-46).

Jesus stated that He had felt power go out of Him: "I know [*egnōn,* second aorist of *ginōskō*] power [*dunamis*] has gone out of Me [*exselēthuian,* perfect active participle of *exserchomai*]" (Luke 8:46). The participle functions as the object of the knowing, His awareness that power was going out.[18] It should be noted that Jesus did not say that He knew who touched Him but simply that someone touched in a special way. He noticed the touching because power (*dunamis,* "force, energy") left His body, and He was aware of this drawing out. The woman's actions were no different from what others had tried (Luke 6:18-19), but her motivation was faith (8:43-48; Matt. 9:22). Hendriksen does not miss the point: "But that is not *Luke's* emphasis. He wants us to rivet our attention on Jesus, whose *power* was enabling him to heal all."[19] Healing was done by power (*dunamis*) that flowed from Jesus—not mere human energy but a force that was resident in His very Person.

Jesus referred to her by the tender appellation "Daughter." Similarly, He had referred to the paralytic as "My son." These were significant terms of paternal care for one as young as Jesus. In stark contrast to the Pharisees, who labeled people and categorized them by artificial standards, He dealt with individual needs and individual faith. Barclay offers an excellent assessment: "As we see Jesus, amidst that crowd, giving the whole of himself to that one, poor, embarrassed woman, we see that he did not think in terms of crowds; he thought in terms of individual men and women. God is like that."[20]

9:23 Matthew now returns to the account of Jesus' raising the official's daughter from the dead. What a contrast between the ruler of the synagogue and a woman excluded from the synagogue by Levitical law because she was unclean. Arriving at the home, Jesus saw the flute players and noisy crowd. Professional mourners and musicians were typical features in a house where death had occurred. Edersheim points out that the Talmud required as a duty for even "the poorest Jew, on the death of his wife, to provide at least two flutes and one mourning woman."[21] The scene was chaotic and filled with both genuine and "professional" grief.

9:24-26 Jesus disrupted the setting by telling everyone to leave the house—an action certainly considered rude and coldhearted by both the family and the friends gathered to share their grief. When He announced that the girl was not dead but asleep (*katheudō* in all three accounts; this can be euphemistic for death but is not to be confused with *koimaomai* in John 11:11), the crowd began to laugh at Him. Luke adds, "Knowing that she had died" (8:53). This is a good reminder that what humans "know" is not limiting to God.

Excluding the crowd, Jesus allowed only the mother, father, and His inner circle of disciples (Peter, James, and John) to be in the room when He raised the girl (Mark 5:37, 40; Luke 8:51). In Matthew's abbreviated version, He simply took the girl's hand and she revived. Mark records the words spoken (probably given to him by Peter, who was present), *Talitha kum,* which is Aramaic for "Little girl, arise." Luke tells us, "Her spirit returned and she rose immediately" (8:55). This informs us clearly that, first, she was truly dead, since the spirit had left her; and second, there was no gradual resuscitation but immediate restoration of full physical energy. Likewise, Mark uses the word "immediately" and states that she began walking around. Mark also records her age as twelve years (5:42).[22] According to Mark and Luke, Jesus instructed her parents to give her something to eat (a very practical injunction; the experience may have been draining on the young girl's body) and not to disclose what He had done, though the crowd had already seen Him enter and knew the girl was dead. He probably wished to have the parents only praise God and not give the details of His actions. Matthew tells us that the news of this event went out into all the land (v. 31).

HEALING OF THE TWO BLIND MEN, 9:27-31

Matthew continues to record other miracles, whereas both Mark and Luke take their narratives in different directions. Matthew's events seem to flow in a sequence that Mark and Luke do not follow for their own reasons.

9:27 Jesus' response to the two blind men appears to have been dramatically different from His response to other appeals for help. The men followed along behind Jesus, crying out to Him, but apparently He ignored them until they followed Him into a house.

Their appeal to Jesus was to "have mercy" (*eleēson,* aorist imperative of *eleēō* or *eleaō*), implying a recognition of some guilt that denied them the right to be healed. Their request was for compassion, not justice—certainly a proper request.

Their appeal addressed Jesus as "Son of David," the first time the title is used of Him. As Carson points out, "There can be no doubt that the blind men were confessing Jesus as Messiah."[23] Meyer notes that what Jesus had already performed was sufficient evidence of His messiahship,[24] and the blind men saw this clearly. The New Testament records, as well as extrabiblical sources, offer ample proof that there was a strong messianic expectation in Israel and that the Messiah would be the Son of David.[25] The testimony of the blind men bears witness to the clear association between the expectations and Jesus' works. In contrast to the blind men's acceptance of Him as the Son of David, the religious leaders in Jerusalem rebuked the crowds for calling Him by that title (21:15-16).

9:28 Jesus entered "the house," probably Peter's home in Capernaum, as in 8:14. Although it is possible that Jesus had taken a house in Capernaum (4:13), He probably did not have His own dwelling place, based on the comment in 8:20. Another possibility regarding the house is that it was Matthew's home (9:10; see comment). However, because of His connection with Peter and the casual way Matthew records that Jesus and the entourage came to Peter's home and began to minister from there, likely Peter's house was Jesus' base of operations in Capernaum. The use of the definite article (*tēn oikian*) implies a particular house of which Matthew assumed the reader would know, as from a previous reference. In Galilee, Peter's home apparently was Jesus' dwelling place; in Judea, the home of Lazarus, Martha, and Mary seems to have been His regular place of residence (Bethany).

Jesus questioned the faith of the two men, even though they had sought Him out and followed Him, begging for mercy. The purpose of His questioning is not stated but the focus is, "Do you believe that I am able to do this?" It is best to assume that Jesus questioned them for the sake of the observers standing by and not that He doubted their faith. They responded in the affirmative, "Yes, Lord." The use of the word "Lord" (*kurios*) may have had no significance beyond recognizing His authority and right to respect.

9:29-31   Jesus took action in two forms. First, He touched the eyes of the blind men, which may have been, as Carson believes, "no more than a compassionate gesture to encourage faith."[26] Second, He declared that their faith would determine the outcome of the touching—"Be it done to you according to your faith" (literally, "according to your faith, let it be to you"). At times Jesus worked privately with an individual, such as the case with Jairus's daughter, and at other times publicly. The point here seems to have been that those observing this miracle should understand that faith in Jesus is the prerequisite for His response to their needs.

The result was that their eyes were opened; there was immediate healing (v. 30). Information concerning how long they had been blind or the cause of the blindness is not given, but one can imagine the excitement resulting from being able to see after having been blind. Thus the "stern warning" (*enebrismēthē*) not to tell anyone seems, from a human perspective, unreasonable. Carson explains: "This rather violent verb reveals Jesus' intense desire to avoid a falsely based and ill-conceived acclaim that would not only impede but also endanger his true mission."[27] Verse 31 may reveal nonadherence to His warnings, as Hendriksen and others assume.[28] Or, to give the men the benefit of doubt, it may simply record that they went about proclaiming their belief that the Messiah had come and that Jesus was Messiah.

CASTING OUT THE DEMON FROM THE MUTE, 9:32-34

9:32   As Jesus and His disciples were traveling, a demon-possessed mute was brought to Him. First, observe that he was brought to Jesus and did not seek out Jesus on his own. His inability to speak may possibly mean inability to hear as well. The word *kōphos* literally means "blunt" or "dull" and may refer to dullness in speech or in hearing (as in Matt. 11:5). In secular Greek the word could mean both at the same time, deaf and speechless.[29] In this particular case, the illness appears to have been caused by demonization. However, from the many accounts of sickness and healing already recorded in Matthew, it is to be understood that there are many causes for illness. No one should assume that demons or God's judgment are the cause for such illnesses.

9:33 Jesus cast out the demon, and the mute was able to speak. Details are not given concerning the casting out, but the aorist passive participle (*ekblēthentos,* "having been cast out") from *ekballō* is the common term used in these events and often implies force (e.g., Matt. 21:39), though not always. Matthew's comments are brief. They simply point out that once the demon was removed, the man's ability to speak was restored.

The response of the people observing the miracle is interesting: "Nothing like this was ever seen in Israel." Hendriksen believes that it is most probable that the comment related to "all the miracles that took place that day (verses 18-33)."[30] Although this may be a logical assumption, there is no grammatical reason to make such a connection. The following verse implies that the issue was the casting out of demons, and the other miracles performed on that day did not involve demons. The amazement must be attributed to the fact that this mute and his condition were well known, and the possibility of his ever speaking again had been considered nil.

9:34 The response of the Pharisees was typical of Jesus' enemies. This verse should serve as a reminder that all the "proofs" offered cannot convince the wicked in heart. The problem the unregenerate have in not accepting Christ is not so much a matter of not having proof of Jesus' power, authority, and truth but having a darkened heart that is unwilling to believe. The blasphemous accusation as to the source of Jesus' power to do the miracle emphasizes that they could not deny its *reality.*

The "ruler of the demons" (*tō archonti tōn daimoniōn*) is identified as *Beelzebul* in Matthew 12:24. The name *Beelzebul* is of puzzling origin. Probably the best understanding is that it derives from *ba'al zibbul,* "from post-O.T. Heb. *Zebel,* manure, dung; *zibbul* meaning an idolatrous sacrifice."[31] Thus the term was used as a slander against the Devil (god of dung), and the Pharisees wished to associate it with Jesus. It was Jesus who linked the name to Satan (Matt. 12:24-26) and pointed out that He was in opposition to such forces.

MOTIVATION FOR THE LORD'S MINISTRY, 9:35-38

9:35 Matthew now adds a summary statement of the miracles performed by Jesus. Certainly the purpose of this record is to correlate His power and authority with the work of the Messiah (e.g., Isa. 35:5-6). The summary is similar to that of 4:23 and may be a literary marker of transition. The itinerant ministry of Jesus is epitomized as teaching, evangelizing, and healing in all the cities and villages of the area.

9:36 As Jesus traveled through the region, the condition of the Israelites stirred His compassion. The expression "felt compassion" (*esplagchnisthē*) indicates the motive behind the next portion of His public ministry, the commissioning of His apostles. Jesus sympathized as He saw the crowds coming with their individual pain and distress. This was in stark contrast to the religious leaders, who only burdened the people with legalistic rituals and traditions (Matt. 23:4; Luke 11:46).

Unlike the scribes, Pharisees, and lawyers, Jesus did not see "sinners" but people who were "distressed" and "downcast." He viewed these Jews as sheep without a shepherd, and Ezekiel 34:1-6 is an appropriate parallel. In the time of Ezekiel, Yahweh viewed the people of Israel in the same way as Jesus viewed them in His day. Those who had the responsibility to shepherd God's flock— that is, to feed and protect them—had fed and protected only themselves, leaving the sheep to the ravaging of wolves and destroyers. Could there be a parallel today with preachers who are more concerned with building churches and reputations than caring for the flock of God?

The analogy to sheep is clearly the most common for God's people, offering the imagery of helplessness, not only physically but also intellectually. Sheep are easily confused and tend to get lost (thus, Isa. 53:6). Not possessing fangs, claws, or powerful muscles, they have no weapon for self-defense and need a shepherd for protection. God sees His people as easily confused and defenseless.

215

He sent shepherds to defend and lead, but the shepherds had betrayed their trust in pursuit of self-interest.

9:37-38 With this view before Him, Jesus turned to the disciples and related the proverb of the harvest. Its main point is that much work needs to be done, but not many are willing to do the work. Many are willing to be religious as long as that brings personal benefit, but few are willing to meet the needs of those who are distressed and downcast. This is not an appeal for social workers but for servants of God who will meet the real (not the perceived) needs of God's people. I am not convinced this pericope is a "soul-winning" passage; the harvest is the scattered people of God who need a shepherd. Unquestionably, the unsaved who become part of God's flock would be included, but one must see more than just soul-winning in Jesus' compassion here.

Critical to this proverb is the application. The disciples were not told to recruit or press into service any warm body to help with the harvest. They were to pray to the Lord of the harvest, asking Him to send the workers. Those harvesting are to be sent from the Owner of the field, not motivated by guilt or glamour. Perhaps one of the difficulties in motivating people to the mission fields is our dependence on human inspiration rather than divine. Sincere prayer will be more effective than professional recruiting.

HOMILETICAL SUGGESTIONS

Not only is this chapter a great demonstration of Jesus' authority and power, which identify Him with the Messiah, but it also reflects the compassion and mercy of the Savior. Emphasis should be placed on the expression of v. 2, "My *son,* your sins are forgiven," and to the willingness of Jesus to be identified with those whom the self-righteous condemned, in order that these needy ones could hear His message of mercy (9:9-13). The great contrast between Jesus and the religious people of His day was becoming more and more evident, as witnessed in His rebuke of their not understanding God's desire for mercy over religious ritual (9:13) and their accusing Him of using demonic power to cast out demons (9:34).

Above all else in the chapter, the significance of v. 36 must not be overlooked. In comparison with Ezekiel 34, this text should serve as a warning to all who would claim the identity of a shepherd (or the Latin, "pastor") of God's people. Jesus referred to Himself as the "good shepherd" (John 10), which stands in dramatic contrast to the hirelings (or self-centered and cowardly shepherds) who desert the flock when danger comes near. This danger lies not in persecution from political forces but from wolves in sheep's clothing (7:15) who spiritually ravage the flock of God. Hirelings refuse to challenge these false prophets or stand against them because it is not socially acceptable to speak against someone in public.

Paul gives a similar warning in Acts 20:28-29 to the elders of the church at Ephesus, "Be on guard for yourselves and for all the flock . . . savage wolves will come in among you, not sparing the flock." The duty of the pastor-teacher is to mature the flock through sound teaching so that they will not be "tossed here and there by waves, and carried about by every wind of doctrine, by the trickery of men, by craftiness in deceitful scheming" (Eph. 4:14). The Jews of Jesus' day heard the traditions and opinions of every rabbi, and every sect of Judaism was driven by error. The Pharisees and scribes in particular perverted the truth by portraying God as a fierce and unforgiving taskmaster.

As the people of Jesus' time were distressed and downcast because of not being tended properly by their shepherds, many today are confused about God and do not have the peace that comes from knowing God because the truth is being perverted by shepherds more concerned with their own careers and needs than caring for the flock. The New Testament church is to be led, protected, and cared for by those whom the Holy Spirit appoints (Acts 20:28-29). Elders are to shepherd the flock and protect it from false teachers, who will only confuse and scatter them (Titus 1:7-9, especially vv. 10-11). In an age having radio and television preachers too numerous to count, books by the hundreds of thousands promoting incredible error (whether intended or not), and clerics preaching sermons rather than teaching Scripture accurately, it is imperative that the shepherds of God's flock recommit themselves to "handling accurately the Word of Truth" (2 Tim. 2:15) and to put the needs (real, not perceived) of the flock above tradition, human loyalties, and self-interest.

Finally in this chapter, the last proverbial teaching of the Lord (which transitions into the next chapter) points to the need for prayer

217

if God's harvest is to be gathered. Once again, the temptation is to follow the world's methodology in achieving God's end. Certainly there are many wonderful and useful things to learn and use for God's glory but not at the expense of ceasing to depend upon Him. Praying for God to send workers will be far more effective than missions conferences, messages on service, or guilt-motivated volunteering. God alone has the right to call His servants to labor, and He must motivate them to serve. A conference, biblical message, or personal and impassioned plea may serve as God's instrument for calling laborers, but one must be careful not to depend upon the instrument rather than the One using it.

MATTHEW
CHAPTER
TEN

COMMISSIONING
OF THE TWELVE

This chapter introduces what may well be considered the beginning of the transition in Jesus' training of the Twelve. Up to this point they had been spectators and not directly involved in the miracles or teaching. Now they were being commissioned and sent out with authority to do what they had seen their Master do. It is also significant to realize that in v. 2 the term "apostle" is used for the first time. Their new authority and new responsibility were matched with a new title. Now they were more than mere disciples; they were apostles.

SUMMONING THE TWELVE, 10:1 (MARK 3:13)

10:1 Jesus' summoning His twelve men is to be viewed as a formal matter and not a casual meeting. The expression "summoned" (aorist participle of *proskaleō*) is more suggestive of an official gathering by notification. It would only be expected that these men were aware that something significant was about to take place. Morison is correct in stating, "The evangelist is not referring to *the original calling of the twelve to be special disciples.*"[1] That event had already taken place in stages; now they were being prepared for a new dimension of their calling.

It is probably best to actually begin the emphasis of the commissioning in 9:37-38. Jesus had instructed His disciples to pray to the Lord (*kurios* used in its more generic sense of "supervisor, foreman, master") of the harvest to send more workers because the harvest was so great. The analogy to a harvest was, of course, highlighting the work of evangelism and discipleship to be done. Jesus did not command them to recruit or persuade others to work in the harvest, but to pray. It is the Lord of the harvest (God the Father) who is responsible for the workers. But those who pray for the harvest may also become part of the harvesting. MacArthur points out, "Those whom Jesus had called to pray for workers, He then called to become workers."[2]

Jesus passed on authority (*exousia*), not just power (*dunamis*). This implies that not only did they possess the force necessary to remove demons and heal physical illness, but they also had the right to do so. There seems to have been no limitation to this authority, but it applied to "every kind" of disease and sickness. Hendriksen notes the major point of the commissioning: "The Twelve are truly representing their Master, for they are doing what he himself is doing and what they have been ordered to do. In the same manner Jesus himself represents the Father (John 5:19)."[3]

10:2-4 (Mark 3:16-19; Luke 6:14-16; Acts 1:13) Matthew uses the title "apostle" in 10:2 for the first time to designate a significant change in the disciples' role. The title does not appear again in the gospel but is used frequently in Luke and Acts (only once in John and twice in Mark). The word basically refers to one who is sent on a mission for another and might be translated "delegate, envoy, messenger."[4] Carson notes that they were already recognized as a distinct group and that "this commission was a stage in the training and preparation of those who, after Pentecost, would lead the earliest thrust of the fledgling church."[5] According to Luke 6:13, it was Jesus Himself who named them "apostles." Luz points out that in Luke and Acts the title "clearly differentiates between the 12 apostles . . . and the *mathētai* who in Acts represents the totality of believers."[6]

The different lists of the apostles reveal certain significant patterns. In each list Peter is always named first; Judas is always last. The lists break down into three groups with four names in each, and the same four are always grouped together. There is even grammatical suggestion in Matthew's list[7] that the groups of four were viewed in pairs, which is also consistent with Mark 6:7, where it is stated, "He summoned the twelve and began to send them out in pairs."

The names in the list are consistent except for a couple of exceptions, which is quite normal in light of the fact that these men, like so many others in that culture, were known by different names. For example, Simon is also Peter, Simon the Canaanite (gospel of Matthew and Mark) is also Simon the Zealot (Luke and Acts), Thaddeus is also Judas the son of James. This writer is officially listed as Lawrence Edwin Glasscock and often receives mail addressed to Lawrence Glasscock. However, those who know me best use the name Ed. This is not a contradiction but normal practice of using the name most familiar to the speaker or most appropriate for the occasion.

It is apparent that those listed were critical components of Jesus' program, and entire books have been written on these twelve notable men. For the purpose of this commentary only a few comments can be offered. Perhaps Thomas sums up the group most appropriately, "Their leading features of mind differ widely from each other. They seem to belong to every specific class."[8] One can only imagine the initial feelings of Matthew and Simon the Zealot,[9] two opponents filled with hate and resentment toward one another prior to their meeting Christ. Now they shared food and slept by the same fire as they traveled the roads in the small band of disciples. This is testimony to the difference Jesus can make in the lives of people when they follow Him. All of the Twelve were individuals who demonstrated weaknesses, personality quirks, and problems typical of any people. Yet, in Christ they became a team of effective witnesses for Him. Hendriksen notes: "What points up the greatness of Jesus is that he took *such men as these,* and welded them into an amazingly influential community that would prove to be not only a worthy link with Israel's past but also a solid foundation for the church's future."[10]

One of these men in particular stands out. Overreacting to the traditional exaggeration of the Roman church in attributing too much authority to Peter, perhaps Protestants have not sufficiently recognized his unique role among the Twelve. Hendriksen asserts, "He was indeed the leader of the group . . . . It is hard to overestimate Peter's meaning for the history of the early church."[11] Carson notes the use of the word "first" (*prōtos,* 10:2) to introduce Peter in the list by saying, "The word cannot mean he was the first convert (Andrew or perhaps John was) and probably does not simply mean 'first in the list,' which would be a trifling comment (cf. 1 Cor. 12:28). More likely it means *primus inter pares* ('first among equals')."[12]

Also of note are the brothers James and John, who along with Peter constituted the "inner circle of disciples." James was the first martyr among the Twelve (Acts 12:2), and John was the last of the apostles to die. These two were named "Sons of Thunder" by Jesus (Mark 3:17), and a clue as to why is seen in Luke 9:54-56.

Judas also should receive some comment. In every list he is mentioned last and as the one who betrayed Jesus. He, like the others, received authority to perform miracles (otherwise some mention would have been made that he was different). Jesus was not as yet marking him out as differing from the others. He would do so later in the Upper Room. This raises the question about the authority and power to do miracles. Is regeneration a prerequisite? Since Jesus Himself labeled Judas the "son of perdition" (John 17:12, *ho huios tēs apōleias,* literally, the "son of destruction") and stated that he "perished" and that it would have been better had he never been born than to reap the consequences of his treachery (Matt. 26:24; Mark 14:21), it is safe to assume that he was not regenerate. It is also clear that he was not a servant of God but of himself. Yet he apparently performed miracles. This, along with Matthew 7:22-23, clearly should warn the naive that claims of miracle-working are not proof that one is speaking for God.

10:5-6   This section reveals Jesus' focus on ministry exclusively to the Jews. His instructions were "Do not go in the way of the Gentiles, and . . . the Samaritans; but rather go to the lost sheep of the house of Israel." Though it may be difficult for Christians to understand this, it is critical to keep in mind that Jesus came not just to save sinners but also to fulfill the promises to Abraham, Isaac, and Jacob. He was the Jewish Messiah, the rightful King of Israel and the anointed Son of David. His mission was first "to the lost sheep of the house of Israel" (15:24), then to the rest of the world. Some commentaries wish to jump to the Great Commission of Matthew 28 to reassure their readers that Jesus was not unconcerned about the Gentiles,[13] but this ignores one of the most critical aspects of His life and ministry. He was the Jewish Messiah come to the nation of God's people. There need be no apology for this focus of His ministry. The Samaritans were despised by the Jews and are specifically named here because they were not yet to receive the work of Messiah. They were a mixed race from the time of the Assyrian captivity, when Gentiles were settled in the area between Galilee and Jerusalem as a part of the deportation and replacement policies of the conquering Assyrians. This mixed race had also established their own cult, recognizing only the Penta-teuch and building their own temple.

The instructions were clear, "Go to the lost sheep of the house of Israel" (v. 6). The term "lost sheep" references back to 9:36 and Ezekiel 34:1-6, calling up the image of helplessness and confusion on the part of the Jews under the religious tutelage of the Pharisees and scribes. Jesus had come to be the Good Shepherd of the people of God. His mission was first to the covenant people, who had been abused by their leaders. He "stood at the nexus in salvation history where as a Jew and the Son of David he came in fulfillment of his people's history as their King and Redeemer."[14] The Jews and the Jews alone were to receive this ministry until the Father directed Him otherwise.

10:7-8   The apostles' ministry would be broadly twofold: first, to preach that the kingdom of heaven was presently being introduced; second, to heal those oppressed by sickness or demons. Neither part of their commission is directly related to the church's mission in the present arena of ministry. To preach (*kērussō*) is not to be under-stood as equivalent to contemporary sermons and homiletical ex-pertise. The word simply means to "make known, proclaim, announce." They were not sermonizing but announcing that the King had come and was to rule according to God's will, not as men rule.

The message was that the kingdom of heaven "is at hand" (*ēggiken,* perfect tense of *eggizō,* "has already come near"). The per-fect tense verb implies that the kingdom was already in the world and therefore does not allow the view that "heaven's reign in the hearts and lives of men . . . was about to begin."[15] The kingdom had come with the King sent from heaven, the One who would rule so that God's will would be done on earth as it is in heaven (6:10; see discussion on 3:2). This kingdom was proclaimed to and subsequent-ly rejected by the Jews, thereby opening the redemptive program of God to the Gentiles, who also will be brought into the glories of the kingdom when Messiah returns to establish His millennial reign.

In addition to declaring that the kingdom was present, they were to emulate the miracles that He had been performing. After listing the varied works of power and authority, Jesus pointed out that they had received this power freely and they were to distribute it freely. The ministry to which the Lord called His servants was bestowed by grace and was not to be merchandised like one's personal property. Paul reminds the church, "We are not like many, peddling the Word of God" (2 Cor. 2:17). The word "peddling" (*kapēleuō*) implies merchandising something for profit and insinuates a selfish motive. Prat says, "These *charismata* are not given to them for their own personal advantage; gratuitous by nature, they are to be used gratuitously in the service for their neighbor."[16] In the instruction following, the Lord would speak to the issue of being supported in ministry.

10:9-10   The next step in the preparation for sending forth these apostles was to focus their attention on God's provision. They were not to acquire gold or any other kind of financial base for their ministry. Some commentators seem to fear this and work around to explaining why it is proper to do what the Lord had just forbidden these men to do. In other places, Scripture certainly does endorse Christ's servants' being paid for ministering, but in this case they were not to look for financial support. For this undertaking, they were to go and minister freely without being concerned for their material well-being. The verb "acquire" means to seek to add to their present goods. He was not telling them to pull off the sandals they were wearing and go barefoot, nor were they to take off their tunics and lay aside their staffs. Mark demonstrates that they were free to use what they already possessed (6:9). The point was that they were not to make provision for this trip in advance.

The phrase "for the worker is worthy of his support" (v. 10) connects His instructions with the anticipation that their needs would be met. They were to have money, clothes, and other needs because their work was honorable and valuable. The issue was, where were these material needs to come from? Now the lesson given in 6:25-34 was to be applied. The disciples of Christ were not to look for guaranteed financial security before going into a ministry; they were to look to God's provision once they were in ministry. This is indeed "faith ministry," moving out to do God's work, not having a support base, and trusting God to provide. How easily

Christian servants talk of faith, yet use this very phrase "the worker is worthy of his support" to justify contracting material substance *before* committing to ministry. This is not to endorse immature and naive irresponsibility in the name of God, but the pendulum has swung to the other extreme of not doing ministry at all without contractual promise of financial sustenance.

The principle of the worker's being worthy of support is not that the worker determines his or her worth and requires adequate compensation, but that God determines worth, and He provides support. Paul sets forth this very principle in Galatians 6:6, "Let the one who is taught the word share all good things with him who teaches." In the instruction following, Jesus suggested that the people who receive the message His disciples proclaim will supply what they need. It is God who will providentially provide through those receiving the blessings of their ministry.

10:11-13   In God's providential care, those receiving the ministry will be used to care for the needs of the servant. Those providing this care are called "worthy" (*axios*, v.11), and the disciples were instructed to inquire (*exetasate*, aorist imperative from *exetazō*, to "make a careful search for, look for") after them. The disciples were to be on the alert for those whom God would use to provide for them. In Christ's plan, each village and city would have a provision for their needs. This pattern had been demonstrated by Jesus already (Luke 8:1, 3), and it gives some insight into how Jesus maintained an itinerant ministry without being a "tentmaker." According to Luke 9:4, when the disciples made contact with these providers, they were to stay with them until the completion of their ministry. Perhaps this was to disciple those who had opened up to them, or perhaps it was just to keep the disciples from moving around too much or looking for "better" provisions. Many homes in this period would be constructed with a room on the roof for housing guests. Usually a staircase was built along an outside wall so that the guest could come and go without disturbing the household.[17] Meyer seems to believe that this mode of provision was to demonstrate "the importance of domestic efforts."[18]

Verse 12 adds that when they entered their supporting house they were to "give it [their] greeting." This probably was to express appreciation for the hospitality afforded by the owner of the house. A house represents the character and nature of its owner, therefore greeting the "house" drew embarrassing attention away from the owner yet still recognized his generosity. The house, then, symbolically represented the household. In v. 13, the greeting is referred to as a "greeting of peace." The typical greeting of the day was similar to "Peace to you," and, coming from the Lord's apostles, it was apparently granting God's peace upon the house by verbally wishing peace for the household (cf. Luke 10:5). The negative was also stated. If the household was not worthy by reason of not heeding the words of the apostles (v. 14), then the greeting was not beneficial to the owner. The greeting would "return" to the apostle, probably meaning that the apostle, upon detecting insincere hospitality, was to withdraw his presence.

10:14-15　　The apostles were to visibly and symbolically reject those who rejected their message. Whether by an individual house or the whole city, rejection of the message meant rejection of that house or city by the King of the kingdom of heaven. Verse 15 speaks of serious condemnation. Not even the wicked and perverted cities of Sodom and Gomorrah would be judged as severely as the city that rejected the Messiah's messengers. The imagery of shaking dust off one's feet emphasized that such defilement was so associated with that place that even the dust was contaminated. It was unacceptable for the servant of the Christ to tolerate any speck of disbelief.

The terrible offense of Sodom and Gomorrah in the eyes of God is well documented in Scripture (Gen. 18:23–19:28), yet the immorality and perversion of the flesh was not to be as severely judged as unwillingness to hear the message of the kingdom. Perhaps part of the reasoning is explained in Luke 12:48: "From everyone who has been given much shall much be required." Israel had the privilege of direct messianic revelation; not so the pagan cities of Sodom and Gomorrah.

10:16　　To relate the dangers involved in being His apostles, Jesus used four creatures of varying natures to parallel their situation. They were sheep: without tools for defense or aggression, easily confused, and not powerful or swift. They would be going into the territory of a pack of wolves: violent, clever, aggressive, and skilled at stalking and killing. They must become shrewd like the serpent: quiet, subtle, difficult to trap, and clever (Gen. 3:1). However, this cleverness/ shrewdness was not to be used to harm others, but only to avoid the destruction of the wolves. Thus the analogy of doves, harmless and symbols of good tidings.

To be shrewd or crafty is not the same as being deceptive. The warning is against being naive and allowing the wolves to destroy them. Christians are not to be unintelligent about the world around them and assume that everyone will appreciate their message or their values. Shrewdness implies not being caught off guard and is demonstrated by Jesus in John 2:24-25, "On His part [He] was not entrusting Himself to them, for He knew all men. . . . He Himself knew what was in man." This is not to be perceived as evidence of divine attribute. Scripture has borne witness to the depravity and treachery of fallen man, and any Spirit-filled believer should be wise enough to know the potential wickedness of those who oppose God's truth.

10:17-18   Jesus then moved from analogy to concrete warning. The wolves were men who would persecute the apostles. He made two predictions about the enemies of the message they were taking to Israel: first, "they will deliver you up to the courts"; second, "and will scourge you in their synagogues." The courts (*sunedria*) were the local councils, which ruled everyday Jewish life. The highest of these was the Sanhedrin, the supreme court of the Jews. The warning of Jesus was that the public proclamation of their message would not be well received among the villages and cities of Israel.

Scourging is a form of flogging. Administered as judgment for crimes in Israel, it was a painful and brutal way of inflicting punishment and could lead to death. The scourge used was sometimes a rod, but the Romans used a whip having leather thongs imbedded with bone or jagged metal. In the Law, an offender could be beaten with thirty-nine lashes but not with forty, because that could be fatal (cf. 2 Cor. 11:24). Jesus was scourged by the Romans, possibly in the hope that the brutality and horrific damage done by the lashes would keep the Jews from demanding His death (Matt. 27:23-26; Mark 15:14-15; John 19:1). Jesus' disciples should have had no misconceptions concerning the negative environment into which they were being sent. This solemn warning would not be accepted today in light of the contemporary view of motivational speeches.

Not only would they be judged and punished in the synagogues but in the secular world as well. The disciples would become witnesses before governors and kings of both Israel and the

Gentiles. It should be noted that their persecution was to be a testimony to these officials. Paul, perhaps better than any other apostle, fulfilled this word, though there is sufficient evidence that Peter and others also experienced this kind of high-level witnessing.

Critical to understanding what was being said is the phrase "for My sake" (*beneken emou*), or, more literally, "because of Me." The apostles would not be convicted of crimes against society such as murder or stealing but for identifying themselves with the Person and work of Jesus. Tasker translates this as "because you are loyal to Me."[19] This passage should not be used to excuse breaking the laws of society, even for good purposes. The persecution would be for doing what Christ Himself had been doing, preaching the kingdom, healing, and casting out demons. None of these things were against the law, Jewish or Roman. The ministry of Christ's disciples was not correcting social evil, or "protecting the innocent," or trying to change immoral laws. They, like their Lord, were to heal the sick and teach that Jesus was the Messiah, a positive, not negative, witness to Christ. This alone would make them enemies to the religious perverts of their world.

10:19-20   Jesus reassured the apostles that the defense of their ministry would not be mere human argument but divinely given testimony. Barnes offers helpful insight into the comfort these words must have given the apostles:

> Poor, and ignorant, and obscure fishermen would naturally be solicitous what they should say before the great men of the earth. Eastern people regarded kings as raised far above common mortals—as approaching to divinity. How consoling, then, the assurance that God would aid them and speak within them.[20]

It should be noted that not all of these men were fishermen, but governors and kings were considered so powerful that any average person would have been totally overwhelmed with being brought before them. Jesus would not depend on the cleverness of human intellect, even of His apostles, to give witness; it would be divinely provided.

10:21-22   The persecution was not going to be confined to mistreatment by strangers and officials. Jesus continued His commissioning speech by pointing out that ministry for Him would make them enemies in their own homes. Brother would be against brother, father against children, and children against parents. This is personal pain for anyone but particularly in cultures such as that of the Jews, who based so much of their personal worth on their heritage and family status. Jesus was not creating a positive image of ministry for these men. The contemporary church, which is frequently told that becoming a Christian will solve one's problems and that people will respect a believer, needs to hear this message. The Lord would soon be even more specific (vv. 34-36) and boldly state, "Do not think that I came to bring peace on the earth; I did not come to bring peace, but a sword." He then pointed out that the conflict He brings is even within families. This passage will be considered later, but the point is clear: the apostles would be rejected and persecuted even in their closest relationships.

"Hated by all" is a phrase that must be accepted by those who follow the One who was hated. The hatred is not to be based upon one's rudeness or other character flaws but "on account of My name." "Name" (*onoma*) is that which represents a person, his nature, authority, or position. It is not just an appellation such as "George" or "Helen" but, rather, a depiction of what the person stands for. To be hated for the name of Jesus meant that His followers would be hated for His rejection of human self-righteousness and for His commitment to the absolute truth of God's Word. Peter, one of the men hearing this frightening message, not only experienced the reality of it but passed on the word to those who were also believers (1 Peter 4:12-16).

The final statement of this verse, "it is the one who has endured to the end who will be saved," is difficult. What is meant by "endure" and "saved" is critical. What "end" is proposed by the Lord here and its connection with being "saved" is also strategic. The context is certainly one of persecution, thus the "enduring" (*hupomenō*) is the enduring or standing firm for the name of Christ in the midst of persecution. And the idea is certainly more than simply staying alive but is, rather, remaining in one's place, persevering in faith in the midst of persecution. This perseverance is until the "end" (*telos*), the completion of some period of time or of some event. It seems best to understand this as the work of preaching Christ, probably beyond the scope of the disciples' immediate mission, considering the comments of v. 18, which might imply the whole age of the church. Of course, the life span of individuals would count as their part of the program, and they are to endure until their work is complete.

One of the most critical features of this comment is that it does not say "one who works to the end" or "doesn't sin until the end." It is referencing standing up in times of persecution. One who perseveres until the end, at his death or at the end of the program, is one who will be saved (future passive verb of *sōzō*). It is unlikely that this refers to being saved out of persecution but to ultimate salvation. The issue is not one's sinlessness or religious busyness but perseverance in persecution. This was not presented to the disciples as a condition for salvation but as a promise that even death and persecution would not affect their ultimate deliverance. Their enemies could only kill the body, but the one who perseveres can know that they cannot do anything beyond that. Calvin explains:

> This single promise ought sufficiently to support the minds of the godly, though the whole world should rise against them; for they are assured that the result will be prosperous and happy. If those who fight under earthly commanders, and are uncertain as to the issue of the battle, are carried forward even to death by steadiness of purpose, shall those who are certain of victory hesitate to abide by the cause of Christ to the very last?[21]

Thus, rather than a qualification for salvation or a burden to bear up under, it is a wonderful promise of victory.

Persevering is not the same as never failing. It is getting back up when one stumbles, continuing the course of life serving Christ even though sin or fear or doubt may occasionally cause the servant to falter. Sin can be confessed and, therefore, not only be forgiven but cleansed out of one's life and record (1 John 1:9). Even verbally denying Jesus at some point is not evidence that one has not persevered and thus is unsaved. Peter is certainly an example of failing and being restored for ministry (John 18:25-27; 21:3, 15-19). Indeed, Scripture lays upon every Christian the burden of restoring a sinning brother (Gal. 6:1), not pronouncing him unworthy of salvation. The exhortation here is to persevere, not so as to be saved but because salvation is sure and the victory is already won.

10:23   Persecution is not to be viewed as the call to martyrdom.

It is not always cowardly to flee molestation, and the Lord was here stating that it may well be His will for His servant to flee. Paul assuredly is an example of this in the book of Acts (13:50-51; 14:5-7; etc.). There was much work to be done in many cities, and the implication was that there was no need (apart from assurance from the Lord to do so) to stay in an environment where the gospel was not being received and where stubborn, rebellious people were resisting Christ's messengers.

The concluding remark of v. 23 is most difficult, "You shall not finish going through the cities of Israel, until the Son of Man comes." Because the term "Son of Man" in relation to coming is most naturally associated with the Second Advent of Christ, it seems best to understand the comment to relate to His return at the end of the church age. The point was that the servants of Christ will not touch all the cities of Israel until He returns. Yet, to our understanding it would appear that all the cities have been visited.

The flow of thought in the discourse had been a warning to His newly appointed apostles that their message might be rejected and that they were to dust off their feet and move on. In vv. 16-22, the warnings change to a broader arena of ministry and persecution. Scripture offers no evidence that the apostles faced any serious opposition on this journey, and certainly none were brought before kings and governors. Therefore Christ's comments in v. 18 are to be understood in terms of future ministry experiences. Some misrepresent the dispensationalists as trying to "detach" v. 23 from its context,[22] when, in reality, their view is the most consistent understanding of the context. The issue is not persecution during the Tribulation period but during the church age. It is also important to remember that the Son of Man had already come and was indeed at work in Israel at that time. Therefore this "coming" had to refer to some event different from that present earthly work. Some, however, take this to mean that Jesus was only promising to join the apostles on their mission before they completed their course. The language of the text and the flow of thought presented does not endorse such a simplistic explanation. It appears that this statement referred to the continuing ministry of evangelism among the Jews and particularly to evangelism in Israel, which was to continue until the Son of Man returns.

10:24-25   Christ summarized His comments about persecution and rejection with a proverbial assertion, "A disciple is not above his teacher, nor a slave above his master." The impact of this statement is difficult to accept in one's daily life. Christ was stating a rule of ministry that may make His servants nervous. The servant should not expect to be treated any better than the master, and Scripture is frighteningly clear as to the treatment our Lord received.

Verse 25 completes the thought by pointing out that whatever reception and treatment the master and teacher received is what the followers will receive. Jesus had just been associated with Beelzebul (see on 9:34 and 12:24-26), and thus the illustration was based upon a recent experience, which should have made a profound impression upon His disciples who had witnessed it. Carson points out the peculiarly offensive nature of Jesus' being called Beelzebul: "Thus the real head of the house, Jesus, who heads the household of God, is being willfully confused with the head of the house of demons. The charge is shockingly vile—the Messiah himself rejected as Satan! If so, why should his disciples expect less?"[23] These verses should challenge any who claim to be serving Christ. What treatment do we expect? Do we hesitate to stand as firmly as Christ because we fear rejection and persecution? Do we have the right to compromise and seek friendship with the world or with religious leaders to avoid being treated as Jesus was treated?

10:26   Jesus' conclusion to His warnings may seem a little inappropriate, "Therefore do not fear them." It is, of course, only natural to fear those who will scourge and kill you. But Jesus was preparing His followers for those hard times by leading them to focus on the ultimate outcome. If one keeps so focused, then fear (as here intended) can be eliminated. The fear discussed here is presented comparatively in light of God's ultimate authority.

The reason for the prohibition (the prohibitive subjunctive mood used is somewhat similar to the imperative force)[24] against fear was stated in the explanatory clause that followed, "for [*gar*] there is nothing covered that will not be revealed." Having told them of the rejection, hate, and violence that awaited His followers, He then exhorted them not to let those facts generate fear. Part of the comfort was that, in the final revelation of all things, they would be the victors. What they could not see immediately, because it would be hidden by the world's resistance to their message, would eventually be unveiled. Their courage and faithfulness to God would be ultimately brought to light. Hendriksen chooses to approach this revealing from the negative, "who these enemies are, what they have done,"[25] but probably it was intended to encourage those who would at times feel deserted and terribly alone. Ryle is correct in his assessment:

> They must be content in this present world to be misunderstood, misrepresented, vilified, slandered, and abused. They must not cease to work because their motives are mistaken, and their characters fiercely assailed. They must remember continually that all will be set right at the last day.[26]

Judgment was coming, and those faithful to Christ would be recognized, the truth would be known, and they would be justified before all those who had slandered and persecuted them.

10:27 Verse 27, therefore, is an exhortation to fulfill their mission. Jesus would privately and personally teach His followers. His mission was to plant the seed, which would grow into the worldwide proclamation of the gospel of God's redemptive program. That program was beginning now, in that remote part of the world, not with fanfare and apparent success but with a presentation to the nation of their Messiah and the nation's subsequent violent rejection. The impact of their work would not be known until the completion of the redemptive work, when the truth of the efficacious work of Christ will be fully revealed. They were to openly proclaim that which their Lord was privately teaching them. At this point, they themselves did not even understand the full significance of their message. The flat roofs of the ancient housetops made excellent platforms from which to speak to large crowds.

10:28 More specific instruction regarding their not fearing is given in v. 28. In this case, Jesus is recorded as using the present imperative (*phobeisthe*) with the negative particle (*mē*), which may indicate His awareness of the fear growing within them. In the world's thinking, killing the body is the most horrible eventuality, yet this is presented here as not the ultimate object for fear. It is the soul (*psuchē*) that is the essence of life, not the body (*sōma*). Therefore fear should be directed only to the One who has authority and power over both—God.

The debates over trichotomy and dichotomy are much too complex to review here. This writer is convinced of dichotomy, that is, that the human creature is composed of two primary components: material and immaterial. The immaterial part of a human is divided into soul, spirit, heart, mind (not to be confused with brain), and other aspects of functional being. The term "soul" (*psuchē*) is probably the most comprehensive in representing human essence,[27] or simply "life" or "person." This is the conscious being who will spend eternity in the loving presence of God or in darkness and torment away from God. The One who holds such power is the One to be feared. This verse is not in any sense a warning about Jesus' followers losing salvation. The point is God's absolute power and authority compared to limited human authorities, which can do no worse than kill the machine that houses the life force within.

The phrase "destroy both . . . in hell [*apolesai en geennō*]" needs some discussion. To destroy (*apollumi*) does not imply annihilation of the soul but primarily to "bring to ruin" or "put to death" (12:14; 27:20). But here not only is the body killed but the soul (*psuchē*) as well. Body and soul are killed "in hell," not annihilated. Meyer offers a good understanding: "to consign body and soul, at the day of judgment, to everlasting destruction in Gehenna."[28] Human ability to destroy is limited only to the body, but God's power and authority give Him the ability to go beyond that to the eternal destruction of both in Gehenna. In Luke, the warning is "Fear the One who after He has killed has authority [*exousian*] to cast into hell (*embalein eis tēn geennan;* 12:5)." The point again is that the one having power to kill the body is not the one to fear, but fear should be shown the One with the greater authority. The implication is not that one should live in fear of going to hell but that those who are Christ's servants have no need to fear mere men, whose ability is limited only to the physical realm. God's authority and power are greater. Therefore, they were to be courageous in completing their commission.

Gehenna is not to be confused with hades. Gehenna is a fiery abyss, symbolic of eternal punishment (Matt. 23:15, 33; 25:41, 46). Perhaps the most vivid and frightening comment about Gehenna is found in Mark 9:43-48, where it is repeatedly described as "unquenchable fire." It is best to equate Gehenna with the "lake of fire" in Revelation 19:20; 20:10-14. Hades (*hadēs*), on the other hand, is a place of dead souls. In the Septuagint it represents the word sheol, which at times referred only to the grave and at others to a place of conscious life but separate from the living. Hades/sheol contained the good and the wicked but in different sections. One portion was a place of comfort and blessing until final reward (sometimes referred to as "Abraham's bosom") and the other portion a place of temporary torment until the final judgment and the lake of fire (cf. Luke 16:19-31; Rev. 20:14).[29]

10:29-31   Christ now offered another reason for comfort. Not only is God more powerful and authoritative than those who can only kill the body, but He cares for those who serve Christ. Sparrows held little value in the marketplace and were largely unnoticed by people busy with daily life. Yet the Father takes note when each one dies. God is concerned with and actively involved with every part of His creation. This truth should motivate Christians to respect the life God has created and also draw comfort from the fact that if God is concerned with these small creatures, how much more He cares for the creatures made in His own image, especially those who are His children. His individual care and attention is further emphasized by v. 30, "the very hairs of your head are all numbered."

10:32-33   The rather strong statement made in vv. 32-33 should not be taken out of the context of this statement concerning God's care. The word "therefore" (*oun*) links this verse to the preceding one with the idea of an application. The idea of "confess" here is to acknowledge and speak truthfully about Jesus, knowing that God cares for us and not fearing those who can only kill the body. In this context, the point was that they were to declare the message to the cities of Israel without fear. This is the "confession" they were to proclaim.

The curious thing is that the Greek text does not simply say "confess Me before men" but confess "in/by Me [*en emoi*] before men." Hendriksen sees the preposition (*en*) as indication of Aramaic influence.[30] Meyer, on the other hand, assumes that "the personal object of confession is conceived of as the one to *whom* the confession cleaves."[31] In other words, the preposition is to mark the object that is being confessed. This explanation seems strained, and Meyer was concerned with not allowing a Hebraism at this point. Since Jesus most probably spoke Aramaic as His daily language, Hendriksen's explanation seems better. To take it otherwise, "confess by Me" implies that the confession was coming from Jesus Himself. This may be theologically correct, but then the parallel phrase that follows would read, "I will also confess *by him* before My Father," which would be nonsense.

Jesus was not speaking of when He returns to heaven[32] but of His intercessory ministry, which was already in effect (Luke 22:31-32). To confess Jesus and His message of the kingdom (10:7-27) meant that they were not to compromise or fail to proclaim Christ as the King of Israel. He was praying on behalf of their work, but if they failed to carry out their task, He would not intercede on their behalf. There is nothing in the context to imply a salvific consequence. This is not a warning that if one fails to give public testimony to his faith in Christ, then Jesus will not claim him before the Father, and therefore he is not saved. Such a view is totally inconsistent with the rest of Scripture and has no support from the context. Neither has the issue "acknowledge him as Lord of one's life,"[33] since no such theme is in the context. The particular issue is fulfilling their commission to proclaim the kingdom to the villages of Israel.

Of course, the same would apply to disciples today. Failure to fulfill Christ's commission results in the Lord's unwillingness to intercede for His servants in their work. The warning did not imply loss of salvation but certainly loss of the peace and victory that would have been theirs. Peter failed to confess Jesus, his failure brought misery and defeat, yet eventually he was restored and used by the Lord in unimaginable ways. Verse 33 is the antithesis of confessing and simply reemphasizes the necessity for faithfulness in doing one's duty.

10:34   What a contrast between the idealized figure of Jesus as the loving, soft-spoken peacemaker of the world and His own description of Himself. He did not come to bring peace but "a sword." Many have trouble accepting the fact that Jesus came not to bring peace to this world, and those whose hope lies in this world are alarmed to think of such a thing. The peace that Christ brought is between individual sinners and the holy God of the universe. The apostles were being sent into enemy territory, and there would be resistance.

Peacemakers are to deliver the message of individual peace with God (such as Rom. 5:1), but making peace with the world is not the aim or goal of Christ. The message of the angels in Luke 2:14 is misunderstood because of older mistranslations and a favorite Christmas hymn based on that older translation. The literal announcement is more accurately translated in the NASB: "on earth peace among men with whom He is pleased." The "sword" was symbolic of the conflict and even violence that would characterize the hostility between Christ's kingdom and the world's kingdom.

10:35-36   The explanatory clause (introduced by *gar*) in vv. 35-36 defines the extent of the hostility. Jesus came to create animosity between family members. This, too, is unpleasant and unacceptable to many, but it is His own statement. The servant of Christ is going to find that even his own family members will oppose Christ and his commitment to Him.

The hostility is not to flow out of personal rebellion or hateful, self-righteous attitudes, but from the Person of Christ directly. He may divide families, but misconduct on the part of those who claim His name is not an excuse for strife. Scripture, both Old and New Testaments, teaches that one is to honor his father and mother, but Christ will introduce tension between parents and their children. The critical truth behind this is explained in the following verses, primarily in v. 37.

10:37   One must choose loyalty to family or loyalty to Jesus. To "love" is not the more specific word *agapaō* but *phileō*, which emphasizes more the emotive, affectionate, attitude. It would be easier to understand Christ's using *agapaō*, since that word is often used of dedication to someone. Jesus was implying that even one's affection is to be first given to Him. Carson points out that this is dedication even above what the rabbis demanded. He concludes, "The saying is either that of the Messiah or of a maniac."[34] Jesus gave Himself for His followers without limitation; for one to be worthy of Him, to come up to His standard, He demands absolute priority. This is not a condition for salvation but dramatically emphasizes the measure of His commitment to His own.

10:38   This is perhaps one of the most abused verses in the New Testament. Every petty ailment, every disappointment, and every frustration of life is considered a cross to bear. Those who so cheaply apply this verse demonstrate their failure to understand the horror of the cross. Crosses were common forms of execution used by the Romans. Roman territories were littered with them and the dead bodies of criminals who dared to disobey the law, and Israel was no exception. Gundry is correct in associating crucifixion with the modern electric chair or gas chamber,[35] except that death by crucifixion took days and was particularly cruel and horrifying. The concept of taking one's cross is repeated by Paul, who uses the term "crucified with Christ" to describe it (Gal. 2:20). The issue is not suffering some unpleasant experience but dying to self. The cross was an instrument of death. Dying to self is the qualification for being "worthy" of Christ. He died for us; to match His standard is to die for Him. One's own choices, comforts, goals, plans, relationships, and so on are to be surrendered for Him.

10:39   Verse 38 is further explained in v. 39. To find one's life— that is, its true worth—is to lose it for Christ. To take up one's cross is to die to self—thus, one's life is lost. The word "life" here is *psuchē* ("soul"), the very essence of one's being. The servant of Christ is to turn loose the right to live as he/she determines and live for Jesus. The great mystery and surprise is that when one turns loose of his own life, he finds true life in Christ. Again, the apostle Paul explains this in Colossians 3:1-4. This material life, with all of its illusions of success and happiness, is to be sacrificed for the spiritual life that will end in the glory of Christ's kingdom, which He chooses to share with His faithful servants.

10:40-41   Christ reminded the apostles that their ministry was not to represent themselves but Him. They were to stand in Christ's place, and to receive them—and, therefore, their message—was to receive Jesus Himself. They were agents of the Messiah. Beyond even that, those receiving the apostles—and thus also Christ—were accepting God the Father as well ("Him who sent Me"). The work of the Son and the Father was so bound with that of the apostles that reception of them was the same as accepting God and His Messiah.

The "prophet's reward" (v. 41) apparently refers to the blessing of the One who sent the prophet. There may be some allusion to 1 Kings 17:8-24 as illustrating the benefit of openly receiving God's prophet. This would complement the remarks in 10:11-15, where Jesus instructs His apostles to bless the houses that receive them. The phrase "in the name of a prophet" refers to the prophet's calling and commissioning to service. His "name" is the position or authority bestowed upon him. One who receives the messenger as such (as one sent from God) will be blessed through the prophet as reward. The parallel expression "a righteous man" is not a second category but is repetitious analogy to emphasize that anyone sent from God carries blessings to those who receive him because he is from God.

10:42 The closing verse enforces what has just been stated in vv. 40-41. The "little ones" must be referring to His servants. These little ones (*tōn mikrōn*) are referred to in endearing terms because they are precious to Christ. But also the term "little" may imply that the world would look upon them as insignificant. Barnes offers his understanding of this phrase: "They are called *little* ones to denote their want of wealth, rank, learning, and whatever the world calls *great.*"[36] Yet, if one recognizes them as disciples and treats them even to a refreshing gift of cold water, it will be remembered and rewarded. Jesus had already told them of their value to the Father (10:29-31), and God's concern is highlighted by rewarding those who care for their needs. This concluded His commissioning speech and offered His apostles a clear, though perhaps discouraging, perception of what to expect on their journey.

HOMILETICAL SUGGESTIONS

The commissioning of the Twelve was a significant event in the ministry of the Lord. These men were unique in that they were the foundation for the universal ministry known as the church (Eph. 2:20) and the perpetuation of Christ's work would rest upon their shoulders. The event marked them as His special representatives and demonstrated that His power and authority would be resident in them. However, the final discourse with these same men reveals that they would not be left to carry on His work in their own power. The Helper, the Holy Spirit, would be sent to replace Jesus and be the director of the church (John 14-17).

In studying the individuals whom Jesus chose to be His apostles, one is impressed with the variety of men called to His service. One of the most critical lessons to be learned from this record is that Christ does not have a mold by which all Christians are shaped. As Joseph was used by God in Egypt, David—a very different personality—was used by God in Israel. Paul was aggressive and austere. Barnabas was patient, by nature an encourager. Yet Jesus used them both. Peter was different from John, Matthew the opposite of Simon. Some were quiet, others outspoken. The point is that there is no one type of Christian. All believers need not have the same tastes, styles, personalities, or methods. Jesus used all kinds. He delights in the varied human personalities He created. As Jesus used that variety, so should those in Christian ministry. Instead of trying to make everyone fit one mold, let the Spirit use individuals as He chooses.

A message the Gentile church needs to hear is that Jesus' ministry and the first commissioned journey of the apostles was focused upon the Jews. Jesus was the Messiah of Israel, King and Son of David. His kingdom work is not to be ignored or played down as though it were insignificant. His faithfulness to His covenant with Abraham, Isaac, and Jacob and the sub-covenant with David give assurance that He will be faithful to the promises made to the church as well. If we understate the Jewish ministry of Jesus, we de-emphasize His faithfulness and thereby weaken the sureness of the promises to us as well. Paul warns the Gentiles not to be arrogant toward the Jews. We are only grafted into their program, and His faithfulness to His people Israel has preserved a remnant that will yet receive their King (Rom. 9-11).

One of the most critical lessons from this chapter is that serving Christ will bring persecution and danger. In an age where people are coaxed into ministry with allusions to successfully reaching the "seekers," the words of Jesus must be confusing. Those who are unprepared to suffer rejection, perhaps even persecution, will stumble when reality confronts them. The image of Jesus as a sweet, nonconfrontational friend of the world does not fit with His statement that He did not come to bring peace but conflict. Jesus' servants must be willing to take up their cross (death to self) and follow Him, even if it means being despised by members of one's own family. What gives comfort in ministry is not popularity or recognition by the unsaved but knowing that they can only kill the body. The peace that the servant of Christ has comes in knowing that the God who has power and authority over both body and soul cares for His own and will compensate their sufferings.

This commissioning is also a call to all who would serve Christ. Take up your cross, follow Jesus, and do not expect better treatment than He received (vv. 24-25). Security will not come from human sources but from God, who sent His Son, who now sends us. If we are received in ministry, it is in the name of Christ. If we are rejected, it is the same. We serve Christ, not self.

240

MATTHEW
CHAPTER
ELEVEN

JESUS CONTINUES
HIS ITINERANT MINISTRY

Following the commissioning and sending out of His twelve apostles, Jesus Himself began a preaching trip. Whether the Twelve had already gone and returned is not stated; but in what some assume to be the parallel passage (Luke 7:18-28), the disciples seem to have been present (Luke 7:11). However, Luke's account may not be inserted chronologically as a counterpart and does not necessarily require the presence of the disciples. While He was on this journey, the imprisoned John the Baptist sent messengers to question Jesus as to His identity. Jesus responded by pointing to His miracles as proof that He was indeed the "Expected One." This query from John's disciples became the platform for Jesus to re-mind the Jews who John was and to introduce the great mystery of John's identity as Elijah in relation to the kingdom offer. Following this explanation, Jesus began to condemn that generation and the cities of Israel for rejecting both John's message and their Messiah. He concluded with an invitation to come for rest from their spiritual struggles, which only He could provide.

JOHN THE BAPTIST'S QUESTION, 11:1-14

11:1   It is possible that the event of v. 1 is only a transition statement to summarize the events between the sending of the apostles and their return. Then in v. 2 the narrative resumes, following their reunion with the Lord. In this case, v. 1 tells us that while Jesus was waiting for the apostles to return from their mission trip, He Himself visited cities for teaching and preaching.

The cities were referred to as "their" cities, not meaning the Twelve's but the cities of the Galileans where Jesus was ministering already. Jesus was "teaching" (*didaskō*), which is to "explain" and "give instruction" (probably about the Scripture concerning Himself), and "preaching" (*kērussō*), which is "proclaiming" or "announcing" (that the kingdom was at hand, 10:7). Such preaching was not the moralizing or sermonizing of our culture but was simply announcing, proclaiming, some event, as did the ancient town criers, who called out current news items. Jesus offered both detailed exegesis of the Old Testament and announcement of the news of the kingdom that had come.

11:2-3 (Luke 7:18-35)   John was already in prison, and here again Matthew offers no explanation for the imprisonment, though previously recording the arrest (4:12) and revealing the details later (14:3-12). Mark, on the other hand, immediately gives details surrounding both John's arrest and his death (Mark 6:16-29). Josephus informs us that John was held in the prison and killed at the castle of Macherus.[1] From his cell, John heard reports of Jesus' works (probably by regular visits from his disciples), and either the reports left him somewhat unsure as to Jesus' actions, or he was aware of his impending death and wanted this confirmation for the benefit of his disciples. John sent two of his disciples (Luke 7:19) with a straightforward question, because the situation was becoming crucial for his own life and the lives of his followers.

In v. 3, the question is simply, "Are you the Expected One?" A more literal translation of the initial question is, "Are You the Coming One [*ho erchomenos*]?" This could be no One other than the Messiah who had been promised to Israel, the Son of David who would sit on the throne, the King of the kingdom that John had announced to be at hand.

The question was John's, and there is no indication that it was really the disciples of John who wanted to know. Apparently John had been incarcerated for a lengthy period and knew death was drawing near. His questioning of Jesus at this point did not decrease his greatness or his faithfulness. The kingdom he had proclaimed did not appear to be growing stronger, nor was there any word that the Messiah was about to march against Herod or overthrow the Romans. From the contemporary perspective, it is clear that Jesus did not plan to overthrow the earthly kingdom to establish the heavenly—but from John's perspective and the anticipation of biblical Judaism, an overthrow was expected. The Messiah was a king, and He was to rule Israel on David's throne. That Messiah would come in like Judas Maccabee and drive out the foreign oppressors was assumed. Therefore John wondered why he was still imprisoned when the King was in the land. Carson's comments are helpful:

> Thematically the three chapters (11-13) are held together by the rising tide of disappointment in and opposition to the kingdom of God that was resulting from Jesus' ministry. He was not turning out to be the kind of Messiah the people had expected. Even John the Baptist had doubts (vv. 2-19), and the Galilean cities that were sites of most of Jesus' miracles hardened themselves in unbelief (vv. 20-24).[2]

John's concern may have arisen because of one of two possibilities: (1) a misunderstanding of Jesus, thus making the incorrect assumption that He was the Messiah; or (2) the erroneous concept that another person would complete Jesus' work. Edersheim seems convinced, however, that the myth of two Messiahs is post-Christian.[3] It is best to assume that John was discouraged and needing reassurance. The humanity of the characters of Scripture should never be spiritualized away, nor should their frailties be ignored. The fact that God uses men even in their weaknesses should encourage each one who is aware of his own weaknesses that God can still use him.

11:4-6 Jesus' response was not a simple straightforward reply but an appeal to let His power and authority answer the question. John had heard the testimonies concerning Jesus' powerful works but wanted confirmation that the proclaimed kingdom had indeed come. Jesus used the present tense verbs ("hearing," *akouete,* and "seeing," *blepete*) in instructing the disciples of John. They were to report what they saw and also what they heard Him teaching. Apparently they had been watching Jesus for some time (cf. 9:10, 14; Luke 7:12-18). It is safe to assume that they had witnessed His miracles, and then Jesus associated the miracles with the Old Testament prophecies.

Jesus listed His miracles: healing the lepers, the blind, the lame, and the deaf, and even raising the dead. He then added that the poor had the gospel preached to them. This was not a reference to the economically deprived—He ministered to the tax collectors and centurion as well—but to the poor in spirit (5:3). His reference connected His work with the prophet Isaiah, who was a primary source for messianic anticipation. Isaiah presented not only the blessings of Messiah referred to here (Isa. 35:5-6; 61:1-2) but also proclaimed the rejection and suffering of the Messiah (Isa. 53:1-12). It is typical of the New Testament's use of the Old not to quote a passage directly but to reference or make allusion instead, so as to bring to mind the whole message of the prophet. Thus, Jesus associated His work with the message of Isaiah, which presents the suffering ministry of Messiah as well as His glorious kingdom. This would give John an understanding of *why* Jesus was not yet establishing His kingdom and offered far more comfort than if Jesus had just simply told John's disciples to go back and say, "Yes, I am the Coming One."

Jesus then added another element to the message for John, "Whoever should not be made to stumble by Me is blessed [v. 6]."[4] For the significance of "blessed" (*makarios*), see 5:3-11. The most significant question here is, what did Jesus mean by "made to stumble [aorist passive of *skandalizō*] "by Me" (*en emoi*)? The idea of stumbling comes from the concept of ensnaring an animal by means of a trap.[5] From there the New Testament developed the meanings of "cause to be caught or fall"; "cause to sin or give offense to"; or "make angry."[6] Jesus was reminding John not to be trapped by unjustified assumptions about Messiah. He was not to be caused to "stumble" (here to lose his blessedness by doubting) because of the false expectations generated by the rabbinical teachings and popular legends of the coming King. Rejection and suffering were part of Messiah's work, and John should not be discouraged by the lack of political movement or by the skeptics who criticized Jesus.

MacArthur understands this closing parabolic challenge thus: "Jesus' closing beatitude was primarily for the sake of John. . . . It was a gentle warning, a tender rebuke. 'Don't doubt,' He said to

John, 'if you want to have the blessing of My joy and peace.'"[7] Carson also makes a good observation: "It is therefore an implicit challenge to reexamine one's presuppositions about what the Messiah should be and do in light of Jesus and his fulfillment of Scripture and to bring one's understanding and faith into line with him."[8] Truly this same warning applies to contemporary Christianity, where Jesus has often been misrepresented and many false assumptions have led to discouragement and stumbling.

DISCOURSE ON JOHN THE BAPTIST, 7-15

11:7-8 Jesus then turned to the people who had witnessed His response to the disciples of John. His questions focused upon their expectations for a prophet. The reference to the wilderness must certainly refer to John's early ministry, when people were curious and amazed at the appearance of this dynamic figure preaching repentance and the kingdom (3:1-6). What did they go to see?

The question was rhetorical, to make a point, not to procure an answer. A "reed shaken by the wind" is a metaphoric way of saying a fickle person who is easily swayed by opinion. Would such a sight have had the impact of a strong prophetic voice such as John? Of course not. Israel was filled with rabbis quoting other rabbis and people shifting from view to view. John had been dogmatic about his message. There was no compromise or uncertainty. Even when approached by the pious religious leaders of the day, he was unbending and unafraid to stand firm in his demand for repentance (3:7-10). In this context it would appear the issue was that John was not vacillating by his seeking confirmation of Jesus' messianic claims. John was not doubting the message he preached but was questioning whether or not he had misunderstood Jesus' being the Messiah.

He continued with another rhetorical question (v. 8), which focused upon John's unique dress. The camel hair robe (3:4) was rugged and not appealing to the eye. It was certainly not the beautiful, comfortable, and expensive garment worn by one in the royal entourage. Though John had come to announce the arrival of Israel's King, the kingdom was not yet instituted. John's garments were appropriate for a prophet. The religious leaders certainly loved their impressive dress, and the wealthy displayed their affluence by glorious robes, but John was not participating in the riches of the present kingdom. His attire, as well as his message, communicated that the announced kingdom was not of this earth.

11:9-10　　The next rhetorical question changed the emphasis to their motive for seeking out John, "Why did you go out?" (more literally, "What did you go out to see? A prophet?"). What drove the Israelites out of their villages and cities to the wilderness area of the Jordan? What were they looking for? Certainly not more of the same religious jargon they had been hearing from the Pharisees, Sadducees, and rabbis. Jesus affirmed that they went out because they had heard that John was a true prophet of God.

Beyond what they were anticipating, however, John was more than just a prophet. He cited Malachi 3:1, to indicate that John was not only a prophet but the very one who would announce the coming of the Messiah (v. 10). More significant is the context of Malachi, which clearly names Yahweh as the One speaking. "Prepare your way before You" distinctly identifies Jesus as Yahweh of the Old Testament. Thus, John's mission took on more critical significance; he was the one signaling the coming of the Day of Yahweh. This helps one understand the urgency of John's message to repent because the kingdom of heaven was at hand.

11:11　　Jesus' praise of John the Baptist was extraordinary in that in doing so He ranked human beings and stated that John was the greatest. Had He said "born of men," there would be little cause for interest; but by saying "born of women," Jesus Himself would be included. However, Jesus used this phrase as a metaphor for mere humanity, which excluded Himself since He is the eternal Logos (John 1:1) and is not to be classified with lesser beings.

"Greater" (*meizōn*) in this context is not speaking of superiority in moral character or worth as a human being. He was greater in the dramatic nature of His ministry. As mentioned in v. 9, he was "more than a prophet." He was the forerunner of the Messiah and as such was more significant than kings, scribes, Pharisees, or whoever else might be compared to him. Carson explains: "While the OT prophets doubtless contributed to the corpus of revelation that pointed to Messiah, they did not serve as immediate forerunners. This is what makes John greater than a prophet (v. 9)—indeed the greatest born of women."[9]

However, in contrast, even the least (*mikroteros*) in the kingdom is greater than John. This was not intended to discredit John, for Jesus had been exalting him, but rather to signify how blessed and honored one is to be in the kingdom. John would, of course, be in the future kingdom, but at this point he was the last of the Old Testament prophets, and the kingdom citizens are of the new covenant. In this sense they are superior (in position and blessing) even to the greatest of the Old Testament prophets, including the forerunner who announced the kingdom. MacArthur adds the perspective that John was great in his role in human history, but the spiritual dimension of the kingdom is greater.[10] Even John himself in the kingdom domain will be greater than John as the forerunner of Messiah. The issue here is one of position and function, not of personal character or nature.

11:12   The next verse introduces the idea of resistance and attack on the kingdom of heaven. Hendriksen seems to move in an opposite direction and views this as an exhortation to violence as qualification for entrance into the kingdom:

> But vigorous and forceful men, people who dare to break away from faulty human tradition and to return to the Word in all its purity, no matter what be the cost to themselves, such individuals are eagerly taking possession of the kingdom . . . . Entrance into the kingdom requires earnest endeavor, untiring energy, utmost exertion.[11]

These arguments certainly raise many problems. This sounds far too works-oriented and contrary to the appeal for those burdened down to come to Jesus because His yoke is easy and His load light (11:28-30). The verb *biastai* is present tense passive (or possibly middle) voice from *biazō* and translates "suffer violence." If it were middle voice, the translation would be "the kingdom of heaven [subject of the sentence] is exercising force [verb]." There is no subject in the sentence except "kingdom of heaven" (*hē basileia tōn ouranōn*), and to insert an artificial subject ("vigorous men"), which does not appear in any text, is to alter the entire focus of the verse. In addition, the second phrase, "and [they] take it by force" (or "attack it with violence"; the same word is used in John 10:12), makes no sense if the kingdom is the one exercising violence. The theological inconsistencies of this proposition are staggering.

Indeed, the religious usurpers were those doing violence to

the kingdom introduced by John and implemented by Jesus. John was in prison, Jesus had just warned that those who preached His message would suffer violence, and His own rejection and death were already being orchestrated. The best understanding of v. 12, then, is "But from the days of John the Baptist [his public introduction to the kingdom] until now [probably the time of Jesus' speech], the kingdom of heaven suffers violence and they ["this generation" mentioned in vv. 16-19] attack it violently."

11:13-14   This section concludes Jesus' teaching on John the Baptist with an explanation (introduced by *gar*) of John's uniqueness. The Old Testament (Law and Prophets often represented the whole Old Testament) prophesied until John came on the scene. He fulfilled the predictions of the Messiah's entrance and set the stage for the next part of God's redemptive program.

Verse 14 introduces one of the most cryptic sayings in the New Testament. If the Jews "care to accept it," John was Elijah. Literally, Jesus said, "And if you are willing to receive it [*dechomai*, "receive, accept"], John himself is Elijah, who must come." Malachi had prophesied that Elijah would precede the coming of the great and terrible day of Yahweh (4:5); thus, the Jews anticipated the return of the great prophet before Yahweh would visit Israel again. John fulfilled that role by coming in the spirit and power of Elijah as the angel had predicted in the announcement of his birth (Luke 1:17). John denied that he was the man Elijah; he was, rather, Elijah-like in function (John 1:21). They were two distinct persons; he was not a reincarnation of or the bodily return of the great prophet. Elijah and Moses appeared at the Transfiguration with Jesus (Matt. 17:3), but Jesus instructed His inner circle of disciples not to tell anyone else until He was crucified and resurrected (v. 9). This puzzled the disciples because they had been taught by Bible scholars that Elijah would return to turn Israel's heart back to God (v. 10), thus preparing the nation to receive Him. Since Jesus was the Messiah, God's vicar upon the earth, and since Elijah had just appeared with Him, they would assume it was time to let everyone know that Elijah had come. Jesus, however, pointed out that Elijah indeed would precede the coming of Yahweh (v. 11) but that, even more perplexing, Elijah had *already come.* This coming was not at the Transfiguration but through John the Baptist (vv. 12-13).

Calvin believed that the identity of John the Baptist is associated with Elijah in his official character, which is what Malachi was intending to convey in Malachi 4:5-6.[12] The Jews took the prophecy of Malachi as meaning a literal, bodily return of Elijah; but Jesus' words, both here and in 17:11-12, imply that John the Baptist was the Elijah-like prophet who would come. And since Israel rejected him, they would likewise reject the One he had come to announce. This is probably the significance of the angel's message about John, "It is he who will go as a forerunner before Him in the spirit and power of Elijah" (Luke 1:17). This does not eliminate Elijah from being one of the two witnesses in Revelation 11:1-19.

11:15 This verse constitutes a parable that may reflect Jesus' characteristic attitude toward His audiences. The same formula appears in Matthew 13:9, 43; Mark 4:9; Luke 8:8, 14:35, always in a context of some ambiguous or parabolic statement. Here it relates to the teaching just offered concerning John the Baptist's being the Elijah prophet had Israel been willing to respond to the message of Messiah. Barbieri describes this as "a solemn call to pay close attention to the Savior's words."[13] It is certainly that and perhaps more, possibly signaling an issue that will be brought to judgment. Everyone normally has ears—thus everyone is responsible to respond to the message. Failure to hear (acknowledge or respond to what was said) will result in judgment.

DISCOURSE ON "THIS GENERATION," 11:16-19

11:16-17 The Lord then entered into a rhetorical discourse to point out the vacillating nature of the people of Israel and their tendency to find fault with God's messengers regardless of their method or character. The oratorical question, "To what shall I compare this generation?" brings the focus upon that particular generation. The same designation ("this generation") is also found in Matthew 12:41, 42, 45; 23:36; 24:34. It almost always related to a warning of judgment connected with the rejection of their Messiah. A "generation" (*genea*) usually refers to the descendants, family, or race bound together by a common origin. However, it can also apply to those born within the same time period.[14] Here, the latter application is used—Jews born in that particular time when Messiah was revealed.

Jesus used the analogy of children playing games (v. 16) to

portray that generation. Like children at play in the marketplace while their parents did business, the Jews were more interested in their own entertainment than in the serious business going on around them. "This generation" of Jews was playing religion but denying the reality of God's redemptive plan.

The comparison to children pretending to play music in the streets portrayed the Jews' fickleness. In their culture, the flute was played for both happy and sad occasions, whether a joyous wedding celebration or a mourning ritual. Verse 17 offers both music types and uses the children's unwillingness to cooperate for illustration. If the music was joyful and celebrating life, they would not dance. But if the music was a funeral dirge, neither would they pretend to mourn (as hired professional mourners). As Barnes points out, "One part are represented as sullen and dissatisfied. They would not enter into the play: nothing pleased them."[15] The Jews of Jesus' time period were wanting to play, but nothing pleased them.

11:18-19   Verses 18-19 bring the illustration to bear upon the ministry of John the Baptist and Jesus' own work. Neither could please the Jews. John came as a solemn, dramatic prophet—austere and stoic. Now that he was in prison, people slandered him with accusations of being demon-possessed. This defamation of character seems to have arisen only after his arrest and lengthy imprisonment. However, the Jews were not satisfied with the powerful works of Jesus either. They slandered Him too, as "a gluttonous man and a drunkard, a friend of tax-gatherers and sinners." Contrary to John, Jesus did not exhibit a rigid and separated lifestyle but drank wine and ate at feasts. He even had been sociable with tax gatherers, who were considered vile offenders of their Israelite heritage. As if that were not serious enough, He also was friendly with sinners who had offended the religious leaders of the day. Thus, two opposite styles and methods of reaching out to Israel were presented, but "this generation" would not respond to either. Like children who make up rules according to their own whims, Israel had developed religious rules. The Jews were not willing to maturely see the difference between the game they were playing and the reality of Messiah's message.

The last phrase in v. 19 is a stinging rebuke to that generation: "Wisdom is vindicated by her deeds." Luke 7:35 has the same account, with the exception that Luke states that wisdom is vindicated by her "children." "Deeds" (*tōn ergōn*) refers to what wisdom has produced, and the product will show the rightness of the wisdom. Likewise, Luke's "children" (*tōn teknoōn*), which represented what was produced, would also show the rightness of the wisdom. Jesus meant that by His product the wisdom of His teaching and ministry would be demonstrated to be right. Unlike the apostate religion of Israel, the power and result of Jesus' work would vindicate both John and Himself.

CONDEMNATION OF THE CITIES, 11:20-24

11:20   Having told His parable, which rebuked the childishness of that generation, Jesus then "began to reproach" the cities (of course, the reference is to the citizens) of Chorazin, Bethsaida, and Capernaum. The idea of reproach (*oneidizōp*) is to "heap insults upon."[16] The same word is used in Matthew 27:44 of the insults hurled at Jesus by the robbers at the crucifixion. It is used in 5:11, where Jesus proclaims that His followers are blessed when enemies insult them for their identification with Him. It also carries the idea of justifiable denunciation, as here, conveying indignation at the rebellion and pride of the people.

His reason for the verbal assault is clearly stated, not leaving any room for misunderstanding. Even though these cities had the privilege of more of His miracles done in them than any others, "they did not repent." Repentance is not to be confused with the modern concept of feeling bad about sin and promising to turn over a new leaf. Biblical repentance is to reconsider or to think differently about something. These cities remained dependent upon the dead religion of Israel with all its traditions and rabbinical legalism instead of recognizing their Messiah and His kingdom standards. The indictments against these cities were justifiable denunciations bringing "woe" (anguish and distress) upon them.

11:21   Chorazin was on the northwest edge of the Sea of Galilee and is mentioned only here and in Luke 10:13 (in the same context). Even though there is no biblical record of the works done by Jesus in this city, apparently they were of great number, enough to bring condemnation for the people's unbelief. Referred to on several occasions, Bethsaida stands out as the city of Peter, Andrew, and

Philip (John 1:44; 12:21) and was a place where Jesus withdrew for retreats (Luke 9:10).

Upon these cities Jesus pronounced "woe" (*ouai*), announcing doom. He declared judgment upon these cities in the form of a solemn warning of coming destruction. This coming judgment was based upon the fact that even pagan cities such as Tyre, targeted in the Old Testament as a city to be destroyed for its pride and Baal worship (Isa. 23:1-18; Ezek. 26-28; Amos 1:9-10), and Sidon, a fellow Phoenician city often associated with Tyre in judgment (Joel 3:4; Zech. 9:2), would have responded to the miracles done in these Hebrew cities. Two important observations can be made here: (1) the statement implies that God knew how those cities would have responded had they been given the same opportunity; (2) God did not give them that opportunity. The main point, however, was to emphasize the guilt of Israel, who rejected *their* opportunity. Sackcloth and ashes were cultural ways of expressing grief and making an appeal for mercy. It should be remembered that often God gave Gentile nations messages of deliverance and at times granted them repentance, but their wickedness would always return, resulting in destruction. It should also be noted that the Gentiles would be the target of the gospel following the Lord's resurrection.

11:22   Jesus further explained that the physical destruction of the cities being discussed, both Gentile and Jewish, would not be the end of the judgment. There appears to be a day coming when another judgment will be dispensed and the Jewish cities will receive worse condemnation than the Gentile. The notion being presented is that the citizens would suffer judgment by the destruction of their cities, but a future judgment still awaits, the Day of Judgment (Rev. 20:11-15). Implied here is the level, or degree, principle of judgment and punishment, as well as the principle "from everyone who has been given much shall much be required" (Luke 12:48).

11:23-24   Jesus' rebuke was intensified for the city of Capernaum, where He had been living and ministering. It had been His base of operations and the center of His teaching and miracles. The rhetorical question, "You . . . will not be exalted into heaven, will you?" is to be understood as irony. Some have understood the reference to heaven and hades as symbolic of exaltation and humility. However, in view of the context and the warning of the Day of Judgment, Carson is correct in saying, "Hades must be given more sinister overtones."[17] It is also assumed, perhaps correctly, that Jesus was consciously using the terms "exalted to heaven" and "descend to Hades" to associate Capernaum with the ancient city of Babylon in Isaiah 14:13-15, which suffered the same faulty attitude and consequence.[18]

The comparison with Sodom is sobering. Few cities have become as infamous and typical of evil and judgment as Sodom, having been so destroyed that even its foundations disappeared because of its repulsiveness to God. Jesus asserted, however, that the wickedness of Capernaum was even worse in that Sodom would not have been judged had that city seen Jesus' miracles. The implication was that they would have responded in faith, which Capernaum refused to do. Verse 24 repeats the same conclusion as was voiced for Tyre and Sidon—Sodom will receive less severe judgment than Capernaum.

JESUS' PROCLAMATION OF DIVINE REVEALING, 11:25-27

11:25-26 The next comment of Jesus is no less difficult or any more palatable than the previous. He offered praise to the Father because the Father sovereignly chooses to reveal His truth to "babes." If we follow Luke's account, this statement is in the context of the seventy's returning from their mission with reports of the powerful works they had done (Luke 10:21-22). The context of Matthew is apparently broken and not intended to flow from v. 24 to v. 25. The phrase "at that time" (*en ekeinō tō kairō*) does not imply sequence from the previous thought, but at some (unidentified) time Jesus said this. Luke gives us the context for the comment.

Jesus praises (*exomologeō*, literally, "acknowledge, confess the same about") the Father for hiding "these things" from the wise and intelligent. The term "these things" refers to the ultimate defeat of Satan and the prevailing kingdom power over the might of the enemy (Luke 10:17-20). The "wise and intelligent" is not referring to biblical knowledge, nor even to wisdom and intelligence that is surrendered to God, but to the wisdom of a worldly system, pseudointelligence that fails to see spiritual reality. In Matthew, Jesus is rebuking the cities of Israel for their willful ignorance of the truth of Messiah. Likewise, in Luke's context, in preparation for the seventy's preaching and miracle-working mission, Jesus sums up their work by saying, "The one who listens to you listens to Me, and the one who rejects you rejects Me; and he who rejects Me rejects the One who sent Me" (Luke 10:16). Thus both contexts imply that the "wise and intelligent" are those who by mere human intelligence are blinded from the truth. In a particular sense, Jesus would later point to the scribes, Pharisees, and Sadducees as examples; but in a broader sense, the "wise and intelligent" must apply to entire villages and cities of Israel who rejected their Messiah. Paul deals with this same proposition in 1 Corinthians 1:18-27; 2:6-16, where wisdom apart from God is said to be foolishness. Christians are to be wise and intelligent but not in the worldly sense of mere human experience and theory.

God chooses the weak and foolish things to frustrate the arrogant and boastful (1 Cor. 1:27-29), and this applies even to the salvation message that the disciples had been sent out to preach. But God does reveal it to "babes" (*nēpioi*), which carries in this context the combined idea of mental naiveté and spiritual need, not tenderness, as some believe.[19] The better idea is probably helplessness and the humility to acknowledge it, which is consistent with 1 Peter 5:5, "God is opposed to the proud, but gives grace to the humble." Carson understands the contrast to be "between those who are self-sufficient and deem themselves wise and those who are dependent and love to be taught."[20]

This revealing and hiding is based upon what is "well-pleasing" to God from His perspective (v. 26). God does not need to explain or justify Himself to humanity concerning His redemptive plan and sovereign work (Rom. 9:20). Carson correctly argues that the concealing and revealing is not an "act of injustice but of judgment."[21] All are sinful and guilty, and God is not obligated to reveal anything to anyone. He has given natural revelation, including inner, intuitive awareness of His presence (Rom. 1). Through John the Baptist He openly proclaimed the coming Messiah. Through Jesus and His disciples He worked miracles for all to see. But He revealed spiritual truth only to "babes" and hid it from the wise, who did not sense a need for spiritual enlightenment.

11:27 Jesus continued His discourse by making the claim that "all things" had now been given over to His authority and control. The connection between His praise of the Father for revealing spiritual truth to babes but not to the self-proclaimed wise, and His statement about knowing the Son is not to be missed. The Father, by doing what was well-pleasing to Himself, had withheld or revealed the truth of Messiah; now Jesus had been given similar authority to reveal the Father to whom He willed. Such a claim of power and equality with the Father was indeed shocking to His audience. This claim to mutual and intimate relationship with the Father led the Jews to attack Jesus as a blasphemer (John 5:18; 10:30-38). All things being handed over to Jesus included the prerogative of revealing the Father to whom He chooses.

THE APPEAL TO COME TO CHRIST, 11:28-30

11:28   After claiming the sovereign authority of the Father and Himself to reveal truth to certain ones, this appeal for people to come to Him may seem incongruous. But it is perfectly logical in the context of the Father's choosing to reveal Jesus' messianic authority and power to "babes." The appeal is to those who are "weary and heavy-laden," not to those who are spiritually strong or in control. Again, the idea is that Christ came for those who acknowledge their need and not for the self-sufficient. The promise here was to give rest or relief (*anapauō*) to those who would come (*deute*, adverbial imperative or exhortation) to Him. He invited those who recognized their weaknesses and needs to come. The idea of "heavy-laden" is certainly to be associated with Christ's condemnation of the Pharisees for tying heavy burdens upon the Jews by their rules, regulations, and artificial standards (23:4; Luke 11:46).

11:29   A yoke was a device that connected two animals for sharing the work of plowing or pulling loads. It also had become a symbol for bondage and abuse (Lev. 26:13; 2 Chron. 10:4, 10-11), which became identified with the freeing work of Messiah (Isa. 9:4). There is also a more positive imagery for a yoke—it is something that binds a person to truth or goodness. Later Judaism associated the Torah with a yoke, as a statement of submission to Yahweh.[22]

Some may assume that since a yoke is usually a bar connecting two animals that Jesus is coupled with the one who comes to Him. However, nothing in the context suggests this. Clement, bishop of Rome, wrote at the end of the first century that Christians have "come under the yoke of His grace" (*ton zugon tēs charitos autou*),[23] which is probably more correct. Calvin, likewise, sees the terminology as referencing the new obligations of being with Christ, "and therefore, Christ, after promising joyful rest to wretchedly distressed consciences, reminds them at the same time, that he is their Deliverer on conditions for their submitting to his yoke."[24] This is not to imply a bargaining for salvation by promising to work for Jesus. Neither is it to intimate that one form of oppression is being substituted for another. Rather, it is to say that service to Christ (the yoke) does not bring weariness or heavy burdens but rest. It is service, however, not freedom from any obligations.

Christ's yoke is not burdensome because His character is "gentle and humble in heart." His service flows from grace, not legalism; from love, not judgmentalness; and from gratitude, not trying to earn what is unattainable by human effort. He does not oppress or require what we are incapable of producing. His gentleness offers us comfort when struggling, and His humility allows Him to know our limitations. Thus, He declares (v. 30), "My yoke is easy, and My load is light." Christianity has struggles: opposition from a fallen world, battles with the flesh, and satanic attacks. But Jesus gives us victory in these, and our struggle is not carrying the yoke He gives. Christians are not burdened down more than the grace given to accomplish individual, God-ordained tasks.

HOMILETICAL SUGGESTIONS

This chapter focuses on comfort in ministry, beginning first with John the Baptist, who sought reassurance from the Lord, and extending to all who are under Christ's yoke. It should be emphasized that the Lord's teaching reassured not only John's disciples but should reassure all believers that His program is at work even if not progressing by *personal* timetables or expectations. Many Christians suffer discouragement because of false expectations based on the erroneous concept that life will be problem-free and financially prosperous. Christ's servants must understand and preach the whole message of Christ, including that there are suffering and hardships for those who would follow Jesus. Joy and peace do not come from conditions in this world but from trusting Christ and understanding His purpose for them.

There is also a critical lesson for the unsaved concerning accountability. A day of judgment is coming, and those having had the privilege of hearing clearly and firsthand the truths of Christ will be judged more severely for rejecting the message than those who never heard. This does not mean that there is no eternal punishment for the latter group. Romans 1 clearly reveals the guilt and condemnation of all, because God has revealed Himself. The cities of Tyre, Sidon, and Sodom will indeed be judged, but the principle "to whom much is given, much is required" is certainly a part of the final judgment.

Jesus and the Father are sovereign over the truth of Christ, but Jesus appeals to all who sense their need to come to Him. More requirements will not be placed upon them nor will they be condemned for their weaknesses. Based upon His own character (gentle and humble), Jesus will give them peace—not irresponsible freedom but responsibility designed under His grace. We are all to "learn from" Jesus the meaning of His grace and comfort, and this should characterize Christianity.

Matthew

CHAPTER

Twelve

Growing Controversy and Tension

In the previous two chapters, Matthew has emphasized the spectacular miracles and public preaching of Jesus as well as the expansion of His ministry by the commissioning and sending of the Twelve. Along with increased activity, Jesus was becoming more aggressive in attesting to His messiahship through both proclamation and miracles. His aggressiveness can also be seen through the distinction He was drawing between Himself and the religious leaders. Perhaps John's imprisonment signaled increasing hostility against the kingdom (11:12), and, rather than seeking to make peace with the enemies of God's program, Jesus intensified His denunciation of Israel's hypocrisy and dead religion.

Chapter 11 ends with condemnation of the cities of Israel that had had the privilege of Messiah's firsthand display of authority. He turned the spotlight of truth on Israel's apathy and apostasy. His uncompromising and harsh words would make many very uncomfortable today. Chapter 12 continues with evidence of growing hostility between people of two realms: those who had been entrusted with the truth but perverted it through their religion; and the Messiah Himself, who had come to proclaim truth and expose the emptiness of the self-righteous religionists.

THE FIRST SABBATH CONTROVERSY, 12:1-8
(Mark 2:23-28; Luke 6:1-5)

12:1 What seems an insignificant event to the modern reader became the focal point of a major encounter between the Messiah and the religious leaders. Once again Matthew introduces this topic by saying, "At that time," not indicating sequence of events but rather the introduction of a major event. The issue here was the first Sabbath controversy.

The Sabbath, by commandment, was to be set aside as holy (Ex. 20:9-11). According to our time reckoning, it began at sundown on Friday (around 6:00 P.M.) and ended at sundown on Saturday. The day was to be a time of rest and reflection. The basic idea was to lay aside the normal daily activities and focus on the Creator. However, through the years the idea of laying aside daily labors for reflection upon the Creator became lost in a strict system of rules and regulations. Laws governing Sabbath-keeping became so confining and rigid that priorities were confused and perverted. Josephus records that about one thousand Jews were slaughtered in the Maccabean revolt because the attack happened on the Sabbath and they would not block a cave entrance for protection, or even fight back, because that was considered work.[1] Regulations covered every aspect of life, including how far one could travel on a Sabbath (only 6/10 mile).[2] The Sabbath commandment (Ex. 20) is the only one of the Ten Commandments not repeated in the New Testament. To presume Sunday is the Christian Sabbath is an error. Because of the resurrection of Jesus Christ being on the first day of the week, both apostolic and early church Fathers set aside Sunday in remembrance of the resurrection ("the Lord's Day"). However, Paul clearly forbids giving slavish loyalty to any particular day (Rom. 14:4-6).

Thus, with fanatical obedience to the traditional rules of the Sabbath in view, the Jews observed the disciples of Jesus breaking one of their laws. A very natural need, hunger, led the disciples to pick some grain, break off the husks, and eat the meat of the grain. This would be like walking through a pecan grove, picking up a handful of nuts, removing the shells, and eating. The religious legalists interpreted this as harvesting a crop.

12:2 It was the Pharisees who challenged Jesus with an "unlawful" act, which is consistent with their reputation of being self-appointed watchdogs over Israel's moral life. The accusation was that the disciples had done "what is not lawful to do on a Sabbath." Picking the grain was not against the Law, for Deuteronomy 23:25 gives permission to do such, whereas it does prohibit using a sickle or harvesting tool to take a neighbor's grain. The issue was the Sabbath, and they could refer to verses such as Exodus 20:10, "You shall not do any work," or Exodus 34:21, "On the seventh day you shall rest; even during plowing time and harvest you shall rest" (also Deut. 5:12-14). Thus by the strictest interpretation of "work," their case against the disciples could be legally argued.

This was not mere empty squabble; the Pharisees could document from Scripture that the death penalty should be exercised for violating the Sabbath (Num. 15:32-36). Nehemiah clearly prohibited the selling of grain and other goods in the marketplace on a Sabbath (10:31; 13:15-22), and the postexilic Jews expanded the restrictions further to make any suggestion of work punishable by death. In the Talmud, volumes are dedicated to the rules and limitations for Sabbath observance. For example, in *Shabbath* there are thirty-nine forbidden "works" listed, including sowing, plowing, reaping, gathering into sheaves, threshing, winnowing, and grinding. Each prohibition in these numerous tracts dealing with the Sabbath is discussed in great detail with hairsplitting definitions. Here, the acts of picking a few heads of grain, rubbing them in the hands to break open the husks, and blowing away the husks were probably interpreted as harvesting, grinding, and winnowing. It is important to note that nowhere in Scripture is such explanation given; the rules applied were extrabiblical. The disciples may have violated the *traditions* of Sabbath law observance, but they did not violate God's Law. Carson points out the fascinating fact that in post-Christian Judaism, the Gemara "expressly permits picking grain by hand and eating it on the Sabbath but merely forbids the use of a tool."[3]

12:3-5 Jesus now gave a response. He made no apology, offered no compromising explanation, and in no way allowed the Pharisees to assume justification for judging His disciples for this act. Instead, He asked an insulting question in their estimation (v. 3), "Have you not read what David did . . ." Insulting indeed, for they were "experts" in the Scriptures, the ones who taught all Israel about the great patriarchs, the covenants, and the Law. To insinuate they had not read this text was to question their authority and integrity. The account was, of course, well known. During David's flight from King Saul, he hid like an outlaw and lacked provisions for his hungry men. One should not miss the connection being made between David and his men and Jesus and His men. The correlation between Jesus and David was significant.

Jesus gave details (v. 4) of how David broke the Law. First Samuel 21:1-6 records that David not only ate consecrated bread and gave it to his men as well, but he lied and deceived the priest Ahimelech, who was later falsely accused by Saul of conspiring with David and was put to death (1 Sam. 22:11-19). The consecrated bread was given to David by the priest, assuming that he was on a mission from the king (v. 2), the vicar of God in the theocratic kingdom, and that David and his men were consecrated themselves (as evidenced by not having been with women, vv. 4-5). Thus, the priest himself, assuming those conditions, did not see a violation of the spirit of the Law.

The connection in the mind of Christ was that *He* was the vicar of God in this world and that His disciples were truly consecrated for ministry. Unlike David, who lied, Jesus had the right to transcend the supposed laws of the Sabbath (though not actually breaking the Law of God). That is the purpose of His claim in v. 8.

Jesus went even further in vindicating His disciples (v. 5). Even the priests broke the Sabbath, yet remained innocent according to the Law. The reference was probably to Leviticus 24:5-9, where God instructs the priest to make the consecrated bread and set it before the Lord every Sabbath and to eat what had sat on the table before. Thus they were instructed to "break the Sabbath." The point is that the Sabbath was not intended to be the apex of all law but was good for its purpose. As Paul says, "The law is good, if one uses it lawfully" (1 Tim. 1:8). The problem arose from a legalistic interpretation and application of the Law. Hendriksen's summary is excellent:

> The trouble with the Pharisees when they found fault with Jesus and his disciples was this, that they not only placed rabbinical tradition on a par with God's written law . . . but that in addition to this they attached an all but absolute value to specific traditions. Not even the divine law as recorded in the Decalog, says Jesus as it were, was to be applied with such rigidity.[4]

12:6   The next statement (v. 6) must have stunned and infuriated the Pharisees, for in their estimation what could be greater than the temple? If the Law could be bypassed by those who work in the temple, because the temple consecrated them, even more could those who served the messianic kingdom be excused, because "something" (*meizon,* neuter) superior to the temple was here, namely the kingdom of heaven. Since the kingdom is superior, those who served the kingdom were superior to those who served in the temple. And if David, not yet king, had the right to feed his men the consecrated bread, then He, the King of Israel, had a right to allow His men to eat grain on the Sabbath. The arguments of vv. 4-5 demonstrate the inconsistency of their judgmental spirit.

12:7   For the second time, Jesus challenged the Pharisees to learn the lesson of Hosea 6:6, "I desire compassion, and not sacrifice" (also see discussion on 9:13). This exhortation to "learn" (9:13), or to "know the meaning of" (12:7), was a rebuke for failing to understand the true meaning of the Law. It was never intended to enslave people or to be the basis of self-righteous standards.

One of the many tasks of the Law was to reveal God's grace. The whole sacrificial system was to emphasize the need for God to forgive, because no one could measure up to the standard of His character. The sacrifices were not intended to be something that earned favor with God but were a testimony of one's need for grace. Thus, the self-righteous who prided themselves in their religious acts missed the point of God's mercy. Had these who prided themselves in their knowledge of the Law understood this, they would not have condemned hungry men for such a minor thing, especially since the Law permitted it (Deut. 23:25) and because no specific biblical law of the Sabbath was violated. Furthermore, the account of Mark offers an explanation for the purpose of the Sabbath, "The Sabbath was made for man, and not man for the Sabbath" (2:27). The Sabbath was to be a benefit for mankind, not a legalistic burden. Therefore compassion, not condemnation, was the proper response even if it did *appear* that these men had broken the Sabbath.

12:8   The conclusion to the whole matter was a claim to authority. The Son of Man (see comments on 8:20) is a title used more than eighty times and seems to have been Jesus' favorite name for Himself. It certainly had messianic overtones (Dan. 7:13-14) and is linked to the Second Advent of Messiah in His power and glory as judge and ruler (Matt. 24:27-31). It is the Son of Man who masters the Sabbath and not the Sabbath that rules over the Son of Man. Therefore He could do as He pleased on the Sabbath. There is no recorded response from the Pharisees.

THE SECOND SABBATH CONTROVERSY, 12:9-14 (Mark 3:1-6; Luke 6:6-11)

12:9-10   According to Luke's gospel (6:6), the next event recorded took place on a different Sabbath. It should not be assumed, therefore, that the controversy of v. 9 followed immediately that of vv. 1-8. This conflict took place in the synagogue where Jesus was teaching (Luke 6:6).

A man with a withered hand set the stage for the conflict. The Pharisees, no doubt still angered over the first confrontation, took the initiative and challenged Jesus concerning the right to heal on the Sabbath (v.10). By asking, "Is it lawful to heal on the Sabbath?" they sought opportunity to accuse Him of being a breaker of the Law. It is safe to assume that an affirmative answer was expected—which would not have been acceptable because of the strong rabbinical teaching to the contrary. That Jesus knew their wicked plans (Luke 6:8) does not imply omniscience but only Spirit-filled wisdom. Jesus "emptied Himself" of the independent use of His divine attributes (Phil. 2:7), and Christians should exercise care in defending the deity of Christ by assuming His use of those attributes. Such inconsistency implies that He "cheated" on the self-emptying, fails to give credit to His dependence upon the Spirit, and ultimately weakens His work as the Second Adam. While not ceasing to be God, He did not rely upon His divine attributes but upon the Spirit (this will be discussed in greater detail later).

12:11   According to both Mark and Luke, Jesus first called the man to come forward. This act deliberately drew attention to the conflict, and the whole assembly watched to see what Jesus would do. The confrontation was a challenge for Jesus to say before the entire synagogue what He had said to the Pharisees earlier—namely, that He was greater than the temple and that the Son of Man was Lord of the Sabbath. The Pharisees knew public sympathy would be with them if the crowd heard such statements.

Instead of directly answering their question, Jesus related a hypothetical incident, which He knew would portray a real-life situation. The average Jew in the synagogue could relate to the problem of having a sheep fall into a pit, then not having access to food or water or the ability to flee from an enemy. The flock owners of that assembly knew what they would do. The Greek text reads "have one sheep," but the NASB is correct in translating it as "a sheep." Carson agrees that the point is not that it was the last sheep a man had but rather that the construction "probably means no more than 'a sheep.'"[5] Thus, the illustration is comparing the value of one animal to the interpretation of the law of the Sabbath.

12:12 Assuming that no one would argue with exerting effort to lift the sheep from the pit (and no argument was given; as Mark records, "they kept silent"), Jesus made His application: "How much more value then is a man?" Carson points out that this was the third time Jesus based His argument upon a comparison of animals to humans.[6] The Jews certainly held to the superiority of the human being, made in God's image, over any other creature. Thus, His conclusion was logical and indisputable, "So then, it is lawful to do good on the Sabbath."

By their silence, they answered their own question. Once again, Jesus had overwhelmed His opposition by wisdom and truth, demonstrating what it means to be "shrewd as serpents, and innocent as doves" (10:16). Mark records that Jesus was looking at them (the Pharisees) with anger (*met' orgēs*) because of the hardness of their hearts (3:5). This view of Jesus is far more common in the Scriptures than contemporary Christianity may feel comfortable with. He was grieved and angered that their concern over rules was greater than their concern for the physical needs of this individual.

12:13 Jesus did not speak any words of healing; He simply instructed the man to put forth his hand. In obedience, the man did as told and was immediately healed. No apparent "work" was done, but the transformation took place before their eyes. The Pharisees could not deny the power or its source, but neither could they account for what He had said or done.

12:14 After the Pharisees had seen the power and compassion of Jesus and the restoration of a man's health, their response was rage (Luke 6:11). Compare Jesus' anger over their hard hearts and lack of compassion with their anger over His compassion and failure to submit to their religion. The Pharisees' response was also significant in that it confirmed the theological proposition of the blindness of the fallen mind. Seeing this great display of power and authority over the damaged hand did not result in the Pharisees' humbling themselves or even acknowledging Jesus as possibly being the Messiah. Instead, they plotted to kill Him. In view of this response, should Christians be surprised that unregenerate people reject the message of Jesus?

CONTINUING FULFILLMENT OF PROPHECY IN HIS MINISTRY, 12:15-21

12:15-16 Jesus was aware of the plot to kill Him and chose at this time to move away from the hostile situation. Later He would willingly face the mob that called for His death, but the time had not yet come for that. Mark records that He went to the sea with His disciples, and a great crowd followed (3:7). Luke omits this next event and begins immediately to recount the night of prayer before sending out His disciples (6:12). Matthew's commentary is very brief, recording only that He healed those who followed Him—those who had witnessed His power and wanted to benefit from it.

Jesus warned the multitude not to spread the news of what He was doing (v. 16). This is certainly contrary to the contemporary church's attitude toward open proclamation any time and any place. Barnes comments, "He was *at this time* desirous of concealment. He wished to avoid their plots and to save His life."[7] While this is true, the purpose has to go deeper, because at a later time He made no effort to "save His life." MacArthur offers a more complete perspective: "Jesus had not come to do His own will but His Father's (Matt. 26:39; John 6:38), and it was not yet the Father's time for the Son's ministry and life to be ended."[8]

12:17 Matthew offers his own explanation by using his familiar fulfillment formula "in order that . . . might be fulfilled" *(hina plērōthē)*. Another reason Jesus did not stay to fight was in relation to Isaiah 42:3, "A bruised reed He will not break, and a dimly burning wick He will not extinguish." This is but one messianic prophecy that Jesus fulfilled. That is not to say that there is not a time when Messiah will speak out and will lift up His voice in the streets, but this was not the occasion for such action.

12:18   In the following verses, the prophecy of Isaiah 42:1-4 is brought into the event to suggest that Jesus' actions were not simply for self-preservation but to demonstrate the desire of Messiah to bring about reconciliation with the nation. Matthew does not quote the Isaiah passage exactly, which has led to unnecessary and unprofitable speculation.[9] Matthew's purpose is to exalt Jesus and not just to explain the reason for His discontinuing the conflict with the Pharisees. Thus, he refers to the whole context of Isaiah 42 rather than to only the verses describing His passive response.

Two titles are used of Messiah in this text. "My Servant" (*pais*, both in Matthew and the LXX) is more than a slave and can refer to a child as well. When used of a servant, it emphasizes the trusted position he holds.[10] He is also referred to as "My Beloved," meaning the object of one's love. Thus, Messiah is the trusted servant who is loved by Yahweh, who sent Him.

Two proclamations are made concerning this beloved and trusted Servant. God has placed His own Spirit upon Him. In the Old Testament context, the Spirit was given to perform specific tasks (e.g., Ex. 35:30-31; Num. 11:16-17) and was not the pledge of inheritance and thus a permanent seal as in the New Testament (Eph. 1:13-14). It was the event of Matthew 3:16 and the claim Jesus made in Luke 4:17-19 that turned the people of Nazareth against Him. The second proclamation is that the Beloved Servant would "proclaim justice to the Gentiles." This, of course, is fulfilled in the post-Ascension commissioning of the church to carry the message of Christ into all the world (Matt. 28:18-20).

12:19-21   These verses explain that Messiah would not quarrel over or forcibly claim the kingdom. Although He had not come to bring peace but a sword (10:34), Jesus was not going to be at this time the warrior-king the Jews had expected. He would neither harm His enemies nor destroy what remained of Israel. Carson offers a good explanation: "The servant does not advance his ministry with such callousness to the weak that he breaks the bruised reed or snuffs out the smoldering wick."[11] Jesus was gentle to the weak and compassionate to the repentant, though He was firm and unyielding in His attack on Pharisaism and other threats to God's truth.

Verse 20 implies that this gentleness has a point of termination —"until He leads justice to victory." This is a reference to the Second Advent, in which He comes not in humble service but as King of Kings to rule with a rod of iron (Rev. 19:11-16). The universal nature of the Messiah's work is implied in this prophecy (v. 18) and is expressly stated to be the hope of the Gentiles in v. 21. In "His Name" forgiveness of sin and reconciliation with God will be found.

A DEMONIAC IS HEALED
AND THE PHARISEES BLASPHEME, 12:22-24

12:22   Even as tension grew between Jesus and the religious leaders, people continued to seek His power and mercy. Someone brought a blind and speechless man for healing. Carson links the blindness and speechlessness to the condition of being demonized.[12] Matthew does not record any words exchanged or physical contact but only the simple statement "He healed him." The healing allowed the man to both see and speak. No mention is made of the demon's being cast out, but v. 24 implies this action. Some commentators see Luke 11:14 as a parallel passage (and it may well be), which focuses upon the casting out of the demon, not the healing.

12:23   The "were amazed" response of the multitude is familiar. The most important feature of Matthew's record is the immediate association of this miracle of Jesus with the title "Son of David." The question is not stated as positively as some commentators assume. Barnes translates it, "Is not this the Son of David?"[13] The question is introduced, however, by the interrogative particle *mēti,* which is used in questions expecting a negative answer.[14] This would indicate some strong hesitancy on the part of the observers to accept Jesus as the Messiah.

Their question was not concerning His power over the demon but was asked probably because the anticipated Messiah was thought to be a warrior-king who would attack not the religion of Israel but the pagan Romans. False expectations often lead to confusion. The Messiah was the promised descendant of David who was to restore the glory of the kingdom. This man, they reasoned, though demonstrating the Isaiah 35:5 type of works, was not demonstrating the glorious kingdom power over the nation's enemies.

12:24   The Pharisees seized the moment, sensing the confusion and doubt of the people. They quickly offered an explanation for the miracle that Jesus had just performed. They could not deny the power of His work, so they slandered the source of His power. On Beelzebul, see 9:34. The ruler of demons was thus given credit for freeing this man from the power of a demon. The reasoning was not logical but was their only way of explaining the power just displayed. Even Jesus' enemies could not deny the reality of His supernatural power, unlike that of many imitators today who use tricks and unverifiable "healings" to simulate power. The expression "ruler of the demons" implied that the Jews held a hierarchical view of the demonic world. Jesus' comments in v. 26 associate this ruler with Satan.

Jesus' Response to the Pharisaical Accusation, 12:25-29

12:25-26 Jesus was "knowing their thoughts," but one should not assume that this meant He was reading their minds. "Thoughts" (*enthumēsis*) refers to their ideas or imaginations expressed in the accusation, meaning that Jesus knew the thinking process that led to their statement. It was a demonstration of His intelligence and wisdom. He knew the presuppositions and disposition of His opponents and understood their reasoning. Thus, He didn't respond with a simple denial of their charge. He proved how desperate their explanation was, being illogical as well as blasphemous.

By use of an example from common sense, He pointed out their fallacious reasoning. "Any kingdom" refers to the consistency of the principle, meaning it would be true of Rome, Israel (they should remember their own divided kingdom era), or even spiritual kingdoms. Not only kingdoms but cities or households will self-destruct if divided and working against their own purposes and needs. Therefore, to assume He was working in opposition to His own kingdom by casting out the demon was totally illogical. Jesus applied this principle to Satan (v. 26). He was not doing the work of Satan because His work was in opposition to the Devil.

12:27 Jesus then turned the accusation against the Pharisees. If (assuming for the sake of argument) Jesus could be exercising demonic power to cast out demons, then the same miracle worked by exorcists of the Pharisees must also be questioned. The expression "your sons" (*hoi hioi umōn*) was not referring to biological offspring but probably to their disciples. Son (*huios*) has a broad range of meaning, including a member of a large group or one in a close relationship.[15] MacArthur points out that the Pharisees would never have claimed that the ability to cast out demons by their own power was ungodly, much less demonic. Therefore to assume such with regard to Jesus demonstrated prejudice, not truth.[16]

The sons of the Pharisees would judge the Pharisees, because their claim would be consistent with Jesus' own claim. Therefore, to accuse Jesus was to accuse them. Instead of Jesus condemning them, their own sons would do so. Gundry comments, "The argument does not necessarily imply Jesus' acceptance of the exorcisms practiced by his antagonists' followers. . . . Rather, the argument points up the hypocritical inconsistency in his antagonists' accusations."[17]

12:28 The argument then took on a more serious tone as Jesus emphasized the magnitude of their accusation. They should consider, what if His miracle was divine, not demonic? Note that He did not say, "Cast out demons by the *power* of God" but by the Person of the "Spirit of God." This point is not to be lost in the casual pneumatology of contemporary Christianity. The power of Christ lay in His endowment of the Holy Spirit, which took place prior to His entry into public ministry (3:15-17). Jesus was the perfect example of the Spirit-filled servant of God. To attack His work was not to attack Him but the Spirit of God, who worked through Him (vv. 31-32).

If it was true that the Spirit of God was working through Jesus, then the only logical conclusion was that the kingdom of God had come. Note here that Matthew uses "kingdom of God" (*hē basileia tou theou*) instead of his usual "kingdom of heaven" (*hē basileia tōn ouranōn*). Perhaps the reason for Matthew's unusual wording is to stress the horrific error of associating Beelzebul with the holy God. The authority and power behind Jesus is God, not Satan. To accuse God's servant of functioning by satanic authority is blasphemy.

12:29 Further evidence was presented in the form of another proverb. The point was simply that if the demon-possessed man was under demonic control, and Satan is the ruler of demons, someone had to bind the demon in order to free the man. The one who binds a strong man must be greater. Jesus demonstrated power over the demon; thus His power was greater. Neither the demon nor the ruler of the demons could prevent His healing the blind and mute man. The servant of God, Messiah, casts out Beelzebul's servant and takes his property.

SERIOUS WARNING TO THOSE WHO OPPOSE HIM, 12:30-37

12:30   Jesus' claim is to be understood in the context of conflict with the Pharisees. It may have been intended for the crowd, who had first raised the question of His messiahship (v. 23), or for the Pharisees themselves. In other places the same idea is stated from the totally opposite perspective, "He who is not against us is for us" (Mark 9:40). Obviously, here the issue is being a part of His kingdom work, which is reflected in the gathering and scattering analogy. Calvin takes this to be pointed specifically against the religious leaders, who should have been assisting Jesus in His kingdom work but resisted instead at every point.[18] Mounce agrees with Calvin and connects this saying to chap. 10 (vv. 6, 16), related to commissioning His men to go to the villages of Israel and gather God's flock.[19]

12:31-32   His next statement was both dramatic and serious. Jesus' assertion that "any sin and blasphemy" shall be forgiven did not come as a surprise, but to actually state that there was a sin that "shall not be forgiven" certainly got one's attention, resulting in two pertinent questions: what is blasphemy, and why is it not forgiven?

Hendriksen suggests that blasphemy (*blasphēmia*) might be defined as "defiant irreverence."[20] The word itself basically means "slander, defamation" or even "reviling judgment."[21] In this context the slander was unquestionably attributing the Holy Spirit's power to Satan (vv. 24-28). Christ's emphasis was on the deity of the Holy Spirit, not on His own deity. Thus, to attribute Christ's work to Satan was to blaspheme God's Spirit, which is unforgivable.

Forgiveness in these verses refers to canceling out the consequences of guilt (*aphiēmi*) and was the common term for forgiving sins (Matt. 9:6). Jesus therefore declared that the consequences of blaspheming the Holy Spirit would not be dismissed, but the penalty would be enforced. Again, Carson's insight is helpful: "His statement is remarkable because one of the glories of the biblical faith is the great emphasis Scripture lays on the graciousness and wideness of God's forgiveness (e.g., Pss. 65:3; 86:5; 130:3-4; Isa. 1:18; Mic. 7:19; 1 John 1:7)."[22] Indeed, this is the theme of many great Christian hymns. But here God's forgiveness is limited, and there is no escaping judgment for blasphemy of the Spirit.

Verse 32 adds even more drama by comparing blasphemy against the Son of Man, which is forgivable, with blasphemy against the Spirit, which is not forgivable. There is a parallelism here that gives additional understanding of blasphemy. Here the Lord refers to it as to "speak against" (*eipē logon kata,* "speak a word against"), which would be to "discredit, slander, contradict," etc., the Messiah. The title "Son of Man" emphasized the messianic role of fulfilling the Davidic covenant. If Jesus' enemies speak against Him in this capacity, there is room for forgiveness. This assumes, of course, repentance that leads to faith in Christ. However, if one attacks the divine power behind Messiah's work, there is no forgiveness. It would have been convenient had the Lord used the present tense verb "is speaking" (i.e., "as long as he is speaking against"), but, instead, He used the aorist (*eipē*), emphasizing the act itself, not the time or continuance of the act.

However, it must be assumed that the act of blaspheming is based upon an unrepentant heart that rejects the evidence presented in the miracles Jesus had worked. Walvoord explains, "Such a sin is not unpardonable in itself, but rather because it rejects the person and work of the Holy Spirit, without whom repentance and restoration are impossible . . . it is not the thought that one seeking pardon will not find it, but rather that one who rejects the Holy Spirit will not seek pardon."[23] An important fact to be considered is that this does not apply to any so-called miracle worker but only to Jesus Himself (cf. Matt. 7:15-23, where false prophets will make similar claims of divine power). It was the claims of Jesus to being God's Son and Messiah that led to this accusation. He alone is the Son of God, who could speak with the authority of Messiah and God, as He alone can forgive sins. The Spirit bears witness to Jesus, and to blaspheme Him is to cut oneself off from the only source of forgiveness. This truth is both for "this age, or in the age to come."

12:33   The parable of the tree and its fruit was to illustrate that one could not separate the product from the source. If Jesus' miracles were good, then He was good. If they were demonstrations of power over Satan, then His source was greater than Satan. The Jews could not deny the reality of His power nor the compassion and mercy He displayed by healing the afflicted. Therefore He Himself must be good and not evil. As an apple identifies an apple tree, good works identify a good person. If Jesus were in league with the Devil as His enemies had claimed, then the product of His life would be evil. This was unquestionably not the case.

12:34-35   Once again Jesus offended the sensitivity of some for His name calling. "Brood of vipers" is literally "offspring of snakes," a descriptive analogy for their harmful character. He also called them "evil" (*poneros;* when used with a definite article, this word is a title for Satan, "the evil one"). The question is, "How can they speak what is good?" The significance of this is to be found in the parable of the tree and its fruit. As the offspring of snakes, and their very nature being evil, their product was therefore not good. Jesus brought the issue down to what they had said and attributed it to their wicked hearts.

Verse 35 continues this theme—a person's heart will determine the product of his speech. The word treasure (*thesauros*) would be better translated "treasure box" (cf. 2:11) or "container in which something is kept." The heart is the treasure box of the soul. If it is wicked, then what comes from it will be wicked. The Pharisees often said good things, because they taught the Law; however, since their hearts were wicked, those good things were perverted into self-righteousness and legalism. In the same way, their accusations against Jesus were the product of evil treasure boxes.

12:36-37   Jesus then warned His accusers to weigh their words carefully. "Every careless word" will be brought up for accountability in the Day of Judgment. Careless (*argos*) actually means "idle" or "useless" and implies words without substance. In this context, with no basis or substance the Pharisees had accused Jesus of using demonic power—idle charges that will be accounted for at the judgment. The warning is that one will be held responsible for what is said, in this case verbally attacking the Son of God.

Verse 37 is a summary statement. The spoken word expresses what is in the heart (v. 35) and justifies or condemns. The standard, or method of speaking against others, that individuals use will be brought back to them. Hendriksen's explanation is excellent: "The judgment passed upon the individual in the final day is going to be 'by,' in the sense of 'in conformity with,' 'in accordance with,' 'in harmony with,' his words, considered as mirrors of the heart."[24]

CONDEMNATION OF THE WICKED GENERATION, 12:38-42

12:38   The lengthy and serious nature of the Lord's response to the blasphemous accusation apparently had an impact upon some of the leaders standing nearby and listening. From accusing Him of being in league with the demons, they now shifted to calling Him "Teacher" (*didaskale*). The partitive genitive used with *tines* implies that certain ones from among the scribes and Pharisees were not so anxious to discredit Jesus. Despite the severe rebuke and the name calling ("vipers" and "evil," v. 34), some were perhaps willing to listen to Him. What they wanted was a "sign" (*sēmeion*), that is, some proof that what He was saying was true. One must certainly be amazed that the healing Jesus had just performed was not sufficient as a sign.

12:39   His answer was typically blunt and to the point. First, He declared that it was an evil (*ponēra*) and adulterous (*moichalis*) generation that craved a sign. He did not credit them with having a desire to know the truth, perhaps because His truthfulness had already been verified many times before. Their evil and adulterous natures were displayed by their stubborn resistance to both what they had seen and His teaching, which was in agreement with messianic prophecies. Second, the issue seems to have been focused on "this generation [*genea*]," referring to the people who were directly involved with His ministry. This may be connected with the idea of a "sign" (*sēmeion*), which Carson understands to mean not just a miracle but "a 'sign' performed on demand."[25] John in his gospel uses "sign" in a more positive sense, as a display of power, whereas here it seems to have been a display of authority. The question goes back to by what authority (divine or demonic) did Jesus work miracles (vv. 24-28). The Pharisees were demanding proof that He was from God. The only sign they would receive was the sign of Jonah the prophet.

12:40-41   These two verses explain what Jesus meant by "the sign of Jonah the prophet." The reference was to His resurrection, but it was veiled in the allusion to His being in the heart of the earth for three days. Some commentators go too far in comparing the experience of Jonah and that of Christ.[26] As with parables, such allusions are meant to draw attention only to the essential components of the comparison. Jonah appeared to have been destroyed by the sea creature (a symbol of God's judgment) but was miraculously brought back after three days to bring the message of mercy. Likewise, Jesus would be swallowed up in judgment but would return in three days with the message of deliverance.

The "three days and three nights" are not to be understood as a literal seventy-two hour period. The explanation for the use of the time will more appropriately be discussed in chap. 27. For now, suffice it to say that in the Jewish culture this expression was a figure of speech intending to convey any part or combination of days and nights to make three days.

Jesus returned to His theme of the severity of Israel's judgment and this generation's condition being worse than that of its pagan neighbors (v. 41; cf. 11:21-24). The people of Nineveh repented at Jonah's preaching, but Israel was not responding to their own Messiah. His statement "Something [neuter] greater than Jonah is here" is somewhat surprising, in that one would normally expect Him to say "someone," comparing Jonah with Himself. The comparison, however, was not between two people, but between two functions—a prophet's and the Messiah's, between a messenger of salvation and the instrument of salvation.

12:42 The idea of "something greater than" was continued in another illustration: the Messiah is greater than Solomon. Solomon was a glorious king, bringing wealth and fame to Israel. Even the Queen of the South (most likely the Arabian peninsula) traveled a great distance to see his glory. Her willingness to exert such effort to see the king of Israel would be a witness against this generation, which was unwilling to see their greater King, the promised Son of David, who would rule the nations.

LESSON FROM THE UNCLEAN SPIRIT, 12:43-45

This next pericope seems unrelated to the previous discussion and certainly is not connected with what follows. It appears to be an aside intended to bring closure to the argument by summarizing the condition of "this evil and adulterous generation." It is a prediction of the consequences of Israel's hard-hearted resistance to the Messiah (v. 45). Their attempt at self-reformation through religious ritual and ceremony would actually make reception of the truth more difficult.

12:43   The main character of the illustration is an unclean spirit (*akatharton pneuma*) who voluntarily leaves the man being possessed and passes through waterless places seeking rest. As fascinating as these tidbits of information about the world of demons may be, the Lord's intention was not to teach a demonology, and one must be careful not to become infatuated with the issue and miss His point. It may be assumed that the spirit left the man to get "rest" from the harassment of exorcists, but it could not find another place to go. Being out of the man's body is compared to being in waterless places, indicating the demon's dependency upon a human host. The "exorcists" would represent the religiousness of Israel, which annoys the spirit but does not subdue it.

12:44-45   The demon determines to return to its host, only to find that the man has cleaned up his life and seems to have the power to resist the unclean spirit. In response to this self-reformation, the demon goes and recruits help from other demons that are even more evil (which may indicate levels of evil intent even in the demonic world), and the eight unclean spirits take over the man's body.

As dramatic and horrific as this story might be, the lesson lies in the phrase "the last state of that man becomes worse than the first." The result of the man's false sense of well-being derived from self-reformation is that even worse evil will come. Thus, Jesus made His application: "That is the way it will also be with this evil generation." These people, who were unwilling to accept the proof of His messiahship, who accused Him of being in league with the Devil (12:24), and who were so proud of their self-righteousness, would be so dominated by the evil they thought they had ejected from their lives that they would be in worse condition than the pagan nations around them. Israel was better off without the false sense of security their empty religion offered.

The True Family of the Messiah, 12:46-50
(Mark 3:31-35; Luke 8:19-21)

As Jesus was concluding His discourse, His mother, Mary, and His brothers arrived and wished to speak to Him. There is no mention of His sisters, which probably indicates that this was not a friendly family gathering but a more serious affair. His brothers were

James, Joseph, Simon, and Jude (Judas); mention is made elsewhere of His having sisters, but they are not named (Matt. 13:55-56).

12:46-47   Mary and the brothers wanted to speak to Jesus, but Matthew does not give any details concerning the content of their intended dialogue with Him. Mark does, however, give some interesting information related to this event: "They went out to take custody of Him; for they were saying, 'He has lost His senses'" (Mark 3:21). It may be difficult to imagine that the family of Jesus could have seriously believed this, but in this context why would they not believe that His claims to deity and His repudiation of the established and respected religious leaders were indications that He had become delusionary? The messenger informed Jesus that His mother and His brothers were outside asking to speak to Him. Perhaps they thought that if they could get Him back home, He could recover from His delusion. Even Mary probably had not anticipated the stress and conflict her Son would create, and, though she had been warned by the angel, watching it unfold was too much for her to comprehend.

12:48-50   His rhetorical question probably caught the messenger off guard. If one takes the question literally, then certainly Jesus may have seemed delusional, because it would be thought that He did not recognize His own family. But the question was indeed rhetorical and was intended to make a significant point—spiritual kinship is more vital than physical kinship. It needs to be emphasized, however, that Jesus was not rejecting His family. Certainly, MacArthur correctly points out, "Jesus was not renouncing His family. He loved them even more than they loved Him. His last request from the cross was for John to care for His mother (John 19:26-27) and through His gracious love His brothers eventually came to believe in Him as their Lord and Savior (Acts 1:14)."[27]

Verse 49 clearly states the principle that His disciples were His family, and then the principle is expanded in v. 50 to include anyone who "does the will of My Father who is in heaven." Some may raise the question as to whether Jesus is saying that obedience to the Father is required for salvation, by which they mean works are required. But the will of the Father is not for one to attempt to earn salvation by religious acts. The Pharisees and scribes have been rebuked for this throughout the last several chapters. The will of the Father is to accept the Messiah whom He has sent. Failure to do this is the basis for the condemnation of the religious leaders that Jesus had just announced. In John 6:40 He says, "For this is the will of My Father, that everyone who beholds the Son and believes in Him, may have eternal life; and I Myself will raise him up on the last day." To obey the Father is to believe in Jesus. To believe in Jesus brings one into a family relationship with Him that is even superior to the biological relationship of His earthly family.

HOMILETICAL SUGGESTIONS

In the first Sabbath controversy (vv. 1-8) Jesus made a most consequential affirmation. His second exhortation for the Pharisees to learn the lesson of Hosea 6:6 is certainly a warning to all who claim the name of Jesus. The church also needs to learn the lesson that God desires compassion, not religious legalism. The hard and fast rules of some churches do not reflect a loving God who forgives and restores but more reflect the Pharisaical attitude that sin is unforgivable and will stain a believer for the rest of his life. Rules that go beyond specific statements of God's Word, no matter how well-intended, may be an indication of Pharisaism, not spirituality. Caution must be exercised in passing judgment in areas not specifically addressed in Scripture.

The second Sabbath controversy emphasized that some people place the rules of their religion over the needs of God's people. Jesus taught that the Sabbath was not intended to be a burden for mankind but was for mankind's benefit. Once again the Pharisees failed to understand the purpose and significance of the Law. Paul tells us in 1 Timothy 1:8 that the Law is good if one uses it lawfully (according to its purpose). The Law was never intended to earn righteousness before God but to help His people understand His nature of holiness and to incite worship. Also it reveals His concern for mankind and man's responsibility to the creatures God Himself entrusted to his care. In the complexity of the Law, man can glimpse what it means to love God with all one's heart, soul, and mind and then to love one's neighbor as oneself (Matt. 22:36-40). But legalism tends to find another purpose, to set standards for people to live by in order to be accepted as holy. God's Word is certainly the authority by which all are obligated to live, but any requirements beyond what is stated by Scripture becomes legalism. Many saints are persecuted and punished for failing to live up to artificial standards extrapolated from Scripture by humanistic assumptions and desires for "protecting high standards." But this is Pharisaism, which Jesus despised. God's people must be trained to exercise grace and love, not rules and regulations. Even when behavior needs to be controlled by covenants of conduct, grace is to be the overriding factor.

Perhaps the most sobering statement in the New Testament is Christ's warning about blaspheming the Holy Spirit. To reject the supernatural power source of Christ's ministry, namely, the Holy Spirit, not His own divine power, is to lose the forgiveness in Christ's redeeming work. Rather than focusing only on the unpardonable sin here, it is suggested that serious consideration be given to the implications of Christ's statements related to the *kenosis* (self-emptying) of Philippians 2:7-8. His works of power were not flowing out of the independent exercise of His divine attributes but from obedience to the Spirit. This is the reason His followers worked the same miracles as He. They too had the Spirit of God. If the Spirit chose to use His power through disciples today, He certainly could do so. However, the consistent teaching of the New Testament is that authority today does not rest in signs of power (even the unsaved appear to be able to perform those, Matt. 7:22-23) but in the Scriptures. Jesus' humility and obedience were demonstrated by His dependence upon the Father and the Spirit; and for this reason He is our example to follow. We cannot hide behind the argument "But Jesus was God." This is the dynamic of the kenosis (self-emptying of the Logos to become one like the creature He came to redeem). This doctrine is one of the most overlooked in the New Testament. Jesus' humanity is weakened by the desire to protect His deity. The motive is legitimate, but the results are not Christ-honoring. The depth of His sacrifice is ignored by downplaying His self-emptying and His humanity.

The final lesson of this chapter is an encouragement to those who feel rejected by friends and family because of their faith in Christ. Jesus recognizes them as a part of His family. Believers may lose the support and friendly association of earthly family members but rejoice that they are members of the great family of God.

MATTHEW

CHAPTER

THIRTEEN

PARABLES OF THE KINGDOM

Chapter 13 seems to mark a shift in the public ministry of the Messiah, demonstrating that a judgment has been passed against this "evil and adulterous generation" (12:39). This judgment is seen in the teaching of parables; only those to whom understanding was granted were able to comprehend their meaning (13:11). Matthew explains this as fulfillment of Isaiah 6:9-10, which indicates judgment has been launched against this generation (13:13-15, 34-35). Walvoord's arguments are legitimate, showing that with the kingdom's having been presented in chaps. 4-10, chap. 11 indicates the Jews were rejecting evidences of Jesus' messiahship and thus judgment was pronounced on the cities of Israel. Chapter 11 closes with an appeal to individual Jews to come to Him for comfort, and chap. 12 climaxes by indicating that a relationship with Jesus must be based on individual obedience to the Father through believing in Christ.[1]

Therefore it would appear that the kingdom of heaven, the messianic reign on the throne of David, was postponed for the time being. This is not to imply that the kingdom had been lost to Israel, but that the gospel would be sent to the Gentiles, and the universal work of Messiah will be the focus until Israel is brought back in repentance. Like the postponement of entrance into the Promised Land while Israel wandered in the wilderness for forty years, so now, once again, Israel's joy was postponed by her rebellion. The parables are intended to hide the keys to the kingdom from all except those granted understanding, which at this point were His disciples.

The focus of a parable should not be on each story detail, as parables are mostly cultural norms without spiritual significance. However, the purpose is to draw attention to key ambient factors (in this case, the seed, the condition of the seed, elements affecting the seed) that focus on the single point of the story. Jesus' use of parables was unprecedented at the time of His ministry. Jeremias states, "Further, Jesus' parables are something entirely new. In all the rabbinic literature, not one single parable has come down to us from the period before Jesus."[2] Albers comments on the importance of the Lord's use of parables, noting that "roughly one-third of the material attributed to Jesus by the Synoptic evangelists comes to us in the form of parables."[3]

FIRST PARABLE: SOWER OF THE SEED, 13:1-9 (Mark 4:1-9; Luke 8:4-8)

13:1-2 Matthew introduces this section with the ambiguous state-ment "on that day." The NIV renders it "that same day" (*en tē hēmera ekeinē*), which may be a better translation and would clearly link the parable teachings with the conflict in chap. 12. It would appear that Jesus left the house where He had been teaching and went down by the sea. No mention is made of His speaking to Mary or His brothers, and they may have left after His response of 12:47-50. Perhaps the house was too confining to accommodate the throng gathered to hear His messages (according to Luke, the crowd was gathering from several villages, 8:4). Because the multitude grew to such a large size (v. 2), to facilitate His speaking Jesus moved into a boat. The lake made an ideal teaching setting since the sloping banks offered an auditorium effect as the sound traveled naturally off the lake.

13:3 Jesus' first parable related to the sowing of seed and the four conditions upon which the seed fell. The designation "parable of the soils" incorrectly places the emphasis. The environment affecting the sown seed extends beyond just the soil. The elements of the parable would be common enough to the audience. A sower walked along his field with bags of seed, took a handful, and scattered the seed with a swinging motion of the arm. The seeds were not carefully placed in holes or plowed furrows as in many kinds of contemporary planting. To compare modern sowing and harvesting analogies to this parable would be incongruous.

13:4   The first sequence related to the sower's work was that the seed landed on the hard, packed-down roadway. Luke adds that the seed was trampled underfoot by passersby (8:5) and did not enter the earth at all but became food for birds. The imagery was clear enough—the seed did not accomplish its purpose and appears to have gone to waste. The spiritual application was given to the disciples later (v. 19), and commentary will be reserved until that point.

13:5-6   The second cluster of seeds landed on "rocky places" (*ta petrdē*) where the soil was shallow and did not allow for roots to anchor into the nutrition resident in deeper earth. The significant element here is the reference to rapid growth, "immediately they sprang up." From a merely human perspective, the immediate results would have led to celebration. From God's perspective, the appearance of immediate success is not important. The shallow roots could not withstand the sun's heat, and what at first looked to be exhilarating achievement was only shallow imitation of vibrant life. The meaning is explained in vv. 20-21.

13:7   The third group of seeds landed among the thorns that grew around the field. Thorns are hardy plants that can easily dominate a field if not removed. Their roots hoard the soil's moisture and nutrients, leaving little to sustain the new life of tender plants. The seed may take hold and produce a plant, but healthy growth or full productivity cannot be attained if thorns are allowed to grow alongside. The Lord later explained this analogy (v. 22).

13:8   The final category was the seed that fell upon good soil. "Good" (*kalē*) in this context refers to having the proper depth, nutrients, and other valuable components to produce fruit. This seed yielded a crop of diverse productivity. Some of the seed produced greater quantities for harvest. The analogy is probably that some parts of the field of good soil were more nutritious than others. Jesus seems to have applied this (v. 23) to an individual life and was not comparing different people. In other words, the same individual might produce different quantities of a variety of crops from the seed.

13:9   Following the first parable, the Lord repeated a proverb that He had used previously (see comment on 11:15). This same charge appears in Matthew 11:15; 13:9; Mark 4:23; Luke 14:35; Revelation 2:7; and 13:9. This proverb warns that what has just been said holds significant accountability.

REASON FOR HIS TEACHING IN PARABLES, 13:10-17

13:10   Since Jesus' teaching in parables was a new approach (though analogy and metaphor were previously used),[4] the disciples appeared confused by His technique. Therefore they asked, "Why do You speak to them in parables?" This was another way of saying, "Why do you not just tell them straight out?" Their confusion indicated that Jesus was not following His usual teaching pattern, and the disciples saw that the crowd had been left bewildered by what was just presented. The term "disciple" here includes more than just the Twelve (Mark 4:10).

13:11   Jesus' response was to inform His followers of their privileged position and that they would receive special grace to understand the meaning of the parables, to "know the mysteries of the kingdom of heaven." The term "mysteries" (*mustēria*) implies secret information and appears only here and in Mark 4:11 (a parallel use) in the Gospels. In secular Greek, it was used for the mystery cults as well as for hidden political agenda. Here it refers to concealment of data related to the kingdom. Paul uses the term twenty-one times in reference to God's program—for example, in hardening Israel (Rom. 11:25) and inclusion of Gentiles in God's redemptive work (Col. 1:27).

It was granted (perfect passive of *didmi*), "given," to His followers to understand these hidden elements of the kingdom, but "to them [the crowd] it has not been granted." Thus, Jesus spoke in coded language. The words were common, everyday words, but the significance behind them was spiritual and of another reality dimension. The question may be raised, then, why speak to the people at all? This will become clear in vv. 14-15—it was an act of judgment for their refusal to acknowledge their Messiah. The secrets of the kingdom were given to no one but the disciples, who received their Messiah by faith.

13:12-13   Christ continued to explain by stating another proverb, "Whoever has, to him shall more be given." This would be repeated as the application of a parable in Matthew 25:29. It is the rule of the privileged that they have and continue to gain, while the ones without are stripped of what little they have. This may seem cruel and lacking of the grace of God, but it was the consequence of Israel's stubborn resistance. Having had the privilege of God's promises and the position as chosen servants of Yahweh, now not only would they not receive the keys to understand kingdom truth, but their privileges would also be taken away.

Verse 13 explains this more clearly. "Therefore" (*dia touto*, literally, "because of this") "I speak to them in parables." This was a straightforward reply to the disciples' question (v. 10). The "therefore" relates back to His explanation (v. 12) that Israel was losing what had been given by virtue of their being the elect people of God, yet stubbornly refusing His Messiah. Hendriksen offers a good observation and links this to Exodus 7:14-22; 8:15 and Proverbs 29:1.[5] Jesus spoke to them in parables because (*hoti*, causal conjunction introducing a clause explaining why) "while seeing, they do not see, and while hearing they do not hear, nor do they understand." This oxymoronic proverb was intended to add guilt to the Jews who saw the miracles but refused to acknowledge what they saw, who heard the teachings but ignored what Jesus said. They did not understand (*suniēmi*, "comprehend, have insight concerning") who Jesus was or what His message meant, because they refused to pay attention to Him and acknowledge His work.

13:14-15   To emphasize the point for the disciples, Jesus referred to Isaiah 6:9-10. Again, the modern reader must not assume that a reference to the Old Testament was intended to be an exact quote. Here Jesus cited Isaiah to bring the condemnation of Old Testament Israel to bear on "this wicked generation"; thus, He did not follow exactly the Hebrew or LXX but changed the tense of the verbs, "you shall," which brought the prophecy up to the Jews of His time. John, likewise, cites this passage to explain why Israel did not believe "though He had performed so many signs before them" (John 12:37-40). The apostle Paul applies the Isaiah passage as the Holy Spirit's speaking to the generation of Jews that rejected his message (Acts 28:25-28). Jesus stated that the prophecy was "fulfilled" (*anaplēro*) in them, implying that even though it was true for Isaiah's generation, completion in full measure would be reached in this generation—the one confronted with the Messiah and who subsequently rejected Him. The double negative repeated before both "hearing" and "seeing" emphasizes their condition, "You shall in no way understand . . . you shall in no way see."

Verse 15 highlights the problem. Their hearts were "dull" (*epachunthē,* aorist passive of *pachunomai*) or, more literally, "had become insensitive." The problem began in their hearts, not their minds. The heart (*kardia*) in Scripture thinks, feels, plans, and even speaks; the inner person interprets what the eyes and ears experience and translates the data for the mind. Thus, unbelief begins in the heart. The eyes and ears are only data receptors; they cannot function properly if the heart is wicked.

Verse 15 also sheds light on the problem by implying willful ignorance: having closed their eyes, "lest they should see . . . and hear . . . and understand . . . and return" for healing. If they had looked and listened with a pure heart, understanding would have been gained. Understanding would then have led to a return to their God (whom they had abandoned for their religion), and by their returning, the Messiah would have healed them. Notice the associations: the eyes see; the ears hear; and the heart understands. But because Jesus was not the type of Messiah expected or wanted, they chose to remain in their ignorance. Meyer sums up their stubbornness: "They are not willing to be instructed by Me, and morally healed."[6]

13:16-17   In contrast, the eyes and ears of the disciples are "blessed" (*makarios;* see comments on 5:3-11) because (*hoti*) they were seeing and hearing. The implication was that their eyes and ears were the recipients of God's good favor, receiving what the other Jews did not. In the broader range of theological truth, it is understood that their hearts were made new for the purpose of receiving and understanding what they were seeing and hearing (e.g., vv. 11, 16, 17). Meyer explains Jesus' statement: "Your intellect, as regards the apprehension of divine truth, is not unreceptive and obtuse, but susceptible and active."[7]

The privilege of the disciples not only exceeded that of the crowd, which heard but did not understand the parable, but even that of the Old Testament prophets (v. 17). Carson puts the comment in proper perspective, "The reference is to OT prophets and others who were just before God—people who looked forward to the coming of the kingdom. Here one cannot help but include Simeon (Luke 2:25-35) and Anna (Luke 2:36-38)."[8] The disciples were privileged to experience and understand what even the prophets could only imagine.

EXPLANATION OF THE PARABLE OF THE SOWER, 13:18-23

13:18   The English versions hardly express the emphasis of Jesus' command. The text is literally *"You* listen to . . ."* The pronoun "You" (*humeis*) is stated separately instead of simply implied by the verbal form and was placed first in the sentence for emphasis. The purpose was to contrast the disciples with those who did not "hear." They were commanded to "hear" (*akousate*) the parable, meaning to learn the lesson of the homily.

13:19   The first part of the story involves the seed eaten by the birds. Jesus explained that this is what happens to the message of the kingdom when people do not understand and the Devil steals the truth. It is interesting that Jesus used "understand" (*suniēmi*) instead of "believe" (*pisteu*). The seed (message of the kingdom) is sown into the heart, but understanding is not gained because the heart is dull ("insensitive," v. 15). The people hearing Christ were not receptive, but the reason is not stated here. Earlier chapters indicate that since Jesus would not endorse their religious activities, His message was not considered desirable. Thus, because of their stubbornness they could not understand the message. While they rationalized and tried to excuse themselves, the Devil came and stole the message from them. Hendriksen explains,

> Verse 19a speaks about the unresponsive, insensible, callous heart, the heart of the person who by persistent refusal to walk in the light has become accustomed hardly even to listen to the message as it is being proclaimed. Under the influence of the devil, whatever it is that this man hears he immediately thrusts away from himself as if for him at least it contained nothing of importance.[9]

13:20-21   The second category is the seed that fell on rocky soil. This represents the one who indicates an immediate response to the message but falls away when persecution comes. Many would assume this teaches the loss of the person's salvation, but neither the context nor words used imply such theology. Many were anxious to follow Jesus, hopefully to capture the benefits of the kingdom. However, they were not genuine in their reception of the King, and the seed could not take root. Judas is probably a good example of this type. Eager to join the band of disciples upon hearing the kingdom was at hand, he assumed that his position as a disciple would guarantee some privileges in the future kingdom. But with the realization that the King must die and the kingdom glories be delayed, Judas betrayed the King. He was never saved and was labeled a devil and the son of perdition from the beginning. His attachment to the kingdom was shallow and selfish; therefore, when he realized persecution was to come, he fell away. MacArthur refers to this kind of response to the message: "When this person hears the gospel it brings a religious experience but it does not bring salvation . . . the gospel truth has not penetrated his heart but only the edge of his mind."[10] The "joy" with which it is received is based on selfish intent (what can the King do for him now?) and not on the eternal value of the King's work.

Jesus says this type "has no root in himself" (*ouk echei de hrizan en heaut*), implying that any apparent growth was only the superficial springing up of a dying seed. Thus, it was "temporary" (*proskairos,* woodenly translated as "toward time"), or only for the moment. Mounce observes, "Unless truth takes deep root in the human heart it will be recanted as soon as it meets any opposition. Thin soil produces superficial commitment."[11] The persecution that exposes this superficiality is not the general problems of life but affliction (*thlipsis*) and persecution (*digmos*) related to the word of the kingdom (*dia ton logon*). Once the person realizes that connection with the kingdom brings suffering, he flees, having never understood the eternal, nonmaterial nature of its blessings.

13:22   The third classification in the parable deals with those who hear the message but are too occupied with the cares of the world to pay attention. Countless people briefly stopped to hear the Lord preach but were too busy "living" to learn of their present death, not lingering to find out more about the message or the Messenger. The thorns represent two areas that prohibit this kind of person from a proper response to the message: first, "the worry of the world," literally, of the "age" (*ain*); second, "the deceitfulness of riches." The idea of worry (*merimna*) is "anxiety, excessive concern." The New Testament has much to say about anxiety, including the famous prohibition of Philippians 4:6 (*mēden merimnate*).

Anxiety was also the focus of one of Jesus' earlier lessons (Matt. 6:25-34, where *merimna* appears six times).

The concerns of the present age and the drive to establish material wealth distract greatly from a kingdom that calls upon its followers to not lay up treasures on this earth (6:19). Riches are "deceitful" in that one may build false security upon temporal goods (Luke 12:15-21). Whereas having wealth may earn respect from other men, that cannot prepare one to stand before God. Pre-occupation with matters of the present life and even the practical reality of providing for retirement might be a hindrance to a proper response to the message of the kingdom.

13:23   The final batch of seeds fell on good soil (*tēn kalēn gēn*), which represents the one who is both hearing (*ho . . . akoun,* present tense participle) and understanding (*sunieis,* also present tense participle). This is the one who bears fruit (the particle *dē* adds emphasis), "who indeed bears fruit, and brings forth, some a hundredfold, some sixty, and some thirty." This diversity of quantity is interesting, because even the least (thirtyfold) is still considered "good soil." Compare Mark 4:20, where the order is reversed: thirty-, sixty-, a hundredfold. Barnes identifies this group as "those whose hearts are prepared by grace to receive it honestly, and give it full opportunity to grow . . . in a heart that submits itself to the full influence of truth, unchecked by cares and anxieties."[12] The most direct application of the good soil would be to the disciples, whom He had promised, "To you it has been granted to know the mysteries of the kingdom of heaven" (13:11), and, "Blessed are your eyes, because they see; and your ears, because they hear" (13:16). In Luke's account these who bear fruit are said to have received the message of the kingdom "in an honest and good heart, and hold it fast, and bear fruit with perseverance" (Luke 8:15). Luke does not list the variant quantities but emphasizes the quality of the one receiving the message.

SECOND PARABLE: THE GOOD SEED AND THE TARES, 13:24-30

13:24-25   Jesus immediately moved into a second parable, which is not found in either Mark or Luke. The analogy of sowing seed was continued, and it may be assumed that He was speaking once again to the crowd (vv. 34-36). Here the point was not the preaching of the kingdom but the growth of the kingdom and the false growth within the kingdom. Jesus drew a comparison between the kingdom and a man (Himself, v. 37) sowing good seed in a field. This was to help envision (1) the evangelistic outreach of the true work of God and (2) the false members of the kingdom. The seed is good (*kalon*), but an enemy sows bad seed. In the early stages it looks like the grain sown by the owner of the field, but actually it lacks the value and life of the true seed. Useless and toilsome to weed out, tares resemble the wheat plant until the point of producing grain. The tare is a type of rye grass. Its seed is referred to as darnel, and it is often host to a smut fungus that can be poisonous to both man and animal.[13] The comment that this was done while men were sleeping (v. 25) is not to imply a failure on the part of the sower but to emphasize the secretiveness of the enemy. His subtle infiltration suggests the craftiness of the enemy of God's work.

13:26-30   The tares become evident with the maturing of the wheat. Although the tares closely resemble the wheat, there is no produce in the head of the plant. The fact that the slaves first question the quality of seed that their master had sown is worth noting, because it would be more naturally assumed that the master would question the slaves. It would appear that the slaves did not first think of an enemy rather than a mistake on the part of the owner.

An "enemy" (*echthros anthrōpos*, a "hated man" or a "hostile man"), here not called the Evil One but something more generic, is blamed by the owner (v. 28). Certainly this must ultimately refer to Satan (see comments on v. 39), but the generic use of "enemy" may be emphasizing the work of false teachers or anyone else who (as Satan's instrument) opposes the truth of God's work by offering substitutes. In v. 38, the tares are referred to as "sons of the evil one" (*hoi hioi tou ponērou*).

The servants' solution is to weed out the tares, but the master instructs them to wait until the end (v. 29), reasoning that a mistake could easily be made and the wheat possibly be destroyed with the weeds. Instruction is given to let the weeds grow alongside the wheat until the harvest (v. 30). Carson states: "'Harvest' is a common metaphor for the final judgment."[14] The parable seems to be teaching that God's work will be permeated with false plants, which appear genuine but do not produce grain. These will be allowed to remain in the field until the judgment. At the harvest, the owner's servants will not be allowed to gather in the crop but "reapers" (*tois theristais;* angels, v. 39) will be sent to gather both tares and wheat. First, the tares will be bundled and burned. Then the true crop will be gathered into the barns for use.

Some earlier scholars attempted to treat this parable as a standard for dealing with church heresy and immorality. The idea seems to have been that sin in the church was to be tolerated until God brought judgment. However, the immediate context and biblical ecclesiology will not permit this view. Carson explains:

> Nowhere in Matthew does "kingdom" (or "reign". . .) become "church". . . . The parable does not address the church situation at all but explains how the kingdom can be present in the world while not wiping out all opposition. That must await the harvest. The parable deals with eschatological expectation, not ecclesiological deterioration.[15]

Although this writer would agree for the most part, there needs to be some adjustment to the idea that the parable is about the kingdom in the present world. The parable is teaching about an enemy coming into God's "field" (not individual churches but His redemptive work in the world) and sowing false religion or imitation believers. The church's duty is not to destroy these weeds (as many Reformers and the Roman church attempted) but to allow God to take them out at the end time judgment. This does not prohibit evicting heretics from assemblies of believers or exercising church discipline, but it does prohibit executing those assumed to be weeds. Christ explained that the "reapers" are the angels sent to execute God's judgment at the end of the age (v. 39-40).

The wheat is gathered into God's "barn" (v. 30). This simply relates the truth that God's elect will be gathered together in God's presence. It is His harvest of redeemed mankind. The barn represents the completion of harvest, when the crop is safely stored away from damaging weather and corruption from the enemy. Further comments on this parable will follow in vv. 36-40, where Jesus offers interpretation for His disciples.

THIRD PARABLE: THE MUSTARD SEED, 13:31-32 (Mark 4:30-32; Luke 13:18-19)

13:31   The introductory formula "The kingdom of heaven is like . . ."

draws a comparison between the known and the unknown. The Jews had not grasped the kingdom of heaven concept, and the mustard tree was a familiar part of their culture. The parable conveyed a truth that should have been comprehensible because of its simplicity, yet there is no indication that the Jews understood. By the interchange of the terms "kingdom of heaven" and "kingdom of God," the parallel passages reveal that the two expressions reference one and the same entity.

13:32   The NASB translates the opening phrase of this verse as "this is smaller than all other seeds." Likewise, the NIV and KJV imply that the mustard seed is the smallest seed (the NIV attempts to justify the statement by adding the possessive pronoun "your," which is not in the text). The problem is that the mustard seed is *not* the smallest seed known to science; therefore some have accused Jesus of making a scientific error. The question is, did Jesus intend to address all seeds or was He speaking in the context of the people of Palestine? In Palestine, the mustard seed was the smallest they could have known. Second, the adjective is a comparative not superlative[16] use with the comparative genitive *pantōn,* "which is smaller among all of the seeds" (*ho mikroteron men estin pantōn tōn spermatōn*). Another reason not to fault Jesus' statement is that according to the Mishnah, the mustard seed was a proverbial norm for smallness;[17] thus, He was simply using a proverb with which they would have been familiar.

The comparison of the parable was between the beginning of the kingdom and its end result. The kingdom would begin as a small, apparently insignificant, event but would grow to a large plant, which would provide nesting and shelter. One should not take the analogy beyond this simple truth. Trying to identify the birds is useless speculation, and to build doctrine from such obscure analogy is dangerous. Christ's point was significant in the context of Israel's expectation that Messiah's kingdom would come in glory and military might; it came instead as a small seed planted in a field. The growth was not portrayed as phenomenal nor did it imply that the kingdom would be vast. Many plants in Palestine were much larger and more impressive than the mustard plant. Jesus was emphasizing the kingdom's insignificant beginning.

Fourth Parable: The Leaven, 13:33

13:33   The fourth parable is logically connected to the third. The parable of the mustard seed deals with the external growth of the kingdom, and the parable of the leaven deals with the internal influence that leads to the growth of the kingdom. Leaven is yeast, which makes dough rise when added to flour. The analogy is that the kingdom is like yeast worked into a lump of dough—it permeates the entire mass. The "three pecks of meal" may symbolize the believer who is given the leaven (the kingdom), which, once internalized, begins to grow until it fills all facets of life. Jesus does not offer any explanation of the features of the parable (the woman, the leaven, the meal), and one must be extremely cautious in attributing interpretations to them. The parable reflects the common cultural cooking habits of a woman. The key ingredient for the parable, the leaven, normally (but not always) represents sin. However, here we are told it represents the kingdom of heaven. The specific quantity of meal (three pecks) is more attributable to a normal amount used in baking than to having any spiritual significance. The meal most naturally represents those in whom the kingdom is placed (believers). The yeast permeates the entire life and is not just a separate part of living, as religion often may be. An alternative understanding would be for the meal to represent the world, but that analogy breaks down. The world may be permeated with the gospel but not with the kingdom.

The Purpose of Parabolic Teaching: Further Explanation, 13:34-35 (Mark 4:33-34)

13:34-35   Matthew seems to repeat himself in explaining the purpose of Jesus' parabolic teaching (vv. 10-13), but the repetition serves to emphasize the judgment being enacted against this generation of Israel. The text reads as a chiastic parallelism.

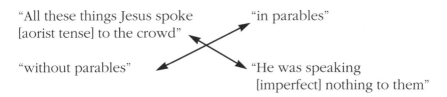

"All these things Jesus spoke [aorist tense] to the crowd"   "in parables"

"without parables"   "He was speaking [imperfect] nothing to them"

The aorist tense and imperfect tense imply that the speaking Jesus was doing was intended to be understood by the series of parables just spoken. To try to apply this to all of His teachings is a mistake. The parabolic messages were to fulfill a promise of God to stubborn Israel.

Jesus cited Psalm 78:2, where Yahweh is speaking to the nation, but the nature of the psalm at first appears to be more positive than the statement in Matthew. However, the psalm goes on to explain how the people of Israel assumed they knew God's words, but there was a wicked generation that "did not prepare its heart, and whose spirit was not faithful to God" (v. 8). Matthew associates this warning with his generation of Jews, who had hardened their hearts against God's Messiah.

EXPLANATION OF THE PARABLE OF THE TARES, 13:36-43

13:36   The disciples were as much confused about the parable of the tares as was the multitude. This was typical of their comprehension, which should not shock the contemporary reader. The Spirit had not yet come to direct them into the truth (John 16:13), and spiritual truth is discernible only through spiritual enlightenment (1 Cor. 2:6-16). Jesus therefore was asked to explain the meaning. This actually demonstrated the proper attitude, and Jesus was willing to help them understand. He had already indicated this (vv. 11, 16-23).

13:37-39   Jesus began by identifying the major characters: the sower is the Son of Man (Himself);[18] the field is the world; the good seed is the sons of the kingdom; the tares are the sons of the "evil one" (v. 38); the enemy is the Devil; and the reapers are the angels (v. 39). These identities should surprise no one and do not require explanation. The point of the parable is that Jesus has planted His elect in the world; they spring up and are growing unto the harvest that He desires. His enemy, the Devil (v. 39), has likewise planted seed in the world, which grows alongside the sons of the kingdom. These appear very similar to the sons of the kingdom. Often Satan's offspring are portrayed as fiendish, grossly immoral, or practicing black magic. Here, however, they are portrayed as religionists who appear godly and resemble the sons of the kingdom. Even Judas did not stand out among the disciples, and Jesus claimed that the pious Pharisees themselves were children of the Devil (John 8:39-44).

The analogy is to portray the "end of the age" (*sunteleia*, "completion"; *aiōnos*, "age, time period") when the harvest will take place. At that point, and not before, the two different crops will be divided.

13:40-43   Jesus' explanation needs no further clarification. The Lord offers lucid detail of the end times judgment of the tares. They are gathered by the angels and burned (v. 40). The false religionists, who were offspring of the Devil and not of the Messiah, are burned, portraying one of the most horrible forms of destruction imaginable. The greater horror is Scripture's teaching that this burning is not temporary, ending in cessation of life, but everlasting (Rev. 19:20; 20:10, 12-15; 21:8) and conscious torture (Luke 16:22-24, 28). This judgment comes at the "end of the age," as the Flood (the first universal judgment against mankind) came at the end of an earlier period of time established by God (Gen. 6:3).

Verses 41-42 offer further details of the statement in v. 40. The Son of Man will send forth His angels to separate the false from the true. This is a divine act and again emphasizes that the duty of the church is not to inflict capital punishment upon heretics or apostates. This is not an inquisition conducted by men but divine judgment executed by supernatural agents. The tares are further identified in v. 41 as "stumbling blocks" (*skandala*, "that which causes trouble or causes others to sin") and "those who commit lawlessness" (*poiountas tēn anomian*). In Matthew 7:21-23, the doers of lawlessness are those claiming to work miracles and cast out demons in the name of Jesus. In 23:27-28, Jesus declares to the Pharisees and scribes that they are full of hypocrisy and lawlessness (same word). In 24:11-12, the spread of lawlessness is associated with the spread of false prophets. It seems best from this passage to identify the tares as self-righteous religionists who outwardly appear godly but pervert the law into a legalistic religion and fail to understand the mercy and grace of God.

Their end is frightful indeed—"Cast them into the furnace of fire . . . there shall be weeping and gnashing of teeth" (v. 42). Barnes observes:

> It is not certain that our Saviour meant to teach here that hell is made up of *material* fire; but it is certain that he meant to teach that this would be a proper *representation* of the sufferings of the lost . . . .

He would not talk of hell-fire which had no existence, nor would the Saviour of men hold out frightful images merely to terrify mankind.[19]

Verse 43 offers the dramatic antithesis of the fate of the tares: "The righteous will shine forth as the sun in the kingdom of their Father." Righteousness is not based upon legalistic adherence to the Law—Jesus' reaction to the Pharisees certainly demonstrated that—but upon faith in Jesus Christ, who came to fulfill the Law and yet pay the penalty of all condemned by the Law (Rom. 3-6). The analogy of shining as the sun depicts the glory of the sons of the kingdom. Those who were commanded to be a light in darkness (5:14-16) will certainly shine at the fulfillment of the work of the Son of Man. Once again, the proverb "He who has ears, let him hear" is to emphasize the importance of the lesson just taught.

FIFTH PARABLE: THE TREASURE IN THE FIELD, 13:44

13:44   The fifth parable is very short. Now the kingdom of heaven is compared to a treasure buried in a field. The primary consideration of the story is the value of the treasure. Its worth was greater than all the other possessions the man owned. He sold these to gain the price of the field, purchasing it to obtain legal rights to its contents—the treasure. Simply stated, the treasure is the only focus in the parable, and the lesson is its great value. Instead of holding onto worldly possessions, one should count the kingdom of heaven of much greater value.

Another possible interpretation, and perhaps the best, is that the kingdom (the treasure) is in the world (the field, v. 38), and Jesus is the one who paid the price for the field so that He could claim the treasure (the church). This makes more sense than assuming a believer must buy the world to own the kingdom. It would also be inconsistent to think that one could buy his way into the kingdom.

SIXTH PARABLE: THE PEARL OF GREAT PRICE, 13:45-46

13:45-46   The fifth parable reemphasizes the same lesson. Some scholars make the treasure in the field represent Israel and the pearl the church.[20] But both parables are about "the kingdom of heaven," and to make one Israel and the other the church is unrealistic. Here the kingdom of heaven is compared to a pearl of such value that everything else the merchant owned was sacrificed to obtain it. Again, the merchant may be seen as portraying Christ paying the great price to purchase the pearl, the elect of God.

SEVENTH PARABLE: THE DRAGNET, 13:47-50

13:47-48   The final parable in the series is taken from the daily routine of life on the Sea of Galilee. The first two parables dealt with sowing and reaping; the last one deals with fishing. The kingdom of heaven is like a giant net used for gathering anything within its range. The expression "of every kind" is important. The thrust of this parable is similar to the lesson of the wheat and tares in that good and bad are allowed to be together and then are separated. The dragnet was thrown into the sea and allowed to sink, then pulled to shore, where its contents were removed. It does not target any particular kind of fish but rather takes anything in its path. The fishermen separate the catch, discarding what is not good for market.

13:49-50   As before (vv. 39-40), the separation is carried out at "the end of the age" and is to be the work of divine instruments (angels). The wicked are taken out from among the righteous and cast into "the furnace of fire." The imagery is of appalling suffering, "weeping and gnashing of teeth," a reminder of the terrible consequences of not being a citizen of the kingdom of heaven. The Jews would naturally have thought that those taken to the fiery furnace were the Gentiles, but, according to Matthew 8:11-12, the "wicked" will include those who had the right to the kingdom but refused their Messiah. The point of the parable is to warn of the finality and horrific consequences of not responding to the Savior of the human race. If one does not fit the category of "righteous," he will be cast into the fire forever.

ANALOGY OF THE SCRIBE, 13:51-52

13:51-52   Jesus had been speaking to His disciples (v. 36) and concluded the lessons by asking if they "understood" (*sunēkate*, aorist of *suniēmi*), to which an affirmative response was given. How much or how well they understood could be debated, but it is safe to assume they were not fearful of asking for help. They had asked for help before (v. 36) and had been enlightened about the kingdom by means of these last few parables, which the crowds did not hear. Yet the rebuke of 15:16 indicates that they were not totally grasping the significance of all aspects of the kingdom message.

Of v. 52 Carson notes, "Interpretations of this difficult verse are legion."[21] The use of a scribe as an illustration of the disciples' responsibility to share what they had learned directed them to become teachers of others. The key features of the parable are: (1) the scribe who becomes a disciple of the kingdom, (2) the head of a household, and (3) the new and old things from his treasury.

Many scholars identify the scribe as "every kingdom worker,"[22] in other words, every citizen of the kingdom who is trained through discipleship. Gundry sees the scribe of the parable as the disciples, who professed to understand what Jesus had been teaching (v. 51).[23] A scribe was basically one who copied and taught the Law and was considered an expert in the Old Testament Scriptures. Here Jesus implied that, since His men had been discipled by Him, they were now "scribes." The emphasis was not on a Jewish scribe's being converted to the kingdom but on the disciples of Christ being scribes in the truest sense. Having just professed to understand His teachings, the disciples acknowledged their status as scribes.

The analogy is to indicate their responsibility in this new position. A house owner was responsible to use his resources to provide for his household. The disciples of the kingdom were to use their resources, their understanding, to provide for kingdom citizens. They, like the house owner, were to draw out of their storehouse (of knowledge). The "treasure" is literally "storehouse" (*thēsaurou*), referring to a deposit box or storage facility, which in this context is certainly their knowledge of the kingdom. They were to "bring forth" (literally, "cast out," *ekballō*) out of this storehouse of knowledge both "new and old." The idea is to share and spread about their knowledge. It was not to be withheld in order to give them a position of power over other people but to be distributed so that they also might understand the things of the kingdom. These things were labeled "new" and "old." The "new" was not a different religion, nor was it contrary to the old—it was the disclosure of that which the "old" had hinted of and anticipated. The new revelation of the Messiah did not replace the revelation given in the Old Testament Scriptures but fulfilled it. The disciples of the kingdom would build on the old to demonstrate that Messiah had come.

JESUS RETURNS TO NAZARETH, 13:53-58
(Mark 6:1-6; Luke 4:16-30)

13:53-54   "And it came about" (*kai egeneto*) is a typical formula Matthew uses to introduce a new pericope. Thus he shifts the emphasis from the teaching of multitudes in parables to the significant event of rejection in Jesus' hometown. Jesus finished the parables, which implied that He had made His point concerning the blindness of Israel (13:13, 35) and was moving to another phase of His work. Mounce observes, "The fourth major section of Matthew's Gospel begins at this point."[24]

Matthew does not mention the name "Nazareth" but refers to it as "His home town" to give emphasis to the shocking response of those who had known Him from childhood. Jesus was raised in Nazareth, a city of questionable reputation. He returned there following His baptism and temptation but left for Capernaum upon hearing of John's arrest (cf. 4:12-13). Perhaps a year later, He returned home and announced His mission through preaching in the synagogue. Luke offers only two short verses concerning the ministry in Galilee to which Matthew gives several chapters. Luke focuses upon the events of Nazareth, giving far more detail than Matthew. As part of this detail, Luke records what Jesus taught in the synagogue that caused the people to be "astonished."

According to Luke 4:16-21, Jesus announced that Isaiah's prediction of the anointed messenger of Yahweh had been fulfilled in Him. The message in the synagogue had been accompanied by a few miracles (Matt.13:58; Mark 6:5), but the Nazarites did not see the miracles as verification of the message and were "astonished," amazed, that He would teach such things. Their skepticism was reflected in their question, "Where did this man get this wisdom, and these miraculous powers?" One would think that, if they recognized His "wisdom" (*sophia*) and "miraculous powers" (*hai dunameis*), they would have accepted His message. But as Luke so carefully records, they tried instead to kill Him. Matthew tells us (v. 57) that they "took offense at Him." Luke explains that at first they "all were speaking well of Him, and wondering at the gracious words which were falling from His lips" (Luke 4:22), but as He continued to teach about the work of God among the Gentiles (Luke 4:25-27) and to associate this with His work as Messiah, they became angry and wanted to kill Him (Luke 4:28-29). The crowd in the synagogue rejected His work and His claims because He implied that Israel was no longer the only focus of God's program.

13:55-56   Their attacks began by ignoring His spiritual calling and reducing Him to a mere human whom they had known from His childhood. He was identified as the carpenter's son, the son of Mary and the brother of James, Joseph, Simon, and Judas as well as unnamed sisters. MacArthur says:

> The facts that Jesus was the carpenter's son and the Son of Mary, that He had brothers . . . who everyone in Nazareth knew, and that He had sisters who still lived there were irrelevant to the issues of His being the Messiah or not. Although the Jews had many incomplete and false notions about the Messiah, they knew He was to come to earth as a man and that He would have to be born into some family and live in some community.[25]

The question in v. 56, "Where then did this man get all these things?" indicates that they were challenging either His authority or the source (*pothen oun*) of His claim that He was the anointed messenger of Isaiah's prophecy. In their eyes He was the son of a common laborer. They had been conditioned to the traditionally pompous roles of the Pharisees and Sadducees. For a common person to claim to be the fulfillment of the great prophecy and then to preach that the Gentiles would be a part of God's redemptive program was more than they were ready to accept.

13:57-58   The people of Nazareth "took offense," or as Luke tells us, "all in the synagogue were filled with rage" (Luke 4:28). To this Jesus responded, "A prophet is not without honor except in his home town, and in his own household." He was not intending to limit where a person can minister but to emphasize the difficulty of separating a prophet from his past. The old proverb "Familiarity breeds contempt" can certainly be applied here. The Nazarites' familiarity with Jesus' family and personal life hindered their acceptance of Him as the Messiah.

Jesus did not work many miracles in Nazareth, and Matthew

explains this as a result of the people's unbelief. The connection between the miracles and their unbelief is not to be construed as inability on the part of Jesus but rather as His unwillingness. The power to work miracles is not based upon a partnership between human and divine but only upon the will of the divine. Mark states that Jesus "could do no miracle" (*ouk edunato ekei poiēsai*) but not because He was dependent upon human participation. Carson points out, "The 'could not' is related to Jesus' mission: just as Jesus could not turn stones to bread without violating his mission (4:1-4), so he could not do miracles indiscriminately without turning his mission into a sideshow."[26] Though the primary issue may not have been Jesus' making His ministry a sideshow, the point of comparison with turning stone to bread is important. Jesus did not work miracles at His own discretion; He was obedient to the Father and did what the Father instructed. What Jesus needed in the time of His temptation was not bread but to obey the Word of His Father. A better understanding of the limitation is that Jesus could not work many miracles because God would not honor Nazareth with such a display of power in light of their unbelief.

HOMILETICAL SUGGESTIONS

The parables make excellent preaching material, but one must be careful not to insert meaning into the symbols that was not originally intended. The key hermeneutical guideline for parable interpretation is to look for the base lesson and identify the major features only in relation to that base lesson. Every parable is intended to communicate but one main point; every other feature is to emphasize that point. Therefore, side issues are not to be forced into the passage. Parables may illustrate some point of theology, but one should not build theology from parables.

The seven parables of this chapter are all specifically stated to represent the kingdom of heaven (five introduced by "the kingdom of heaven is like," one by "the kingdom may be compared to," and one He explains as "when anyone hears the word of the kingdom"). One must not substitute the term "church" for "the kingdom of heaven." The kingdom of heaven is a broader term, which covers God's full redemptive program.

Perhaps one of the most significant lessons to be learned from this chapter is that the disciples' were enlightened to understand the mysteries of the kingdom. First Corinthians 2:6-16 explains that only through the Spirit can one understand spiritual truth. This is certainly consistent with what Jesus taught His men in the lessons from the parables. Other critical lessons to be learned from these parables are the dangers of religion, the counterfeiting work of Satan, and the value God places on the kingdom of heaven.

MATTHEW
CHAPTER
FOURTEEN

RETURN TO THE
AREA OF GALILEE

Ancient Near Eastern narrative was not as concerned with chronological sequence as is the Western mind set. Therefore, though all the synoptics record the following events, their differing context placement seems odd to contemporary readers. However, the biblical narratives conform to the normative style of recording history, and each testimony is consistent with the other accounts, presenting the reader with historical information in the order relative to the purpose of each gospel writer.

THE ACCOUNT OF JOHN'S MARTYRDOM, 14:1-13
(Mark 6:16-29; Luke 9:7-9)

14:1-2 Jesus was working mostly in and around the region of Galilee, which was under the rule of Herod the tetrarch. This was Herod Antipas, son of Herod the Great, who had died a few years after the birth of Jesus. His title, "tetrarch" (*tetraarchēs*), originally referred to ruling one-fourth of a kingdom, but later it became a title for a ruler of lower rank than a true king. At the death of Herod the Great, the struggle between his sons to gain control of the kingdom ended in the territory's being divided among Philip, Herod,[1] and Archaelaus. Archaelaus was banished because of his rash cruelty, and the kingdom was redivided between Herod and Philip, each being given a tetrarchy[2] (and both bearing the title *Herod*). Herod

Antipas, as tetrarch over Galilee, thus gained regular information about the miracles and power of Jesus.

In v. 2, Herod's assumption that Jesus was actually a resurrected John the Baptist is revealed. According to Mark, the people of the area also assumed that Jesus was John the Baptist. They had certainly heard of John and his unjust murder by Herod and believed that Jesus was John himself (Mark 6:14). There were also rumors that Jesus was Elijah or the predicted prophet who would be like Moses (Mark 6:15). The superstitious nature of the people and the unjustified murder of John fueled the rumors that brought fear to Herod. According to Luke's account, Herod was trying to see Jesus to determine for himself whether He was the resurrected John (Luke 9:7-9).

14:3-5   John had been arrested and imprisoned for condemning the immoral relationship between Herod and Herodias, former wife of his half-brother Herod Philip (not necessarily Philip the tetrarch; there appears to have been another half-brother Philip by a different wife[3]). Josephus offers some historical account of John's murder, which was discussed in chap. 3.[4] He explains that Herod Antipas had fallen in love with Herodias.[5] John condemned the marriage (v. 4), which angered Herodias and caused her to seek his death (Mark 6:18-19). John was most likely preaching from Leviticus 8:16; 20:21, and he appears to have preached this message repeatedly (the text literally reads "John was saying," imperfect tense, *elegen*, implying continuous action in past time.

In v. 5, Matthew records that Herod was afraid to put John to death, as does Mark 6:20, which adds that in other areas "he [Herod] used to enjoy listening to him." It may seem strange that, in an environment known for brutal tyrants, one man such as John could strike fear in the heart of Herod. Mark informs us that Herod considered him "a righteous and holy man" (6:20). Matthew adds that his fear of killing John was based on the opinion of the Israelites, who considered him to be a prophet. To openly execute a righteous man, especially one who was regarded as a prophet, would most likely bring on a riot. Herod locked John in prison, hoping to silence him (cf. Matt. 11:2-3). Josephus records a similar account of these events (see chap. 3).[6]

14:6-7   Something as simple as a birthday party became Satan's instrument to attack the imprisoned servant of God. Herodias used her daughter to manipulate Herod into ordering John's execution. According to Hoehner, the daughter was Salome,[7] who may have been as young as twelve years or no more than fourteen.[8] Her dance was exhilarating to both Herod and his leaders (Mark 6:22), and in his passion Herod vowed to give her anything she wanted. It is useless to speculate as to how all of this took place, but it was not unheard of in the ancient world for tyrants to make such rash oaths.

14:8   Herodias, the mother, took advantage of this state of affairs to wreak her vengeance upon the prophet of God who had so boldly proclaimed her to be in sin. Mark offers much more detail: Herod promised to give the young temptress up to half of his kingdom (6:23). The girl went to her mother for advice (6:24), and the mother instructed her to ask for the head of John the Baptist (6:24).

Something of man's depraved nature can be seen in the action of each of the three main players in this sad drama: the young girl used her seductive skill to lure the king into a vulnerable position; Herod foolishly promised, before witnesses, to give away up to half of his kingdom; and Herodias was so bent on revenge that she chose to kill a man who was already in prison rather than to capitalize on the wealth and control of Herod's kingdom.

14:9   The "ethical" behavior of Herod is interesting. He would rather execute a man whom he knew to be righteous and holy (Mark 6:20) than to break his irrational oath. Matthew and Mark both note that it was because of his dinner guests that he fulfilled his promise (v. 9; Mark 6:26). The "haste" and "immediately" and "right away" statements in Mark's account emphasize that Herodias was anxious to take advantage of the situation. Had young Salome not demanded that it be done "right away" (*exsautēs,* "at once"), Herod might have been able to wait for a period and let the promise pass away unfulfilled. Matthew records that Herod was grieved (*lupētheis*) to execute John (Mark uses the compound form, *perilupos,* "very grieved") but carried through with his oath regardless.

14:10-13   These few verses appear to be an unseemly summary for the end of such a significant life. The martyrdom of John was a rather quiet and somber event. Only the claiming of the body by his disciples served as an indication of any proper closure to this powerful ministry. But such is true in the lives of many saints who labor and die for the kingdom, almost unnoticed by the world or, sadly, as here, as victims of depraved power. It is ironic that

Matthew records that the head was given to "the girl" (*korasiō*, diminutive of *korē*, "girl," thus more literally, the "little girl"; see comment on her age in vv. 6-7) to emphasize how this powerful king had been manipulated by this young seductress. Even the most powerful humans are incapable of controlling their own depraved nature.

The disciples of John went to the prison and claimed the body. Whether his head was recovered and buried with the body is not stated. The disciples had been prepared for John's departure through his constant focus on the growing ministry of Jesus and the diminishing of his own (John 3:22-30) and probably also by the event recorded in Matt. 11:2-7. Matthew informs his readers that the disciples of John buried him and then went to report to Jesus (v. 12). They well knew of the connection between these two and that Jesus was now the sole spokesman for the kingdom that John had announced.

This led Jesus to withdraw to a "lonely place" for solitude before continuing His ministry (v. 13). Carson does not associate the withdrawing with the report of John's death,[9] and this would be questionable if one assumes v. 13 begins the next narrative instead of closing the last. It is to be remembered that chapter and verse divisions are a modern addition to the text. The aorist participle "heard" (*akousas*) and the conjunction "now" (*de*) seem much more likely to be bringing the prior narrative to closure: "Now when Jesus heard [their report], He withdrew from there in a boat, to a lonely place by Himself," where He was joined by His disciples. His presence was discovered, and a crowd began to gather. This leads into v. 14.

THE FEEDING OF THE FIVE THOUSAND, 14:14-21 (Mark 6:30-44; Luke 9:10-17; John 6:5-15)

14:14   According to Mark and Luke, this next event followed the return of the Twelve from a mission of preaching and casting out demons (cf. Matt. 10:1-7). Jesus heard their report of victories, but the gathering crowd forced a retreat to a private area around Bethsaida. Before long, however, the people again discovered their location, and once more they were surrounded by curious and needy throngs.

The Lord did not respond with resentment because of deprived privacy but "felt compassion for them, and healed their sick." The miracles worked here were not stated as proof of any claim of Jesus but were the result of His compassion (*esplagchnisthē*, "moved inwardly and emotionally") because of their physical needs. This same compassion was what led to the miracle of feeding the five thousand. According to Mark's record, Jesus also felt compassion because they were like sheep without a shepherd, and He used this opportunity for teaching (Mark 6:34).

14:15-16   Jesus' healing of the sick appears to have taken most of the day. As evening came the people were not prepared for a meal, perhaps having never assumed they would be in this remote area for this length of time. According to John, Jesus raised the question first to Philip (who was from this area) as to what would be the source of food for these people (John 6:5). Of course, contemporary Christians realize that the spiritual answer would have been "Well, Lord, You are the Bread of Life; You could feed them." But in reality, when we are faced with overwhelming circumstances (such as having more than five thousand people to feed), our answer is very much like Philip's, "We don't have the resources!" John also tells us that He asked the question of Philip not to get advice but "to test him" (John 6:6). Jesus already had a plan. The answer of the disciples (v. 15) seemed to be "Let them take care of themselves"—"send the multitudes away, that they may go into the villages and buy food for themselves." Jesus had other plans and a lesson for His disciples to learn. He said, "They do not need to go away; *you* give them something to eat" (v. 16). Barbieri notes that the emphasis was on the disciples ("you") providing the food.[10] What a shock this must have been to them. Philip calculated that it would take more than two hundred denarii (about eight months' wages) to feed the crowd (John 6:7), which he assumed was well beyond their resources.

14:17-18   Jesus had them search and find what food was available, and John tells us that Andrew found a young boy with five loaves of barley bread and two fish (John 6:8-9), which would not be sufficient to feed even Jesus and the Twelve. The barley loaves indicated the economic status of the young boy—barley was the most common grain and was used primarily to feed livestock. It was a "symbol of poverty and scorn."[11] The poor often mixed it with wheat or other more expensive grains to make the bread last longer.

Jesus simply required the disciples to bring the scant supplies to Him (v. 18). If one considers the report of John, it becomes apparent that Jesus was going to use this opportunity to teach His disciples a valuable lesson, not concerning their responsibility to feed the poor (there is no indication that the multitude was poor, other than the boy who supplied the meager amount of food) but concerning His power to provide when His followers are willing to trust Him. A saying often attributed to Hudson Taylor might be given as the theme of the lesson, "The Lord's work, done the Lord's way, will never lack the Lord's supply."

14:19   The disciples were told to divide the people into smaller groups of 100 or 50 people per group. Knowing that there were 5,000 males (the gender sensitive *anēr* emphasizes males) "aside from women and children" (v. 21), one could assume that probably one hundred or more groups of people were scattered along the hillside. The fact that "grass" or "much grass" is mentioned is indication of the time of year, which is consistent with John's statement that the Passover was near.

Jesus, "looking up toward heaven," blessed the food and broke the loaves for distribution. Pate sees a strong allusion to the institution of the Lord's Supper, believing that the blessing and breaking of bread to meet the physical needs of the crowd fore-shadowed the Lord's Supper in meeting the spiritual needs of people.[12] However, Jesus' actions were common enough that no spiritual significance beyond thanking God for the blessing of His provision should be sought. Carson rightly notes, "The actions—looking up to heaven, thanking God, and breaking the loaves—are normal for any head of a Jewish household."[13] The disciples saw the insufficient supply of food, witnessed Jesus acknowledging God's provision (John 6:11), and witnessed, to their amazement, that the supply never ran out. They would carry an armload of food to a group of people and return to be loaded up again. What a lesson to learn in preparation for their ministry.

14:20   As Jesus promised, when one seeks God's kingdom first, even his material needs will be met (Matt. 6:25, 31-33). However, as this verse states, not only were the people satisfied but there was even surplus. The young boy who gave his single basket of five loaves and two fish perhaps went home with twelve baskets.

14:21   The statement concerning the number of men as well as women and children is recorded for the reader to grasp the magnitude of this miracle. The number of people was probably between 7,500 to 10,000, though only speculation can arrive at any figure. Modern readers may stagger over this number of people being gathered in one place to see a person, but there is no reason to doubt the account. Secular records also have references to such large numbers being assembled to see a person of importance.

WALKING ON THE SEA, 14:22-27 (Mark 6:45-52)

14:22-23   Both Matthew and Mark record that "immediately" (*eutheōs/euthus*) after feeding the great multitude, Jesus "made" (*anagkazō*) His disciples get into a boat and cross the sea. Carson notes that "the verb is very strong and might be translated 'compelled.'"[14] Why would Jesus want to send His disciples away and leave Him with the crowd, and why He would be so forceful about it?

Apparently, upon witnessing the spectacular miracle just performed, the people were excited and determined to declare Jesus to be their king (John 6:14-15)—but for the wrong motives. Mounce offers good insight by saying, "It suggests that the disciples would have liked to stay and share in the excitement of the crowd."[15] Jesus, however, had other intentions. Neither the time nor the conditions were right for Him to be king. Therefore He quickly ("immediately") sent away His disciples and stayed behind to disperse the crowd. The scene may have been one of exhilaration and confusion for the disciples as well as for the multitude.

With the disciples gone and the crowd dispersed to their own villages and homes, Jesus walked up into the mountain for solitude. Finding seclusion for a time of prayer was not out of character for Him, and one can imagine that after such an intense day of healing the sick, performing the profound miracle of feeding the multitude, and then dealing with those wanting to make Him king, He welcomed the silence and aloneness.

"When it was evening" is a reference to the later part of the evening. The term "evening" covered a broad range of time normally divided into two periods. Early evening was around sunset

(v. 15); later evening was the time following darkness until the late night hours (v. 23). Thus, in the dark on the mountain, Jesus was by Himself for a time of prayer. The Scriptures do not emphasize these moments alone and rarely record Jesus' isolating Himself to pray, as preachers have often heralded. But He did find occasions to be alone for prayer. He also prayed in front of His disciples and with crowds of people. The probable reason for so little information concerning His private prayer life is just that—it was private and not for show or sermon illustrations.

14:24   Matthew records that the boat had traveled "many stadia away from the land" and, Mark states, was in the "midst of the sea." A stadia is the equivalent of approximately 200 yards (607 feet). Thus the fanciful accounts of Jesus' walking along the shore beside the boat and then wading out to get in is unbiblical. The boat was also being battered by waves, and the wind was creating great difficulty in their making progress. Comments related to Jesus walking on the sea in the storm as a picture of His coming to comfort the church in times of trials[16] are to be ignored as extreme allegory.

14:25   The "fourth watch" refers to the time period of about 3:00 to 6:00 A.M. The Hebrews divided the night into three periods of time (early, middle, and late, cf. Judg. 7:19), but the Romans used four divisions (6:00-9:00 P.M.; 9:00-12:00 P.M.; 12:00-3:00 A.M.; and 3:00-6:00 A.M.). Matthew, perhaps because of his career as a Roman tax gatherer, uses the Roman time reference.

Jesus came to them, "walking on the sea" (*peripatōn epi tēn thalassan*). Mounce mentions some arguments that the preposition *epi* should be translated "toward [by its use with the accusative case] the sea" and in v. 26 as "by the sea" (by its use with the genitive).[17] But the context clearly indicates that Jesus did indeed walk upon the raging sea, and the case use with prepositions is not so rigidly structured as to require any change in the translation from "on." Jesus, as the perfect, Spirit-filled man, was able to overcome the physical laws of nature. God was demonstrating through Him that natural things are subject to Him and not vice versa.

14:26   Some hold the view that Jesus was just walking along the seashore and waded in shallow water to get to the boat. But the disciples (some veteran seamen) would then appear rather stupid. They assumed that they were far out to sea (which Matthew states to be the case, v. 24) and were surprised to see the figure of a person moving across the tossing waves. Their fear is emphasized by two expressions, *etarachthēsan,* aorist passive of *tarassō,* "to be terrified," and *phobos,* "fear" (from which we derive the English "phobia"), which caused them to cry out.

They believed they were seeing a ghost (*phantasma,* our "phantom"). This conclusion was probably drawn from the way the figure moved. The sea was churning, but it is not likely that Jesus was having difficulty keeping His balance, since the waves would be subject to Him. Out of the darkness, in the middle of the sea, a lone figure moved steadily across the water. It is easy to understand why they would panic and assume this must be a ghost.

Mark records that Jesus "intended to pass by them" (Mark 6:48, *zethelen parelthein autous*). Why Jesus would have walked past is uncertain. But He had told them to go to the other side of the lake (Matt. 14:22; Mark 6:45). Perhaps He planned to meet them there. Mark notes that Jesus had seen them struggling against the wind even before He left the shore. Barbieri suggests more than a mere passing by, understanding this as a special manifestation like an Old Testament theophany, to "pass by" as used in to "show one-self."[18]

14:27   The voice of Jesus came out of the midst of the storm to bring peace to their hearts, "Take courage, it is I" (*tharseite, egō eimi*). The comfort came from knowing He was near and there was no ghost. Therefore they were to be confident rather than fearful. He also commanded, "Do not be afraid," or perhaps, more literally, "Stop being afraid" (*mē phobiesthe*). The present imperative gives a command to do something constantly or, when an imperatival prohibition as here (*mē*), forbids the continuance of something or "an interruption of an action already begun."[19]

PETER WALKS ON THE WATER, 14:28-33

14:28-29   Mark does not include the account of Peter's walking on the sea, but the anecdote is certainly typical of Peter's daring and impulsive behavior. Peter's statement "Lord, if it is you" is not so much indicating doubt as it is expressing a confident request. It could correctly be translated, "Lord, since it is You, order me to come to You upon the water." Peter, no doubt, had confidence in the Lord's power, and as one who had spent years upon the sea in boats, this phenomenal display of the Lord's capacity to overcome nature thrilled him to courageous action. It is important to notice that Peter did not just climb out of the boat. He knew the normal laws of physics were not going to be canceled by mere human enthusiasm. He knew he needed the Lord's command to perform this miracle. This was a step of faith.

Peter stepped out of the boat and found himself standing on water (v. 29). This was a miracle perhaps more difficult to understand than the healings that Peter and the others had witnessed. No mention is made of the distance traveled or the amount of time Peter spent on the water, but the text does state that he took some steps ("walked on the water and came toward Jesus.")

14:30 The walk ended in a display of fear and a loss of the faith that had encouraged him to leave the safety of the boat. It must be remembered that Peter's experience is not an analogy to saving faith, nor is it intended to demonstrate anything other than the little faith of the disciples though they had so much visible evidence of Jesus' supernatural endowment. Matthew reveals the downfall of Peter: "But seeing the wind." The wind was representative of the raging storm that was creating towering waves and other frightening visual circumstances surrounding him. In other words, though Peter had seen Jesus' power over this storm and had been given His specific command to step out, the danger of his immediate circumstances overwhelmed him. Peter began to sink while watching the storm rather than the Lord. He became aware of his danger and cried out for help. This alone is worth noting; he still knew of Jesus' power to deliver him.

14:31 Matthew uses the term "immediately" (*eutheōs*) to imply that the Lord did not hesitate to rescue His zealous but weak disciple. What may strike the reader as odd is that He also quickly (before they even got into the boat) rebuked Peter, saying, "O you of little faith." One lesson here is that a little faith can accomplish much; he did walk on the water. But the rebuke must have struck the others severely since they had not even gotten out of the boat.

The rhetorical question, "Why did you doubt?" was to draw attention to the fact that Peter had begun well but then doubted the power that Christ had given him. The command of the Lord should have been sufficient to sustain him, and even seeing that he did not immediately sink should have been proof of the security of Christ's servant when in the will of the Lord. Carson points out, "It was not that he had lost faith in himself, but that his faith in Jesus, strong enough to get him out of the boat and walking on the water, was not strong enough to stand up to the storm."[20]

14:32-33   When the Lord and Peter entered the boat, the wind ceased. The connection is probably that the wind was deliberately employed by the Lord. It had created an environment where His men would be tested and taught the lesson of His power over every kind of circumstance. When the test was over, the wind ceased without any command from the Lord. One would assume that they should have learned this lesson from the event of 8:23-27. Reality, however, is that all human beings struggle with daily physical existence and easily lose sight of God's power and plans.

Verse 33 offers an excellent explanation of true worship. Worship is not generated by songs or other religious activities but flows from within, driven by awe and fear of the One who is worshiped. The word "worship" (*proskuneō*) means to "fall down before and worship." It is the natural result of gaining a true view of just how powerful and good God is. Seeing Jesus' mastery of even the forces of nature brought forth amazement and veneration on the part of His disciples. In Mark's account, worship is not mentioned, but it reads "they were greatly astonished" (6:51), which reflects a similar attitude.[21] Matthew and Mark both record the disciples' failure, but Mark makes it more severe and places the assessment at the end of the story (6:52), explaining that their fear in the boat was because they had not learned the lesson of Christ's power from the miracle of feeding more than five thousand people. However, in spite of the hardening of their hearts, their conclusion was "You are certainly God's Son!" The expression "God's Son" actually implies One who comes forth from God and who is of God's nature.

14:34-36   They landed in Gennesaret (the northwest side of the sea of Galilee), and Jesus continued (presumably the next day) to heal all those brought to Him. His reputation had become so dynamic that, once word spread that He was in the region, crowds began to gather, bringing their sick to be healed (v. 35).

Perhaps the request to "just touch the fringe of His cloak" was related to the spreading of the news about the woman who had suffered from a hemorrhage for twelve years and was healed by simply touching the "fringe of His cloak" (9:20-22, same wording).

That woman had reached out without asking, not having any promise from Him, yet found mercy because of her faith. Now others, having heard the story, were asking for the same privilege and receiving the same results: "as many as touched it were cured." His blessings continued to flow to the individuals who sought Him and trusted Him.

HOMILETICAL SUGGESTIONS

The account of the martyrdom of John is vivid testimony to the depravity of man. John, who was innocent of all except speaking the truth of God's Word, was killed to gratify the spite and vengefulness of a bitter person. Herod, who knew of John's holy life and feared him as a true prophet, was manipulated and victimized by his own undisciplined lust and impulsive boasting. His foolish promise and prideful determination to honor it regardless of the injustice, serves as a warning of the extent to which sin can carry a person. Herodias's willingness to use her young daughter to entice her husband in order to get what she wanted is another horrific testimony to the wickedness of the fallen human creature.

Jesus offered us an example of unselfish ministry when He found His solitude interrupted by people desiring to have their own needs met. He could have ignored them or sent them away because of the terrible news of John's death, but He willingly left His seclusion and took care of them. He even worked one of the most spectacular miracles performed in Galilee to demonstrate His concern for their needs and to help His disciples to understand that neither He nor His work is restricted by limited human resources. Too often God's servants hesitate to step into ministry because they have calculated their resources and do not see any way to accomplish what is needed. Perhaps we need to learn the lesson of the disciples and commit what is available to Christ and trust Him to work according to His power, not our riches.

Possibly the most significant lesson to be learned from this chapter is the one Peter had to learn the hard way. We are to focus on Jesus and not circumstances. Peter's walk on the sea came to an abrupt end when he took his eyes off Jesus and began to look at the state of affairs around him. From the human standpoint it was impossible for Peter to walk on water, and the storm was certainly violent and dangerous. However, as long as he was watching Jesus, who had overcome all the circumstances that Peter feared, he walked in perfect safety and victory. The author of Hebrews makes this point clear in 12:2-3, "Fixing our eyes on Jesus . . . consider Him . . . so that you may not grow weary and lose heart."

Some serious consideration needs to be given as well to the response of the disciples to Jesus' walking on the sea. Worship cannot be generated from external activity; it flows from an inward attitude toward Christ. Too often worship is associated with music or some other human activity. The people of God need to see His awesomeness, His power, His incredible grace—then they will worship Him. Let the preacher focus on the God of Scripture to bring forth genuine worship, that which is in spirit and in truth.

MATTHEW

CHAPTER

FIFTEEN

CONTRASTING THE PHARISEES WITH THE CANAANITE WOMAN

As Jesus continued to minister around Gennesaret, He was confronted by some Pharisees and scribes who had come from Jerusalem, perhaps for that very purpose. What is most significant in this section is the contrast between these religious leaders and the Canaanite woman. Their challenge of Jesus and subsequent offense by His contemptuous answer reflects unrepentant hearts and stubborn resistance to His claim to messiahship. In strong contrast, the woman is seen as seeking Jesus for help, not to criticize— a Gentile with no rights to the Messiah but totally convinced of His power and authority. When He refused the request to heal her daughter, she persisted, arguing against His stated reasons. Not offended at being referred to as a "dog," she called Him "Lord" and continued her appeal. Jesus responded by granting her request and praising her for her great faith. This is a marvelous chapter, offering insight into the heart of Jesus and His ministry.

ARGUMENT WITH THE PHARISEES AND SCRIBES, 15:1-6
(Mark 7:1-23)

15:1-2 Matthew continues his narrative with a steady, flowing train of thought. The "then" (*tote*) is not intended to show sequence as much as it is a general indication of continuation of the growing conflict between Jesus and the religious leaders. Hendriksen states,

"It is evident that the opposition against Jesus is increasing in intensity."[1] These Pharisees and scribes were not local leaders but "from Jerusalem" (*apo Ierosolumōm*), apparently having come for the very purpose of challenging Jesus. Matthew specifically states that they "came to Jesus" (*proserchontai tō Iēsou*). Jesus' reputation had grown to the point of creating insecurity and fear in those whom He challenged. Bruce suggests that the local religious leadership had invited these Jerusalem dignitaries to help them refute the teachings of Jesus.[2]

The question asked (v. 2) could be easily misunderstood without a proper understanding of the ritual-washing tradition. The "washing of hands" was ceremonial for religious purification, not hygienic. The synagogue inscription of Theodotus at Jerusalem (prior to A.D. 70) implies that supplies of water for ritual washing were provided in the synagogue.[3] This indicates the importance of ritual washing to the religious Jews of that time. Edersheim states, "To neglect it was like being guilty of gross carnal defilement. Its omission would lead to temporal destruction, or, at least to poverty. Bread eaten with unwashen hands was as if it had been filth."[4]

It is also important to note that the Pharisees did not accuse the disciples with breaking the Law of Moses; they were well aware that the violation was against "the tradition of the elders." The "elders" were the great rabbis of the past whose oral teachings had come to be viewed almost equal in authority to that of the Law itself. These teachings were detailed explanations of rules of conduct. Whereas the Law may only record "Remember the Sabbath to keep it holy," the oral traditions listed specific rules to fulfill this commandment. Some rules were so fanatical that only the most committed would practice them, thus creating the hierarchy of spirituality in which the Pharisees reveled. Although noble and good intentions were often behind the Halakah (the body of oral discourse on the Law), the Pharisees erred by honoring it almost on a par with Mosaic Law. Following the time of Christ (ca. A.D. 35-200), the Halakah was inscripturated to form the Mishnah.

15:3 Jesus' response was probably shocking and offensive to His attackers. Having accused them of transgressing "the commandment of God," which even the Pharisees would have to admit was more serious than transgressing the tradition of the elders, Jesus added that God's commandment had been broken by their adherence to their tradition. His point was that tradition, no matter how noble the intent, had caused them to violate the Law that God Himself had specifically given.

15:4 Jesus then gave explanation ("for" is an explanatory *gar*) of the commandment violation. He referred to Exodus 20:12, which Paul called the "first commandment with a promise" (Eph. 6:2). Jesus' stark comment was to draw attention to the disparity between their concern for human traditions and the Word of God. The Pharisees were transgressing (*parabainō*) the commandment of God, which implied a leaving behind or turning away from by their enthusiastic pursuit of traditional interpretations of minute points of obscure law.

The Law of Exodus 20:12 says to honor one's mother and father. The word "honor" (*timaō*) primarily meant to "place a value upon," but it also meant to "revere" or show the value of someone or something. Jesus was emphasizing the divine attitude toward parents and the family structure. This attitude was serious enough to demand the death penalty for any insolent child who cursed his mother and father. Such respect for parental roles is certainly foreign to contemporary thinking.

15:5 The Pharisees, however, taught that giving money to the temple took priority over caring for one's parents. The phrase "given to *God*" (*dōron*, "gift, offering"—Mark uses *Korban,* which translates the Hebrew word for "a gift set apart for God") indicates their rationalization. The prepositional phrase "to God" is not in the text but is properly assumed from the context. Mark records the Lord's rebuke: "You no longer permit him to do anything for his father or his mother" (Mark 7:12), which points to the tradition of giving the "offering to the Lord" instead of taking care of parents, thus being in conflict with Exodus 20:12. Hendriksen offers an excellent explanation of this, concluding,

> If either father or mother, noticing that a son had something which was needed by the parent, asked for it, all that was necessary was for the son to say, "It's *dōron*" . . . he is really saying, "it is consecrated to God," and by making this assertion or exclamation he, according to Pharisaic teaching based on tradition, had released himself from the obligation of honoring his parents.[5]

15:6   The point Jesus desired to make was that traditions may conflict with the divine Word and that people had to choose which was more authoritative. Although the ceremonial washings may have been a good practice, the Pharisees erred by elevating them to the level of Scripture. The traditions often did not reflect the heart and mind of God and were therefore wrong.

CHRIST DEFINES "VAIN WORSHIP," 15:7-11

15:7   Jesus boldly called them hypocrites (*hupkritēs*), a term used eighteen times in the Gospels (fourteen in Matthew) and applied most directly to the scribes and Pharisees by Jesus Himself. The first usage directly addressing the Pharisees occurs in this passage. Coming from Greek drama, the word referred to one who played a part, and it became a metaphor for "pretender."[6] The word clearly has a negative connotation in New Testament use. Jesus then linked these hypocrites to Isaiah 29:13, which speaks of God's judgment against Israel—"rightly did Isaiah prophesy of you."

15:8   Verse 8 identifies the factor that earned the name "hypocrite": they offered God honor with their lips (verbally) but did not honor Him in their hearts (the internal, essential quality of one's being). The heart (*kardia*) is a term commonly used in both Testaments to reference the character of a person. Ascribed the attributes of thinking (Luke 2:19), feeling (John 14:1), believing (Rom. 10:10), and directing the person (Heb. 4:12), the heart is to be understood as more than just an emotive factor. What the Pharisees really believed and chose to accept about God did not honor Him. Their religion had replaced their relationship with God.

15:9   Then Jesus went even further to condemn and expose their failure. Despite all of their ceremony, religious words, and pious attitudes, their worship was vain (*matēn*). The word "vain" implies to be of no purpose—their worship had no substance but only empty ritual. True worship requires spiritual communing with God, intimacy, and truth. To ascribe glory to God and to honor His holy name (worship) requires action in accordance with His Word (truth). Jesus Himself proclaimed that those who worship God must do so in spirit and in truth (John 4:23-24).

The participial phrase in v. 9 indicates the means by which they worshiped God in vain: it was by teaching human precepts as being equal to God's Word. Even with all their rules and regulations and pomp and pious activity, true worship was not achieved because it was not according to His truth but according to their traditions.

15:10-11 Jesus then took this opportunity to teach the multitudes what He had just tried to teach the Pharisees. His calling of the crowd together probably indicates that the conversation with the Pharisees was private, and He wished to make the issue a public one. Peter refers to the teaching as a parable (v. 15), but Jesus' response does not seem to indicate that the meaning was cryptic. The instruction to "hear and understand" (*akouete kai suniete*) intimates that He expected attention and application of what He was going to say to them.

Verse 11 presents a terse and forceful proverb reflecting a deeper understanding of defilement of the human creature. Eating with unwashed hands (v. 2) cannot create defilement, because man is not defiled by things entering his body. Here defilement (*koinoō*) is to make something "unclean" or "profane." The noun form is *koinos, ē, on,* from which we get Koine Greek, meaning "common" and referring to the Greek used in everyday life as well as in New Testament writings. Rather than one's being concerned with ceremonial cleanliness, which was both artificial and vain, Jesus pointed out that he should be more concerned with what comes forth from within. In chap. 12, Jesus says that one speaks what is in the heart (vv. 34-35); thus, defilement in the heart will flow from the mouth (v.18).

EXPLANATION OF THE DEFILEMENT TEACHING, 15:12-20

15:12 The disciples' response gives insight into the reaction of both the Pharisees and the disciples themselves: the Pharisees were offended, the disciples shocked. Mark does not record their comment but informs us that the disciples and the Lord had apparently gone into a house for this private conversation (Mark 7:17). The use of "offended" (aorist passive of *skandalizō*, "cause to sin" or "have doubts") means that the Pharisees were angered or shocked, stumbled over, and were troubled by what Jesus said. The implication is that they took personally the lesson of defilement. They correctly understood the intent of His rebuke. Barnes comments, "They were so zealous of their traditions that they could not endure that their absurdities should be exposed."[7] Hypocrisy is always offended by the truth.

Some seem concerned with proving that Jesus did not offer "a personal attack on the Pharisees rather than on their use of the law,"[8] but such distinction is unnecessary. It is clear that Jesus was not concerned with offending. He addressed them as "hypocrites" (v. 7) and referred to them as "blind guides" (v. 14). In contemporary culture, where political correctness is considered a sign of spiritual maturity, Jesus would certainly seem unspiritual. Mounce judiciously observes from the disciples' question "the timidity of the disciples, who apparently did not wish to offend the religious rulers."[9] Jesus wished His followers to see that the offense against God for laying aside His truth for the sake of tradition (cf. Mark 7: 8-9) was far more serious than an offense against religionists who were misleading people.

15:13   In response to the disciples' question about offending the Pharisees, Jesus used a gardening metaphor—the point being that the Pharisees were not from God (they were ones whom the Father had not planted) and would be uprooted like weeds extracted from a garden. This comment is reminiscent of the parable of the tares in 13:24-30. It must be assumed that if the Father did not "plant" them, then the enemy did. The powerful implication of this must not be overlooked. These plants were to be "rooted up"—not just cut down—dug out by the roots and cast from the program of the heavenly Father. Such is the fate of those who replace God's truth and true worship with legalistic religion.

15:14   Jesus now added another derogatory appellation to the Pharisees and scribes, "blind guides of the blind." Because they could not see to lead those who could not see, Christ instructed His disciples to "let them alone" (*áphete,* imperative from *aphiēmi,* "leave behind, dismiss, forsake" them). The insinuation was probably that Jesus' followers were to divorce themselves from them by complete disassociation. Interestingly, a reference from Paul (a former Pharisee), addressing the Jews, speaks of their considering themselves "guides to the blind" (Rom. 2:19). Here Jesus did not deny that they were leading the blind but pointed out that they themselves were blind as well. He used a sad but descriptive proverb, they "both will fall into a pit" (cf. Luke 6:39).

15:15-16   Peter, apparently speaking as the representative of the whole group of disciples ("us"), asks for explanation of the parable. A parable (*parabolē*) is normally considered to be a short pithy story with a single moral, but the term here evidently referred to Jesus' short, weighty statement of v. 11.

Peter's request seems reasonable, and one would think that Jesus would be pleased with his desire to understand. However, His response (v. 16) reflected great displeasure with the question. The word "also" (*kai*) implied a grouping together with those whom He had just called "blind guides." Thus Carson states, "The disciples' failure to understand shocks Jesus."[10] There were other times when Jesus expressed disappointment and agitation with the disciples for their lack of understanding (John 14:5-9). Their privileged position and contact with Him certainly gave them an advantage over others, yet they did not seem to appropriate this benefit.

15:17-20 Jesus explained the meaning of His rebuke to the Pharisees with a simple lesson in biology (v. 17). The digestive process and elimination of waste answered the question of eating foods. There was no need for the ceremonial washing of hands to prevent defilement. However, the explanation was not intended to answer biological questions but rather to reemphasize the point that defilement before God is not a physical issue but an issue of the heart. Ceremonial hand washing cannot affect that.

Jesus then made the point that defilement before God is defilement in the heart, which proceeds out of the mouth, not that which enters through the mouth (vv. 18-19). The heart motivates the mouth to speak; therefore, if the heart is defiled, the mouth will be a fountain of defilement. The heart is the center of a person's essence, the term that best portrays the total person (see comment on 15:8). Verse 19 is a rather severe and discouraging view of the human heart. Nonetheless, it is the divine declaration of its wicked condition. The list of sins provided is certainly not complete nor intended to be a total catalog of offenses against God. Mounce offers a helpful comment on this list:

> Matthew then lists seven evils (v. 19). After the first (evil thoughts), they follow in the order of the sixth through the ninth commandments (murder, adultery, sexual immorality, theft, false testimony, slander). It is interesting that the listing of evils from the second half of the Decalogue follows the discussion of the violation of the fifth commandment in verses 4-6.[11]

"Slander" is not found in Exodus 20, and the prohibition against coveting is omitted in Christ's statement. Otherwise, it is interesting that Jesus did begin at the fifth item of the Decalogue and went through the ninth in His rebuke of the Pharisees. The things that proceed from the heart defile a person (v. 20), not ignoring a ritualistic cleansing rite. Christ wanted His followers to understand that they needed to cleanse their hearts and not be concerned with, or deceived by, external acts of cleansing.

DIALOGUE WITH THE CANAANITE WOMAN, 15:21-28 (Mark 7:24-30)

15:21   Jesus entered the Gentile territory of Tyre and Sidon on the Mediterranean coast, north of the Sea of Galilee. The reason for His going here is not revealed; perhaps He was simply retreating from the constant pressure of conflict, knowing Israel's religious leaders would not follow into a Gentile region. Mark reveals His desire for obscurity (7:24), but His reputation had obviously already penetrated this region as well.

15:22   Perhaps the woman living in the area and seeking help from Jesus was called "Canaanite" because her ancestral roots were from the Canaanite tribes. Or perhaps Canaan once included territory extending that far north. Meyer leans toward the latter explanation.[12] She was also identified as Greek and Syrophoenician (Mark 7:26). The Greek term *hellēnis* was sometimes generic, referring broadly to educated Gentiles (Greek-speaking), which is why Mark adds "of the Syrophoenician race," indicating that she was not of the Greek (Hellenistic) race. "Syrophoenician" referred to the area of Syria and Phoenicia that would include both cities of Tyre and Sidon.

This Gentile woman had heard of Jesus' power and sought Him out to heal her demon-possessed daughter. Her salutation reveals much: first, she asked for mercy, not a miracle or proof of power; second, she called Him "Lord" (which at the least showed great respect for Him and humility on her part); third, she called Him "Son of David." Perhaps this last element was most significant, because it implied recognition of His messianic authority. Her exposure to Judaism and her expectations of Messiah are unknown, but her faith toward God's Anointed/One is revealed—she knew to whom she was appealing.

Her daughter was "cruelly demon-possessed." A good term for this condition is "demonized" (*daimonizetai*). The demon did not own the girl but apparently controlled, tormented, and injured her. Scripture offers many details about demonism, but not much information is given here. Demons appear able to occupy the mind and to control (or at least affect) the physical predicaments of their victims. However, much of the modern phenomena of demon/spiritual warfare is not consistent with biblical demonology but is founded on myths, experiential misdiagnosis, and hypersupernaturalism. Too often the modern exorcist employs secret methods and rituals more in line with ancient voodoo practices than with the healing and cleansing power of Christ. One must question not only the methods but even the motives of those who make sensationalistic drama out of such sad affairs. Demons often get credit where simple human sin is the culprit, and the reputation of demon "exorcists" is substituted for glorifying Christ's power. The condition of this girl is not specifically stated, nor are any details about family history or other popular "causes" offered.

15:23-24   Christ's immediate response may seem coldhearted and shocking: He basically ignored her. "He did not answer her a word." This would be another teaching moment for His disciples. His silence toward her was to make the point He would later state (v. 24). The disciples were disturbed because she was causing an incident by following them and shouting for help. One can only imagine the scene: the hysterical woman following Jesus and His entourage, yelling out to Him for help, and He not even acknowledging her. The disciples were not moved with pity for the woman or her daughter but were, most likely, personally embarrassed at the spectacle she was causing. Whether their intent was that He answer her request and then send her away or just send her away is unclear.

Jesus responded to their demand (vv. 23-24). There is a general failure to recognize the true Jewishness of Jesus' Person and mission, and often this extremely important aspect of His ministry is overlooked by Christians. His mission was stated here as "I was sent *only* to the lost sheep of the house of Israel." This response may imply that the disciples assumed Jesus would send her away with her request[13] and that His refusal was based upon His mission to Israel. Even though He had already healed Gentiles, that work was performed in the context of Israel; now they were in Gentile territory. He was the Jewish Messiah, King of Israel, not a missionary to the world. Kingsbury points out that in "Matthew's scheme, it is precisely such 'no-accounts' (social outcasts such as the Gentile woman) as these persons who are the ones in Israel who correctly perceive that Jesus is the Son of David."[14]

15:25   Once again the woman appealed to Jesus with humility and persistence. One is reminded of Jesus' own teaching on prayer: keep on asking, seeking, and knocking (see comments on Matt. 7:7-11). Her request was simple, "Help me." Her love for and commitment to her daughter were commendable, but her situation was still that she had no rights to the benefits of messianic power and authority, which belonged to Israel.

15:26-27   His response to her direct appeal was based upon that understanding. The proverbial reply has Israel represented as the children and the truth that Messiah brought as the bread that was rightfully theirs. It would not be "good" (*kalos,* "proper, right, fitting") to take that which rightfully belonged to one and give it to another, especially a dog. "Children" was a proper term for Israel, since they were the chosen children of God and were by covenant heirs to the His kingdom upon earth. The term "dog" is *kunarion* and most likely refers to a lapdog or family pet,[15] an assumption supported by her referencing eating crumbs that fall from the table. This is to be contrasted with *kuōn,* also meaning "dog" but in the more severe and negative connotation of an unclean street animal, which was to be despised and rejected (see Matt. 7:6). Jesus was certainly letting the woman know she did not have the privileges of the "children," but neither was He associating her with outcast dogs. In Mark's account, the Lord seems to have provided her with some hope by stating, "Let the children be satisfied first." This does not imply a contradiction of Matthew's record but offers additional insight into the conversation. She understood that "first" (*prōton*) indicated priority but not necessarily exclusivity. It is possible that the Lord was implying the later opening of His work among the Gentiles.

In v. 27, the woman's response is witty and bold but not insolent, "Yes, Lord" (*nai kurie*). She was not objecting to being referred to as a dog, and she followed through with the analogy to make an application appropriate to her needs. By pointing out that it was acceptable to let dogs eat what fell from the table, she was not asking to be brought into the family but to benefit from being in the house. She did not seek equal status with Israelites but only blessings that they lost by their carelessness.

15:28   The response pleased Jesus and sparked an exclamation of praise, "Your faith is great." This is similar to the praise of the centurion in Matthew 8:5-10, "I have not found such great faith with anyone in Israel." The magnitude of her faith can be seen in her persistence in appealing to Christ. She knew deep within herself that He and He alone could help her daughter, and because she believed this so intensely, even in the face of being ignored and then refused, she kept asking (Mark 7:26). This was faith—total commitment to the object of faith even when outward facts did not appear agreeable. Hendriksen makes an interesting comparison:

> She triumphed in spite of *a.* the initial silence of Jesus, *b.* his seeming (never real!) coldness and his words of seeming reproach, and, *c.* the indifference of the disciples ("send her away"). Now was it not a very similar manifestation of determined perseverance in the face of opposition ("I will not let thee go except thou bless me," Gen. 32:26) that changed a "Jacob" into an "Israel" (Gen. 32:28)? This woman, then, was in that sense a true Israelite![16]

As a result of this woman's perseverance, driven by true faith, her daughter was healed and the demon expelled. There is no record that Jesus went to the girl. Scripture simply says, "Because of this answer go your way; the demon has gone out of your daughter" (Mark 7:29), and that the daughter was healed at once (Matt. 15:28). There was no formula, no confrontation with the demon, no claiming territory, no steps to be followed. Just at the word of Christ, it was so.

THE FEEDING OF THE FOUR THOUSAND, 15:29-39 (MARK 7:31-8:9)

15:29-31   Jesus now returned to the territory around the Sea of Galilee, specifically the area of Decapolis (Mark 7:31), a predominately Gentile district near the locality of the earlier demoniac healing and other signs. He went into the mountain and was visited there by many who brought friends and family suffering from a great variety of illnesses (v. 30). There is no mention in these verses about casting out demons, and the ailments (crippled, blind, and mute) seem all to have been purely physical disorders. Details concerning the healing of one man in particular is found in Mark 7:32-35. The man was deaf and had a serious speech impediment. Mark offers perhaps more details on this healing than on any other in the New Testament. Again, there was no casting out of demons but rather the simple touching of the man's ears and tongue. This was the first of two great healing miracles involving saliva (Mark 7:33 and 8:23-24). Matthew does not focus on any particular miracle but only records that He healed.

The multitude "marveled" (*thaumazō*), "were amazed," at the healing of all these people (v. 31). For three days (v. 32) they witnessed the blind receiving sight, the crippled (those having useless and withered limbs) being "restored" (*hugiēs*, "made whole or healthy"), and the lame (those unable to walk) walking. Their response was absolutely correct—"they glorified the God of Israel." This last statement points to three facts concerning this healing ministry. First, no one could deny the reality of His power or authority. Second, He was not giving credit to Himself but to God, who sent Him. Third, these Gentiles knew Israel's God was bestowing this great outpouring of mercy into their lives.

15:32-39   Some commentators believe the events of 15:32-39 and 14:14-21 are the same, but this view presents numerous difficulties. Mounce offers some explanation but does not adhere to this view.[17] One simple argument is Christ's own statement in Mark 8:19-21, where He reminds the disciples of *both* events. Other obvious differences demonstrate a few of the difficulties:

MATT. 14	MATT. 15
5 loaves of bread	7 loaves of bread
2 fish	a "few" small fish
12 baskets left over	7 baskets left over
"baskets" (*kophinos*)	"large baskets" (*spuris*)
5,000 men	4,000 men

Carson offers a longer list,[18] but these points are sufficient here. These were two separate events.

15:32   As with the feeding in chap. 14, Jesus stated that His reason for the miracle was His compassion for the multitudes (14:14).
Both Matthew and Mark note that the crowd had been with Jesus
for three days, being amazed at the miracles He was performing.
Apparently they had not brought food or taken opportunity to purchase any in the village. Knowing they would experience hunger
and physical weakness on the journey home, and that some had
traveled great distances (Mark 8:3), Jesus indicated to the disciples
His intent to feed them. This is certainly a glimpse into the practical, real world in which these events took place.

15:33   Again, the disciples questioned the intelligence of such a
"rash" comment. Their perspective was mere human reaction: they
were in a "desolate place" (*herēmia,* "desert, uninhabited area").
They failed to remember who wished to feed these people. How
quickly forgotten was the similar miracle of chap. 14. Carson suggests that perhaps the problem was that even though they accepted
the miracle among Jews as anticipation of the kingdom banquet, a
similar provision for these Gentiles was not expected.[19]

15:34-36   This time there was no young boy to provide bread
and fish for the miracle. The supply of seven loaves and a few fish
was probably from the ration that the disciples carried for their own
journey. Some look for significance in the number seven, but there
is no exegetical reason for this. If any importance is to be found, it
may be in the seven loaves entrusted to the Lord increasing to a
quantity requiring seven "large baskets."

As before, the crowd was instructed to sit on the ground (v. 35),
but neither Mark nor Matthew give crowd grouping details as on
the first occasion (Mark 6:40). However, a similar strategy can be
safely assumed.

15:37-39   Several key details are worth noting. First, they all ate.
Four thousand men, with women and children in addition, were
fed. Second, they were satisfied—not only did Jesus make sure
everyone ate, He also provided so that they were content (*chortazō,*
"eat one's fill"). Third, the remaining pieces were collected as
before so that the ministry was done without sacrifice to those who
had provided the original source. Fourth, for each loaf of bread
provided, one large basket filled with bread was returned. The
"large basket" (*spuris*) was large enough to hold a person (cf. Acts

9:25). This is typical of the way the Lord blesses those who release their resources for His use.

The closing verses of the chapter simply recount the large number of people fed with such scanty supplies and that the Lord moved on to another location. Having fed the people, He dismissed them, letting them know that His miracles and ministry in this area were finished, and then He went to Magadan. This city or region is not known to us now, but many scholars believe it was an area on the western shore of Galilee. If so, Jesus returned to the land of Israel.

HOMILETICAL SUGGESTIONS

This chapter begins with the conflict between Jesus and the religious leaders (Pharisees and scribes) over the violation of their traditions. It must be remembered that the Pharisees, though hypocrites, were sincere in their desire to serve God. Their main problem seems to have been that they had lost sight of the heart and mind of God by becoming committed to tradition. Rabbinic instruction and application of Scripture had become associated with the Scripture itself. The Halakah (rabbinic explanation and application of the Law) was based on good and noble intentions but unintentionally became confused with authoritative Law. Thus Jesus and His disciples appeared to be lawbreakers, because they did not observe the traditional interpretation.

The question is, do individual Christians, churches, and Christian institutions have their own "Halakah"? Sad to say, the answer is yes. Well-intentioned explanations and personal interpretations of Scripture are sometimes taught and defended with the fervor that should be limited to Scripture. Every believer must guard against substituting his *opinion* of what God intended for the clear statements that God gave. Women's being prohibited from wearing pants because of an obscure statement in the Old Testament, at a time when both men and women wore robes (men wearing skirts, so to speak) is only one of numerous illustrations. Christians must honestly, humbly, and openly question what issues they divide over and determine upon what basis they condemn other believers for not being on their spiritual level.

Another key lesson to be learned from this chapter is the

importance of adopting the attitude Christ reflected toward offending religious leaders. In an age where pressure, even in Christian environments, is to be politically correct, those who want to be Christlike should consider this posture of our Lord. His concern was not whether He offended men but whether He offended God. Paul tells us that to seek to be "men pleasers" means that one cannot be a God pleaser (Gal. 1:9-10; 1 Thess. 2:4-6). This is not to imply that Christians should be arrogant and hateful toward others. Believers are to seek to live at peace with all men and to prefer others above self. But to ignore or alter God's truth to win the favor of men is sin.

What a contrast can be drawn between the Pharisees, who were offended because Jesus would not condone their self-righteousness, and the Syrophoenician woman. She even accepted being called a dog and endured the initial "coldness" of Jesus because, by faith, she understood that He alone could meet her need. Her humility and perseverance in coming to Him for mercy is a lesson for all sinners to learn. Jesus' compassion in healing and feeding the four thousand also reflects His desire to minister to those who seek Him out and rely upon Him. Once again, one should not overlook this in contrast to the self-righteous religious leaders.

MATTHEW
CHAPTER
SIXTEEN

BEGINNING PREPARATION
FOR HIS DEATH

Jesus returned briefly to the land of Israel and immediately was confronted with opposition again. This time the Sadducees joined forces with the Pharisees in an attempt to trap Him into a blasphemous claim and discredit Him. The Pharisees and Sadducees were political and religious enemies, holding antagonistic views on major issues (such as supernatural beings and the resurrection) and having little respect for one another. However, the Sanhedrin was composed of both sects, and often they would join together against a common foe—in this case, Jesus.

Following this brief encounter, Jesus left Israel once again. This time, along with His disciples in a private retreat, He began to prepare them for His eventual betrayal and death. The Lord's ministry began to focus on the impending "cup" that the Father had set before Him.

JESUS' REFUSAL TO GIVE A SIGN FROM HEAVEN, 16:1-4
(Mark 8:10-13)

16:1 The fact that both the Pharisees and Sadducees confronted Jesus is worth noting. The two nouns (Pharisees and Sadducees) are governed by one definite article, which links them together as a pair, indicating corporate action, not separate groups. Thus this may have been an official delegation for the Sanhedrin. Mark men-

333

tions just the Pharisees, probably because of his intention to focus on major issues and people and since the Pharisees tended to dominate the religious scene.

Matthew records that they came specifically to test Him (*peirazō*) but certainly not in the legitimate sense of trying to determine whether or not He was the genuine Messiah. It would appear from chaps. 12-13 that He had already pronounced judgment upon them because they would not believe. Unlike the testing in Matthew 12:38, they now challenged Him for a sign "out of heaven" (*ek tou ouranou*). This may have been due to the influence of the Sadducees, who denied any supernatural element, or they may have been acknowledging His claim to authority and power from heaven. Hendriksen may be correct in interpreting their demand as trying to make Jesus compete with the great Old Testament saints who had given spectacular "heavenly signs" during their ministries (cf. Ex. 16; Josh. 10:12-14; 1 Sam. 7:10; 1 Kings 18:30-40).[1]

16:2-3[2]   The Lord's response appears to have been a colloquial proverb. It was not the intention of Jesus to teach a universal law of meteorology but to recite a well-known adage to make a point. Even in contemporary times, an old maxim is "Red sky at night, sailor's delight; red sky in the morning, sailors take warning." This may have been a common view of those who lived along the shores of the Sea of Galilee. Note that He stated, "You say . . ." (v. 2). They had asked for a sign "out of heaven," and Jesus pointed to common signs in the heavens, which they claimed to be able to understand. For a similar discourse, see Luke 12:54-56.

•   Christ's rhetorical question again implied that they made the claim of being able to read the sky in order to predict weather. Now, however, He turned their claim back to them. If they were skilled at seeing signs, then His miracles, teachings, and fulfillment of Old Testament messianic prophecies should have been recognized as "signs" of the kingdom. The "signs of the times" (*ta de sēmeia tōn kairōn*) might more literally be translated "the indications of the appointed time or occasion," referring, of course, to the appointed time of the Messiah. All the indications of the kingdom were in place—John the Baptist had announced His arrival, the Romans had desecrated the Holy Place, miracles were flowing from Messiah as predicted in the Old Testament, His teachings were righteousness and truth in strict accordance with Scripture—yet they could not discern these things.

16:4   His condemnation of the generation that sought a sign was intended as an additional insult. Rather than being spiritual and wanting to see God's miracles, the generation was "evil" (*poneros,* a word used to personify Satan himself) and "adulterous" (*moichalis,* a feminine word applied to both male and female and indicating horrific unfaithfulness). God should not be required to prove Himself by signs and wonders—His Word is sufficient for the faithful. All of God's works demonstrate His faithfulness and sovereignty; and He is not obligated to prove His love, commitment, and faithfulness beyond the cross and empty tomb.

The "sign of Jonah" (already mentioned in 12:38-41) was clearly a reference to His own burial and resurrection. With the Sadducees being present for this statement, the impact must have been even more significant. They rejected the resurrection and life beyond the flesh; thus, pondering the message of Jonah, they were more perplexed and probably more cynical than before. Hendriksen's comment is excellent, "What a sign this death and resurrection would be for the Pharisees, who were constantly planning Jesus' death, with no fear that he would ever be able to conquer death; and for the Sadducees, who did not even believe in any resurrection!"[3]

Mark records that Jesus, "sighing deeply" (*anastenaxsas tō pneumati,* literally, "gave a deep groan in the spirit"), left them (Mark 8:12-13). This expressed the deep agony and exhaustion He felt at being constantly in conflict with the faithless, self-righteous religious leadership. His personal anguish did not begin in Gethsemane.

JESUS REBUKES THE DISCIPLES FOR FAILING TO UNDERSTAND HIS WARNING, 16:5-12 (Mark 8:14-21)

16:5   The "other side" apparently referred to the lake, which meant a return to predominantly Gentile territory. Jesus knew His time was drawing near for a final confrontation with the religious leaders at the Passover feast in Jerusalem, and temporarily He sought rest away from the turmoil. Apparently the disciples were responsible to make provisions for any journey, and on this occasion they failed to do so. According to Matthew's account, they forgot to take bread. However, while in agreement, Mark adds they did have one loaf (8:14), hardly enough for all.

16:6-7   Jesus made a comment, intending to use the aftermath of His conflict with the Pharisees and Sadducees as another teaching opportunity for the disciples. He warned them to be aware of the danger of the leaven of the Pharisees and Sadducees. The disciples, however, were more concerned with the discovery that they had failed to provide provision for the journey. They did not seem remotely aware of the intense inner struggle that the Lord was feeling (Mark 8:12; also see comment on 16:4).

The two commands, "watch out for" (*horate,* present imperative of *horaō,* "perceive, notice, recognize") and "beware" (*prosechete,* present imperative of *prosechō,* "pay close attention to, be on guard against") are serious indications of how offensive and dangerous the influence of these religious leaders were. Leaven (yeast) was a catalyst to make dough rise for cooking purposes. It is used symbolically in Scripture for any agent that brings influence into a situation. Most often, it has a negative connotation and usually represents sin. Carson offers a good summary of the biblical use of "leaven": "'Yeast' (v. 6) was a common symbol of evil (see on 13:33) and could therefore be applied to different kinds of wickedness (e.g., Luke 12:1; cf. Exod 34:25; Lev 2:11; 1 Cor 5:6-8), but always with the idea that a little of it could have far reaching and insidious effect."[4]

The disciples reflected their misunderstanding of Jesus' warning but apparently did not respond directly to Him: "they began to discuss among themselves" (v. 7). Their minds were typically focused on the temporal and immediate situation rather than on the more significant spiritual battle going on around them. In their defense, it must be acknowledged that all believers have this tendency—to be so involved with present needs that the spiritual perspective is overlooked. Barnes also points out that the metaphor of leaven representing doctrine would have been unknown to them because there is no record of its having been used that way.[5]

16:8-10   Jesus did not seem to be so quick to excuse them however. His stinging rebuke, "you men of little faith," indicates His displeasure with their discussion among themselves. Jesus was "aware" of their conversation over the failure to bring a supply of bread and appears to have been angered over their private discussion. The rebuke emphasized their lack of faith related to not having bread. "Little faith" was the issue, because after just witnessing the miracles of feeding the five-thousand-plus (14:19-21) and then again the four-thousand-plus (15:32-38), they worried about their lack of bread. If He was able and willing to feed the masses before, why should they be troubled? Verses 9 and 10 record the reminder that twice He had miraculously provided food for the hungry; only a "little faith" could have so easily forgotten the grace and power displayed by those miracles. How many times would the disciples need to see Him provide before they would believe?

16:11   The rhetorical question (of v. 11) brought the issue back to a failure of understanding: "How is it that you do not understand?" Because they had not grasped the conflict between Jesus and the religious leadership, their failure to understand was based upon their major concern for physical nourishment rather than the spiritual truth Jesus was presenting.

16:12   Finally, the truth became clear to the disciples: the issue was the teaching of Israel's religious leaders. As leaven permeates and influences a whole lump of dough, the teachings of the Pharisees and Sadducees had permeated the whole of Israel. Their human traditions, rabbinic additions to the Law, and legalistic religion had become the normative views. Jesus warned His followers against their doctrine. They were to recognize and avoid the traditions of the Pharisees and Sadducees as neither group represented the truth about God, though both claimed to be protectors of the truth. Jesus' followers were to separate God's truth from religious error, so that they could lead others to the true faith. Here Matthew defines the leaven as "the teaching of the Pharisees and Sadducees." Luke 12:1 records Jesus' giving another warning to His disciples concerning leaven, referring to Pharisaical leaven, which is defined as "hypocrisy."

Mark's parallel passage has "the leaven of the Pharisees and the leaven of Herod" (Mark 8:15). The addition of Herod and the omission of the Sadducees in Mark's record is easily explained when one keeps in mind that most Sadducees were Herodians, that is, supporters of the political dynasty of Herod. Mark's use of "Herod" rather than "Sadducees" was probably to emphasize the differing dangers in the two groups. Barbieri explains:

Perhaps that is why Jesus referred to Herod here rather than the Sadducees as a group. The Pharisees were hypocritical and very proud, with a legalistic spirit surrounding their laws and traditions. The Herodians on the other hand were very worldly and had an intense interest in political power. Jesus warned His disciples to be careful of both attitudes.[6]

PETER'S CONFESSION, 16:13-20
(Mark 8:27-29; Luke 9:18-21)

16:13   Jesus led His men to the mostly Gentile area of Caesarea Philippi (about twenty-five miles north of the Sea of Galilee and not to be confused with Caesarea on the coast). The area was noted for the majestic Mount Hermon, which may have been the site of the Transfiguration. Though Matthew does not record the story of the healing of the blind man in Bethsaida (Mark 8:22-26), and Luke records none of the events of Matthew and Mark immediately following the feeding of the five thousand (Luke 9:12-17), all three Synoptic Gospels record the confession of Peter with varying amounts of detail.

In this somewhat remote area where Jesus came for prayer and isolation (Luke 9:18), He began to question the disciples about the multitudes' opinion as to His identity. Matthew records Jesus' reference to Himself in the inquiry as "Son of Man," but both Mark and Luke record "Who do people say that *I* am?" However, in the immediate context of both Mark and Luke, "Son of Man" was used by Christ in reference to Himself (Mark 8:31; Luke 9:22). This variation is easily understood in normative historical narrative.

16:14   The people of Israel were trying to understand who Jesus was, and opinions ranged from a resurrected John the Baptist, to Elijah, to one of the prophets—in particular the prophet Jeremiah. It is interesting to note that each of the people named, and even the generic "one of the prophets of old," referred to someone deceased. Somehow the people found it easier to believe that Jesus was a resurrected prophet than a separate Person, the Messiah. His works and teachings were obviously so powerful and impressive that it did not seem possible for a "mere human" to do them.

John the Baptist had made a tremendous impact on the nation. His death had been both shocking and offensive to Israel. Many had assumed he would introduce a king like Judas Maccabee, and his death discouraged some concerning the messianic hope. The messages of Jesus and His conflict with the religious leaders were both similar to John's (though no records indicate that John ever worked miracles). Thus, rumors of Jesus could have easily sparked new optimism that John was not really dead—perhaps he had been resurrected to finish his mission. Upon hearing of Jesus' work, Herod Antipas feared this (14:1-2).

The belief that Jesus might be Elijah was probably based upon Malachi 4:5, "Behold, I am going to send you Elijah the prophet before the coming of the great and terrible day of the Lord." The powerful works of Jesus, coupled with His condemnation of the nation's apostasy, may have created an expectation that His was the last warning before the "great and terrible day of the Lord," and that created the association with Elijah. This identification would indicate that some of the crowds perceived Jesus to be the forerunner of the Messiah and not Messiah Himself.

Jeremiah was the third name mentioned. This is interesting from the standpoint of Jeremiah's rejection and suffering at the hands of Israel's leaders. Perhaps the people witnessed the conflict between Jesus and the Pharisees, scribes, and Sadducees and remembered Jeremiah's similar ministry. Possibly they had heard rumors of a plot to get rid of Jesus even as there had been against Jeremiah. They may have assumed that Jeremiah had returned to once again call Israel to repentance in order to avoid being destroyed by her enemies. Some Jewish tradition may indicate that the Jews expected Jeremiah to return with power and authority for restoration of Judah's glory.[7] If He was not Jeremiah, then it was assumed He could be one of the other prophets.

16:15-16   Jesus then turned to what was most important to Him—who did His own men think Him to be? The opinion of His followers was of supreme importance at this point. If they were as blind and confused as the rest, then His work would suffer a setback. Hendriksen indicates the significance: "In the original enormous stress is placed on 'But *you.*' This personal pronoun, second person plural, stands at the very head of the question. It appears first as a word all by itself, and is then included again as an element in the verb."[8]

Peter answered on behalf of the group (v. 16) by denoting two aspects of Jesus' identity: first, "You are the Christ"; second, "You

are the Son of the living God." Each title was critical to His Person
and His work. To identify Him as Messiah ("the Christ," *ho Christos*)
was to recognize that He was the long-anticipated servant of Yahweh. As "the Anointed One," He would be the One to suffer and
die for the sins of the people but also the One to rule the world as
Israel's king (Isa. 52-53; Dan. 7:13-14; etc.). As the "Son of the living
God" (*ho huios tou theou tou zōntos*), He was unique among men.
Gundry is correct to argue, "The title 'Immanuel . . . God with us'
(1:23) and the whole account of the virgin birth demand in
Matthew the stronger connotation of essential deity."[9]

The term "son" (*huios*) refers to relationship, whether a literal
biological connection (paternal and even ancestry, e.g., "son of
David") or metaphoric (e.g., "my son in the faith"). The connection
implies that one is dependent upon or the product of another. Theologians are correct to apply this title to the incarnation of the
Logos by the work of the Holy Spirit.[10] By virtue of His supernatural
conception in the womb of Mary, the child born was out of God
Himself. The eternal Person of the Logos became Son of God
through incarnation (the taking on of flesh) as described in John
1:1-14. He was out of God, sent from God, dependent upon God
(for His earthly work), and obedient to God, His Father (in His
incarnational work), and thus uniquely the Son of God. "Living
God" is to mark the contrast between the true God and the deities
of the surrounding cultures. He is alive and active, not a lifeless
myth or superstition of man's making.

16:17   Jesus' response to Peter was to declare him "blessed"
(*makarios;* see discussion on Matt. 5:3), here probably meaning
"fortunate, the recipient of God's favor." The reason stated was that
what he had just declared had not been perceived by others (thus
proven by responses to the question in v. 13) and, indeed, was the
result of divine illumination. Jesus' use of Peter's formal name,
"Simon, son of John" (*Simōn Bariōna—Bar Iōna,* from the Aramaic, *bar* = son, *Iōna* = John). Alford explains:

> The name Simon Bar Jonas is doubtless used as indicating his fleshly
> state and extraction, and forming the greater contrast to his spiritual
> state, name, and blessing which follow. The same "Simon son of Jonas"
> is uttered when he is reminded by the thrice repeated enquiry,
> "Lovest thou me?" of his frailty, in his previous denial of his Lord.[11]

There is a powerful contrast between the revelation from his heavenly Father and the natural status of his human father. The main point here lies in the fact that Peter's understanding, and confession of, the Person of Jesus was not the product of human wisdom or cleverness but the result of the heavenly Father's choosing to reveal to him this reality (cf. John 5:37; 6:44-45, 65; 8:47). There is no record of any audible voice, dream, vision, or other conscious method of revelation. It is best to assume that Peter was not even aware his view was anything but his own. The Father unveiled Jesus before Peter's heart that he might know He was the Messiah, the only true Son of God (for further information concerning this same concept, see 1 Cor. 2:6-14).

16:18   This verse could certainly be considered one of the most controversial statements in Scripture. One of the official "approved sources" for the lives of the saints of the Roman church claims, "So Our Lord chose him, and fitted him to be the Rock of His Church, His Vicar on earth, the head and prince of His Apostles, the centre and very principle of the Church's oneness, the source of all spiritual powers, and the unerring teacher of His truth."[12] Such views are common in the Roman Catholic faith, but Protestants have long argued that such application of the statement in v. 18 is unwarranted and unbiblical. Calvin argues that the claim does not even warrant a response because it is obvious that the Scripture does not substantiate the Roman assertion. He concludes, "I willingly concede to Peter the honor of being placed among the first in the building of the Church . . . but I will not allow them to infer from this that he has a primacy over others."[13] Calvin's view was that the words spoken to Peter were intended for all the disciples.[14]

The arguments related to the nuances of word meaning and grammatical features of this verse are so numerous that to offer fair representation and evaluation is simply not possible. Hendriksen offers a concise presentation and evaluation of some major views.[15] For the purpose of this commentary only a few key observations will be made.

First, the wording itself is important, *kagō de soi legō,* "and I now say to you." The pronoun "you" is singular, and in the flow of discussion from v. 17, this is obviously intended to be a direct address to Peter, Simon Barjona, and not generically to the group. The next clause is the most confusing, *hoti su ei Petros, kai epi tautē tē petra oikodomēsō mou tēn ekklēsian,* "that you are Peter [a rock], and upon this rock I will build my church." The implication is assumed that Peter (*petros*) is the same as "this rock" (*tē petra*), and therefore, the church of Jesus Christ is built upon Peter. This view presents several problems.

First, Paul explains that the church is built upon the foundation of the apostles (plural, not singular), Jesus Himself being the chief building stone (Eph. 2:20). Second, no other verse refers to Peter as the foundation of the church. Third, Paul claims equal authority with Peter, but placing emphasis on his work among the Gentiles whereas Peter's work was primarily with the Jews (Gal. 2:7-8). Since the church is primarily Gentile, this would place Paul's work in priority over Peter's if one wanted to compare their position as foundational to the church. Fourth, the words themselves are significant. The Greek word used to refer to Peter is *petros,* which means a "stone."[16] The masculine form may not be intended to be a personal name at this point (though this could be the place where it became a name for Simon) and would naturally be translated "a stone." The feminine form used next (*petra*) often refers to a large rock or even rocky ground; tombs were carved from *petra* (Matt. 27:60). Some scholars wish to weaken the differences between these two words,[17] but there is no reason to do so. Some assume what the underlying Aramaic words used here were, but to step beyond the text to build doctrine is not the intention of this commentary. True, the distinction of these words alone is not sufficient to build doctrine, but to assume the two forms represent a desire to preserve a pun[18] is also more speculative than required. Jesus could easily have used the same word and avoided great confusion had He intended to make Peter the object of the action of building His church. Other objections follow.

The conjunction *kai,* though normally and most naturally translated "and," has far more significance than just connecting phrases or words. There is an adversative sense of the word as seen in many contexts, e.g., John 7:19, "Did not Moses give you the law, and yet [*kai*] none of you carries out the law?" Another example is John 16:32, "[I am alone], and yet [*kai*] I am not alone." It is also likely that the conjunction is emphatic, "indeed, in fact," to create a dramatic contrast between Peter, whose confession had come not from his own cognitive skill, and the Messiah Himself. With these considerations, it is possible to translate this as "I say to you that you are a stone, and yet I will build my church upon this foundation rock." Not only is this translation a legitimate possibility, but it also is far more consistent with the rest of Scripture.

Another possible understanding is that not the person of Peter is the foundation of the church but rather his confession, "You are the Christ, the Son of the living God." This view is perhaps the most popular among Protestant evangelical scholars. While less objectionable, it is again unclear. Christ's church is not based upon a man's testimony but is founded upon the reality of the Person and work of Christ. So why attribute it to what Peter said? More correctly stated, the church is founded upon the truth that Christ brought into the world.

The best understanding of this passage is that Jesus was making Himself the foundation of the church. His statement was in the context of Peter's proper identification of His Person, but He was not rewarding Peter for His correct assessment (He quickly told Peter it did not originate within his own mental exercises.) The word *petra* does not represent or refer to the man Peter in any other verse of Scripture or to any "confession," but is used elsewhere to refer to the teachings or the Person of Jesus Christ. In Matthew 7:24, *petra* refers to His teachings, metaphorically used as a foundation stone upon which a person's life is to be built. In Romans 9:33, *petra* is used of Christ as the "stone of stumbling" upon whom we are to believe. Peter references the same teaching, not referring to himself but to Jesus in 1 Peter 2:8, a "rock of offense" (*petra skandalou*). In 1 Corinthians 10:4, Christ is referred to as the "spiritual rock" (*pneumatikēs . . . petras*), and Paul says, "And the rock [in Ex. 17] was Christ [*hē petra de ēn ho Christos*]." Thus, at least in the use of *petra,* Jesus or His truth is always the object represented. There is no need to associate the rock with Peter, as though Jesus were going to build His universal work upon him or upon any testimony he offered. Jesus was clear that *He* would build *His* church and it would built upon the foundation of His own Person and work.

The next statement is the victory proclamation "the gates of Hades shall not overpower it." His church would not be overcome by the gates of hades (*pulai hadou*). One must avoid misusing this verse to claim "victories" Jesus never intended. Carson mentions that "the 'gates of Hades' have been taken to represent the strength of Satan and his cohorts,"[19] but there is no reference to hades being the domain or kingdom of Satan. Hades (*adēs*) appears in the LXX more than one hundred times, mostly translating the Hebrew *sheol,* the "place of the dead, death," or possibly on occasion "the grave." In the New Testament, the word is used only ten times, referring to much the same idea as the Old Testament *sheol.* In Revelation 20:13, hades and death itself will "give up the dead in them" for judgment. The best concept seems to be that the boundaries, or means of access and exit, of death cannot prevail over the church that Christ was going to build. Jesus Himself holds the keys to the gates of hades (Rev. 1:18). The One who overcame death gives victory to the church He is building so that death cannot hold those who belong to it.

16:19   This next statement is no less complicated or controversial than v. 18. Keys give authority and power to someone. As keys open doors, those who hold the keys are wielding authority; thus, Christ promised Peter that He would give him authority of the kingdom of heaven. The "you" (*soi*) is again singular, and the flow of thought can hardly refer to anyone but Peter. The general idea is that the person holding the keys (Peter) has the power to exclude or include entrance as he deems fit. This is the reason for the many stories about St. Peter's gate, about Peter as the gatekeeper of heaven, and for the appeals to St. Peter to let someone into heaven. It certainly contributes to Peter's position in Roman Catholic theology. However, the better explanation is to be found in Peter's role as the one who opens the door of the kingdom message to both Jews (Acts 2:14-41; 3:12-26) and Gentiles (Acts 10:9-45). Peter's role as chief among the Lord's disciples was to open the way for the gospel to be preached. Thus Peter does not possess authority in relation to who enters or does not enter the kingdom, but rather his authority was to begin the worldwide ministry, beginning with Jews but spreading to the Gentiles as well.

When Jesus said, "Whatever you shall bind on earth shall be bound in heaven," He was not giving Peter authority to determine individual salvation, which then would be binding upon heaven; rather, He was declaring Peter's role in speaking as heaven's representative. An alternative and very probable translation (though rather wooden in English) would be "And whatever you should bind [*dēsēs,* aorist active subjunctive] on earth shall have been bound [*dedemenon,* perfect middle/passive participle] in heaven and whatever you shall loose [*lusēs,* aorist active subjunctive] on earth shall have been loosed [*lelumenon,* perfect middle/passive participle] in heaven." Both perfect tense participles are preceded by the future tense verb *estai,* "it shall be," thus making the construction a periphrastic perfect (i.e., a more complex way of stating a tense, here using the future of *eimi* with the perfect participle). Turner indicates that the participles in Matthew 16:19 are examples of future perfect periphrasis and that they "take the place of the normal future perfect."[20] Perschbacher notes, "The future forms of *eimi* join with an anarthrous participle, either present or perfect, and give emphasis to the present progressive action, or to the perfect complete action."[21]

This grammatical discussion is to point out that Jesus was telling Peter that he would be the voice of what had been previously determined in heaven, not that he would be declaring what heaven would then confirm. Carson states:

> The periphrastic future perfects are then perfectly natural: Peter accomplishes this binding and loosing by proclaiming a gospel that has already been given and by making personal application on that basis (Simon Magus). Whatever he binds or looses will have been bound or loosed, so long as he adheres to that divinely disclosed gospel. He has no direct pipeline to heaven, still less do his decisions force heaven to comply; but he may be authoritative in binding and loosing because heaven has acted first.[22]

In light of this interpretation, it is fitting to note that Peter was not the only apostle to receive this promise. In 18:18, Jesus gives the same promise but this time He uses the plural pronoun (*humin*) and second person plural verbs (*dēsēte, lusēte*). The context makes clear that primarily He is addressing His disciples but indirectly indicating that the church as a whole has the same prerogative. An interesting parallel in John 20:21-23 features the same use of the perfect tense in association with the coming of the Holy Spirit. Thus the divine prerogative of forgiving, binding, or loosing is expressed through the heavenly message of the church as the instrument of the Holy Spirit. Clearly, no papal authority is given to Peter in this verse.

16:20   After the questioning and subsequent promise of the victory and authority of the church, Jesus made a rather confusing
statement: they were to "tell no one that He was the Christ." In light
of the bewilderment and erroneous views of the people of Israel
(v. 14), it would be assumed that Jesus would send His men out to
proclaim His messiahship. Yet He warned them not to do that.
Some argue that the purpose of this prohibition was to "guarantee
(1) that the decisive factors in the conversion of men are not
nationalistic fervor and impenitent messianic expectation but faith,
obedience, and submission to Jesus; and (2) that the events leading
to the Cross are not to be short-circuited by premature disclosure."[23] Mounce points out that since the disciples did not fully
understand as yet all of what His messiahship involved, He did not
want the rest of Israel to rashly react to Him as Messiah until everything was in place.[24] Although these are good reasons, another
must not be overlooked: part of the judgment against Israel was
that they should experience blindness (13:13-15), which is a significant part of Pauline theology of redemption (Rom. 11:7-11, 22-32).

CHRIST PREDICTS HIS SUFFERING AND DEATH, 16:21-28 (Mark 8:31-33; Luke 9:22)

16:21   Matthew's comment "from that time . . ." (*apo tote*) indicates a shift or beginning point (aorist middle of *archō* also indicates a beginning point) of a new attitude in the ministry of Jesus.
Something new had begun (see 4:17, where the same expression is
used at the inauguration of His public ministry). The context implies that this was the beginning of His preparation of the disciples
for His departure. Whereas there had been allusions to His future
suffering (e.g., 12:39-40), now He would speak directly to the issue.

He "showed" (*deiknumi*, "point out, explain, reveal, prove")
His disciples four specific events of the immediate future: He would
go to Jerusalem, thus far not a major focus of His ministry; He
would suffer many things at the hands of the religious leaders; He
would be killed; and He would be raised from the dead after three
days. The particle *dei* ("must, it is necessary") used here indicates
the finality of these events. They were decreed and thus "must"
take place.

It is vital to note that the suffering would be at the hands of the religious leadership, specifically, the elders, chief priests, and scribes. Elders were the spiritual and communal leaders. Unlike "elders" (*presbuteros*) in Greek society, who were mere political figures like modern-day city councilmen, Israel's leaders were viewed as godly men having spiritual insight. Their tradition can be traced back to Numbers 11:16-30, where it is recorded that the Spirit of God descended upon chosen elders of the nation to assist Moses in ruling. Their betrayal of Messiah would be a breach of faith that affected the whole nation. Not only had the elders failed the people, but the chief priests, those who interceded for them, would also betray and murder the Anointed One. The third group named was the scribes, a professional office, not a religious party. They were experts in the Scriptures and were mostly composed of Pharisees, even though Sadducees also had their scribes. Called "lawyers," or experts in Mosaic Law, these men who should have seen the Messiah in the Scriptures became His accusers. Alford points out that all three classes made up the Sanhedrin, the high court of Israel.[25] Meyer notes, significantly, that what Jesus predicted was "not being stoned to death by the people, but judicial murder through the decision of a court of justice."[26] Israel's spiritual leaders would kill their Messiah.

For the first time, the disciples were confronted directly with the frightening truth that their leader was to die. They had witnessed the hostility of the Pharisees and Sadducees, had heard His denunciation of the scribes and Pharisees, and knew of the anger it had generated; but now they were told that Jesus would be killed. Jesus knew and would not try to avoid what "must" happen. The promise of the resurrection after three days now specifically defined the allusion made in 12:40.

16:22   Peter's response was typical for this natural leader of the disciples, "God forbid it, Lord!" (more literally, "Mercy to you, Lord, this shall not be to you"). The horror of the words just heard so overpowered him that he actually "rebuked" (*epitimaō*, "command order, rebuke, scold") his "Lord." He took Jesus aside, apparently for private counsel, assuming the Lord had misspoken. Peter's confession of v.16 seemed now to fall by the wayside as he corrected what he assumed to be a mistaken notion on the part of the Lord. Peter's understanding of the Messiah's destiny was severely lacking. Like the majority of his day, he anticipated that Messiah would establish a glorious kingdom, but Peter's hopes were shattered by what he heard.

16:23   The Lord's response to Peter was not an outwardly compassionate understanding of Peter's fear but a stern rebuke for his selfish motives and lack of faith. The remark "Get behind me, Satan!" (*hupage opisō mou satana*) can be compared to His dismissal of the real Satan (Matt. 4:10), "Begone, Satan!" (*hupage satana*). The term "Satan" (*satana*) means an "adversary," and Peter was now opposing Jesus' mission. Satan is the opponent to God's redemptive plan; and Peter, by his selfish response, was aiding Satan, not Jesus.

Jesus called Peter a "stumbling block" (*skandalon*), because he was at the moment an obstacle to Christ's mission, creating a strong contrast to the declaration of v. 18, "You are a rock." Peter unknowingly was acting as Satan's tool. Jesus explained why Peter was a stumbling block. His attitude was an obstacle. His motive was the offending factor. "For [*hoti*, "because"] you are not setting your mind on God's interests, but man's." Not concerned about God's program or the mission of the Messiah, Peter centered on the consequences to himself and the other disciples if Jesus should die. Again, the contrast should not be missed. In v. 17, Jesus points out that Peter's confession was revelation from God; in v. 23, Peter's expression is purely human. Hendriksen observes:

> From God's point of view it was necessary for the Savior to suffer, die, rise again, etc., in order to save his people. From the human point of view, the two concepts *Messiah* and *suffering* were wholly incompatible. Peter, allowing himself to be influenced by Satan, was speaking from the foolish human point of view . . . . He did not realize that he was asking for his own eternal damnation.[27]

16:24-26   Jesus then addressed all His disciples about discipleship. While they were still in shock over His terrifying prediction, He disclosed the consequences of their identification with Him. Jesus' remark was stated in a conditional form, "If one wishes [or is willing] to follow Me . . ." which implies a volitional act.

The two requirements to following Jesus are self-denial and death. "Let him deny himself" is a foreign concept in contemporary society, even in Christian circles. Hendriksen defines self-denial as "to renounce the old self. The self as it is apart from regenerating grace."[28] But this is not adequate in and of itself since even the renewed self is still self. To "deny" (*aparneomai*) means basically to "give up ownership, disown" or to "renounce claim" to something. One who follows Jesus must realize that his life is not his own to do with as he pleases (cf. 1 Cor. 6:19-20). Thus, career, location, comforts, pleasures, and material goods, and so on, are not a matter of personal choice, but must be based upon the Lord's claim to one's life.

The second qualification was to "take up his cross, and follow Me." The idea of "cross bearing" has been degraded to any inconvenience or disappointment in life. But the cross was a well-known symbol of disgrace, torture, and death. It was an instrument of execution used widely by the Romans to kill any they considered unfit to live under Roman rule. The cross was so disgraceful as a method of death that it was forbidden for any Roman citizen, no matter what the crime. Thus Paul was decapitated (according to tradition) rather than being crucified as were Peter and thousands of other "enemies of the state." Consequently, Christ's statement indicated that His followers must assume themselves to be dead, crucified with Him (cf. Gal. 2:20). A disciple is to have the attitude that says, "I do not have the right to determine my own course of life or the elements of it: I am dead, crucified with Jesus. I live to serve Him only." When one talks about being a disciple of Christ, let him remember His standards of discipleship.

Jesus explained (explanatory *gar* introducing the statement in v. 25) that the one who is trying to "save his life," that is, cling to it and preserve it for himself, will forfeit his life. The word for "life" is *psuchē*, normally translated "soul," which might lead some to jump to the wrong conclusion. *Psuchē* is used of the whole person as well as for that inner quality of essence known as the soul. One example of this use is 1 Peter 3:20, where it is said that "eight persons" (*oktō psuchai*) were saved through the Flood waters. Of course the verse is referring to their whole being, including the physical, not just their souls. Jesus' warning is for those who are afraid to follow Him and who try to cling to their lives. They will "die" regardless of how they compromise and try to avoid it. In contrast, those who willingly let go of their lives and lay them down for Jesus ("for My sake") will find a life so abundant and rich that it is unknown to all but the faithful.

Verse 26, like v. 25, offers an explanation for the preceding statement (second explanatory *gar*), which indicates a building argument. Thus this verse is offering rationale for the proclamation just made in v, 25. It is a puzzle as to why the translators of the NASB and NIV translated *psuchē* as "life" twice in v. 25 but suddenly changed to "soul" in v. 26 for the same word. Carson assumes the change is based on a shift from a physical emphasis to a spiritual one.[29] Justification for this, however, cannot be found in the context. What makes v. 25 physical and v. 26 spiritual? Verse 26 explains the rationale for v. 25.

The first rhetorical question dealt with the final outcome of one's efforts in life. If one gives priority to gaining all the wealth the world has to offer, yet in the end loses (*zēmioō*, "suffers loss, forfeits") his life, what is his profit (*ōpheleō*, "achievement, gain")? The perfect parallel teaching is the parable of Luke 12:15-21, which warns about greed and making material gain the priority rather than being "rich toward God." Hendriksen points out the irony of Satan's similar temptation of the Lord to gain the kingdoms of the world by worshiping him rather than by dying, as the Father wished (Matt. 4:8-10).[30]

The second rhetorical question pointed out the foolishness of exchanging the value of a life lived for God for the sake of temporal material gain. This is not unlike Esau's trading his birthright for a bowl of beans. Mounce explains:

> Though Jesus' statement is ultimately eschatological, there is a profound sense in which self-interest destroys life here and now. Each decision of life is making us into a certain kind of person, and the opportunity to relive life is not open to us. Life is lost (or gained) in living.[31]

Jesus was not warning about the loss of salvation but the loss of reward and good favor with God by forfeiting the spiritual things for the material. The New Testament is replete with similar warnings in light of ultimate accounting to the Lord for the use of our lives (e.g., 2 Cor. 5:10).

16:27-28   Another explanatory *gar* brought closure to the Lord's thesis. He Himself was the example of self-denial and willingness to take up the cross. It was the "Son of Man" who would reward the faithful. The title, Christ's favorite for Himself, emphasizes both His messianic work and His identification with the human race. He is the Second Adam, the Second Man, who came to redeem man by His obedience and sacrifice. As the Son of Man He suffered, obeyed, died, and was resurrected. Now Jesus was saying that, as the Son of Man, He will also return to reward those who followed Him. The promise was not a proclamation of how to be saved but a pledge to reward those who suffer for Him (cf. Rom. 8:17-18).

The comment in v. 28 is perplexing if one tries to make it woodenly literal. If understood to mean that some of the disciples would not die until the millennial kingdom is established, then much of New Testament chronology must be reinterpreted. Carson believes the meaning lies in the postresurrection appearances and in the sending forth of the church to evangelize the world. Some of these men would see the foundation of the kingdom through world evangelization.[32] There is some merit to this view, but it seems not to sufficiently fulfill the expression *en tē basileia autou,* "in His kingdom."

In light of the testimony of all three synoptics that the next recorded event was the Transfiguration (17:1-8; Mark 9:1-8; Luke 9:27-36), it might be best to understand that His comment was predicting that preview of the kingdom glory of the Son of Man. The Transfiguration was a glimpse of Jesus in glory, which Peter, James, and John (the inner circle of disciples) would be privileged to witness. In this way these three did not die before they saw the Son of Man coming in His kingdom. Their vision was a preview of what was to come. Following His death, they were to encourage the others by telling what they had seen.

HOMILETICAL SUGGESTIONS

This chapter records the intensification of the conflict in the Lord's ministry. The antagonism of the religious leadership is emphasized in vv. 1-4 and 21. One should note that the Lord's response was not amiable or tolerant but forceful and unyielding. His refusal to give a sign to the Pharisees and Sadducees was highlighted with stern condemnation. He called them an adulterous and evil generation—not exactly the world's model for winning friends and influencing people. Perhaps the Lord was trying to communicate to

His followers that being popular and accepted by the world or its religious leaders is not the highest goal.

The disciples, by failing to understand what He meant by the "leaven of the Pharisees and Sadducees," demonstrated the danger of being too focused on material things and needs. Their misunderstanding was the result of putting human need at the center of their concern. The metaphor of leaven warns against the infiltration and influence of bad teaching. Like yeast in dough, wrong teaching spreads and affects every part. One is to be on guard against false teaching from religious leaders (cf. 7:15; 1 John 4:1; etc.).

The promise of Jesus to build His church, which will overcome the hold of death and which will be built upon Himself, should offer comfort to every believer. Certainly Peter was the Lord's key man and one who wielded much authority in the early church, but the power and victory of the church is not dependent upon him. The apostles, like the church today, were spokesmen for heaven and were to proclaim forgiveness or condemnation based upon the decrees of heaven. The mandate to carry the message of the kingdom is for all believers, not just Peter.

Verses 21-28 compose a most critical segment of the gospel record. The Lord began to focus on His upcoming death, and the apostles did not want to hear it. Like many today, they wanted good news, comfort, assurance. Instead, they were told that for them to be true followers of Jesus, ownership of their lives must be relinquished and a willingness to follow Him in death to self must be present. The Lord's message is repeated by Paul in 1 Corinthians 6:19-20, Romans 14:9-15:4, and Galatians 2:20, as well as other places in the New Testament. Being a follower of Christ is a serious commitment to live as He lived and die as He died.

MATTHEW
CHAPTER
SEVENTEEN

TRANSFIGURATION AND
RETURN TO CAPERNAUM

Matthew 16:21, "from that time," marks the point where Jesus began to focus soberly on His upcoming betrayal, suffering, death, and resurrection. This chapter continues that intense focal point as Jesus began His journey up to Jerusalem. He stopped in Capernaum, His base of operations, and persisted in preparing His men for the time when He would leave them behind and they would continue His work. The Transfiguration account may well be the fulfillment of the last comment in chap. 16, "There are some of those who are standing here who shall not taste death until they see the Son of Man coming in His Kingdom." Indeed, the three "inner circle" disciples did see Jesus in His glory, accompanied by Moses and Elijah. Elijah was the prophet designated to prepare the people for the coming Day of the Lord (Mal. 4:5; also note the reference to Moses in v. 4). Thus chap. 17 continues the theme introduced in chap. 16—the earthly ministry of the Lord was drawing to a close.

THE TRANSFIGURATION, 17:1-9
(Mark 9:2-9; Luke 9:28-36)

17:1 Some have found an intended parallel between the events of the Transfiguration and the experience of Moses in Exodus 24.[1] Although there are certain interesting similarities that perhaps could make a connection between Jesus and Moses, one should be cautious in depending upon such creative interpretation for the event's meaning and significance. One of the errors of rabbinical interpretation was that imagination, bordering on fantasy, became central in finding the meaning of a text rather than a literal, historical, and grammatical interpretation. The context of Matthew 17 should not be influenced by embellished associations with former events.

There is an *apparent* contradiction between the records of Matthew and Mark and that of Luke. Both Matthew and Mark state that it was "six days later" (Matt. 17:1; Mark 9:2), but Luke records, "some eight days after" (Luke 9:28). The answer is one of common sense as well as careful scrutiny of what was said. The expression "six days later" does not identify the antecedent of "later." There is only the assumption that it was after the statement of the Lord concerning the viewing of the coming of the Son of Man (16:28). This is logical and creates no problem in itself. Luke's account records "some eight days after these sayings," without clarifying what sayings. The plural (*tous logous toutous*) could be referring to the whole period of discourse from the conflict with the Pharisees up until the Transfiguration. How many days were involved is not stated, but often Scripture condenses events of several days into a simple statement. Luke's wording clearly implies no intent to be specific about the time, *ōsei* ["about, approximately"] *hēmerai oktō* (eight days). Meyer correctly summarizes, "This *ōsei* makes it unnecessary to have a recourse to any expedient for reconciling the numbers."[2] Thus, rather than assuming a contradiction, it must be acknowledged that the specific time frames stated are not in conflict but only intentionally imprecise.

Jesus took only three of His disciples on the mountain with Him. Barbieri does not accept the idea that there was "favoritism" toward these men and speculates that "these three had shown themselves especially spiritually responsive to what illumination they had already been given."[3] Certainly it must be agreed that favoritism as exercised by mere humans is not the issue. However, how can Peter who had just been called Satan and who would deny His Lord vehemently be considered more spiritually responsive? Mark 5:37 and Matthew 26:36-37 also reveal these three received privileged treatment and responsibility. For whatever reason, the Lord singled out these men as special in His program.

Because of their prominent roles in post-Ascension ministry, the selection of Peter and John is easily understood. However, James was killed early in the mission (Acts 12:2) and did not function in a key role in building the church. Considering its proximity to Caesarea Philippi (16:13), the mountain these three men were taken to was probably Mount Hermon.

17:2 The word "transfigured" (*metemorphomai*) means "to be changed in form." The English word "metamorphosis," which refers to a change in the form or structure of an animal such as a butterfly from a caterpillar or a frog from a tadpole, comes from this Greek word. Thus it should be understood that this refers to a dramatic and supernatural change in the Lord's appearance. The attempts of some to weaken the dramatic change in His form are both inadequate and unnecessary.[4] Matthew records that part of the transformation was that "His face shone like the sun" and also that even "His garments became as white as light." Mark adds that the whiteness was beyond what human laundering could accomplish (Mark 9:3), and Luke records that His clothing had the appearance of lightning flashing (Luke 9:29). Luke also says that His face "became different" (*heteros*, "another"), that is, different in appearance. Lenski's comments are excellent:

> The body and nature of Jesus were glorified . . . . When the disciples looked at the countenance of Jesus they looked at a refulgence that was as brilliant as the sun itself. This extended to Jesus' entire form, for his very garments had the translucent whiteness of pure light. Instead of thinking of Moses (Ex. 34:29; 2 Cor. 3:13), we have far more reason to think of John's vision of Jesus in Revelation 1:13–15.[5]

17:3 Not only was the Lord transformed before their eyes so that they could view His glorious essence, but the disciples also saw two heroic and significant Old Testament persons join the Lord for a conversation. Moses and Elijah were significant for their roles in preparing the kingdom: Moses, the lawgiver for the kingdom, and Elijah, the prophet who would come before the Day of the Lord. Penner is representative of several scholars who see Moses and Elijah as representing the Law and Prophets and thereby "indicative of the entire Old Testament."[6] Matthew simply records that these two prophets were "talking with Him," but Luke specifies that their conversation was about His "departure" coming up in Jerusalem (Luke 9:31), obviously a reference to His death. Therefore one purpose for the Transfiguration may have been to encourage and comfort Jesus regarding the forthcoming trials, which the disciples had failed to see was needed.

17:4　　Typical of Peter, he spoke up with a suggestion based upon a wrong assumption. The suggestion to build three tabernacles (*skēnē,* "tent, temporary shelter") was based upon the Old Testament Feast of Tabernacles (Lev. 23:33-44). Peter seemed to have been overcome with the supernatural nature of this event and meant the booths to symbolize divine blessing through the presence of these three glorious persons. Mark informs us that Peter spoke out of fear and being overwhelmed (9:6). Luke adds that Peter spoke as Moses and Elijah were about to depart, "not realizing what he was saying" (9:33).

17:5-6　　While the words were still coming out of Peter's mouth (*eti autou lalountos*), a voice from heaven interrupted. The "bright cloud" is reminiscent of the Shekinah glory of God (Ex. 13:21-22; 16:10; 19:16; 40:34-38), indicating His presence. The words spoken reflected a rebuke, not encouragement in their time of fear. Penner observes that the suggestion of building three tabernacles "put the three on equal standing,"[7] which was not only erroneous but almost blasphemous. Thus, the heavenly Father spoke to these men and corrected their weak view of Jesus. "This is My beloved Son," not just another prophet like Moses or Elijah. Carson says, "The rebuke . . . is administered solely because what Peter blurted out compromised Jesus' uniqueness."[8]

That the voice was a rebuke and not a comfort can be seen clearly by the response of the trio of disciples: "they fell on their faces and were much afraid" (v. 6). It should not be assumed, however, that fear was a wrong response. Fear is a key element of worship. When one is confronted with the reality of who Jesus is and with the majestic Person of God, fear is only natural. Terror (irrational fear) has no place in a healthy relationship with God, and indeed this is the significance of 1 John 4:18. However, fear (*phobos*) in the proper sense is a part of the Christian attitude (2 Cor. 7:1; Eph. 5:21; Phil. 2:12-13; 1 Peter 1:17).

17:7-9　　Jesus acted with compassion toward His men. Matthew records three actions. He came to them; He touched them; and then

He spoke to them. The coming indicated a separation of some distance between Jesus and the prophets, and the disciples. Jesus did not speak loudly from a distance but came near to them.

He then touched the men (aorist participle of *haptō,* "took hold of them, touched"), creating a dramatic contrast to the transcendence of the majestic voice, which brought fear. Jesus' touch brought assurance and a stirring view of His tender mercy. At other times, His words had been sharp and stinging; but here they were comforting and compassionate, "Get up, and stop being afraid." There was no need to fear when Jesus was with them, when He "came near."

As they lifted their eyes (v. 8), the prophets and the glory that had transformed Jesus could no longer be seen. They saw only their Lord. The purpose for which they had been brought to this place was completed (cf. 16:28–17:2), and now they were told to keep this sensational experience to themselves until after His resurrection (v. 9). Probably the secret was to be maintained until His victory over death was proclaimed, and then the vision was to be made known to verify the messianic glory of the risen Lord. Carson points out that this was the fifth and last command for the disciples to remain silent about His Person. He suggests that it was, first, to prevent "superficial political messianism" and, second, because such news would not "only foster false expectations but [His subsequent crucifixion] would also quickly disillusion those who held to them."[9]

PRIVATE INSTRUCTION CONCERNING THE MYSTERY OF ELIJAH, 17:10-13 (Mark 9:11-13)

17:10   The question the disciples raised about Elijah was certainly based upon the anticipation created by Malachi 4:5, "Behold, I am going to send you Elijah the prophet before the coming of the great and terrible day of the Lord." What is interesting is why the disciples made the connection between the coming of Elijah and the Transfiguration experience.

As with all Old Testament references in the New, it is critical to consider the full impact of the context of the Old to insure proper application of the New. Malachi 4 is a promise of final justice and the establishment of true righteousness. The disciples had been hearing their Master preach this message (beginning in particular with the Discourse on the Mount, chaps. 5–7) and had been prepared through the early ministry of John the Baptist. Also in the context of Malachi 4 is the reference to Moses, "Remember the law of Moses My servant," which precedes the reference to Elijah. Therefore, when the disciples witnessed the Transfiguration, having heard the repeated messages of true righteousness and being confronted with both Moses and Elijah, to associate this with the promise of Malachi was natural. The disciples demonstrated a good theological process by connecting the event with Malachi's promise. Their confusion came with the reference to His death. Elijah was coming to "restore the hearts of the fathers to their children" (v. 6)[10] and this was the time for judgment against the evil world and the establishment of righteousness (vv. 2-3). Therefore how could He die?

17:11-13   Jesus answered by affirming what the rabbis had been teaching for centuries—yes, Elijah would come before the completion of the Messiah's work. Jesus used the present tense verb "is coming (*erchetai,* v. 11), best understood as a futuristic present "to describe vividly a future event"[11] and the future "will restore" (*apokatastēsei*), which implies events yet to come. However, in v. 12, He uses the aorist tense with the indicative mood, indicating a *past* event, "Elijah came already." By this deliberate grammatical structure Jesus presented the Elijah event from two perspectives: that which will be and that which has already been. It is possible that the future Elijah event is that described in Revelation 11:3-11, where Elijah the Tishbite is one of the two witnesses. Certainly the context of the events would be consistent of the great and terrible Day of the Lord.

In v. 12, Jesus deals with the Elijah event as already past, "Elijah already came." The disciples understood this as a reference to John the Baptist (v. 13) and rightly so, since Jesus Himself had already clearly made the statement that John was Elijah, "From the days of John the Baptist . . . he himself is Elijah" (11:11-15). But the Jews had rejected John's prophetic message ("they did not recognize him," v. 12), and the hearts of the people were not turned. Thus Messiah would also be rejected and murdered. This also answers any questions the disciples might have had about how Jesus could be the Messiah if Elijah had not first come to bring repentance.

However, the resurrection and future return of the Messiah,

not as humble servant but as glorious Son of Man, is certainly as real as His first advent, and it too will be preceded by the prophetic declarations of an "Elijah." There is no reason that he could not be the original prophet, Elijah the Tishbite, but neither is it impossible that the future Elijah will be a prophet in the "spirit and power of Elijah" even as John was. This "spirit and power of Elijah" was the reason that John denied being *the* Elijah (John 1:21). He was not the Old Testament prophet but a separate messenger from God who would only fulfill the role of Elijah, warning men to repent in Elijah's spirit and power. This may lead one to assume that the next Elijah event will be the Tishbite prophet himself.

THE DISCIPLES' INABILITY TO CAST OUT A DEMON, 17:14-21 (Mark 9:14-29; Luke 9:37-43)

17:14-16   According to the parallel passages, Jesus and the inner circle of disciples descended from the mountain the next day (Luke 9:37). They found a crowd gathered around the other nine disciples as the scribes argued with them (Mark 9:14). Upon seeing Jesus approaching, part of the crowd ran to meet Him. Jesus inquired regarding their discussion with His disciples (Mark 9:15-16). Amid a tense and confusing scene, the crowd anxiously waited to see what Jesus would do.

Matthew's account focuses on the man who petitioned Jesus to heal his son. The man fell on his knees or, more literally, "knelt" (*gonupeteo*). Carson states, "The word . . . has no overtones of worship,"[12] and its other uses in the New Testament (Matt. 27:29; Mark 1:40, and 10:17) indicate that it was a display of respect (or feigned respect as in Matt. 27).

Verse 15 records the man's request, "Lord, have mercy on my son." The appeal for mercy (*eleaō*) implied that he assumed Jesus had the power to help his son if He were only willing (but there is some doubt concerning his faith; see Mark 9:22). He then added as reason (*hoti*) that the son was a "lunatic" (*selēniazomai,* literally, "moonstruck"; *selēnē* = "moon"). This word is used only twice in the New Testament, here and 4:24 (where it is translated "epileptics"). The NIV interpretation is "has seizures," which may be acceptable when compared with Mark 9:18, describing the phenomenon as being thrown to the ground, foaming at the mouth, grinding his teeth, and stiffening out. This description is also the likely cause of the NASB rendering "epileptic" in 4:24. However, this was not the physical disorder of epilepsy but demonic oppression, as is clearly shown in v. 18, Mark 9:25, and Luke 9:42. It is incorrect to say that the Scripture here associates the physical disorder of epilepsy with demonization; again, the term used was, literally, "moonstruck," and any similarity of condition is not a medical diagnosis but descriptive of a malfunction. Here the malfunction was spiritually induced, not physical. Epilepsy is controllable with medication, but demonism is not.

Verse 16 indicates that in the absence of Jesus, the nine disciples were still recognized as having power, probably from the reports of their ministry recorded in 10:1-8. The NASB's "could not cure him" is, literally, "they did not have power to heal him." They appeared to lack power; Jesus said they lacked faith (v. 20).

17:17-18   The first response from Jesus was anger with the crowd. His reply (v. 17) indicated frustration and disappointment: "How long shall I put up with you?" His address to the "unbelieving [*apistos*] and perverted [*diastrephō*] generation" included all standing there (perhaps including His own disciples; see v. 20). Hendriksen explains that it included the disciples who failed, the father who seems to have questioned Jesus' power (Mark 9:22), the scribes, and all His contemporaries.[13] The Lord's indignation ("How long shall I be with you? How long shall I put up with you?) is easily understood when one remembers the glory of the Transfiguration and now His descent to this dismal scene. He commanded the boy to be brought to Him.

Matthew simply records (v. 18) that the Lord "rebuked him" (the demon), and he came out of the boy. Mark offers more detail, explaining that the boy had been afflicted with the demon from his youth (9:21), indicating a period of some years. Mark and Luke both record that the demon reacted to the presence of Jesus by dashing the boy to the ground in a convulsion.

Mark 9:22 indicates that the father's faith was wavering. Perhaps the failure of the disciples had created doubt in his mind about Jesus' power. To the father's "if you can do anything" Jesus retorted, "If you can!" The NIV is probably more correct in translating this as a question, "If you can?" with emphasis on the "if." The grammar allows for either a statement or a question. The context lends more credibility to the latter. Jesus was again expressing frustration at unbelief by quoting what the father had just said but phrasing it to emphasize His annoyance with the doubting of His power. Jesus turned back the father's remark, saying that what He was looking for was faith. There was no question as to His power, but whether He would heal the boy or not seemed dependent upon whether the father would trust Him. This was not dissimilar to Jesus' response to the Syrophenician woman or the centurion, who, though being Gentiles, received what they requested because of their faith. Would the father, in the midst of this unbelieving and perverted generation, have faith in Jesus? Mark 9:24 indicates he did, and Jesus healed his son. "The boy was cured at once" (17:18) without any further discourse or inquiry.

17:19-20   Matthew and Mark both record the question of the disciples (Mark 9:28), but Matthew alone records His rebuke concerning their lack of faith. In Mark the answer is related to the "kind" (*kenos,* "sort, family, category"), but in Matthew the issue is the "littleness" of their faith (v. 20), though the explanation of the "kind" is given in v. 21, if one accepts the textual support for it. The disciples came to Jesus "privately," and Mark adds that it was once they were in the house (9:28). This is understandable in light of the disciples' public failure and His apparent anger at the crowd's interest.

The rebuke in Matthew is not recorded in Mark, but this does not justify questioning its authenticity. Mark's focus is on the need for dependence upon divine strength (prayer and fasting), and Matthew focuses on the weakness of the disciples' faith. These are not contradictory but closely related issues. Faith, characterized by prayer (seeking God's power) and fasting (humbly waiting upon Him), were the necessary elements for dealing with this well-entrenched demon. The disciples had perhaps forgotten that the power to cast out demons was not theirs but God's alone. Rather than praying and fasting, acts showing dependence upon God, had they tried to remove the demon by words or commands on their own authority? Matthew's emphasis on faith indicates they were not trusting in God. The Jews had professional "exorcists" (*exsorkistēs,* Acts 19:13) who depended upon incantations and magic formulas[14] (as do many contemporary exorcists), which possibly influenced these disciples. But the Lord used the authoritative word from heaven to expel them without debate or steps or formulas. Jesus was upset because His men lacked the faith and spiritual character to accomplish what He had to do for them—command the spirit to come out of the boy.

The hyperbolic illustration of the mustard seed, the smallest seed known to this time and culture, made the point that their faith was even smaller than that. By possessing even that much faith, they could have moved mountains, much less a demon. Some believe the reference to the mustard seed was to encourage them to continue in faith, because a mustard seed starts small but grows large.[15] However, nothing in the wording or context supports this perception. There is no implication of anything planted and growing, only a quantitative illustration as to the smallness of their faith. In contrast, the father's faith was sufficient to find favor with Christ and to rid his son of the demon. Calvin aptly remarks, "There is none of us that does not experience both of them [belief and unbelief] in himself. As our *faith* is never perfect, it follows that we are partly *unbelievers;* but God forgives us, and exercises such forbearance towards us, as to reckon us believers on account of a small portion of faith."[16]

17:21 Though some significant manuscripts omit this verse, enough support exists to justify keeping it. Based on its similarity to Mark's comment (9:29), some speculate a later scribal copying into Matthew's account. This is understandable and does occur in other pericopes. See the discussion on v. 20 for an explanation of the significance of prayer and fasting as demonstrations of faith.

SECOND CLEAR PREDICTION OF HIS DEATH AND RESURRECTION, 17:22-23 (Mark 9:31; Luke 9:44-45)

17:22-23 The second prediction of Jesus' death and resurrection follows closely on the miracle just performed. The wording of the three synoptics give a picture of the crowd being deeply impressed with the miracle and giving glory directly to God, not even to Jesus (Luke 9:43). They record that He subsequently moved His men away from the area to spend time explaining His upcoming trials and death (Mark 9:30-31). The disciples failed to understand, as the full impact of the event was deliberately hidden from them (Luke 9:45).

Their being afraid to ask Him for clarification is also recorded (Mark 9:32; Luke 9:45). This fear-inspiring aspect of Jesus may be unappealing to some Christians who misunderstand the true nature of the Lord, but it is consistent with the whole revelation of Jesus Christ. The disciples were used to rebukes for their lack of understanding (Matt. 15:15-16; 16:11, 21-23). Matthew simply records that they were "deeply grieved," which is certainly understandable.

LESSON FROM THE TWO-DRACHMA TAX, 17:24-27

17:24   Matthew alone records this event, which may not have been significant to the purpose of the other writers but offers a valuable lesson as to the Lord's attitude. The two-drachma tax (about two days' wages) was the largest source of income for the temple treasury during this period and was compulsory for every male over the age of nineteen. Most likely this tax was based upon Exodus 30:12-14. The month of Adar was set apart for this "offering," and if a person had not paid the tax by the end of the month, legal action was taken against him.[17] The question of v. 24, therefore, carried great weight in relation to Jesus' reputation. Had He failed or been unwilling to pay the tax, the implication would have been that He did not support the temple and therefore could not be God's Son. Note that the tax collectors (of the temple, not Rome) did not approach Jesus but went to Peter. Perhaps His having outwitted and embarrassed the religious leadership made them afraid to approach Him.

17:25-26   Peter's response was "Yes," even without asking the Lord. The basis for this reply could have been the past experience of seeing Jesus pay the tax or simply that Peter could not imagine any true Jew not supporting the temple.

Jesus spoke to him "first" (*prophthanō*, "come before"), implying that, before Peter had the chance to tell what had happened, Jesus already knew (whether by overhearing or by supernatural means is not stated) and wanted to use this as a teaching opportunity. Jesus used a rhetorical question, one of His favorite teaching methods, to raise the question of "rights" to not pay the tax. Note that He called him Simon (five uses in Matthew) rather than Peter (twenty-three uses in Matthew). The reason for using this name is not apparent. Perhaps the lesson was not intended for Peter only, and this formal address alerted others to listen as well.

The question about civil taxes was not to detract from the religious tax under discussion. The analogy taught that taxes were intended to exclude the ruler's household members—for example, Caesar's sons would never be asked to pay taxes to Rome. Peter's response (v. 26) was correct, and Jesus built upon it to make His point, "The sons are exempt." Since He was the Son of God, whose temple was supported by the tax, then He too was exempt from the temple tax. Thus Jesus was not under obligation to pay it.

17:27   Understanding the point of v. 26 is critical to comprehending His counter point in v. 27, "But, lest we give them offense . . ." He would pay the tax. One does not need to expend much time to locate numerous occasions where Jesus knowingly and willingly offended the Jews (e.g., 15:3-12; 16:1-4; 23:13-33), so the question is, why was He concerned about it here? The major consideration was that the temple was considered holy by Jesus Christ (Matt. 21:12-13); thus, supporting it was honorable. Another important factor was that this tax, unlike so many of the traditions that Jesus opposed, was based upon Exodus 30 and therefore was a scriptural practice. Jesus realized this was not an issue over which one should fight. To refuse to pay would certainly cause more controversy, of which Jesus was not afraid, but it was not an issue that needed to be controversial. He chose His battles well.

Thus Jesus willingly relinquished His "right" to be exempt from the temple tax in order not to "offend" (cause others to fall into sin). Then, to indicate how easily God takes care of such needs, Jesus sent Peter on what must have seemed a foolish errand in order to provide not only Jesus' tax but Peter's as well. Carson sums up this lesson adeptly, "Perhaps, too, we are reminded again of Jesus' humility: he who so controls nature and its powers that he stills storms and multiplies food now reminds Peter of that power by this miracle, while nevertheless remaining so humble that he would not needlessly cause offense."[18]

HOMILETICAL SUGGESTIONS

The Transfiguration account is somewhat mysterious, and one should be careful in making applications to current situations. However, there are some important aspects that will help formulate a more complete picture of Jesus' method of discipleship. The three disciples chosen to accompany Him, not only here but in other situations as well, were indicative of a principle of discipleship. There was hierarchy even among the disciples. Even more deliberately, Jesus would separate out Peter for special attention and responsibility among the rest. Too often in contemporary Christianity, favoritism is charged when a pastor sees key men into whom he can build special tools for ministry. As Paul showed with Timothy and Titus, discipleship often involves giving special attention to men who will be aides and even successors in ministry. The inner circle of disciples is a good example of our Lord's discipleship method. These three were not allowed to speak of the Transfiguration experience, even to the other disciples, until after His resurrection. They also were given details about the ministry of Elijah and John the Baptist.

The faith lesson learned by the nine is also critical. The point of vv. 14-21 is not how to cast out demons but that faith is necessary for doing the Lord's work, and past success does not guarantee future accomplishments. When difficulty is confronted, prayer and fasting should be the first response. A change in program or method may be needed, but until prayer and fasting reveal this, one should not just rely on human wisdom to act. The disciples were rebuked for their littleness of faith, not for their lack of effort or creativity.

A final lesson to be learned in this chapter is that one should be willing to forfeit "rights" in order to avoid causing others to stumble. Notice that Jesus was not saying that every issue should be compromised in order to keep peace but that some issues should not be a cause of conflict. Jesus willingly entered into conflict to protect the people from religious heresy and to defend the truth. But He was unwilling to cause stumbling over matters of personal "rights." One should consider Romans 12:17-18; 13:1-7 and Romans 14:13–15:2 in light of this principle.

MATTHEW
CHAPTER
EIGHTEEN

ADDITIONAL TEACHINGS
ON KINGDOM VALUES

Matthew's message certainly centers on the Lord's teachings of the kingdom, and this chapter continues that flow of thought. It is incorrect to view these lessons as random teachings about children or church discipline. All are connected in the kingdom values theme. All the issues are presented within the context of the "greatest in the kingdom" opening question. One should not try to understand the significance of the lessons (e.g., vv. 15-20 as "church discipline") apart from the context ("greatest in the kingdom" discussion).

THE GREATEST IN THE KINGDOM, 18:1-6
(Mark 9:33-37, 42; Luke 9:46-48)

18:1   Matthew sets the context for the discussion on the greatest in the kingdom, "at that time" (*en ekeinē tē hōra*). Hendriksen correctly states, "There is a close *temporal* connection between this chapter and the preceding paragraph . . . [and] there is probably also a *material* or *thought* connection."[1] Both chronological and conceptual circumstances create the environment of the discussion. Jesus had just raised the issue of the sons of earthly kingdoms being exempt from taxes; thus, the disciples were thinking of kingdom privileges.

But they seemed oblivious to an even more dramatic contextual issue (17:22-23; Mark 9:30-34; Luke 9:44-46). Apparently, between the last miracle (17:14-21) and the lesson of the two drachma tax (17:24-27) Jesus had explained the news about His coming suffering and death. The disciples, however, failed to understand and feared asking for clarification (Mark 9:32; Luke 9:45). Instead, they began to entertain the question of who would be greatest when He established His kingdom. The events of the Transfiguration (17:1-12) in which the three had received special privileges was also a likely catalyst for the discussion. They may also have been thinking about Jesus' statement to Peter (16:18-19). Then, when they heard the two-drachma lesson and the allusion to the sons of the kingdom being exempt, they apparently assumed their conversation was justified.

18:2-4 Jesus' response was as shocking and unexpected as one could imagine. Calling a child to Himself (perhaps one of Peter's own, since some believe they were more than likely in his home[2]), Jesus made the point that the primary issue was entering the kingdom, not being the greatest (v. 3). The qualification for entering the kingdom was to be converted (*straphēte*, aorist passive subjunctive of *strephō*, "be turned around") and become as the children (*ta paidia*).

The emphasis on entering and turning around are not to be misunderstood. He was not telling the disciples how to be saved; He was bringing their lofty discussion back into proper perspective. The "turning around" contrasted the attitude of the self-sufficient with the attitude of childlike dependence. Their concern for preeminence in the kingdom reflected a proud spirit inconsistent with kingdom membership. He then moved to answer the question (v. 4): the one with the childlike attitude was the greatest. Jesus seemed to be challenging the motive behind the question. Carson rightly observes, "The child is held up as an ideal, not of innocence, purity, or faith, but of humility and unconcern for social status."[3] Humility and servanthood mark greatness in the kingdom. The "greatest" (*ho meizōn*) in the disciples' mind was the one with the most rank and power. To Jesus, it is the one who most clearly demonstrates character consistent with those in the kingdom, humility.

18:5-6 Jesus then took His lesson to the next step. Even though there is no direct statement to this effect, the emphasis was now upon those who were kingdom members, true believers, represented by the child. Believers are like children and to receive (*dechomai*, "receive, accept, welcome") one of them is equal to receiving Jesus

Himself. This equating certainly offers witness to the "greatness" of all kingdom children. Another dimension to the discussion was that others, not yet believers, could enter the kingdom only by being humble like a child, not proud and self-sufficient. This may have been intended to include all of Israel, who were invited to come to the kingdom.

In v. 6, the converse situation is presented. Jesus issued a severe warning to those causing one of the kingdom children to stumble. "Stumble" (*skandalizō*) is used of causing someone to sin by influence and of causing one to doubt by teaching error. Mounce, following Beare, sees this as leading weak Christians into apostasy and "is probably aimed at 'false teachers who lead simple Christians into error or unbelief.'"[4]

The warning states that drowning in the sea is better than reaping the consequences of causing one of God's children to stumble. A millstone was a large, wheel-shaped stone, which rested on a stone pad. Grain was poured on the pad, a donkey turned the millstone, and the stone crushed the grain, producing meal usable for making bread. One need not become too concerned about details of the millstone analogy, as the point was simple—a drowning in the sea depths was to be preferred to being guilty of subverting even one of God's children.

PARENTHETICAL WARNING, 18:7-9

18:7   "Woe" (*ouai*) is a common expression denoting a serious warning of impending doom. The object of the warning is the world (*tō kosmō*). The term *kosmos* ("world") implies an order or system and in this context certainly refers to the whole realm of humanistic involvement. Hendriksen is probably correct to understand its use here as making a distinction between those of the kingdom and those who "belong to 'the world,' to mankind alienated from the life of God."[5] The NASB ("because of its stumbling blocks") and NIV ("because of the things that cause people to sin") both interpret the prepositional phrase *apo tōn skandalōn* as causal. This is a remote yet acceptable use of *apo* with the genitive/ablative case.[6] The world, humanity apart from God, will be judged because it places stumbling blocks before the children of God.

The warning becomes more personalized by the statement "Woe

to that man through whom the stumbling block comes!" The point seems to be that though stumbling blocks certainly are going to be in this world, one must not just excuse himself but understand that personal accountability is still God's method of judgment. Thus, the individual must avoid being a stumbling block.

18:8-9   The Lord next used hyperbole to show the seriousness of causing someone to stumble, but here He changed to emphasize one's bent to self-stumbling. Certainly, to be lame, crippled, or blind would be a grievous burden, yet Jesus stated that even these conditions were preferable to being cast into "the fiery hell." The same sober thought is found in Matthew 5:29-30. The emphasis here is on the personal application of Jesus' warning. "If your hand or your foot causes *you* to stumble" reminded His followers that the danger did not just lie in enticement to sin from outsiders but from one's own body. This is not to imply that the physical body is evil in and of itself but that the body can be an instrument for sin (Rom. 7:18-23).

Proper interpretation of this passage requires one to understand Christ's statement as hyperbole, a common figure of speech that overstates a situation in order to accentuate a critical lesson. The Lord was not commanding or endorsing self-mutilation but was dramatically illustrating the horror of being cast into eternal fiery hell. As painful and destructive as limb amputation might be, it was to be preferred to hell's torment. The point of the Lord's statement was not to describe a salvific method (bodily mutilation) but, again, to emphasize the severity of eternal judgment. One cannot save himself by plucking out an eye, but the severity of hell is worse than plucking out an eye.

The place of torment is described as "eternal fire" (*to pur to aiōnion,* v. 8) and "fiery hell" (*tēn geennan tou puros,* v. 9). Barnes says, "This is compulsive proof that the sufferings of the wicked will be eternal."[7] The horror of eternal punishment is motivation not to stumble and not to cause others to stumble. Mark 9:42-48 further defines this "fiery hell" as a place of "unquenchable fire" (v. 44) and Jesus quoted (v. 48) Isaiah 66:24, "For their worm shall not die, and their fire shall not be quenched," a reference to the destiny of those who transgress against God.

To try to make this passage a warning that the disciples might lose their salvation is inconsistent with the immediate context and the rest of Scripture. Rather, a comparison is made between the inconvenience and discomfort of detaching from the body anything that can cause stumbling and the perpetual pain of eternal fire. Temporal denial of those things that cause sin is minor compared to the consequences of being cast into fire. Again, this is not a passage teaching salvation, but one that teaches the fearsomeness of eternal torment and the seriousness of causing others—or self—to go there. Salvation from this terror is clearly spelled out in numerous passages (John 3:16; Eph. 2:8-9; etc.) as being by God's grace through faith, not through self-denial and sinlessness.

VALUE OF THE INDIVIDUAL, 18:10-14 (Luke 15:3-7)

18:10   Jesus then refocused on the "little ones" who had been the topic of vv. 4-6. (Verses 7-9 have been parenthetical; the issue of causing innocent believers to stumble digressed to the danger of allowing one's own physical indulgences to be a stumbling block.) Christ returned to the thought of childlike faith and warned against despising (*kataphroneō,* "treat with contempt, think nothing of") these little ones (those humble enough to be great in the kingdom).

The reason not to despise their childlike faith is expressed by the "for" (explanatory *gar*) in "for I say to you." Christ explained that the angels of these little ones were in heaven constantly beholding the face of the Father. This comment has led to many theories concerning angels, some of which are so fanciful as to be blasphemous. It must be remembered that the "children" are the believers who express childlike faith. Jesus has not been giving a discourse on childhood but on faith and entering the kingdom (vv. 3-4). It was the angels of believers that were being discussed. It must also be noted that no reference was made to guarding, protecting, watching over, or any other of the popularized myths. The essence of these angels was not specified, neither was any special function attributed to them. The Jews had numerous legends about angels, many of which were without scriptural basis. Jesus' reference simply stated that the angels of believers were in heaven beholding the face of God. The best understanding seems to be found in Hebrews 1:14, "Are they not all ministering spirits, sent out to render service for the sake of those who will inherit salvation?" No scriptural reference mentions an angel's being appointed to watch over a particular person. However, when one of God's children has a need, and God chooses to meet that need, an angel may be sent to minister. The emphasis is on God's care for His children, not that some angel is responsible to watch over them. Such care demonstrates the value of these "little ones" (believers); thus, they must not be despised by those who think they are "great" in the kingdom.

18:11 Very little textual support exists here for including "For the Son of Man has come to save that which was lost." However, the statement is both true and biblical, as it appears in this exact form in Luke 19:10.

18:12-13 Jesus' next lesson reinforced what He had just stated about the worth of these "little ones," and this lesson is not to be isolated from the issue of belonging to the kingdom. Monetarily, ninety-nine sheep are far more valuable than one sheep. But the value of the "little ones" is so great that God is unwilling to allow even one to stray off and will seek the wandering sheep to bring it back to the fold.

Verse 13 is not implying that God does not care for the ninety-nine but that any one of the hundred that has wandered off is the object of His intense concern. God preserves His whole flock, and even one member who is led astray becomes the focus of His shepherding heart. Barnes notes, "If God thus loves and preserves the redeemed, then surely man should not despise them."[8]

18:14 The Father does not will (*thelō*) that any one of the little ones perish. Carson summarizes this lesson of God's care for His sheep very well: "If this is his will, it is shocking that anyone else would seek to lead one of 'these little ones' astray."[9] The Lord has taken upon Himself this responsibility (John 6:37-39). The "little one," the one who comes in humble faith, will enter the kingdom and is kept by the Lord, the Good Shepherd (John 10), to fulfill the Father's will.

DEALING WITH SIN IN THE BROTHERHOOD, 18:15-20

18:15 This discussion of dealing with sin cannot be properly understood apart from the context of the kingdom. The warnings of vv. 6-14 deal with not making others or even oneself stumble. Then Jesus emphasized the desire of God to protect and restore His wandering children. Moving on, He next addressed the matter of interpersonal responsibility in light of sin within the brotherhood.

Determining the proper text here is a problem. Some manuscripts contain the phrase "against you" (*eis se*), and many others do not. The question is whether the instruction of v. 15 is to be understood as a brother sinning in a general sense or if it particularly states, "If your brother sins against *you.*" Arguments for a more generic sense of sinning can be offered; but because of Peter's question at the end of the discussion, "How often shall my brother sin against me?" the disciples apparently understood it to be sin against them in particular.

It is important to understand that the issue is not someone's hurting your feelings or doing something with which you disagree. The issue is sin (*harmartia,* "departure from righteousness"), that is, someone's committing some unrighteous deed against you. What has been done must be a violation of some standard of God, for sin (*hamartia*) "is always used in the NT of man's sin which is ultimately directed against God."[10] The principle of confrontation is not to be applied in matters of personal taste (e.g., style of music, style of clothing) but when one violates the Word of God in some way that directly affects you (lying, stealing, etc.).

By going to the brother privately, the sinning brother is not encumbered with pride and thus not so prone to self-defense. The idea of "listen" (*akouō*) implies a proper response to what is heard, not just auditory capacity. Such use of *akouō* is common in the New Testament. With proper confrontation and response, the brother is "won" (*kerdainō*), or "won over." Rather than sin's disrupting the relationship and the sinning brother's being overcome by his sin, he becomes an object of God's joy (v. 13).

18:16-17   If the sinning brother does not properly respond to the exhortation, then others are to be included in the process. The use of two or three others is to protect a person from being falsely accused (cf. Deut 19:15). Two brothers should be able to reconcile differences, but where such cannot be done, others are to be brought in for the confirmation of guilt or innocence of the one charged. The wisdom of this procedure is evident. If the accused brother is not guilty, his name is cleared; if he did sin, then no opportunity is given for a claim of being falsely accused.

Verse 17 brings in a final stage of dealing with the sinning brother. If the sinner stubbornly refuses to respond to the exhortation of the three or four who see his guilt, then the whole assembly is brought into the action. The word "church" (*ekklēsia*) only refers to an assembly of people and should not be understood here in the later sense of the local church. Of course, the principle is the same because the pattern set forth applies to all His kingdom people. Any assembly of God's people, not just a local church in the modern sense, has authority to excommunicate an offending brother.

The church is to treat the stubborn sinner as a "Gentile and a tax-gatherer." These two designations bring the exhortation back into the Jewish, pre-Gentile church context. Both Gentiles and tax collectors (not to be confused with contemporary IRS employees) were despised and rejected by the orthodox Jews of Jesus' culture. In the mind of the Jews, Gentiles did not have a covenant with God, were not the chosen people, and had no part in the messianic promises. Thus, if the brother rejected the authority of the community of believers, he was to be treated as one outside the covenant and the blessings of God. Tax collectors, likewise, were despised and rejected, being viewed as traitors who sold out to the Romans for their own profit. Thus, the treatment of an unrepentant offending brother was to be severe, which also reflects being within the warning context of causing a "little one" (a believer) to stumble. Sin, here being connected with that which could cause stumbling, was not to be excused or tolerated.

AUTHORITY OF THE MESSIAH'S COMMUNITY, 18:18-20

18:18   Whereas 16:19 states the same promise, the "you" in the earlier passage is singular and refers to Peter (see 16:19). In this verse, Jesus changes to the plural (*humin*) and uses plural verbs (*dēsēte*), indicating that the group of disciples was now given the same privilege as Peter. As in 16:19, the binding and loosing on earth was what had already been determined in heaven. The followers of Christ were to carry out the determinations of heaven, including the act of discipline within the community.

18:19-20   The promise of v. 19, "Anything that they may ask, it shall be done for them," is not to be taken as a blank check. Understanding the truth of any biblical doctrine is dependent upon all that is said related to that topic. Prayer is a major topic in Scripture, and conditions are always assumed with regard to a promise of receiving answers (e.g., 21:22; James 4:3; 1 John 5:14). It is the Father who responds with the answer because He is still the authority behind the work of the Son. The great promise of v. 20 is causal, "for" (*gar*) the gathering "in My name" is a condition for receiving the request of v. 19. To gather in the name of Christ is to gather for His benefit. To do something in the name of someone else is to do it as that person's representative or for his benefit. To pray in the name of Jesus is to ask that God will act on His behalf. When Jesus' servants gather "in His name," He is among them. This insures that what is asked is in accordance with His will, and therefore it will be done. Carson is probably correct in insisting the context is that when the witnesses against the sinning brother are gathered together, Jesus will be in their midst.[11] Thus, the primary focus of the promise is in executing judgment against a sinning brother.

WARNING AGAINST NOT FORGIVING, 18:21-35

18:21-22   Peter's question now reemphasized the personal element of the discussion. Jesus had spoken of procedure concerning those who do not respond to confrontation by the offended brother; Peter now brought in the other aspect. If he does correct the sin, how many times should this process be exercised? The question about "seven times" reveals something of the human mind-set concerning forgiveness—there is a limit. According to Carson, rabbinic teaching was that a sinner might be forgiven a repeated sin three times, but there was no forgiveness for the fourth.[12] Perhaps Peter was thinking of Proverbs 24:16, "For a righteous man falls seven times, and rises again," or perhaps seven just seemed a generous round number. Luke 17:3-4 records Jesus' lesson of forgiving seven times in one day, which was probably symbolic of the completeness of forgiveness, not a literal number.

Peter apparently felt he was being overly merciful in assuming seven times, but the Lord's response soon brought him to reality. Jesus used a figure of speech to make the point of not keeping count (v. 22) . It may seem the Lord was saying that the limit of forgiveness is 490 times, but, in fact, His point was that one should not limit forgiveness. Some see a connection to Genesis 4:24, where the LXX reads exactly the same number, "seventy-sevenfold" (*hebdomēkontakis hepta*), but more than likely it was a figurative way of expressing that one should not worry about the quantitative equation. The principle of pure Christian love is that it does not keep account of wrongs done (1 Cor. 13:5, NIV). One who wishes to keep count of how many times he has forgiven someone fails to understand how many times God has forgiven *him* for offenses. Jesus' subsequent parable illustrated this point.

18:23 The parable depicted the wickedness of not forgiving, because to not forgive reflects a lack of appreciation for the mercy one has himself received from God. "For this reason" (*dia touto*) introduced a comparison between the kingdom of heaven's attitude toward an unforgiving saint and the attitude of an undeserving servant shown mercy by an earthly king, who then failed to exercise the same mercy toward others.

18:24 A slave owed a king ten thousand talents. A "talent" (*talanton*) was the highest denomination of money and was worth around 6,000 denarii.[13] A denarius was considered fair pay for one day's work (Matt. 20:2-9). The sum owed for just one talent, then, was equivalent to about sixteen years of labor. The expression "ten thousand" is not precise since *murios* basically means "countless" or "thousands." For the contemporary reader, one might figure the total amount owed to be around $66 million or, as Carson estimates, considering inflation, "this could be over a billion dollars in today's currency."[14] This was clearly a hyperbolic parable not relating a true account. The point was that the sum owed was so ridiculous that there could be no hope of repayment. Speculation on how a man could incur such a debt to a king would be useless.

18:25-27 Among the Jews, a slave owner was not permitted to sell a slave's wife or child, though for a man to sell himself or even members of his own family into indentureship was common (Lev. 25:39; Neh. 5:5).[15] However, among the Romans such treatment of a slave (*doulos*) by a master (*kurios*) was commonplace. Though the meager amount realized by the sale of the slave could never repay his debt, it would represent some gain on the part of the master and would serve as a warning to other slaves.

The slave followed his only possible course of action—to beg for leniency (v. 26). Reflecting total humility, he prostrated himself, knowing that he was helpless before the master and totally dependent upon mercy, not justice. The slave besought his master to be patient and also promised to repay "everything." Of course, patience, even if granted, would not help since repayment was impossible. Perhaps the servant has not grasped the overwhelming profoundness of his debt. The master's response (v. 27) was gracious beyond human precedent: he felt compassion, released the man from slavery, and forgave (*aphiēmi,* "cancel out, dismiss") his debt. Through the mercy of the master, the slave received far more than he could ever have hoped for—not just time to repay (which in any case could never have been done) but total release from his debt. And beyond that, he was released from slavery. Now the one who had been in danger of being sold and losing his family was a free man and debt free.

18:28-30   The second point of Jesus' lesson is found in the slave's failure to grasp the reality of his privileged status and to learn from the king's good example of grace. The 100 denarii owed by his fellow slave would be equivalent to 100 days' pay, not just a few dollars or "twenty dollars" as some have said.[16] By contemporary American standards, the value would be approximately $10,000, a trifling amount, however, by comparison. Hendriksen calculates this to be "one six-hundred-thousandth" of what the first slave owed his master.[17] Actually, the percentage was probably much more dramatic. The point was that the sum was insignificant in comparison to what the other slave had owed.

The forgiven slave's violent response to the second slave demonstrated that his heart had not been touched by the grace extended to him. The second slave did exactly as the first had done (v. 29). He asked for patience and promised to repay what was owed, but the response was very different. The forgiven slave was unwilling to be patient for repayment (much less release the man from the debt) and had the second slave thrown into prison (v. 30). His act of greed and lack of mercy stood in stark contrast to the tremendous act of grace shown him. This lack of mercy toward a peer who owed so little (by comparison) demonstrated a wicked heart and absolute failure in learning the lesson of grace.

18:31-34   The conclusion to the Lord's lesson serves as a serious warning. Verse 33 encapsulates the anecdote's main point, "Should you not also have had mercy [*eleaō*]?" Even the human king understood that his act of grace should have affected the life and attitude of the slave. The natural response to receiving grace should be to give grace. The consequences of failing to respond properly came back upon the ungrateful slave, and his end was according to his judgment on his fellow servant.

18:35   In conclusion, the Lord made application to His listeners. He was not warning of loss of salvation but answering Peter's question (18:21)—not on a superficial level but on the level of the need of Peter's heart. Peter needed to understand that forgiveness is not to be limited or conditional. If one approaches forgiving others without understanding the enormous grace God has bestowed upon him, then there will be only self-righteous judgment of those who fail us. The wicked servant's heart was not affected by the mercy shown him. Christ's servants must not make the same mistake.

It is poor hermeneutics to build doctrine solely from parables, and those who see v. 35 as a threat of losing one's salvation miss the point of the parable. The statement in this verse must be interpreted consistently with other revelation. This issue is not eternal salvation. This is a lesson on the magnitude of God's forgiveness and the pettiness of Peter's question. John 6:37-40 and numerous other verses teach that the believer's salvation is established upon Christ's faithfulness and sacrifice, not upon any works or worth of the believer. Verse 35 is only a graphic way of expressing the accountability of those who have accepted grace to display grace. If one wants judgment upon others, he must realize he is inviting judgment on self. This again was one of the messages to self-righteous Israel and part of the warning against the leaven of the Pharisees (16:6).

HOMILETICAL SUGGESTIONS

Like the disciples, many Christians become concerned with their rank and reputation in the church. With today's promotion of books and conferences, the attention paid to some well-known Christian speakers has a damaging influence on one's perspective of "greatness." A primary lesson for contemporary Christianity is that what is often recognized as "greatness" is no more than popularity, fame, and humanistic definitions of success. Publishers promote their authors, conferences publicize their key speakers as success figures and "experts," and the world's view of greatness is often the measure of one's worth. However, Jesus defines greatness by one's humility and trust in the heavenly Father. Christians need to focus on the standards set by Christ.

This chapter also warns those who would adversely influence the servants of Christ. Even self-delusion that causes one to stumble must be avoided. If one considers mutilation of the body as a horrific event, then let him understand that spiritual destruction is even more serious and offensive to God. Romans 14 and 15 offer excellent guidelines concerning not causing others to stumble. Temporal fulfillment of physical desires is discussed, using the analogy of the hands, feet, or eyes leading one away from the truth. Even these critical parts of life are to be sacrificed if they interfere with one's entering the kingdom with the faith of a child.

A great comfort offered in this chapter is the reassurance of God's commitment to seek out His lost sheep and bring them back to His flock. He rejoices over every child who returns after straying. Not only that, but the parable of the lost sheep also emphasizes God's aggressive pursuit of the one who wanders off. A comparison with John 10 is helpful in completing the analogy of the Shepherd's concern for and attention to His flock.

In light of the discussion on stumbling blocks and God's searching for His wandering sheep, Jesus moved into the idea of how sin affects interpersonal relationships and the responsibility of brothers to deal with sin between them. The process of confrontation is a pattern for believers to follow—not as a mechanical process to bring judgment but as an act of concern and love. Galatians 6 is a perfect parallel, and James 5 likewise offers some input as to the attitude to be expressed in the community dealing with sin in its midst.

The discussion on sin in the community raises the question as to personal expressions of forgiveness. Christians must understand the unlimited nature of forgiveness in their own lives. Victorious Christian living is based upon the fact that God's grace is undeserved and cannot be earned. But that grace is to flow from the one who has received it. If one truly grasps the forgiveness of God and just how unworthy he is, then forgiving others is more natural and easy. An unforgiving spirit reflects a failure to understand the magnitude of the forgiveness received. This is Pharisaism in its purest form. The Pharisees are portrayed in the New Testament as missing out on the Messiah's kingdom because of not seeing their need for forgiveness. Their estimation of their own spiritual worth was reflected in their condemnation and demand for punishment of those violating their religious traditions. Recipients of grace are to be instruments of grace.

MATTHEW

CHAPTER

NINETEEN

JESUS' MINISTRY IN THE REGION OF JUDEA

Having finished His discourse on forgiveness (18:21-35), Jesus moved closer to Jerusalem. The central points of this chapter seem to focus upon two questions: (1) is it lawful to divorce one's wife for any cause at all, and (2) what must one do to obtain eternal life? The Lord's answers to these questions may make some Christians uncomfortable, but they are as relevant and as authoritative today as when first spoken. One must not underestimate, however, the significance of the original context, and caution must be used not to read into the text the values and assumptions of contemporary Christianity.

TRAVELING TO JUDEA, 19:1-2 (Mark 10:1)

19:1-2 There is some difficulty in understanding exactly where Jesus went and what route He took to get to Judea. Luke's narrative adds numerous events not recorded by Matthew or Mark. Also, the expression "came into the region of Judea beyond the Jordan" is not as clear as the English version would imply. Some suggest that Jesus traveled down the eastern side of the Jordan River and entered into Judea so as to avoid Samaria. The reading of the parallel text (Mark 10:1) inserts (in some dependable manuscripts) the conjunction *kai* ("and"), which might be taken to imply that Jesus traveled down the eastern side of the Jordan and then crossed the river to enter Judea.[1] Since Matthew later relates that "as they were going out *from Jericho*" (20:29, which is on the western side of the Jordan), this could well be the proper view.

Verse 2 reveals that the crowds were still following Jesus and that He was continuing to minister to their needs. He healed them "there" (*ekei*), implying that He had set up some kind of temporary base. Establishing that the events recorded in Luke took place during His time here is not critical, as Luke followed a logical rather than chronological order when recording his narrative. However, in the synoptics, the overlapping of many events is always likely.

DIALOGUE RELATED TO DIVORCE, 19:3-12
(Mark 10:2-12; see discussion on 5:31-32)

19:3   The discussion on divorce began with a question raised by the Pharisees to test Jesus (*peirazontes auton,* "testing Him"). As Barnes points out, "This means to get him, if possible, to express an opinion that should involve him in difficulty."[2] The same expression is found in 16:1 and 22:18, 35, where attempts are made to draw Jesus into controversial responses so that they might accuse Him of error or blasphemy (see also Mark 8:11; 10:2; 12:15; Luke 11:16; 20:23; John 8:6). The question was loaded with deliberate treachery and not intended to honestly seek an answer.

The question dealt with the reason for divorce and not whether divorce was permissible. Too often contemporary scholars are looking for an absolute answer to the modern debate rather than allowing the text to speak to the issue at hand. Here the question is whether divorce is permissible (*exsestin,* "proper, permitted, lawful") for any cause at all (*kata pasan aitian*). As pointed out in 5:32, the famous and influential rabbi Hillel taught that almost any failure or weakness in the wife was sufficient cause for divorce,[3] whereas Shammai, an equally influential and famous rabbi, taught that sexual immorality alone was sufficient for divorce.[4] The Pharisees were obviously hoping to catch Jesus aligning with one or the other and then debate the opposite side. It seems that Jesus would have been in agreement with Shammai, and that would have been adequate to open the debate. However, Jesus did not wish to enter a debate about rabbinical viewpoints; instead, He pointed to Genesis and God's original design (v. 4).

19:4-6   Jesus answered by appealing to Scripture (Gen. 1:27), not to rabbinical dogma. His opening comment was intended to offend and provoke a response. He attacked the very thing of which the Pharisees were so proud, their knowledge of Scripture. They had, however, unknowingly become so concerned with the religious opinion of the rabbis that they had lost sight of the Word of God (15:3). Jesus did not side with either Shammai or Hillel—He reminded the Pharisees of God's design for marriage. God created the genders from the beginning. The more literal translation of Jesus' statement is "The One who created from the beginning, made them male and female." This is not only a more accurate translation of Jesus' words but also is more consistent with the Genesis record, which points out that God created Adam and then from him made Eve (Gen. 2:21-22). Eve was fashioned for a purpose, to be a "helper suitable for him" (or a "helper corresponding to him," Gen. 2:20). Adam and Eve were to bear children and rule the earth for the glory of God. Edwin Yamauchi concludes, "This means that marriage is not viewed primarily as a tribal affair designed to continue the clan as in some societies, but as a relationship between two individuals for companionship and intimate fellowship."[5] The key issue here was that arguments of Law and legal exceptions were not to be the point, but the integrity and purpose of God's design was to be upheld. The focus was not on divorce but on the marriage.

Jesus continued to refresh their memories concerning the design of marriage as God prescribed (v. 5; Gen. 2:24). His commentary is added in v. 6, "Consequently, they are no longer two, but one flesh," indicating that two people who join together in marriage are not only legally bound but are now actually physically joined. They have become "one flesh" (*sarxs mia*). Carson astutely connects this with Genesis 1:27: "The 'one flesh' in every marriage between a man and a woman is a reenactment of and testimony to the very structure of humanity as God created it."[6] Jesus' central point, therefore, emphasized the sanctity of marriage, not the rabbinical reasons for divorce (of which Josephus says, "Many such causes happen among men").[7]

His conclusion was "What, therefore, God has joined together, let no man separate (v. 6)." The emphasis is not on individual cases. But as a general rule, God ordained marriages, not man—therefore man is not to separate (*chōrizō*) the union of male and female. The separation of male and female, husband and wife, is not a human prerogative, since the union is God-ordained. The implication is certainly that God's design is for permanence in the marriage relationship. This then led the Pharisees to ask the second question.

19:7   Their question related to the purpose of Deuteronomy 24:1-4, "Why then did Moses command to give her a certificate of divorce?" In Deuteronomy 24:1, Moses sets the context for writing the bill of divorcement: "She finds no favor in his eyes because he has found some indecency in her." The fact that the wife "finds no favor in his eyes" (*'im lo' thim^eṣa' ḥēn b^e'ēnayn*) is not to be taken apart from the next phrase. The idea of *ḥēn* ("grace, favor," perhaps even "pity") not being in the eye of the husband was because some "indecency" (*'r^ewath*) had been found in her. Identification of this "indecency" has been the center of innumerable scholarly debates and writings but still eludes any certain denotation. According to some Mishnah statements, if a man likes another woman better than his wife, or if his wife goes into the street with her hair loose, if she spins in the street, or if she is noisy, lawfully he can divorce her.[8] The word "indecent" comes from *'rwh* and basically means "nakedness" or "genitals."[9] The idea of shame seems to be connected with its use consistently. In Leviticus 18:15-19, it is used repeatedly in prohibitions against unlawful sexual relations. To understand its use here as the discovery of some sexual impurity in his wife seems best. However, since execution was the penalty for adultery, Moses must have understood this to be sexual promiscuity of some lesser degree, perhaps in the wife's flaunting of her sexuality before other men or a situation involving intimacy with another man without actually experiencing sexual intercourse. Upon discovery of this shameful matter, the husband had the recourse of divorcing her.

The question related to the certificate of divorce (*biblion apostasiou*, a "book of sending away" or the Old Testament *sēpher c^e rithuth*, a "book of cutting off") that Moses instructed the Jewish husbands to give to the wife when he sent her away. Two things should be noted: the wife was given no procedure to divorce her husband; and this is not a betrothal situation since he "sends her out *from his house*" (Deut. 24:1). Josephus states that for a woman to divorce her husband "was not according to Jewish laws . . . but a wife, if she departs from her husband, cannot of herself be married to another, unless her former husband put her away."[10] The certificate allowed the wife to remarry without being condemned for adultery. If she married another but did not have the certificate, her remarriage would be adultery. The Deuteronomy provision also protected the woman from legal wife-swapping, because she was not allowed to go back to the first husband under any circumstances. A man could not divorce his wife, let her marry another man who would then also divorce her, and then take her back. Such was abomination in the sight of God.

The official divorce certificate in Judaic religious law is referred to as a *Get. The Jewish Encyclopedia* describes the content of a typical *Get:* "Even in the times of the Mishnah, the form seems to have been very simple, requiring, besides the date, place, and the names of the parties, the phrase 'thou art free to any man.'"[11] Leo Trepp also describes a *Get* and states that the woman is free to remarry ninety days after receiving it.[12] Thus, in the *Get* as well as in Deuteronomy 24:2, the implication is that the certificate permitted the woman to remarry without being guilty of adultery.

19:8   The question raised was, "Why did Moses command [*entello-mai*] . . ." but Jesus responded that Moses "permitted" (*epitrepō*). This author is not convinced that this is a major issue, because it would only be natural for the Jews to refer to Mosaic instruction as a command. Jesus' answer, however, did emphasize that it was an option and not a requirement and was permitted because of "your hardness of heart."

The hardness of heart references back to the Deuteronomy contexts, and the certificate of divorce should be understood as a provision to protect women from the hard-hearted treatment of husbands. They could not dismiss their wives as easily as the Egyptians (to whom the Israelites had been in bondage for four hundred years, the context from which they had just fled) but instead must have legitimate cause and follow the procedure of writing a certificate, freeing the wife to remarry without being stoned for adultery. If guilty of adultery, she was not to be divorced but put to death (Lev. 20:10).

Jesus again reminded them that the issue was neither what was permitted nor what the rabbis taught but God's original plan. "From the beginning" there was no provision for divorce because in God's original design there was to be fidelity and loyalty to one another, which bonded two into one flesh. Jesus held up the ideal, though acknowledging the imperfect world and human failure.

19:9   Jesus continued by offering His interpretation of "indecency in her [Deut. 24:1]." The Hebrew phrase is very difficult and can only best be understood as implying some unclean or impure behavior. "But I say to you . . ." is to be taken as an explanation of the Mosaic code and not a replacement of it. He explained that whoever should divorce his wife without the reason of fornication was violating the Mosaic provision. Thus Jesus interpreted the "indecency" (*'r*ᵉ*wath*) of Deuteronomy 24 as "fornication" (*porneia,* Matt. 19:9). Fornication is not the same as adultery (*moicheia*). The first is sexual immorality in a broad sense, the latter sexual intercourse of a married person with someone other than his/her marriage partner. By the natural sense of the word, sexual immorality or impurity, even short of adultery, is an acceptable cause for divorce. Though this may be offensive to the "Christian" concept of the sin of divorce, it is the clear statement of the Lord.

Some try to play down the statement and refer to Matthew 5:32 and 19:9 as the supposed exception clauses. But no supposed condition exists; the statement itself is an exception clause. To list and discuss all the arguments that attempt to discount or redefine the Lord's statement is practically impossible. In current thinking, the dignity and spiritual analogy of marriage is not nearly as important as the evil of divorce. Thus, whereas Scripture protects the pureness of marriage to the point of capital punishment, some in contemporary religion promote marriage at any cost. Though perversion, abuse, infidelity, and so on, might characterize a marriage, some believe the sin lies in divorce. The unnatural and unrealistic (as well as unbiblical) argument that one can divorce (or separate) but not remarry violates all that marriage is to symbolize and also disobeys 1 Corinthians 7:3 and Ephesians 5:23-33. Jesus acknowledged that in the case of sexual promiscuity, divorce may be an accepted transaction. Carson offers an excellent consideration of the primary objections to this view as well as a legitimate response.[13]

Some versions add, "And he who marries a divorced woman commits adultery," but this is most likely a scribal addition taken from 5:32 and does not have sufficient manuscript support to be considered a part of the original text. However, its addition does not alter the main point of the text.[14] Fornication is legitimate reason for divorce and permits remarriage, but it is not God's desire. God's design is the permanence of the marriage, which honors Him. Thus, the most God-honoring course is forgiveness and restoration, even in the case of sexual promiscuity (including adultery), where reconciliation and restoration are possible. Lowery is correct when he concludes, "Sometimes the 'offending' partner does not seek forgiveness, nor is reconciliation always accepted. . . . When divorce occurs in such a situation, the exception grants the aggrieved partner the right to remarry."[15]

19:10   Jesus clarified God's design in this matter for the disciples (vv. 10-13), particularly how one should not attempt celibacy apart from possessing God's gift. The statement of the disciples "It is better not to marry" is clearly in relation to the Lord's answer concerning divorce "for any cause at all" (v. 3). "If this is the case" (*ei houtōs estin hē aitia*) indicates the seriousness of the matter, and the context clearly indicates that if fornication is the only permissible reason for divorce, it would be advantageous not to marry at all. When one considers the attitude of the Jews toward marriage and divorce (such as Josephus's comment that there were many reasons for divorcing one's wife, and the fact that some reasons offered by the rabbis were as frivolous as finding a more attractive woman), to hear the disciples respond in this manner is not surprising. Since Jesus took a narrow view of the reason for divorce (only in the case of sexual impurity), a man with a wife who became overweight or senile or was barren and so on must remain faithful to her. The disciples seemed almost sarcastic in saying that it was better not to marry than to have to continue in a marriage with a woman no longer attractive or capable of satisfying the husband's every whim. Hendriksen states: "They, along with many other people of that day and age—and of today!—seem to have been obsessed by the idea, 'what can I get out of marriage for myself?' . . . These men did not as yet fully understand that the spirit of love, service, and sacrifice . . . must be applied to every relationship of life, also to that of marriage."[16]

19:11-12   Jesus then warned the disciples that celibacy was not to be taken lightly and that not everyone was capable of being single. More specifically, He warned that only some who were eunuchs (castrated males who were overseers of harems in the Far and Middle East) either from birth or made so voluntarily would be able to accept such a challenge. Certainly there are some who are eunuchs in spirit (as circumcised in heart), which is probably what He intended by "made themselves eunuchs for the sake of the kingdom of heaven," men who are free from the normal sexual drives (though it is also very likely that some may have been castrated to guarantee their sexual purity). Carson offers a good summary:

> Jesus, like Paul after him (1 Cor 7:7-9), is prepared to commend celibacy "because of the kingdom" (not "for the sake of attaining it," but "because of its claims and interests". . . . But it is important to recognize that neither Jesus nor the apostles see celibacy as an intrinsically holier state than marriage (cf. 1 Tim 4:1-3; Heb 13:4), nor as a condition for the top levels of ministry (Matt 8:14; 1 Cor 9:5), but as a special calling granted for greater usefulness in the kingdom. Those who impose this discipline on themselves must remember Paul's conclusion: it is better to marry than to burn with passion (1 Cor 7:9).[17]

Marriage as God's normative design is both good and holy. However, some individuals may be called to so focus their minds on ministry for the kingdom that castration (either literal or through the gift of celibacy) may be necessary to ensure no distractions. But the avoidance of marriage to eliminate living with a woman who no longer pleases her husband is not an option, and neither is divorcing her "for any cause at all" (v. 3)—the question that started the whole discussion.

REMINDER OF CHILDLIKE FAITH, JESUS BLESSES THE CHILDREN, 19:13-15 (Mark 10:13-16; Luke 18:15-17)

19:13   Mark and Luke point out that children (*paidion*) were brought to Jesus, whereas Luke records that infants (*brephos*) were brought to Him. This difference in terminology should not be a matter of concern. The term *paidion* is broad enough to be a synonym for *brephos*. Had Matthew or Mark used *pais* (a child between seven and fourteen years of age[18]), there would be more difficulty.

The purpose was so that Jesus "might lay His hands on them." Among the Jews, such action was representative of a blessing from a patriarch. These blessings were to declare the benefits of inheritance or to confer certain qualities on those receiving the blessing (i.e., Gen. 48:14-20). Meyer points out, "The *laying on of the hands* (Gen. 48:14) was desired, not as a mere symbol, but as *a means of communicating* the blessing prayed for."[19] Here, however, the issue was most likely not the desire for patriarchal blessing but was the people's response to the teaching and power of Jesus. They recognized His power and authority, though He did not hold any official office or community title, and wished His blessings upon their children.

The disciples rebuked those who brought the children to Jesus, apparently considering His time too valuable to be taken up with these little ones who could not further the kingdom. Mounce believes that the disciples were annoyed because "their journey to Jerusalem was being slowed down."[20] However, no reason is given to believe they were that anxious, especially in light of the hard lessons about the upcoming agony and death of their leader (16:21).

19:14-15 Jesus' response was not only for the benefit of the children but was also to remind the disciples of a major point already made (18:1-4). He explained the reason He wanted the children brought to Him: "For the kingdom of heaven belongs to such as these." This was not to imply that children make up the kingdom but that childlike faith is characteristic of those who are great in the kingdom. Jesus ministered to these children as requested, then left to continue His trip to Jerusalem.

LESSON ON OBTAINING ETERNAL LIFE, 19:16-26
(Mark 10:17-27; Luke 18:18-27)

19:16 Matthew simply mentions that "one came to Him," but Luke adds "a certain ruler" (*tis auton archōn,* either a civil official or perhaps a synagogue leader). Other information about the man includes that he was youthful (v. 20; still, as a ruler he was probably over thirty years of age), wealthy (v. 22-23), and committed to the Law of Moses (v. 20). Mark tells us that he "knelt before Him," indicating recognition of Jesus' honored status as a teacher and healer. Thus, his approach reflected a sincere spirit. According to Mark 10:17 and Luke 18:18, his respect for Jesus could also be seen in the address of "Good Teacher" (*didaskale agathe*).

The question reflected the concern of the young ruler for *earning* eternal life ("What good thing shall I *do?*") The young man's confidence that he had already done everything the Law demanded became apparent from the discussion (v. 20).

19:17   Before answering his question, Jesus asked a question of His own, "Why are you asking Me about what is good?" Mark and Luke both record the question as, "Why do you call Me good?" (In their accounts the young ruler calls Him "Good Teacher.") The synoptics often offer different aspects of the same event, which are not contradictory but complementary, and since only pieces of the conversation are recorded, it is to be assumed that what was said included both the complementary "Good Teacher" and a question about what good works could earn eternal life.

Jesus' response in all three accounts leads to one conclusion—only One is good. The question, "Why do you call Me good?" is to draw attention to the fact that only God is good (Mark 10:18; Luke 18:19), and He is the determiner of what is good. Therefore, when Jesus went on to answer the ruler's question, He was demonstrating His authority to answer for God. This may not have been a direct claim to deity, but at the least it certainly asserted His role as the Messiah, God's Anointed One.

Jesus' answer, "If you wish to enter into life, keep the commandments," shocks today's Christian. It would be assumed in contemporary evangelical circles that Jesus would have laid out some "packaged form" of the gospel. Unquestionably, to make keeping the commandments a requirement to be saved would be considered heresy. Thus, the contemporary reader is required to keep the original context in mind to properly understand the Lord's comments. First, the young man's problem lay in his assuming he was righteous, having kept all the Law (v. 20). Second, the Law was the requirement for righteousness by God's standards, but no one except Messiah could always keep the Law; thus, the Law pointed to everyone's guilt (Rom. 3:19-23; Gal. 3:21-23). The reason for the Lord's answer was to make the young man, and those around who could hear, understand that no one is capable of earning eternal life.

19:18-19   The confidence of the young ruler was seen in his desire for clarification: "Which ones?" Jesus responded by listing the sixth, seventh, eighth, ninth, and fifth commandments (Ex. 20). Mark adds, "Do not defraud," which may have been an appendage to "Do not bear false witness," but otherwise he follows the same order. Luke reverses commandments seven and six but otherwise lists the same as Matthew. Matthew adds, "And you shall love your neighbor as yourself" from Leviticus 19:18 and thereby demonstrates that the Law extended beyond the Ten Commandments. Mark and Luke may have omitted this reference because it was unnecessary in order to make the Lord's point and complicated the story beyond their purpose.

Speculation as to why these particular commands were chosen or why the fifth was put after the others is useless. To the human mind, commandment ten would have been more appropriate for a rich man, "You shall not covet your neighbor's house . . ." because material wealth can easily breed even more greed. However, Jesus certainly knew the young man's heart better than later readers of the event. The overall story relates to the failure of legalism to earn righteousness.

19:20   The young man boasted, "All these things I have kept," with Mark and Luke adding "from my youth up." Thus, he was confident in his ability to keep the Law. He then asked, "What am I still lacking?" Hendriksen notes, "What is important is that this young man realized that he had not as yet attained everlasting life, not even in principle."[21] Carson agrees, adding, "The man's further word, 'what do I still lack?' show his uncertainty . . . as well as his notion that certain 'good works' are over and above the law."[22] Whereas these are true observations and may reflect the heart of the young man, another possibility is that he wished to hear that he lacked nothing. Perhaps he approached the Lord, knowing His reputation as a teacher, and sought recognition from Him as being worthy of eternal life.

19:21-22   Rather than commending the young man, the Lord added yet another test. The idea of "perfect" (*teleios, a, on*) is "completion" or "successful end results." Though this man had admirably kept the Law, he was not complete in the requirements for eternal life. This should not be viewed as a second stage, or level, of earning salvation but only as a demonstration that keeping certain laws was not adequate. Christ chose the weakest area of this man's life to challenge his worthiness: "sell your possessions and give to the poor . . . and come, follow Me." The man responded as Jesus knew he would; "he went away grieved."

The promise of "treasure in heaven" for selling everything and giving to the poor was also a test to determine the seriousness of his concern for eternal life. If truly interested, the young ruler had to understand that eternal treasure is of greater value than temporal wealth. Selling and giving away his wealth was not an Old Testament requirement, and certainly doing such would not merit eternal life. Jesus was not stating a method of earning eternal life but demonstrating to the young man that he was not as righteous as he assumed. He went away "grieved" (present passive participle of *lupeō*) or "being grieved" by the prospect of having to give up his wealth. Having come to seek praise from this notable teacher because of his Law-keeping, the young ruler left having been informed of some things he could not or would not do. The rabbis taught that poverty was "worse than all the curses of Egypt combined"[23] and actually forbade giving away all one's possessions.[24]

19:23-24   Jesus drew a conclusion from this event, summarizing it as "A rich man enters the kingdom of heaven with difficulty." The rich man had come feeling blessed by God (wealth in the Old Testament was taken as God's blessing) and confident that he had sufficiently kept the Law. Christ, however, had demonstrated that he lacked heart for the kingdom or its King. The problem was that material wealth hinders some from choosing that which is far more valuable. The pursuit of or protection of material goods too easily keeps one from seriously being concerned about spiritual matters. Fortunately, Jesus did not say that it is impossible for the wealthy to be saved, but only difficult. Abraham, Solomon, Joseph of Arimathea, and Zacchaeus are only a few examples of God's chosen men who were wealthy.

The illustration of the camel in v. 24 is a hyperbolic proverb to emphasize this difficulty. Some argue that the illustration refers to a gate in Jerusalem called "the eye of the needle" or that Jesus was referring to some narrow pass, but that is more allegory than fact and loses the proverbial intent of Jesus. Meyer correctly states, "To render this word by *a narrow gate,* a narrow *mountain-pass,* or anything but a *needle* is simply inadmissible."[25] Likewise Carson remarks, "Attempts to weaken this hyperbole by taking 'needle,' not as a sewing needle, but as a small gate through which an unladened camel could just squeeze—and only on his knees—are misguided."[26] The Mishnah relates a similar proverb with the exception that it uses an elephant rather than a camel: "A man, not even in his dreams, sees an elephant pass through the eye of a needle."[27]

19:25-26   Hearing this proverb startled the disciples. The assumption that wealth was indication of God's blessings, as with Job, Abraham, Isaac, and the other great heroes of Judaism, was common among the Jews. Their question, "Who then can be saved?" revealed the connection in their mind between entering the kingdom of heaven (v. 23) with being saved (v. 25). The misunderstanding was that material blessing was an indication of God's approval of one's spiritual life. If those receiving material blessing were hardly saved, how could common people be saved?

Verse 26 sums up the point. For men to save themselves is impossible, but God is able to save anyone. God is the One who takes the initiative in salvation for He alone has the power to save. That nothing is impossible with God is a common theme in the Scriptures: Gen. 18:14; Job 42:2; Jer. 32:17, 27; Zech. 8:6; Matt. 19:26; Luke 1:37. Though a person cannot possibly save himself, God is capable and willing to save.

REWARDS FOR FOLLOWING JESUS, 19:27-30
(Mark 10:28-31; Luke 18:28-30)

19:27   Peter's question is not to be taken out of the context of the overheard discussion with the rich young ruler. Jesus had told the young man that he must give up everything and follow Him (v. 21). Peter seemed suddenly to realize that this was exactly what he and the others had done. Note that Peter used the plural "we" (*hēmeis*) and was not just selfishly looking out for himself. This was not an empty boast (cf. 4:19-22; 9:9). They had really left behind careers and other obligations in order to follow Him. The question now came to Peter's mind, "What is in it for us?"

19:28-29   Notice that Jesus did not in any way seem upset with Peter for asking this question. He did, however, make clear that the reward was future and not for the present. The expression "in the regeneration" (*en tē paliggensia,* literally, "in the rebirth"; see Titus 3:5) is not to be identified with the previous clause, "you who have followed Me," since Jesus certainly did not need a rebirth, but with the clause following, "shall sit upon twelve thrones." The promise was that those who had followed Him (referring here to His twelve disciples) in the present life would receive their reward (thrones) in the next life, which could be entered only by a new birth (John 3:3-6).

When Jesus is exalted (the "Son of Man will sit on His glorious throne," cf. Dan. 7:13-14), then (and not before) these disciples will be likewise rewarded, each with his own throne. The twelve disciples will govern the twelve tribes of Israel in the messianic kingdom. This is not allegory or parable or symbolism but a promise of future reward for faithful service. Barnes attempts to relegate this promise only to an honorable title,[28] but his understanding flows from a theological bent away from an actual millennial kingdom rather than from any normative interpretation of the text.

The question must be raised about Judas in relation to this promise. Scripture bears witness that Judas was a false apostle, the son of perdition, and one who cheated the other disciples by stealing money from their treasury (John 6:70-71; 12:6; 17:12). Alford assumes the election recorded in Acts 1:20-26 filled the empty throne,[29] but God nowhere endorses the decision of the eleven, who resorted to casting lots instead of waiting for the giving of the Spirit. Paul, certainly the Lord's choice (Acts 9:1-15; Gal. 1:1, 10-15), will be the twelfth judge over Israel.

Not only did Jesus answer the question about the disciples who had followed Him in His earthly ministry, but (v. 29) He continued to point out that there are rewards for all who follow Him. Simply put, anyone who has given up anything for the Lord will be repaid "many times as much." This means, Mark explains in 10:29-30, that even in this life, family and resources (not necessarily personal property) will be provided a hundred times more than if one seeks to cling to his possessions. The possessions and houses, brothers and sisters are the community of believers who are to share with one another when any has need. Barbieri points out that Mark "did not repeat the expression 'father' because the Father of the believer is God Himself."[30] Mark also mentions that persecution would be part of this life (10:30), even as Jesus reminds His disciples in John 15:18-21.

19:30   This last statement is somewhat enigmatic but is related to the promise that though they would now be rejected by the nation, they would in the regeneration be rulers. The implications of the proverb are spelled out in particulars in chap. 20, vv. 1-16, where they are repeated in reverse form. Hendriksen offers a summary of the proverb's meaning: "The 'first' are those who because of their wealth, education, position, prestige, talents, etc., are highly regarded by men in general, sometimes even by God's children. . . . But since God sees and knows the heart many of these very people are by Him assigned to a position behind the others."[31] In light of the discussion with the wealthy young ruler who outwardly kept the Law, this is a plausible explanation. Certainly the world would look at him as a leader and prominent person, but he did not even get invited into Christ's kingdom. The disciples, who had forsaken all worldly goods, would be rulers over the tribes of Israel. Such irony is reflected in this short proverbial statement.

HOMILETICAL SUGGESTIONS

The first major topic of this chapter is not only controversial but divisive, and the issue is critical to understanding God's design for marriage. When approaching this text, it is critical not to allow emotional arguments to cloud the meaning. Note first that the question was not whether or not one can divorce his wife—permission was already determined by Mosaic Law. The question raised was whether or not the divorce could be for "any cause at all." The only point of discussion here is the cause for divorce under the Law, and Jesus answered with a twofold reply dealing with (1) the hardness of the human heart and (2) sexual promiscuity. God's design is that divorce not take place unless sexual misconduct is continued without contriteness; but if divorce is the result, there is no reason to punish the divorced person. Too often divorce is treated as the unpardonable sin, and numerous unbiblical restrictions are placed on individuals already suffering the pain of a failed marriage. Where committed, sin must be dealt with; but to punish a person simply because he/she is divorced is not exercising God's mercy or healing restoration.

The second key lesson focuses on the danger of self-righteousness by highlighting the rich young ruler's confidence in his ability to gain eternal life by his own worthiness. The strange response of Jesus reflected His awareness of the attitude of the young man who seemed so earnest. Jesus placed before him the one commandment he did not obey, "Love the Lord your God with all your heart and with all your soul and with all your might" (Deut. 6:5), since the man treasured his riches more than serving the Messiah. The message of the dialogue of vv.16-22 is not that one must give away all possessions to gain eternal life, but that one cannot claim perfection and thus earn eternal life. Jesus just led this man into the realization that neither his good intentions were enough nor was his desire to gain eternal life. Whether the young rich man ever came to understand his need to depend upon God is not revealed, but the lesson certainly struck the hearts of the disciples (vv. 25-26).

Connected to the lesson of the insufficiency of self-righteousness is the encouragement of Christ's promise. He will reward all those who follow Him. In this life the reward will be the blessing of homes and families beyond those that could be accumulated by wealth. In the future life of the regenerate, other rewards are not as yet specified but are certainly promised in Scripture (Matt. 6:18-20; 1 Cor. 3:11-15; 2 Cor. 5:10; 1 Tim. 6:17-19).

MATTHEW
CHAPTER
TWENTY

KINGDOM REWARDS
AND HONORS

Chapter divisions in the English Bible should always be approached with the understanding that the dividing point was not inspired but determined by scholarly opinion. This writer usually agrees with such chapter division but disagrees here; the first part of the discussion is certainly a continuation of the Lord's answer in 19:28-30. More specifically, the parable of 20:1-16 is an explanation and illustration of the remark of 19:30, "Many who are first will be last; and the last first." Beyond this, chap. 20 recounts the journey continuation to Jerusalem along with another prediction of the Lord's death and resurrection, a lesson on honors to be given in the kingdom, and the healing of two blind men.

PARABLE EXPLAINING THAT THE LAST WILL BE FIRST, 20:1-16

The word "for" (*gar*) continues the thought from the preceding clause (19:30). Jesus was explaining the meaning of the enigmatic phrase concerning the last and the first. The context is reward for service (19:27), and the parable in these verses relates to the concept of receiving rewards for the sacrifices made to follow Christ. **20:1-2** Jesus built the parable around His common theme of the kingdom of heaven. Here He compared the kingdom to a landowner who hires laborers for his field work. The overwhelming lesson of the parable is that this landowner is generous beyond any normative human expectations. The landowner can be none other than God, who takes upon Himself to hire and send out the workers into His vineyard. This may have reminded the disciples of His instructions when He sent out the seventy: "Beseech the Lord of the harvest to send out laborers into His harvest" (Luke 10:2).

The opening scene is "early morning," emphasizing the eagerness of the owner to get the workers started and the fact that they were hired for a full day's work. The owner and the workers made an agreement for one denarius for one day's work. This appears to have been considered fair wages as no one complained or bargained for more.

20:3-7   The following verses explain how the owner continued to send workers into the field throughout the day. According to Jewish reckoning of time, the third hour (v. 3, *tritēn hōran*) would be 9:00 A.M.[1] The assumption would be, then, that these joined the labor force some three hours after the first group went into the field. In v. 4, no payment amount is mentioned. The workers simply went to work on the landowner's word of giving "whatever is right."

The same event took place at the sixth hour (noon), ninth (3:00 P.M.), and eleventh (5:00 P.M., only one hour before dark) hours. Again, no payment amount is stated. The first group of workers had been in the field for twelve hours, the last group for one hour. In the interpretation of parables, attempting to make every detail represent some deep truth is not fitting. The details given in vv. 5-7 are not to be analyzed beyond a simple communication of the inequity of the hours worked.

20:8-9   When evening came (around 6:00 P.M.), the workers gathered together to receive pay for their work. The foreman was to distribute the pay, though the landowner had actually hired and sent out the different groups. Hendriksen asserts that the word "evening" (*opsios, a, on,* literally, "becoming late") "indisputably points to the evening of the world's and of the church's history, the great day of the final judgment, and of the manifestation of God's kingdom in all its glory."[2]

However, this meaning is not as clear as assumed. At the end of the age, angels, not human laborers, are sent to harvest the field (13:39). Also, nothing in the context points to an end of the age message. Carson correctly states, "Some take 'when evening came'

(v. 8) as an allusion to the judgment, but this is doubtful. It is essential to the story in a time when laborers were customarily paid at the end of each day (cf. Lev 19:13)."[3] Thus, "evening" was simply the appropriate time for paying the laborers.

The instructions were to call the laborers and "give them the wage," not give them "*their* wages" as the NASB and NIV translate. "The wage" (*ton misthon*) is articular singular, implying only one wage. The point is that only one amount was going to be paid; payment would not be on a scale based on number of hours worked. The steward was also instructed to begin with those who came last. This may have been to guarantee that those who began work first would witness these later workers receiving the same amount of money. Verse 9 states that each received one denarius, the same amount the first group had been promised (v. 2). Had the early workers received their pay first, they would have left happy, and there would have been no point to the parable.

20:10-12   As the earliest laborers watched the latter groups' payment, they assumed receipt of a higher wage than promised for themselves—a logical assumption from a human perspective. That seems only fair. Instead, they received the same amount as those who only worked one-twelfth of their work time. However, the amount received was exactly the amount promised (v. 2).

Not surprisingly, these laborers began to grumble (*gogguzō*), making a simple and correct complaint: those who came in the late afternoon, a cooler part of the day, and worked only one hour received the same pay as those who labored for twelve hours in the heat. Humanly speaking, they had every right to complain. Undoubtedly, no one reading this today would tolerate such treatment. Lawsuits, union strikes, and every kind of action to receive fair treatment would be initiated.

20:13-15   The response of the landowner was neither apologetic nor sympathetic toward the complaint. He addressed one of the complainers as "friend" (*hetairos,* "companion, friend"), which, as MacArthur points out, was "not the term for a close friend but rather a casual companion."[4] Perhaps its use was to highlight the landowner's goodwill, indicating that he was not looking down upon or minimizing the man's worth.

Then the landowner made the most important point, "I am doing you no wrong." It is critical to realize that the landowner kept his promise. The laborers were not cheated but paid as promised. He reminded them of their agreement to work all day for a denarius, a typical one-day wage. The wording clearly indicates that they made the agreement (*sumphōneō*) with him; the landowner did not trick them. Then he dismissed the complainers by saying, "Take what is yours and go away" (*hupage*) (v. 14). His "wish" (*thelō*) was to give the last workers the same as the first—not what he owed them, but what he wished to give them.

Verse 15 argues further that his actions were lawful. He kept his promise to the first workers, so the law was not violated; therefore, they had no right to protest. The landowner condemned their complaining spirit. Further, he pointed to the evil within them. The NASB and NIV read similarly, "Is your eye envious?" or, "Are you envious?" The word translated "envious," however, is *ponēros*, "evil." Literally, the question is, "Is your eye evil?" The evil lay in the fact that the landowner was "generous," literally, "good" (*agathos*). The contrast is good versus evil. His payment to the last workers was "good." For the first workers to earn a denarius for a day's work was appropriate, but their greed after seeing what the others were paid was "evil." Instead, they should have praised the landowner for his goodness to the other workers. Giving a full day's wage for only an hour's work was grace extended, generosity. One who gives grace should not be criticized; to do so is evil.

20:16   The conclusion was "Thus the last shall be first, and the first last," even as stated in 19:30, though in reverse order. Those receiving grace and bounty beyond what is deserved will be first in the kingdom. Those who labored for a set price will get only the set price. The major emphasis is the grace of God, who gives beyond what is earned. Therefore, the disciples should not be worried about what will be for them (19:27). The day will come when they will be paid, not according to what is deserved, but according to what the gracious God wishes to give.

REMINDER OF HIS COMING DEATH AND RESURRECTION, 20:17-19 (Mark 10:32-34; Luke 18:31-34)

20:17-19   The NIV translates "As Jesus was going up to Jerusalem"; the NASB renders "As Jesus was about to go up." The participle "going up" (*anapainōn*) could possibly be translated as the

NASB has it, but too much is assumed, and the NIV more accurately translates the verb. Jesus took the disciples "aside by themselves," which implies that this message was intended only for them. This involved more than just a secret that He wanted kept; it was a private moment. The news He gave was not a callous and impersonal prophecy but a tremendous burden for Him to bear. Quite likely He was seeking comfort and a time of intimate praying with His small band of men. This was not the first time He had mentioned this awful destiny (16:21).

Verse 18 recounts specific details of this appalling coming event. The "Son of Man" (Jesus' favorite designation of Himself, involving strong messianic implications) was going to be delivered up (*paradidōmi,* "given over, betrayed") into the power of the religious leadership (chief priests and scribes), who would condemn Him and sentence Him to death (see 26:57–27:1). After the Jewish council condemned Him, He would be turned over to the Gentiles (the Romans), who would abuse, mock, and kill Him (v. 19; see 27:11-31). The pronouncement ended with the joyful promise that after three days He would be "raised up" (see 28:1-10).

HONORS IN THE KINGDOM—
THE FATHER'S PREROGATIVE, 20:20-28 (Mark 10:35-45)

20:20-21 The sad event that followed was made even more tragic by the fact that it appears to have directly come after the Lord's news of His impending suffering and death. Mark and Matthew relate the same event, but Matthew adds the detail that the mother of James and John accompanied her sons and spoke first in relation to the issue. The Scripture refers to women traveling with Jesus and His disciples, and at times there appears to have been a sizable entourage. Thus, to have their mother present was not unusual. Also, Mark's not mentioning the mother does not discredit Matthew's story, since the synoptics typically include various details unique to each writer. She may have introduced the issue and then her sons offered opinions as to their right to be placed in the seats of authority.

Jesus was asked to declare that one son would sit on the right side and one on the left side of His throne when He had established His kingdom (v. 21). The NASB "command" is too strong for the word *eipe* (aorist of *legō*); she was asking Him to proclaim their positions to the other disciples. Hendriksen credits the mother with great faith. He explains:

> The basis for it may well have been the saying of Jesus reported in 19:28, according to which he promises that one day he would be seated on the throne of glory, and that each of The Twelve would then also be seated on a throne. She believes that this is actually going to happen. She is convinced of this in spite of the fact that right at this moment there is very little to show that events are moving in that direction.[5]

Hendriksen's observation is correct, and her faith was shown to be even stronger by the fact that Jesus had just announced His upcoming death and resurrection. She therefore either ignored His prophecy or believed in His victory over death. Mark's account relates that the sons took up the request, asking to share in His glory (10:37) which also tied the request to the comment in Matthew 19:28.

To sit on the immediate sides of a throne was to indicate special privilege and power. Such proximity to the King suggests a sharing of His prerogatives and influence. There is little reason to interpret this request as anything but selfish. Why James and John thought they had rights to these preeminent positions over the other disciples, especially Peter, is not stated, but such is typical of humanistic politics. How calloused these followers of Jesus were to the terrible news of the suffering that awaited Him in Jerusalem. They were concerned only for their own glory.

20:22   Jesus was patient, and His response was not intended to be a rebuke. First, He pointed out the magnitude of their request, "You do not know what you are asking," indicating a far more complex issue than just His declaring seating arrangements. Carson identifies their problem: "It is often ignorance that seeks leadership, power, and glory: the brothers do not know what they are asking. To ask to reign with Jesus is to ask to suffer with him."[6] Thus Jesus asked the question, "Are you able to drink the cup that I am about to drink?"

The "cup" is a symbol of taking what is served to you in life. For Jesus, the cup was humiliating and painful suffering at the hands of His enemies and, ultimately, His death. Did James and John think that they were able to share this experience with Him? Their rather flippant answer was yes. This reflected not their courage but their inability to grasp the horror yet to come.

20:23 The Lord made two major points in His response: first, indeed they would drink of His cup; second, to appoint the ranking of the kingdom thrones was not His prerogative. The seats of honor not being Christ's to give may seem strange, but when one remembers that He came to do the Father's will and that His messianic mission was one of serving the Father, it is logical to assume that the Father would reward those who serve His servant, Messiah. These places of honor have been prepared (perfect passive of *etoimazō*), indicating they were previously made ready for the ones the Father chose.

20:24 The natural response of the remaining disciples was jealousy and anger. The designation "the ten" (*hoi deka*) emphasizes division between the disciples—the two (James and John) and the ten. Their jealousy was indicative of attitudes not much different from that of the two brothers. Apparently none had taken to heart the lesson that to be greatest in the kingdom required humility and trust (18:1-4).

20:25-28 Recognizing that the earlier lesson had not been understood and internalized, Jesus reiterated the point by using a different metaphor from the Roman culture, where rulers flaunted their positions by demanding obedience. He called His twelve together and presented the lesson again.

The "rulers of the Gentiles" certainly referred to the Romans and their levels of government. Their complex system of authority operated with the highest positions being determined by birth and wealth.[7] The characteristics of this earthly leadership were "lording over" (perhaps, "lord against them" or "lord down upon them") and "exercising authority over" their subjects. The Romans took from, demanded from, and abused their subjects. Rulers held envious positions since they acquired both the most and the best. Everyone else was forced to give them honor and obedience.

Jesus clearly stated that this leadership style was not a role model for His servants (v. 26). In contrast, the greatest among Messiah's servants would be the one who gave and served others. This contrast is marked by the strong adversative conjunction *alla,* which emphasizes the antithetical nature of the two kingdoms. The difference in attitude between secular leadership and spiritual leadership rests in the attitude of servanthood. What a shock to these men who had grown up in a world of Roman pomp and circumstance, where powerful men were esteemed, flattered, and waited on. Verse 27 summarizes the lesson in a phrase reminiscent of 19:30 and 20:16, "Whoever wishes to be first (*prōtos*) among you shall be your slave (*doulos*)." This was another way of saying the first shall be last, or that the one who wants to be first must make himself last. Servanthood will result in the reward of priority in the kingdom.

The standard of this servanthood was demonstrated by Jesus Himself. The "just as" (*hōsper;* v. 28) attests to the degree to which one is to become a slave of others. The Son of Man, the Messiah Himself, did not come to be served, that is, to be waited upon by others. He did not sit in the chief seats of the synagogue, nor did He refuse to pay taxes or charge money for His ministry. Instead, He freely gave, healed, and taught. Ultimately, He gave His very life. The word translated "life" here is not *bios,* which refers to basic biological or material life, but *psuchē* (soul). The use of "soul" does not intend to convey the idea that He gave up His soul in torment but rather His very life essence. Peter uses this word to refer to "life" in reference to Noah and his family, "eight persons [*psuchai*], were brought safely through the water" (1 Peter 3:20)—the lives of these people were spared. The connection is that *psuchē* can simply refer to the breath of life, the energy of life, and not necessarily to the spirit that is in mankind. Scripture says animals also have souls (Gen. 1:20, 30, LXX).

In contrast to coming to be served, He came to give His life as a ransom for many. The word "ransom" (*lutros*) is found in ancient manuscripts as a term for buying of freedom for slaves. Deissmann points out that this word is found in documents "for a slave's redemption money" several times.[8] Christ's very life was paid out to ransom ("buy the freedom of") "many" (*pollōn*). He, then, is held up as the standard by which those who wish to be great in the kingdom are to measure their service. Jesus served even to the point of dying for others.

HEALING THE BLIND MEN, 20:29-34
(Mark 10:46-52; Luke 18:35-43)

The three accounts of this incident differ in three primary areas: first, Matthew records that there were two blind men, but both Mark and Luke list one blind man; second, Matthew has the blind men calling Jesus "Lord" (*kurios*), whereas Mark and Luke say "Jesus"; and third, Matthew and Mark have the event taking place as Jesus was "going out from Jericho" (*ekporeuomenōn autōn apo Ierichō*), whereas Luke has "approaching Jericho" (*tō eggizein eis Ierichō*).

It is to be remembered that the synoptics often present variety in reporting, offering augmentation, not contradiction. Thus, whether there was one or two blind men is not critical, since both Mark and Luke do not insist on *only* one blind man—their accounts just concentrate on the one. Carson suggests that Matthew, because he was an eyewitness, remembered not just the well-known Bartimaeus but another beggar as well.[9] Jesus being called "Lord" or "Jesus" is not important since both are correct and both could have been said; however, there is some reason to question the textual legitimacy of the word *kurios.*

20:29   The detail of approaching or departing Jericho is a significant issue. Possibly two healing events took place, one of the blind man as Jesus entered the city (Luke 18:35), and the other of Bartimaeus (only Mark uses the name of this beggar) as Jesus left the city (Matt. 20:29-30; Mark 10:46). However, accepting two events with such similar details is difficult, and to understand all three accounts to be referring to the same episode is best. Barbieri suggests two cities of Jericho, the ancient and the one occupied in Christ's day, and concludes, "If the miracle occurred between the two sites, both accounts are satisfied."[10] Calvin offers another possibility:

> My conjecture is, that, while Christ was approaching to the city, the *blind man cried out,* but that, as he was not heard on account of the noise, he placed himself in the way, as they were *departing from the city,* and then was at length called by Christ. And *so Luke,* commencing with what was true, does not follow out the whole narrative, but passes over Christ's stay in the city; while the other Evangelists attend only to the time which was nearer to the miracle.[11]

This may be a bit contrived, but it is legitimate to say that the events of Christ's life and ministry were often condensed to record only the lesson material the Spirit of God desired. Mark states, "And they came to Jericho. And as He was going out from Jericho . . ." which may be intending to relate two stages of His visit. Thus, Calvin may be correct. Luke's account is the record of His research (Luke 1:1-4);

therefore, having read Mark's statement "And they came to Jericho" (*kai erchontai eis Ierichō*), he may have recorded the detail of the event without being concerned with whether it was as Jesus entered or left the city. The account stands as a true record of the miracle.

20:30-31   Two blind men, one of whom was Bartimaeus (perhaps a well-known roadside fixture), heard that Jesus was passing by. Obviously, the large crowd following Him made a lot of noise, and this caught their attention (Luke 18:36-37). Use of the title "Son of David" is significant, as Pate explains: "The title 'Son of David' seems to have been associated in Judaism with the Messiah (see *4 Ezra 12:32; 4Qflor 1:11; Ps. Sol. 17:23*). It is difficult to escape the conclusion, therefore, that the usage of the title by the sightless man indicated his belief that Jesus, the Son of David, was the Messiah."[12] The appeal to their Messiah was for mercy.

The multitude's response reflects the low value placed on the handicapped during that era, though Israel was responsible to share their blessings with the less fortunate. Obviously the crowd believed that Jesus of Nazareth, apparently traveling to Jerusalem for the great Feast of Passover, was too important to be bothered by blind beggars. The beggars, however, persisted in their cries for mercy though the crowd tried to silence them.

20:32   In spite of the crowd's efforts to protect Him from being inconvenienced by worthless beggars, Jesus heard their cries and stopped His journey. The whole parade of followers and supportive entourage, as well as curious crowds, also came to a halt. Jesus, interestingly enough, did not go to the beggars but called for them. Perhaps this was to draw them into the midst of the crowd. His question did not reflect lack of attention to their apparent need but allowed for verbalization of their faith in His ability to care for their physical problem.

20:33-34   Neither shy nor selfish, the men gave a simple reply—they wanted the ability to see. Rather than being annoyed by their hindering His travel, Jesus felt their pain and desperate need. His dramatic response (being "moved with compassion") becomes even more touching when one remembers His cognizance of what awaited Him in Jerusalem. Rather than being overly occupied with His own woes, Jesus was concerned with theirs. This was a vivid demonstration of what He had just said to the disciples, "The Son of Man did not come to be served, but to serve" (v. 28). Jesus granted their request with direct and spectacular power and healed them immediately. Scripture is not clear as to whether they followed Him permanently or only on this journey to Jerusalem (cf. Mark 10:52, "on the road"). It is possible that Bartimaeus became a disciple, and this would account for His name's being used by Mark.

HOMILETICAL SUGGESTIONS

The main point of this chapter is the teaching related to kingdom rewards and honors. The parable of the laborers indicates that God is gracious in payment for service rendered for Him. Those who labor for God's kingdom should not be concerned with what they will receive for their efforts, since the reward received will not be according to what is deserved but according to the graciousness of God—which is much greater.

Jesus' prediction of His upcoming suffering and death serves as a warning as to how calloused the human heart can become. Having just heard of what faced their Lord, His key men seemed to overlook His needs and saw only their own hopes and concerns. To identify with this situation, imagine telling a friend of your impending painful death from a terminal illness and then hearing his request that you submit his resume to your employer, along with a personal recommendation that he take over your job once you are gone. This is how the Lord felt, though His response was gentle. A most interesting feature here is that Jesus will not be the One to make the decision concerning what they sought. The rewards for those who faithfully serve the Lord will be handed out by the Father, not the Son.

Jesus had already promised that the Twelve would sit upon thrones (19:28), but James and John sought special recognition over the others. The ten became jealous and angry. This very human aspect of the disciples is important because we see that human nature is the same in every age. Their attitudes provided a platform for Jesus to teach one of the most critical lessons of Christianity: leadership is for serving, unlike the world's view of wielding power and rank over others. Servant-leadership is a unique aspect of spiritual reality in the body of Christ. One must constantly evaluate his motives in desiring to be a leader in Christian ministry, especially in consideration of Mark 10:42-45.

MATTHEW

CHAPTER

TWENTY-ONE

JESUS ENTERS JERUSALEM

Jesus then entered Jerusalem for the last time, and this final week of the Lord's earthly life was filled with stress and conflict. Five major episodes in the Jerusalem area are covered in this chapter: the Triumphal Entry (where the people welcomed Him as a prophet and the Son of David); the second cleansing of the temple (which sparked additional conflict with the chief priests and elders); the lesson of the fig tree outside Jerusalem; the second day of temple conflict related to Jesus' authority; and the parable condemning Israel's religious leaders.

ENTRANCE INTO JERUSALEM, 21:1-11
(Mark 11:1-11; Luke 19:28-38; John 12:12-19)

According to John 12:1 and 12, this entrance was only six days before the Passover. Hendriksen offers adequate argument that Jesus reached Bethany on Friday in time to rest on the Sabbath. On Saturday evening (following the Sabbath), Martha, Mary, and Lazarus hosted a meal in Jesus' honor at Bethany, and the next day, Sunday, Jesus went into Jerusalem.[1]

21:1-3 Matthew does not record the visit to Bethany or the meal with Lazarus, as his concern is to demonstrate yet another fulfillment of prophecy in the life of Jesus. Thus Matthew's account begins with the sending of two disciples to the village of Bethphage. Jesus told the men to enter the village and "immediately [they would] find a donkey tied there and a colt with her"(v. 2). Details as to how the disciples would identify the designated animal pair are not given—only the "immediately" time factor and the notation of gender with "colt." Though both Mark and Luke mention only the colt, Matthew offers additional information. Mark and Luke also state that the colt had not as yet been ridden. It is interesting that the disciples were not to ask anyone's permission but simply to untie and bring the animals to the Lord. This appears to have been a prearranged situation.

Jesus raised the possibility that someone might question their actions, and their response was to be "The Lord has need of them," following which the questioner would immediately relinquish the pair. Again, it can only be assumed that some unnamed follower of Jesus had agreed to put the animals at the Lord's disposal. The fact that the term "the Lord" (*ho kurios*) was sufficient authority to allow these men to walk away with the animals is interesting. Meyer notes that this implied a preunderstanding and dependability on the part of the animals' owner: "The people of the place are so loyal to Him as perfectly to understand the meaning of *ho kurios, k.t.l.,* and to find in those words sufficient reason for at once complying with His request."[2]

21:4-7 Matthew associates this event with the fulfillment of Zechariah 9:9. As is often the case, the writer of the New Testament is not quoting but referencing the Old Testament passage. In vv. 4-5, Matthew's concern is connecting this event with the promise to the inhabitants of Jerusalem that their deliverer would come and His entrance would be on the "foal of a donkey." That emphasized His humility and that He would come in peace, not as a military conqueror (cf. 1 Kings 1:32-35). Carson comments, "Jesus was not only proclaiming his messiahship and his fulfillment of Scripture but showing the kind of peace-loving approach he was now making to the city."[3] The disciples obeyed the Lord (v. 6) and found the animals as predicted. Then they covered the animals with their garments (v. 7) to provide a makeshift saddle for the Lord.

21:8 The next event was most remarkable in that it indicated the openness of the people of Jerusalem to Jesus. Their subsequent turning against Him can be directly linked to the strong and hateful attack against Him by the religious leadership. Matthew records (v. 8) that "most" (*pleistos,* superlative adjective), but not all, of the crowd began to join in the procession by spreading either their garments or branches of palm trees (John 12:13) in front of the donkey on which Jesus was riding. This reception was typical of ancient Near Eastern cultures as a display of welcome to an important dignitary. Barnes notes that the palm branch was an emblem of joy and victory and used as an emblem of peace.[4]

21:9   The crowd (*ochloi*) was led by the disciples (Luke 19:37), but these were probably the seventy and not just the Twelve. It may have included even other "disciples," who had joined the procession in Galilee expecting establishment of the kingdom. The entourage would have been impressive—a crowd in front of Jesus, spreading garments and branches, and a crowd behind Him, all singing praises. The scene certainly would have stirred the inhabitants of Jerusalem and drawn attention from visitors in the city for the Passover Feast.

The chant "Hosanna to the Son of David" was certainly a loud, public proclamation of the Messiah's entrance. The word "Hosanna" (*Hōsanna*) is taken from the Hebrew words *hōshi'a na* in Psalm 118:25, "Save, I pray" (Hiphil of *yasha',* "save, deliver," and particle of entreaty, "I pray," or urgency, "now").[5] Note that the chant was addressed to the Son of David, which implies that the messianic expectations for the Son of David were being recognized in Jesus. The people were crying out for deliverance. However, the word "deliver" should not automatically be taken in the sense of saving them from sin. Judas Maccabeus was also a son of David who had delivered Israel, purged the temple, and thus became a legend among the people. His deliverance was, however, a military victory. Many who hated the Romans would likewise sing hosanna to Jesus in anticipation of their being driven out of Jerusalem, even as Maccabeus had driven out the Greeks.

The rest of the song, "Blessed is He who comes in the name of the Lord; Hosanna in the highest" also should be understood as having two dimensions. To some, Jesus did come in God's name, that is, with His authority and power. But to others the cry implied only that this "prophet" (v. 11), like numerous other prophets, had been sent on a mission from God. More than an appeal to God in heaven for deliverance, "Hosanna in the highest" may indicate a form of praise. Carson notes, "'Hosanna in the highest' is probably equivalent to 'Glory to God in the highest' (Luke 2:14). The people praise God in the highest heavens for sending the Messiah."[6] However, most likely the majority of the crowd would not have understood the spiritual mission of Messiah and would have assumed this to be a possible sign of God's deliverance from oppression.

21:10-11   The grand entrance into the city drew an even larger crowd of spectators caught up in the majesty of the moment. Curious, the newcomers sought the identify of this person receiving such adoration and generating so much excitement. Matthew used hyperbole, "all the city," to emphasize the attention His entrance spawned, and the word *seiō* (NASB "stirred"), which is used of earthquakes and could be translated "shaken," to emphasize how this event created a serious disruption in Jerusalem. The question, "Who is this?" indicates a suspenseful atmosphere and expectation of some significant event, especially for the dispersed Jews who had returned to Jerusalem for Passover.

Luke records other events that occurred between Bethany and Jerusalem. The Pharisees demanded that Jesus make His disciples stop stirring up the crowd by their shouts of "Hosanna," but Jesus responded that the message must be proclaimed and, if men failed to praise Him at this moment, "the stones will cry out" (Luke 19:39-40). Luke also records the emotional impact of this event on Jesus. Though He had entered Jerusalem many times, this entrance was different. Viewing the city as He approached, Jesus wept—not for His own suffering about to come but because He knew the coming destruction of this beloved city (19:41-44).

Matthew records Jerusalem's opinion of Jesus as "the prophet" who was from "Nazareth in Galilee" (v.11). It is interesting that He was thus identified, since Nazareth was a city of bad reputation (John 1:45-46), but it is certainly consistent with Matthew's earlier statement that He would be called a Nazarene (2:23). Jesus was routinely referred to as a Nazarene or "of Nazareth" (cf. Mark 10:47; Luke 4:34; John 1:45; Acts 10:38; etc.). For people of public note to be identified with their home city as a means of distinguishing them from others with the same surname was not uncommon.

CONFLICT IN THE TEMPLE, 21:12-17
(Mark 11:15-18; Luke 19:45-46)

21:12-13   One would assume that Jesus, having experienced such a grand entrance into the city, would relish the glory and take time to enjoy what appeared to be a victorious moment. On the contrary, He entered the temple and began to create conflict.

The temple should not be thought of as a single building but a complex of buildings built on a hill and covering approximately thirty-five acres. The temple mount itself was about 750 feet square and surrounded by a wall. Steps inside this wall led to the platform on which the temple was built. The outer area was the first division of the temple mount and was referred to as the "court of the Gentiles." Non-Jews were allowed to come into this area for worship and possibly to open shops for trading.[7] Between this area and the next temple division was an inner lattice partition, which held warning signs. "Heathens and those who had contracted uncleanness by contact with the dead were not permitted to proceed further than that point."[8] Inside this area were dozens of rooms for keeping everything from firewood to musical instruments: dressing rooms for priests, complete with "lockers" for storing their serving garments, council chambers for the Sanhedrin and the Great Sanhedrin, class space for learning to play temple music, bathing areas for priests, meeting rooms, latrines, to name a few. The women's court faced the temple but was separated from both the men's and priests' courts. It was approximately 200 feet square, having a balcony area for viewing certain festival activities. The main area outside the temple proper was called the court of Israel and the court of the priests. This area contained the bowl for ritual washing, the altar of sacrifice, and the entrance to the Holy Place, where only the priest could enter. Beyond the Holy Place was the Holiest of Holies, an area only the high priest could access and then only once a year with an acceptable sacrifice.

The temple section that housed the money changers and animal sellers can be debated. Edersheim believes it was the court of the Gentiles (fn. 7), but this cannot be positively demonstrated. The question is whether tradesmen being set up outside the temple compound proper would have so upset the Lord. The temple (*to hieron*) referred to the whole complex, which would have included not only the outer court (of the Gentiles) but also the numerous colonnades completely surrounding the temple proper. The local businessmen possibly set up their profit-making enterprises within these multitudinous chambers.

Jesus' aggressive and passionate behavior in throwing these profiteers out of the temple certainly destroys the passive and weakling image of Him that so many have tried to create. The term "cast them out" (*exebalen*) implies force and not just persuasion, and the phrase "overturned the tables . . . and seats" (of those doing business) reflected His passion. Mark adds, "He would not permit anyone to carry goods through the Temple" (11:16). Jesus seems to have taken control of the area, and, possibly because of His intensity and because so many had joined His entourage, the religious leaders were afraid to challenge Him.

This was not the raving of a religious fanatic but the divine wrath against blasphemers in the temple. This was not a church building or some secular institution. Israel's temple was to honor God and was symbolic of His presence among Israel (2 Chron. 5:1-14; 6:1-10; 7:1-3; 11-12). But these merchants had turned it into a place of commercial enterprise for personal gain. This was the second cleansing of the temple (John 2:13-17).[9] Thus, at the beginning of His earthly ministry, Jesus demonstrated His "zeal" (*zēlos*), which "ate Him up" (*kataphagetai,* future middle of *katesthiō,* "consumed") concerning His Father's house (John 2:17), and at the end of His earthly ministry He demonstrated that the passion had not decreased. Neither changing money from foreign currency to coins used in Israel nor selling doves for sacrifice was wrong—but placing these profit-making enterprises within the perimeters of the holy temple was wrong and totally unacceptable.

Verse 13 offers an explanation of Jesus' actions. He referred to Isaiah 56:7, in which the temple is called "My house of prayer" (*beyth-thepilathi*), and Yahweh declared that it was to be called ("recognized as") a house of prayer. But these blasphemers had converted it into a "robbers' den," literally, a "cave of robbers." The imagery is that of a hillside hideout for road bandits. Because of their using the holy ground for making profit, Jesus declared them no better than highway outlaws, and He drove them out to purify the place. Indeed, this event was somewhat similar to what Judas

Maccabeus had done, but it was Israel's own and not foreigners that Jesus purged from the temple.

21:14   Jesus moved from condemning the greedy merchants to caring for the needy. He seems to have established a place for Himself in the temple for conducting ministry, perhaps the very place from which He drove the moneychangers and dove sellers. Matthew tells us that the blind and lame "came to Him," and He healed them. Hendriksen's observation is insightful, "What a scene! While some are expelled, others are welcomed."[10] The contrast between these two groups gives clear testimony of the holy attitude toward those who use God's place for selfish ends and those who are in serious need. Those handicapped in life were welcomed; those who took advantage of the religious habits of God's work were not.

21:15-16   Verse 15 offers sad testimony to the hardness of unrepentant hearts. After witnessing the gracious and powerful works of Jesus, the chief priests and scribes did not fall down to worship Him. Neither glory nor credit for the good He was doing was offered; instead, they "became indignant." To add to their anger, the children in the temple area continued to cry out, "Hosanna to the Son of David," as the crowds had chanted when Jesus entered Jerusalem (v. 9). The religious leadership's indignation stemmed from three major events in the temple: first, Jesus' expulsion of the merchants, whom they had allowed; second, Jesus' healing of the blind and lame crowding into the temple; and third, the children's verbal praise, identifying Jesus with the Son of David.

Their exasperation was expressed in the question, "Do you hear what these are saying [v. 16]?" "These" is emphasized in the text and probably denotes the low regard these "important" men had for children. Jesus first responded directly with "Yes" (*nai*), and then used one of His favorite methods for making a point—He asked a question. "Have you never read?" He followed this up by quoting part of Psalm 8:2 from the Septuagint (8:3 in the LXX and Hebrew text). It is interesting to note that 1 Corinthians 15:27; Ephesians 1:21-22; and Hebrews 2:6-8 all refer Psalm 8 to Jesus. The Lord's question would certainly be an insult to these proud men assumed to be experts in Scripture. His point was that God draws honor even from babes when they sing of Him. The reference in Luke to the stones crying out (19:40) joins with this verse to demonstrate that God will receive His deserved glory even if the self-righteous religious leaders fail to offer it to Him.

21:17   Jesus ended His first day in the temple by returning to Bethany, where He most likely lodged with Lazarus, Martha, and Mary, though the home of Simon the Leper (26:6) could have been another option. Significantly, Jesus did not stay overnight in the city but took His rest in the more tranquil setting of Bethany, returning to the temple daily to engage in teaching, healing, and debating with the religious leadership. Luke's simple summation states, "He was teaching daily in the temple" (19:47).

LESSON OF THE FIG TREE, 21:18-21
(Mark 11:12-14, 20-26)

Mark places this story before the cleansing of the temple and then brings the apostles' reaction into discussion the day following the cleansing. Matthew simply relates the story as a whole and does not bother with details of when the tree was withered or when the disciples actually learned the lesson. Mark's intent is to give chronological order; whereas, Matthew merely makes the point of the lesson. Undoubtedly Mark's sequence of events is the literal account. Carson sums it up: "If the Triumphal Entry was on Sunday, then, according to Mark, the withering was on Monday; and the disciples' surprise at the tree's quick withering, along with Jesus' words about faith, were on Tuesday."[11]

21:18   "He became hungry" is the significant statement in v. 18 —first, a reminder of His humanity. Jesus felt the same physical needs that every human has felt. His deity did not exclude Him from the normal biological necessities of life. The *kenosis* (Phil. 2:7) was when the Lord laid aside the independent exercise of His divine attributes, including self-sustenance, and became dependent upon the Father to provide His every need (Matt. 4:3-4; 11). Scripture ascribes other human attributes to Jesus, such as anger, fear, disappointment, and physical exhaustion; He indeed knows what His human creature feels. His hunger could be connected to possibly having arisen early for prayer and then departing prematurely in eagerness to return to the temple before the hosts provided a meal.

21:19   The miracle of withering the fig tree stands alone in the marvelous works of Jesus for several reasons. First, this display of

power was a negative demonstration—rather than healing and restoring, He took life from the tree. Second, this use of His power
was in relation only to Himself, not as a ministry to others. These
two unusual facts dictate that close attention be given to this event
so that the lesson intended can be learned.

The scenario has Jesus, hungry and eager to get to Jerusalem,
seeing at a distance a fig tree having leaves. In Palestine, the early
figs often appeared before the leaves;[12] therefore, the Lord's expecting figs to be on the tree was not unreasonable, even though it was
not the normal time for fruit (Mark 11:13). The premature leaves
indicated the possibility of figs. Some concern may be raised regarding Jesus' omniscience and His not knowing the barren nature
of the tree. Again, the point of the *kenosis* (Phil. 2:7) was His refusal
to call upon divine attributes. He, like any other human being, saw
the leaves and correctly assumed that figs might be present.

Christ spoke directly to the tree and pronounced judgment.
Hendriksen does not believe this was an act of punishment: "It is
impossible to believe that the curse which the Lord pronounced
upon this tree was an act of punishing it, as if the tree as such was
responsible for not bearing fruit."[13] But the point is that the tree was
displaying leaves, which indicated the possibility of fruit. Jesus then
took advantage of the tree's deceptive appearance to teach a valuable lesson to His disciples concerning the nation. Israel also put
on a display of being fruitful for God, but the outward appearance
was deceiving—closer scrutiny revealed the absence of fruit.

However, this must be gleaned from the whole context and
allusions to references such as Isaiah 5:1-5 and John 15:1 (the "true"
vine contrasted with the unfruitful vine of Israel). A more immediate application was made by the Lord regarding faith and prayer (v.
21-22; Mark 11:22-24). Often overlooked is the fact that Jesus came
into the world as a man, the Second Adam, or Second Man (Rom.
5:12-19; 1 Cor. 15:45-49). What He did was no different from what
Adam, in his pre-Fall role as ruler of his domain could have done.
Mastery over nature is the prerogative of mankind, a divine commission forfeited by rebellion. What Jesus did would be within the
realm of unfallen mankind and is still possible with faith and prayer.
The qualification for receiving answers to such prayer, however, must
fall within the other God-given conditions, such as if God wills, and

so on. Restored humanity in the kingdom age will execute similar control over nature.

The statement "At once the fig tree withered" was not to imply that the whole tree at once turned brittle and brown. But the tree immediately began the process of dying and started to wither. Mark 11:20 records the disciples' observation that the tree withered "from the roots up," indicating the drying began at the roots and progressed to the top. The withering process began immediately at the Lord's curse.

21:20-22   The emphasis on the lesson to the apostles must not be overlooked. Mark 11:14 makes note that the disciples "were listening," which indicates they were a primary consideration in the event. Then Peter (Mark 11:21), seeing the tree, was "reminded" (*anamnēstheis,* aorist passive of *anamimnēskō*) and, upon remembering the lesson, brought the Lord's attention to the tree. The question as to how it could have happened so quickly relays the effectiveness of the Lord's lesson. It got their attention.

The lesson the Lord brought out was not Israel's lack of fruit (though certainly the analogy could have been implied) but, rather, the power of faith and prayer. Jesus stated that if one has faith, then even more powerful demonstrations of human preeminence over nature would be possible. The calming of the storm and withering of the tree were displays of ruling, and the human creature as God intended him to be was ruler over the natural world. What is lacking in the fallen creature is the faith to exercise this rule. This author does not believe that apart from being redeemed from this sinful body (Rom. 8:20-23) any human other than Jesus will exercise such control; but if faith and prayer were what they should be, such power is possible when in harmony with the purpose of God. Otherwise, the words of Jesus (v. 21) are deceptive and meaningless. Barbieri is certainly correct in concluding, "The object of faith is always the key, and Jesus' admonition was for them to keep their faith focused on the sovereign Lord."[14]

The promise in v. 22, "All things you ask in prayer, believing, you shall receive," is not to be taken as a blanket statement. Other scriptural qualifiers regarding prayer and, using proper hermeneutics, the context of all teachings on prayer must be considered. "All things" are to be understood as all things that are in harmony with the will of God (1 John 5:14) and not asked with the wrong motives (James 4:3).

SECOND DAY IN THE TEMPLE, 21:23-27
(Mark 11:27-33; Luke 20:1-8)

21:23   This would appear to be Tuesday, the day following the tense and stormy cleansing of the temple. The first event of the day seems to have been the religious leadership's challenge to Jesus' authority. "These things" probably refers to the driving out of the merchants as well as to His healing and teaching. On the first day the leaders apparently did not know how to respond and had since counseled together and decided to challenge His authority. The word "authority" (*exousia*) implies one's right to do something and not the power (*dunamis*) to do it. Carson observes, "Their concern in asking who gave him this authority sprang less from a desire to identify him than from a desire to stifle and perhaps ensnare him."[15]

21:24   Jesus' answer, as in so many other confrontations with the religious leaders, reflects His disregard for their right to challenge Him. His response turned the pressure back upon them. He was notifying the crowd and the leadership that He was not under any compulsion to answer them if they were unwilling to answer His question first. Pate points out that this form of counter-question was typical in rabbinical debates[16] and was thus not begging the question.

21:25-26   The question of John's baptism was to force the leaders to commit to one of two actions: either (1) acknowledge John's divine message, which included identifying Jesus as the Messiah (Matt. 3:1-17; John 1:19-34); thus their comment, "He will say to us, 'then why did you not believe him'" (v. 25); or (2) to openly deny John's status as a prophet and thereby draw the crowd's anger upon themselves. In their deliberations (v. 26) they confessed that the people believed John to be a true prophet from God. Luke reveals their fear of being stoned if they denied that John was a prophet (20:6). But their reputations were of more concern than the truth about either John or Jesus. Their own hypocritical politicking had them trapped.

21:27   Their response, "We don't know," exposed their weakness. As leaders, they should have known. Such a response certainly disappointed the people standing by and left Jesus with the stronger position from which He simply refused to answer them. If incapable of determining John's authority, they would not be able to discern His either. The question is, why would Jesus not delight in announcing the basis of His authority? But the people had already acknowledged that He was a prophet, the Son of David, to whom they called out for deliverance (21:9). Jesus did not have to prove His authority to them. He also knew the leaders' corruptness and didn't concern Himself with their approval. Thus, no answer.

PARABLE OF THE TWO SONS, 21:28-32

21:28-30   Matthew alone records this parable. The primary elements are two sons (literally, "children," *tekna*): one who at first refused but then actually did what was asked, and one who immediately gave verbal consent but did not follow through in obedience. The point of a parable is to offer a seed truth, not to allegorize truth, and one should not look for hidden meanings here. The point is, which of the sons did what the father asked? Is obedience to agree verbally but not to do? Or is obedience to do, even if resisted at first? The first son refused, regretted it (*metamelomai,* "have remorse"),[17] and then did the father's work. The second gave lip service but felt no compulsion to do what he was told.

21:31-32   Jesus' question was simple and straightforward, "Who obeyed the father?" Even these hypocrites knew the right answer— the one who ultimately did what the father asked. This was the response Jesus wanted to hear, because it led to His next assault on their self-righteous attitude. "Truly I say to you" opens a shocking proclamation. The tax gatherers (hated by the Jews as greedy traitors) and harlots (whores) would have access to God's kingdom before them (literally, "will go before you into the kingdom of God").

Verse 32 explains the Lord's reasoning. Those rejected by the religious leaders for apparent refusal to obey God (or the leaders) responded to the message of John the Baptist. Jesus said they "believed" (*episteusan*) him, and thus the way of true righteousness was opened for them. On the other hand, the religious leaders did not believe (*ouk episteusate*), failed to gain the way of righteousness, and were therefore themselves the disobedient ones. The kingdom is open to those who obey (that is, those who believe in God's Son as He commands), not to those who give lip service to God but reject His provision of righteousness.

PARABLE OF THE VINEYARD OWNER, 21:33-46
(Mark 12:1-12; Luke 20:9-19)

21:33-39   The details of this parable were not intended to be heavily analyzed for hidden meaning but simply to tell a story of rebellion and arrogance. The landowner (*oikodespotēs*) developed property as an investment and equipped it for rental to make a profit. The vine-growers (*geōrgois,* "tenants, farmers") rented the property and thus entered into a contractual agreement with the owner.

The term "another" (v. 33) connects this parable with the previous one, where Jesus told the chief priests and elders that tax collectors and prostitutes would enter the kingdom before them. The first parable was told in response to their unwillingness to acknowledge John the Baptist's authority as being from God. This parable continued that theme but moved in a direction emphasizing their rebellion and hostility toward God. The parable elements clearly represent God, Israel, and the religious leaders, but attempting to attach metaphoric significance to items such as the long journey or other small details is useless. The point hinges on the landowner's preparation, the contractual agreement, and the owner's anticipation of profit.

Verses 34-36 recount the treachery of the tenants. The time for harvest came, and the landowner sent servants to collect the profit due him. The disloyal farmers, however, beat and murdered the servants. A second force of servants was dispatched and, likewise, was rejected and killed. Again, given the nature of parabolic teaching, trying to find some group to assign to each set of servants would be inappropriate. It is best to simply understand these servants as representative of the sending of prophets to Israel. The two groups of servants sent reflected the landowner's giving the tenants more than one opportunity to do what was right. This possibly refers to the "former and latter prophets" or perhaps to the Law requirement of two or three witnesses being required to bring guilt upon the accused.

Finally, Jesus added the climactic feature that the landowner sent his own son for a final appeal to the farmers to do what was honest (vv. 37-39). This act communicated the seriousness of the situation. The tenants should have naturally respected the owner's son and paid what was due. Instead, their plotting and subsequent murder of the property heir revealed the incredible evil nature of these unworthy tenants. In their twisted sense of reality, they assumed his murder would somehow give them rights to the land. Neither respect for the son nor any remorse for their greed and cruelty was shown—they killed the son, even as they had the servants.

21:40-41   Jesus next called upon the priests and Pharisees to draw a conclusion to the story. The question was simply, what will the owner do? He left it to the instinctive response of those listening to condemn such corrupt behavior. Not yet sensing this to be a lesson about them, even these wicked religionists knew the owner would not tolerate the murder of his son. They referred to the tenants as "wretches" (*kakos,* "evil, bad") and played off that term, predicting a "wretched end" (*kakōs apolesei,* "destroyed severely"). The owner would then, of course, rent the property to others who would pay him when the crops were harvested. Ironically, their correct answer had just described their own fate. Jesus pointed out that the kingdom of God was going to be "taken away from" Israel and given to others, who would produce what God wanted and give God His due produce (v. 43).

In Mark's (12:9) and Luke's accounts (20:16), Jesus Himself gave the answer to the parable, with Luke recording apparent shock on the part of the religious leaders. Neither Mark nor Luke actually state that Jesus Himself answered the question, though that certainly seems most probable. The leaders' response, "May it never be!" (*mē genoito*), implied their horror at the prospect of the tenants' fate. The *mē genoito* may be more of a verbal confirmation of horror at their fate than a response of disbelief to Jesus' story. Matthew offers specific details of how Jesus made His point, whereas Mark and Luke simply record the answer.

21:42   For the fourth time in Matthew's record, Jesus questioned their reading of Scripture, highlighting a certain text (cf. 12:3; 19:4; 21:16, 42). Contemporary Christians may have difficulty in understanding the insulting nature of such a question. It was addressed to those who presented themselves as experts in the Law. Once again

Jesus brought to their attention that their knowledge of Scripture was not as profound as presented to others.

On this occasion Jesus referenced Psalm 118:22-23, which is probably a testimony of David, who was at first rejected and spent his early years living in the wilderness fleeing Saul (1 Sam. 16:10–2 Sam. 2:4). Hendriksen argues that the psalm refers to the nation of Israel, which was looked down upon by other nations but became the head of all nations, and Jesus is the representative of the whole nation.[18] The better reference seems to be to David and then to the "Son of David" (i.e., Jesus, cf. 1 Peter 2:7)—but that is not really critical in understanding the point of the reference. Men may reject Him, but God has already established Him as the chief stone in His program. The connection with the parable is found in the idea of greed for self-gain rather than the desire to honor God, which led to rejecting God's Son. But as the psalm reminded them, God takes what is rejected by rebellious man and crowns His work with it.

21:43-44   Jesus then made applications both to the parable and to the psalm. In the parable, "therefore" more literally is "because of this" (*dia touto*), referring to the reason the kingdom was going to be taken away from these leaders. The causal statement drew an application from the parable in which the tenant farmers did not give the owner his due and even killed his servants and son. Likewise, Israel had rejected and killed the prophets of God and now were about to kill His Son as well. Even as the landowner would rightly take away the land and rent to others, so God would cast out these religious leaders and draw all nations into His kingdom. Carson notes that "the building metaphor makes no explicit allusion to the church: the point is christological not ecclesiastical."[19] The scribes, Pharisees, Sadducees, elders, and priests had rejected God and attempted to establish their own glory. Jesus now came to tear the kingdom away from them and give it to others. The disciples of Christ would now carry out the work of God.

The second application, v. 44,[20] referenced the stone of Psalm 118:22-23. There are two results to rejecting the stone: some fall upon it (*ho pesōn epi ton lithon*), and it falls upon others (*ephē hon dē an pesē*).The first group is "broken to pieces" because of the religious leadership's false teaching—they stumble and fall against the stone, and brokenness and severe judgment result. The second group's being "scattered like dust" was probably a reference to the winnowing process where the chaff was separated from the wheat and scattered by the wind. The second group, then, would be those upon whom the vengeance of the Messiah will fall, exposing them as false prophets and separating them from the true prophets of God. It is a scene of judgment, predicted first by John the Baptist (Matt. 3:12): "His winnowing fork is in His hand . . . and He will gather His wheat into the barn, but He will burn up the chaff with unquenchable fire."

21:45-46   The chief priests and Pharisees now realized that they were the target of His lesson. The more specific term "Pharisee" here simply designated the religious section to which the elders (v. 23) belonged. The idea of their "hearing" (*akouō*) was to "comprehend the meaning." Finally, they understood that the parable was announcing their judgment by the Messiah and that they had pronounced their own doom (v. 41).

Even after comprehension, their response was neither repentance nor remorse but anger and defensiveness. They wanted to get rid of Jesus for His words. How ironic this was in light of the point of the parable (vv. 38-39). However, they "feared the people" and knew an attack upon Jesus would bring assault from the crowds. The people still viewed Jesus as a prophet (even as some religious groups do today) but had not yet recognized Him as the Messiah.

HOMILETICAL SUGGESTIONS

This final week of Jesus' life provides dynamic and challenging insight into the heart and mind of the Lord. As He experienced the exhilarating welcome of the crowds into Jerusalem, He soberly reflected on the necessity of such praise. This was another fulfillment of the Old Testament's allusion to the coming Messiah, and His coming needs to be kept in that original context. Christians often fail to understand that Jesus was the Son of David and that His coming demonstrated God's faithfulness to His promises to David. The Jewish nature of Jesus' mission should not be overlooked in one's zeal to talk about the salvation of all people.

The message of the cleansing of the temple should not be weakened to comply with modern views of Jesus' "gentleness." The passion the Lord felt for this temple reflected the passion we should have for God's work and God's truth. In contemporary Christianity there seems to be far more concern for not offending man than for not offending God. If we are to be Christlike, perhaps we too should be less concerned with political correctness and more concerned with God's name. Studying this part of the life of Christ should be a realistic portrayal of the holy Messiah, who was zealous and aggressive toward the temple.

Clear distinction should be made between the temple and the contemporary church. The temple involved clear covenant responsibilities and was symbolic of Israel's worship and God's presence among His people. Church buildings do not have the same significance.

The conflict with the priests and elders is typical of religious resistance to the work of God. Christians should guard against falling into the trap of becoming so focused on religious tradition and self-righteousness that the true Jesus or the true mission of the church is missed. Today, many Christians fail to see the mission field around them because of their anger over decaying American values or the gross immorality in their midst. This was the mistake of Pharisaism—these men, too, were upset with the sinners of their day and did not see themselves as responsible for bringing the saving knowledge of God to the lost.

MATTHEW
CHAPTER
TWENTY-TWO

FURTHER CONFRONTATIONS
WITH THE RELIGIOUS LEADERS

This chapter continues recording the events of the last week of the Lord's earthly ministry. The dialogue proceeds from chap. 21, where Jesus tells parables of the kingdom to the very ones having the kingdom taken away from them. The tension revealed in 21:45-46 and the first parable of chap. 22 indicate that Jesus was not going to back down from the religious leadership's hostility. Following this parable, they attempted on three occasions to trap or discredit Jesus before the people. The Pharisees and Sadducees, usually enemies, conspired to destroy Him for His condemnation of them. The chapter ends with Jesus putting to silence His enemies.

PARABLE OF THE WEDDING GUESTS, 22:1-14

22:1-2   Matthew alone records this parable, though some suggest that the same parable is recorded in Luke 14:15-24. However, Hendriksen correctly concludes, "It must not be confused with that of the Great Supper (Luke 14:15-24)."[1] The parable fits with the other two relating why the kingdom would be taken from the religious leaders of Israel. The language of v. 1 also indicates a connection, "spoke to them again" (*palin eipen*).

Verse 2 begins the story of the invitation to a great wedding feast, which represents the kingdom of heaven. The king (God) was giving a wedding feast for his son (Christ). Scripture contains several references to Messiah's coming being similar to a marriage (9:15; 25:1; John 3:29; Eph. 5:25-32). The wedding feast was a time of great celebration and joy, and the king obviously wanted to share this great event with those who appeared to be the most worthy.

22:3-6 The invitations were sent, but those first thought worthy rejected the offer. Verse 3 simply states they were "unwilling" to come. "Unwilling" is from *thelō* (here a descriptive imperfect tense indicating nothing more than a factual statement—they did not want to come). The king gave his invited guests a second opportunity (v. 4). Perhaps if they understood that preparations had already begun, the urgency of coming would be realized. This is reminiscent of the previous parable (21:35-37), where more than one attempt to draw the rightful persons to the kingdom was made. The animals were already slaughtered and other foods prepared; thus, the feast could not be delayed. This second appeal indicated the seriousness of the invitation. To refuse at this point insinuated that the invited guests were not concerned for the king or for joining his celebration.

In v. 5, "paid no attention" to his appeals (more literally, "and, they, disregarding [this] went away") indicates that they were too busy with their own interests to have interest in the gracious invitation of the king. What is worse, the messengers who had been sent to invite them were abused and killed (v. 6). In each parable the pattern is evident—the religious leaders were refusing to obey God and were violent toward His servants (the prophets) and even to the Son Himself.

22:7-8 The king's response was retaliation against the obstinate and thankless guests, which is also consistent with the point of the previous parable. The armies ("his armies") would be in reality the Romans, who would come to destroy them and "set their city on fire"—indeed, the very fate of Jerusalem in A.D. 70 under Titus.[2] The king declared these guests "unworthy," though they outwardly had appeared to be the proper guests (v. 8). Their selfish and rude behavior indicated a lack of proper respect for the king, and they were therefore deemed "unworthy" (*ouk . . . hagioi*). Their unworthy status was not based upon their social standing or their religious merit but solely upon their unwillingness to come to the king's feast.

22:9-10 The king sent his servants to find other guests for his feast, instructing them to go to the "main highways" (*tas diexodous* *tōn hodōn,* perhaps major intersecting roads), implying places most people would travel. The broad invitation, "as many as you find there," implies that neither credentials nor achievements were required for the privilege of being at the feast. Verse 10 reveals that both "evil and good" (*ponērous te kai agathous*) were brought in. Thus, not even moral worth was the criterion for entry. This aspect of the story neatly connects back to the first parable, where tax collectors and whores were said to enter the kingdom before the religious leaders (21:31).

22:11-12   Though no qualifications are stated, there was obviously one requirement—the right "wedding clothes." Even though both evil and good guests were in the banquet hall, one person stood out as not being properly attired. The wedding clothes reflected a proper attitude toward the affair, and the other guests obviously knew this and dressed appropriately. Barnes suggests that during this time frame the host customarily provided robes for the meal. He appeals to Genesis 45:22; 2 Kings 10:22; and Esther 6:8; 8:15 to substantiate the practice. He concludes, "This renders the conduct of this man more inexcusable."[3] The verses referenced by Barnes do not prove the assumption; nevertheless, the suggestion may have merit in that it would explain the king's high displeasure with the improperly dressed man.

With formality and cordiality, the king addressed the guest as "friend" (*hetaire,* v. 12), not implying intimacy (more naturally, *philos*) but only politeness. The question dealt with the manner in which, or perhaps the audacity with which, he came without the proper garments. Carson hesitates in identifying the wedding garments as "righteousness," since the wedding party was made up of both "evil and good" guests.[4] While it was true that the guests were "evil and good," this designation was not intended to relate to their moral status before the king since both were present. But if the king granted the garments, as Barnes suggests, that could imply that this guest was not given "righteousness" as were the others. Thus the question, why was he different? Perhaps, rather, the garment was indicative of realizing the privilege and reality of the invitation. Thus, the analogy would be that faith is represented by the garment. Hendriksen proposes that the offense was that this guest turned down the host's provision of a robe because of self-satisfaction or pride.[5]

However, no specific answer is given in the parable. As Hendrickson states, "It is better to leave the symbolism a little vague and say no more than that the man, though invited, did not prepare acceptably for the feast."⁶ The fact that he was speechless attests either to his lack of understanding of what was required or to his sudden realization of the insult to his host.

22:13   The man was not only ejected from the feast but was bound and thrown into a place of torture. Binding "hand and foot" was certainly indicative of severe judgment from which the man had no means of escape. Being thrown into "outer darkness" (*to skotos to exōteron,* "the outmost darkness") can be paralleled with 8:12, where Jesus says "the sons of the kingdom shall be cast out into the outer darkness . . . there shall be weeping and gnashing of teeth" (see also 25:30). The weeping and gnashing of teeth is to portray the horrors of the suffering (cf. 13:42, 50; 24:51).

22:14   The conclusion and lesson to be learned were expressed by the Lord following an explanatory *gar* ("for"). The "many" (*polloi*) represent those "called" (*klētoi*) or invited (as to the feast), and the "few" (*holigoi*) represent those "chosen" (*eklektoi*), those who are actually chosen to stay. The expression could also be understood as "the invitation is general, but the selection of who is accepted is few." This would seem to clearly teach that the kingdom will not be filled with all who are invited (the gospel is preached to all) but only with those who are chosen (those with the proper garments).

THE PHARISEES TRY TO TRAP JESUS, 22:15-22
(Mark 12:13-17; Luke 20:20-26)

22:15   Matthew begins this part of his narrative with the temporal adverb *tote,* which denotes a sequence of events. Having heard the parables and knowing that Jesus was pointing to them—yet, fearing the crowd because the people believed He was a true prophet (21:45-46)—the religious leaders set out to discredit Him. The word "trap" means to "ensnare," as a hunter would set a snare and wait for an animal to step into it. The "snare" was to be His own teaching. Thus these men plotted an intricate question to prompt a radical answer from Jesus that would provoke the Jews against Him.

22:16   The Pharisees sent their disciples to try and catch Jesus off guard, probably assuming He would be suspicious if they them-selves asked the question. The "Herodians" were a branch of Phar-isees who were politically loyal to Herod's dynasty. The poll-tax question demonstrated their desire for the Romans to be against Jesus as well. The Romans had always been favorable to the Hero-dian line, and the loyalty was somewhat mutual.

The disciples of the Pharisees approached Jesus with a typical-ly deceptive tactic—flattery. Calling Him "teacher" (*didaskalos*) not "rabbi" (*rabbi*), they offered feigned respect by acknowledging that He was truthful (but He claimed to be the truth, John 14:6) and that He taught the "way of God in truth." If this had been actually believed, they would not have come with malice in their hearts. Satan often uses flattery to take God's servants off guard. By recog-nizing that He would not "defer" to any man, they meant that He would not compromise God's truth to win the favor of anyone (lit-erally, "it is not of concern to you regarding anyone, for you do not see any person's appearance"). Unlike these men, Jesus neither flat-tered nor ignored people because of their rank or wealth. What these men said was totally correct, but the spirit with which they said it made them hypocrites.

22:17   Their question in and of itself was not wrong. The Jews did argue over whether or not taxes should be paid to a foreign power. The leaders understood, however, the people's resentment regarding the taxes and the unfair treatment by tax collectors. Their devised snare seemed foolproof: if Jesus said the Jews should pay taxes, the people would turn against Him; and if He said the Jews should not pay taxes, the leaders could turn Him in to the Romans for insurrection.

22:18   Jesus was deceived neither by their flattery nor by their pretended concern over payment of taxes. "Malice" is literally "evil intent" (*ponēria*). Rather than playing their coy game, Jesus con-fronted them head on by asking, "Why are you testing Me?" and added further offense with "you hypocrites!" The idea of a hypocrite is one who plays a part, like an actor reading a part in a play while hiding behind a mask. Jesus again demonstrated that He was not concerned to any degree with offending those who rejected Him.

22:19-20   By asking for the show of a coin, Jesus shifted the focus back to them. They presented a denarius, which was appar-ently the coin used for paying the Roman government tax. It should not be confused with the temple tax of 17:24-27. The question (v. 20) was simple enough but equally clever. The image on the coin in their possession was Caesar's, which could have been a violation of their law against graven images.

22:21-22 Minted Roman coins bore the current emperor's image on one side, bore other government emblems on the reverse side, and thus was quite similar to American currency having both presidential images and governmental emblems. His answer was therefore simple: if Caesar's image is on the coin, it is rightfully Caesar's (by virtue of his image representing his government's financial status). Jesus answered the question by pointing to responsibility toward human government—obedience and payment of what was due (cf. Rom. 13:1-7)—but also added the responsibility of giving to God what was due Him. How could they condemn Him for this answer? They could not spring their trap and were forced to leave without having accomplished their goal.

SADDUCEES ATTEMPT TO EMBARRASS JESUS, 22:23-33 (Mark 12:18-27; LUKE 20:27-40)

22:23-24 Matthew records Jesus' next challenge as happening that same day. This time His opponents were the Sadducees. "On that day" (NASB; or "that same day," NIV) is, more literally, "in that hour," (*en ekeinē tē hēmera*).

Sadducees were the more liberal and rationalistic of the religious groups. Though recognizing the Pentateuch as divine Scripture and verbally endorsing its authority, the Sadducees did not give equal recognition to the rest of Scripture and openly denied any value to oral tradition.[7] In matters of the supernatural (even as recorded in the Pentateuch), especially the resurrection of the dead, this sect refused to accept biblical teachings. Other tendencies included being very materialistic, more relational toward the Romans, and legalistic, believing in the severe exercise of the judicial system. Josephus (a Pharisee) said, "The Sadducees are able to persuade none but the rich, and have not the populace obsequious to them, but the Pharisees have the multitude on their side.[8] Marvin Pate offers an excellent summary of this particular religious sect.[9]

Their question (v. 24), like that of the Pharisees' disciples and the Herodians, was not a sincere seeking of truth. They proposed a hypothetical situation that reflected their commitment to the legal code of Moses, but also which they believed would make Jesus look foolish because of His resurrection teachings. After all, these rationalists and materialists could hardly imagine a more ludicrous view of reality than one woman being fought over by all these husbands. Their view would not permit the possibility of life beyond this physical existence. The Sadducees made reference to Deuteronomy 25:5, where the Law gives a man the option to marry his brother's widow to provide her with a child.

22:25-28 The situation was exaggerated to seven brothers to make feasibility look more ridiculous. The possibility that not one of the seven husbands could give her a child was not only highly improbable but certainly not a real-life situation. Without warrant of any Old Testament verification, they also assumed the marital state would continue beyond this life. There was also an indication they held to the view that a woman could not have numerous husbands. The question, "Whose wife of the seven will she be" (v. 28) was stated to indicate that she could have only one. The comment "they all had her" suggests their view that the marital relationship indicated ownership. They thought this would make Jesus commit the blunder of trying to make her the wife of all seven (adultery) or else confess that there must not be a resurrection. One wonders if this was a favorite argument the Sadducees used against the Pharisees to disprove the resurrection.

22:29 Jesus' response was once again blunt and unflattering. "You are mistaken" (present middle indicative, second person plural of *planaō*) might also be translated "You have deceived yourselves" or "You misled yourselves." He explained why they went astray in their thinking: "not understanding the Scriptures." Had they recognized the authority of all the Scriptures, such as Isaiah 26:19, Daniel 12:2, and Job 19:25-27, they would have known that resurrection was clearly taught.

Their other problem was not understanding the "power of God" (*tēn dunamin tou Theou*). The idea of "power" is the exertion of a dynamic force, and they were ignorant of God's dynamic energy, which is greater than even the force of death. Their view of God was too small. They believed His authority or influence was limited to the realm of the material world—thus, part of their failure lay in a weak view of God. The Sadducees were ignorant of the fact that

He was "capable of raising the dead to an existence quite unlike this present one."[10]

22:30   Here is one of Scripture's rare insights into postresurrection life. Jesus explained (explanatory *gar*) how they erred concerning the resurrection. In the resurrected life, people neither marry nor are given in marriage (*gamousin oute gamizontai*). This clause reflects both male (do not "marry") and female (not "given in marriage") roles. It is important to note that attempting to transfer earthly standards to the resurrected life can only lead to ignorance of the reality of the immortal life. Most seem to assume that the issue of marriage is related to reproduction;[11] that is, since there will be no death, there will be no need for procreation and therefore no need for marriage. While not totally objectionable, this view does not treat marriage with the full dignity required. The purpose of marriage is not only procreation. Certainly, the Sadducees were focusing on the obligation of a man to impregnate his brother's widow, but Jesus' answer was not limited to that aspect. God designed male and female to be partners and intimate companions, not just reproduction units. Marriage, the legal contractual element with which the Sadducees would be concerned, was the key question here: "Whose wife of the seven shall she be?" In other words, who had claim to her? Jesus' answer implied that such associations would be no longer binding (with which Paul agrees, Rom. 7:1-2).

The next statement, "but they are like the angels in heaven" (*hōs angeloi en tō ouranō*), is difficult simply because so many misconceptions about angels and so little real information concerning their nature and essence exist. This commentary cannot provide a full angelology and must here concentrate only on the possible meaning in Christ's words. The most obvious reason for the comparison with angels is that the Sadducees denied their existence in any form (Acts 23:8). Jesus therefore was emphasizing their ignorance of all nonmaterial creatures and was doubling His rectification of their error. To be "as the angels" does not require being of the same essence, since they are incorporeal spirits, but resurrected humans will have material (though glorified) bodies. Jesus statement was merely a clear assessment that angels are not bound by marital relationships. Scriptural analysis does not indicate angel reproduction; furthermore, angels are only referred to in the masculine gender. Angels are not the spirits of departed humans and do not have normative human qualities. Therefore, to assume Jesus was saying that resurrected humans will not reproduce because of angelic likeness is to be too concerned with only one aspect of the marital bond and jump to the conclusion that resurrected people will be either sexless or all males.

Angels[12] are totally and exclusively dedicated to God, and in the resurrection glorified human beings will be totally and exclusively dedicated to God. No human relationship will impede one's unqualified intimacy with Christ. One's love for other human beings will not be depleted, but the only "marriage" relationship will be with God in His pure form.

22:31-32   Jesus, knowing the Sadducees acknowledged only the Pentateuch as authoritative Scripture, challenged them concerning their failure to know of the Pentateuchal assumption of the resurrection. Notice that He says it was written "to you [it was their responsibility to know and acknowledge] by God" (attributing to Exodus, and thus to Moses, divine authority) concerning the resurrection (v. 31). Therefore, they were accountable for their erroneous view of the resurrection.

The reference (v. 32) was to Exodus 3:6, part of the Scripture recognized by the Sadducees as inspired text, where God tells Moses that He is the God of Abraham, Isaac, and Jacob (the triad of patriarchs upon whom the Jews depended for identity and covenant with God). His point was, is God's domain only over formerly existing beings? Is His rule only to be applied to people who no longer exist except in a people's writings? How ridiculous. The Sadducees realized the implication of the lesson—Abraham, Isaac, and Jacob, though dead hundreds of years before Moses, were being held up as proof that God had not forgotten His covenant with them. If they no longer existed because their material life had ended, then how could He be their God?

22:33   The people listening to the discussion were impressed with the logic of Jesus' answer. It is worth noting that even though the conversation was between Jesus and His opponents, the crowds were always listening (as in 5:1-2–7:28). Their reaction was as in the past: "they were astonished [*ekplēssomai,* "amazed"] at His teaching." Not the content, as most Jews believed in the resurrection, but His style of argumentation and the irrefutable wisdom of His answers generated this amazement. The best understanding of this is given in Matthew 7:29, "For He was teaching them as one having authority, and not as their scribes." In other words, Jesus did not present numerous views of popular rabbis and depend on tradition to prove His points. He went directly to Scripture and based His arguments upon the authority of God's Word, not upon contemporary or past opinion.

ANOTHER TEST, THE LAWYER'S QUESTION, 22:34-40 (MARK 12:28-34; LUKE 10:25-28)

22:34-35 Attempts to discredit or condemn Jesus continued. Even after hearing that He silenced the Sadducees as He had them, the Pharisees immediately "gathered themselves together" and apparently devised another plan. A lawyer (*nomikos,* an expert in Mosaic Law) came to Jesus with yet another question, though having the same motive, "testing Him."

22:36 The lawyer addressed Him as "Teacher" (*didaskalos*), not rabbi, which indicated recognition of His skill in teaching and the presence of a following but at the same time not giving Him the dignity of being a recognized leader among the Jews that "rabbi" would imply. The question attempted to lead Jesus to choose a "favorite" law or the most significant law in His estimation. More literally, it could be translated, "Which commandment is great in the Law?" or possibly, "What sort of commandment in the Law is great?" "Great" (*megalē*) is not a comparative in the form used here, but the dative, *en tō nomō,* would indicate a comparative use. The idea would be "Among the commandments in the Law, which is greatest?"

22:37-38 The Lord answered with no apparent hesitation: the greatest is Deuteronomy 6:5, which places one's attitude toward God as the most important commandment. Jesus did not quote one of the Ten Commandments, but such designation is more a Christianized nomenclature than a true understanding of the Law. The Mosaic Law contains 613 commandments, and the rabbis often debated as to which were great and which were rather insignificant.

Deuteronomy 6:5 instructs Israel to love God with their whole being. This may not be the kind of commandment the lawyer had in mind, but Jesus was reminding the Jews that God wanted their hearts, not religious observances. Yahweh commanded the Jews to love (*'hb*) Him (their God, *'loheycha*) with all their heart (*lēbab*), which refers to their inner being, mind, or heart, and with all their soul (*nepscha*), that is, with all their life energies, and with all their might (*me'odecha*), which is one's "abundance, force, might." This was a descriptive way of saying that God demanded the whole being—everything that made a person a living being was to love Yahweh his God.

In application, Jesus altered the wording. Instead of "might" as the last aspect of one's being, Jesus stated "mind" (*dianoia,* "mind, understanding"). The LXX translates the Hebrew *me'odecha* by the Greek *dunameōs* ("power"), which would be a good translation, but Jesus used the word for mind, or understanding, to make a point. The Jews were zealous in their religious life and pursued God with great fervor (Rom. 10:1-2). Jesus noted that their zeal was misguided and that they were to love God with their understanding also. Religious zeal is not a substitute for correct theology.

Jesus simply stated (v. 38), "This is the great and foremost commandment." Thus He concluded that Deuteronomy 6:5 is "great" (*megalē*) or "remarkable in magnitude" but then also added that the first (*prōtē*) meaning has priority. The word "great" is artic- ular (having the definite article, *tē megalē*), which individualizes or particularizes it: "the great commandment" among the command- ments. The word "first" is an adjective ascribing prominence or superior importance to its antecedent ("commandment"). Therefore Jesus was stating that the commandment to love God with one's whole being is the most distinguished and preeminent of all the commandments.

22:39 Jesus added a second great commandment, which was "like" the first. "Second" (*deutera*) suggests a listing in rank of importance or significance, and this would be number two. He ref- erenced Leviticus 19:18, and its similarity ("like it," *homoia*) lies in the qualification for love. The primary responsibility of God's peo- ple is to love God; the second is to love one's neighbor.

The most significant issue in this command is understanding who one's neighbor would be. The word (*plēsion*) basically refers to one who is close by. This nearness does not need to be taken in the sense of actual physical proximity but may refer to nearness in some connection of spirit or nature. An example is Matthew 5:43, by showing contrast, "Love your neighbor, hate your enemy." An enemy may live next door, but the status of "enemy" lies in animosity of spirit or cause. A neighbor is one with whom a common alliance has been formed.

It is incorrect to reach *prima facie* conclusions from Luke 10:29-37, where the point is not that a neighbor is whoever is in need. Rather, being a neighbor is not based upon social, religious, or economic status but upon loving others and giving of oneself. The parable is not defining "neighbor" but teaching an attitude of neighboring, which was to be demonstrated by loving another, regardless of ethnic or social station.

Clement of Alexandria seems to use the term in his letter to the Corinthians in reference to the community of Christ.[13] This is consistent with New Testament use as well where the Old Testament concept of fellow Hebrews being "neighbors" is related (Acts 7:26-27). It is also consistent with the context to which Jesus referred (Lev. 19:18) and of fellow Christians as "neighbors" (Rom. 15:2; Eph. 4:25; James 4:11-12). Thus, one should not allow the humanistic view of anyone's being a "neighbor" to weaken the implication. This passage must be considered as directly applied in John 13:34-35. Should one understand the command to love (*agapaō*) one's neighbor as to love every human being, then there would be nothing significant or unique about John 13:35, which is to mark Christians as Christ's disciples. Though every person, having been made in the image of God and therefore having worth, should be treated with respect and concern, the love Christians have for one another is to be unique, standing as a living testimony to our connection with Jesus.

To love a fellow believer "as oneself" does not mean that one must learn to love oneself. The assumption is that self-love (not self-esteem or liking oneself) is an intuitive drive to take care of oneself. To protect oneself and to care for one's own needs is instinctive. Love, *agapaō*, is a self-sacrificing giving of oneself—as Jesus gave Himself without reservation for us. This second command is to care for others even as one cares for self. Agape love is not an emotion but a commitment to give what others need. This is illustrated in 1 John 3:14-18. To be willing to give sacrificially to the needs of a fellow believer is the second greatest commandment.

22:40 Jesus' concluding remark is truly phenomenal. The purpose and intent of all the commandments (613 by most rabbinical count) is fulfilled in keeping these two: love God with all your being, and love your neighbor in the same way you love yourself. If one loves both God and his/her neighbor in this manner, the purpose and intent of any law will not be broken. For example, if a man loves his God and his wife, there is no need for a commandment not to commit adultery. Adultery offends God and causes pain and shame to his wife. Love (*agapē,* commitment to sacrifice for others, not the emotion) will forbid him to commit an act that causes such pain. Therefore, the purpose of the commandment is fulfilled in the act of loving.

JESUS CHALLENGES THE PHARISEES, 22:41-46
(Mark 12:35-37; Luke 20:41-44)

22:41-42   Then the Lord reversed the situation by asking the Pharisees a question to trap them. The comment "while the Pharisees were gathered together" (*sunēgmenōn*) is to help the reader envision the huddling body of Pharisees trying to plot a way to ensnare Jesus. Matthew alone mentions that Jesus directed His question to this particular group.

Jesus questioned them in relation to Messiah (v. 42). The word "Christ" (*Christos,* "Anointed One") is the Greek equivalent of the Hebrew *mashiach* or the Greek *Messia* (John 1:41), the "Anointed One," that is, "the Messiah." He asked them to identify who they anticipated the Messiah to be. The question, "Whose Son is He?" refers to His biological lineage. Their response was correct—the "Son of David" (cf. 2 Sam. 7:12-13; Isa. 11:1-10; Jer. 23:5-6).

22:43-45   Even though correct, their answer was not sufficient for understanding the true nature of Messiah. As Carson notes, "This view, though not wrong, is too simple because, as Jesus points out, David called the Messiah his Lord (v. 43)."[14] It is also significant that Jesus emphasized that David spoke by the Spirit (*en pneumati kalei*), calling the Messiah Lord (*kurios,* "master"). The Lord's question implied that David recognized his descendant as being of greater significance than himself. Since David was speaking in the Spirit of a person not yet born and calling Him Lord, it must be acknowledged that this Messiah was superior to David and not just a human descendant.

Jesus quoted Psalm 110:1 (v. 44),[15] where the Lord ("Yahweh" in the Hebrew) is speaking to David's lord (*adonai,* "my master"), promising to make his enemies his footstool. The point is, who is David calling his lord (v. 45)? It would have been improper and inconsistent with views of patriarchal protocol to address a mere descendant in such a manner. Barnes notes that if the person being addressed as "lord" was not already in existence, then how could David make this statement? He questions, "If he was then David's lord—if he was his superior—if he had an existence at that time— how could he be descended from him?"[16]

22:46   The Lord's question achieved two objectives: (1) the Pharisees could not answer the question concerning Messiah's superiority over David, which meant that their assumptions about Him needed to be reevaluated; (2) the attempts to trap Him with hypocritical questions were stopped. Hendriksen rightly summarizes, "Jesus had vanquished these foes so completely that rebuttal had become impossible."[17]

HOMILETICAL SUGGESTIONS

For many, the concept of being Christlike is limited to pleasant thoughts of His feeding, healing, and forgiving. Truly these actions demonstrated what Christ is like, but this is only one dimension of Christ's Person and work. This chapter continues from chap. 21 to emphasize another aspect of His being, which is His unwillingness to accept religious hypocrisy. Jesus' primary target of condemnation was not the immoral people of His day but rather the self-righteous Scripture-quoters.

Jesus was anything but politically correct in His time and place. He was committed to upholding truth even if it angered and brought persecution from the religious leadership. Jesus upset their religious system, which had a foundation of truth but had been subtly conformed to the standards of pious zealots. These leaders were failing to represent God as One who cares for sinners and was willing to forgive. By emphasizing their own holiness and being unwilling to deal lovingly and compassionately with sinners, they had made themselves enemies of the Messiah. He did not hesitate to expose their failure to correctly represent God.

Some condemn this aspect of Christlikeness in Christianity today, because dealing with failure within the church makes people uncomfortable. Pointing at homosexuality, abortion, drug use, sexual promiscuity, and numerous other sins and condemning those involved is easier than examining our own hearts and motives. Yet this is the lesson of the last week of Christ's life. He focused on the need for God's people to remain humble and to seek out the lost. The message of the church is the "good news" of hope for the lost—not just when they quit sinning but while yet sinners (Rom. 5:8). This is not to imply excusing or ignoring sin but to draw attention to maintaining the focus of Christ, not excusing or ignoring self-righteous religion.

The religious leaders of Jesus' time tried to trap Him, publicly embarrass Him, and turn the people away from Him. Christians need to see this ugly side of self-righteous religion. Is a church pharisaical? Let the church examine its attitude toward the lost. Is a church actually in conflict with Christ's mission? Let the church examine its outreach efforts and its willingness to be open to dialogue with the unsaved. Has the church become so pious that the unsaved would feel unwanted if invited to meetings or home Bible studies? Has the church forgotten that we are no more than sinners saved by grace? Challenge the church to be humble and to realize that apart from God's undeserved mercy, believers are no better than the worst sinner.

MATTHEW
CHAPTER
TWENTY-THREE

WARNINGS RELATED TO SCRIBES AND PHARISEES

This chapter follows closely on the revelation that Jesus had put to silence the religious leaders who sought to trap Him in some teaching that might bring Him into disfavor with the populace. The topic of the chapter relates directly to that final mastery over His enemies and centers on warnings about and to the scribes and Pharisees. Verses 13-33 contain a powerful condemnation of the failure of these men who tried so hard to be religiously perfect. The chapter concludes with a tender and compassionate song of lament over the Holy City, which had killed its prophets and was unwilling to be gathered back to God.

INSTRUCTIONS RELATED TO SCRIBES AND PHARISEES, 23:1-12 (Mark 12:38-40; Luke 20:45-47)

23:1-2   Matthew again uses the temporal adverb *tote*, suggesting a chronological connection between these sayings and what preceded. Having silenced His enemies, Jesus now turned His attention to those who had been standing near and listening. He spoke to the crowd (*ochlois*) and to His disciples. Thus, this warning was to those who considered the scribes and Pharisees as teachers of the Law and also to His disciples, who would become the primary teachers of the new assembly of followers after His ascension. Carson points out that this was not His first denunciation of these religious hypocrites, "Perhaps a year earlier Jesus had begun to denounce the Pharisees (15:7)."[1]

The "seat of Moses" (v. 2) refers to the position of Moses as the leader of Israel. France suggests, "The expression "Moses' seat" (Matt. 23:2) may therefore be figurative, indicating the authority of the teacher who, like Moses, speaks in God's name."[2] This position of authority had been claimed by "the scribes and the Pharisees" (*hoi grammateis kai hoi Pharisaioi*). The repetition of the definite article before each group indicates that Jesus was separating them into two distinct parties. This was unusual in that the scribes were nearly always Pharisees and thus grouped together with them. Here the emphasis was probably to distinguish both scholars and religionists, such as saying "theologians and pastors" in our setting. This would not mean that some theologians could not also be pastors (or vice versa), but it emphasizes two aspects of ministry.

23:3 Because of this position of authority ("therefore," *oun,* indicates to draw a conclusion), attention was to be given when they spoke (*eipōsin,* second aorist subjunctive, third person plural from *legō*) the Scriptures. The main point of the Lord's argument should not be missed. The instruction was not to give blanket endorsement of whatever these religious leaders said; it was to recognize the authority of Moses but also to expose their hypocrisy. There was a strong contrast between what they said and what they did, and this was the Lord's way of drawing attention to their lip-service.

The second part of the instruction was *not* to do what they did. Whereas the crowd and disciples were to keep the words of Moses that these men spoke, they were also to realize that the works (*ta erga autōn*) of these religious leaders were not examples of how to keep the Law of Moses. One must not think that Jesus was implying that the Pharisees got drunk or were immoral. Their "works" were self-righteous efforts to attain religious perfection. These leaders read the words of Moses but failed to understand the lesson of dependence upon God and the need to confess their sin. Instead, they created a religious system to display their moral superiority.

The stated reason for not imitating the religious deeds of the scribes and Pharisees was that they said the right things but did not practice the things preached. The expression was literally "They are saying but not doing" (*legousin gar ou poiousin*). The first warning related to the Pharisees and scribes, then, was not to be like them.

Those who follow Christ must not just talk about Scripture but do what it says.

23:4   Verse 4 begins a list of three major illustrations as to why these leaders were not to be imitated. First, they burdened others. The illustration portrays creating burdens rather than assisting people with their already oppressive loads. Instead of helping mankind find God's grace and mercy, their religious legalism abused their position of sitting "in Moses' seat." The contrast between the religious leaders and Jesus can be seen in His own attitude and this condemnation of their practices. Matthew 11:28-30 records Jesus' appeal for the religiously exhausted to come to Him and find rest because He did not demand the impossible legalism of the self-righteous. The religious leadership felt no compassion for those oppressed by sin and failure, and the comment "are unwilling to move them with so much as a finger" reveals their hard-heartedness.

23:5   The second charge leveled against the scribes and Pharisees was that their motives for religious zeal were purely egotistical. They did all their deeds (*erga,* same as in v. 3) to be seen (*theaomai,* "noticed, as to put on display") by men. To attract attention to themselves, they "broadened their phylacteries." Phylacteries, small leather boxes attached to the forehead and left arm with leather straps, are not mentioned in the Old Testament, but their use seems to have derived from a very literal application of Exodus 13:9-10. Small scrolls containing a portion of Scripture (Ex. 13:1-10; 13:11-16; Deut. 6:4-9; 11:13-21) were kept in the boxes. Increasing the size of the phylacteries more readily drew attention to the wearer and also aided in identification from a distance. Apparently, the original intent of this practice was to prompt observance of the Law; but, like so many other well-intentioned religious practices, it soon became an empty symbol. Edersheim offers some helpful discussion on this topic.[3]

These religious leaders also "lengthened the tassels of their garments" (literally, "make greater their fringes"). Many Jews wore prayer shawls or attached fringe to their outer garments in obedience to Numbers 15:37-41 and Deuteronomy 22:12. Jesus appears to have worn such tassels on His garments as well (9:20; 14:36). The tassels were to serve as a reminder to obey the Lord's commandments (Num. 15:39). But once again the Pharisees and scribes perverted the purpose, and the tassels became demonstrations of their confidence that they did keep the commandments. Thus, their length was exaggerated that they might appear even more spiritual. **23:6-7** The third display of arrogance was seen in their competition to be recognized and in the public arena, evidenced by being fond of (*phileō*) the prominent seats at banquets and in the synagogues. Having the privileged positions was important to their sense of worth. Chief seats in the synagogues were benches located at the front, closest to the scrolls and in full view of anyone entering the assembly. These men loved public attention and eagerly sought to place themselves in positions coveted by others. James warns Christians against being guilty of giving "important" seats to the wealthy and influential (James 2:2-3), and Jesus parabolically warned against coveting such places (Luke 14:8-10).

Verse 7 indicates that they loved public recognition, even in common settings such as the marketplace. Their being greeted implied having been singled out and recognized as important persons among commoners. These leaders also coveted the title of rabbi, which was more than just "teacher." Rabbis were viewed as wise, superior to others, and spiritual advisers. Their disciples served them and sat at their feet with great reverence and gratitude. Thus, these religious frauds loved being classified as the elite in their community, and for this Christ condemned them.

23:8-10 Jesus next gave a list of restrictions connected with His last denunciation, "They love . . . being called rabbi." Their failure related to their desire to be recognized as someone significant. Carson notes the emphatic "you" (*humeis,* not translated in the NASB) and recognizes that Jesus was probably speaking directly to His disciples instead of to the whole crowd.[4] The use of rabbi (*hrabbi*) in this context along with teacher (*didaskalos*) connotes a connection between the two terms. A rabbi was viewed as one having authority beyond the material taught, and Jesus' disciples were forbidden to take this title. The reason was that there was only one teacher (*didaskalos*), Jesus Himself. The disciples were brothers (implying equals). The major point here was that no individual disciple would be superior, but all would be equal. The Lord Himself was the only one recognized as rabbi. Since "teachers" are later listed as a gift that Christ gives His universal church (Eph. 4:11), apparently the use here was in the sense of prideful position, not the genuine function of teacher of God's truth.

A second prohibition (v. 9) applied to the designation "father." This term, like "teacher" or "rabbi" in the previous verse, related to a religious title and not to the familial nomenclature of everyday use. The disciples were forbidden to call any man "father" in the sense of recognizing him as their spiritual authority. The reason stated was that only one Father exists, and that is the heavenly Father. The father was the ultimate authority over the household and in patristic terms was the primal source of the family. For any man to presume to be the fountainhead of those in the faith or the ultimate authority over God's flock was to usurp a position that only God is to occupy. Terms have both a generic meaning and a specialized meaning in particular contexts (such as "apostle," "deacon," "elder," and here "teacher" and "father").

The third restriction was on being called "leader" (*kathēgētai*, "teacher, leader, master"). Once again applying the basic hermeneutical principle of harmony of Scripture, it is understood that being a leader was not forbidden, but desiring the recognition of being a leader was being discouraged. The overall emphasis was on the Pharisees' and scribes' error of coveting prominence. Thus a proper understanding of these prohibitions must relate to this theme of seeking self-glory.

23:11-12   The conclusion was a reiteration of the lesson already presented (vv. 20:26)—to be significant in the kingdom requires a humble spirit of servanthood. If one is concerned with titles (such as teacher, rabbi, father, or leader), then apparently he has failed to understand this basic principle of the kingdom. Jesus' conclusion was stated in simple terms, "The greatest among you shall be your servant." The word "servant" is *diakonos,* which later became a technical term for the church office of "deacon." Here, however, it simply meant an attendant.

Verse 12 takes the form of a warning. Self-exaltation is the beginning of a humbling process that will degrade the proud to a position of lower standing. Proverbs 29:23 states a similar principle, "A man's pride will bring him low, but a humble spirit will obtain honor." Carson points out, "The principle enunciated in these verses reflects not natural law but kingdom law."[5] The secular world recognizes and rewards self-assertiveness, and humility is often interpreted as weakness. Peter, who was hearing this, apparently learned the lesson and passed it on to his readers (1 Peter 5:6). In the present context, it is worth noting that the passive voice is used, "shall be humbled" and "shall be exalted." The ultimate act of humbling or exalting is determined by God, not the individual. God's action in this context is based upon the attitude demonstrated by the person.

WARNINGS TO THE SCRIBES AND PHARISEES, 23:13-33

This passage should not be confused with a similar, yet different, passage in Luke (11:42-47). There is no justification for ignoring the different contexts or the differing content of the two accounts. Jesus' method of dealing with the religious leadership may make some uneasy, because He was extremely caustic and aggressive in His condemnation. Seven times Jesus used the expression "scribes and Pharisees, hypocrites." Four times He referenced them as being blind, once as fools, and twice as serpents or vipers. These forms of address are unacceptable in today's politically correct world.

The formulaic warnings began with "woe" (*ouai*), which is an interjection denoting pain or displeasure.[6] Here the interjection denoted strong condemnation and a warning of impending judgment. Some scholars[7] desire to weaken the "woe" to an expression of grief for these men, but this view stems more from a contemporary value system of "gentleness" than from a contextual understanding of Jesus' righteous indignation at these "hypocrites," "blind guides," and "snakes." Seven times the warning was addressed to the scribes and Pharisees in particular, identifying them as hypocrites (*hupocritai*). This label indicated their characteristic of being pretenders. In light of the instructions in vv. 2-7, the word must have referred to their desire to be viewed as spiritual giants rather than sinners saved by God's grace.

23:13-14 The first condemnation was based upon their cutting off the kingdom of heaven from men. The accusation dealt with their culpability as the teachers and spiritual leaders who, by their rejection of Messiah and their opposition to His truth, had shut off the way into the kingdom. By their stubborn resistance to Jesus, they not only kept themselves out of the kingdom, but, worse, even those apparently seeking the kingdom (those who were "entering") were turned aside by the leadership's perversion of the truth.

There are strong reasons for doubting the textual credibility of v. 14. Even in manuscripts that contain the verse, numerous variants suggest some confusion. To assume that a later scribe inserted this verse, borrowing from Mark 12:40, is best. Being taken from another passage means that it is still truth, though not actually a part of Matthew's record. What is said in Mark is that the religious leaders took advantage of widows (who had no male head) by long prayers, which gave the appearance of spirituality. For this abuse, a more severe condemnation will be faced.[8]

23:15   This verse condemns the leaders for not being satisfied with perverting the Jews only but going also on missionary expeditions to convert others to their false brand of Judaism. By converting these to their religion, they made them "twice as much a son of hell" as they were themselves. Barnes explains, "To be a child of hell was a Hebrew phrase signifying to be deserving of Hell."[9] Meyer suggests the phrase "twice as much . . . as yourselves" should be understood as "because superstition and error usually appear with a twofold greater intensity in the taught than in the teachers."[10]

23:16-17   The next woe was targeted at the same group, but He addressed them as "blind guides" to point out their leading others astray. "Guide" here does not refer to the professional service of guiding but probably just to one who leads another, such as one would lead a blind man (15:14). Their own blindness was demonstrated by their perversion of the truth of the superiority of the temple over the things within it. The "temple" (*naos*) refers to the sanctuary, or the inner part, of the structure.

Their argument was that the gold used in the temple was superior to the temple itself. Alford believes the gold was not the ornamental gold that decorated the building but rather the Corban (treasury gold).[11] Meyer also points out that expressions such as "by the gold which belongs to the temple" is frequently found in the Mishnah and concludes that it refers to "the ornaments, the vessels, perhaps also the gold in the sacred treasury."[12] It is best to understand the reference to be to any gold in the temple. In other words, the material worth of the temple was viewed as more valuable than the function of the temple.

The implication was that swearing an oath obligated (*opheilō,* "put one in debt to") the one making the oath to the person or object called upon to verify the oath. Thus, the leaders were teaching that the gold was more binding than the temple itself. For this devaluing of the temple, Jesus pointed out their blindness and pronounced this woe upon them.

Jesus also called them "fools" (*mōroi,* "foolish, stupid," v. 17), which sometimes also bears the connotation of being obstinate or godless, and He again referred to their being blind. The word "fool" is used ironically by Paul, who calls himself a fool compared to the "prudent" (*phronimos,* "wise, sensible, thoughtful") Corinthians (1 Cor. 4:10). This contrast would indicate that a fool was a person who was not sensible (did not think rationally or with "common sense"). God's wisdom, in contrast to human "wisdom," is "foolish" (1 Cor. 2:14). The religious leaders could not see the logical outcome of His work; therefore to them it was foolish.

Perhaps the most perplexing use of the word "fool" is in 5:22: "Whoever shall say, 'you fool,' shall be guilty enough to go into the fiery hell." The apparent contradiction comes from the fact that the One who makes the statement of 5:22 is also the One who has just called these men fools. The context of 5:22 is condemnation of a wicked heart that sought to slander or otherwise injure another person. But here, as also in 7:26, the word is used to indicate the lack of common sense demonstrated by opposing God's truth and His Messiah. It points up the foolishness of confusing the worth of material things with the worth of God's temple. Jesus was not attacking His opponents out of a wicked heart (as is warned against in 5:22) but was speaking for the benefit of all those around: those who view God and His temple with such carnal values are fools. The rhetorical question ("Which is more important?") was intended to communicate this.

23:18-19   Jesus continued pronouncing the same woe, using another example of their backward value system. Verse 18 again references what the Pharisees taught—to swear an oath on the altar was not binding; it was the object sacrificed that bound the one taking the oath. Again Jesus used the address "blind [men]," which carried the accusation of being unable to realistically view the situation. He pointed out that the altar was superior to the offering by use of the rhetorical question, "Which is more important?" Offerings burned up and were gone, but the altar was that permanent tool that presented the offering to God. In addition, the altar was a part of the temple itself and was therefore more important. Their failure to understand this demonstrated their blindness.

23:20-22 Jesus' conclusion to this section was introduced by "therefore," indicating that He was going to offer the correct teaching that these blind guides had failed to see. They had established a false dichotomy between the things of God and the offerings to God. The issue was God—the One who received the offering and the One who owned the temple and everything within it. Jesus also pointed out that God dwelt in His temple (v. 21), which was a reminder to the Jews of their great heritage and the covenant made with Solomon regarding the temple (1 Kings 8:12-53; 9:1-9).

A unique building, the temple had specific blessings and warnings attached to it, and Christians have no right to equate their local church building with the temple. Such confusion takes away from the significance of Christ's words and the promises made to Israel. Taking an oath was to be a sobering act (note Christ's instruction to His followers, 5:34-37), not some formulaic ritual as these had made it. One should also notice the identification of heaven (*ouranos*) as the "throne of God." God sits upon heaven as a throne. Those who swear by heaven call upon God to verify their words, and God regards this as a serious affair. Thus, woe to those who were blind to what oath-taking required.

23:23-24 The next woe was related to their fanatical practice of tithing. The word "tithe" is from the Middle English and correctly translates the Greek *apodekatoō,* "to give a tenth." Tithing was a form of tax used by rulers as far back as ancient Babylon, Persia, and Egypt. Prior to the Law of Moses, Abraham paid a tenth of the spoils of war to Melchizedek (Gen. 14:20). Contemporary Christian tithing usually requires church members to give ten percent of weekly or monthly income to the church. But tithing in the biblical sense was actually far more complicated. The tenth was not based just upon income (some today even tithe only net income, not the gross) but on all properties and livestock. One should carefully study Leviticus 27:30-33 and Deuteronomy 14:22-29 for some understanding of the practice. Josephus explains that the purpose of the tithe was to provide for the Levitical priests, who were not given a portion of the land upon which to grow crops or raise herds.[13] Numbers 18:20-24 clearly states that the tithe of Israel was to go to the priests because they had no other source of income, not being allowed to own property, raise herds, or inherit any other portion of Israel's material wealth. Freeman offers a good discussion on this topic.[14] The temple itself was supported by taxes and offerings. Contemporary tithing to maintain church property and staff salary is not truly a representation of tithing. However, the principle is not wrong as long as the practice does not become a legalistic measure of obedience to God. Nowhere does the New Testament require or even assume a tithe. Giving is to be done as a freewill offering to God to perpetuate the ministry and to support those who have dedicated their lives to Christ's service. The amount given is to be based on one's view of God's gracious provision (e.g., 2 Cor. 8:1-8; 9:6-13).

The hypocrisy of the scribes and Pharisees was demonstrated by the fanatical tithing of even their household herbs, while they overlooked the more crucial points of the Mosaic Law. This is certainly typical of legalism—focusing on minute details of external religious acts but failing to act upon the more important principles behind the Law. Christ did not tell these men to stop tithing their herbs (the law actually required tithing of even seeds, Lev. 27:30) but to not neglect (*aphiēmi*, "dismiss, lay aside") the "weightier provisions of the law." Note that these "weightier provision" ("more serious matters") were named: justice, mercy, and faithfulness. Justice (*krisin*) is a forensic term indicating fair treatment from the law. God's Law is designed to protect the helpless or disadvantaged (which is why loving one's neighbor fulfills the Law), but the religious leaders used it to take advantage of the weak. Mercy (*eleos*) is characteristic of God's dealing with sinful mankind, yet these who claimed to be God's spokesmen failed to be merciful. They instead created heavy burdens for others and refused to bear anyone else's burden (v. 4). Faithfulness (*pistis*), also characteristic of God, implies trustworthiness and dependability. These hypocrites were too busy taking care of themselves (vv. 5-7) to be concerned with being available and responsible for others.

Jesus said they should do both: tithe as the Law required but not dismiss as less important the attitudes that represent the purpose and function of the Law. Jesus once again called them "blind guides," a rebuke for failing to see and lead others according to God's standards. Their legalism blinded them to the "weightier matters" of the Law and made them shallow religionists. The ironic proverb "Strain out a gnat and swallow a camel" emphasized how they fanatically worried about meaningless detail of ritual but missed the much larger consideration of the proper attitude and spirit that God was looking for. It is always easier to give outward imitation of holiness than to maintain the heart attitudes that are the foundation to true godliness.

23:25-26　　The next rebuke came in the metaphor of cleaning cups and plates, and the analogy was simple and straightforward—these leaders were more concerned with outward appearance than inner contents (cf. v. 5). The utensils represented their lives—the outside looked admirable, but the inside was filled with corruption and defilement. Jesus mentioned two points of defilement: "robbery" (*harpax*), which referred to forcible confiscation of property or grasping something greedily,[15] and "self-indulgence," which basically meant a lack of self-control,[16] implying not being able to control their passion for self-glorification.

The metaphor certainly represented the Pharisees (Luke 11:39), who worked so hard to look clean outwardly, and that is indeed how they appeared to those who saw only external behavior. The now familiar rebuke "blind" (v. 26) reminded them that they did not see the real issue. He warned them to "first clean the inside of the cup," which testified to the priority of inward cleansing. Also, cleansing is an act acknowledging the presence of that which requires cleansing. Thus, this group was to first acknowledge their need and then seek to clean defilement from their inward being. The consequence (*hina*, indicating consequential condition) of that inward cleansing (of the heart) would be a clean exterior. He was not rebuking their desire to display righteousness but only their concern for external appearance rather than internal reality.

23:27-28　　The next "woe" was related to the same problem—their concern for external appearance rather than concern for internal character. This time, the Lord used the analogy of whitewashed tombs. Tombs were considered places of defilement and symbols of uncleanness because of the decomposing bodies within, the stench of death, and the fear of disease from decaying flesh. But tombs were a necessary part of life. The facades of tombs in many cultures were decorated with paintings or carvings of family life or of the deceased; however, in the Jewish culture tombs could not be decorated with images, so whitewash was applied for a cleaner and more attractive appearance.

Another factor was perhaps even more critical. The Law stated that anyone touching a dead body or a grave was unclean (Num. 19:16). Hendriksen believes that with Passover pilgrims flowing into Jerusalem, the religious leaders feared someone might inadvertently walk across a grave and be defiled. Thus the tombs were whitewashed using powdered lime dust to make them conspicuous, "lest any pilgrim should render himself ceremonially unclean by coming into contact with a corpse or a human bone."[17] Carson, likewise, points to the tradition of whitewashing tombs in the month of Adar, just before Passover.[18]

Jesus applied the principle to the scribes and Pharisees (v. 28). He made the analogy that these religious hypocrites defiled others who come in contact with them even as people who made contact with a tomb were defiled (Luke 11:44). Whereas in v. 25 He is seen condemning them for being full of robbery and self-indulgence, in v. 28 He condemns them for being full of hypocrisy (*hupocritēs,* "pretense, deception") and lawlessness (*anomia,* behavior depicting lack of authority). The irony of this is that these who prided themselves in the Law were condemned for not being under control of the Law. Jesus denounced not their lack of religious discipline but their ignorance of the true purpose and function of the Law.

23:29-33   The Lord's pronouncements against the leadership continued with the serious charge that they were participating in the death of God's prophets. Building off the analogy of tombs, Jesus targeted as their next condemnation the practice of adorning the tombs of the prophets and the "righteous" (referring to those pronounced righteous by God and not the self-righteous). This rebuke was not intended to criticize the practice of caring for tombs, but their condemnation flowed from their hypocrisy in doing so.

Their pretension consisted of the claim that they would have been more righteous than their fathers and would not have participated in killing the prophets. Verse 30 attaches their hypocritical boast to the act of adorning the tombs. Jesus pointed out (v. 31) that since their fathers' guilt was acknowledged and since so much emphasis was placed on their traditions and heritage, the guilt of their predecessors must also be shared. Verse 32 distinctly makes them guilty by association. Jesus literally said, "And you make complete the measure [of guilt] of your fathers." However, their heritage was not what made them guilty. The evidence of their shared guilt was in their seeking to kill Jesus (John 7:19), rendering them just as guilty of killing God's prophets as their fathers. This connects with the parable Jesus had just taught (21:33-39) and also led to the prophetic utterance of vv. 34-39.

Verse 33 reflects the anger of Jesus toward those who hated God and sought to silence His prophets. "Serpents" were symbols of evil. The Evil One had used the serpent to deceive Eve and is called "the serpent of old" (Rev. 12:9). "Brood of vipers" was most likely a parallelism to make His statement more dramatic and forceful. Perhaps Jesus was thinking of Psalm 58:3-4 in relation to lies told the people that poisoned their hearts. His question was a terrifying promise: "How shall you escape from the sentence of hell?" The implication was that there is no escape from the consequences of rejecting God's truth. "Hell" translates *geenna,* "valley of the sons of Hinnom,"[19] which was the valley south of Jerusalem. This valley had been the scene of unspeakable sacrificing of children by fire (2 Chron. 28:3; 33:6) and thus became infamous as a place of burning destruction. Mark 9:43 characterizes *geenna* as a place of "unquenchable fire." This is the destiny of those who reject God's messengers.

JUDGMENT PREDICTED UPON THOSE
REFUSING GOD'S MESSENGERS, 23:34-36

23:34-36 This section is not a warning but rather a prediction as to the continuation of the same wickedness that had been in the fathers. "Therefore" is more literally "because of this" (*dia touto*), referring forward to v. 35. Those rejecting the prophets of God, including the Jews to whom He was speaking, were guilty along with all those who had ever persecuted the messengers of God.

Notice that Jesus was talking about prophets, wise men, and scribes whom He Himself (emphatic *egō*) was sending (the present tense, *apostellō,* is to be understood futuristically, from this time onward). Meyer points out that this was "uttered not by God . . . but by *Jesus,* and that under a powerful sense of His Messianic dignity, and with a boldness still more emphatically manifested by the use of *idou.*"[20] The statement "you will kill" was to draw attention to their guilt, even as their fathers were guilty of killing those sent them from God. Their boast of v. 30 was thus exposed. This prophecy of persecution of Christ's servants was clearly fulfilled in the book of Acts.

Verse 35 is intended to link their viciousness toward Christ's servants with the hateful and violent rejection of God's Old Testament servants, going back to the killing of Abel. Abel was the first human victim of man's depraved nature and his murder the first bloody act of man's rebellion. Zechariah "the son of Berechiah" (Zech. 1:1) would certainly be the great prophet of the postexilic time, but since no record of his death exists, some assume this must not be referencing him. MacArthur points out that the Old Testament refers to more than twenty men named Zechariah, which indicates that it was a popular name.[21] But here the identification is "son of Berechiah." Hendriksen and others suppose that an early copyist mistakenly inserted this apposition,[22] but no manuscript evidence suggests this. Carson offers some helpful discussion on the issue,[23] but this writer is not convinced that Jesus was referring to any Zechariah other than the prophet of Zechariah 1:1. Not knowing about his death, one should not assume that Jesus was unaware of the means of death. The fact that a similar fate befell one who presumably was his grandfather (2 Chron. 24:20-21) is not sufficient reason to impose this name on that character. However, the reference is ambiguous and should be treated as such. There is no clear or simple answer except that Jesus was referring to a real event that somehow capsulized the murderous heart of mankind from Genesis to the close of the Old Testament canon.

The forceful "whom you murdered between the temple and the altar" most likely referred to their guilt by being descendants of those who displayed similar character by killing the prophets (thus the point of His dialogue in vv. 29-34). It is possible, however, that a recent priest with this traditional name was martyred by this generation for preaching against them, but the first explanation is more conceivable.

"All these things" (v. 36) that would come upon this generation (the generation to which He was speaking) were the consequences of murdering the prophets and righteous men of God. Lenski comments, "All these deeds of blood will descend like an avalanche on 'this generation,' the one now living. Many who were standing before Jesus would see it all. In only a few years Jerusalem would be in ruins, the Jewish nation would be destroyed."[24] Truly, the destruction of Jerusalem in A.D. 70 by Titus was the beginning of judgments. Israel was so brutally oppressed that it ceased to exist as a nation between Titus's destruction and its reestablishment in 1948. That generation did witness the horrific judgment of God via the Roman conquest and sacking of the city.

JESUS' LAMENT OVER JERUSALEM, 23:37-39

23:37-39   As Lenski astutely points out, "The entire chapter has been one of stern denunciation—calm, measured, irresistible, fortified with absolute proof at every step, final. Now at last, the note of tenderness breaks into that stern judgment, and the hope that still continues to the last moment sends forth its ray of light to penetrate the midnight gloom."[25] The Lord did not overlook the sin of His people or play down their wicked hearts or detestable deeds, but He declared that He still cared for them and grieved on their behalf because of the judgment coming.

"O Jerusalem, Jerusalem" was a form of direct address showing great emotion. Jesus reiterated their guilt: "who kills the prophets and stones those who are sent to her." The Holy City here personified the whole of the nation, but literally only Jerusalem was sacked by the Romans. The Lord "wanted to gather" the Jews as a hen gathers her chicks under her wings for protection. "Wanted" is the word *ēbelēsa* (aorist active indicative, first person singular of *thelō*), which indicated His desire as well as His willingness to do so. Even though Jesus knew and had experienced their rebellion and violence, His desire was to protect them from what He knew was coming. This was grace! The problem was that the Jews were "unwilling." Jesus used the same word (*thelō*) with a strong negation to express the state of their hearts (*ouk ēthelēsate*).

Verse 38 states the predictive conclusion of their refusal to respond to His grace. Their "house" referred not only to the temple or the Holy City but to all those dwelling in Israel. The house of Israel was about to be made desolate. "Desolate" (the term included in many important manuscripts) implies to be "barren, empty." Verse 39 explains their desolation: they would not have their Messiah or God's promised kingdom until they called out, "Blessed is He who comes in the name of the Lord!" The expression "from now on" (*apē arti*) verifies that from the time of His departure from the earth at the hands of this murderous generation, the nation would not see their Messiah until they called out for salvation from Him. Jesus alluded to Psalm 118:26, a context He had previously identified as prophesying His coming (21:42). Announcing a new era in God's dealing with the nation of Israel, this is one of the most tragic texts of Scripture. The expression "until you say" (*heōs an eipēte*) indicates a point at which He will reappear to this people to restore their blessed position with Him. This event is prophesied in Zechariah 12:10–13:9.

HOMILETICAL SUGGESTIONS

In an age of political correctness, this chapter may prove difficult for Christians to appreciate. The church, however, needs to see the Lord expressing His strong aversion to the religious hypocrisy of the Pharisees and scribes. In the first section, the Lord drew the attention of both His disciples and the crowd that had been witnessing His debates with their leaders. Jesus despised hypocrisy, as it led people away from the truth. To better understand His response to the leaders, Christians need to understand the three major characteristics of Pharisaism: they put heavy burdens on people through mandatory observance of minute rules and regulations; they loved appearing to be pious; and they loved public recognition and prerogatives of honor (i.e., special treatment).

In light of this, believers should also be reminded of three prohibitions stated here by the Lord: do not be called rabbi; do not call any man your (religious) father; and do not seek to be called the leader. These prohibitions all must be kept in the context of the religious arrogance of the religious leadership just condemned. The major point of these prohibitions is stated in v. 11—the greatest in the church is the one who is the servant. Humility is the key to being exalted by the Lord. Those who exalt themselves to positions of prominence will be put in a lower place when the Lord rewards His servants.

The second major portion of this chapter focuses on the eight (or seven) woes pronounced upon the religionists. A series of messages could easily flow from these severe warnings in order to provide believers with a sober view of the things that bring the Lord's rebuke. Every person is subject to the same hypocritical pitfalls as the scribes and Pharisees. Paul reminds us that their zeal was "for God" but "not according to knowledge" (Rom. 10:2). Likewise, many well-intentioned Christians can become zealous of righteousness to the point of becoming judgmental of others and prideful regarding their own morals. The four references to being blind indicate that these men had lost sight of their own spiritual needs.

A study could be made of the names that Jesus used for these who failed to understand God's grace or their need for it. *Hypocrite* was a term that referred to playing a part. As actors in the ancient Greek theaters held up clay masks and recited lines, these leaders put forward a facade of being righteous but were not righteous in their hearts. Christians need to be challenged to quit pretending and be willing to admit to fellow believers their burdens and sins, in order to receive help in overcoming their weakness (Gal. 6:1-3; James 5:16). *Blind* was another term to describe the self-righteous, who were oblivious to their own needs and the grace of God in the lives of others. Being blind meant that, as they tried to lead others, both would fall. The servant of God must help Christ's followers to see their own needs and the grace and mercy of God. The final term was *snakes* or *vipers*. This implied the danger of the poison of self-righteousness. Like a snake's venom, a self-righteous and judgmental spirit destroys hope and brings only death. The church must become conscious of the destructiveness of religious hypocrisy.

Finally, the chapter exposes God's mercy and tender heart. The grief expressed by Christ (vv. 37-39) was comforting to those who struggled with the truth of impending judgment. God loves and desires to draw all people to Himself so that they might be saved (1 Tim. 2:4), and He, as demonstrated here, grieves over those who refuse. The church must be challenged to love even those who reject Christ and blaspheme Him, having the same compassion as Jesus Himself. This does not imply that the judgment on the unregenerate will be lessened or forgotten. God's judgment and their condemnation is set, as they will be cast into the lake of fire (Rev. 20:10-15). The justice of God will be enforced, but this is to be understood only in conjunction with His great compassion.

MATTHEW

CHAPTER

TWENTY-FOUR

CHRIST'S EXPLANATION
OF COMING TRIBULATION

This chapter begins what is normally referred to as the Olivet Discourse, which continues through chap. 25:46 and is best known for its eschatological content. The primary contextual element of this discourse is Christ's response to His disciples regarding three questions: When will the temple be destroyed? What will be the signs of Jesus' second coming? What will be the signs of the coming end of the age? The Lord's answers may be divided into three sections: first, the pretribulation symptoms, which are not to cause fear; second, the "abomination of desolation" as predicted by Daniel; and third, the events following the Great Tribulation.

THE OPENING PROPHECY, 24:1-2
(Mark 13:1-2; Luke 21:5-6)

The events of this chapter follow the series of confrontations between Jesus and the religious leaders in the temple compound. Matthew omits the account of the widow's offering, which, had he included it, would have been between 23:12 and 13 or perhaps at the very beginning of chap. 23. Hendriksen points out that these events probably occurred the Tuesday before Passover.[1]

24:1-2 Matthew simply remarks that some of the disciples were pointing out the buildings of the temple complex (v. 1), but this is not to be understood as a guided tour. According to Luke, the disci-

461

ples are simply referred to as "some" who "were talking" (21:5), commenting on how the temple was adorned with beautiful stones and votive gifts. Mark records that a disciple was remarking on the wonder of the temple with its impressive buildings and elaborate layout (13:1). In light of the tense confrontation just experienced, Jesus' denunciation of Israel's religious leaders, and especially the depressing prediction of Jerusalem's coming destruction, it might be best to understand this comment about the temple as an awkward attempt to calm Jesus or to shift the conversation to something more positive. Jesus, however, did not wish to focus on the beauty of stone blocks and the different symbols of vows taken in the temple (the "votive gifts" of Luke).

Christ's response was less than encouraging to His disciples (v. 2). He first asked the question, "Do you not see all these things?" The grammatical structure makes identification of "these things" somewhat difficult. "These things" is in neuter form, but "building" is feminine. Pronouns agree with their antecedents in gender and number. If "buildings" was the antecedent of "these things," then the latter would be in feminine form. However, if the question was to refer to His previous teachings and predictions (which appears the most logical), then the Lord would have used the negative particle *mē,* which anticipates a negative response rather than *ou,* which anticipates a positive response. It is not likely that Jesus would have asked if they could see these things, assuming they could, and then begin the explanation of chaps. 24-25. If they could "see" (metaphoric use of *blepō*), then His explanation would be unnecessary. The answer lies in a combination, "Can't you see these buildings [neuter to include the entire temple complex]? Of course you can, but can you see the reality of their temporalness?" The prediction was that the temple was to be destroyed completely, even disassembled stone by stone. There would not even be a ruin to come to or to rebuild. Josephus offers a vivid description of the battle around the temple and how it was burned and sacked by Titus's army in A.D. 70.[2] The statement was not strictly hyperbole, because the temple was literally torn down soon after its destruction, and the massive, artistically cut stones were used by the Romans in other structures. Josephus says, "Caesar gave orders that they should now demolish the entire city and temple . . . it [the whole city] was so thoroughly laid even with the ground by those that dug it up to the foundations, that there was left nothing to make those that came thither believe it had ever been inhabited."[3]

THE PRETRIBULATION SYMPTOMS, 24:3-14
(Mark 13:3-13; Luke 21:8-11)

24:3   Jesus crossed the Kidron Valley and chose a place to sit with His disciples on the side of the Mount of Olives, where He had a commanding view of Jerusalem. There Peter, James, John, and Andrew (according to Mark) asked three questions. The first, "When will these things be?" was apparently directly related to the destruction of the temple. One can only imagine the fear building within the hearts of these men as they looked across the valley to the magnificent golden-roofed temple and its large complex of impressive buildings, the very symbol of their religious heritage and faith, and pondered the prediction of its destruction. If God would allow the temple to be destroyed, what of the rest of the city or of the nation itself? This answer would come within the lifetime of almost all the men sitting on the hillside with the Lord.

The second question, "What will be the sign of your coming?" was the natural sequence if one understands their comprehension of the Lord's predictions up to this point. They correctly assumed that the destruction of the temple and city would lead to His return in glory (cf. 16:27-28) but did not understand the time factor between the two events. They also assumed that some sign (*sēmeion*) would indicate His coming (*tēs sēs parousias*). Speaking of His coming (*parasouia*) indicated they had faith in His prediction of His death and resurrection. This desire for a sign prompted the warning of v. 4. Though *parousia* was a common word used for anyone's arrival, there can be little doubt as to its theological significance within the church and as the major focus of the church's hope (1 Cor. 15:23-24; 1 Thess. 2:19; 3:13; 4:15; 5:23; James 5:7-8; 2 Peter 3:4-15; etc.).

The third question, "And [what is the sign] of the end of the age?" indicated their belief that the Lord's coming would bring the completion of a particular program of God. The "end" (*sunteleias*) implied the completion of something. The term "age" (*aiōnos*) defined that completion as the closing of a time period set off by a distinct beginning and ending. One may understand the word better by the expression "era," a chronological designation of major events within a certain time frame, such as the Renaissance era. The "age" as these disciples understood it would have been their own time frame. It could be a reference to the "end of the world" as contemporary writers would understand the term. To the disciples, it would have indicated the closure of Israel's rebellion and the beginning of the glorious kingdom.

24:4-5   Jesus' response was first to warn the disciples about being deceived. This warning was prompted by their eagerness for a sign. The danger of being misled (*planēsē*) was increased if one was too enthusiastic or anticipated some symbolic indication of the event. The warning was also provoked by the fact that "many" would come in the name of Jesus (v. 5). Often the expression "to come in the name of" implied to come as a representative of or with the authority of, but here the warning was against false messiahs ("I am the Christ"). History is filled with examples of the truthfulness of this prediction. The success of this false claim ("and will mislead many") is also sadly verified in history.

24:6-8   Jesus began to give the disciples some idea of the intervening time between the destruction of Jerusalem and His return, admonishing them not to be frightened by the coming catastrophes or impending dangers. There would be wars and rumors of wars. Ironically, this phrase is used by sensationalist preachers to point to the end of the world. In fact, Jesus said this was not to alarm His followers (*mē throeisthe*, "do not be alarmed or startled"). His commentary was that these kinds of events would certainly happen (*dei*, "to be necessary"), but He also added, "The end is not yet," or, "This is not the end." Wars and reports of war are simply normative in human history. No matter how personally threatening such conditions may appear and no matter how great the threat to one's life or nation, this is not proof of the end of the age.

Jesus continued by adding that national wars and struggles among empires would perpetuate throughout the age and were not symptomatic of the end times (v. 7). He said that famines and earthquakes were likewise a part of human history and not to be seen as "signs." There is therefore no justification for taking "earthquakes" as prophetic language referring to political unrest.[4] These human tragedies are consequences of man's rebellion against God, proof that the world is in a fallen state, but are not prophetic portents of eschatalogical consummation.

Thus Jesus said (v. 8), "These things are merely the beginning of birth pangs," early indications of what is coming. World wars, famine, and phenomenal natural catastrophes are not the end but serve as reminders of greater calamities yet to come. A preview of the Great Tribulation can be seen in the localized and smaller-scale tribulations such as wars, famines, and earthquakes.

Matthew used the temporal particle *tote* in v. 9 and again in v. 10, possibly to indicate sequence of events or perhaps to indicate happenings while these other world tragedies are being experienced. Jesus warned against being anxious about wars, famines, and earthquakes, because these are simply a part of the human condition, but "then" (following or during these normal tragic events) other things will be coming into the world that will directly affect them.

24:9 The prediction of the destruction of the temple and the city of Jerusalem gave the disciples cause to fear, but now they themselves were specifically named as targets of tribulation (*thilpsin*). This same message would be repeated in the Upper Room Discourse, where Jesus would remind them of His warning (John 15:20–16:3). The prediction included martyrdom and rejection, not only in Israel but "by all nations," which implied the broader field of their mission compared to Jesus'. The disciples, targeted "on account of my name" (*dia to onoma mou*), would not be victims of random violence and tribulation but marked for persecution because of identity with Jesus. His "name" implies His Person and mission. As His name is preached in all the world, those carrying His name will be rejected and murdered. This related back directly to the condemnation of the religious leaders and the destruction of Jerusalem (23:34-39).

24:10-12 The forewarnings in these three verses may present three arenas of activity: internal betrayal (v. 10); the influx of false prophets (v.11); and the callousness of the general population (v.12). The Lord set the events as during "that time" (*tote,* v. 10), which certainly referred to the time when the followers of Jesus were being persecuted. During times of persecution, many "will fall away" (*skandalisthēontai,* future active indicative of *skandalizō*) or, rather, will be "offended" and withdraw. Parallels can be seen in Matthew 11:6 where Jesus uses it in relation to people being offended by His ministry, and in 13:57, where the people of Nazareth are offended at His teaching. Jesus even predicted this very attitude in His own closest followers on the eve of His betrayal (26:31), implying that because of the rejection of the gospel some would be offended or intimidated into becoming enemies of the truth. Thus, some would be betrayed and turned over to the persecutors, resulting in internal strife (hating one another). That treachery within the ranks of family and even fellow believers (or some who profess faith) was indicated by the reciprocal pronoun "one another" (*allēlous*).

External factors will bring another level of troubles for the followers of Christ. The influx of false prophets (*pseudoprophētai*) will create confusion and pseudo-Christian cults. Jesus warned of many false prophets, not just one. John the apostle points to the fulfillment of this prediction (1 John 4:1) and warns future generations. Paul, likewise, warns of false apostles (*pseudoapostoloi*) who deceive by disguise (2 Cor. 11:13). The result is that "they will mislead many." Unlike danger from pagan religions or blatant enemies of the truth, the danger of a false prophet is the half-truth spoken and use of the same vocabulary as true prophets. This should serve as a warning to Christ's servants to help believers discern truth from subtle distortions.

Verse 12 continues this segment of warning by previewing the world's callousness. Jesus said literally that because (*hoti*) of lawlessness (*anomia*, "being without restraint of law"), which is increased (*plēthunthēnai*, aorist passive infinitive of *plēthunō*, "had spread"), the love of many will die out (*psugēsetai*, future of *psuchomai*, "grow cold, "die out"). Thus the growing lack of restraint will produce a coldness in concern for others. This seems more related to the general condition of the world than to the followers of Jesus. It is also consistent with Paul's prophetic description of the unregenerate world in the "last days" (2 Tim. 3:1-4).

24:13   This verse has been widely used to teach the erroneous doctrine that loss of faith means that one cannot be saved. The problem begins with the superficial hermeneutic of giving "saved" the same meaning in every context, which is not true for any word. Words have no specific meaning apart from context. Here, "saved" (*sōzō*) means basically to "deliver" or to "rescue"—from what and in what manner is dependent upon the context. Paul encouraged the Philippians that their prayers would bring about his salvation (*sōzō*) (Phil. 1:19), but from prison, not eternal torment. Contextually, the salvation being discussed here was not eternal redemption but deliverance from the persecutions and wretchedness of the world. Hendriksen explains, "He, who, in spite of all these disturbances and persecutions, remains loyal to Christ shall enter into glory. For himself the period of persecution and trial will last until death delivers him from this earthly scene (John 16:33; 2 Tim. 3:12)."[5]

Note that this was a promise, not a warning. There was no conditional clause but rather a simple statement, "the one enduring (*ho upomeinas*) until the end [the end of the trial] will be delivered out of the trial" either by death into glory or rescue. The words "the end" are not to be taken as the end of the age but as the end of the individual's trial, since the context speaks of periods of tribulations. As Carson notes, "Individual responsibility persists to the end of life."[6] One's eternal destiny is not determined by resistance to torture or to being deceived by false prophets, as that would certainly require human effort for salvation and thus violate clear teachings such as Ephesians 2:8-9; Titus 3:5; etc.

24:14   The most positive prediction of the Lord's discourse was that the gospel of the kingdom will be preached worldwide, beyond the borders of Israel. "This gospel of the kingdom" (*touto to euangelion tēs basileias*) is literally "this good news of the kingdom." The phrase is first mentioned in 4:23 with the inauguration of the Lord's earthly ministry and again in 9:35 in a summary statement, "Jesus was going about all the cities and the villages, teaching in their synagogues, and proclaiming the gospel of the kingdom." The "kingdom" is not to be taken from its normal contextual meaning, which in Matthew must be understood as the "kingdom of heaven." This phrase appears thirty-four times in Matthew and is used synonymously with "kingdom of God" (19:23-24), which appears three times in Matthew. The point is that this was not a general preaching of the gospel of salvation but a proclamation of the kingdom of Messiah to all nations. The faithfulness of God to His people Israel was proclaimed in the good news of the coming messianic kingdom. Hendriksen defines this kingdom as "the reign of God in heart and life."[7] But such a definition is not consistent with Jesus' expressed expectations of the kingdom. This proclamation is to continue until the end.

THE ABOMINATION OF DESOLATION, 24:15-28
(Mark 13:14-23; Luke 21:20-24)

24:15 The next section of the Lord's discourse began with an inferential particle, "therefore" (*oun*), functioning as a transitional conjunction to move the listener to the ensuing warning. It could be understood as "consequently." In addition, He used a temporal particle (*hotan,* "when, whenever"), indicating the conditions upon which Israel should be alarmed (vv. 16-21). His discourse then moved toward answering the direct question, "What will be the sign of . . ."

The "you" directly referred to the disciples (vv. 1, 3) but owing to the eschatalogical context should be understood figuratively as the people of Israel. Carson understands the reference to be limited to the destruction of Jerusalem.[8] Luke's account seems to be more focused as such, but both Matthew and Mark appear to emphasize more than that localized tragedy. The eschatological nature of the warning is seen in v. 21 (Mark 13:19), a tribulation unlike anything else in history or the future. The sacking of Jerusalem in A.D. 70 could not qualify, since Jerusalem had previously been totally sacked and the great Solomonic temple destroyed (Babylonian captivity). The nature of eschatalogical revelation allows for a typological fulfillment at one level with a more complete fulfillment at another. This will be seen in the reference to Daniel's abomination of desolation.

The "abomination of desolation" (*to bdelugma tēs eramōseō*) is here specifically stated as the one spoken of by the prophet Daniel. This immediately informs the reader that the act of Antiochus Epiphanes (168 B.C.)[9] was not the ultimate fulfillment of Daniel 9:27, 11:31, and 12:11, since Jesus was implying that it is yet future. The idea of an abomination (*bdelugma*) is to be "detestable" or "disgusting." In the Old Testament the word referenced things used in idolatry. In the New Testament this same word is used in Luke 16:15 of the self-righteous religion of the Pharisees. Here it is the disgusting thing that brings "desolation" (*erēmōsis*) or "destruction." A major cognate idea is the desolation of a desert or barren area. This disgusting thing takes its place (or is "positioned," perfect passive participle, accusative neuter singular from *histēmi*) in the "holy place" (*topō hagiō*), which is most likely the temple rather than the Holy City. This "abomination" brings on the "desolation."

According to Daniel 9:27, following the cutting off of Messiah a covenant will be made with Israel in which their offerings are stopped and abominations come in the person of one who will bring desolation and total destruction. In Daniel 11:32, the placing of the abomination of desolation is followed by smooth words to detract from the covenant, but "the people who know their God will display strength and take action." The final reference in Daniel is 12:11, where the context implies that wickedness would be allowed to continue and a purging and refining will be taking place during which sacrifices would be stopped. Between the stopping of the regular sacrifices and the abomination of desolation, there will be 1,290 days. Scholars have offered a wide variety of interpretations to these "days." One popular view has it represent three and a half years. The arguments for all the diverse views are too numerous for the purpose of this commentary. For this reason, this writer prefers here only to say that Daniel's message would *prima facie* be identified with the action of Antiochus Epiphanes IV around 168 B.C. But in light of all the chronological details of Daniel and Christ's own words that this was yet to be seen, it must be referring to events yet to come in relation to Jesus' teaching. That such an event was described by Josephus[10] prior to the fall of Jerusalem has some validity. However, Daniel's prophecy implies that it is a person who desecrates the Holy Place and then subsequently pours out desolation on the people. This was not the case of the renegade Jews who took control of the temple mount. The parenthetical exhortation to the "readers" certainly seems to refer to those who read the prophecy of Daniel.

24:16-18   The next few verses are symbolic of the immediacy and peril of the coming desolation. Again, this certainly had immediate fulfillment in the destruction of Jerusalem in A.D. 70. It is not necessary, however, to limit the warning to that event. Verse 21 implies that this will be an incident of far greater magnitude than that of sacking a city. Some wish to attach v. 21 to the verses that follow rather than to the preceding verses,[11] but the wording would seem too awkward. Those in Judea are to flee to the mountains. This geographic reference is only typical of the fleeing to be done in every region. It is but natural that this familiar region would be used to emphasize the reality of the danger.

Those on the housetop are to flee without entering the house

(v. 17). This depicts something of the ancient world lifestyle. Homes in this region often were built with flat roofs to serve as eating and sleeping areas during the summer heat. A stairway constructed alongside an external wall gave access to the roof. If one is on the roof and sees the impending destruction, no time is to be taken even to get goods from the house. The severity of the desolation will be such that escape is to have highest priority, not the comfort or provisions within the house. The danger is to be viewed as so perilous that a worker should flee without even retrieving his cloak at the edge of the field (v. 18). Again there may be a parallel to the fleeing of the city in A.D. 68-69 before Titus laid siege, but if so, it is no different from Antiochus's unknowingly fulfilling in a partial way the prophecies of Daniel. The context here is that when this blasphemous and destructive person desecrates the Holy Place, appalling tribulation will break out, this time "such as has not occurred since the beginning of the world" and such as will not "ever" occur again (v. 21).

24:19-22   Verses 19-20 continue the illustration as to how serious the plight will be of those who are living during this tribulation. The word "woe" (*ouai*, v. 19) indicates great cause for alarm. But instead of reflecting pain resulting from impending judgment (as in 23:13-29), this "woe" more than likely attests to pity on the part of the Lord. The extra hazard of having a small child creates even greater cause for alarm. Likewise (v. 20) the conditions of winter would create extra burdens for those trying to flee. This draws attention to the practical nature of Jesus' warning. He was not speaking of some fanciful religious story but the real prospect of trying to escape a harrowing fate in the difficult circumstances of bad weather and poor road conditions. Furthermore, if the flight is on a Sabbath, the escape would be made more difficult due to the lack of provisions that would be available on other days or because religious fanatics might stone those fleeing or impede their escape in order to enforce observance of their holy day. There is no cause to look for any significance to this last statement other than it emphasized to these Jews, conditioned to reverence the Sabbath, as to how serious this situation will be.

Verse 21 offers an explanation (*gar*) for the illustrations of urgency just presented and uses the temporal adverb *tote* ("then") to connect the previous statements with the prediction of the worst tribulation ever, which will also be worse than anything to follow. Again, the primary reason for believing this tribulation is yet future is because the destruction of Jerusalem and even the Holocaust could not be described in such superlative terms. Pentecost correctly distinguishes the different uses of the word "tribulation" (*thilpsis*):

> It is used in a non-technical, non-eschatalogical sense in reference to any time of suffering or testing into which one goes. . . . It is used in its technical or eschatological sense in reference to the whole period of seven years of tribulation, as in Revelation 2:22 or Matthew 24:29. It is also used in reference to the last half of this seven year period, as in Matthew 24:21.[12]

This verse clearly states that this will be a one-time-only kind of event. This expression connects with Daniel 12:1, which certainly refers to a period too great for the destruction of Jerusalem in A.D. 70.

Verse 22 introduces a twist to the prophetic proclamation, as the tense of verbs changes from the last verse and even within the verse itself: "Unless those days *had been shortened*" (*ei mē ekolobōthēsan*). The aorist passive indicative verb "cut short" is understood in a past tense, yet the "great tribulation" is spoken of in the future (*esthai,* "there *will be,*" v. 21). Then the Lord shifted back to the future tense, "For the sake of the elect those days *shall be* cut short [*kolobōthēsontai*]." Probably the statement relates to the sovereignty of God's plan. In His decreed will, He set the limit of days of the Great Tribulation so that all human flesh (*pasa sarx*) would not be destroyed. Specifically for the sake of the elect, they will in actual time (yet future) be shortened. MacArthur understands this as a shortening of the number of daylight hours so that "the Antichrist's forces are compelled to operate in total darkness. God will use that darkness for the sake of the elect, using it to hide them from their would-be destroyers."[13] Nothing grammatically or contextually leads to this assumption, however. The best understanding is that the number of days was set at a limit beyond what would destroy all flesh. The issue is not necessarily that the number was reduced from a previous number but was limited, shortened, from a greater possible number that would annihilate the human race.

The elect (*tous eklektous*) would first refer to the nation, which had been thus designated for centuries (Isa. 45:4), and then to all who believe in Jesus (Eph. 1:4). In this context, it is most likely used regarding the nation. Daniel identifies this time as "decreed for your people and your holy city," indicating that Israel, not the church or mankind in general, will be the center of the Tribulation suffering. Thus, if God had not limited the number of days "for the sake of" (*dia* with the accusative) the elect, then all flesh would perish from the horrors being poured out on the world.

24:23-28   Jesus then returned to the warning concerning imitation Christs. Characteristically, Matthew introduces these next verses with *tote*,[14] denoting a sequence of but not necessarily chronological succession. Verses 21-22 jump to the time of the Great Tribulation, and the subject of v. 23 is the next topic for discussion, not the next event in chronological order. Thus, returning to the thought of vv. 4-5, Jesus again pointed to the rise of false Christs. He simply said, "Do not believe them."

Verse 24 gives two aspects of warning: one is against false Christs; and one is against false prophets. The false Christs are those who claim to be the Messiah. The false prophets are those who proclaim the arrival of these false Messiahs or proclaim false teachings. The false prophets will show "great signs" (*sēmeia megala*) and "wonders" (*terata*), which should send a warning to believers today who are impressed with the "signs and wonders" movement. Apparently such phenomena are no indication that the prophets are from God or that they are representatives of Messiah. The future signs and wonders will be so dramatic and powerful that even the elect will be misled—"if possible" (*ei dunaton*). The reassurance is that apparently such deception is not achievable. The point of v. 25 is that the disciples are not to be shaken when these things happen. The happenings only prove that Jesus had advance knowledge of coming events and all is a part of His plan (John 15:18–16:4).

Verse 26 repeats the warning of vv. 23-24. The wilderness reference may be a reflection on the previous appearance of John the Baptist (Matt. 3:1-3), but the second coming of Messiah will not be to such a remote location. Thus, "do not go forth" seeking Him. The next reference, "the inner rooms," suggests the concept of secret societies. Hendriksen points out, "As if the Christ were only for a few initiates, the Head of a private fraternity, revealing himself to no one else."[15] On the contrary (v. 27), there will be no secrecy or hidden meetings. His coming will be visible from coast to coast. The analogy of lightning from the east to the west pictures the brilliance and expansiveness of His coming (*hē parousia*) in contrast to the secluded "wilderness" or "inner rooms." The significance is that "every eye will see Him" (Rev. 1:7). "The coming of the Son of Man" (*hē parousia tou huiou*) is a clear reference to the Lord's second coming, since "Son of Man" was Jesus' favorite title used of Himself.

Verse 28 is not only ambiguous, but it also references an obscure citation in Job 39:30 describing the "hawk" (*nes*, "bird of prey") as one that feeds on slain, decaying human bodies. The most probable meaning of this reference is that along with the spectacular appearance of the Son of Man, there will also be the carnage of the Tribulation.

FOLLOWING THE GREAT TRIBULATION, 24:29-41 (Mark 13:24-27; Luke 21:25-28)

24:29 The next section deals with the major events following the tribulation of "those days." This is surely the same tribulation mentioned in v. 21 and not the general tribulation of v. 9 as some suggest.[16] Verses 22-28 may be seen as parenthetical, explaining why the Great Tribulation would be shortened and that false Christs will be on the scene. Verse 29 then resumes the discussion of the events following the Tribulation.

The astronomical events may be taken as hyperbolic, symbolic/ figurative, or actual: the sun will be darkened; the moon will not reflect light; the stars will fall from heaven; and the powers of heaven will be shaken. In contrast to Ridderbos, Berkouwer believes that these events are "not purely figurative since the description refers to the real end."[17] Luke's parallel passage (21:25-26) indicates that the events will create panic upon the earth. Therefore, the incidents are certainly real enough to be witnessed by the earth's inhabitants and to terrorize them. Isaiah 13:9-13 describes a similar scene and characterizes it as the time of God's wrath, "the day of the Lord."[18] Likewise, Peter predicts the disruption and destruction of heavenly bodies and order (2 Peter 3:7-12), which is associated with the return of the Lord (2 Peter 3:3-6).

The "powers of the heavens" (*hai dunameis tōn ouranōn*) may refer to the "greater heavenly bodies, which rule the day and night"[19] or, as a better understanding, may refer to the fact that "all the forces of energy . . . which hold everything in space constant, will be in dysfunction."[20] Christ "upholds all things by the word of His power," and this is what in the natural world would be known as the laws of physics. This word of His power will be loosed so as to shake the very foundations of the universe.

24:30   Following these unprecedented astronomical phenomena, "the sign of the Son of Man" will appear in the sky. It should first be noted that "sign" is singular (*to sēmeion*) and not plural, a series or group of signs. Second, this sign will be in heaven (*en ouranō*), not on the earth, and would appear to be different from the sun and moon's being blacked out and the universe shaken. In the darkness left by the dysfunctional luminaries, this sign will appear.

MacArthur believes that the sign is the Son of Man Himself: "The sign of should be translated as a Greek subjective genitive, indicating that the sign will not simply relate to or point to the Son of Man (as with an objective genitive) but will indeed *be* the Son of Man."[21] Though such an opinion is not totally objectionable, it seems redundant to say the "sign" will appear and that the sign is "the Son of Man." The object of the verb "will appear" (*phanēsetai*) is "the sign" (*to sēmeion*, accusative indicating direct object) and not "the Son of Man" (*tou huiou to anthrōpou;* this genitive construction may be objective or subjective or a genitive of description or numerous other types of genitive). Whatever Jesus intended by the "sign," it must be consistent with the question in v. 3, "What will be the sign of your coming?" This "ensign" or "standard" (*sēmeion*) will announce the return of the Lord and may be the trumpet of v. 31 or the "sound of the mighty peals of thunder" and the opening up of the heavens ("heaven opened") of Revelation 19:6-18, which is certainly appropriate to the prediction "They will see the Son of Man coming on the clouds of the sky with power and great glory."

24:31   The event of the coming (*parousia*) of the Son of Man (the Messiah and Second Adam) to rule the kingdom of God on earth will begin with His sending angels to gather His elect. These elect are those still left in the world, having survived the Great Tribulation, and might best be identified as the 144,000 sealed Jews (Rev. 7:4-8) and the innumerable saints of every tribe and nation (Rev. 7:9-14).

This event is not to be confused with the Rapture of the church

in 1 Thessalonians 4:16-18. As Benware points out, this verse "contains no reference to the resurrection or glorifying of any saints,
which is a critical part of the Rapture."[22] Wood, likewise, demonstrates the differences between this event and the Rapture of 1 Thessalonians.[23] The reference to a trumpet in both passages (Matt. 24:31
and 1 Thess. 4) is hardly sufficient reason to link the two events. A
trumpet blast was a common symbol for introducing a major dramatic event. The Rapture is not the gathering work of angels but
the summoning of the church saints by the Lord Himself (1 Thess.
4:16). Here, however, angels gather these together with the saints
already present with the Lord.

24:32-33   Jesus then referred to the parable of the fig tree (*tēs
sukēs . . . tēn parabolēn*) and told His disciples to learn (*mathete*)
its lesson. Nothing is hidden or complex in this parable—when the
leaves appear, one should know that summer is near. Verse 33
makes application by stating, "When you see all these things, you
know that it is near" (NIV). Identifying "all these things" (*panta
tauta*) is primarily a matter of staying with the flow of contextual
thought. Carson concludes, "The more natural way to take 'all these
things' is to see them as referring to the distress of vv. 4-28, the
tribulation that comes on believers throughout the period between
Jesus' ascension and the Parousia."[24] The only disagreement this
author has is that the focus is not on what comes upon believers
but rather on Israel, culminating with horrific astronomical signs
(vv. 21-29). Since these disciples would not be on the earth when
these events take place, for them to see and know exemplifies the
awareness of those saints on earth at the time (Rev. 7). The NASB's
"*He* is near, at the door" is interpretive; the NIV is correct to follow
the Greek more naturally as "it," referring to the Parousia.

24:34-35   The "generation" (*genea,* "race, nation, people") to
which Jesus was referring is the generation that sees the signs just
given for the Parousia. Once the unveiling of this "great tribulation"
(v. 21) begins, that generation will not pass away until everything is
brought to completion. To add weight to what He had just said, the
Lord added the proclamation that His words were more lasting than
even the universe itself. The heaven and the earth will be taken
away, but what He has proclaimed will last eternally.

24:36-39   Again, in response to the desire of the disciples to
know the time of His coming, Jesus stated that only the Father

knows. That information is accessible neither to the heavenly realm nor to humans, thus all sensationalistic preaching predicting the time of the Lord's coming is fraudulent. Even more startling, the Son Himself did not know the day or the hour.[25] Some mistakenly believe that Jesus had to be omniscient in order to be Deity. This shallow view of the Lord's humanness indicates a failure to understand either the powerful declaration of the kenosis (Phil. 2:7) or the fact that His followers worked miracles just as spectacular as His own (including raising the dead). The Lord did not attempt to display His deity but rather, in contrast, emphasized His humanity. As an obedient servant in His humanity, Jesus did not know the day or the hour of His return. That was the Father's responsibility and prerogative. In the kenosis (self-emptying), Jesus laid aside the independent use of His divine attributes and submitted Himself to know and do only what the Father revealed.

The Lord added explanation as to the character of the secret time. He referenced the Flood of Genesis 6 as an illustration of how sudden the coming will be (v. 37). In the days of Noah, the prophet had been preaching and building the ark. Everyone could see the development of Noah's work, but the people continued "eating and drinking" and "marrying and giving in marriage" as though nothing was going to change. In other words, the warnings of Noah were ignored, and the people continued living as always until the very day he entered the ark. This is similar to the conditions of the last days according to 2 Peter 3:3-7. Like the people of Noah's time being oblivious to the coming judgment until too late, in the same way the unbelieving will be caught off guard by the coming of the Son of Man (v. 39).

24:40-41 These two verses have often been misapplied to the Rapture of the church. But the context deals with coming judgment and the gathering of the elect at His coming. The term "taken" is *paralambanō,* "to take, take with or along, receive, accept,"[26] and, for the most part, is a positive concept, not negative. However, in John 19:16 (v. 17 in the NASB), it is used of the Romans taking Jesus to His crucifixion. The phrase "took them all away" in v. 39 (definitely referring to their destruction) is a different word (*ēren,* aorist of *airō,* "take away, conquer, kill"). Referencing a parallel teaching in Luke 17:26-37, Pate comments that the "taking" might be as

"Noah and Lot were taken and, therefore, saved from judgment while the rest were left for destruction."[27]

It might be best to understand the taking of these as the collecting of the elect of v. 31 (not the Rapture of the church, but the gathering of the sealed Jews and faithful Gentiles of the Tribulation) and leaving the others behind for the judgment about to come on the earth.

BEING PREPARED FOR THE LORD'S RETURN, 24:42-51
(Mark 13:33-37; Luke 21:34-36)

24:42-44 Verse 42 makes the application (*oun*) that His followers are to be alert (*grēgoreite,* "keep awake, watch out, be alert") so that the event will not catch them off guard. Considering the lesson of vv. 45-51, the meaning would be that as long as the saints remain on the earth, they must be faithful to the Lord's task because there will be no way to anticipate in advance when they will be called into His presence. This is further illustrated in v. 43. One should be cautious in assigning the analogy to the coming of Christ by saying Jesus is a thief who comes in the night. The parable is simply saying that if sufficient warning were given, there would be no surprise to take advantage of the house owner. Everyone would be prepared if a date and time were set, but the main point of the parabolic warning is that one must be prepared day in and day out because no such warning is provided. Jesus then began a series of parables, all pointing to the necessity of watchfulness. As Hendriksen points out, "common to all these passages is the idea of the suddenness and unexpectedness of the coming, and consequently the danger of unpreparedness on the part of those for whom that parousia has significance."[28] "For this reason" (v. 44), that is, since no warning or sign will be given until the Lord actually appears, the disciples were to be faithfully doing what He has told them to do. Thus, the message was that instead of worrying about signs, one is to just be faithful to his assigned duties. Even though the Tribulation will clearly be in process, the overwhelming circumstances will so distract from focus on the Lord's promises (not unlike the despair of the disciples after the Resurrection, Luke 24) that even those who are sealed and who are faithful will not be able to predict His appearance. Luke's account adds the warning, "Be on guard, that your hearts may not be weighted down with dissipation and drunkenness and the worries of life, and that day come on you suddenly like a trap" (21:34).

24:45 Another parable followed to highlight the dangers of not living with awareness of the Lord's coming. Jesus was not concerned with the time of His return and did not want His disciples to focus on it either. Whether He was coming back in a week or in a millennium, His followers were to be busy doing what He had left for them to do. The main character of this parable was the "faithful and sensible ["wise, prudent, judicious"] slave" who was trustworthy enough to be put in charge of the feeding and caring of the household in the master's absence. The "who is . . ." question is answered in v. 46 as the one "so doing when he [the master] comes."

24:46-47 The reward for the faithful and sensible servant who does what his master told him to do is that he is "blessed" (*makarios,* cf. comments on Matt. 5:3-11). The word implies one worthy of praise or one treated with good fortune. Jesus declared that the faithful and sensible servant who is found doing what he was told will be promoted, put in charge of all his master's possessions (v. 47). One might think of the account of Joseph and his experiences in Egypt. His diligence and faithfulness were rewarded with rank and authority; likewise, the faithful servant of Jesus will be rewarded with rank and authority in the kingdom.

24:48-49 The negative counterpart to the blessed servant was the "evil slave." In his heart (*en tē kardia autou*), that is, in the deepest recesses of his being, he determined that his master was going to be gone a long time. His conviction was that he had free rein to do as he pleased because the master would not be back for a long time. Since he was evil (*kakos,* "bad, wrong, one who does harm," not *ponēros*), his natural instinct was to take advantage of the situation. Verse 49 portrays this bad slave as violent toward others and self-indulgent, using his position to serve himself rather than serve his lord. This selfishness, intrinsic to his being "evil," was manifested because he had no concept of a coming day of accountability. The evil slave lived only for immediate gratification.

24:50-51 The consequences of his conduct came upon him when the master returned. There was no announcement of the master's intention to return, thus no warning to prepare. It was assumed that the servant would be prepared every moment to give an account of his use of the privileges given him by the master. The severity of his punishment (v. 51) emphasized the seriousness of doing the master's work. "Cut into pieces" (*dixotomeō*) was hyperbolic and dramatic, indicating severe retribution. The wicked slave was to be treated like an outcast.

The point of the illustration is clear: the Lord expects His disciples to be serving Him and not themselves, and His return is not going to be announced in advance. Therefore, in anticipation of that return, every moment should be spent in doing what is required. However, the illustration of the "evil slave" needs to be addressed with caution. One point of the parable was to separate the faithful from the wicked. It does not teach that a servant of Christ will be thrown out into the place of hypocrites where there is weeping and gnashing of teeth. The "evil slave" represents not a true disciple but one who professes to serve the master. His wicked heart was revealed by his selfish life and abuse of power. His lack of anticipation of his lord's return demonstrated that he was not genuine.

HOMILETICAL SUGGESTIONS

This section of Matthew's gospel is critical for believers of today. The attractions and distractions of the world have become so strong that many are losing sight of the imminent return of the Lord. The disciples' three questions provide relevant messages for the church.

The destruction of the temple in A.D. 70 and the subsequent horrors that fell upon Israel are a reminder of the truthfulness of the words of our Lord. His prediction of the temple's being torn down and the incredible destruction of the Holy City serve as historical testimony to the Lord's authoritative words and to God's willingness to judge even His beloved chosen people.

Perhaps one of the most significant lessons is the reminder not to get caught up in sensationalistic preaching about the end times. Pointing to natural catastrophes, wars, and atrocities as an indication of the end times is misleading teaching, because Christ stated that these are only normal conditions for mankind. The beginning of birth pains was the destruction of Jerusalem, and the subsequent horrors of human history are only testimonies of the fallen world in which we live.

The Great Tribulation is unprecedented in human history and will never be repeated. The destruction of Sodom and Gomorrah, the universal Flood, the devastation of Jerusalem during the Babylonian captivity and again in A.D. 70., and even the Holocaust of World War II cannot measure up to the torment and destruction of this appointed time. The main focus of the Great Tribulation will be the nation of Israel, which was not a possibility until after its reestablishment in 1948. For the church, the importance of this truth does not relate to warning of going through this tribulation, as this designated time is appointed against Daniel's people, not the church (Dan. 9:24). Rather, the church should know that God is not through with His people Israel. They need to hear the message of their Messiah and be prepared to call upon His name (23:37-39).

Perhaps the most important lesson is the warning about being a faithful and sensible servant. The last section compares two kinds of slaves: the faithful and wise in contrast to the evil and selfish. The true servant of Christ anticipates His soon return and is busy doing what He left His servants to do. We have great privileges as His servants, having an understanding of the coming destruction of the world, eternal values, and rewards. Luke 12:48 warns that to whom much is given, much is required. Many Christians fail to realize that their responsibility is to be doing the Master's work. The unsaved have no hope beyond this present material world and no motivation beyond immediate gratification. The believer has eternal hope, not based upon the temporal or frail securities of this life. May our lifestyle and attitude be a witness to our anticipation of the Lord's return (1 Peter 3:15; 1 Cor. 15:19; etc.).

MATTHEW
CHAPTER
TWENTY-FIVE

CONCLUSION TO
THE OLIVET DISCOURSE

This chapter continues the discourse on the Mount of Olives and offers two more parables to emphasize the importance of being prepared for the Lord's return. It closes with the teaching of the judgment of the sheep and goats, which left the disciples with a completed picture of events leading to the inauguration of the kingdom. As the Lord closed these lectures, the record of Matthew shifts back to the tension and drama of the temple and then leads to the intimacy of the Upper Room. Chapter 25 is eschatological and provides the completed revelation of God's program to establish the kingdom of the Son of Man.

PARABLE OF THE TEN VIRGINS, 25:1-13
(not found in Mark or Luke)

25:1-2   The key to this parable, as in the previous two, lies in its offering a contrast, being prepared and being unprepared. The kingdom is compared (*homoioō*, "has similarity to") to ten virgins, five described as foolish and five as prudent. The elements of the parable were common cultural items. According to Edersheim, ten witnesses were the required number "to be present at any office or ceremony, such as at benedictions accompanying the marriage ceremonies."[1] The virgins accompanied the bride as she went with her bridegroom to the wedding, and the lamps (often mounted on poles)[2] were to light the way if the ceremony was at night. Jesus stated (v. 2) that five of the virgins were "foolish" (*mōrai*), as no advance plans were made for the possibility of an extended wait. Five were "prudent" (*phronimoi*), that is, demonstrated foresight or insight.

25:3-5   The foolish had lamps, but were too shortsighted to prepare for a possible lengthy delay and, thus, did not carry extra oil. In contrast, the prudent took along extra oil in flasks (v. 4). The contrast was simple: the foolish did not make ready for the delay possibility, while the prudent thought ahead and prepared. Note that all the virgins slept, not just the foolish. Here the analogy of sleeping does not carry a negative connotation, as in some other passages (1 Thess. 5:6-7). In interpreting parables, one should keep focused on the main point and not be distracted by the peripheral particulars of the story. The point here was failure to anticipate unforeseen events and make advance provision.

25:6   The term "midnight" has no eschatological significance but simply conveys the inconvenience and unexpected hour for the event. How unusual it would be to begin the wedding parade at midnight. This dramatically emphasized what Jesus said (24:44), "The Son of Man is coming at an hour when you do not think He will." His coming will not be at a convenient or logical time. All artful and sensationalized predictions are useless because no sound, analytical scheme is within the range of human perception. The coming of the bridegroom was announced with a "shout" (*kraugē*) by a public crier who called out to summon all the members of the wedding party. The assumption was that the bridegroom had traveled from a great distance and thus arrived at an unusual hour. The wedding party was to be waiting for his arrival.

25:7-9   With the "shout" the virgins arose to meet and accompany the groom to the bride's home and from there to accompany both back to the groom's home. To "trim" (*kosmeō*) their lamps meant cutting the wicks and refilling the bases with the extra oil. Here the distinction between the two groups is evident (v. 8). The foolish, having already used the oil in their lamps, did not have an adequate amount now that the celebration procession was beginning. Seeing the extra oil brought by the prudent, the foolish asked to use their supply. The response in v. 9 is not intended to teach principles of sharing or stewardship but to make the point that the prudent were not responsible to cover the foolish virgins' lack of foresight. This was not the appropriate time to be concerned with one's supply of oil. That need should have been anticipated and planned for at the proper time.

25:10-12   More as an act of desperation than an indication of commitment, the foolish virgins went to find oil, regardless of the hour. Not only were they in danger of missing the significant social event, but they also risked public humiliation. During their desperate search, the bridegroom arrived, and those who were prepared participated in the feast.

"The door was shut" was a dramatic way of saying that, once the feast had begun, no one was allowed in to disrupt the proceedings. The foolish virgins finally arrived at the location of the feast (v. 11) but could not enter. Their cry, "Lord, lord, open up for us" was sad testimony of their failure to grasp the consequences of their foolishness. "Lord" is *kurios* ("lord, master"), the disciples' familiar appellation for Jesus. However, the word was also common as a polite form of address and more correctly translates here as "sir." The response of the gatekeeper was "I do not know you," which probably denotes their lack of individual significance and their not being included with the original group of virgins. Though interesting parallels with 7:22-23 could be drawn, there is no theological connection between the two contexts, and no attempts should be made to conjoin the different teachings of the two pericopes. So, even though originally invited to participate in the festive occasion, the foolish virgins lost their opportunity by not being prepared.

25:13   Once again, the application was straightforward: in regard to the kingdom of heaven (v. 1), one should be on the alert as its inauguration is approaching, though the day and hour are unknown. No time will be given to prepare, so one must stay in the preparation mode. Regardless of the day or hour, those who expect to be a part of the kingdom must be ready to welcome it.

It is important to note a significant feature of this parable that may lead to some confusion—there is no mention of the bride. Some late and weak manuscripts add a reference to the bride, but as Carson concludes, those words "may have been added out of a sense of propriety, a desire for a well-rounded story in which the bride should be present . . . . On external evidence alone, omission is more likely the original."[3] Thus, the church, the "bride of Christ," is not the focus of this parable, and the issue is not the rapture of the church. The parable is about being prepared. The Jews of Jesus' day were not prepared to join in the feast of the King because of not being prepared for the coming of the Messiah. That generation was foolish and unprepared.

THE PARABLE OF THE TALENTS, 25:14-30 (see also Luke 19:11-27)

Matthew and Luke have different contexts for this parable. In Luke's account, the Lord was proceeding up to Jerusalem; in Matthew's, He had been in Jerusalem for a few days and had already gone through a series of confrontations with the religious leaders. It is possible that either Jesus told this parable twice, relating the different features to the uniqueness of the different contexts, or that Luke records it out of sequence to emphasize the drama about to take place in Jerusalem. To relate events in logical sequence rather than chronological to emphasize certain aspects of their accounts was not unusual for ancient narrators. The variances in the two accounts reflect two purposes in telling their stories, and the language differs enough to allow for two parables of very similar nature. As Carson observes, "The few parallels are well within the bounds of the speech variation of any itinerant preacher. Moreover, the emphasis in each of the two parables is somewhat different . . . . On the whole it seems best to side with certain older commentators (Plummer, Zahn) who discern two separate parables."[4]

25:14-15 "For just like the man . . ." introduces the parable, which continued discussion of the kingdom of heaven. In the same way that a man leaves his possessions in the care of others, the Messiah, having left the seeds of His kingdom in the care of His servants, expects a profit when He returns. Here, rather than coming for the first time, the King is portrayed as coming again to reap His investment left in this age to the care of His followers. The term "entrusted" is not to be taken lightly. *Paradirōmi* means to "give something over to others for their use or care." In the negative sense, it can mean "betray" but here apparently portrays the stewardship of some of the man's material wealth. Verse 15 reveals that different amounts of "talents" (*talanton*) were given to three different servants, representing one who did exceptionally well, another who did well, and a third who failed by not making a profit. The point was not maintaining what was given but making increase from what was entrusted. A *talanton* was a measure of money (either in coins or bars of silver or gold) worth between 5,000 and 6,000 denarii. Depending upon whether the talent was silver or gold, its worth could have been as much as twenty years' salary to a common laborer (the NIV's note suggesting that a talent was worth more than $1,000 is far too conservative).

To give a servant five talents, then, was to entrust him with a notable fortune. To another was given two talents, likewise a very large amount of money; and to the third, a lesser though still significant amount of currency. Jesus carefully clarified that the amount given was "according to his own ability," which implies a thoughtful and personal stewardship based on the rich man's evaluation of his servants.

25:16-17 The first servant went out ("immediately," according to some manuscripts) and invested (*ergazomai*) the talents and doubled his master's money. The action may have involved some risk, but he used the honor of being entrusted with such a great treasure to make a profit for his lord. In the same way, the second slave doubled his money as well. Thus these two servants earned their master 100 percent profit with what had been entrusted to them.

25:18 In contrast, the third wasted his opportunity by being protective of that entrusted to him. He simply dug a hole and buried the money, a common practice in the ancient world assumed by the reference to "a treasure hidden in a field" (13:44). Though some might praise the act because of the no-risk factor for such a large sum, this did not please his master.

25:19-21 The Lord's expression a "long time" before the master returned implies that the servants must have been investing and trading over a length of time rather than engaging in just one quick moneymaking scheme. The master came to "settle accounts" with these servants and wanted a report of his investment. The servant with the five talents came first (v. 20) with the good report of doubling the money and drawing attention to his achievement with "See [*ide,* "behold," expressing a dramatic sight], I have "gained five more talents."

The master expressed pleasure in the efficient and thoughtful work of his servant, attributing goodness and faithfulness to him. However, referring to him as a slave (*doulos*) indicated this was not a partnership and that profit was expected. The master could have taken his profit without commendation, but instead recognized the servant's worth and rewarded him not only with kind words of praise but with material compensation. This reward is not to be understood as personal finances but as added responsibility, which increased the servant's authority and prestige. The expression "few things" is an intended understatement to demonstrate how the master viewed his material things in comparison to the value placed on the faithfulness of the steward. In addition to being given public praise and a promotion, the faithful servant was also brought into an intimate and warm relationship with his master ("the joy of your master").

25:22-23 The exact expressions of vv. 19-21, on the part of both the servant and the master, are repeated in these two verses. The amount of money was apparently not the issue, since the servant doubling two talents received the same praise and reward as the one doubling five. The key feature was goodness and faithfulness, evidenced by making profit for their master from the stewardship received.

25:24-25 The third servant presented a completely opposite scenario. When summoned, this steward offered an excuse for failing to make a profit. One can only imagine his frantic thoughts as he observed the first two presenting their increase and receiving praise and rewards. Then, standing before the master, he attempted to shift the blame. "I knew you to be a hard man" implied that if the master had not been so hard, then the servant would have taken the risk and invested his money. Hendriksen summarizes, "In order to invent an excuse for his own dereliction of duty, this fellow has the audacity to accuse his master of being 'hard.'"[5] This was not unlike Adam, who tried to shift the blame of his failure onto God for giving him a wife (Gen. 3:12), or Saul, who blamed the people he was supposed to be leading for disobeying God's instructions (1 Sam. 15:15).

The wicked servant literally said, "Lord [or Sir], knowing you, that you are a hard man . . . I buried your talent in the earth." The term "hard" (*sklēros*) means "difficult, harsh, terrible" and is described here as meaning that the master had a reputation for tough business practices, "reaping where you did not sow, and gathering where you scattered no seed." The truthfulness of this charge must be questioned because (v. 15) the master entrusted his great fortune to others and did so "according to his [each servant's] own ability." He also showed great generosity in both praise and reward to the servants who performed well.

The third servant then simply offered back what had been initially given to him (v. 25). "See, you have what is yours." Alford makes an important observation related to this comment, "This is also false—it was not *to son* (what is yours)—for there was his lord's time, and his own labor which was his lord's too—to be accounted for."[6] MacArthur correctly points out, "Although he had been given fewer resources than the other two slaves, he had the same obligation to use what he had to his maximum ability."[7] As with the other two, this servant prefaced his presentation with "See" (*ide*); however, the effect was far less impressive.

25:26-27 The master's response was not to defend himself but rather to point the accusing finger back to the slave. In contrast to "good and faithful," which ennobled the first two, this servant heard "You wicked and lazy slave." The word "wicked" is *ponēros,* which in a moral concept implies something ethically reprehensible.[8] Though the servant had failed to do what was ethically expected of him, even worse was his attempt to excuse himself by blaming the character of his lord. The label "lazy" (*oknēros*) indicated that the motive for burying the talent was actually an unwillingness to exert the effort required for trade or investment in the marketplace.

When the master said, "You knew that I reap where I did not sow," he was not accepting the accusation as true but, rather, using the claim as a logical argument to show that the slave was lying. If the slave actually believed that the master possessed such a greedy and demanding nature, then why was the money buried instead of placed in the bank to earn interest (v. 27)? This interest-bearing factor likewise indicated the master's journey to have been lengthy. Even the small gain of bank interest would have pleased the master, but this slave was too lazy to even make the deposit. Though the Old Testament forbade charging interest to another Israelite on loans (Ex. 22:25), it was perfectly legal to earn interest from Gentiles (Deut. 23:20), such as in Roman banks or in business dealings with Gentiles. Thus Jesus, even in His parable, was not violating the Law.

25:28-30 The one talent was taken from the third slave, and he was not given a second opportunity to please the master. Rather, he suffered immediate judgment. Some are confused by the lord's giving the one unused talent to the man who had originally been given five; but considering the statement that the initial stewardship was based on ability (v. 15), this servant logically would make the best use of it.

The summary of v. 29 is not intended to offer explanation as to why the one talent was given to the servant who originally had five. Nevertheless, the *gar* ("therefore") was used emphatically rather than in an illative sense (introducing a reason): "Indeed! Take the talent from him." The same principle is used in relation to kingdom standards in 13:12. In the Matthew 13 context, the issue was insight into kingdom truth, which the disciples received, but the people were taught in parables, which they did not understand. The disciples were given more truth and insight, while the people were kept in darkness by the parables (13:11-15). In the present context, the issue was the stewardship of the king's property. The good and faithful servant received more, and the wicked and lazy lost everything entrusted to him.

Verse 30 presents a severe and climactic end to the parable. The wicked and lazy servant was cast out of the "joy" of his master (vv. 21, 23) and called "worthless" (*achreion*), meaning of no use. The "outer darkness" along with "weeping and gnashing of teeth" has already been referenced in 8:12 and 22:13 as a place for those rejected from the kingdom. This appears to be extreme harshness toward one who did not lose the talent but merely preserved it. However, the Lord's point was that the kingdom (v. 1, context of this parable) was calling servants to honor and glorify its King. Those who failed to do so demonstrated they were not true servants but wicked, lazy, and useless usurpers of the prerogatives of the kingdom. Their fate was expulsion from the kingdom (of light) into darkness, torment, and remorse. Primarily this parable relates to Israel, who claimed a desire to serve their King but in reality squandered His blessings. Any attempt to relate this to the church or associate the "talents" with skills or abilities, especially spiritual gifting, is eisegesis. Though the principle may apply in some way, it is not the point of the parable. The Jews rejected their Messiah, which led to the pronouncement of judgment upon city and nation (23:37-39). The disciples, hearing this message, were being alerted to the severity of that judgment to come. As with all parables, to become rigid in associating every element with some particular feature of the church or the life of the Lord is to most likely miss the primary point. Here, the "journey" (v. 15) is not to be taken as the Lord's return to heaven following His resurrection, as it is not the focus of the parable. The entrusting of valuable property to "good and faithful" servants in contrast to "wicked, lazy, and useless" servants is the point. The religious leaders claimed to be servants of God and wanted to be in the kingdom, but in reality they were wicked, lazy, and useless to the King. Therefore, as in 8:12 and 22:13, they would be stripped of their part of the kingdom and cast out into outer darkness.

THE JUDGMENT OF THE SHEEP AND GOATS, 25:31-46

25:31-32   Jesus then moved into discussion of the specific details of His return. The connection between the lesson of the parables and this subsequent discussion might best be seen in that the parables related to those privileged to be Israelites, specifically His servants, and how they were to anticipate His return. The latter referred to the nations. Jesus took the disciples mentally to the time when He will return and establish His glorious kingdom. His angels will be with Him. This reference to angels should not be taken in the generic sense of "messengers," as though referring to the prophets or the apostles, but in its more natural sense of spirit beings. Their presence emphasizes that this will be no mere earthly kingdom, but the Son of Man is going to be revealed in His glorious state, including accompaniment by these glorious beings.

In v. 32, imagery is created of a universal court. The nations (*ethnē*) are gathered before His throne, and all the peoples of the earth are separated into one of two categories. This judgment must not be confused with the Great White Throne judgment of Revelation 20:11-15 (to declare the everlasting state of the unsaved), or with the *bēma* ("judgment seat") of Christ in 2 Corinthians 5:10 (for believers). The nations are gathered before the messianic throne following the return of Christ. This is to be associated with 24:30-

31; when the Lord comes again in His glory and the elect (Rev. 7:1-9; the 144,000 Israelites and the faithful Gentiles who are saved through the Great Tribulation) are gathered to Him. Then the remainder of the nations are gathered for this judgment.

The analogy of the shepherd is an appropriate metaphor for the Son of Man, who is the Good Shepherd (John 10). He separates the peoples of the nations as a shepherd would go through a flock and separate the sheep from the goats. The practice of separating sheep from goats in the ancient world had practical values, but one should not assume any more significance here than the idea of two categories of people who survived the Great Tribulation.

25:33   The nations are divided and then separated. The "sheep," who apparently find favor in His sight, are placed on the right. The "goats," who are being rejected, are placed on the left. Earlier the mother of James and John had approached Jesus, trying to secure these positions for her sons (20:20-21) to demonstrate their honor and significance in His kingdom. Here, apparently, the left side would not be considered a place of honor but, on the contrary, a symbol of rejection. Most likely the positions (left and right) simply reflect the separation.

25:34   The sheep, those on the right, are invited into the kingdom. These are "blessed of" the King's Father. To be blessed (*eulogeō*, not *makarios* of 5:3-11 or 24:46) in this context is to have received some gracious benefit. The Father has bestowed this benefit before the invitation to enter His Son's kingdom, but specifics are not given here. The invitation is to "come . . . inherit the kingdom," which means literally to "take possession of, take a share of" (*klēronomeō*).

The most fascinating aspect is that the statement addresses the "nations," not the Jews. The Gentiles are therefore invited to share in the kingdom. Even more intriguing is the last phrase, "prepared for you from the foundation of the world." The kingdom Messiah is establishing will include the Gentiles, and not as a last-minute adjustment to God's plan but determined from the very foundation of the world (*katbolēs kosmou*). The messianic kingdom, therefore, was predetermined, before the world was put into operation, to be a place for the human race to experience the divine kingship of God's Anointed. This is not to detract from the Davidic covenant, where David's "Son" would rule the world in peace; but it means that in God's pre-creation decree, all those "blessed by God" would be a part of the Golden Age. Israel will head the nations, and the Messiah will rule the whole earth from the Davidic throne, which will fulfill the promises to David and the nation. The church will be joint heirs with Christ in this age, being His servants with full kingdom power and glory. And the Gentiles who live through the Tribulation, those who are labeled "sheep," will be permitted to enter the kingdom to experience the blessings of God's sovereign, direct rule on earth.

25:35-36   The next two verses offer explanation (explanatory *gar*, v. 35) as to why they have received this wonderful privilege. Here the exegete must be careful not to read into the text any more than what is said. Jesus listed six specific needs to which these "sheep" responded with compassion and acts of mercy: hunger; thirst; being a stranger; nakedness; sickness; and imprisonment. Carson says, "The reason for admission to the kingdom in this parable is more evidential than causative."[9] This may be correct, but the major thrust is that these acts of compassion were performed while unaware of earning favor with God or of any significant benefit to them personally (v. 37).

25:37-39   The sheep are here called the "righteous" (*hoi dikaioi*), which is to be understood as a forensic term indicating imputed righteousness rather than intrinsic character. However, possibly it is also a title of honor respecting their "right behavior" in feeding and caring for the brothers of the King (v. 40). Their question, "When did we . . ." attests to surprise in hearing that they had performed such things for *Him.* Barnes sees their response as "indicative of humility—a deep sense of their being unworthy of such commendation."[10] However, their surprise is not in that they were recognized for doing good things, but in that He is saying they did it to Him.

25:40   The King's response to their question leads to a greater understanding of the mystical union of Jesus and the people of Israel: "these brothers of Mine." Many excellent scholars assume that the brothers must be Christians.[11] There is certainly truth in stating that the disciples are referenced as brothers of Christ, as are all believers (12:46-50), but it is assuming too much to say that "Jesus never speaks of Jews as his brothers."[12] The disciples and the crowd to which He pointed spoken of in 12:46-50 were Jews. They were those who believed Him and followed Him, but they were

Jews. The term "brother" (*adelphos*) did become (post-Ascension) an almost technical term for those joined together in Christ, but it also had normal meanings within the context of Jesus' time. Calling another Jew a brother was common. Peter, a believer, referred to the crowd of Jews (nonbelievers) as "brothers" (Acts 2:29); and Paul, a believer, referred to his fellow Jews (nonbelievers) as his "brethren" (Rom. 9:3). Thus, it is not so strange to hear the Messiah of Israel refer to the Jews as His brothers.

The context would certainly be strained to attempt to place the church in this event. The Great Tribulation, a period of unparalleled suffering (24:21), is a time appointed for Israel (Dan. 9:24-27), not the church, and the sequence of events just described by Jesus best places this judgment after that tribulation. The best understanding of "brother" in this context is that they are the faithful Jews who are suffering in anticipation of their Messiah's return. The term would also include the faithful of all nations (Rev. 7:4-14). But the focus is on those converted during the Tribulation period and primarily on the Jews (the 144,000).

25:41-45　　The next category (the goats) is brought forward, given the reason for their condemnation, and the exact opposite scenario is presented. In this instance the group is addressed as "accursed ones" (*hoi katēramenoi,* "those having a curse put upon them"), here implying that these have been pronounced guilty and sentenced to torment. The destination of the goats is "away from" the King and into the "eternal fire" (*to pur to aiōnion*), their everlasting destiny. "Eternal" might best be understood as "everlasting." Eternal implies no beginning as well as no ending. The fire of destruction was "prepared" and therefore had a beginning.

It is important to note that the fire was prepared not for humans, but for Satan and the angels that followed his rebellion. Yet, these human beings are condemned to share this place of torment with him (cf. Rev. 20:10, 15). This implies that they are categorized with Satan's rebellion. The reasons stated here are the antithesis of the reasons for the blessings above. The hunger, thirst, being a stranger, naked, sick, and in prison were conditions of the Messiah's brothers, and the goats did not offer aid. Again, the context of the Great Tribulation and the suffering of God's chosen people is the major point. One cannot avoid everlasting torment by meeting the material needs of people; the issue here is the acceptance or rejection of Messiah's chosen people. Carson states, "As people respond to his disciples, or 'brothers,' and align themselves with their distress and afflictions, they align themselves with the Messiah who identifies himself with them."[13] These ask the same question as the sheep, "When" did this happen? (v. 44). Unless people understand the connection between the Messiah and His people, they would not be aware of their acceptance or rejection of Him (v. 45). Jesus identifies with His people to such a degree that actions toward them are taken personally by Him. This statement is certainly reminiscent of the words of the risen Lord to Paul (Acts 9:4), "Why are you persecuting Me?"

25:46   The conclusion to the judgment of the sheep and goats is summarized by the appointment of their separate destinies. The goats "go away into eternal punishment" (*kolasin aiōnion*), but the sheep, "the righteous," enter into "eternal life." Thus, the fate of these two groups is determined by their response to the needs of the persecuted people of the Messiah. It should also be remembered that not only do the "righteous" (declared to be so by their right response to the needs of the messianic people) enter into eternal life, but they are also welcomed into the kingdom that is about to be established on the earth (vv. 31, 34).

HOMILETICAL SUGGESTIONS

This whole section may be seen as a presentation of the dichotomy between those who are a part of the messianic kingdom and those who are not. The context is the kingdom, first in two parables describing features of preparedness for the coming King and, second, in the prediction of the judgment of the nations. Three pairs of antonymous persons are set up to demonstrate the contrasts between the true servants of Christ and the false, as well as those who will be accepted and those rejected by the Messiah at His return.

The first parable should be used to illustrate the necessity of anticipating the Messiah to come at any time and not just when one thinks He should come. The oil does not represent the Holy Spirit or any other feature of the Christian life, but only symbolizes the lack of preparation on the part of the foolish. The lack of foresight and preparedness for the great event is the main point. How Christians remain prepared for the Lord's appearance would be a good focus for study of this parable.

The second parable does not represent the giving of spiritual gifts or special artistic abilities. The point is investing in the Lord's work and being ready to demonstrate that the valuable truth of His coming kingdom has been wisely used for His glory. This parable demonstrates the accountability of Christ's servants and might best be applied with the proverb "To whom much is given, much is required" (Luke 12:48). Those who have been given the freedom to live openly for Christ, having access to Bible colleges, Christian bookstores, numerous study tools, and so on, will certainly be held more responsible than those in less privileged areas. Though these principles can be illustrated from the parable, it is also likely that the primary focus is on the nation of Israel, who squandered their privileges by not serving the Lord when He came. This is the reason for the severe judgment meted out at the end of the parable.

The judgment of the sheep and goats is significant in the flow of the Lord's argument. The event is stated to occur when He comes in glory and establishes His kingdom. The judgment of the nations is based upon their treatment of Israel and all believers during the Tribulation. This is not to be confused with the Great White Throne judgment of Revelation 20. That judgment is of "the dead" (Rev. 20:12), and the heavens and earth "flee" (Rev. 20:11), which is not a factor in Matthew 25. The judgment of the Great White Throne will be determined by whether or not individual names are written in the Lamb's book of life (20:15) and not by their care for the Messiah's brothers. This account is not a parable for teaching a lesson but a prophetic declaration closing the Lord's teaching on the kingdom of heaven and bringing to closure the Olivet Discourse.

MATTHEW
CHAPTER
TWENTY-SIX

EVENTS LEADING
TO HIS ARREST

This chapter contains the saddest record of human depravity. One of the Twelve betrays the Lord; the religious leaders, under the leadership of the high priest Caiaphas, blaspheme and physically abuse their Messiah; and even the most vocally dedicated of the disciples, Peter, denies his Lord three times and is brought face to face with his own weakness and failure. This chapter also records some of the grandest qualities of the human experience as the Son of Man was faced with the horror and shame of His coming death but stood firm in faith and loyalty to the Father. Later in life, Peter, the one who denied his Lord, would write that this courageous act of Jesus was to be an example for all who claim to be His servants (1 Peter 2:21-23).

TWO DAYS BEFORE PASSOVER, 26:1-5
(Mark 14:1-2; Luke 22:1-2)

26:1-2   Jesus concluded His lessons on the side of the Mount of Olives and began to move toward Bethany. Matthew and Mark specifically state that the events here were only two days before Passover (v. 2). Meyer identifies this as being Tuesday; the Feast would begin on Thursday.[1] The Passover Feast was on Nisan 14 (Ex. 12:1-14), beginning at sundown. Hendriksen points to the climactic nature of the Lord's comments: "Something new is added when Jesus now designates the very day when this being handed over for crucifixion would take place, namely, during the night from Thursday to Friday, with the crucifixion itself to occur on Friday."[2]

The Son of Man was not just to be arrested but "handed over" (*paradidotai*), implying betrayal. This should have prompted the disciples to think about possible treachery among their own group or, at least, that the religious leaders would turn Him over to the Gentiles. The reference to crucifixion, likewise, had to create some frightening thoughts for them. Crucifixion (*stauroō*) on the infamous Roman cross (*stauros*) was designed to be a slow and painful form of death. This form of execution was so degrading and agonizing that Roman law prohibited any Roman citizen's being crucified.[3] Christ first mentions this horrible destiny for Himself in 20:18-19.

26:3-5   Verse 3 begins with the temporal particle *tote* ("then"), but this is not to imply the beginning point of the plotting to kill Jesus (see 12:14). Carson is correct in seeing the statement following vv. 1-2 as Matthew's way of indicating that all the coming events were under God's sovereign control.[4] The "chief priests and the elders of the people" was most likely a reference to the Sanhedrin. Though the third major group (the scribes) is missing in Matthew's record, Mark does include the scribes. Thus this was a gathering of the primary elements of the Sanhedrin, the same body that would meet later to hold the "trials" for Jesus. The meeting was held in the "court" (*tēn aulēn,* more likely the "courtyard" since this was an unofficial meeting) of the high priest Caiaphas. The true high priest was Annas (Luke 3:2; Acts 4:6), the father-in-law of Caiaphas. Annas (also spelled Ananus) was removed as high priest by the Romans (who probably thought he had too much power over the people), and Caiaphas was placed in the position.[5] Jesus' being first taken to Annas (John 18:13) implies that the Jews still looked to him as the true high priest.

This meeting was not a trial but a conference for making a plan to rid themselves of this One who dared challenge their authority and reputation. They "plotted together" (*sunebouleusanto,* "took counsel of one another") as how best to dispose of their enemy. The meeting was not to consider the possibility that His accusations against them might be true, that perhaps somehow religious error had unconsciously crept in. Neither was a public defense being devised to openly respond to His charges. Instead, they plotted to "seize" Him by "stealth" (*dolos,* "treachery, deceit") and kill Him.

Verse 5 indicates that they knew the people were seriously considering the things Jesus claimed and also that during this holy time (the "festival" was the week of Passover) messianic expectations were always high. Moreover, the Galileans who widely followed Jesus might stir up trouble while so many visitors were in Jerusalem. From this statement, apparently, the decision was made to wait until after Passover to kill Him. These plans changed, however, when Judas (one of His own) devised a plan to arrest Jesus apart from the crowd's attention (vv. 14-16). Once again, this demonstrated God's sovereign control over every detail of the Lord's coming sacrifice.

ANOINTING OF JESUS' HEAD; THE BETRAYAL PLANNED, 26:6-16 (Mark 14:3-11)

26:6-7   This anointing should not be confused with the account in John 12:3-8 or Luke 7:37-50. The anointing of John 12:3-8 took place six days before Passover in the home of Lazarus, Martha, and Mary, when Mary anointed Jesus' feet, upsetting Judas, who received the same rebuke as the disciples received here in the house of Simon the Leper. The Luke 7:37-50 event occurred in the home of a Pharisee apparently named Simon as well. Identifying Simon the leper is difficult, as the name "Simon" was quite common, and "leper" referenced a known condition (or former condition) rather than a family name. Simon must have been cured by the Lord, because, if still a leper, Jesus and His disciples would have violated the Mosaic Law by being in his home. Perhaps this was the leper of Matthew 8:2-3, or he may have been yet another leper since their healing was a trademark of His ministry (10:5-8; 11:4-5).

In the house of Simon, an unidentified woman approached Jesus and poured expensive perfume over His head, an act symbolizing extreme reverence, sometimes performed to honor great rabbis. Perfume specifics are limited (John gives a detailed description) to its being very expensive and stored in an alabaster container. To access the perfume, the slender neck of the container had to be snapped off to open the vial.

26:8-9   The disciples' response was typical at this point of their training. They saw only the perfume's material value and not the spiritual value in the act of worship. Mark records that only some of the disciples were upset. But these were speaking among themselves (not to the Lord or in open discussion) and rebuking the woman for waste (Mark 14:4-5). Mark also sets the perfume's value at 300 denarii, equivalent to a common laborer's annual wage (14:5). In contrast to Judas (John 12:4-6), some of the disciples were truly concerned for the poverty-stricken, since their ministry included reaching out to Israel's poor (11:5).

26:10-11　　The Lord did not respond with a stern rebuke but used the opportunity to reinforce a previous lesson (John 12:8). Teachers often teach the same lesson a second or third time to emphasize some critical doctrine. Jesus was "aware" of their discussion, most likely not by any supernatural power but by having been attentive to their mumbling and their comments to the woman. His question, "Why do you bother the woman?" implies that He overheard their remarks.

Jesus labeled her act as a "good deed to [or "for"] Me." This must have thrilled her. She certainly stung from the rebuke of the disciples, only to be vindicated by the Lord Himself. The incident also demonstrated how the disciples, who knew Jesus more intimately than anyone else, still often failed to understand His Person or His true mission. The words of v. 11 were not intended to belittle concern for the poor but to place them in proper perspective to the Lord Himself. Worshiping Him was of far greater value than feeding the poor. This does not mean that constructing a beautiful church building is more important than providing for the needs of those who make up the church but that He has priority in every aspect, including material needs. In contrast to the poor, Jesus' time with them was limited. He soon would be gone from their presence, and the disciples would no longer be able to personally and physically demonstrate reverence to Him.

26:12-13　　Whether the woman knew of and understood Jesus' crucifixion predictions is not stated, but Jesus attributed her act to one anticipating His death and burial. In the burial process, bodies were washed, anointed with fragrant oils and perfumes, and wrapped in linen. To Jesus, this perfuming was symbolic of future events. Therefore, throughout the centuries wherever the gospel is preached, this gesture will remain as a memorial to her faith and commitment to Him. The use of "gospel" (*to euanggelion*) is significant here in that the pronoun "this" must identify it with His death and burial, which would lead to His glorious resurrection, and this is good news for the world.

26:14-16   It would appear that when Judas witnessed this second "waste of money," he determined to betray Jesus. John 12:6 reveals his greedy and corrupt character by his theft of ministry money. Matthew's wording "one of the Twelve" emphasizes his treachery and indicates the fulfillment of Psalm 41:9. Matthew also records his full name, which has since become synonymous with cowardly betrayal.

Judas met secretly with the chief priests and bargained for money. He apparently realized that Jesus was serious about His coming death and that his selfish motives for following Him were not going to be fulfilled. Therefore he sought to cut his losses by getting something for his investment in Jesus. Undoubtedly, like most of Israel, Judas expected Messiah to drive out the Romans and establish a new Israelite kingdom, much like Maccabeus had done. Now, though Jesus had demonstrated great power and influence, it was apparent that there would be no revolution and no new kingdom from which to profit. Pity or justification for his actions are unnecessary as Judas was a cowardly, greedy man who sought only his own welfare. "Thirty pieces of silver" was not just a random figure. It most likely was derived from the legal reimbursement requirement for an injured slave (Ex. 21:32), perhaps reflecting a low view of Jesus. More significant, however, is the connection of which the priests would have been ignorant. In Zechariah, the Lord sends the prophet to act the role of a shepherd who breaks his staff in refusing to protect a rebellious flock. There the wages of the shepherd were weighed out, thirty shekels of silver (Matthew uses the LXX terminology), which the prophet then took and threw to the potter in the house of the Lord (Zech. 11:12-13). Once the bargain was struck, Judas began to seek opportunities for betraying Jesus into the vicious hands of His enemies. That such an act of treachery should follow on the wonderful act of worship of v. 7 was divine irony.

THE LAST PASSOVER AND
INSTITUTION OF THE LORD'S SUPPER 26:17-30
(Mark 14:12-26; Luke 22:7-23; John 13:21-30)

26:17   The next temporal marker was "the first day of Unleavened Bread," and this phrase would make it Thursday morning. This was the traditional preparation day for sacrificing the household lambs and arranging the food and drink necessary for the Passover (Mark 14:14). The disciples' question indicated their expectation for the Lord to lead them in the Passover meal rather than their participating in family feasts. The question in Matthew's account is apparently in response to Jesus' instructions for Peter and John to go and prepare a place for them to eat Passover (Luke 22:7-8).

26:18-19   Matthew omits details on how they were to recognize this "certain man," but both Mark and Luke offer some interesting information. The disciples were to enter Jerusalem. They would meet a man carrying water, a unique circumstance as such tasks were usually relegated to females. They were simply to follow into whatever house he entered and then inquire of the owner as to where preparations were to be made (Mark 14:13-14; Luke 22:10-11).

The two were to say that "the Teacher" asked regarding the room for the feast. Here the term "teacher" (*ho didaskalos*) was used as a recognizable title to designate this particular teacher as Jesus. Undoubtedly, the house owner must have been a follower of Jesus or else the title would not have been significant. Also this reveals that Jesus had already made preliminary arrangements apart from the knowledge of the Twelve. Hendriksen suggests that this mysterious process, rather than just naming the man and telling the disciples exactly where to go, may have been intended to keep Judas from having advance knowledge, allowing private time with the disciples before His arrest.[6]

That Jesus would send a message to this man stating that "my time is at hand" is also noteworthy, perhaps implying this man understood the importance of this particular Passover. Carson, however, believes it was ambiguous to both the man and the disciples.[7] The owner of the house showed them a large room above his own house (Mark 14:15; Luke 22:12). Typical of many homes of this period, the main dwelling was on ground level, and a banquet or guest room was built on an upper level, accessible by a stone stairway built alongside the building. The disciples (Peter and John) did as told, and the arrangements were made.

26:20   That Thursday evening, Nisan 14, the Lord ate the Passover meal with His Twelve. A cultural feature often overlooked is the "reclining" at the table. A beautiful Renaissance painting known as *The Last Supper* incorrectly depicts certain aspects of this meal. In this culture, the low tables were arranged in a U-shape for such occasions. Instead of sitting, diners reclined on grass mats placed around the tables, each person propping on an elbow with his feet pointing away from the table. Insight into other significant features of the Passover is critical to properly understand this event, and the pastor or teacher desiring to fully comprehend it would do well to research the topic thoroughly. Pate's brief but helpful description[8] is recommended.

26:21   The action within this chapter probably took place following the events recorded in John 13:4-21. In Luke, Jesus stated His eagerness to eat "this" particular Passover (22:15), specifically because it would be His last on this earth (22:16). While eating the meal, which began sometime after sundown (thus Friday by Jewish reckoning[9] though Thursday evening according to current time frames), Jesus made the alarming announcement that one of the men around the banquet table would betray Him. How far the meal had progressed before the statement was made cannot be determined, but to assume near the end is probably safe, as Jesus soon sent Judas out and no one protested that he would miss the meal. Luke implies that Judas was present for institution of the Lord's Supper and, therefore, heard the explanation of the bread and wine representing His body and blood (22:19-21). This makes the betrayal of the Lord even more amazing.

26:22-23   With the exception of Judas, each man responded with sincere grief and fear ("surely not I"). An amazing factor is the questioning of themselves first. It reflects their own inner struggle and fear that the growing hostility might cause them to break and fail their Lord. Nothing indicates accusations against anyone else, including Judas. Matthew records Judas's question separately from the others (v. 25). Hendriksen points out the "loathsome hypocrisy" of his response and notes that it was "probably after considerable hesitation."[10] In John's account, Peter prompted John to personally ask Him who it was (13:21-25).

The Lord's answer, "He who dipped (aorist participle) his hand with Me in the bowl," (v. 23) was not as obvious as appears to the modern reader. As the meal was served, the serving dishes located in the middle of the tables were passed around. "He who dipped" could have been any one of the men around the table; indeed, this is more clearly stated in Mark 14:20, "It is one of the Twelve, one who dips with Me in the bowl." The point was that it would be one who had just shared this meal with Him. In John's account, note that Jesus was speaking directly to John when the future tense (*egō bapsō*) was used: Jesus Himself would dip and hand the sop to the traitor. Thus, John did not record exactly the same conversation. Why John did not understand or reveal the traitor was not explained.

26:24 Jesus once again used the third person reference to Himself, "the Son of Man," and stated that His "going" (a familiar euphemism for death) would be in accordance with what had been written of Him. Thus, for the Messiah to die in this manner was predetermined by the will of God. This may be intended as an allusion to Psalm 41:9 or more broadly to Isaiah 53:4-12. Luke more clearly states, "As it has been determined" (22:22). Barnes points out that the phrase might more literally be "marked out by a boundary— that is, in the divine purpose."[11]

"But woe to that man by whom the Son of Man is betrayed" indicates the other side to divine purpose. The human element was not excused by one's falling into a fatalistic view of sovereignty. Judas was responsible for his actions and would pay a terrible price. "It would have been good for that man if he had not been born," sobering and terrifying words in view of the reality that must have struck Judas's heart at hearing them. Judas was not an innocent victim of a sovereign plan: his wickedness and greed had set him up as the person to fulfill this role of betrayer. MacArthur's summary is good: "Contrary to the perverted reasoning of some interpreters, the fact that this sinful act was used by God to provide salvation from sin did not justify Judas by making evil good. God's sovereignly turning evil to His own righteous purposes does not make a sin any less sinful or the sinner any less guilty."[12]

26:25 Judas's hard heart must certainly be seen in this hypocritical response. Already having bargained for the betrayal, he had the money in his possession. Only one depraved of any sense of conscience could look the Lord in the face and ask this question, "Surely it is not I?" It may be significant that Matthew records that Judas called Him rabbi (*hrabbi*) whereas the other disciples called Him Lord (*kurios,* v. 22). Jesus' response was direct and chilling, "You have said it yourself." There could be no doubt in Judas's mind that his treachery was known. Jesus sent Judas away, but the others still do not make the connection to his being the traitor (John 13:27-30). John also reveals that at this moment the wickedness of Judas was compounded by Satan's filling his heart (John 13:27).

26:26 Jesus then moved into the unique feature of this last Passover. Connecting the Passover meal with the upcoming events of His death, He instituted the memorial supper commonly referred to as Communion. First, He took the bread (*artos*), which in the Passover meal would be unleavened matzos, and used it as a symbol of His body. The significance of its being unleavened cannot be overstated, since leaven normally represents hypocrisy and sin (e.g., 1 Cor. 5:1-8). Therefore, to celebrate the Lord's Supper with the improper symbol of leavened bread does not rightly portray or honor that being represented.

Jesus "broke" (*klaō*), not cut, the bread. The matzo used in Passover was baked in thin sheets much like crackers and was broken or torn when distributed. It symbolized the breaking of His own body. As the bread was consumed, the participants were certainly aware that it symbolized the sustenance of their spiritual lives, even as bread was the most basic food sustenance for physical life. As the bread was passed, each broke off a piece to symbolize the taking of His life so that they might live. The words "This is My body" (*touto estin to sōma mou*) was actually the dividing wall between the German and Swiss Reformations. Luther demanded that it be taken literally, whereas Zwingli understood it figuratively. Of course, the expression can be no more literal than when Jesus said, "I am the door."

26:27-28 Next, Jesus took the cup (*potērion*), which symbolized the pouring out of His blood (v. 28). None of the gospel writers uses the word "wine," though the drinking of wine at the Passover cannot be denied. Some modern efforts to remove "wine" from this context and replace it with "grape juice" reflect immaturity and error. This culture did not have the capacity to stop natural fermentation, and the fruit of the vine was processed by pressing the grapes, which produced the wine (Isa. 16:10). The vessel bearing the wine—the cup—was used repeatedly of Christ's suffering (e.g., 20:22-23; 26:39). The shed blood represented here was passed among the disciples, and they were told to drink to demonstrate participation in this great sacrifice, the symbol of the New Covenant (Luke 22:20).

That the blood is poured out "for many for forgiveness of sin" was indicating that through the shed blood of Messiah, sins would be forgiven. Though the death of Jesus was sufficient for all sins and the sacrifice was made for all, the forgiveness is not automatic for all, since faith is required to appropriate the sacrifice personally. The New Testament clearly defines the "many" as those who believe in Him. This blood covenant was explained in great detail in Hebrews 9-10. It was "poured out" as an offering before God and deemed sufficient to compensate for the offense against God's holiness. Therefore, those who partake of the body and blood, by faith, are forgiven of their sins. The ceremony itself does not save but is performed as a memorial to the Lord's sacrifice (Luke 22:19; 1 Cor. 11:23-26).

26:29-30   Jesus' next comment (v. 29) was to reassure the disciples this was not the last time He would celebrate this meal with them. He promised not to drink the wine again until reunited with them to celebrate this feast in His Father's kingdom. By this statement, He not only reflected confidence in His own resurrection but in theirs as well and their joining Him in the Father's kingdom.

Most likely the hymn sung was the "Hallel" (Pss. 114-18), traditional at Passover. The sections most appropriate to their situation would be part of Psalm 116, concerning God's faithfulness to keep His vows; Psalm 117, praising Yahweh for His covenant love; and Psalm 118, rejoicing in triumph over those who reject Him. Upon completion, they left for the familiar Mount of Olives to pray and prepare for the Lord's great ordeal.

ON THE MOUNT OF OLIVES, 26:31-46
(Mark 14:27-42; Luke 22:31-46)

26:31-32   Their journey took them out of the city through one of the eastern gates, down into the Kidron valley, up Mount Olivet, and finally to the garden spot called Gethsemane. As they walked, Jesus made another startling prediction—all of His men would desert Him that night. Note, not just Peter but "all of you" (*pantes humeis*) "will fall away," or, more literally, "be caused to stumble" (*skandalisthēsesthe,* future passive of *skandalizō*). The idea was to be overcome by the terror and confusion of the coming events and temporarily "lose faith" and flee.

Jesus associated this panic with a statement in Zechariah 13:7, an Old Testament context that promised "a fountain will be opened for the house of David and for the inhabitants of Jerusalem, for sin and for impurity" (v. 1) but which also promised to inflict judgment on the people before ultimate restoration (vv. 7-9). By Jesus' correlating the Zechariah prophecy with the scattering of His own men, He indicated that Israel's salvation, judgment, and eventual restoration was about to begin. Carson also notes, "Yet Jesus' words 'for it is written' show that the disciples' defection, though tragic and irresponsible, does not fall outside God's sovereign plan."[13]

As an encouragement, Jesus quickly added the reassuring statement "After I have been raised" (v. 32), which focused back on the ultimate victory rather than the momentary defeat. The passive voice, "have been raised," indicated that the resurrection was not only His prerogative but both the Spirit and the Father would be involved in the process as well. Jesus was not only reassuring the disciples of His resurrection but also of their victory. Though having just predicted their falling away because of panic, He clearly implied a reunion with them in Galilee. They would fail in a moment of weakness but would not be cast aside. Rather, Jesus would have them perpetuate the work after His ascension.

26:33-35   One should be cautious about too quickly condemning Peter's response. Not so much arrogance but sincere loyalty and zeal prompted his remarks. Any serious student of the New Testament must surely realize that Peter's words were from his heart. The passion that drove him was often misguided but not here—he simply did not take into account the limitations of human flesh. One should admire both Peter's desire to stand firm and his "commitment" to do so, as he only expressed what was truly felt deep within. However, bold professions of loyalty and impassioned testimonies of commitment are not sufficient to successfully carry one through the trials of life.

The Lord's answer (v. 34) must have cut deep into Peter's soul. The word "truly" (*amēn*) was an emphatic way of stating an important proposition and was a signal for Peter to listen carefully. The Lord then predicted that Peter would deny Him three times before the cock crowed (twice according to Mark 14:30) to announce the new day. Luke adds dialogue between the Lord and Peter, revealing that Satan sought opportunity to attack the disciples. But the Lord reassured Peter of His intercession and that Peter would strengthen the others (Luke 22:31-32).[14] Pate observes, "Peter now becomes the actor on center stage, with Satan accusing him on the one hand and Jesus defending him as his advocate on the other hand. Jesus' intercession for Peter would eventually reestablish the apostle's faith."[15] The Lord knew in advance where His servants would struggle and even fail, but He interceded that they might be victorious.

Peter reinforced his claim to faithfulness, "Even if I have to die with You, I will not deny you" (v. 35). Here bold commitment had digressed into stubborn pride. Peter directly and confidently denied the very words of His Lord. The other disciples joined in, affirming their loyalty as well. Again, considering the tense emotion of all that had been said (see John 13-17 for more Upper Room dialogue) and with the Lord repeatedly confirming His upcoming death, one must appreciate the disciples' passionate desire to stand firm with Him during this time. Jesus did not expend any more time or energy trying to convince them of their own weakness. They would discover it soon enough.

26:36   Jesus reached a familiar spot on the mount called the Garden of Gethsemane ("oil press"), and Luke 22:39-40 indicates that it was the custom (*ethos,* "regular practice") for Jesus to come here. This accounts for Judas's being able find Him (John 18:2). The disciples were instructed to sit down and wait while He separated from them for prayer (about a stone's throw away, Luke 22:41). Matthew, Mark, and Luke record this event, but John, who was in the inner circle and went the extra distance (v. 37), did not. However, John records the "high priestly" prayer spoken before the Garden (John 17), which the other three omit.

26:37-38   Once again, the three key disciples were separated for special privileges. Peter and the sons of Zebedee (James and John) were taken with Him the "stone's throw." Here Jesus began to display the grief that must have been so intense within His soul. He "began to be (*ērxsato,* aorist middle of *archō*) "grieved and distressed," or began to express His inward agony. "Be grieved" (*lupeisthai*) and "distressed" (*adēmonein*) cannot truly communicate the depth of His sorrow and troubles. MacArthur offers a good perspective, "We cannot comprehend the depth of Jesus' agony, because, as sinless and holy God incarnate, He was able to perceive the horror of sin in a way we cannot."[16]

It is difficult to comprehend how these three mere men must have remembered this event in later, more spiritually mature years and meditated on their Lord's opening His hurting heart to them. Verse 38 reveals the most vulnerable moment of our Lord's life recorded in Scripture, as He confessed that His very soul (the deepest recess of human awareness) was "deeply grieved" (*perilupos,* intensified form of "grieved" in v. 37). God wants us to see the agony of His Son as a real person facing the horrors of torture and death and, even greater, the full weight of all humanity's sin. Anticipating the coming rejection of His people (who sang hosannas to Him a few days earlier) and the brutality of Roman execution, Jesus groaned within. As He contemplated feeling the guilt and consequences of sin, His soul cried out in anguish. The oppression of death weighed heavily upon Him. How fitting that Isaiah should say of Him "man of sorrows, and acquainted with grief" (Isa. 53:3). His request of these three inner-circle disciples, His most intimate friends, was simply to "keep watch with Me" (*grēgoreite metē emou,* "keep awake and be alert with Me").

26:39 Jesus again separated Himself but this time only "a little beyond," which probably meant within hearing range of His prayers and crying. The phrase "fell on His face" indicates the intensity of the moment, and His posture reflected helplessness and total surrender to the Father whom He addressed. Mark records the address as "Abba! Father!" (*abba ho patēr*), indicating intimacy and affection. His request was to let the cup (symbol of His suffering and death) pass by without His having to take it. Two conditions were put upon the request: first, "if it is possible," and second, "not as I will, but as Thou wilt."

The first condition incorporates some complicated and serious theological issues. Primarily, to resolve humanity's sin problem apart from this suffering and death must have been impossible or else the Father would have granted His request. Since this book is a commentary and not a theological treatise, suffice it to say only that God, in His unlimited wisdom and knowledge, had no other alternative to compensate for mankind's attack on His holiness or to redeem the creature made in His own image other than to become man and suffer the awful consequences of this sin Himself. Thus, to let the cup pass from His Son was not possible.

The second, "not My will but Yours," likewise has some profound theological implications. It is apparent that two wills (*thelō*) were at work in this scene. The "will" (*thelō*) was not a reference to the decreed plan of God but rather to a preference in relation to choice. "Desire" might better express the intent. Because of the shame, suffering, and ultimate pain of separation from the Godhead, Jesus did not desire to take the cup, but the Father did desire it, for He, representing the fullness of the Godhead, knew what was necessary for the conclusion of the redemptive program. God "desires" (*thelō*) all men to be saved (1 Tim. 2:3-4) and, thus, desired this cup to be taken by His Son. There was no conflict in the divine decree or the ultimate "will" of the Godhead. The statement indicated the personal preference of the Lord, which He, as an example for all God's servants, surrendered to the ultimate will of God. Meyer states it well: "The wish, to which in His human dread of suffering He gave utterance, that, if possible, He should not be called upon to endure it, at once gives place to absolute submission."[17]

26:40-41   Jesus returned to the inner circle of disciples (seen by His addressing Peter) and found them sleeping. How long Jesus had prayed is difficult to say, but these men had failed to do what He had asked, "Keep watch with Me" (v. 38). Those who boasted of dying for Him could not even keep awake for Him. He addressed Peter, again indicating his position as leader of the group, and rebuked them all with the rhetorical question, "Are you [plural] not able to keep watch with me for one hour?" The "one hour" (*mian hōran*) is not to be understood as our modern concept of a precise number of minutes but indicated an unspecified length of time that would have been more than a few minutes.

Before returning to another period of personal prayer, He exhorted them to keep alert and pray so that (*hina* indicating purpose) they might not enter into "temptation" (*peirasmos*), or testing trial. The idea was to not yield to the temptation of failing their mission. The last clause was neither condemnatory nor offering an excuse for their failure but simply a statement summarizing the reality of the situation. Peter and the others certainly had good intentions and a willingness to do right ("the spirit," human not divine), but being subject to the flesh will bring failure because the flesh is weak ("sickly"). The human condition is one of inability to do what the spirit may desire. Good intentions are not sufficient, as the flesh must be empowered by God Himself to make God's servant what he needs to be.

26:42-44   Matthew records that Jesus went away a second time and repeated the prayer, requesting to bypass this suffering if possible. Once again He expressed the surrender of His will to the Father's. Mark simply says that He prayed, "saying the same words" (14:39). For the second time, Jesus returned to the inner circle and found them sleeping (v. 43). Matthew makes no reference to Jesus' addressing the three, but Mark records, "They did not know what to answer Him" (14:40), which suggests another rebuke for their lack of watchfulness. Mark simply states, "Their eyes were very heavy" (14:40), meaning overcome by exhaustion. It was probably midnight or later. Luke also adds that sorrow (*apo tēs lupēs,* "from the grief/sorrow") or emotional exhaustion contributed to their inability to stay awake (22:45). One can only imagine the weariness of soul from the experiences of this final week and especially these last few hours. For a third time, Jesus left to return to His solitude and repeat the same prayer (v. 44).

Luke alone records the phenomenal physical agony of His praying, being so fervent that "His sweat became like drops of blood" (*hōsei thromboi haimatos,* 22:44). The particle *hōsei,* "like, approximating," would tend to support Pate's view that the language is figurative: "Jesus did not literally sweat drops of blood. Rather, His perspiration was so profuse that it was like blood spilling on the ground."[18] Again, only Luke records that an angel was sent to comfort and strengthen the Lord (Luke 22:43), reflecting both the intensity of the ordeal and the Father's concern.

26:45-46   For the third time, Jesus came to the trio of sleeping disciples and asked, "Are you still sleeping and taking your rest?" The question may have been more compassionate than it sounds. He awoke and prepared them for the next event, "The hour is at hand." The expression "the hour" (*hē hōra*) refers to the moment of action rather than a specific chronological point of reference. The moment had come, "at hand" (*ēggiken,* perfect tense), meaning "already drawn near and being consummated."

The "hour" began with the event of being "betrayed into the hands of sinners" (v. 45), and the sinners must have included both the Jews and the Romans. Jesus seemed calm as He stirred up His followers to go out and meet His betrayer (v. 46). Rather than hiding, cowering back, or staying prostrate on the ground until they pulled Him away, Jesus reflected the peace and dignity of One content with the Father's will.

Judas's Betrayal, 26:47-56
(Mark 14:43-50; Luke 22:47-53; John 18:3-12)

26:47   Even as Christ was speaking to His men, the mob came to arrest Him. Judas (note, "one of the twelve") led the band of temple guards and other armed men into the darkness of the garden and found Jesus with the rest of the (loyal) disciples. The mob, armed with clubs and swords, obviously anticipated resistance from the disciples. It would have been only natural to expect a fight since this arrest would certainly end in a guilty verdict and execution. Judas may have warned as well of the disciples' sworn allegiance to Jesus and their commitment to die rather than let Him be arrested. Judas may have anticipated violence from Peter in particular. The mob also came with authority from the Sanhedrin, represented here by the reference to the chief priests and the elders.

26:48-49   Judas prepared to identify Jesus for the mob by kissing Jesus, a commonly used mode of greeting one who was respected. Such an act of treachery has become infamously known as the "Judas kiss." Judas's instruction to "seize Him" (*kratēsate auton,* "take hold firmly, restrain") suggests that Judas really did not understand the Lord at all or perhaps remembered how supernaturally He had eluded His enemies before. Without hesitation ("immediately") Judas carried out his mission, greeting Jesus with "hail" (*chaire*), from *chairō,* "rejoice, be glad," reflecting a sad, ignorant irony. He also called Him "Rabbi," or teacher, indicating submission to Him, which again is ironic. Whether the kiss was on the cheek or the hand (both were common for greeting a rabbi) is unimportant. Identification of Jesus was the point.

26:50   Jesus responded by addressing Judas as "friend," and this should not be misunderstood or romanticized. The word *hetaire* does mean "friend, companion" but is used in less affectionate and mere association environments. It is used only in Matthew and on only two other occasions (Matt. 20:13 and 22:12), neither use indicating any more than polite cordiality. Had Jesus used *philos,* there would have been a significant nuance of intimacy and concern. But He used only the polite form of address with no indication of affection.

Luke offers more dramatic and profound dialogue (Luke 22:48). Jesus called Judas by name and pointedly asked him, "Are you betraying the Son of Man with a kiss [a sign of affection and respect]?" One must wonder if Judas's heart sank and if he recalled Jesus' words of the previous meeting, "But woe to that man by whom the Son of Man is betrayed! It would have been good for that man if he had not been born" (Matt. 26:24).

26:51   All four Gospels record the brief and violent attempt by Peter (John gives his name, 18:10) to defend the Lord. He drew a sword and attacked one of the men in the mob. Although it may be considered a foolish and unspiritual act, what he did was in keeping with Peter's character (a man of action) and, to his credit, with his promise "I will die with you" (vv. 33, 35). Peter is often treated as foolish and wicked for this outburst, but there is need to offer respect to Him. Peter's spiritual understanding was limited at this point, but his loyalty, bravery, and willingness to die shine as a bright light in this dark moment. The temple guard and the Roman cohort (John 18:3, 12) were not only far greater in number but were also trained in combat. Peter, a fisherman, though knowing there were only two swords, launched an attack that required both love and faith toward the Lord.

26:52-53   The Lord Himself had told the disciples to get the swords (Luke 22:36-38), and to Peter it would have seemed that this was the purpose for having them. However, the Lord's point was more long-term; the kingdom of heaven was not to be defended with human instruments or power. Verse 52 records, "All those who take up the sword shall perish by the sword." Hendriksen notes, "This proverbial saying must not be interpreted in an absolute, unqualified sense, as if use of the sword were always wrong. . . . But rashly swinging the sword, without even being willing to wait for Christ's answer to the question, 'shall we strike with the sword?' (Luke 22:49) is always wrong, and will mean retribution for the one who does it."[19] Alford, likewise, puts it into the proper context: "Our Lord does not say '*Cast away* thy sword;' only in His willing self-sacrifice, and in that kingdom which is to be evolved from His work of redemption, is the sword altogether out of place."[20] More specifically, the proverb is to be understood as a general principle; those who depend on the sword to defend themselves are destined to die by it.

The Lord put it all into a more dramatic perspective (v. 53). If He wanted to be defended, He would not depend upon an untrained, though zealous, fisherman; He would ask and the Father would send twelve legions of angels (approximately 72,000) to protect Him. This brings up two interesting points. First, neither the kingdom nor the name of Christ is to be propagated, protected, or enforced with human weapons. One angel is capable of destroying an entire army of soldiers (2 Chron. 32:21); therefore, what would twelve legions be able to do? God does not need the might of men to accomplish His will. Second, though to "drink the cup" was the Father's will, it is here suggested that had the Son asked, the Father would have sent the angels to defend Him. Thus, His surrendered will was not forced, but volitional.

26:54   But angels would not come, they would not be requested. The Son was on course to complete the redemptive plan of God. Neither foe nor friend would interfere with Christ's determination to complete His mission. God's truth, spoken centuries before, was now being fulfilled: "It must happen this way." The word "must" (*dei*) implies a certain necessity, a divinely decreed event that is obligated by the very virtue of God's Word to take place. What God has decreed is going to take place. No amount of human emotion (even well-intended) or human energy will impede its fulfillment.

26:55   Jesus healed the wound (a fact only Luke records, 22:51) and turned to speak to the mob who came to arrest Him. He questioned their use of arms. From a human perspective, they probably expected resistance from the disciples and perhaps from Jesus Himself. But Jesus reminded them of who He was, One who had been in their midst daily. The statement "I used to sit in the temple teaching and you did not seize Me" was to point out their cowardly nature and the inconsistency of their action. Carson states, "The implication is that there is no need to arrest him secretly and violently, except for reasons in their own minds that reveal more about them than about him."[21]

26:56   Jesus told them they were a part of the fulfillment of

Scripture. What was happening was the fulfillment of the prophets. Jesus was not intending to point out any one verse of Old Testament prophecy; but the betrayal (Ps. 41:9), the abuse about to follow (Isa. 53:3-9), the desertion of His disciples (Zech. 13:7), and His crying out to God from the cross (Ps. 22:1) were only a few of the prophetic utterances related to the Messiah's death. Mark (14:50) records briefly that the disciples fled. Matthew, Luke, and John do not record that action, but the contexts indicate it.

TRIAL BEFORE CAIAPHAS, 26:57-68 (Mark 14:53-65; Luke 22:54-71)

John does not give details about the trial before Caiaphas but clarifies that there was first an unofficial visit to Annas, the true high priest who had been removed from office by the Romans (18:13-24). The significance of their first going to Annas is that, though according to Rome he had no official power, he was still viewed by the Jews as the high priest. Matthew skips the appearance before Annas, probably because it was unofficial and was not the trial before the Sanhedrin. The variance in the records is not a contradiction but a multidimensional presentation of the events. Each Gospel writer contributed to the full picture according to the purpose divinely assigned him.

26:57   Matthew records the trial before Caiaphas, the Roman-appointed high priest, Annas's son-in-law.[22] The members of the Sanhedrin were present (scribes and elders, and Mark mentions the chief priests as well, 14:53). This mock trial (the second, if one includes the appearance before Annas, John 18) took place sometime after midnight and before sunrise (27:1). Edersheim points out that "all Jewish order and law would have been grossly infringed in almost every particular."[23] The Sanhedrin met in unprecedented hours, and their meeting was not held at the normal location. The members who met were probably forewarned to be ready, which is why these could be present on such short notice. Any who might protest this kangaroo court were most likely simply not told. There was no opportunity for Jesus to summon witnesses on His behalf, and the people were not told of the hearing so that they could witness the proceedings. Testimony to their heinous criminal act is given in 26:4 and 26:14-16. This was no more than a mock trial to justify killing Him.

26:58   Though the disciples fled into the night, Peter could not resist following behind the mob to see what was happening. John tells us that one other disciple followed along as well (John 18:15). Many scholars assume this "other disciple" was John himself. Peter entered the outer courtyard and sat down with "officers" (*hupēretēs,* "attendants") of the court. These were not authoritative officers but those who ran errands and dealt with unruly people in trials. Peter was waiting to see the outcome, yet surely he knew it already. One should appreciate Peter's loyalty, though later he failed even as His Lord predicted. Had he not been here, there would have been no occasion for him to deny the Lord. But he could not stay away. His heart was gripped with the dread of what was happening, and he could not casually walk away.

26:59   This verse reinforces what was said above, that the purpose of this gathering was not to hold a fair trial but rather to legalize their plot to kill Jesus. They "kept trying" (*ezētoun,* imperfect active indicative of *zēteō*), the imperfect tense indicating a continual process, to find false witnesses (*pseudomarturōn*), not just witnesses. Matthew states that the purpose of the false testimony was to find cause for putting Him to death. The conjunction *hopōs* connotes purpose. They sought false witnesses because true witnesses would not give them cause to kill Him.

26:60-61   Verse 60 states that they were having difficulty in finding false witnesses. This implies that it was not sufficient to just make up lies about Him. The charges needed to sound legitimate, or the Romans would not allow them to have Jesus executed and the people might riot. Hendriksen points out:

> The verdict must be made official and reasons must be formulated, so that the sentence that subsequently will be based upon it can be justified before the Jews, and so that the indispensable co-operation of the Gentiles—especially of Pilate—can be obtained.[24]

Amazingly, these religious Jews who meditated, prayed, memorized Scripture, fasted, and preached righteousness were able to block out statements in Scripture such as Proverbs 6:16-19, which emphasizes that God hates "a lying tongue," a "heart that devises wicked plans," and "a false witness who utters lies."

Finally, two witnesses came forward with some information that gave the Sanhedrin their needed charge. The quantity "two" is significant because at the word of only one witness no one was to be put to death (Num. 35:30), and "on the evidence of two witnesses or three witnesses, he who is to die shall be put to death; he shall not be put to death on the evidence of one witness" (Deut. 17:6).

The accusation (v. 61) was a perversion of a comment Jesus had made to the Jews early in His ministry (John 2:13-22). Their testimony was that Jesus claimed He would destroy the temple. Their statement was that He said, "I am able to destroy the temple of God." In fact, Jesus said, "[You] destroy this temple [His body], and in three days I will raise it up" (John 2:19). Jesus did not correct their error or attempt to defend Himself.

26:62-64   The high priest, Caiaphas, wanted a chance to further incriminate Jesus, but His silence frustrated his expectations. The question, "What is it that these men are testifying against you?" was hopefully to induce Jesus into making more elaborate claims. "But Jesus kept silent" (v. 63) offers a powerful testimony to His inner strength and resolve to let the eternal program continue. He easily could have refuted their charge, as He had done many times in the past, but He chose not to defend Himself (cf., Isa. 53:7).[25]

The last part of v. 63 is crucial in understanding the claims of Jesus to deity and the Jewish concepts of Messiah. Caiaphas asked straight out, "Are you the Messiah, the Son of God," indicating that Messiah was understood to be the Son of God. "Son of God" to Caiaphas would not refer to the triune conception of Messiah's deity but as One empowered by God with the privileges of divine blessing. Jesus had publicly accepted the title "Son of David" (Matt. 21:15-16), which was undoubtedly a messianic title, and had openly proclaimed Himself as Messiah to the Samaritan woman (John 4:25-26).

Jesus' answer was twofold: a direct and positive affirmation of the question of His messiahship and an additional revelation that the Jews who sat in judgment of Him here (plural, "you shall see") would see the Son of Man in His glory. The affirmative "You have said it" (*su eipas*), is stated even more clearly in Mark's account, "I am" (*egō eimi,* 14:62). There can be no serious doubt that He unhesitatingly claimed to be the Messiah with all the attendant implications of power and glory, regardless of the agonizing circumstances in which He found Himself.

The "hereafter" (*apē arti*) means "from this point on." Alford takes this to refer to His postresurrection glory, which even His enemies will eventually see: "The glorification of Christ is by Himself said to *begin with his betrayal,* see John 13:31: from this time— from the accomplishment of this trial now proceeding. In what follows, the whole process of the triumph of the Lord Jesus even till its end is contained."[26] The title "Son of Man" was the appellation Jesus used of Himself more than any other and was also a common designation for Messiah. He combined Psalm 110 and Daniel 7:13-14 to forcefully affirm that He was the Messiah, the Son of God, the Son of Man, whom these very men would eventually see in His glory. Carson's summary is excellent: "Jesus is telling the members of the Sanhedrin that from then on they would not see him as he now stands before them but only in his capacity as the undisputed King Messiah and sovereign Judge."[27]

26:65-66 The response of the high priest was sufficient evidence that he both understood and resented the claim of Jesus to being the Messiah, the Son of God, and the Son of Man, who was to receive the glorious kingdom of Daniel. He "tore his robes" in conjunction with the cultural symbolism of grief and sorrow. Here it seems to have been a public display of horror at Jesus making such claims for Himself. Barbieri points out that the Law forbade the priest to tear his garments (Lev. 21:10, meaning the high priestly garments), and thus "he may have torn some of his undergarments as a sign that he indeed had heard blasphemy and was expressing his indignation."[28] It may also be that due to the unofficial (illegal) nature of the trial, he may not have been wearing the garments of his office, or possibly he simply broke the Law, being too caught up in his anger to think about it. He had certainly violated God's Word in many other ways already.

Caiaphas brought the trial to an end by declaring no further need for witnesses; he had enough to charge Jesus with blasphemy, which could bring the death penalty. The question, "What further need . . . " was rhetorical and was not looking for an answer to close the case. The next question, "What do you think?" was calling for a vote from the court. The sentence seems to have been unanimous, "He is deserving of death!" Finally the religious leaders had attained the goal they had set, to "seize Jesus by stealth and kill Him" (26:4).

26:67-68   Having accomplished their purpose, they began to celebrate by abusing their quarry. The language describes brutal treatment—spitting into the face of the One who would die for them, slapping and beating Him with their fists. The term "slapped" (*hrapizō*) may be better understood as "struck Him with sticks." The hatred being expressed by this treatment was senseless if one was truly looking for justice. This was revenge for the times He had outwitted them in public and called them hypocrites, snakes, and whited sepulchers. The mocking challenge of v. 68 is terribly frightening when one realizes that, indeed, God did know their names. Luke informs us that they had blindfolded the Lord when they began their sport of beating this bound prisoner who had never tried to resist them (Luke 22:63-65).

PETER'S DENIAL, 26:69-75 (Mark 14:66-72; Luke 22:56-62; John 18:15-18, 25-27)

26:69-70   Matthew then returned to Peter, who was sitting in the courtyard with the trial attendants (v. 58). From this vantage point, he could hear and perhaps even see some of the events of the mock trial. From the Gospel record, it does not seem likely that Peter could see everything; but at one point, he apparently made eye contact with the Lord (Luke 22:61). It is also possible that the look took place as Jesus was being led out of that trial and taken to Pilate.

One of the female servants recognized Peter as being associated with "Jesus the Galilean." The designation "the Galilean" was normal enough for the culture since regions or cities were often attached to personal names for more specific identification. Galilee might best be identified with what in contemporary circles would be labeled a blue-collar area and was looked down upon by the pseudo-intellectuals of Jerusalem. Mark adds that the girl more specifically went on to identify Him as a Nazarene (14:67); and in the second identification of Peter with Jesus, she said, "Jesus of Nazareth" (v. 71). Nazareth was a city of very bad reputation (John 1:46). Thus this identification must have sounded ominous at this tense moment around the fire. From the human perspective, it is easy to sympathize with Peter when he said, "I do not know what you are talking about" (v. 70). Imagine the sounds of mocking and brutality during the trial, the cries of blasphemy coming from the high priest, and the early morning hour (probably shortly before daybreak) after a long and emotionally draining night, and one surely will not be too quick to condemn Peter. The whole context created a dark and foreboding atmosphere, and Peter was undoubtedly both emotionally and physically exhausted.

26:71-72   The second denial took Peter even further into the blackness of failure. The first denial was more general, "I don't know what you are talking about," but then he intensified his denial with an oath and denied knowing "the man" (*ouk oida ton anthrōpon*, v. 72). Had Peter used *ginōskō*, the implication would have been no knowledge of Jesus intimately or experientially; but by using *oida*, he denied even having any knowledge about Him. This would have stood out as an apparent contradiction to his wanting to be in the courtyard.

26:73-74   The third denial came when another bystander, probably provoked by the second servant girl's persistence, recognized his Galilean accent: "The way you talk gives you away." The region of Galilee was known for its unique accent, much as an American regional location can be determined by the inhabitants' accent (a Southern drawl or New England nasal tone). Since he was from Galilee, how could he possibly not know (*oida*) of this person who had created such a stir among the people? Now Peter's denial peaked, resulting in a violent, panic-driven response. He began to curse and swear and repeated, "I do not know the man!" His intensity reflects the terrible struggle of his broken spirit and also his love for the man on trial. The fierce reality of the moment had generated fear that replaced the confidence of the Upper Room (26:33, 35). Which of us would dare to think that in the same situation we would have acted any differently?

"Immediately" (*eutheōs*) the cock crowed (for the second time, Mark 14:72), the signal Jesus had given concerning his denial. Luke records that at this time, perhaps this very moment, "the Lord turned and looked at Peter and Peter remembered the word of the Lord" (22:61). How tragic and yet how beautiful was this profound moment. In the midst of all the horrific suffering of the Lord, He found Peter's face and looked into His eyes (*strapheis ho kurios eneblepsen tō petrō,* literally "turning, He looked straight at [*emplepō*] Peter"). Anyone who has studied the Lord's heart and attitude toward this man Peter knows that this was not a look of anger or resentment but certainly of pity. But as Peter looked into the bruised and bloody face of Jesus, perhaps with blasphemous spittle still on His face, his heart was crushed.

26:75   The prophetic words of Jesus began to burn in the mind of Peter, "Truly I say to you that this very night, before a cock crows, you shall deny Me three times" (v. 34). His self-assured answer probably also echoed in his head, "Even if I have to die with You, I will not deny You" (v. 35). Peter's desire, his zeal, and his commitment can never be denied, but now he was faced with the real problem of humanity—the weakness of the flesh. He came face to face with the ugly, selfish, wickedness of the human heart. He had failed because no flesh is capable of itself to stand against such pressures.

The bright spot in this dark moment comes from remembering the comment Jesus made following His prediction of Peter's failure. Pate observes, "The first part of Jesus' prophecy had come true; Peter did deny his Lord. But so would the second part eventually come true—Peter would be restored" (Luke 22:32).[29] Peter's bitter weeping reflected a man who faced his own cowardice and defeat. He was so utterly devastated that he required very special attention from the Lord to be restored (John 21:15-17).

HOMILETICAL SUGGESTIONS

This is the longest chapter in Matthew's gospel and, in some ways, the most difficult to work through. One must not ignore nor play down the intense emotion that is expressed in these verses. The other extreme will be to overplay the emotions and romanticize the dialogue and events to the point of drifting into a hyperspiritual drama that loses touch with reality.

The anointing of Jesus' head (vv. 6-16) provides an opportunity to remind Christians that worship of the Lord takes priority over even the most crucial acts of charity. The church should certainly care about the poor, especially any within the body of Christ, but not to the point of distraction from honoring and worshiping the Lord. The material needs of people are not to take priority over the

spiritual realm. The focus of the church is to be heavenly, not earthly, and Christocentric, not anthropocentric.

The institution of the Lord's Supper (vv. 17-30) will best be
understood in the context of the Passover meal. Any teacher would
be wise to call upon the numerous resources available to provide
the body of Christ with a clear image of the Jewish customs and
events of this great occasion. The addition of the breaking of the
bread and the drinking of the final cup of wine becomes so much
more meaningful in the context of the Passover meal. The primary
focus in this memorial service must be on the significance of the
symbols. Understanding the meaning behind unleavened bread and
the fruit of the vine is critical in understanding the sinless body of
Christ as that which sustains our very eternal life and our purification
by the blood of Christ. First Corinthians 11:20-34 is a crucial cross-
reference to understanding the spiritual significance of participating
in the holy meal. Above all, one must avoid making this a meaningless or flippant ceremony. It must be a dramatic reminder of the
suffering and selfless giving of our Lord for our "free" eternal life.

The stress and growing fear of the Upper Room and the Mount
of Olives must be seen. These are not players acting out a story, but
real people with fear and doubt as well as physical and emotional
exhaustion tearing away at them. After almost a week of confrontations and threats, the disciples were stressed beyond imagination.
The Lord Himself was reaching a climax of emotional turmoil. This
section should be taught with proper consideration for the historical context and the very human pain and fear being demonstrated.
Courage, cowardice, fear, faith, hate, and love are all strong emotions
in this passage of Scripture.

The trials (vv. 57-67) are a reminder of religion's hate for true
spirituality and how the self-righteous can be vindictive toward
those who expose them. The lies, secrecy, plotting, and finally the
brutality are reminders of the hardness of fallen hearts, even among
those who have the Scriptures, the religious lifestyle, and the verbal
profession of worshiping God. Every Christian must feel the pain of
the brutality inflicted upon our Lord and must pity the tragic realization of Peter's own weakness. Let each of us take care not to
judge Peter any harder than we would want to be judged if in the
same situation. Peter's defeat is a warning to all who think too high-

ly of themselves because they do not understand the powers of evil or their own intrinsic sinfulness.

The glory of this dark night lay in the fact that it was not the end of the story. The gloom of the moment made the glory of the subsequent victory more radiant. Peter was restored and became chief among the apostles. He faced the potential of martyrdom once again, but after receiving the promised "helper" (John 14-16; Acts 2), he stood firm and bold in proclaiming the name of His Lord (Acts 2:14-36; 3:1-4:31). The lesson is that the power not to "deny Christ" does not lie in the determination of the person, his religious zeal, or his personal loyalty (for Peter certainly had all of these) but upon being filled with and dependent upon the Spirit of God.

Peter spoke more directly to this horrible event than any of the non-Gospel writers. He spoke with great confidence of the Lord's example, which we are to follow (1 Peter 2:21-23) and seems to have learned one of the most important lessons for any who would aspire to being a servant of Christ—humility (1 Peter 5:5-7). Peter's denial did not mean his being cut off from Christ's program. Unlike many Christians who believe that if you fail once you are no longer qualified for service, Jesus was in the business of restoring and using His servants regardless of their failures. Peter is an example of His patience and cleansing power. Peter could not go back and retract the cursing, oaths, and vehement denials, but he could accept the Lord's forgiveness and restoration and go on to glorify Him (especially in testimony to this mercy) by his life and eventually by his willing martyrdom. Too often the church fails to reflect God's wonderful power of restoration and forgiveness because of a misguided sense of holiness. Standards are erected that do not allow for human failure and therefore do not allow for God's amazing grace and cleansing capability. Galatians 6:1-2 are often overlooked as a part of the Christian experience. Yet Peter, before the instruction was written to the church, experienced it from the Lord.

MATTHEW
CHAPTER
TWENTY-SEVEN

THE CRUCIFIXION
AND BURIAL OF THE LORD

Matthew now records the final stages of the Lord's human work. Having endured the shameful treatment and condemnation of the Jewish high court, Jesus was brought before the Gentile magistrate, Pontius Pilate. John's gospel covers the dialogue with Pilate in detail and provides an interesting contrast to the Jewish "trials" of the night before. Up to this point, according to all the gospels, Jesus had been paraded before Annas and Caiaphas, and now it would be Pilate.

JESUS TAKEN TO PILATE, 27:1-2
(Mark 15:1; Luke 23:1-2; John 18:28-32)

27:1-2   The next morning, Friday, the plot to rid themselves of Jesus was carried to the next level. Having obtained (though illegally) the Sanhedrin's condemnation of Jesus, the religious leadership now plotted ("took counsel") how to present this judgment to the Roman authority, namely, Pilate, the governor (v. 2) so as to win his approval for Jesus' execution.

According to Luke's record, they "began to accuse Him" of instigating the people to quit paying taxes and of creating a rebellious attitude among the people (23:2). Of course, no evidence of these false charges could be produced, but these men knew that Rome would not execute a man simply for having religious views contrary to the Jewish religious leadership's. Therefore charges were fabricated (during their plotting, v. 1) to gain Roman sympathy for their hatred of this man. Apparently any consciousness of the Mosaic prohibitions against lying and bearing false witnesses had become so suppressed that these men no longer sensed conviction for these overt sins.

JUDAS'S REMORSE AND DEATH, 27:3-10

Only Matthew records the last events of this miserable man's life, but Luke gives a poetic summary of his death in Acts 1:18-19. Matthew details the self-inflicted consequences of Judas's treachery, describing him as the one "who had betrayed Him," which became the permanent notoriety attached to his name.

27:3 Upon hearing of the condemnation of the Sanhedrin, Judas "felt remorse" (*metamelomai*), implying regret for his actions. This is not the same as repentance (*metanoeō*), which implies changing one's mind. Though he underwent feelings of guilt, no indication is given that Judas now viewed Jesus as the true Messiah but only as an "innocent" man (v. 4).

27:4 His penitence led to a return of the thirty pieces of silver to the chief priests and elders. Along with returning the money, Judas also confessed his sin (aorist of *hamartanō*) of betraying "innocent blood," v. 4 (*haima athōon*). The religious leaders' response revealed even more of their coldhearted nature. No attempts were made to reason with Judas or even rebuke his wavering. Rather, they simply said, "What is that to us? See to that yourself!" This response vividly expressed their lack of concern for the man and his struggle or, more important, for the innocence of Jesus. Judas was no longer needed, and his stroke of conscience was of no interest.

27:5 Judas threw the coins into the sanctuary, perhaps because none of the religious leaders cared to touch the soiled money (v. 6). Having found no comfort from those who had so quickly embraced him to gain assistance in arresting Jesus, Judas went out and "hanged himself" (*apēgxsato*). Peter's account of Judas's death (Acts 1:18) varies but not so much as some skeptics would imagine. "Falling headlong" might be translated "having become swollen" (*prēnēs genomenos*). The word "headlong" (*prēnēs*, "headfirst, forward") can also possibly mean "swollen, distended."[1] From the same root, the word *prēthō* means "to blow up, to swell out by blowing."[2] Since this is the only New Testament use of *prēnēs,* a word comparison is not possible. Motyer states the possibility that *prēnēs* could mean to "swell up, burst," or even "crack."[3] Bruce also acknowledges, "There is evidence, however, that *prēnēs* may be taken here in the sense of 'swelling up' as if connected to *prēthō* or *pimprēmi.*"[4] In addition, the word that the NASB translates "falling" is the aorist participle of *ginomai,* meaning "come to be, happen, come, go"[5] and does not naturally mean "fall." This writer suggests that Acts 1:18 be translated "Having become swollen, he burst open in the middle and his bowels poured out." This would be a graphic description of the demise of Judas, who hung until his body swelled and burst open from decay, which implies that no one even bothered to cut down the body.

27:6-8   Curiously, then the chief priests seemed concerned for what was "lawful" (v. 6). After violating numerous laws in the fake trials, encouraging false witnesses, and not allowing time for the accused to gather a defense, they wanted the application of this returned money to be "lawful." The coins could not be put in the temple treasury after having been used to buy the blood of Jesus. Hendriksen associates their concern with Deuteronomy 23:18,[6] which may be the closest reference, though not pertaining to blood money but to offerings from prostitutes and sodomites. This legalistic concern for money while ignoring laws related to the fair treatment of Jesus highlights their hypocrisy.

Their counsel concluded with a decision to purchase the "Potter's Field" for burying strangers without money or family to take care of their burial. The field may have been purchased from a particular potter or, as Carson suggests, may have been a field where potters dug their clay.[7] The singular designation "the potter's" lends credibility to the first view. Matthew states that the field became and remained known as the "Field of Blood" (v. 8), implying widespread knowledge of the prior use of this money. Luke records that the field was named "Field of blood" in Aramaic, "their own language"[8] (Acts 1:19).

27:9-10   Matthew again appeals to the Old Testament to indicate that the events in the life of Jesus were not random but anticipated in the prophetic Word of God. He references Zechariah 11:12-13 to demonstrate the predetermined end of the Messiah's traitor. It is interesting that the death of the wicked betrayer led to provision for the burial of strangers. Zechariah 11 figuratively portrays the price of betrayal as being cast to the potter in the house of the Lord, and this symbolically represents the money being returned to the sanctuary (v. 5) and being given to the potter for the field (v. 7). Thus this implied the rejection of the Messiah, and the ultimate price of the shepherd's life went to the potter (v. 10).

THE TRIAL BEFORE PILATE, 27:11-26
(Mark 15:2-15; Luke 23:3-7, 13-25; John 18:28–19:16)

27:11   The "governor" (*hēgemonos*) was the highest authority in Israel. Pilate was next under the Syrian legate to whom he ultimately answered. Pilate tried at one point to shift the trial to Herod, the Jewish king (Luke 23:6-7). Jesus disappointed Herod by not being willing to entertain him with a miracle, answer any of his questions, or enter into a debate with the religious leaders in self-defense. Therefore He was sent back to Pilate (Luke 23:8-12). To this point, Jesus had been taken to Annas and abused; sent to Caiaphas and abused; then taken to Pilate; sent to Herod and abused; and then sent back to Pilate.

Pilate's question (v. 11) related to the issue of most concern to Rome, "Are You the King of the Jews?" It is doubtful that Pilate really feared this bruised and bloodied man was a threat to Rome. But as an official of that government, he was responsible to know all the political tensions of his territory. The question regarded the religious leaders' accusations made before him as to why Jesus should be executed—"We found this man misleading our nation . . . saying that He Himself is the Christ, a King" (Luke 23:2). Jesus' claim to being the king of Israel was not so much a threat to Rome as to the Herodian line of puppet kings under Rome's control, but it would be viewed as a potential revolt and inter-Jewish struggle, which Rome would not welcome.

Jesus' answer was clearly affirmative, "You have said" (*su legeis*). As Meyer observes, "There is nothing ambiguous in such a reply."[9] Indeed, it was a typical response to a direct question. The discussion in John's gospel offers more detail. In response to the inquiry, Jesus actually asked Pilate a question, "Are you saying this on your own initiative, or did others tell you about Me [John

18:34]?" and did not answer Pilate's question (until v. 37). Laney understands the Lord's question as clarifying whether Pilate asked because of concern about an Israelite revolt or because of provocation by the Jews.[10]

27:12-14   Matthew notes that the religious leaders were present and continued to give Pilate reasons for executing Jesus, but the Lord made no attempt to defend Himself. Confused by His silence, Pilate offered Jesus the opportunity to defend Himself. The religious leadership accused Jesus of "many things" (v. 13), trying to build a case that would guarantee conviction. Pilate witnessed their intense hostility, and, because he knew that Jesus' life was certainly at stake, the accused's silence perplexed him (v. 14). It is obvious that Jesus did not remain silent because of having nothing to say in defense; however, He had already surrendered His will to the Father's, and this was part of the plan.

27:15-16   Matthew adds details concerning a Passover Feast tradition. The governor customarily released one prisoner at that season as a sign of good will. The choice of which prisoner was made by the crowd. Mark 15:8 indicates that the people had already approached Pilate for this favor. Interestingly, in connection with this, Pilate had apparently already declared that he found no guilt in Jesus (John 18:38-39), which was the first of three pronouncements by the governor regarding Jesus' innocence (18:38; 19:4, 6). In contrast to the innocent Jesus, Pilate offered Barabbas, a "notorious prisoner" (v. 16) and a murderer involved in an insurrection (Mark 15:7), as well as a highway robber (John 18:40).

27:17-18   Pilate made the offer to release either of the two. There can be little doubt that he assumed the Jews would rather have Jesus back on the street than a robber and murderer; however, he failed to anticipate the hatred of these depraved hearts and the certainty of God's plan. While perhaps assuming the charges against Jesus had been spawned only by petty jealousy (v. 18), Pilate soon discovered the seriousness of their execution attempt. The chief priests busily began recruiting voices to call for the release of Barabbas (Mark 15:11).

27:19   While sitting on the "judgment seat" (*bema;* see 2 Cor. 5:10), Pilate received a warning message from his wife not to get involved with this person. She is identified by Hendriksen as Claudia Procula,[11] and her presence was significant because some Romans protested wives' accompanying their husbands when engaged in overseas duty.[12] There is no reason to assume that her dream was a God-given, prophetic communication. The Romans were well known for their omen and dream superstitions. Her frightening premonition may have been caused by growing tension over the last week in Jerusalem or perhaps by overhearing both Jesus' name and the commotion early that morning when the Jews came to see Pilate. Hendriksen points out that the Coptic churches and the Greek church honor her as a proselyte,[13] but no substantial reason exists for giving credence to any such theory.

27:20-21 The chief priests and elders were busy stirring up the crowd present for the trial. Others possibly began to gather after realizing that Pilate was holding court and that the miracle worker from Galilee was the One on trial. One wonders what the chief priests said to make the mob prefer Barabbas over Jesus. In any case, when Pilate offered the choice, the crowd picked the murderer and robber (v. 21), not the One who had raised the dead, healed the sick, fed the multitudes, and cast out demons.

27:22-23 Pilate was probably taken aback by the choice. His question, "What shall I do with Jesus?" reflects confusion. According to Luke's record, Pilate declared, "You brought this man to me as one who incites the people to rebellion, and behold, having examined Him before you, I have found no guilt in this man regarding the charges which you make against Him. No, nor has Herod, for he sent Him back to us; and behold, nothing deserving death has been done by Him" (23:14-15). Thus the two highest legal authorities in the land of Israel had declared Jesus to be innocent.

The mob answered Pilate's question with the mindless chant "Let Him be crucified." Perhaps unable to believe their response, Pilate asked, "What evil has He done?" The crowd continued to demand His crucifixion (v. 23). Pilate even offered to "punish" Jesus and then release Him (Luke 23:16); but this would not satisfy the people, and they cried out for Barabbas to be released (Luke 23:18). Matthew records, "They kept shouting all the more . . . Let Him be crucified!" At this point, the Jews were intoxicated with the chief priests' hate and slander. The contrast between this shouting at the trial and the cheering a few days earlier as Jesus rode the donkey into Jerusalem is phenomenal. The only explanation is the depravity of the human heart and the wickedness of the spirit forces being turned toward this end. But behind this human madness and spiritual darkness, the divine plan was being brought to fruition (see Acts 2:23).

27:24   Pilate saw that "he was accomplishing nothing." Reason had left the people, and a riot could erupt if he did not fulfill their wishes. The Romans had seen the Jews revolt many times before. Indeed, when first appointed to Jerusalem, Pilate underestimated their religious zeal and brought Roman banners inside the temple compound, inciting a riot. From that and other unfortunate miscalculations, Pilate learned firsthand how volatile this people could be.[14] A. H. M. Jones says of Judea, "The Jews and Samaritans were, it is true, a turbulent people, addicted to riots, brigandage and even rebellion."[15]

In what has now become a famous symbolic act, Pilate washed his hands to indicate that he was not personally taking the guilt of executing an innocent man. This is consistent with Roman ideals of law and justice. Though brutal in combat and political intrigue, the Romans held a high view of legal procedure. According to John, Pilate "made efforts to release Him," but the Jews threatened to accuse him before Caesar as being disloyal (John 19:12). At this point, Pilate gave in to their request, and in the name of Rome "Pilate pronounced sentence that their demand should be granted" (Luke 23:24).

27:25   In response to Pilate's claim to being "innocent of this Man's blood" (v. 24), the Jews made a tragic boast, "His blood be on us and on our children!" This idiomatic expression implied taking responsibility for the death of a person. David said, "Your blood is on your own head, for your mouth testified against you," when condemning the Amalekite who boasted of killing King Saul (2 Sam. 1:16). These Jews were saying that not only would they accept responsibility for killing the Messiah, but that responsibility would also pass on to the next generation. This was most likely the point of Peter's appeal to the Jews (in Acts 2:14-40) to repent (change their thinking about Jesus as the true Messiah) and be baptized because of the forgiveness of sins, and thus be saved "from this perverse generation" (2:40), that is, the generation that took responsibility for killing the Messiah.

27:26   The trial concluded with three rulings from Pilate: the release of Barabbas; the scourging of Jesus; and the dispatching of

Jesus for crucifixion. The governor reluctantly freed Barabbas, knowing his habitually criminal nature would probably result in future arrest. Since Pilate had declared Jesus innocent three times (John 18:38; 19:4, 6), the scourging may seem strange, but the action may have been more compassionate than first thought by modern minds. First, Pilate may have anticipated that the Jews would have compassion on Jesus after witnessing the frightful results of the scourging. Second, if Jesus was to hang on the cross, severe flogging would produce blood loss and perhaps a quicker death.

But these theories must be treated as such; the fact remains that the scourging was insanely cruel and vicious. The scourge was a whip constructed of a short stick (about twelve to fourteen inches long) having several strips of leather (about three feet long) attached. Often the leather strips had stones, metal particles, or bone fragments imbedded so as to tear into the flesh. Josephus describes the victim's appearance as "their inward parts appeared naked."[16] This form of punishment often resulted in death, and to this our Lord submitted in fulfillment of Isaiah: "By His scourging we are healed" (53:5; also 1 Peter 2:24). With this dreadful abuse completed, Pilate then turned Him over to be crucified.

ABUSE AND MOCKERY OF
THE ROMAN SOLDIERS, 27:27-31 (Mark 15:16-20)

27:27-28 The sadistic nature of the Roman soldiers has sufficient verification in secular history to make this event commonplace. The Praetorium, part of the old Herodian palace, was obviously large enough for this extensive gathering (perhaps as many as 600, "the whole cohort") to hold their own perverted celebration of the trial's conclusion. Before time to take Him to crucifixion, the soldiers stripped off His outer garment and replaced it with a scarlet robe (v. 28), which was probably one of the Romans' cloaks. The robe (*chlamuda*) was usually about waist length and normally red. "Scarlet" (*kokkinos*) can mean "red," and the "purple" (*porphurous*) of Mark 15:17 and John 19:2 also can describe a color ranging from rose to deep purple. Carson notes, "The ancients did not discriminate among colors as closely as we do, and BAGD (p. 694) adduces a reference in which a Roman soldier's cloak is said to be "purple."[17]

27:29-31 The cruelty continued. A fake crown was placed upon Jesus' head to mock His claim to being King of the Jews (Luke 23:3; John 18:33-37). Thorns in this region, unlike our domesticated rosebush thorns that have a length of between one-quarter to perhaps one-half an inch, these barbs could be two to three inches long. Small animals trapped in their strong, razor-sharp grip could die. The crown placed upon Jesus inflicted great pain and caused profuse bleeding. The mockers then turned to buffoonery, giving Him a makeshift king's staff (a reed) and kneeling before Him to feign respect. For those who know the Person who was treated in this horrific manner, a better understanding is gained of the overwhelming grace of God—toleration for such inhumane and despicable treatment only magnifies His love for His lost creatures.

Spitting into an enemy's face (v. 30) showed hate and utter contempt. Why these Roman soldiers[18] displayed such vehement behavior is not clear; but perhaps the forces of darkness were exulting in the vulnerable position of the One who created them. Following the humiliation and torture by these Gentiles, Jesus was finally led to the outer courtyard where His cross (probably the cross-beam only) lay waiting to be carried by Him to Golgotha. The cape was removed and replaced with His own garment before they "led Him away to crucify Him."

THE CRUCIFIXION, 27:32-56
(Mark 15:21-41; Luke 23:26-49; John 19:17-37)

27:32   Verse 32 records the requisitioning of Simon to carry Jesus' cross, but John 19 states that Jesus carried His own cross, at least for a while (v. 17), which produces two potential scenarios. First, possibly upon leaving the palace grounds, the Romans recruited a man named Simon, from the city of Cyrene located 800 miles from Jerusalem along the Mediterranean coast (west of Egypt and today known as Libya). A large number of Cyrenean Jews must have resided in Jerusalem since a large synagogue there was associated with them (Acts 6:9) and since their dialect was listed in the "tongues" phenomenon of Acts 2:10. Upon reaching the hillside of Golgotha, Jesus was forced to carry the cross the last few yards to the crucifixion site. The second possible scenario would have Jesus carrying the cross initially, but, because of the severe abuse during the long twelve-hour ordeal, He collapsed "coming out" of the city, and the Romans coerced Simon into completing the task for Him.

The cross carried through the city may have been the entire crucifixion instrument. Most likely the unit would have been shaped in the traditional "dagger" form, since the charges were nailed above His head, and as such would have been extremely heavy and awkward to drag. Another possibility is that only the cross-beam to which His hands would be nailed was carried. This beam would have been approximately five to seven feet in length, rough-hewn from a single timber and also very heavy and awkward. Some have attempted to romanticize the story, making Simon a compassionate hero, but the text does not permit this. He was a victim of the Roman prerogative of "requisitioning," as the verse says: "whom they pressed [*aggareuō,* "forced"] into service." The remark in Mark 15:21 may possibly indicate he was known to the church, perhaps being converted after the Resurrection.

27:33-34   The hillside where the Romans publicly executed those condemned by the state was called Golgotha, which is Hebrew for "place of the skull." No record suggests that the name was derived from the hill's shape, and the "discovery" of a skull-shaped hill during the eighteenth or nineteenth century (after so many wars on the site, its appearance was undoubtedly changed) has no relevance to the true location of Golgotha. The name would be appropriate for a place where death was common and bodies would decay on their crosses if unclaimed. The Greek word for "skull" is *kranios* (English "cranium") and was translated into the Latin by *calvarius,* from which comes the name Calvary.

Jesus was given a stupefying drink to diminish His struggling during the nailing process (v. 34). The soldiers mixed wine with "gall" (*cholē*), a bitter-tasting substance. The term was often used in referring to bile secreted from the liver. Mark refers to the mixture as wine and myrrh, which is more specific as to what kind of "gall" (bitter-tasting substance) was used. This mixture apparently acted as a narcotic to restrain a prisoner's resistance. After tasting the drink, Jesus recognized the substance and therefore refused to take it, not wanting to dull His senses at this critical moment in the redemptive program. He preferred to suffer the fearful pain than sacrifice these last hours of His work—His intercession, demonstration of victory, care of His mother, and other critical events yet to come. The famous seven sayings from the cross would be meaning-less had He been affected by the drugged wine. If not offered as a narcotic, it could have been a taunting of the guards, mocking His thirst (cf. Ps. 69:21).

27:35-36   The crucifixion process was brutal and devastating for the human body, involving twelve-to-fourteen-inch spikes being driven into the hands and feet to secure the victim. Not the palm, but probably the wrist or carpus bone area was used to hold the hand spike. Even with this, ropes were often used to help hold the weight of the body so that the spike would not tear loose. The feet were placed together on a small, wedged-shaped lip built near the bottom of the cross, and another spike was driven through both feet to hold them in place. The Lord, therefore, having been beaten, slapped, mocked, spit upon, and laughed at, now endured the unimaginable pain of rusty iron spikes being driven into His body.

The prisoners who suffered crucifixion were treated with cal-lousness and were assumed to have no rights whatsoever. Even Jesus' garments were taken from Him as they laid Him out on the cross, and then the Romans divided them up as booty for their work. The practice of "casting lots" was a form of gambling and is not to be confused with the biblical practice of casting lots. The soldiers had His outer robe, inner tunic (seamless, John 19:23-24), belt (sash), and sandals. To crucify victims totally nude was customary, but the Jewish sensitivity to such crude display may have allowed Jesus to keep at least a loincloth. After determining the allotment of His cloth-ing, the soldiers sat down to guard their prisoner (v. 36), ensuring that no one aided an escape or ended His suffering prematurely.

27:37   It was customary to publicly post the crimes of the one crucified. On the part of the cross extending above the cross-beam, Pilate ordered to be written "This is Jesus, the King of the Jews." John records that the inscription was in Hebrew (Aramaic), Latin (the official language of Roman courts), and Greek (the common language of the Roman Empire), so that all who passed by could read it (19:20). Further, John notes that the Jewish leaders did not like the inscription, but Pilate refused to change it (19:21-22). Pilate may have kept the inscription more as an aggravation to the Jews (whom he despised) rather than from any conviction of the mes-sianic claims of Jesus. Even if he believed Jesus to be the "King of the Jews," that would not mean much to this Roman who controlled the puppet kings of Israel.

27:38   Jesus was crucified between two "robbers" (*lēstēs*), or insurrectionists. This same word (*lēstēs*) was used of Barabbas (John 18:40), and one can only wonder if he had been a partner of these two. If so, Jesus very literally took his place between these other two. The two robbers suffered as much as did Jesus, though only in the physical realm, but they deserved the death penalty (see v. 44 for more commentary on this). How different was this Man in the middle.

27:39-40   The verbal abuse continued even at the cross. "Those passing by" appear to have been simply people walking along the road, who are separated out by Matthew from the religious leaders (v. 41). They were "wagging their heads," or shaking their heads in contempt,[19] displaying their utter rejection of who He claimed to be (cf. Ps. 22:7). Both their gestures and verbal blasphemy ("hurling abuse") added to His anguish. Those whom He came to save were vulgar and cruel to Him in His suffering. In Psalm 22:6-7, 12-18, David prophetically revealed what was in the mind of Jesus as He hung on public display, hearing the hateful words.

The taunt "if you are the Son of God" (v. 40) was not the first time He had been challenged to prove His claim to being God's Son (Matt. 4:3, 6). Thus, at the beginning and then at the end of His earthly ministry, attempts were made to get Jesus away from God's will by this challenge. Coming down off the cross would not have proven that He was the Son of God; rather, staying when He certainly could have come down was the greater proof.

27:41-43   The religious leaders joined in the heckling. All three groups of the Sanhedrin are named—chief priests, scribes, and elders —as "mocking" (*empaizō*) or, more specifically, "making fun" of Him, "ridiculing" Him. Their first blasphemous accusation was "He saved others; He cannot save Himself." The reference to "saving" (*sōzō*) was certainly in reference to deliverance from demons, illness, and even death. They could never challenge His supernatural powers and made no attempt to deny them but simply pointed out that He was now suffering and about to die. Of course, the issue was not that He could not save Himself but that He *would* not save Himself. Had he selfishly rescued Himself from this death, then there would be no salvation for any human being. Thus He chose not to save Himself. As Mounce states, "It was the power of love, not nails, that kept Him there."[20]

The second slander was "He is the king of Israel [or so He says]; let Him now come down from the cross, and we shall believe in Him" (v. 42). These mockers do not appear to have been speaking directly to Jesus but to one another within His hearing, perhaps mockingly reading the charge written over His head (v. 37). But since plenty of witnesses to His other miracles did not lead to belief, why would they believe now? According to Luke, the Roman soldiers seemed to be caught up in the sport of insulting Jesus and also cried out for this proof (23:36-37). Actually, the kingdom was going to be established by His not coming down (Phil. 2:8-11).

The third hateful chiding from the religious leadership (v. 43) came in the form of paraphrasing Psalm 22:8. How paradoxical that in their ignorance they actually called to bear upon this situation a clearly messianic psalm. Indeed, the Lord did commit Himself to the Lord as the psalm says, but such commitment was not in order to receive His personal preference but to do as the Lord desired. The Lord would certainly deliver Jesus from the hold of death, raise Him for hundreds of witnesses to see, take Him into glory, and someday return Him to the earth to establish the kingdom—all of this because the Father does delight in Him and because He is indeed the Son of God.

27:44   Last, even the two dying robbers slandered and blasphemed. Matthew's comment seems to imply that both men started off participating in the heckling. But according to Luke, at some point one began to realize there was something unique about this Man (23:39-41). This second robber appears to have come to genuine faith in Christ and asked, "Jesus, remember me when You come in Your kingdom" (Luke 23:42). When one considers how ridiculous this must have sounded from the human point of view, it can only be explained in terms of genuine faith. He apparently had complete trust that this Man dying next to Him would have a kingdom and that death would not be able to keep Him from it. Jesus' response (His second saying from the cross)[21] verified the sincerity of his faith, "Today you shall be with Me in Paradise." Note first that this robber was to be with Jesus that day. Second, he would join Jesus not in heaven but in paradise. Paradise was the part of hades also known as "Abraham's bosom" (Luke 16:20-25), where departed saints received comfort until taken into God's presence following the resurrection of Christ.

27:45   Matthew records that darkness fell upon the earth about the "sixth hour" as Jesus hung on the cross, whereas John records that at the "sixth hour" Jesus was still on trial with Pilate (John 19:14). This seeming discrepancy has caused some confusion for those unfamiliar with the two methods of reckoning time in this historical setting. The Jews calculated the new day as beginning at 6:00 P.M. and divided the day into four watches of three hours each or into two parts of twelve hours each. The expression "sixth hour" had two possible meanings for the Jews, either midnight (sixth hour from the new day starting at 6:00 P.M.) or twelve noon (sixth hour from daybreak, assumed to start at 6:00 A.M.). For the Romans, the day was also broken into four watches of three hours each or two parts of twelve hours each. The major difference was that the new day began at midnight in their computation system. Therefore the sixth hour was either 6:00 A.M. or midnight (dependent upon its being the first or third watch).

Matthew, Mark, and Luke use the Jewish time calculations and, therefore, when using the "sixth hour" they refer to noon (12:00 P.M.). John, however, uses the Roman time calculation because of writing much later and to the predominantly Gentile church. Therefore, in John the term "sixth hour" means 6:00 A.M. Thus, in Matthew 27:45, darkness came upon the earth at noon (12:00 P.M.), "the sixth hour," and remained until 3:00 P.M., the "ninth hour." But in John 19:14, when Jesus was in the courtroom of Pilate, the time was 6:00 A.M. (Roman time). God very carefully recorded the times of the major events:

1. Jesus arrested on Thursday after midnight
2. Jesus condemned before Pilate by 6:00 A.M., Friday (John 19:14, "sixth hour," Roman)
3. Jesus on the cross by 9:00 A.M. (Mark 15:25, "third hour," Jewish)
4. Darkness covered the earth from 12:00 noon until 3:00 P.M. (Matt. 27:45, "sixth hour . . . ninth hour," Jewish)
5. Jesus dismissed His spirit (died) around 3:00 P.M. (Luke 23:44- 46, "ninth hour," Jewish)
6. After 3:00 P.M. but before 6:00 P.M. (Jewish Passover began at 6:00 P.M.), Jesus removed and placed in the tomb.

27:46   This prophetic saying of Jesus occurred near the end of the darkness, about the "ninth hour," that is, about 3:00 P.M. His comment was naturally spoken in Aramaic, the common language of the Hebrews, recorded in that language, and then translated for the reader. Matthew, however, retains the Hebrew in His first expression, "*Eli, Eli*" ["My God, My God"], whereas Mark transcribes to Aramaic, "*Eloi, Eloi.*" Mark may just translate the first words into Aramaic for harmony with the rest of the statement, but Matthew maintains the Hebrew to reflect what Jesus actually said. It is noteworthy that Jesus did not cry, "My Father, My Father," but rather, "My God, My God." As the Second Adam, the human sin-bearer, He could not address the One judging the sin of the world as Father but as God.

Jesus was quoting from Psalm 22:1, a hymn of David having several parallels to the crucifixion experience. Thus Psalm 22 is a messianic-prophetic text, where David, a type of the coming Messiah, expressed the agony of the coming One. To "forsake" (*egkatelipes*) is to "abandon" or "desert" someone and expresses one of the greatest mysteries of the Christian faith. How can one Member of the Triune Being abandon or desert another Member? The Hebrew text of Psalm 22 uses the word '*zb,* which also means "leave behind, forsake, abandon."

This writer does not believe that the expression must be understood ontologically but rather forensically. Sin, which Jesus "became" (2 Cor. 5:21) and which He bore in His body (1 Peter 2:24) became a barrier separating the conscious union of God and Messiah (even as David, the anointed king of God, sensed the absence of communion with God in his time of oppression). The abandoning was not a splitting of the Person of God but was the segregation of the holy from the sinful to the degree that the Son could not sense the presence of and communion with the other Members of the Godhead. Christ's experience was expressed by David (Ps. 22), whom Jesus then quoted to signify the depth of His agony and sorrow. God neither broke off His essential being from the Son nor stopped loving Him; but the Father did turn His holiness away from participating in the Son's human experience at this time of sin-bearing. To Christ in His human awareness, God had abandoned Him (Ps. 22:1). Jesus felt that loneliness as His enemies mocked Him (22:6-7, 16). With His aching body totally drained of energy and strength (22:14-15), He felt the "curse" of sin (Gal. 3:13) as He lived out the horrifying prophecy of Isaiah (53:4-11).

27:47-49   Those standing nearby responded not only with confusion but with curiosity. They thought He was calling on Elijah, the great prophet taken in spectacular fashion from the earth (2 Kings 2:11-12) and who was to reappear before the Day of the Lord (Mal. 4:5-6). Hendriksen believes this pericope describes not genuine curiosity but "the mockery of those heartless persons who tried to make others believe that they heard Jesus cry to Elijah for help."[22] However, there is no evidence for this,[23] and His calling on Elijah would not have discredited Him but rather created further messianic identification. The years of ministry and miracles, the dramatic scenes of the last week in the temple, and now the supernatural darkness could well have created concern among some observers for what was happening.

It should also be remembered that others were at the foot of the cross. The disciple John, Jesus' mother, and other women were present (John 19:25-27). Probably many Jews who had followed Jesus out of curiosity were present as well. Amid the shouting and mocking, He cried in a loud voice, *"Eli, Eli."* In light of the tumult— the two robbers groaning, the crowd yelling abuses, and the soldiers noisily active in games and conversation—the cry could have been misunderstood as the somewhat similar *Eliyah.*

One of those standing alongside ran to get something for Jesus to drink (v. 48), perhaps to refresh His throat so the crowd could better understand His cries, or even as a compassionate response to His fifth saying from the cross, "I am thirsty" (John 19:28-29). The "sour wine" (*oxsos*) was not the same mixture of wine and gall offered earlier. Most commentators believe this act was intended to be mockery, but this author disagrees. Hendriksen, likewise, views this as "genuine sympathy."[24] The jar of wine was present (John 19:29) because the soldiers and most of the poorer citizens drank it. *Oxsos* "relieved thirst more effectively than water and, because it was cheaper than regular wine, it was a favorite beverage of the lower ranks of society and of those in moderate circumstances."[25] Jesus "received the sour wine" (John 19:30), which implied He did not perceive its being offered as an act of malice or disrespect.

The rest of the witnesses wanted to "see whether Elijah [would] come to save Him" (v. 49), suggesting that a miracle was expected.

This statement was possibly intended to mock the crowd as well as the Lord, but no clear evidence indicates whether it was mockery at this point or expectation of some spectacular event. Some major manuscripts (including Sinaiticus and Vaticanus, both fourth century, and the Vulgate) have a variant reading stating that a soldier standing by thrust a spear in Jesus' side and both water and blood flowed out. The most common view is that later editors corrupted these manuscripts by taking this account from John 19:34.

27:50 Considering Matthew's detailed account of other events, the Lord's death being summarized in such simple words is poetically striking: "Jesus cried out again with a loud voice, and yielded up His spirit." Both Luke and John give details of what was said in this loud voice. He made two final statements: first, "It is finished!" (John 19:30), and second, "Father, into Thy hands I commit My spirit" (Luke 23:46). The first of these statements is profound beyond any other human words. What was finished? Just His agony on the cross? No. He had finished the work He came to do. "It is finished," *tetelestai* (perfect passive indicative of *teleō*), was the public proclamation of what Jesus had already sensed in His being. Exactly the same verb form is found in John 19:28, "Jesus, knowing that all things had *already been accomplished.*" The use of *tetelestai* meant that the price had been paid and all that remained was the giving up of His physical life to gain the ultimate victory for man by His resurrection. The verb can also mean to "pay"[26] as in Matthew 17:24 and Romans 13:6. In the perfect passive form, as here, it would mean "to have been paid." Laney explains that this same word was written on receipts "indicating that the debt had been paid in full."[27] The wages of sin is death (Rom. 6:23), and Jesus Christ paid that wage. Indeed it was "paid in full!"

The second part of His final words on the cross, "Father, into Thy hands I commit My spirit" (Luke 23:46) used the significant address "Father" after the lonely agony of "My God, My God." This was surely proof that all was paid in full, His work was completed, and His high-priestly prayer for restoration was fulfilled: "I glorified Thee on the earth, having accomplished the work which Thou hast given Me to do. And now, glorify Thou Me together with Thyself, Father, with the glory which I had with Thee before the world was" (John 17:4-5). Jesus quoted yet another psalm of David, 31:5 (v. 6 in the Hebrew) to bring His earthly work to closure. As Pate observes,

"Jesus' committal of His spirit to the Father encapsulates His *dependency* on God, a reliance that carried Him all the way through life and, now, death."[28]

Jesus then "yielded up His spirit," an expression that obviously communicates His sovereign control over His death. The term "yielded" is from *aphiēmi,* which means here to "release, dismiss." Dismissal of His spirit (*pneuma*) implied that the power or energy that drove His physical being was separated from the flesh. The body then became a lifeless shell as His being was transported into paradise (Luke 23:43) to await His resurrection. Death by crucifixion was usually a long and painful process, and the Lord's death occurred earlier than the Romans expected (Mark 15:44; John 19:32-34). Ordinarily, the victim suffocated or died from the extreme pressure placed on the heart.

27:51-53   Matthew alone records all the supernatural events that occurred with the Lord's death. Both Mark and Luke record the tearing of the veil, but only Matthew notes the opening of the tombs and the dead being raised bodily. The ripping of the veil visually symbolized the author of Hebrews' comments concerning the Lord's death, "We have confidence to enter the holy place by the blood of Jesus, by a new and living way which He inaugurated for us through the veil, that is, His flesh" (10:19-20). The veil was a heavy curtain separating the Holy Place from the Holiest Place. Only priests could enter the Holy Place, and only the high priest could enter the Holiest of Holies—and then only once a year and only with blood. By His death Jesus opened the way for all those covered by His blood to enter directly into God's presence. The veil being torn from top to bottom symbolized God Himself opening the way from heaven down to the earth.

Concurrent with the death of Christ, a great earthquake apparently shook the area, which may have caused some fear among the witnesses. Could it have just been coincidence that the death of the One who claimed to be the Son of God should be accompanied with the shaking of the earth? This may explain the ambiguous statement in Luke 23:48, "When they observed what had happened, [they] began to return beating their breasts [a sign of grief]." With the earthquake the tombs opened, and this event probably was, in itself, not a miracle but a providential act brought about by the tremors. The events following, however, were miraculous and not providential.

Not to be associated with the earthquake, the most bizarre and difficult to understand event took place—"many bodies of the saints who had fallen asleep were raised; and coming out of the tombs, after His resurrection they entered the holy city and appeared to many" (vv. 52-53). The most critical phrase is "after His resurrection." The dead saints were not raised until after the Lord's resurrection. Carson argues, "Matthew does not intend his readers to think that these 'holy people' were resurrected when Jesus died and then waited in their tombs till Easter Sunday before showing themselves. . . . The 'holy people' were raised, came out of their tombs, and were seen by many after Jesus rose from the dead."[29] Matthew leaves many unanswered questions as to the identity of these saints (*hagios*), but Carson's guess is as good as any: "They were certain well-known OT and intertestamental Jewish 'saints,' spiritual heroes and martyrs in Israel's history."[30] These raised saints entered Jerusalem and appeared to many witnesses. After this occurrence, no additional information is given, and it can only be assumed then they were translated into heaven. Most likely they were on the earth until the point when Jesus first ascended to His Father following the Resurrection or at least by the time of His final ascension (Acts 1), fifty days later.

27:54 The response of the Roman centurion (an officer in charge of 100 men) is recorded in Matthew, Mark, and Luke. Observing the three-hour darkness, an earthquake, rocks splitting, and tombs opening had an effect on this warrior, causing him to make some interesting declarations. Matthew records that the centurion became "very frightened" but also made the statement "Truly this was the Son of God." MacArthur believes this is evidence of saving faith, not only of the centurion but of all the soldiers: "I believe the soldiers' confession of Jesus' deity gives witness to the possibility of their salvation. Both their fear and their confession were spiritual responses to Christ."[31] But this view has some problems. First, the Romans were very superstitious, and "great fear" would be the expected response, not from a knowledge of the deity of Jesus but from the myths concerning the way the gods worked through such natural phenomena as earthquakes and darkness (e.g., an eclipse).[32] Second, the centurion did not specifically say,

"This was *the* Son of God." What he said was just "This was a son of a god." The Romans believed not only in many gods but that these gods had offspring, sometimes half-human, half-deity, that interacted with humans in daily life. The same would apply to Mark 15:39.

The Luke 23:47 statement also was complimentary of Jesus, "Certainly this man was innocent," but certainly was not a confession to His deity or saving power. The word "innocent" (*dikaios*) is often translated "righteous" in the New Testament but only in theologically oriented contexts. In a judicial sense, the NASB correctly translates it as "innocent." It is highly unlikely that this pagan soldier would have the theological discretion to make a spiritual declaration of Jesus' intrinsic character. He obviously felt (from his superstitious background) that the supernatural events testified to this man's innocence. The strongest argument is that the centurion began to praise God (*edoxsazen ton theon*), yet one cannot read Christian significance into this person's mind and heart. Perhaps he understood the Jewish God well enough to really worship Him, though quite possibly he was praising a pagan god; or his experience could have been similar to those who praise God without understanding the salvific nature of Jesus. Neither the language nor the context implies that this man or his soldiers became Christians.

27:55-56 Matthew then comments on the activity of others near the cross. These women "who had followed Jesus from Galilee, ministering to Him" (v. 55) are named in Matthew, Mark, and John: Mary Magdalene; Mary the mother of James and Joseph; the mother of the sons of Zebedee (Matt. 27:56); Salome; Mary the mother of James the less and Joses (Mark 15:40); Mary the mother of Jesus; Jesus' aunt; Mary the wife of Clopas; and John the apostle (John 19:25-26). The question is whether some of the women identified differently in the multiple lists are the same ladies. For example, it is possible that Mary the mother of James and Joseph in Matthew was the same Mary whose sons are called James the less and Joses in Mark. If these references are to the same woman, then quite possibly she was also called Mary the wife of Clopas (in John). Carson suggests that this could also be Mary the mother of the Lord (cf. Matt. 13:55).[33] However, it is not likely that James, the Lord's half brother, would be James "the less." It is also possible that the name of the mother of James and John, sons of Zebedee (in Matthew), is Salome in Mark. Thus a list of people near the cross would be:

Mary the Lord's mother; Mary Magdalene; Mary the wife of Clopas (mother of James and Joses); Salome (mother of James and John); John (the apostle); and Jesus' aunt (Mary's sister).

THE BURIAL, 27:57-66
(Mark 15:42-47; Luke 23:50-56; John 19:38-42)

27:57   Arimathea was a currently unknown location that Luke refers to as "a city of the Jews" (23:51). Along with Matthew's comments of Joseph being rich and a disciple, both Mark and Luke note his godly character, anticipation of the kingdom, and prominent membership in the Sanhedrin (Mark 15:43; Luke 23:50). Luke also adds the critical note that he had no part in the Sanhedrin's decision to condemn Jesus (23:51), which supports the theory that certain Sanhedrin members were not notified of the late night trial. John clarifies that Joseph was secretly a disciple (19:38).

27:58-60   Joseph came and asked for the body of Christ "when it was evening," that is, some time after 3:00 p.m. on Friday but before 6:00 P.M., which would begin the high Sabbath of Passover (Luke 23:54). According to Deuteronomy 21:22-23, a criminal executed and hanged on a tree was not to be left hanging overnight. Since the coming day was a Sabbath, and a special Sabbath at that, the Jews would not allow removal of the body after sunset. Thus the task had to be done soon.

Joseph went to Pilate and asked permission to take the body of Jesus. Mark pointed out that he "gathered up courage," as this act would certainly anger fellow Sanhedrin members, whom he had feared up to this point (John 19:38). Pilate ordered that the body be given to Joseph but only after verifying that Jesus was dead (Mark 15:44-45). The centurion knew Jesus was truly dead because of personally watching Him die (Luke 23:46-47) and afterwards witnessing the soldiers break his legs, a measure used to accelerate the dying process and ensure death before sundown because of the coming high Sabbath (John 19:31-34).

Joseph wrapped the body in a clean linen cloth (v. 59), which he had purchased (Mark 15:46), most likely for this occasion. John added that Nicodemus (John 3:1-21) joined Joseph in preparing the body for burial (John 19:39-40). The use of spices and perfumes in preparing the body was important in the Jewish traditions. Joseph then placed the body in his own tomb (v. 60), fulfilling Isaiah 53:9 (cf. v. 57). The "large stone" should not be envisioned as just a big rock, since this tomb was a man-made cave (Mark 15:46, "hewn out in the rock"), but should be understood as a cut stone, much like a coin standing on edge. It was approximately five feet in circumference, about six inches thick, and was designed to roll in a track built in front of the tomb. The track sloped so that the stone could be rolled to seal the entrance to keep out animals and grave robbers.

27:61   Matthew hardly mentions the women watching this entombment, but their roles were significant. Mary Magdalene and the "other Mary" (the mother of James and Joses, Mark 15:47) were apparently waiting to see where the body of Jesus would be laid. An interesting side note is that there had been no time to plan or make proper burial preparations, though Jesus had often given warning of this coming event. These two ladies followed to find the tomb location and then joined the other women in preparing the spices and burial cloths. The burial procedure was interrupted because of Passover (Luke 23:55–24:1). Thus Jesus was in the tomb before 6:00 P.M. Friday.

27:62-64   On the next day, Saturday, a Sabbath, the religious leaders went to see Pilate. There must have been genuine fear in the hearts of these hypocrites for them to violate their own strict Sabbath observances to meet with the governor. They remembered Jesus' prediction of rising again after three days (v. 63). However, their fear was not that He would actually do this but that His disciples would counterfeit a resurrection (v. 64). This certainly reflected a lack of understanding of just how disillusioned the disciples were.

27:65-66   The remark "you have a guard" may refer to Pilate's granting permission to use Roman guards or just the opposite, "You have your own guards and don't need the Romans." Carson prefers this second view,[34] which may be supported by the fact that following the Resurrection the guards reported to the chief priests, not to Pilate (28:11). The cynical statement "Make it as secure as you know how" implies that Pilate may have taken personal delight in the apprehension of these religious hypocrites. The temple guard was stationed and the seal placed on the stone. Now any attempt at fraud would certainly be detected.

HOMILETICAL SUGGESTIONS

In presenting the death of Judas, one must avoid either of two extremes. One should not seek to overlook his wickedness and believe that somehow in the end he was saved. Jesus called him the "son of perdition" and declared that it would be better had he never been born. Though to have sympathy for Judas may be natural, one must remember that his remorse was not repentance and his guilt no more than what any normal person should have felt. On the other hand, Judas, though influenced by Satan in the end, was not any different from any other unregenerate soul. Driven by greed and the human desire for immediate gratification, Judas is an illustration of how one can focus hope on this earthly existence and miss the eternal blessing Jesus offers. Many professing Christians follow Jesus only to get His "blessings." They extend "worship" to Him only because they lead happy, prosperous lives or need a religious crutch when tragedy strikes. Christians need to follow Jesus with the realization that hope in Him is not for this world only (1 Cor. 15:19); in this world, believers will be rejected, hated, and persecuted for identification with Him (John 15-16).

The trial of Jesus before Pilate needs to be studied with the gospel of John as the primary source. The dialogue between Pilate and the Lord reveals that Jesus showed more respect and patience with Pilate than He did with the Jewish high priest. This is consistent with His intolerance of pseudo-religious leaders and His patience and pity toward those not having the privileges of the religious elite. Jesus' comment in John that His kingdom is not of this world speaks volumes as to the purpose and mission of the body of Christ. He is not building a kingdom in this perverted world but is drawing out the elect to populate His kingdom when established.

Pilate's resistance to having Jesus crucified and his three declarations of His innocence add to the heinousness of Israel's crime. Even though the highest legal office declared Him innocent three times, the Jews refused to accept this verdict and forced His condemnation by means of rioting and threatening to appeal to Caesar. Their choice to have a murderer released onto the streets rather than the One who healed, cast out demons, raised the dead, and fed the multitudes highlights the doctrine of depravity. Such stubborn resistance emphasizes the wickedness of the human heart and the unfailing completion of God's sovereign plan using their wickedness (Acts 2:22-23). Likewise, the abuse by the Roman soldiers confirms that such depravity is to be found not just in the Jews but in all human hearts. These men knew Pilate had declared Him innocent, yet they entertained themselves by inflicting pain and humiliation.

The spectacular events accompanying His death (earthquake, tombs opened, veil torn) are testimonies to the magnitude of His last moment of sacrifice, but almost as amazing was the stepping forth of Joseph of Arimathea. Up to this point he had kept his faith in Christ a secret for fear of the Jews, but now, when all looked bleakest, he stepped forward to care for his Lord's body. When others were denying and hiding, Joseph proclaimed his faith. This was faith at its best. Jesus had just died a horribly disgraceful form of death, but Joseph knew that there must be more. When to the human eye it looked as though all was over, he was willing to be identified with Him.

The events of the crucifixion are appalling and depressing, yet even here God's glory is seen. Jesus, with resolute conviction, endured shame and suffering from the worst of human treatment, yet demonstrated compassion ("Forgive them because they don't understand what they are doing") and concern for others ("Woman, behold your son . . . behold your mother"). He continued to extend mercy to those who turned to Him ("Today you will be with Me in paradise") and never retaliated against those slandering or abusing Him. Peter later looked back on this event and told the church that Jesus is our role model for suffering (1 Peter 2:20-24).

MATTHEW

CHAPTER
TWENTY-EIGHT

RESURRECTION

The events of chap. 28 separate Christianity from the false religions of the world. The resurrection of Jesus Christ announced that God had accepted the payment of the Second Adam and now there was provision for overcoming the wages of sin. It also promised that death itself cannot hold the believer and that life is eternal in Christ. This last chapter of Matthew contains the pericope commonly labeled the "Great Commission," which gives direction and purpose for the followers of Jesus. His disciples are to be making disciples, a perpetual commission until He returns to take the church from this corrupt world.

ANNOUNCEMENT OF THE RESURRECTION, 28:1-10
(Mark 16:1-8; Luke 24:1-10; John 20:1-10)

28:1 The next morning, early on Sunday, the women returned to the tomb for completion of the body preparation for proper burial, which had been cut short by the coming Sabbath (Luke 23:54-56). Matthew expresses this time as "after the Sabbath, as it began to dawn" (NASB). But some scholars stumble over his wording, seeming overly concerned with finding a way to show complications in the time frame of the events rather than allowing for normal forms of expression.[1] The construction of the language can easily be taken exactly as rendered by the NASB. The consistent testimony of all four records reveals that the Sabbath had ended (after 6:00 P.M. Saturday). Early the next morning before the sun had risen, the ladies went to the tomb. All the Gospels indicate an early arrival time, as dawn began to filter light into the darkness. The "first day of the week" was Sunday and would become somewhat of a focus day for the early church (Acts 20:7; 1 Cor. 16:2).

Matthew mentions that two of the Marys came to the tomb; Mark adds that Salome was also there (16:1); Luke names Joanna, perhaps the aunt mentioned in John 19:25 (24:10); whereas John simply focuses on Mary Magdalene (John 20). This group may have traveled together, or possibly they left from different homes to meet at the tomb at sunrise. Note that these women did not go expecting to witness the Resurrection but to finish the burial customs on the body of Jesus.

28:2-4   What they found instead was shocking—the tomb was open, and an angel sat upon the stone that had sealed the opening. This earthquake was another dramatic witness to the significant event that had taken place. Probably localized and accompanying the appearance of the angel, the earthquake did not, however, open the tomb. Matthew indicates that the angel rolled away the stone.

The events of vv. 2-4 seem related to events prior to the women's coming. The angel sitting outside on the stone is described as having the appearance of lightning. One can only speculate as to what this was to convey. Lightning is seen as bright flashing light, therefore, his "appearance" (not his clothing) was like brilliant flashes of light (shining skin?). In addition to this brilliance, his clothing was "as white as snow." The whole of his appearance meant this was not a human in common robes but certainly a supernatural being. The guards were terrified at his sudden appearance and apparently fainted or went into shock (v. 4).

The four gospel accounts offer some variations requiring comment. Matthew states that the women saw the angel sitting outside on the stone, whereas Mark records that they entered the tomb and saw the angel sitting inside (16:5).[2] Luke also records their entrance into the tomb but places two angels standing next to them (24:3-4). By combining all of the accounts, the events would be as follows: the women arrived at the tomb, saw that the stone had been rolled aside, and an angel sitting on the stone greeted them with the news of the Resurrection. Stunned and in disbelief, some of the women (if not all) stepped into the tomb at the invitation of the angel on the stone (28:6). Possibly some left the scene immediately. In particular, it is quite feasible that Mary Magdalene never entered the tomb but ran to notify Peter of what she had seen (John 20:1-2). Once inside, the group saw another angel sitting where the body should have been, and the victorious message was repeated (Mark 16:5-7). Also, other angels standing within the tomb asked why they would seek the living among the dead (Luke 24:3-7). Narrative literature must be understood as a fluid account of events, and the fact that one author records only part of an event does not require an exclusive view of what happened. By juxtaposing the accounts, one sees this event as a dramatic and dynamic episode: the open tomb; the angels proclaiming the message of His resurrection; the stunned group of women, some running off immediately, some going into the tomb.

28:5-6   The first angel encountered gave the message of the Resurrection. His exhortation to "not be afraid" was to inform them he had no intention of doing them harm. Matthew uses the emphatic construction (includes the pronoun *humeis,* "you"), indicating not to be like the guards who fainted. The angel revealed that he was aware of their reason for coming (to tend to the body) and their expectation to find the crucified body of Jesus.

Undoubtedly, this heavenly creature must have taken some delight in proclaiming to these mortals "He is not here for [*gar,* "because"] He is risen" (v. 6). Knowing more experientially the reality of Jesus' identity, the angels must have been shocked that these humans who knew Him so well had overlooked the actuality of His resurrection. Thus, perhaps as a mild rebuke, the phrase "just as He said" was added. Hendriksen is correct in saying, "We might have expected a different message, for example, a stern rebuke, in view of the fact that these women showed by their action that they had not taken seriously enough Jesus' prediction of rising on the third day. But . . . a gentle admonition, a loving reminder—comes at the very end of the angel's message."[3] The angel then encouraged the ladies to enter the tomb and see where He had been lying. Both Mark and Luke pick up the story here and describe the details of their entering the tomb.

28:7-8   The message was not just that Jesus had bodily risen from the dead but that He was going to meet them in Galilee. The women were to tell the disciples to return to Galilee (they were obviously still in Jerusalem) and be prepared to see the resurrected Lord. "Behold, I have told you" is a declaration that the angel had done his job and now these women had the responsibility to carry the message to the others.

Matthew records that the ladies left "with fear and great joy" (v. 8), reflecting not so much two different emotions as a combination of anxiety over the reality of what had been witnessed, with so many unanswered questions, and inner exhilaration stemming from the announcement. From Mark's account, it seems they began to be overcome with fear as they traveled along the road—"trembling and astonishment had gripped them" (Mark 16:8). The women may have determined to forgo their mission and return to their homes. If so, this would explain why Jesus appeared to them (28:9). Even though the angels had sent them with a clear mission, Jesus stopped them and repeated it. If they were not overcome with growing doubts and fears as Mark records, this would not have been necessary.

28:9-10   The obvious gap between vv. 8 and 9 is best explained by Mark 16:8. Jesus stopped the women from returning home. His greeting was cordial and probably familiar, *chairete,* "greetings." Their response of dropping before Him and taking hold of His feet in veneration was most likely the effect of shock from seeing Him, as well as the overwhelming joy of now realizing the truthfulness of the angel's message.

Jesus repeated the message of the angel (v. 10). First, He told the women to stop being afraid (*mē phobeisthe*). The negative particle *mē* used with the present tense imperative means to stop what is already in progress or to not continue an action.[4] They were overwhelmed with fear, and Jesus instructed them to cease from being controlled by that fear. Second, He repeated the instruction to relay to the disciples the word that He would meet them in Galilee. Jesus referred to them as "My brethren," which may designate any who believe in Him (Matt. 12:50) but here most likely meant His disciples (see v. 7). Barnes makes an appropriate observation: "There is something exceedingly tender in the appellation here used—'my brethren.' Though he was risen from the dead, though about to be exalted to heaven, yet he did not disdain to call his disciples his brethren. This was calculated still farther to silence the fears of the women and to inspire them with confidence."[5] The appointment in Galilee did not negate the possibility of prior meet-ings with them in Jerusalem, and He did meet two along the road to Emmaus (Luke 24), ten disciples assembled without Thomas (John 20:19-24), and again later when Thomas was with them (John 20:26-30). Of course, admission must be made that Jerusalem was not specifically stated as the location of these meetings, but it seems the best assumption. Luke mentions that the women did deliver the message (24:9).

REPORT TO THE CHIEF PRIESTS, 28:11-15

28:11-15   Concurrent with the women's taking their message to the disciples, some of the guards were making their way to the high priests to report this supernatural event. Interestingly enough, the chief priests did not seem to dispute it, and their response was typi-cal—a meeting was held to scheme their way out of the truth (v.12). The counsel resulted in bribing the guards to keep quiet about what had actually happened and to lie about their unfaithful-ness to duty. It took "a large sum of money" because the leaders' whole reputation would be damaged. Had these been Roman sol-diers guarding the tomb, execution could have resulted from failing to carry out their assigned task.

The story they were to tell (v. 13) was based on the fear expressed to Pilate (27:62-66). The idea that the disciples could actually have broken the seal and moved the huge stone without waking the guards was ridiculous, but it was the only response offered to account for the open tomb. Verse 14 is even more inter-esting in that the religious leadership promised a cover-up if Pilate discovered what actually happened at the tomb and that the guards had failed in their duty. The guards agreed to lie and took the money (v. 15). "To this day" indicates that the story was still circu-lating when Matthew wrote his gospel about thirty years after the events. Indeed, the report still seemed to be going around when Justin Martyr (A.D. 100-165) wrote *Dialogue with Trypho.*

MEETING IN GALILEE, 28:16-20

28:16-17   Matthew omits the other meetings with the disciples (Luke 24:36-51; John 20:19-29); the appearances to Mary Magdalene

551

(John 20:11-18); and the Emmaus road account (Luke 24:13-35). His purpose is to emphasize the commissioning of the eleven to carry on His work, so he proceeds directly to that event. In v. 16, Matthew mentions that "the eleven disciples" proceeded to Galilee, bringing the focus on them and not all the followers of the Lord. It is possible that a large crowd accompanied them, and many scholars believe this would be the occasion for the five hundred witnesses Paul references (1 Cor. 15:6).

Details of the prearranged meeting are not recorded in the Gospels. The men went to the mountain "designated" (*etaxsato,* from *tassō,* "appointed, set aside, directed"). Which mountain is not specified. One could certainly appreciate the significance if it were the same mountain on which the Transfiguration had occurred. Galilee was the chosen area for this meeting probably because it had been the focus of Jesus' earthly work and His disciples were originally from that area. Before His death, Jesus had told His disciples that, following His resurrection, He was returning to Galilee (26:32).

Even though they had already seen Him on a few other occasions, the disciples' immediate response was to worship (*proskuneō,* "fall down before") Him (v.17). This should be noted by those who treat Jesus as their "good buddy." Seeing the resurrected Lord brought instinctive humility and adoration, not a flippant hand shake or back-slapping celebration.

It is most consistent grammatically to understand "they" as the "eleven," which is the nearest antecedent. However, it is difficult to understand how any of the eleven could be doubtful (*edistasan,* aorist third person plural of *disazō*), especially considering the events of John 20:19-30. Barnes, however, does believe the reference is to the eleven: "As for example, Thomas, John 20:25. The disciples had not expected his resurrection; they were therefore slow to believe."[6] MacArthur points out that "exactly what was doubted is also not specified."[7] It is quite possible that these men were not doubting the Resurrection itself but whether the Person now standing before them was the real Jesus or some impostor. Perhaps something more like the Transfiguration was expected. And in light of the comment of v. 18, Jesus may not have first appeared to them in close proximity. Seeing Him from a distance, some immediately fell to the ground and began to worship; others hesitated, being uncertain of His identity. The integrity of Scripture is upheld by recording these doubts rather than portraying everyone as hyperspiritual. It is also likely that those who doubted were not of the eleven. Rather, they may have been the followers of 1 Cor. 15:6, those who had not yet seen the risen Lord but came here because word had spread that the Lord was meeting with the eleven.

28:18 Jesus came nearer (*proserchomai*, "approached, come toward") to the eleven and spoke to them. Once again, the natural antecedent of "them" is the eleven, though it is possible that He was addressing the larger crowd. However, even though there may have been a crowd of several hundred, He had specifically appointed this meeting to be with the eleven and, therefore, was most likely speaking to them.

Jesus' first statement related to His own authority (literally, "It has been given to Me, all authority in heaven and upon [the] earth"). Emphasis was placed upon the authority's being given to Him. He did not take it Himself, but it had been presented to Him. This authority was obviously a presentation from the Father as reward for His obedience (Phil. 2:8-11). What was given was "authority" (*exsousia*), which differs from power (*dunamis*). *Dunamis* is "force, power." Jesus always had the *dunamis*. *Exsousia,* more than just power, includes the right to exercise that power. Jesus as the Son of Man did not exercise His power but rather was totally submissive to the Father and dependent upon the Spirit. However, having accomplished His work as the obedient Son, He was then delegated the right to exercise His power in heaven and upon the earth. The designation "earth" (*tēs gēs*) rather than world (*kosmos*) may also be significant in that it refers to a material domain rather than the system operating within that domain. He certainly had power and authority over the *kosmos,* but "earth," *gēs,* was intended to be a spatial and material designation to compare with heaven.

28:19 The Great Commission is often misrepresented by the emotive call to "*Go.*" In reality, the commission is not to "go" but to "make disciples." The word "go" is translated from *poreuthentes* (aorist passive participle from *poreuomai*) and would be just as well translated "having gone." It assumes the going as having already taken place and is certainly part of the commission (Acts 1:8). Matthew places His emphasis on what is to be done when one has gone. As the main verb, he uses *mathēteusate* (aorist imperfect imperative from *mathēteuō*), "make disciples," which is the heart of the commission.

The authority by which one makes disciples is Christ's authority. The "therefore" (*oun*) meant that on the basis of the authority given Christ, His followers were to go and make other disciples. These disciples were not to be Jews only but were to come from "all the nations." Christ's authority was over all the earth, and now His ministry was not to be confined just to Israel but to extend to all the nations. This is consistent with the instructions of Acts 1:8. Christ had a plan by which He was going to make disciples all over the world, and these eleven men were only the seeds of the great work of world evangelization and discipleship.

The first step in this global disciple-making is baptism. The word "baptize" (*baptizontes*) is a present tense participle indicating a continual process in the making of disciples. Baptism does not save anyone but is public identification with a person or cause and testifies to one's salvation. John baptized the Jews to identify them with the coming Messiah and His kingdom. Here, the baptism is to identify with the Father, the Son, and the Holy Spirit. The term "name" (*to onoma*) implies one's character, nature, authority, rank, and purpose. To do something in the name of someone is to do it as his representative and as acting within his authority or purpose. It is very similar to the contemporary idea of "power of attorney." Thus, to pray in the name of Jesus means to ask as His representative and for His purpose, not simply attaching His name at the end of a request list. The baptism was to publicly identify the new convert with the salvific work of the Triune God. The expression *"the name"* is singular and articular (having a definite article) and is qualified by the three genitive modifiers, "Father," "Son," and "Holy Spirit." Thus (by the name's being singular but modified by three distinct Persons) one authority, character, and purpose is implied—that is, one God who saves. The mode of baptism is never specified in Scripture, but the word itself (*baptizō*) basically means to "plunge under, submerse." Only disciples are to be baptized. A disciple is a follower of Jesus, one who has submitted to Him as teacher. It is those "who [have] received His word" who are to be baptized, not infants or those simply wanting to be religious (Acts 2:41).

28:20   Another part of the discipleship process is education. A second present tense participle (*didaskontes,* "teaching") is connected with the main verb, "make disciples." To teach, *didaskō,* is to inform and also to commit truth to someone else. The practical nature of biblical teaching can be seen here in that what is taught is obedience, not just facts. Discipleship involves teaching the converts to "observe" (*tērein,* literally. "keep, guard, obey, pay attention to") *all* that Jesus commanded His disciples. Thus, making a disciple is not just leading someone to faith in Christ (though that is certainly the first step) but also requires teaching that one to live according to all that Jesus commanded His original disciples.

One should not overlook the important qualifier "all." It is not a fulfillment of the Great Commission just to lead someone to Christ or just to teach them basic moral principles of godly living; they are to be instructed in the practical outworking of all of Jesus' commandments. The "all that I commanded you" is critical in being a Christian. Thus, the early believers were "continually devoting themselves to the apostles' teaching" (Acts 2:42). What Christ had taught His twelve disciples was to be passed down through the church so that wherever the name of Jesus was preached, His value system, His program, and His truth were to be propagated and preserved. This is the Great Commission. Carson points out, "Jesus does not foresee a time when any part of his teaching will be rightly judged needless, outmoded, superseded, or untrue: *everything* he has commanded must be passed on to 'the very end of the age.'"[8] The biggest danger here is that some do not understand the historical context and meaning of Christ's teachings within their literary contexts. Some misuse His teachings because of failure to understand the Lord and His mission, primarily as the Messiah of Israel. To take His teachings and make application in a different context is not teaching to "observe" them. His truths are eternal, and a proper understanding of these requires a consistent hermeneutic and sound knowledge of all the doctrines.

Jesus closed this meeting with the great promise "I am with you always, even to the end of the age," referring to completion of the redemptive program. The "you" here must extend beyond the eleven since they would be unable to live until the "end of the age." Jesus promised to be with His disciples until the end. No period of the church age has ever found His servants without the presence of their Lord. Hendriksen points to the emphatic construction "I myself am with you."[9] The great promise of the sending of the "other comforter" (the Holy Spirit) who would empower and direct the church (John 14-16) was not negating the fact that the Lord Himself would still be actively involved with His servants (John 14:16-20). He is called the "head to the church" for this reason (Eph. 1:20-23). As disciples spread throughout the world, making other disciples, Jesus is right in the midst. His servants are never alone and never abandoned to the task without divine guidance, comfort, and strength. As the Father was with the Son, step by step, so the Lord is with His servants, step by step.

HOMILETICAL SUGGESTIONS

When preaching the Resurrection, one should not become so focused on that glorious outcome that the turmoil and tension of the event is missed. The women did not come to watch the Resurrection occur, but came expecting to find a dead body, badly bruised and contorted from the agony of crucifixion. Even when confronted with angelic messengers, there was doubt and fear. All four gospels portray faithless and frightened disciples, and this fact is not to be covered up in an attempt to celebrate this great event. The reality of Jesus' brutal death was overwhelming, and their inability to grasp the truth lets us know that even today Christians can struggle with fear and doubt when faced with the harsh realities of life. Too much spiritualization has been done to God's Word. These were real people, hurt, confused, and terrified.

The fact that Jesus appeared to the women is also significant. Some theologians have perverted this truth to suit their "rights crusades," but, in reality, the disciples were hiding because their lives were at stake. In the ancient world, if a rebel was captured, his key men were also hunted down and executed. These men who stood with Jesus in the temple as He debated the religious leaders were certainly in danger. However, one should not play down the great privilege of these women in being the first to hear the message and the first to see the risen Lord. Their faithful and humble service was rewarded. Mary Magdalene was a very special case, as she actually saw the Lord first (Mark 16:9) and received some tender, loving care from Him (John 20:11-18). Preaching this resurrection section requires approaching the four gospels as a whole, not just one testimony. The varying accounts are not contradictory but parts that complete the contributions of others. If one approaches the Gospels with diligent study and an open mind to allow for fluid history and a dynamic story, then the drama of this greatest event will not be lost.

The Great Commission needs to be presented in a more responsible manner than in past generations, where emotive preaching has ignored the responsibility of full obedience to the command. Making disciples is a serious obligation and must be viewed as a process of transforming new converts into mature disciples. One cannot claim to be carrying out the Great Commission if no provision has been made for teaching and developing the convert. Neither is it sufficient to teach elementary Bible lessons and pretend that one has taught the disciple to keep all that Christ commanded. The author of Hebrews scolds his readers because of their continuing to be babes in understanding (Heb. 5:12–6:3). The responsibility of the pastor-teacher is to equip and mature the saints so that they are no longer "children, tossed here and there" by false doctrine and deceitful men (Eph. 4:11-14). Too many missionaries and pastors think that preaching the gospel and having people walk an aisle, raise their hands, pray a prayer, or sign a card is fulfilling the Great Commission. This is one reason that more than three hundred Christian denominations and thousands of cults exist in the world. The teaching aspect of the Great Commission has been greatly neglected.

Focus needs to be placed on the last statement of Matthew's commentary as well. Christians are not left alone in this world to carry out the Lord's work. He is ever present and always involved with His disciples. What a comfort to those entering hostile environments to preach the gospel, and for those suffering for the name of Christ. He is with us, until the end.

NOTES

INTRODUCTION

1. Eusebius, *Ecclesiastical History,* trans. Kirsopp Lake, 2 vols. (Cambridge, Mass: Harvard Univ. Press, 1975), 3:39; 16. The Greek text of the critical comment reads, *Matthaios men oun Hebraidi dialektō ta logia sunetaxsato, h'rm'neusen d' auta hōs 'n dunatos hekastos.*

2. Ibid., 6:25; 4.

3. Ibid., 3:24; 6.

4. Ibid., 5:10; 3.

5. Ibid., 5:7; 2.

6. William Hendriksen, *New Testament Commentary on Matthew* (Grand Rapids: Baker, 1973), 85.

7. R. V. G. Tasker, *The Gospel According to St. Matthew,* Tyndale New Testament Commentaries (Grand Rapids: Eerdmans, 1981), 12.

8. Robert H. Stein, *The Synoptic Problem* (Grand Rapids: Baker, 1987), 129.

9. This writer once had a professor who actually believed the only way to understand the New Testament was to translate from the Greek into Aramaic and then into English.

10. Hendriksen, *Matthew,* 85.

11. Ibid., 91.

12. Eusebius, EH, 3:39; 16.

13. Henry Alford, *The Four Gospels,* vol. 1, *The Greek Testament* (Chicago: Moody, 1968), 29.

14. Tasker concludes, "Most modern scholars find it very difficult to believe that our Gospel of Matthew is a translation of an Aramaic document." (*Matthew,* TNTC, 1:13.)

15. D. A. Carson, *Matthew*, EBC (Grand Rapids: Zondervan, 1984), 8:12.

16. Ibid., 4.

17. Eta Linnemann, "Is There a Gospel of Q?" BR, August 1995, 19.

18. Stein, *The Synoptic Problem*, 43.

19. Ibid.

20. Linnemann, "Is There a Gospel of Q?" 19.

21. Jeff Lyon, "Gospel Truth," *The Chicago Tribune Magazine*, 17 July 1994, 10.

22. Ibid.

23. Linnemann, "Is There a Gospel of Q?" 22.

24. Carson, *Matthew*, 8:6.

25. Ibid., 8:13.

26. Eusebius, EH, 6:25; 4.

27. Ibid., 3:24; 6-7.

28. Robert H. Mounce, *Matthew*, NIBC. (Peabody, Mass: Hendrickson, 1991), 1:2.

29. Alford, GT, 1:24.

30. Carson, *Matthew*, 8:17.

31. Heinrich A. W. Meyer, *The Gospel of Matthew* (Peabody, Mass: Hendrickson, 1983), 2.

32. Ibid., 33.

33. Hendriksen, *Matthew*, 96.

34. Mounce, *Matthew*, 1:2.

35. Meyer, *Matthew*, 1.

36. Carson, *Matthew*, 8:19.

37. Alfred Edersheim, *Sketches of Jewish Social Life* (Peabody, Mass: Hendrickson, 1994), 51.

38. Daniel Sperber, "Tax-Gatherers," in EJ, ed. Cecil Roth, 16 vols. (New York: Macmillan, 1972), 15:873.

39. A. H. M. Jones, *Augustus* (New York: W. W. Norton, 1970), 122.

40. Ibid., 119. For this last comment, compare Luke 2:1-2.

41. Sperber, "Tax-Gatherers," 15:873.

42. Alford, *Four Gospels*, 1:24.

43. Meyer, *Matthew*, 2.

44. *Lives of the Saints,* compiled from *Butler's Lives* and other approved sources, and officially approved by Pope Leo XIII (New York: Benziger, 1922), 464.

45. Kenneth Scott Latourette, *The First Five Centuries* (New York: Harper, 1937), 101. However, his documentation from Eusebius is not correctly noted.

46. Meyer, *Matthew*, 2.

47. Eusebius, EH, 3:24; 6.

48. Ibid., 5:7; 2.

49. Mounce, *Matthew*, 1:3.

50. Hendriksen, *Matthew*, 97.

51. Carson, *Matthew*, 8:21.

52. James Straham, "Antioch," in *Dictionary of the Apostolic Church*, 2 vols., (Edinburgh: T. & T. Clark, 1926), 1:69.

53. Ibid., 8:21.

54. Strahan, "Antioch," DAC, 1:69.

55. Carson, *Matthew*, 8:21.

56. Ibid., 8:79.

57. Eusebius, EH, 6:25; 5.

58. Alford, *Matthew*, 1:30.

59. J. W. Scott, "Matthew's Intention to Write History," WTJ, (1985), 70.

60. Alford, *Matthew*, 1:31.

61. Mounce, *Matthew*, 1:3.

62. Carson, *Matthew*, 8:17.

63. Mounce, *Matthew*, 1:4.

64. William Barclay, *Gospel of Matthew, The Daily Study Bible* (St. Andrews, 1975), 36.

65. Carson, *Matthew*, 8:17. The comment references passages that are difficult to interpret and are often targets of debate.

66. Steve Willis, "Matthew's Birth Stories: Prophecy and the Magi," ET (November 1993), 44.

CHAPTER ONE

1. Biblical genealogies do not necessarily include every person but link significant persons. For a helpful discussion on the gaps in genealogies see B. B. Warfield, "The Antiunity and Unity of the Human Race," in *Studies in Theology* (Edinburgh: Banner of Truth, 1932), 235-58.

2. Some might argue that 2 Samuel refers to Solomon rather than to the Messiah. It is not unusual in OT prophecy to use an individual who serves as a type of the Messiah. Certainly God's promise had significance beyond Solomon. Jer. 23:5-6, adds that the Lord will "*. . . raise up for David a righteous Branch; and He will reign as king . . . and this is His name by which He will be called, 'the Lord our righteousness.'*"

3. Edersheim offers a helpful discussion from rabbinic literature to demonstrate the almost divine position attributed to Abraham by the teachers of Israel. Alfred Edersheim, *The Life and Times of Jesus the Messiah* (Grand Rapids: Eerdmans, 1972), 1:271-72.

4. Merrill F. Unger, "Genealogy," in *The New Unger's Bible Dictionary* (Chicago: Moody, 1988), 463.

5. Meyer, *Matthew*, 38.

6. BAGD, 887.

7. Meyer, *Matthew*, 43.

8. The name "Jesus" is omitted from the Vulgate and the Syriac versions but is probably best retained as it reads.

9. Edersheim, *Life and Times*, 3:354.

10. C. Marvin Pate, *Luke*, Moody Gospel Commentary, 62.

11. Ibid.

12. Robert H. Gundry. *Matthew*, 2d ed. (Grand Rapids: Eerdmans, 1994), 22.

13. D. A. Carson, *Matthew*, 8:74.

14. Flavius Josephus. *The Works of Flavius Josephus,* trans. William Whiston (Grand Rapids: Baker, 1980) 2:274.

15. The word for "wanting" (to disgrace her) is *theio,* but the word for "desired" (to send her away) is *boulomai.* Both imply to desire something or express a personal inclination toward. However, at times, and certainly here, *boulomai* refers to decisions made or a determination toward something, that is ". . . of decisions of the will after previous deliberation," BAGD.

16. Meyer, *Matthew*, 50.

17. It is possible for neuter nouns to refer to persons, but even in these cases "the emphasis is less on the individual than on some outstanding general quality." Nigel Turner, "Syntax," in *Grammar of the Greek New Testament* (Edinburgh: T. & T. Clark, 1963), 3:21.

18. Ibid., 3:86.

19. For example see Arno C. Gaebelein, *The Gospel of Matthew, 33.* (Neptune, N.J.: Loizeaux, 1910).

20. Acts 7:45 uses the same name, *Iēsou* (Jesus) for Joshua.

21. Gundry, *Matthew*, 24.

22. William Hendriksen, *New Testament Commentary: Matthew* (Grand Rapids: Baker, 1973), 80-81.

23. Ibid., 133.

24. Matthew references the LXX more than any other gospel writer: Matthew, 40 times; Mark, 19; Luke, 17; John 13.

25. Some late minuscules (9th century and later) changed the LXX to conform to Matthew.

26. Carson, *Matthew*, 8:78.

27. Ibid.

28. The word *ginōskō* implies intimate or experiential knowledge.

CHAPTER TWO

1. Gundry, *Matthew,* 37.

2. Raymond Brown, *The Birth of the Messiah* (Garden City, N.J.: Doubleday, 1977), 189.

3. For a more complete look at this fascinating character of history see Josephus, *Wars of the Jews The Works of Flavius Josephus* (Grand Rapids: Baker, 1980), and A. H. M. Jones, *Augustus,* for a better understanding of the political environment of this time period.

4. Gundry, *Matthew,* 26.

5. Some would find such reference in Psalm 72:10-11.

6. Brown, *The Birth of the Messiah,* offers a detailed review of the mythological traditions that grew up in later centuries of Christian tradition.

7. Josephus records details of his brutal protectiveness in *Antiquities* and *Wars.*

8. Jones, *Augustus,* 71.

9. See Carson, *Matthew,* 85-86; Brown, *The Birth of Messiah,* 171-74.

10. Carson, *Matthew,* 86.

11. Hendriksen, *Matthew,* 155.

12. Idumaea is the Greek form for the country of Edom, which is associated with the descendants of Esau. Refusal to allow the Israelites passage through their land during the Egyptian Exodus (Num. 20:14-21) resulted in bitter animosity between the two nations. Both Saul (1 Sam. 14) and David (2 Sam. 8) fought against the Edomites.

13. Calvin, "Harmony of the Evangelists," 16:131. Vol. 16 of *Calvin's Commentaries.* Translated by William Pringle (Grand Rapids: Baker, 1981).

14. See BAGD, 886-87.

15. Alfred Edersheim, *The Life and Times of Jesus the Messiah,* appendix IX, 710.

16. An interesting name for metaphoric purposes since Jesus called Himself the Bread of Life (John 6:32-35).

17. BDB, *ts`yr,* 859.

18. BAGD, *oligos,* 563.

19. Gundry, *Matthew,* 29.

20. Calvin, "Harmony," 16:135.

21. Some have suggested that *oikia* should be translated "village" rather than "house," but this is a weak argument as *oikia* is consistently used for "house."

22. Although gold is a well-known substance in contemporary culture, frankincense and myrrh are undefinable to the average person. Frankincense, a gum taken from balsam tree bark, has a fragrant aroma and is used in perfumes, in religious rituals, and as a medicine. Myrrh comes from a shrub in Arabia and is used in making spices and medicine and also ceremonially used in burial rites (John 19:39).

23. William Barclay, *The Gospel of Matthew*, 1:33.

24. Gundry, *Matthew*, 32.

25. Ibid., 33. See also the defense of his rationalistic hermeneutic in the second edition preface.

26. Hendriksen, *Matthew*, 179.

27. Carson offers a more complete discussion in *Matthew*, 8:91-93.

28. Josephus, *Antiquities* XIV.XV.12 (or 3:343).

29. Hendriksen, *Matthew*, 183.

30. Carson, *Matthew*, 8:94.

31. Not to be confused with Ramah in Naphtali, which is north and west of the Sea of Galilee.

32. This parenthetical statement referencing Bethlehem is believed to be a scribal gloss. Cf. L. Elliott Binns, *The Book of the Prophet Jeremiah* (London: Methuen, 1919), 234. A tomb near the present city of Bethlehem is ascribed to Rachel, but it is not likely the genuine burial site.

33. Ibid.

34. Carson, *Matthew*, 8:95.

35. See Josephus, *Antiquities*, 17:6, 5–17:8,1.

36. F. F. Bruce, "Matthew," in *Understanding the New Testament* (Philadelphia: A. J. Holman, 1970), 10. The date of 4 B.C. is difficult because the standardized Western calendar originated in A.D. 525 at the request of Pope John I, and the Scythian monk Dionysius miscalculated the dates of the Roman calendar, setting 754 A.U.C. (*anno urbis conditae*—754 years after the founding of the city of Rome) as A.D. 1 of the Christian calendar. See Harold Hoehner, *Chronological Aspects of the Life of Christ,* (Grand Rapids: Zondervan, 1977), 11-27.

37. Josephus, *Antiquities* 17:8; 2.

38. Ibid., 17:8; 3–17:11; 1.

39. Ibid., 17:11; 4.

40. Ibid., 17:13; 1-2.

41. John Calvin, "Harmony," 16:163.

42. Ibid., 16:164.

43. Carson, "Matthew," EBC, 8:97.

CHAPTER THREE

1. See Pate's discussion on this topic, *Luke*, 95-96.

2. Josephus, *Antiquities* 18:5. 2.

3. A monastic commune of religious Jews, the Essenes lived in the Qumran area on the northwestern border of the Dead Sea from about 2 B.C. to A.D. 2 and were the most likely source of the Dead Sea scrolls.

4. Josephus, *Antiquities* 13:5. 9.

5. BAGD, *metanoēō*.

6. H. E. Dana and Julius R. Mantey, *A Manual Grammar of the Greek New Testament* (Toronto: MacMillan Company, 1927), 108.

7. F. Blass and A. Debrunner, *A Greek Grammar of the New Testament,* rev. by Robert W. Funk (Chicago: University of Chicago, 1961), 62.

8. Carson, *Matthew,* 8:99.

9. John F. Walvoord, *Matthew: Thy Kingdom Come,* 30. (Chicago: Moody, 1978).

10. Ibid.

11. Carson, *Matthew,* 8:102.

12. Julius A. Bewer, *The Prophets,* 628. (New York: Harper, 1955).

13. Calvin, "Harmony," 16:183.

14. BAGD, 277.

15. Abba Eban, *My People: The Story of the Jews,* 80. (New York: Random House, 1968).

16. M. Man, "Pharisees," in *Encyclopedia Judaica,* 365. (New York: Macmillan, 1971).

17. Eban, *My People,* 80.

18. Pate, *Luke,* 98.

19. Meyer, *Matthew,* 1:79.

20. Josephus, *Antiquities* 18:5. 2.

21. Edersheim, *Life and Times,* 1:271.

22. Perschbacher correctly points out that "anarthrous nouns modified by pas . . . refer to the whole class." Wesley J. Perschbacher, *New Testament Greek Syntax,* (Chicago: Moody, 1995), 68. The point is that any tree fitting that category is to be cut down. This writer is not convinced that Carson or Turner are correct in making a sharp distinction between "every" and "any." See Carson, *Matthew,* 104; and Turner, "Syntax," in *Grammar of New Testament Greek,* 3:199.

23. Carson, *Matthew,* 105.

24. Hendriksen, *Matthew,* 213.

25. Tasker, *Matthew,* 49.

26. The word *peristera* is translated both as "dove" (Matt. 3:16) and "turtledove" (Luke 2:24).

27. This passage is traditionally seen as one of the evidences of the tri-unity of God, with the divine Son, the Holy Spirit, and the Father all appearing at the same time and place, each separately participating in this inauguration of the redemptive program.

28. The last public childhood appearance of Jesus was at the age of twelve in the temple. He returned to Nazareth at that time and remained in obedience to His earthly parents. Now eighteen years later, He begins His public ministry.

CHAPTER FOUR

1. The old Latin theological terminology is "peccable" ("able to sin") and "impeccable" ("not able to sin") from peccare, "to sin."

2. Hendriksen, *Matthew*, 223.

3. It should be noted that fasting is not commanded in the New Testament and, in comparison with so many other subjects, Christ said very little concerning the issue. His most direct teaching on the subject simply warns about fasting in order to have others know one is fasting (Matt. 6:16). True fasting is not a ritual but a commitment to lay aside any distraction, even food and drink, in order to focus on an issue God has made a concern. Those who brag about or flaunt fasting certainly need to heed Christ's warning. Fasting was required under the Old Testament Law (Lev. 16:29-31). The Hebrew *tsûm*, "humble your souls," NASB, is the act of fasting) and was thus assumed in the New Testament.

4. For a nice synopsis of this very broad topic see, "Fasting," in the *Zondervan Pictorial Bible Dictionary*, ed. Merrill C. Tenney. (Grand Rapids: Zondervan, 1967).

5. Meyer, *Matthew*, 94.

6. Ibid.

7. J. Dwight Pentecost, *The Words and Works of Jesus Christ*, (Grand Rapids: Zondervan, 1981), 100.

8. Carson, *Matthew*, 113.

9. Christ quotes the LXX, not the Hebrew text.

10. BAGD.

11. Everett F. Harrison, *A Short Life of Christ*, (Grand Rapids: Eerdmans, 1991), 87.

12. Meyer, *Matthew*, 95.

13. Israel Lipschutz, "Appendix to the Temple," in *Encyclopedia Talmudica*, (Jerusalem: Talmudic Encyclopedia Institute, 1992), 615.

14. Ibid.

15. Josephus, *Antiquities* 15:11; 5.

16. Meyer, *Matthew*, 1:98.

17. Hans Conzelmann, *The Theology of Luke*, (New York: Harper & Row, 1966), 27.

18. Pate, *Luke*, 117.

19. Donald Guthrie, *A Shorter Life of Christ*, (Grand Rapids: Zondervan, 1970), 82.

20. John Calvin, "Harmony," 16:222.

21. Carson, *Matthew*, 8:117.

22. Tasker, *Matthew*, 1:57.

23. This writer does not take Luke 5:1-11 as a parallel account but a separate event in which Jesus is confirming His call of these men. Luke 4:38 clearly indicates that Jesus was already involved with Peter before entering his boat.

24. Carson, *Matthew*, 8:119.

25. Ibid.

26. Meyer, 1:105.

27. Adolf Deissman, *Light from the Ancient East,* trans. Lionel R. M. Strachan (Grand Rapids: Baker, 1978), 440.

28. Leo Trepp, *Judaism: Development and Life* (Belmont, Calif.: Dickenson, 1966), 149.

29. Carson, *Matthew,* 1:249.

30. Robert Mounce, *Matthew,* 1:34.

31. Hendriksen, *Matthew,* 250.

32. The ten cities are normally considered: Damascus, Kanata, Dion, Hippos, Gadara, Abila, Scythopolis, Pella, Gersea, and Philadelphia.

CHAPTER FIVE

1. C. H. Dodd, *The Bible Today,* 84.

2. John R. W. Stott, *The Message of the Sermon on the Mount,* BST, (Downers Grove, Ill.: InterVarsity, 1978), 24.

3. See Gundry, *Matthew,* 65-66.

4. Hendriksen, *Matthew,* 260.

5. Carson, *Matthew,* 1:126.

6. Ibid., 1:123.

7. Meyer, *Matthew,* 1:111.

8. Stott indicates that Augustine was the first to use the term *sermon* (BST, p. 24). It does not appear in Matthew's record.

9. Carson, *Matthew,* 1:128.

10. Stott, *Sermon on the Mount,* 29.

11. Carson, *Matthew,* 1:129.

12. See F. Hauck, *"Makariōs,"* in TDNT, 4:367-70.

13. Even though v. 11 also begins with *makarioi,* the pattern breaks because Jesus personalizes it for His disciples, *makarioi este hotan.*

14. Mounce, *Matthew,* 38.

15. Henry Alford, "Matthew," in *The Greek Testament* (Chicago: Moody), 1:37.

16. Carson, *Matthew,* 8:133.

17. BDB, 777

18. Gesenius' *Hebrew and Chaldee Lexicon.* See *'ny.*

19. Meyer, *Matthew,* 1:114.

20. Carson, *Matthew,* 8:134.

21. Stott, *Sermon on the Mount,* 47.

22. R.C.H. Lenski, *St. Matthew's Gospel,* 191.

23. See "Pure," DNTT, 3:102-7.

24. Hendriksen, *Matthew*, 277.

25. Carson, *Matthew*, 8:135.

26. Alford, *Matthew*, 1:39.

27. It seems that the term "sons" is frequently used in a forensic sense of legal heirs and not specifically related to gender in such cases.

28. See for a defense of this view, Stott, *Sermon on the Mount*, 52.

29. Meyer, *Matthew*, 1:117.

30. Stott, *Sermon on the Mount*, 57.

31. Hendriksen, *Matthew*, 282.

32. Liddell and Scott's *Intermediate Greek-English Lexicon*, "*mōrainō*." (Oxford: Clarendon, 1959).

33. Merrill F. Unger, *The New Unger's Bible Dictionary*, 868.

34. Carson, *Matthew*, 8:138.

35. Attempts to connect this statement with Isa. 2:2-5 as a messianic reference is too artificial. The comment concerning the city on a hill was to illustrate, not predict or fulfill any OT reference.

36. Lenski, *St. Matthew's Gospel of Matthew*, 202.

37. Meyer, *Matthew*, 1:119.

38. Carson, *Matthew*, 8:140.

39. Ibid.

40. Ibid.,141.

41. BAGD, *kataluō*.

42. The term *teleological* refers to bringing something to completion or accomplishing a goal.

43. Carson, *Matthew*, 8:142.

44. Hendriksen, *Matthew*, 289.

45. Ibid.

46. *plēroō* indicates "fill, complete, fulfill, accomplish," NIDNT, 1:733.

47. See *parerchomai*, BAGD.

48. See *iōta*, BAGD.

49. See *keraia*, BAGD.

50. See *luō*, BAGD.

51. John Brown, *Discourses and Sayings of Our Lord Jesus Christ*, (Winona Lake, Ind.: Alpha Pub. Reprint, 1981), 1:176.

52. Josephus, *Antiquities* 13:10; 6.

53. It should be remembered that the Old Testament distinguished between murder and justifiable homicide such as war, self-defense, and capital punishment under the law.

54. Hendriksen, *Matthew,* 295.

55. BAGD, *Raka,* 733.

56. Carson, *Matthew,* 8:149.

57. Josephus offers explanation of the laws of adultery in *Antiquities* 4:8; 23.

58. Horst Reisser, *"moicheuō,"* NIDNTT, 2:582.

59. Carson, *Matthew,* 8:151.

60. Stott, *The Message of the Sermon on the Mount,* p. 86.

61. Carson, *Matthew,* 8:151.

62. Clifford A. Wilson, *Jesus the Teacher* (Victoria, Australia: Word of Truth, 1974), 99.

63. Carson, *Matthew,* 8:151.

64. Ovadiah ben Yaacov Sforno, *Sforno: Commentary on the Torah,* trans. Raphael Pelcovitz (Brooklyn: Mesorah Pub., 1993), 829.

65. Hillel was born in Babylon around 30 B.C. and is claimed by some to be the most influential Jewish teacher of the first century B.C. (cf. Dagobert D. Runes, "Get" or "Divorce" in *Concise Dictionary of Judaism* (New York: Philosophical Library,1959), 112.)

66. "Divorce," in *The Jewish Encyclopedia,* ed. Isidore Singer (New York: Funk and Wagnalls, 1903), 4: 624-25.

67. Josephus, *Antiquities* 4: 8; 23.

68. Reisser, *"porneuō,"* 1:497.

69. Josephus, *Antiquities* 6:6; 5.

70. Josephus, *Wars,* 2:8; 6.

71. See Hendriksen, *Matthew,* 311.

72. Alford, *Matthew,* 1:54.

73. Gundry, *Matthew,* 96.

74. Carson, *Matthew,* 8:157.

75. D. Martyn Lloyd-Jones, *Studies in the Sermon on the Mount* (Grand Rapids: Eerdmans, 1979), 303.

76. See the discussion by Nigel Turner, "Syntax," in vol. 3 of *A Grammar of New Testament Greek* (Edinburgh: T & T Clark, 1963), 93-94.

77. See *teleios, a, on,* BAGD.

78. Carson, 8:161.

79. It is of concern to this writer that much of contemporary Christianity measures spirituality by being disciplined to get up early and spend thirty minutes in prayer and Bible reading. Evangelism is carried out as a duty, and being at church is a test of commitment. We are to force ourselves to pray and read our Bibles even if we don't "feel like it." This is Phariseeism. The Pharisees too prided themselves in such discipline. If one does not want to pray, he should pursue why and deal with that, not force insincere prayer as though it were the external act that counts (6:5-7). How many husbands or wives would be

pleased if their spouse spoke to them only out of being disciplined? What kind of empty relationship is produced by forced duty rather than a desire to be with another person? God is not impressed with "spiritual discipline" but rather with children who delight to be in His Word and who delight in speaking with Him.

CHAPTER SIX

1. Stott, *The Message of the Sermon on the Mount,* 125.

2. Josephus, *Antiquities* 3:12; 6.

3. That these "have their reward in full" (*apechousin ton misthon autōn*) is a most significant declaration. The expression "to have in full" is taken from the technical secular Greek use of *apechō*, found in numerous papyri and ostraca receipts indicating that nothing else was owed; the bill was paid in full. This is not to be confused with the term used in John 19:30, "It is finished" (*teleō*). Deissmann states, "I think we may say, therefore, that this technical meaning of *apechō*, which must have been known to every Greek-speaking person, down to the meanest labourer, applies well to the stern text about the hypocrites: 'they have received their reward in full,' *i.e.,* it is as though they had already given a receipt, and they have absolutely no further claim to reward." (Adolf Deissmann, *Light from the Ancient East,* trans. Lionel R. M. Strachan [Grand Rapids: Baker, 1978], 111.)

4. Stott, *Sermon on the Mount,* 130.

5. LS, *hypokritēs.*

6. See William Barclay, *New Testament Words* (Westminster), 140-43.

7. The real Lord's Prayer can be found in Matthew 26:39, 42 and John 17:1-26.

8. Gundry, *Matthew,* 104.

9. A comparison of the two versions is found with commentary in the appendixes.

10. Meyer, *Matthew,* 146.

11. Erich Tiedtke and Hans-Georg Link, "*opheilō*" in NIDNTT.

12. Lenski's argument concerning justification and a final remission is both inappropriate to this context and inconsistent with biblical teaching on the necessity of continual forgiveness from daily sins. See R. C. H. Lenski, *Matthew,* 269. The aorist tense in and of itself does not imply a once-or-all or final act. See Frank Stagg, "The Abused Aorist," JBL (1972), 221-31.

13. See Perschbacher, *New Testament Greek Syntax,* 87. Other grammars agree.

14. Stott, *Message of the Sermon on the Mount,* 149-50.

15. Meyer, *Matthew,* 149.

16. "*Didache,*" in *Apostolic Fathers,* Loeb Classical Library, trans. Kirsopp Lake (Cambridge, Mass: Harvard Univ. 1977), 1:321.

17. See Carson's discussion, *Matthew,* 8:176.

18. Though the events are not parallel, the subject matter of Luke 12 is very similar to that of Matthew 6.

19. Perschbacher, *New Testament Greek,* 103-4. Also Dana & Mantey, (Toronto: Macmillan, 1957), *Manual Grammar of the Greek New Testament,* 301; and Turner, "Syntax," 76.

20. Ibid., 159-60.

21. Stott, *Sermon on the Mount,* 155.

22. Carson, *Matthew,* 8:179.

23. Ibid.

24. Tasker, *Matthew,* 1:77.

25. Hendriksen, *Matthew,* 353.

26. See Carson, *Matthew,* 8:182.

CHAPTER SEVEN

1. Stott, *Sermon on the Mount,* 174.

2. Ibid.

3. Carson, *Matthew,* 8:183.

4. Tasker, *Matthew,* 79.

5. Meyer, *Matthew,* 162.

6. Stott, *Sermon on the Mount,* 176.

7. Carson, *Matthew,* 8:184.

8. Stott, *Sermon on the Mount,* 177.

9. BAGD, *katanoeō.*

10. Meyer, *Matthew,* 163.

11. Hendriksen, *Matthew,* 358.

12. Albert Barnes, "Matthew and Mark," in *Notes on the New Testament* (Grand Rapids: Baker, 1955), 76.

13. Gundry, *Matthew,* 122.

14. "Didache," *The Apostolic Fathers,* trans. Kirsopp Lake (Cambridge: Harvard Univ., 1977), 323.

15. Chiastic parallelism is syntactical structure with four corresponding parts set up like an X. The structure is made up of two lines, each having two parts: line one, part A and B; line two, part A and B. Line one part A relates to line two part B. Line one part B relates to line two part A.

16. Though the teaching is similar, as stated in chap. 5, Luke's account and Matthew's account are not to be confused as taking place at the same time. Jesus is simply repeating the same lesson to a different audience.

17. Carson, *Matthew,* 186.

18. Ibid.

19. Hendriksen, *Matthew,* 361.

20. See *aiteō,* NIDNTT, 2: 855-59.

21. Hendriksen, *Matthew,* 362.

22. See Perschbacher, *New Testament Greek Syntax,* 290-91.

23. This is a significant theological point. Christ is stating in clear language that mankind is evil by nature because in Adam every human is fallen and spiritually dead until regeneration. Even in the regenerate state, humanity is still plagued by intuitive sinfulness.

24. The LXX reads *kai ho miseis, m'deni poi's's.*

25. Shabbath 31, a.

26. Take notice that Jesus does not say *"in* the Law and Prophets" but *is* the Law and Prophets. In other words, the Law and Prophets might be summed up as "treat people in the same way you wish to be treated." The Law and the Prophets were not given to oppress people, as the scribes and Pharisees had done, but to teach people how to live with proper consideration of others. This is dynamically joined with Christ's other summary statement about the Law, "You shall love the Lord your God . . . You shall love your neighbor as yourself . . . On these two commandments depend the whole Law and the Prophets" (Matt. 22:37-40).

27. Carson, *Matthew,* 8:188-89.

28. Gundry, *Matthew,* 128.

29. Ibid., 129.

30. Carson, *Matthew,* 8:191.

31. Ibid.

32. Tasker, *Matthew,* 83.

33. J. C. Ryle, "Matthew-Mark," in *Ryle's Expository Thoughts on the Gospels,* 4 vols. (Grand Rapids: Baker, 1979), 1:70.

34. An ostracon from Thebes dating to A.D. 63 refers to Nero as "the lord" (*Nerōnos tou kuriou*), and similar references are found in papyri dating to A.D. 66. Wilcken listed 27 ostraca referring to Nero as "the lord." (Deissmann, *Light from the Ancient East,* 105; 173.)

35. Ibid., 179, "Apion to Epimachus his father and lord, many greetings" (an Egyptian soldier to his father, 2d cent. A.D.).

36. Some assume this connection; see Meyer, *Matthew,* 168.

37. Carson, *Matthew,* 8:192.

38. Ibid.

39. Hendriksen, *Matthew,* 377.

40. Stott, *Sermon on the Mount,* 206-7.

41. See Carson, *Matthew,* 8:195, for an excellent discussion on the structure of the Greek text indicating Matthew's style of communication.

CHAPTER EIGHT

1. Carson, *Matthew,* 8:196.

2. For an idea of the complexity of the harmony of the different gospel accounts one might refer to *Synopsis of the Four Gospels,* ed. Kurt Aland (United Bible Society, 1982). A helpful tool would be A. T. Robertson's *A Harmony of the Gospels for Students of the Life of Christ* (New York: Harper, 1950).

3. The Luke 5:12-14 account is not necessarily the same event.

4. See also, Josephus, *Antiquities,* 9:4, 5.

5. BAGD.

6. Carson, *Matthew,* 8:198.

7. Tasker, *Matthew,* 87.

8. Ibid.

9. It is possible that this is the same event recorded in Luke 7:1-10. There are significant similarities but also significant differences. If the same event, Matthew just omitted the "middlemen" (the elders) because the point of the story contrasts the faith of the non-Jewish centurion to Israel's lack of faith. Compare the events:

MATTHEW 8:5-13	LUKE 7:1-10
Centurion's child (*pais*)	Centurion's slave (*doulos*)
Came personally	Sick and about to die
Paralyzed, suffering great pain	Sent Jewish elders
Jesus states He will come	Elders offer reasons for worthiness
Centurion stops Him	Jesus on the way
	Additional friends sent to stop Him

The similarities are too strong to assume coincidental occurrences, though several centurions being in any military area such as Capernaum should be acknowledged. The somewhat similar event recorded in John 4:46-54 is not to be confused with this event.

10. Carson, *Matthew,* 8:200.

11. See *pais, paidos, ho* or *hē,* BAGD.

12. Calvin, *Calvin's Commentaries,* 16:382.

13. Carson, *Matthew,* 8:203.

14. According to John 1:44, Bethsaida was "the city of Andrew and Peter." This could possibly mean their birthplace or relocation to Capernaum as a more central location to follow Jesus in ministry.

15. Hendricksen, *Matthew,* 401.

16. Carson, *Matthew,* 8:207.

17. Luke places this event, or perhaps a similar experience where Jesus taught the same lessons, on the journey to Jerusalem (Luke 9:57-62). Except for the repetition of the burial request for the father, the two events simply could be deemed

different occasions. It may be possible that the request to bury the father reflected cultural attitudes, meaning that he would be willing to follow Jesus as soon as his father died and thus ended responsibility to his father. If this were the case, the repetition of the request would not be unusual. The other circumstances of the two accounts would imply that these were two similar but separate incidents where Jesus repeated the same lessons.

18. U. Luz, "The Son of Man in Matthew: Heavenly Judge or Human Christ," JSNT 48 (1992), 4.

19. Ibid., 18. This writer appreciated Luz's work but must disagree with his conclusion that "it is not possible to interpret *ho hios tou anthrōpou* as a christological title." Luz's arguments along this line were too narrow, and it seems legitimate to conclude that Jesus and His followers used it as such.

20. Carson, *Matthew*, 8:213; See discussion, 209-13.

21. BAGD, *tote*.

22. Ferdinand Prat, *Jesus Christ: His Life, His Teaching, and His Work*, trans. John J. Heenan (Milwaukee: Bruce, 1950), 332.

23. BAGD.

24. Dr. John A. Sproule used this illustration in Greek exegesis classes.

25. BAGD.

26. Hendriksen offers a good discussion of this issue; *Matthew*, 413.

27. Edersheim offers an insightful discussion on the difference between Jewish traditions concerning demons and the New Testament revelation regarding them. See Edersheim, *The Life and Times of Jesus the Messiah*, appendix 8, 759-63.

CHAPTER NINE

1. Hendriksen, *Matthew*, 418.

2. Carson, *Matthew*, 8:221.

3. BAGD, *teknon*.

4. Calvin, "Harmony of Matthew, Mark, and Luke," 16:393-94.

5. Edersheim, *Life and Times of Jesus the Messiah*, 1:93.

6. Hendriksen, *Matthew*, 419.

7. Lenski, *St. Matthew's Gospel*, 358.

8. Carson, *Matthew*, 8:222.

9. Pate, *Luke*, Moody Gospel Commentary, 138.

10. For further information on this person and the use of these names, review the Introduction, 19-24.

11. Blendinger, "Disciple, Follow, Imitate, After," NIDNTT, 1:480.

12. Hendriksen, *Matthew*, 424.

13. Feinberg, *The Minor Prophets*, 32.

14. Hendriksen, *Matthew,* 428.

15. Carson, *Matthew,* 8:227.

16. Pate, *Luke,* Moody Gospel Commentary, 142.

17. Lenski, *Matthew,* 372.

18. See Ernest DeWitt Burton, *Syntax of the Moods and Tenses in New Testament Greek* (Grand Rapids: Kregel, 1976), 176.

19. Hendriksen, *Gospel According to Luke* (Grand Rapids: Baker, 1978), 336.

20. William Barclay, *And He Had Compassion* (Valley Forge: Judson, 1976), 51.

21. Edersheim, *Life and Times of the Messiah,* 1:555.

22. An interesting side note is the fact that the girl was born the same year the woman's hemorrhaging began.

23. Carson, *Matthew,* 8:233.

24. Meyer, *Matthew,* 203.

25. See Jack Dean Kingsbury, "The Title 'Son of David' in Matthew's Gospel," JBL 95/4 (1976), 591-602.

26. Carson, *Matthew,* 8:233.

27. Ibid.

28. Hendriksen, *Matthew,* 436.

29. BAGD.

30. Hendriksen, *Matthew,* 438.

31. H. Bietenhard, "Satan," NIDNT, 3:469.

CHAPTER TEN

1. James Morison, *Gospel According to the St. Matthew* (Minneapolis: Klock & Klock, 1981), 151.

2. John MacArthur, Jr., *Matthew 8-15, The MacArthur New Testament Commentary* (Chicago: Moody, 1987), 119.

3. Hendriksen, *Matthew,* 450.

4. BAGD, "*apostolos.*"

5. Carson, *Matthew,* 8:236.

6. Luz, "The Disciples in the Gospels According to Matthew," in *The Interpretation of Matthew,* ed. Graham N. Stanton (Edinburgh: T & T Clark, 1995), 127.

7. The first four are connected by *kai.* After that the article is omitted between pairs but appears again before the next pair. This is only a possible inference, not a certain pattern.

8. David Thomas, *The Gospel of St. Matthew,* ed. William Webster (Grand Rapids: Baker, 1956), 148.

9. The Zealots were also called Sicarii after the daggers they used to assassinate the perceived enemies of Israel. Josephus records that the Sicarii called them-

selves Zealots because they saw themselves as zealously pursuing the protection of the nation. Josephus, however, considered them thugs and brutes who deserved to be destroyed by the Romans. According to Josephus, they cut the throats of priests and any others whom they determined were willing to submit to Rome. Tax gatherers in particular were hated by the Zealots because they stole money from the Jews to pay Rome and to live in luxury. The famous siege of Masada was Rome's last major blow against the Sicarii. See Josephus, *Wars*, 7:8, 1.

10. Hendriksen, *Matthew*, 455.

11. Ibid., 452.

12. Carson, *Matthew*, 8:237.

13. See Hendriksen, for example, *Matthew*, 456.

14. Carson, *Matthew*, 8:244.

15. Hendriksen, *Matthew*, 457.

16. Ferdinand Prat, *Jesus Christ*, trans. John J. Heenan, 2 vols. (Milwaukee: Bruce, 1950), 1:348.

17. Edersheim, *Sketches of Jewish Social Life*, 92.

18. Meyer, "Matthew," in *Meyer's Commentary on the New Testament*, 1:210.

19. Tasker, *Matthew*, 1:108.

20. Barnes, "Matthew," in *Notes on the New Testament*, 112.

21. Calvin, "Harmony," 16:456.

22. Carson, *Matthew*, 8:252.

23. Ibid., 253.

24. See, Turner, "Syntax," 3:74-77.

25. Hendriksen, *Matthew*, 469.

26. Ryle, "Matthew," in *Expository Thoughts on the Gospels*, 102-3.

27. It should be noted that "soul" is not that which separates humans from animals because even animals apparently have souls (Lev. 24:18, Hebrew *nephesh*; Rev. 16:3).

28. Meyer, *Matthew*, 1:216.

29. For more information see DNTT, 2:206-9.

30. Hendriksen, *Matthew*, 473, n. 456.

31. Meyer, *Matthew*, 1:216.

32. Ibid., 1:217.

33. Hendriksen, *Matthew*, 473.

34. Carson, *Matthew*, 8:257.

35. Robert Gundry, *A Survey of the New Testament* (Grand Rapids: Zondervan, 1994), 127.

36. Barnes, "Matthew," in *Notes on the New Testament*, 116.

CHAPTER ELEVEN

1. Josephus, *Antiquities,* 18:5; 2.
2. Carson, *Matthew,* 8:260.
3. Edersheim, *Life and Times of the Messiah,* 1:79, note 1.
4. The NASB is not as accurate here as the NIV: "Blessed is the man who does not fall away on account of Me." However, the most literal rendering is provided above.
5. J. Guhrt, *"skandalon; skandalizō,"* DNTT, 207-10.
6. BAGD.
7. MacArthur, *Matthew 8-15,* 246.
8. Carson, *Matthew,* 8:262.
9. Ibid., 8:264.
10. MacArthur, *Matthew 8-15,* 255.
11. Hendriksen, *Matthew,* 490.
12. Calvin, "Harmony of Matthew, Mark, and Luke," 16:2;16.
13. Louis Barbieri, *Mark,* 98.
14. See Colin Brown, "Generation," DNTT, 2:35-39.
15. Barnes, "Matthew and Mark," in *Notes on the New Testament,* 1:120.
16. BAGD.
17. Carson, *Matthew,* 8:273.
18. Hendriksen, *Matthew,* 496.
19. Ibid., 499.
20. Carson, *Matthew,* 8:275.
21. Ibid.
22. *"zugos,"* DNTT, 3:161.
23. Clement, "The First Epistle to the Corinthians," in *The Apostolic Fathers,* trans. Kirsopp Lake, 2 vols. (London: Harvard Univ. Press, 1977), 16:17.
24. Calvin, "Harmony," 16:44.

CHAPTER TWELVE

1. Josephus, *Antiquities,* 12:6; 2.
2. Ibid., 13:8; 4. See footnote.
3. Carson, *Matthew,* 8:280.
4. Hendriksen, *Matthew,* 515.
5. Carson, *Matthew,* 8:284.
6. Ibid.
7. Barnes, "Matthew and Mark," 1:129.
8. MacArthur, *Matthew 8-15,* 294.

9. See Carson for discussion; *Matthew,* 8:285-87.

10. BAGD.

11. Carson, *Matthew,* 8:286.

12. Ibid., 8:287.

13. Barnes, "Matthew and Mark," 130.

14. BAGD.

15. Ibid.

16. MacArthur, *Matthew 8-15,* 309.

17. Gundry, *Matthew,* 235.

18. Calvin, "Harmony of Matthew, Mark, and Luke," 16:73.

19. Mounce, *Matthew,* NIBC, 118.

20. Hendriksen, *Matthew,* 528.

21. BAGD.

22. Carson, *Matthew,* 8:291.

23. Walvoord, *Matthew, Thy Kingdom Come,* 89.

24. Hendriksen, *Matthew,* 531.

25. Carson, *Matthew,* 8:294.

26. Hendriksen, *Matthew,* 535.

27. MacArthur, *Matthew 8-15,* 339.

CHAPTER THIRTEEN

1. See Walvoord, *Matthew,* 95-96.

2. Joachin Jeremias, *The Parables of Jesus* (Scribner, 1954), 12.

3. Robert H. Albers, "Perspectives on the Parables—Glimpses of the Kingdom of God," *Word and World,* IV:4, 438.

4. This writer does not agree with Carson (*Matthew,* 304) that Matthew 7:24-27; 9:15-17; and 16-19 are parables. Parables are stories that require some key to understand whereas analogy and metaphor are illustrations comparing one thing to another.

5. Hendriksen, *Matthew,* 554.

6. Meyer, "Matthew," 1:254.

7. Ibid., 1:255.

8. Carson, *Matthew,* 8:311.

9. Hendriksen, *Matthew,* 559.

10. MacArthur, *Matthew 8-15,* 358.

11. Mounce, *Matthew,* 1:129.

12. Barnes, "Matthew and Mark," in *Notes on the New Testament,* 1:143.

13. See ZPBD, 668.

14. Carson, *Matthew*, 8:316.

15. Ibid., 8:316-17.

16. The superlative form is rare in the NT, and the comparative form took its place. However, there is not grammatical reason in this passage to force the "smallest" interpretation. It is rather being compared to other seeds, and among them it is one of the smaller. See Blass, Debrunner, and Funk, paragraphs 60, 244, and 245.

17. *Niddah* 5:2.

18. As explained earlier, "Son of Man" was Jesus' favorite self-identification. It referenced His humanity and His role as the "Second Adam." It had definite messianic implications.

19. Barnes, "Matthew and Mark," in *Notes on the New Testament,* 1:147.

20. Walvoord, *Matthew,* 105.

21. Carson, *Matthew,* 8:331.

22. Hendriksen, *Matthew,* 580.

23. Gundry, *Matthew,* 281.

24. Mounce, "Matthew," 137.

25. MacArthur, *Matthew 8-15,* 410.

26. Carson, *Matthew,* 8:336.

CHAPTER FOURTEEN

1. Several rulers were named Herod, and the reader must be careful to distinguish which particular Herod is being referenced.

2. Josephus, *Antiquities,* 18:2; 1.

3. See Harold W. Hoehner, *Herod Antipas* (Cambridge: Univ. Press, 1972), 131-36.

4. Ibid., 18:5; 2.

5. Ibid., 18:5; 1. Herod was visiting his brother Philip and fell in love with Philip's wife, who apparently also fell in love with Herod. They agreed to break from their present spouses and to marry, which led to the war with Aretas (the father of Herod's wife) in partnership with some of Philip's army and the defeat of Herod's army.

6. Ibid., 18:5; 2.

7. Josephus offers a list of the complicated family line and names Salome as the daughter of Herodias by Herod Philip, whom she divorced. See *Antiquities,* 18:5; 4.

8. Hoehner, *Herod Antipas,* 151-56.

9. Carson, *Matthew,* 8:339.

10. Louis Barbieri, *Mark,* 148.

11. ZPBD, 661.

12. Pate, *Luke,* 204-5.

13. Carson, *Matthew,* 8:342.

14. Ibid., 8:343.

15. Mounce, *Matthew,* NIBC, 1:144.

16. See Gundry, *Matthew,* 296-98.

17. Mounce, *Matthew,* 1:144.

18. Barbieri, *Mark,* 153.

19. Turner, "Syntax," 3:75.

20. Carson, *Matthew,* 8:344.

21. See Carson' s discussion, ibid., 8:345.

CHAPTER FIFTEEN

1. Hendriksen, *Matthew,* 608.

2. Bruce, "Matthew," in *Understanding the New Testament,* 50.

3. Deismann, *Light from the Ancient East,* 440.

4. Edersheim, *Life and Times,* 2:9-10.

5. Hendriksen, *Matthew,* 613.

6. LS, "*upokritēs.*"

7. Barnes, "Matthew and Mark," in *Notes on the New Testament,* 1:161.

8. Carson, *Matthew,* 350.

9. Mounce, *Matthew,* 151.

10. Carson, *Matthew,* 8:351.

11. Mounce, *Matthew,* 151-52.

12. Meyer, "Matthew," 1:284.

13. See Carson, *Matthew,* 8:354.

14. Jack Dean Kingsbury, "The Title 'Son of David' in Matthew's Gospel," JBL 95/4 (1976), 599.

15. BAGD, *Kunarion, ou, to.*

16. Hendriksen, *Matthew,* 625.

17. Mounce, *Matthew,* 1:154.

18. Carson, *Matthew,* 8:358.

19. Ibid.

CHAPTER SIXTEEN

1. Hendriksen, *Matthew,* 635.

2. These two verses are omitted from some important manuscripts, primarily Vaticanus and Sinaiticus. Many scholars agree, however, that there is ample reason

to accept them as original and authentic. This commentator agrees that their authenticity should be recognized.

3. Hendriksen, *Matthew,* 638.

4. Carson, *Matthew,* 8:362.

5. Barnes, "Matthew," in *Notes on the New Testament,* 168.

6. Barbieri, *Mark,* 180.

7. One such statement is found in 2 Maccabees 15:15-16. This author's translation would allow only a very obscure reference, but it could be seen as some foundation for eschatological hope. Hendriksen, *Matthew,* 642, suggests it might be the reference in 2 Macc. 2:4-8, which implies that Jeremiah had hidden the ark and altar of incense in a cave.

8. Hendriksen, *Matthew,* 642.

9. Gundry, *Matthew,* 330.

10. E.g., Louis Berkhof, *Systematic Theology* (Grand Rapids: Eerdmans, 1984), 334-35.

11. Alford, *Matthew,* 1:172.

12. Benziger Brothers, comp. *Lives of the Saints* (New York: Benziger, 1922), 331.

13. Calvin, *Institutes* (MacDill, Fla.: MacDonald, n.d.), 4:6, 5.

14. Calvin, "Harmony," 16:291.

15. Hendriksen, *Matthew,* 645-49.

16. BAGD.

17. Hendriksen, *Matthew,* 646.

18. Carson, *Matthew,* 8:368.

19. Ibid., 8:370.

20. Turner, "Syntax," 89.

21. Perschbacher, *New Testament Greek Syntax,* 295.

22. Carson, *Matthew,* 8:373.

23. Ibid., 8:375.

24. See Mounce, *Matthew,* 1:163.

25. Alford, *Matthew, Greek Testament,* 1:175.

26. Meyer, "The Gospel of Matthew," 1:301.

27. Hendriksen, *Matthew,* 656.

28. Ibid.

29. Carson, *Matthew,* 8:379.

30. Hendriksen, *Matthew,* 658.

31. Mounce, *Matthew,* 1:165.

32. Carson, *Matthew,* 8:382.

CHAPTER SEVENTEEN

1. See Pate, *Luke*, 210-11.

2. Meyer, "Matthew," 1:308.

3. Barbieri, *Mark*, 194, quoting R.A. Cole.

4. Hendriksen, *Matthew*, 665-66.

5. Lenski, *St. Matthew's Gospel*, 652.

6. James A. Penner, "Revelation and Discipleship in Matthew's Transfiguration Account," *BibSac* (April-June 1995), 204.

7. Ibid., 207.

8. Carson, *Matthew*, 8:386.

9. Ibid., 388.

10. Thomas Moore explains this cryptic phrase very well: "The hearts of the devoted ancestors were to live again in the obedience of their repentant posterity, and that the backslidden sons were to be restored to the piety of their fathers." (Thomas V. Moore, "Malachi," *A Commentary on Haggai, Zechariah and Malachi* [Edinburgh: Banner of Truth, 1979], 423.) Compare this with Gabriel's prediction, Luke 1:16-17.

11. Ernest DeWitt Burton, *Syntax of the Moods and Tenses in New Testament Greek* (Grand Rapids: Kregel, 1976). See also Turner, "Syntax," 3:63.

12. Carson, *Matthew*, 8:390.

13. Hendriksen, *Matthew*, 674.

14. For illuminating documentation of this see Josephus, *Antiquities*, 8:2; 5. Speaking of Solomon's wisdom in discovering all manner of cures and scientific facts, he writes, "God also enabled him to learn that skill which expels demons . . . he left behind him the manner of using exorcisms, by which they drive away demons" He then gives an example of a dramatic exorcism by a certain Eleazar, who used a special root and ring while "reciting the incantations which he [Solomon] composed."

15. Hendriksen, *Matthew*, 675.

16. Calvin, "Harmony of the Evangelists," 16:325-26. Parenthetical clarification is the author's.

17. Alfred Edersheim, *The Temple:Its Ministry and Services* (Peabody, Mass.: Hendrickson, 1944), 45.

18. Carson, *Matthew*, 8:395.

CHAPTER EIGHTEEN

1. Hendriksen, *Matthew*, 684.

2. Carson, *Matthew*, 8:396.

3. Ibid, 397.

4. Mounce, *Matthew*, 1:174.

5. Hendriksen, *Matthew*, 691.

6. Turner, "Syntax," 3:258.

7. Barnes, "Matthew and Mark," in *Notes on the New Testament*, 1:186.

8. Ibid., 187.

9. Carson, *Matthew*, 8:401.

10. W. Ghnther, *"hamartia,"* NIDNTT, 3:579.

11. Carson, *Matthew*, 8:403.

12. Ibid., 405.

13. *"Talanton,"* LS.

14. Carson, *Matthew*, 8:406.

15. Among the Hebrews, selling oneself or family members into indentureship was not the same as slavery, because they were making a contract of labor for money. Thus, those who bought these labor contracts were to treat the persons as "hired men," not personal property (Lev. 25:39).

16. Mounce, *Matthew*, 1:178.

17. Hendriksen, *Matthew*, 707.

CHAPTER NINETEEN

1. See, Carson, *Matthew*, 8:408.

2. Barnes, "Matthew and Mark," in *Notes on the New Testament*, 1:194.

3. Runes, "Get," in *Concise Dictionary of Judaism* (New York: Philosophical Library, 1959), 112.

4. "Divorce," in *The Jewish Encyclopedia*, 4:624-25.

5. Edwin M. Yamauchi, "Cultural Aspects of Marriage in the Ancient World," *BibSac* 135 (July-September 1978), 248.

6. Carson, *Matthew*, 8:412.

7. Josephus, *Antiquities* 4:8, 23.

8. See W.W. Davies, "Divorce in the OT," ISBE vol. 2, edited by James Orr (Grand Rapids: Eerdmans, 1974), 2:863-64, and Runes, "Get" or "Divorce," in *The Concise Dictionary of Judaism*, 112.

9. *'rwh*, BDB.

10. Josephus, *Antiquities*, 15:7; 10.

11. *"Get,"* in *The Jewish Encyclopedia*, ed. Isidore Singer, 5:646.

12. Leo Trepp, *Judaism: Development and Life* (Belmont, Calif.: Dickenson, 1966), 191.

13. Carson, *Matthew*, 8:413-18.

14. See Hendriksen, *Matthew*, 716-17 for more discussion.

15. David K. Lowery, "A Theology of Matthew," in *A Biblical Theology of the New Testament*, Roy B. Zuck, ed. (Chicago: Moody, 1994), 59.

16. Hendriksen, *Matthew*, 717.

17. Carson, *Matthew*, 8:419.

18. George Braumann, "Child," NIDNT, 1:280.

19. Meyer, "Gospel of Matthew," 1:342.

20. Mounce, *Matthew*, NIBC, 1:182.

21. Hendriksen, *Matthew*, 724.

22. Carson, *Matthew*, 8:423.

23. Mishnah, *Babha Bathra*, 116a.

24. Talmud, *Arakhin*, 8:4.

25. Meyer, "Matthew," 1:345.

26. Carson, *Matthew*, 8:425.

27. Mishnah, *Berakoth*, 55b.

28. Barnes, "Matthew and Mark," in *Notes on the New Testament*, 1:200.

29. Alford, *Matthew*, 1:199.

30. Barbieri, *Mark*, 231.

31. Hendriksen, *Matthew*, 732.

CHAPTER TWENTY

1. The Jews reckoned time in four parts: 6:00 P.M. to midnight; midnight to 6:00 A.M.; 6:00 A.M. to noon; and noon to 6:00 P.M. Daybreak was generally considered to be around 6:00 A.M.

2. Hendriksen, *Matthew*, 738.

3. Carson, *Matthew*, 8:428.

4. MacArthur, *Matthew 16-23*, 212.

5. Hendriksen, *Matthew*, 745.

6. Carson, *Matthew*, 8:431.

7. Jones, *Augustus*, 134-43 offers an excellent explanation of this structured society.

8. Deissmann, *Light from the Ancient East*, 328, n. 1.

9. Carson, *Matthew*, 8:435.

10. Barbieri, *Mark*, 240.

11. Calvin, "Harmony of Matthew, Mark, and Luke," 16:429.

12. Pate, *Luke*, 348.

CHAPTER TWENTY-ONE

1. Hendriksen, *Matthew*, 759.

2. Meyer, *Matthew*, 362.

3. Carson, *Matthew*, 437.

4. Barnes, "Matthew and Mark," in *Notes on the New Testament*, 1:216.

5. BDB.

6. Carson, *Matthew*, 439.

7. Edersheim, *The Temple*, 22.

8. Israel Lipschutz, "Appendix to 'The Temple,'" *Encyclopedia Talmudica*, 604.

9. Some try to argue that John 2 is the same account as Matthew 21, but the differences in the two accounts are too numerous to give credibility to the theory.

10. Hendriksen, *Matthew*, 771.

11. Carson, *Matthew*, 8:444.

12. John L. Leedy, "Plants," ZPBD, 663.

13. Hendriksen, *Matthew*, 774.

14. Barbieri, *Mark*, 256.

15. Carson, *Matthew*, 8:447.

16. Pate, *Luke*, 376.

17. There is some mss. variance relating to which son is the first and which is the second; the NASB follows one reading, placing the obedient son as the first and the remorseful, disobedient son as the last. The NIV and KJV follow the UBS[4] and have the disobedient son as the first.

18. See Hendriksen, *Matthew*, 785-86.

19. Carson," *Matthew*, 8:454.

20. Some scholars, such as Hendriksen, *Matthew*, 787, believe v. 44 to be an interpolation from Luke 20:18 and that no strong support exists for its inclusion; however, textual support includes Sinaiticus (4th C.E.) and Vaticanus (4th C.E.) the early Latin mss., the Vulgate, the Byzantine text, and the church Fathers: Chrysostom, Cyril, Jerome, and Augustine. Thus, this writer would include it as original text.

CHAPTER TWENTY-TWO

1. Hendriksen, *Matthew*, 791.

2. An interesting look at the reality of the fulfillment of this can be found in reading Josephus, *History of the Jewish Wars*, books 4-6.

3. Barnes, "Matthew and Mark," in *Notes on the New Testament*, 232.

4. Carson, *Matthew*, 8:457.

5. Hendriksen, *Matthew*, 798.

6. Ibid.

7. Josephus, *Antiquities*, 13:10, 6.

8. Ibid.

9. Pate, *Luke*, 384.

10. Carson, *Matthew*, 8:461.

11. See Hendriksen, *Matthew*, 805-6; and Mounce, *Matthew*, 1:209.

12. Excluding, of course, those who betrayed God and are sealed in their doom.

13. Clement, "First Epistle of Clement to the Corinthians," 2:6, 38:1, and 50:7–51:2, in vol. 1 of *The Apostolic Fathers*, trans. Kirsopp Lake (London: Harvard Univ. Press, 1977).

14. Carson, *Matthew*, 8:467.

15. Carson points out this is the most frequently quoted chapter in the Old Testament; ibid.

16. Barnes, "Matthew and Mark," in *Notes on the New Testament*, 1:238.

17. Hendriksen, *Matthew*, 813.

CHAPTER TWENTY-THREE

1. Carson, *Matthew*, 8:471.

2. France, "Sit," NIDNTT, 3:589.

3. Edersheim, *Sketches of Jewish Social Life*, 202-6.

4. Carson, *Matthew*, 8:474.

5. Ibid., 8:476.

6. BAGD, *ouai*.

7. Tasker, *Matthew*, TNTC, 1:217.

8. See, Barbieri, *Mark*, 280, for an explanation of the crime against widows.

9. Barnes, "Matthew and Mark," in *Notes on the New Testament*, 1:242.

10. Meyer, "Matthew," 1:392.

11. Alford, *Matthew, The Greek Testament*, 1:229.

12. Meyer, "Matthew," 1:393.

13. Josephus, *Antiquities*, 4:4; 3-4.

14. Freeman, "Tithe," ZPBD.

15. *Harpag', BAGD.

16. *Akrasia*, BAGD.

17. Hendriksen, *Matthew*, 834.

18. Carson, *Matthew*. See also Mishnah Shekalim 1:1 and Mishnah Kelim 1:4.

19. *Geenna*, BAGD.

20. Meyer, "Matthew," 1:397.

21. MacArthur, *Matthew 16-23*, 394.

22. Hendriksen, *Matthew*, 838.

23. Carson, *Matthew*, 8:485-86.

24. Lenski, *St. Matthew's Gospel*, 920.

25. Ibid.

CHAPTER TWENTY-FOUR

1. Hendriksen, *Matthew*, 850.

2. Josephus, *Wars*, 6:4; 5-7.

3. Ibid., 7:1;1, parenthetical comment added. Josephus does say that one wall was left for the Romans to use as a garrison protection and that the most impressive towers of the city were left intact to show how great the city had been at one time.

4. See the suggestion in Barnes, "Matthew and Mark," in *Notes on the New Testament*, 1:252.

5. Hendriksen, *Matthew*, 854.

6. Carson, *Matthew*, 8:499.

7. Hendriksen, *Matthew*, 855.

8. Carson, *Matthew*, 8:499.

9. See, MacArthur, *Matthew 24-28*, 34, for a good summary of Antiochus.

10. Josephus, *Wars*, 4:3; 6-8.

11. Carson, *Matthew*, 8:501-2.

12. Pentecost, *Things to Come*, 170.

13. MacArthur, *Matthew 24-28*, 45.

14. Matthew uses *tote* more than ninety times, twenty-seven times in this discourse.

15. Hendriksen, *Matthew*, 861.

16. Carson, *Matthew*, 8:504.

17. Berkouwer, *The Return of Christ*, (Grand Rapids: Eerdmans, 1972),166, fn. 60.

18. A partial execution of this judgment took place in Israel by the invasion of the Medes, but the heavenly phenomena did not happen at that time and are yet future.

19. Alford, *Matthew*, 4:243.

20. MacArthur, *Matthew 24-28*, 51.

21. Ibid., 54.

22. Paul Benware, *Understanding End Times Prophecy*, (Chicago: Moody, 1995), 209.

23. Wood, *The Bible and Future Events*, (Grand Rapids: Zondervan, 1973), 42.

24. Carson, *Matthew*, 8:507.

25. Attempts to discredit this statement because of omission in later copies of Matthew is not acceptable. Sufficient textual support exists, and it is also supported by Mark 13:32, where there is not a variant. It apparently was changed later because of the assumed theological difficulties.

26. BAGD.

27. Pate, *Luke*, 332.

28. Hendriksen, *Matthew*, 871.

CHAPTER TWENTY-FIVE

1. Edersheim, *The Life and Times of Jesus the Messiah,* 2:455.

2. Ibid.

3. Carson, *Matthew,* 8:514, n. 1.

4. Ibid., 8:515.

5. Hendriksen, *Matthew,* 882.

6. Alford, *Matthew, The Greek Testament,* 1:253.

7. MacArthur, *Matthew 24-28,* 102.

8. Ernst Achilles, *"Ponēros,"* NIDNTT, 1:565.

9. Carson, *Matthew,* 8:521.

10. Barnes, "Matthew—Mark," in *Barnes's Notes,* 271.

11. See Hendriksen, *Matthew,* 889; and Carson, 8:520.

12. Carson, *Matthew,* 8:520.

13. Ibid., 8:522.

CHAPTER TWENTY-SIX

1. Meyer, "Matthew," 1:451.

2. Hendriksen, *Matthew,* 895.

3. W. F. Boyd, "Cross, Crucifixion," in *Dictionary of the Apostolic Church,* ed. James Hastings, 2 vols. (Edinburgh: T. & T. Clark, 1926), 1:286.

4. Carson, *Matthew,* 8:523-24.

5. See Josephus, *Antiquities,* 18:2;2.

6. Hendriksen, *Matthew,* 904.

7. Carson, *Matthew,* 8:533.

8. Pate, *Luke,* 421.

9. The Jewish reckoning started the new day at 6:00 P.M.

10. Hendriksen, *Matthew,* 905.

11. Barnes, "Matthew and Mark," in *Notes on the New Testament,* 1:281.

12. MacArthur, *Matthew 24-28,* 148-49.

13. Carson, *Matthew,* 8:540.

14. In Luke 22:31, the "you" is plural. Satan demands to sift the disciples, but every "you" of v. 32 is singular. Jesus prayed for Peter ("Simon, Simon") so that Peter's faith would not fail; when Peter turned again, he was to strengthen the others.

15. Pate, *Luke,* 429.

16. MacArthur, *Matthew 24-28,* 167.

17. Meyer, "Matthew," 1:472.

18. Pate, *Luke,* 434.

19. Hendriksen, *Matthew,* 925.

20. Alford, *Matthew, The Greek Testament,* 1:278.

21. Carson, *Matthew,* 8:548.

22. Josephus, *Antiquities,* 18:2; 2.

23. Edersheim, *Life and Times of Jesus the Messiah,* 2:553.

24. Hendriksen, *Matthew,* 928.

25. For an interesting evangelistic use of this prophecy, see Acts 8:29-35.

26. Alford, *Matthew, The Greek New Testament,* 1:282.

27. Carson, *Matthew,* 8:555.

28. Barbieri, *Mark,* 334.

29. Pate, *Luke,* 438.

CHAPTER TWENTY-SEVEN

1. *Prēnēs,* BAGD. See discussion.

2. *Prētbō,* LS.

3. J. A. Motyer, "Akeldama," NIDNTT, 1:94.

4. F. F. Bruce, *The Acts of the Apostles* (Grand Rapids: Eerdmans, 1975), 77.

5. *Ginomai,* BAGD.

6. Hendriksen, *Matthew,* 945.

7. Carson, *Matthew,* 8:562.

8. Luke was a Greek making reference to the Jews' language, Aramaic.

9. Meyer, "Matthew," 1:496.

10. Laney, *John,* 331.

11. Hendriksen, *Matthew,* 953.

12. See Carson, *Matthew,* 8:569.

13. Hendriksen, *Matthew,* 953.

14. See Josephus, *Antiquities,* 18:3; 1-2.

15. Jones, *Augustus,* 103.

16. Josephus, *Wars of the Jews,* 2:21; 5.

17. Carson, *Matthew,* 8:573.

18. Mercenaries from many ethnic groups formed the legions of Rome, so all of the soldiers were not Romans.

19. Hendriksen, *Matthew,* 966.

20. Mounce, *Matthew,* 1:258.

21. The sayings of Jesus appear to be made in this order: "Father, forgive them; for they do not know what they are doing" (Luke 23:34); "Today you shall be with

Me in Paradise" (Luke 23:42-43); "Woman, behold your son . . . behold, your mother" (John 19:25-27); "My God, My God, why hast Thou forsaken Me" (Matt. 27:46; Mark 15:34); "I am thirsty" (John 19:28); "It is finished" (John 19:30); "Father, into Thy hands I commit My spirit" (Luke 23:46).

22. Hendriksen, *Matthew*, 973.

23. Alford seems to think there is evidence, "but it was replied in intended mockery, as *houtos,*—'this one among the three,'—clearly indicates." (Alford, *Matthew, Greek New Testament*, 1:295.

24. Hendriksen, *Matthew*, 973.

25. BAGD.

26. Ibid.

27. Laney, *John*, 350. See also Moulton and Milligan, *Vocabulary of the Greek New Testament*.

28. Pate, *Luke*, 457.

29. Carson, *Matthew*, 581-82.

30. Ibid., 582.

31. MacArthur, *Matthew 24-28*, 280.

32. This is not to imply that the darkness was an eclipse, as the descriptive terms are not consistent with an eclipse, but only that the Romans had strong religious views of such phenomena.

33. Carson, *Matthew*, 583.

34. Ibid., 586.

CHAPTER TWENTY-EIGHT

1. Gundry, *Matthew*, 585.

2. Mark says "a young man" wearing a white robe spoke to them; angels are often portrayed appearing as men (Acts 10:3, 30).

3. Hendriksen, *Matthew*, 990.

4. Perschbacher, *New Testament Greek Syntax*, 104.

5. Barnes, "Matthew and Mark," in *Notes on the New Testament*, 1:320.

6. Ibid., 1:322.

7. MacArthur, *Matthew 24-28*, 337.

8. Carson, *Matthew*, 8:599.

9. Hendriksen, *Matthew*, 1003.

SELECTED BIBLIOGRAPHY: FOR FURTHER STUDY

Aland, Kurt, ed. *Synopsis of the Four Gospels*. Stuttgart: United Bible Societies, 1982.

Alford, Henry. *The Four Gospels*. Vol. 1 of *The Greek Testament*, revised by Everett F. Harrison. Chicago: Moody, 1968.

Bacon, Benjamin W. *Studies in Matthew*. London: Constable, 1930.

Bacon, Gershon. "Idolatry." In vol. 8, *Encyclopedia Judaica*. Jerusalem: Macmillan, 1971.

Barbieri, Louis. *Mark*. Moody Gospel Commentary. Chicago: Moody, 1995.

Barclay, William. *And He Had Compassion*. Valley Forge: Judson, 1975.

_____. *The Gospel of Matthew*. Vol. 1 of *The Daily Study Bible*. Saint Andrews, 1975.

Barnes, Albert. *Matthew and Mark*. Vol. 1 of *Notes on the New Testament*. Grand Rapids: Baker, 1955.

Bauer, Walter. *A Greek-English Lexicon of the New Testament*. Translated and augmented by William F. Arndt, F. Wilbur Gingrich, and Frederick W. Danker. Chicago: Univ. of Chicago, 1979.

Benware, Paul N. *Understanding End Times Prophecy*. Chicago: Moody, 1995.

Berkhof, Louis. *Systematic Theology*. Grand Rapids: Eerdmans, 1984.

Berkouwer, G. C. *The Return of Christ*. Grand Rapids: Eerdmans, 1972.

Bewer, Julius A. *The Prophets*. New York: Harper, 1955.

Bietenhard, Hans. "Diabolos." In *New International Dictionary of New Testament Theology*, vol. 3. Grand Rapids: Zondervan, 1979.

Binns, L. Elliott. *The Book of the Prophet Jeremiah*. London: Methuen, 1919.

Bock, Darrell, L. "Current Messianic Activity and OT Davidic Promise: Dispensationalism, Hermeneutics, and NT Fulfillment." *Trinity Journal* 15:1 (Spring 1994).

Boyd, W. F. "Cross, Crucifixion." In *Dictionary of the Apostolic Church*. Edited by James Hastings. Edinburgh: T. & T. Clark, 1926.

Brandon, G. F. "Zealots." In vol.16 of *Encyclopedia Judaica*. New York: Macmillan, 1972.

Brown, Francis, S. R. Driver, and Charles A. Briggs. *A Hebrew and English Lexicon of the Old Testament*. Oxford: Clarendon, 1978.

Brown, Raymond E. *The Birth of the Messiah*. Garden City, N.J.: Doubleday, 1977.

Bruce, F. F. *The Acts of the Apostles*. Grand Rapids: Eerdmans, 1975.

_____. "Matthew." In *Understanding the New Testament*. Philadelphia: Holman, 1970.

Bullock, C. Hassel. *An Introduction to the Old Testament Prophetic Books*. Chicago: Moody, 1979.

Burton, Ernest DeWitt. *Syntax of the Moods and Tenses in New Testament Greek*. Grand Rapids: Kregel, 1976.

Calvin, John. *Harmony of the Evangelists*. Vol. 16 of *Calvin's Commentaries*. Translated by William Pringle. Grand Rapids: Baker, 1981.

_____. *Institutes*. MacDill, Fla: MacDonald., n.d.

Carson, D. A. *Matthew*. Vol. 8 of *The Expositors Bible Commentary*. Edited by Frank E. Gaebelein. Grand Rapids: Zondervan, 1984.

Carson, D. A., Douglas J. Moo, and Leon Morris. *An Introduction to the New Testament*. Grand Rapids: Zondervan, 1992.

Chafer, Louis Sperry. *He That Is Spiritual.* Revised. Grand Rapids: Zondervan, 1967.

Clement. *First Epistle of Clement to the Corinthians.* Vol. 1 of *The Apostolic Fathers.* Translated by Kirsopp Lake. London: Harvard Univ. Press, 1977.

Conzelmann, Hans. *The Theology of Luke.* Translated by J. C. Mohr. New York: Harper, 1966.

Dana H. E., and Julius R. Mantey. *A Manual Grammare of the Greek New Testament.* Toronto: Macmillan, 1957.

Davies, W. W. "Divorce in the Old Testament." In vol. 2, *The International Standard Bible Encyclopedia,* edited by James Orr. Grand Rapids: Eerdmans, 1974.

Deissmann, Adolf. *Light from the Ancient East.* Translated by Lionel R. M. Strachan. Grand Rapids: Baker, 1978.

Dodd, C. H., *The Bible Today.*

Eban, Abba. *My People: The Story of the Jews.* New York: Random House, 1968.

Edersheim, Alfred. *The Life and Times of Jesus the Messiah.* Grand Rapids: Eerdmans, 1972.

_____. *Sketches of Jewish Social Life.* Peabody, Mass.: Hendrickson, 1994.

_____. *The Temple.* Peabody, Mass. Hendrickson, 1994.

Eusebius, *The Ecclesiastical History.* Translated by Kirsopp Lake. Cambridge, Mass.: Harvard Univ. Press, 1975.

Feinberg, Charles L. *The Minor Prophets.* Chicago: Moody, 1980.

Fraser, Alexander. *The Return of Christ in Glory.* Scottsdale, Pa: Evangelical Fellowship, 1953.

Gaebelein, Arno C. *The Gospel of Matthew.* Neptune, N.J.: Loizeaux, 1910.

Gesenius' Hebrew and Chaldee Lexicon. Translated by Samuel Prideaux Tregelles. New York: John Wiley, 1885.

Grant, Michael. *From Alexander to Cleopatra.* New York: Charles Scribner's, 1982.

Grogan, Geoffrey W. *What the Bible Teaches About Jesus.* Wheaton: Tyndale, 1979.

Grudem, Wayne. *Systematic Theology.* Grand Rapids: Zondervan, 1994.

Gundry, Robert H. *Matthew.* Grand Rapids: Eerdmans, 1994.

_____. *A Survey of the New Testament,* 3d ed. Grand Rapids: Zondervan, 1994.

Guthrie, Donald. *A Shorter Life of Christ.* Grand Rapids: Zondervan, 1970.

Harrison, Everett F. *A Short Life of Christ.* Grand Rapids: Zondervan, 1991.

Hartman, Geoffrey H. "Midrash As Law and Literature." *Journal of Religion* 74 (1994): 338-55.

Hendriksen, William. *Matthew. New Testament Commentary.* Grand Rapids: Baker, 1973.

_____. *Luke. New Testament Commentary.* Grand Rapids: Baker, 1978.

Hoehner, Harold W. *Herod Antipas.* Cambridge: Univ. Press, 1972.

Jewish Encyclopedia. Edited by Isidore Singer. New York: Funk and Wagnalls, 1903.

Jones, A. H. M. *Augustus.* New York: W. W. Norton, 1970.

Jones, John Mark. "Subverting the Texuality of Davidic Messianism: Matthew's Presentation of the Genealogy and the Davidic Titles." *Catholic Biblical Quarterly* 56:2 (April 1994): 256-72.

Josephus, Flavius. *The Works of Flavius Josephus.* Translated by William Whiston. 4 vols. Grand Rapids: Baker, 1980.

Kingsbury, Jack Dean. "The Title, 'Son of David,' in Matthew's Gospel." *Journal of Biblical Literature* 95/4 (1976): 591-602.

Laney, J. Carl. *John.* Moody Gospel Commentary. Chicago: Moody, 1992.

Latourette, Kenneth Scott. *The First Five Centuries.* New York: Harper, 1937.

Liddell, H. G., and Robert Scott. *A Greek-English Lexicon.* Revised by Henry Stuart Jones. Oxford: Clarenden, 1968.

Linnemann, Eta. "Is There a Gospel of Q?" *Bible Review* (August 1995).

_____. *Is There a Synoptic Problem?* Translated by Robert W. Yarbrough. Grand Rapids: Baker, 1992.

Lipschutz, Israel. "Appendix to 'The Temple.'" In *Encyclopedia Talmudica*. Jerusalem: Talmudic Encyclopedia Institute, 1992.

Lives of the Saints. Compiled from *Butler's Lives.* New York: Benziger: 1922.

Lloyd-Jones, D. Martin. *Studies in the Sermon on the Mount.* Grand Rapids: Eerdmans, 1979.

Luz, Ulrich. "The Disciples in the Gospels According to Matthew." In *The Interpretation of Matthew,* edited by Graham N. Stanton. Edinburgh: T. & T. Clark, 1995.

_____. "The Son of Man in Matthew: Heavenly Judge or Human Christ." *Journal for Study of the New Testament* 48 (1992): 3-21.

Lyon, Jeff. "Gospel Truth." *The Chicago Tribune Magazine* (July 17, 1994): 8-15.

MacArthur, John F., Jr. *The Gospel According to Jesus.* Grand Rapids: Zondervan, 1988.

_____. *The Legacy of Jesus.* Chicago: Moody, 1986.

_____. *Matthew.* 4 vols. *The MacArthur New Testament Commentary.* Chicago: Moody, 1987.

Macaulay, J. C. *Behold Your King.* Chicago: Moody, 1982.

Man, M. "Pharisee," in *Encyclopaedia Judaica.* New York: Macmillan, 1971.

Manson, T. W. *The Servant Messiah.* Grand Rapids: Baker, 1977.

Meyer, Heinrich August Wilhelm. *The Gospel of Matthew.* Peabody, Mass.: Hendrickson, 1983.

Moore, Thomas V. "Malachi." In *A Commentary on Haggai, Zechariah, and Malachi.* Edinburgh: Banner of Truth, 1979.

Morison, James. *Gospel According to St. Matthew.* Reprint. Minneapolis: Klock & Klock, 1981.

Morris, Leon. *The Gospel According to Matthew.* Grand Rapids: Eerdmans, 1992.

Motyer, J. A. "Akeldama." In *The New International Dictionary of New Testament Theology.* Edited by Colin Brown. 2 vols. Grand Rapids: Zondervan, 1975.

Moulton W. F., and Milligan. *Vocabulary of the Greek New Testament*. New York: Gordon Press, 1977.

Mounce, Robert H. *Matthew. New International Biblical Commentary*. Peabody, Mass: Hendrickson, 1991.

McNeile, Alan Hugh. *The Gospel According to St. Matthew*. Grand Rapids: Baker, 1980.

New Dictionary of Theology. Edited by Sinclair B. Ferguson and David F. Wright. Downers Grove, Ill.: InterVarsity, 1988.

Overman, J. Andrew. *Matthew's Gospel and Formative Judaism*. Minneapolis: Fortress, 1990.

Pate, C. Marvin. "Luke," in *Moody Gospel Commentary*. Chicago: Moody, 1995.

Pentecost, J. Dwight *The Words and Works of Jesus Christ*. Grand Rapids: Zondervan, 1981.

_____. *Things to Come*. Grand Rapids: Zondervan, 1958.

Perrin, Norman. *The Resurrection According to Matthew, Mark, and Luke*. Philadelphia: Fortress, 1980.

Perschbacher, Wesley J. *New Testament Greek Syntax*. Chicago: Moody, 1995.

Plummer, Alford. "The Gospel According to S. Luke" in *The International Critical Commentary*. Edinburh: T & T Clark, 1977.

Prat, Ferinand. *Jesus Christ*, 2 vols. Translated by John J. Heenan. Milwaukee: Bruce Publishing Co., 1950.

Robertson, A. T. *A Harmony of the Gospels for Students of the Life of Christ*. New York: Harper and Row, 1950.

Runes, Dagobert D. "Get" and "Divorce." In *Concise Dictionary of Judaism*. New York: Philosophical Library, 1959.

Ryle, J. C. *Matthew and Mark*. Vol. 1 of *Ryle's Expository Thoughts on the Gospels*. Grand Rapids: Baker, 1979.

Sanders, J. Oswald. *The Incomparable Christ*. Chicago: Moody, 1971.

Scott, J. W. "Matthew's Intention to Writer History." *Westminster Theological Journal* 47 (1985): 68-82.

Sforno, Ovadiah ben Yaacov. *Sfrono: Commentary on the Torah*. Translated by Raphael Pelcouitz. Brooklyn: Mesorah, 1993.

Spencer, William David, and Aida Bescançon Spencer. *The Prayer Life of Jesus*. Lanham, Md.: Univ. Press of America, 1990.

Sperber, Daniel. "Tax Gatherers." In vol. 15, *Encyclopedia Judaica*. New York: Macmillan, 1972.

Stein, Robert H. *The Synoptic Problem*. Grand Rapids: Baker, 1987.

Stott, John R. W. *The Message of the Sermon on the Mount*. Downers Grove, Ill.: InterVarsity, 1978.

Straham, James. "Antioch." In *Dictionary of the Apostolic Church*, edited by James Hastings. Edinburgh: T. & T. Clark, 1926.

Tasker, R. V. G. *The Gospel According to St. Matthew*. Vol. 1 of *Tyndale New Testament Commentaries*. Grand Rapids: Eerdmans, 1981.

Thomas, David. *The Gospel of St. Matthew*. Edited by William Webster. Grand Rapids: Baker, 1956.

Trepp, Leo. *Judaism: Development and Life*. Belmont, Calif.: Dickenson, 1966.

Turner, Nigel. *Syntax*. Vol. 3 in *A Grammar of New Testament Greek*. Edited by James Hope Moulton. Edinburgh: T. & T. Clark, 1963.

Unger, Merrill F. *The New Unger's Bible Dictionary*. Chicago: Moody, 1983.

Walvoord, John F. *The Blessed Hope and the Tribulation*. Grand Rapids: Zondervan, 1976.

_____. *Matthew: Thy Kingdom Come*. Chicago: Moody, 1978.

Warfield, B. B. "The Antiquity and Unity of the Human Race." In *Studies in Theology*. Edinburgh: Banner of Truth, n.d.

_____. *The Person and Work of Christ*. Philadelphia: Presby. and Reformed, 1950.

Wenham, John. *Redating Matthew, Mark and Luke*. Downers Grove, Ill.: InterVarsity, 1992.

Willis, Steve. "Matthew's Birth Stories: Prophecy and the Magi." *Expository Times* (November 1993): 43-45.

Wilson, Clifford A. *Jesus the Teacher*. Victoria, Australia: Word of Truth Production, 1974.

Wood, Leon J. *The Bible and Future Events.* Grand Rapids: Zondervan, 1973.

Yamauchi, Edwin M. "Cultural Aspects of Marriage in the Ancient World." *Bibliotheca Sacra* 135 (July-September 1978): 241-52.

Zondervan Pictorial Bible Dictionary. Edited by Merrill C. Tenney. Grand Rapids: Zondervan, 1967.

Zuck, Roy B., ed. *A Biblical Theology of the New Testament.* Chicago: Moody, 1994.

INDEX OF SUBJECTS

INDEX OF AUTHORS

INDEX OF SCRIPTURE
AND ANCIENT WRITINGS